C A N A D I A N
MACROECONOMICS

Problems and Policies

FOURTH EDITION

BRIAN LYONS
Sheridan College

PRENTICE HALL CANADA INC.,
SCARBOROUGH, ONTARIO

Canadian Cataloguing in Publication Data

Lyons, Brian.
   Canadian macroeconomics: problems and policies

4th ed.
ISBN 0-13-177585-5

1. Macroeconomics. 2. Canada – Economic
conditions. I. Title

HB172.5.L96 1995   339'.0971   C94-931269-X

Prentice-Hall, Inc., Englewood Cliffs, New Jersey
Prentice-Hall International (UK) Limited, London
Prentice-Hall of Australia, Pty. Limited, Sydney
Prentice-Hall Hispanoamericana, S.A., Mexico City
Prentice-Hall of India Private Limited, New Delhi
Prentice-Hall of Japan, Inc., Tokyo
Simon & Schuster Asia Private Limited, Singapore
Editora Prentice-Hall do Brasil, Ltda., Rio de Janeiro

ISBN 0-13-177585-5

Acquisitions Editor: Jacqueline Wood
Developmental Editor: Linda Gorman
Production Editor: Valerie Adams
Production Coordinator: Anna Orodi
Cover Design: Carole Giguère
Cover Image: Phototone by Letraset
Page Layout: Phyllis Seto

1 2 3 4 5   99 98 97 96 95

Printed and bound in Canada.

For Barbie, Marnie and Amber

TABLE OF CONTENTS

CHAPTER 20 Introduction to macroeconomics   421

CHAPTER 21 Our basic economic objectives and how we measure them   429

CHAPTER 25 *Stabilizing the economy: Government fiscal policy   554*

CHAPTER 28 *The nature and causes of inflation* **645**

CHAPTER 29 *Dealing with inflation: Policies and problems* **667**

CHAPTER 30 *The nature of unemployment* 692

CHAPTER 31 *Economic policy in perspective* 718

CHAPTER 34 The Canadian dollar in foreign exchange markets   809

CHAPTER 35   *The international monetary system*   845

CHAPTER 36 *Into the future* 874

PREFACE

This book is an introductory macroeconomics text that addresses itself to the major economic problems facing Canada and Canadians today, and the policy choices confronting governments in dealing with these issues. It is not oriented toward rigorous, abstract or elegant economic theory, nor to a mathematical approach to economics—students of introductory economics neither want nor need these. Rather, its approach tends to be practical and pragmatic, introducing theory not for its own sake so much as to contribute to an understanding of the problems being discussed.

The organization of the book follows the evolution of economic problems and policies over the years, starting with the problems of *depression, recession* and *unemployment* that dominated much economic thinking and policy-making from the 1930's until the 1960's. The focus then shifts to the problem of *inflation* that dominated much of the 1970's and the *stagflation* that became associated with it. Increased coverage is devoted to the problem of unemployment, not only because of the long and severe recession of the early 1990's, but also because of the changing nature of unemployment in Canada and the trend toward more long-term unemployment as well as higher unemployment rates as the economy undergoes fundamental structural change. Finally, consideration is given to the trend toward economic "globalization" in general and the Canada–US Free Trade Agreement in particular, as Canada is faced with the challenge of how best to adjust to an economic environment that is changing in fundamental ways. The intention of this approach is to gain a better understanding of current economic problems by viewing them in the perspective of recent problems and policies.

Throughout the book certain basic concepts and themes appear and reappear for emphasis. Some of these are: the fundamental importance of *productivity* (output per worker) to prosperity, the contribution of *saving and investment* to prosperity, the *role of markets* in promoting prosperity through effective and efficient use of economic resources, the real nature of *inflation* and its effects upon our prosperity, and the economic realities of the *international environment*. In analyzing macroeconomic problems throughout the book, the concept of the interaction between *aggregate demand* and *aggregate supply* is used. These frames of reference for analysis are more appropriate for the introductory student, as they are easier to grasp intuitively than some of the more commonly used theoretical approaches.

Economically, Canada is a very fortunate country in many ways, which has made it possible for Canadians to enjoy great economic prosperity without concerning themselves very much with basic economic principles. In fact, until fairly recently, economic progress occurred so readily that some of the "basics" of economics were seemingly forgotten or ignored by Canadians and their governments.

However, as this edition was being prepared, Canadians' "free ride" was coming to an end as various fundamental economic realities were asserting themselves, not the least of which were the importance of productivity and competitiveness and the limitations imposed by excessive debt. In this new and much more challenging economic situation, it is more important than ever that "the basics" be remembered and emphasized: only by doing this can Canada achieve its tremendous economic potential and outgrow the saying that "The next century is Canada's—and always will be."

The relationship between government economic policy and the public's understanding of economic issues is fundamentally important here. If political necessity dictates that government policy must be framed to appeal to the public, the present economic situation makes it vital that the public understand economic realities, issues and policies. Only such knowledge can ensure that economic policy will be directed toward the long-term economic advantage of Canadians rather than framed for short-term political expediency. If governments must be more responsive to the public than to their economic advisers, perhaps the time has come when economics is too important to be left to the economists, and the public must become more economically literate.

Some people believe that this task is impossible—that economics is too difficult a subject to be comprehended by most people, and must therefore be left to the experts. This view is not correct. Economics is not a particularly difficult subject at all—the real task in teaching introductory economics is to organize many things that people either already know or can grasp quite readily into a systematic framework that promotes greater understanding of important economic problems. Hopefully, this book can help people to do this in a readable, not unduly painful, and maybe even occasionally enjoyable way.

A person undertaking a project such as this is indebted to a great number of people. In particular, I would like to express my gratitude to Bill Trimble, who said I should do it, Len Rosen, who didn't let me say I wouldn't, and all those instructors and students who used the first three editions and offered helpful comments and suggestions. I would also like to thank the people whose reviews of all four editions of the manuscript were so helpful: for the first edition, Ray Canon, Gord Cleveland, Ward Levine, Jim Thompson and Ian Wilson; for the second, Alan Idiens and Chuck Casson; for the third, Linda Nitsou, Bo Renneckendorf, Gord Enemark, L.W. Van Niekerk, Stephen Wise and Ann Dunkley; and for the fourth, Carol Ann Waite, Izhar Mirza, John Parry and Byron Eastman. In addition, I would like to express my appreciation to the many excellent Prentice Hall editing people whose help and support have been indispensable, most recently Linda Gorman and Valerie Adams for the fourth edition, and to Prentice Hall's excellent marketing people. Finally, I want to acknowledge my indebtedness to my family—Barbie, Marnie and Amber—who have provided support and understanding over unduly long periods of time.

I have no doubts that there are many improvements that can be made to this book, and welcome any suggestions from teachers or students. Please write to me at Sheridan College, Box 7500, McLaughlin Road, Brampton, Ontario, L6V 1G6.

Brian Lyons
Sheridan College, 1995

CHAPTER 1

What is economics?

What is "economics"? To the householder, economics is the difficult task of balancing the family budget, so that there is not too much month left over at the end of the money. To the business leader, economics is the problem of producing a product at sufficiently low cost that it can be marketed profitably in competition with the products of other producers. To a government leader, economics means difficult policy choices between goals that often conflict with each other, making it impossible to please everyone and thus ensure re-election. To the general public, economics is usually associated with vague, incomprehensible and often contradictory pronouncements by people called "economists," concerning matters of great national and international importance that seem rather depressing and impossible to understand, much less resolve.

While each of these views may be in its own way accurate, each is only a part of the real meaning of economics, because each represents only the viewpoint of a particular group (householders, business leaders, government leaders, voters). From the viewpoint of the economist, however, economics covers a broader field, dealing in the widest sense with how well a society's economic system satisfies the economic needs and wants of its people. Since the basic task of an economic system is to produce goods and services and to distribute them among the people of a society, the most commonly used definition of **economics** is

> the study of the decisions a society makes concerning the production of goods and services and how the society distributes these goods and services among its members.

This somewhat dull and simple definition leads us into a variety of areas of much broader concern and greater interest, such as:

- Must a million Canadians be unemployed?
- Why are economists so concerned about government budget deficits and debt?

1

- How can Canadian governments deal with their deficits/debt problems?
- Will the severe inflation of the 1970's return to the Canadian economy?
- Will there be another severe recession before the turn of the century?
- Why did the international value of the Canadian dollar fall by over 13 percent from 1991 to 1993, and what does this mean for Canadians?
- Will the North American Free Trade Agreement with the United States and Mexico bring prosperity or hardship to Canadians?
- Will the relaxation of Canada's restrictions on US investment under the Canada–US Free Trade Agreement mean more jobs for Canadians, or US domination of the Canadian economy?
- In what industries and occupations will there be the greatest growth of job opportunities in the future, and why?
- Why are some people paid hundreds of thousands of dollars per year, while others receive less than one percent of that?
- How many Canadians are really poor?
- Would a sharp increase in the minimum wage rate help to reduce poverty among Canadians?
- How could Canada's social welfare system be improved?
- How big is the male–female "pay gap," why does it exist, and what can and should be done about it?
- Should the government "police" the prices and profits of business?
- What can be done about the cost of government?
- Are strikes severely damaging to the Canadian economy?
- Should the government place legal limits on the rent charged by landlords?
- Why are governments been cutting back on the services they provide to the public?
- Can we have economic growth without destroying our environment?

Some aspects of economic matters such as those above raise *philosophical* questions; for instance, should the government restrict or reduce social welfare benefits as a matter of policy? Other aspects of economics, however, involve more *technical economic analysis*. For example, if the government undertakes to combat inflation, by how much will the unemployment rate probably increase? In many cases, also, economics becomes involved with *value judgments*. For example, suppose that if the government restricts imports of shoes in order to protect jobs in the Canadian footwear industry, higher shoe prices in Canada will cost consumers roughly $120 000 for every job saved through this policy. Is this a worthwhile price to pay for the jobs that are saved? This question involves a value judgment, in the sense that even people who agree concerning the economic analysis of the issue may disagree on what policy the government should follow. One may be more concerned about the effect of layoffs in the Canadian shoe industry, while another may place greater emphasis on the higher prices that Canadian consumers will have to pay for shoes.

Folklore versus economic analysis

Probably the greatest obstacle to the effective learning of economics is not what people *do not know* so much as what they *think that they do know* about the subject. In fact, much of this "knowledge" consists of widely believed but not necessarily accurate ideas, such as:

- If the rich paid a fairer share of the tax burden, the rest of us could pay much lower taxes and the government would have no budget problems.
- Government budget deficits and debt don't matter.
- Government borrowing and increases in government debt are always bad.
- Canadians cannot compete with low-wage industries in other countries.
- The government should always balance its budget.
- If the government used its economic policies more effectively, both unemployment and inflation could be eliminated.
- A higher international value of the Canadian dollar is economically good for all Canadians.
- The way to eliminate poverty is to increase the minimum wage dramatically.
- Keeping out imports will increase the prosperity of Canadians.
- Strict government controls on labor unions and strikes would cure many of the nation's economic problems.

None of the above statements is true, but they are widely believed by the public. The objective of this book is to replace this type of folklore about economics with the tools for accurate analysis of economic issues of importance to Canadians.

The limitations of economic analysis

Because it deals with the behavior of people (consumers, business people, government policy-makers), economics cannot be a precise science such as physics or mathematics. Similarly, economic analysis does not provide clear and simple answers to important questions, such as whether the government should reduce taxes. However, economic analysis can do a great deal to illuminate the consequences of reducing (or not reducing) taxes, thus *clarifying the choices* to be made. Therefore, while economic analysis does not provide us with decisions, it provides us with a much better basis for making decisions.

Can economists agree on anything?

"Ask five economists what should be done about a problem and you'll get six different recommendations" is a jibe frequently directed at economists, whose credibility is often considered in the same category as that of weather forecasters. Given the disagreements among economists (and others who describe themselves as such) on matters of importance, it is easy to get the impression that the field of economics involves more unsubstantiated opinion than systematic analysis. In fact, economics is in considerably better condition than seems to be generally supposed. First, to add color to news coverage the media often seek out dissenting opinions on economic issues, giving such opinions the appearance of a legitimacy that they neither possess nor deserve. Second, many public pronouncements on economic matters are made not by economists, but rather by politicians whose goal is not to discuss economic issues rationally, but rather to score (or obscure) points politically. Disagreements among economists arise not from *economic analysis* of issues but rather from differences concerning *policy recommendations* (value judgments) that arise from that analysis. In fact, there are many generally accepted facts, concepts and theories that constitute a sort of "mainstream" of economic thought that is less publicized but much more important than disagreements between individual economists. This book attempts to build around this mainstream of thought, while considering the major alternatives to it where these are important.

What is economics about, then?

Economics came to be known as the "dismal science" because of the economic theories of Thomas Malthus (1766–1834). Malthus, an English clergyman, theorized that because population could grow faster than the world's food supply, humanity was destined to live with a constant struggle with starvation. While no one can say what the future will bring, a combination of lower birthrates and modern production technology has raised living standards in many societies far beyond anything dreamed of in Malthusian theories, and has brought the study of economics to matters which, while serious, are much less depressing.

Economics, then, is about many matters both small and large. On a small scale, *microeconomics* (after the Greek word *micro*, for small) focuses on particular aspects of economics, such as consumer demand, supply, demand and prices under various conditions, the role of big business, labor unions and government in the economy, and the economics of particular industries such as agriculture and oil.

On a large scale, *macroeconomics* (based on *macro*, for big) deals with broader matters pertaining to the performance of the economy as a whole, such as recession, inflation and unemployment, and matters of international trade and finance. The purpose of this book is to develop an understanding of these economic matters which are of importance to all Canadians. Before examining these issues, however, we will consider the basic problems of economics and the various types of economic systems that exist, in Chapters 2 and 3 respectively.

Isn't this all terribly difficult?

Not really. Probably the most insightful observation ever made about economics as a field of study is that it is a *complex* subject but not a *difficult* one. Unlike nuclear physics or differential calculus, there is little in economics that many people find conceptually difficult. Rather, economics deals with people and their behavior and decisions as consumers, business people and government policy-makers. Much of this behavior is already known to the student of introductory economics; what needs to be done is to organize these fragments of knowledge into a framework for analyzing and understanding economic events. This book attempts to do this in a way that eliminates the use of abstract theories and higher-level mathematics, instead focusing on developing an understanding of real and relevant Canadian economic problems in a readable and, hopefully, enjoyable way.

QUESTIONS

1. What has economics meant to you? From what viewpoints have you viewed the economic system?
2. How well does Canada's economic system fill the needs and wants of Canadians? What shortcomings do you perceive, and what do you think could be done about them?
3. The inability of economists to make accurate economic forecasts shows that they know so little about the workings of the economy that their advice on economic matters should be disregarded." Do you agree with this statement? Why?
4. What are some of the specific developments that have enabled us to escape the dismal predictions of Malthus? Do you believe that Malthus's theories will eventually come true? Why?

The economic problem

In Chapter 1, we saw that **economics** is basically the study of how a society makes decisions regarding the production of goods and services and how these will be divided among its people. As we shall see, different societies make these decisions in very different ways. However, all societies, whether they are capitalist, socialist, communist, industrialized or developing, are faced with essentially the same basic economic problem—how to use their limited economic resources to the best possible advantage.

Using economic resources to satisfy human wants

As we said in Chapter 1, economics is not a difficult subject but it can be a complex one. A modern industrial economy involves a bewildering number of factors, such as consumers, small businesses, big businesses, labor unions, governments, exports, imports, the level of output, employment, unemployment, the money supply, interest rates, prices, the international value of the nation's currency, government tax revenues, government spending, consumer spending and saving, banks, profits, stock markets, and many others. Furthermore, each of these factors is related to the others in ways that are often subtle and complex. It is no wonder that many people find economics confusing and have difficulty "seeing the forest for the trees." Worst of all, such complexities often make it difficult to understand an issue because they obscure the basic economic principles involved in the problem.

In order to better understand an economic situation, it can be very helpful to eliminate the many complexities associated with a modern economy that tend to obscure the basic economic principles involved. In order to do this, suppose that we are part of a group of people stranded on a desert island. With none of the complexities of a modern economy to distract us, our group must come to grips with the most basic economic problem: we have people with economic needs and wants, and we have available to us certain economic resources. Our people need and want things such as food, shelter, clothing, security and so on. To produce these things, we have available to us the three basic types of economic resources, or **inputs**—the skills of our people, the equipment we have, and the natural resources of the island.

(a) The skills of people ("labor")

The largest and most important single economic resource available to any society is the skills of its people, which economists refer to as **labor**. This includes all types of skills: manual labor, skilled work, management and professional employment. In our desert-island mini-society, people will have various skills appropriate to the situation, such as hunting, fishing, building, managing, planning and organizing.

(b) Capital equipment

Another vitally important economic resource is society's stock of **capital equipment**, by which we mean its tools, equipment, machinery, factories, computers and so on. Capital equipment is of crucial importance because it increases *output per worker*, or *productivity*. And when each worker produces more, the society can enjoy more economic prosperity, or a higher material standard of living—more goods and services per person. Figure 2-1 illustrates this fundamentally important point.

While a modern industrial economy possesses a vast array of factories, machinery, equipment and tools, our desert-island mini-society will only have a few basic tools, such as spears, fish nets and plows. Thus, its people may wish to increase their stock of capital equipment, in order to increase their productivity and thus their standard of living.

FIGURE 2-1   *The Importance of Capital Equipment*

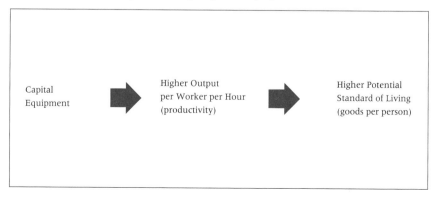

> Labour productivity is probably the most telling measure of economic performance. Unless productivity grows, living standards stagnate.
>
> *The Economist*, February 13, 1993, p. 67

(c) Natural resources ("land")

The third economic resource available to a society is *natural resources*, which economists refer to as **land**. In our desert-island mini-society, these natural resources would likely be few and simple—waterways, fish, land, trees, plants and so on. In a modern economy, natural resources are often a much more complex matter, involving high technology and sophisticated energy resources such as oil, natural gas and atomic energy.

There is a tendency to think of natural resources as depletable (and depleting); however, this is not always the case. Some natural resources, such as forests and fish, can be renewable if managed effectively, while technology is capable of creating entirely new resources, such as oil, natural gas and nuclear power. For example, until the development of nuclear reactors, uranium could not reasonably be considered an economic resource. The Athabasca Tar Sands of Northern Alberta represent an enormous energy resource if the technology can be developed to extract oil from them at an economical cost. Thus, while some natural resources become depleted, new resources can be developed through technology.

The task of an economic system

The task of any economic system is to organize and use these economic resources, or productive inputs, to produce goods and services (**output**) of the types and quantities that will best satisfy the needs and wants of the people of the society. This process is shown in Figure 2-2.

FIGURE 2-2   *The Basic Operation of Any Economic System*

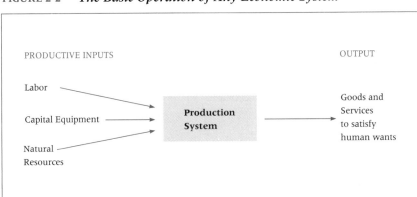

In our desert island mini-society, the process shown in Figure 2-2 will be quite simple: people with various basic skills will be using simple tools such as spears, nets and plows to produce products to satisfy basic needs such as food, shelter and security. In a modern economy, this process is much more sophisticated, involving the use of a wide range of skills and "high-tech" equipment and resources, especially energy, to produce a tremendous volume and variety of both goods and services. However, the basic task is the same in both economies: how can we use our economic resources to our best advantage?

THE BASIC "ECONOMIC PROBLEM" OF SCARCITY

This is a particularly important question because we do not have enough economic resources to produce everything that we would like to have. This is the basic "economic problem" of **scarcity**: the economic resources (inputs) on the left side of Figure 2-2 are in limited supply, while the amount of goods and services wanted by people on the right side of Figure 2-2 seem to be unlimited. Since we cannot have everything that we want, we are forced to make choices, some of which might be difficult.

THE PRODUCTION-POSSIBILITIES CURVE

One way of illustrating the problem of scarcity is with a **production possibilities curve.** Suppose our desert islanders can only produce two items—vegetables and fish. If all their economic inputs were devoted to producing vegetables, they could produce 15 kilograms of vegetables daily, but no fish. This option is shown as combination **A** in Figure 2-3 which indicates vegetable production of 15 kg and fish production of 0. If the desert islanders went to the opposite extreme and used all their productive inputs to produce fish, the result would be fish production of 5 kg and vegetable production of 0, as shown by combination **F** in Figure 2-3.

Of course, it is more likely that the islanders would choose to produce some combination of fish and vegetables, such as combinations **B** (14 kg vegetables and 1 kg fish), **C** (12 kg and 2 kg), **D** (9 kg and 3 kg) or **E** (5 kg and 4 kg). In making their choice, however, they will be restricted by the limitations of the production-possibilities curve: since their economic resources are limited, *producing more of one product necessarily means being able to produce less of the other*. The islanders may want to have 4 kg of fish and 12 kg of vegetables (combination **X**), but they will not be able to. Resource scarcity dictates that if they want 4 kg of fish, they can only have 5 kg of vegetables, and if they are to have 12 kg of vegetables, fish production can only be 2 kg. Thus, while it is possible to produce 4 kg of fish or 12 kg of vegetables per day, it is not possible to produce this much of both on the same day. The islanders must make choices among various combinations of products, and the production-possibilities curve reflects the limitations that resource scarcity imposes upon their choices.

FIGURE 2-3 *Production-Possibilities Curve*

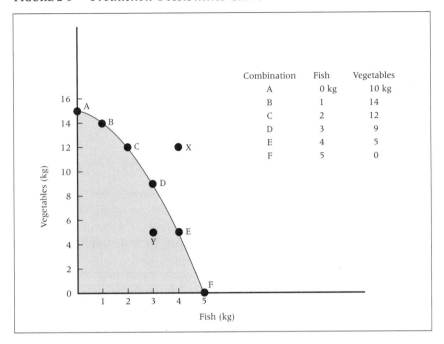

Combination	Fish	Vegetables
A	0 kg	10 kg
B	1	14
C	2	12
D	3	9
E	4	5
F	5	0

However, the combinations shown by the production-possibilities curve are based on two important assumptions—that the islanders use all of their available productive inputs, and that they utilize them as efficiently as possible. If some of their productive inputs were not used (if, for instance, some of the workers were sick, or one of their fish spears was broken) output would be below the potential level shown by the production-possibilities curve. Point **Y**, at which fish production is 3 kg and vegetable production is 5 kg, reflects such a situation. With fish production at 3 kg, vegetable production could be as high as 9 kg rather than 5 kg, and with vegetable production at 5 kg, fish production could be as high as 4 kg rather than 3 kg. However, if the islanders do not employ all of their productive inputs, their production will be below its potential. In fact, even if all inputs are employed, production may fall short of its potential. If the islanders' inputs (labor and capital equipment) were not producing fish and vegetables as efficiently as possible, production could be below its potential level and the islanders could still wind up at point **Y**.

It is important to recognize that the production-possibilities curve indicates the economy's *potential* output, assuming that economic inputs are fully employed and efficiently utilized. Production can be at any point on the production-possibilities curve (if inputs are fully and efficiently utilized) or within the shaded area (if they are not), but cannot be outside the curve.

However, the islanders need not live forever within the limitations imposed by the curve shown in Figure 2-3. This curve represents the sit-

FIGURE 2-4   *Economic Progress: Shifting the Production-Possibilities Curve Outwards*

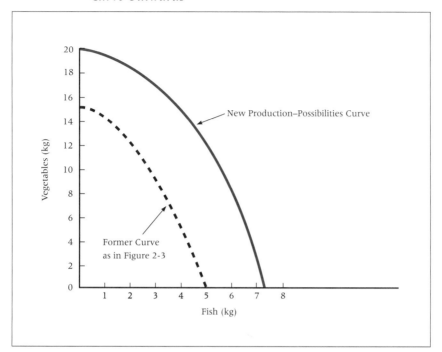

uation at a particular point in time, given the economic resources available to the islanders at that time. If, in the future, they were to add to their economic resources, say, by building *new capital equipment* or developing *new technologies*, their potential output of both fish and vegetables could increase. Figure 2-4 shows the new production-possibilities curve that could be created by additions to or improvements in the islanders' economic resources.

The inquisitive reader may wonder why the production-possibilities curve is bowed outward as it is, rather than following a straight line. The shape of the curve reflects the *changing efficiency* of resources as they are shifted from one use to another. For instance, in Figure 2-3, the table shows that to increase fish production from 0 to 1 kg, we must sacrifice only 1 kg of vegetable production. But as we push fish production higher, we must forego ever-higher amounts of vegetable production to achieve the same increases in fish production. The second kilogram of fish costs 2 kg of vegetables, the third kilogram of fish requires the foregoing of 3 kg of vegetables, and so on.

To produce the first kilogram of fish, we would shift resources (labor and capital) out of their *least efficient use* in vegetable production (say, from the least productive land or using the least efficient capital equipment) into their *most efficient use* in fishing (say, using the best available equipment to fish the most productive waters). However, as we push fish production higher and higher, the trade-off between fish and vegetable production becomes less attractive. Increasingly, we have to shift labor and capital out of more efficient uses in vegetable production and into less efficient uses in fishing. The fifth kilogram of fish production is particularly costly in terms of vegetable production lost (5 kg of vegetables), as it requires that we shift labor and capital out of our last (and most efficient) use in vegetable pro-

THE CONCEPT OF OPPORTUNITY COST

The trade-offs between fish and vegetable production as shown by the production-possibilities curve are referred to by economists as opportunity costs. The opportunity cost of using economic resources to produce any item is the amount of any other item that those same economic resources could have produced instead. The production-possibilities table in Figure 2-3 provides a good illustration of this concept.

The opportunity cost of producing the first kilogram of fish is the loss of 1 kg of vegetable production, which declines from 15 to 14 kg. The opportunity cost of the second kilogram of fish is the 2 kg of vegetable production lost when their production falls from 14 to 12 kg, and so on, as shown by the following table.

Combination	Fish Production	Vegetable Production	Opportunity Cost of:
A	0 kg	15 kg	
B	1	14	The 1st kg of fish = 1 kg vegetables
C	2	12	The 2nd kg of fish = 2 kg vegetables
D	3	9	The 3rd kg of fish = 3 kg vegetables
E	4	5	The 4th kg of fish = 4 kg vegetables
F	5	0	The 5th kg of fish = 5 kg vegetables

We can express opportunity cost in terms of vegetable production foregone for *each additional kilogram* of fish, as shown in the table. Alternatively, we can calculate the opportunity cost of *any given amount* of fish production. For instance, the table shows that the opportunity cost of the third kilogram of fish production is 3 kg of vegetables, while the opportunity cost of 3 kg of fish production is 6 kg of vegetables, because if the entire 3 kg of fish had not been produced, vegetable production could have been 15 kg rather than 9 kg.

To calculate the opportunity cost of anything, ask yourself, "What could have been produced instead of it?" For instance, the opportunity cost of building a $15 billion oil and gas pipeline is not the $15 billion, but rather the other products (housing, roads, machinery and so on) that could have been produced by the inputs used to produce the pipeline. And, to a student, the opportunity cost of riotous living on the weekend could be viewed as the 16 extra marks that he or she could have obtained on the economics test on Monday if the time had been spent studying.

duction and into our least efficient use in fish production. As a result of these factors, the production-possibilities curve is not a straight line, which would reflect a constant trade-off between fish and vegetable production, but rather a curve which reflects *changing efficiencies* and trade-offs.

We have used a very simplified situation, involving a production-possibilities curve for only two products, in order to illustrate the basic nature of the problem of scarcity. While the real world is much more complex, involving many more inputs and outputs, the basic reality shown by our simple production-possibilities curve still exists. Because our economic resources are limited, our output of goods and services is also limited, and society must somehow make choices between various goods and services: we cannot have as much of everything as we would like.

EFFECTIVENESS AND EFFICIENCY

Because we cannot have everything that we would like, it is very important that we use our scarce economic resources wisely. This brings us to the concepts of *effectiveness* and *efficiency*. These are the two most basic measures of the performance of any economic operation, from an individual business to a nation's entire economy.

- **Effectiveness** relates to performing a task well, in the sense of meeting your objectives. For instance, if the objective of a business is to produce top-quality running shoes for the elite athlete and that business' shoes sell well in this particular market, it is considered "effective." On the other hand, if another business has the objective of producing low-quality, low-cost running shoes for the "low end" of the market and that business' shoes are among the best sellers in that particular market, it is also considered to be "effective."

  When we speak of an entire economy rather than a single business, the concept is broader but basically the same—if the economy produces goods and services that are needed and wanted, it is said to be "effective."

- **Efficiency** refers to using the economic resources available to you to produce a *high volume of output at a low production cost per unit*. The most common measure of efficiency is "productivity," or output per worker. Societies with efficient economies that produce a high volume of goods and services per worker tend to have a high material standard of living, or consumption per person.

To recap, it is important that an economy be *both* effective *and* efficient. The more efficiently and effectively a society uses its economic resources, the more successful it will be in making available to its people larger volumes of goods and services that are needed and wanted and at lower prices. As a result, its people will enjoy a higher material standard of living.

The three basic questions of economics

As we have seen, the task of any economic system is to use its scarce economic resources efficiently and effectively, so as to best satisfy the needs and wants of its people. Since economic resources are scarce and we cannot have everything that we want, we are forced to make certain very basic choices:

- What goods and services should we produce?
- What production methods should we use to produce them?
- How should we divide up our output of goods and services among ourselves?

These are the three most basic economic questions that every society must face, regardless of whether it is capitalist or communist, industrialized or developing.

(A) WHAT TO PRODUCE?

Because economic resources, or productive inputs, are scarce, no society can have all the goods and services it would like to have. Instead, it must *make choices*, or set priorities. For example, the people in our desert-island mini-society would have to decide whether to produce fish, vegetables, shelter, nets, spears, traps, plows or other things that they want.

Because economic resources are scarce, these choices will not be as easy to make as they might seem at first. If we decide to use people to farm vegetables, those people will not be available to catch fish or build shelter. Thus, a decision to produce more of one thing necessarily means accepting less of other things. This forces us to set priorities, or decide what is most important to us. Obviously, this relates to the goal of effectiveness as discussed in the previous section, because the priorities we set will reflect our needs and wants, or how useful each product is to us.

Consumer goods versus capital goods

One of the most basic "what to produce" decisions that must be made is whether *consumer goods* or *capital goods* will be produced. Consumer goods (such as food, clothing and automobiles) can be enjoyed now, but are used up quickly and do not contribute to longer-term economic prosperity. Capital goods (such as tools and equipment), on the other hand, provide less immediate enjoyment but will contribute to society's production and prosperity in the future, by increasing our productivity for the many years that they will last. Figure 2-5 illustrates this choice.

These decisions will have a crucial influence on the prosperity of a society both in the present and in the future. If our desert-island mini-society emphasizes the production of consumer goods, its people will enjoy a higher standard of living in the present. However, if they emphasize consumer-goods production to the point of neglecting capital-goods production, they

FIGURE 2-5   *Consumer Goods and Capital Goods: the Choice*

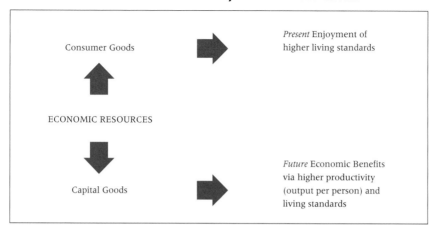

will enjoy less prosperity in the future. On the other hand, if its people are willing to do with fewer consumer goods in the present in order to build more capital goods, they can look forward to higher levels of economic prosperity in the future. Over the past few decades, Japan and Germany are noted for placing a high emphasis on building capital goods for the future, while North America has tended to place a greater emphasis on consumer goods and services for enjoyment in the present.

(B) HOW TO PRODUCE IT?

Once we have decided *what* we want to produce, we must decide *how* each product or service is to be produced. This is a question of production methods: how should we combine our scarce inputs of labor, capital equipment and land for use in production?

As a simple example, suppose our desert-island mini-society has decided to produce (cultivate) vegetables. The next question is, how should it do this? Should it cultivate them by hand? Or use simple tools such as hoes? Or more sophisticated equipment such as plows? Before the vegetables that we want are produced, we will have to make a decision about how to produce them.

Generally speaking, production methods that result in higher output per worker (productivity) will prove beneficial to a society's economic prosperity. However, the decision may become more complicated if we need to use economic resources to build capital equipment in order to increase output per worker. Obviously, in deciding the answer to this question, we are pursuing the goal of efficiency as discussed earlier. By being efficient, we avoid wasting our scarce economic resources, and thus increase our economic prosperity.

This search for efficiency can lead in quite different directions under different circumstances. For example, farming in North America uses a great deal of capital equipment and very little labor, while farming in Southeast Asia uses a great deal of manual labor and very little capital equipment. Yet both production methods make economic sense, because labor is relatively scarce and thus costly in North America while capital equipment is scarce and labor is plentiful in Southeast Asia. So both production methods are "efficient," in the sense that they economize on the use of those inputs which are most scarce relative to the others: capital equipment in Asia and labor in North America.

Thus, production methods vary greatly from product to product and from economy to economy; some are almost completely manual while others are almost totally automated. In general, we try to use inputs in the most efficient way possible, so as to get the *maximum output per unit of input*. This avoids wasting our scarce inputs and thus increases our economic prosperity.

(C) WHO GETS HOW MUCH? (HOW TO DIVIDE UP THE "ECONOMIC PIE"?)

The final basic question is this: how will our mini-society divide up our output of goods and services among its members? Who will receive what share of the output?

Should everyone receive the same share? Or should some people receive more than others? If some are to receive a larger share, why should this be the case? Should each person get only as much as he/she produces? But what if some people cannot produce enough to survive without help from the others? But if we take too much from the most productive people in order to help the less productive ones, might the productive people lose their incentive to produce and contribute, leaving us all worse off?

This question is also known as "how to divide up the economic pie?" It is certainly the most controversial of the three basic economic questions. Somehow, our mini-society must find an answer to this question, as must every society.

In a modern economy such as Canada's, this question becomes somewhat more complex than in our desert island mini-society. A person's share of the "economic pie" depends on his or her *income*. If an accountant's income is twice as large as a laborer's, the accountant's share of the economic pie will be twice that of the laborer.

But how should a society *decide* who gets what share of the pie? Should hockey players receive a larger share than doctors? Should lawyers have larger share than social workers? Should teachers get a larger share than nurses? Somehow, every society has to work out the question of how to divide up the economic pie.

Answering the three questions

In this chapter, we have considered the three basic questions of economics that every society must answer—what to produce, how to produce it and how to divide up the economic pie.

Different societies answer these questions in very different ways. In the next chapter, we will examine the different types of economic systems that exist, and how these systems deal with the basic questions.

DEFINITIONS OF NEW TERMS

Economics The study of the decisions a society makes regarding the production of goods and services and the division of these among its people.

Inputs Economic resources such as labor, capital equipment and natural resources that are used to produce goods and services.

Labor The largest single productive input available to any economy, labor includes all of the productive talents of the people of a society, mental as well as physical.

Capital (Equipment) The tools, equipment, machinery and factories used by labor to increase production per person and, thus, living standards.

Land Short form for all the natural resources available to a society's economy as economic inputs.

Output The goods and services produced by a society using its productive inputs.

Scarcity The problem that, while economic inputs (and thus potential output) are limited in availability, people's wants and needs are apparently unlimited.

Production-Possibilities Curve A graph showing the maximum possible output of one product that can be combined with any given output of another product, assuming full and efficient utilization of all available productive inputs.

Opportunity Cost The concept that the real economic cost of producing something is the foregone opportunity to produce something else that could have been produced with the same inputs.

Effectiveness A measure of how well the goods/services produced meet the needs/wants of people—a "quality concept," in the sense of usefulness.

Efficiency A measure of the volume of goods/services produced relative to the inputs used to produce them—a "quantity concept."

CHAPTER SUMMARY

1. The basic task of an economic system is to use its productive *inputs* (labor, capital equipment and land) to produce goods and services so as to satisfy the wants and needs of the people of the society.

2. This task encounters the problem of *scarcity*: whereas society's economic resources are limited in quantity, people's wants and needs are apparently unlimited; thus, not all wants and needs can be satisfied.

3. The task of an economic system, then, is to make the best possible use of its scarce economic resources by providing answers to the following three questions:

   (a) *what* to produce

   (b) *how* to produce it, and

   (c) *how to divide it* among the people so as best to satisfy the needs and wants of the society.

QUESTIONS

1. In the affluent society of Canada today, have we overcome the problem of scarcity or do we still face it?

2. Of the three productive inputs (labor, capital and land), which is the most important today? Which is gaining in importance the most rapidly?

3. In some societies, old people who are unable to work any longer are left to die. What might explain such a custom?

4. How does the custom referred to above compare to Canada's attitudes toward those who are unable to support themselves? What might explain this difference?

5. It has been suggested that the highest paid people in industry and government should receive no more than two-and-a-half times as much take-home pay as the lowest-paid workers. Do you agree with this suggestion? Why? What do you believe would happen if such a policy were implemented?

6. Following is a table showing the production possibilities for widgets and reemistrams.

Combination	Number of Widgets	Number of Reemistrams
A	0	20
B	1	18
C	2	14
D	3	8
E	4	0

What is the opportunity cost of producing:

(a) the first widget?		**(e)**	three widgets?
(b) the second widget?		**(f)**	the fourth widget?
(c) two widgets?		**(g)**	four widgets?
(d) the third widget?			

7. While all economic resources are scarce in the sense of being in limited supply, the problem of scarcity is particularly dramatic when the physical amount of a resource is actually diminishing, as with some agricultural land.

   According to a government inventory of Canada's land resources carried out in the 1960's and 1970's, only 11 percent of Canada's land is capable of sustaining agriculture of any kind, less than 5 percent is capable of sustaining crops and less than 0.5 percent is valuable, class-one land capable of sustaining the whole range of Canadian crops. Thirty-seven percent of Canada's class-one agricultural land and 25 percent of the nation's class-two land can be seen from the top of Toronto's CN Tower. Under pressure of "urban sprawl," this prime agricultural land continues to be converted to residential, commercial and industrial uses.

   (a) Why does this high-quality agricultural land continue to be converted to other uses?

   (b) Should the government permit this to happen?

   (c) What could be done to arrest this trend and protect our agricultural land?

8. The following table shows production possibilities for two commodities—fradistats and kadiddles.

Combination	Fradistats	Kadiddles
A	0	6
B	8	5
C	15	4
D	21	3
E	26	2
F	30	1
G	33	0

   (a) What is the opportunity cost of producing:

   (i)   the first kadiddle?

   (ii)   the second kadiddle?

   (iii)   the third kadiddle?

   (iv)   the fourth kadiddle?

   (v)   the fifth kadiddle?

   (vi)   the sixth kadiddle?

   (b) Draw the production-possibilities curve for fradistats and kadiddles on a graph, placing kadiddles on the vertical axis and fradistats on the horizontal axis.

(c) If the economy achieved greater efficiency in the production of kadiddles, how would the production-possibilities curve change?

(d) If a more efficient method of producing fradistats were developed, how would the curve change?

(e) Suppose more economic resources (labor, materials and capital) became available. How would the curve change?

9. Fred's Fradistats Ltd. can produce fradistats using either of two production methods: manual or mechanized. Using the manual production method, 10 employees are required, working 8 hours per day at $10 per hour. Overhead costs (rent, office, etc.) are $200 per day and material costs are $5 per fradistat. The manual method produces 50 fradistats per day.

   Using the mechanized production method, 5 employees are required, working 8 hours per day at $10 per hour. Overhead costs (rent, office, etc.) are $200 per day and material costs are $5 per fradistat. Depreciation expenses on the fradistat-forming machine are $300 per day and the machine uses $150 of energy per day. The mechanized production method also produces 50 fradistats per day.

   (a) Use the table below to calculate the cost of producing each fradistat using each of these two production methods.

	Manual Method	*Mechanized Method*
Labor cost per fradistat	$	$
Material cost per fradistat		
Overhead cost per fradistat		
Depreciation cost per fradistat		
Energy cost per fradistat	_____	_____
Total cost per fradistat	$_____	$_____

   According to the above figures, which production method would be chosen as the most efficient method?

   (b) Suppose wage rates increased to $12 per hour. What effect would this have on:

   (i)   production cost per unit under the manual method.

   (ii) production cost per unit under the mechanized method.

   (iii) the choice of production methods.

   (iv) the number of workers employed.

   (c) Suppose wage rates were still $10 per hour and energy prices declined by 40 percent. What effect would this have on:

   (i)   production cost per unit under the manual method.

   (ii) production cost per unit under the mechanized method.

   (iii) the choice of production methods.

   (iv) the number of workers employed.

(d) Suppose a new fradistat-forming machine is developed which still requires 5 workers, costs twice as much as the old machine (making depreciation expenses $600 per day), uses $320 of energy per day (compared with $150 for the old machine), and produces 80 fradistats per day. Would it be economical for the company to introduce the new machine?

(e) Sections (b), (c) and (d) show that the most efficient production method depends on _____ , _____ , and _____ .

10. The text notes that over the past few decades, Japan and Germany have emphasized the production of capital goods more than North America, which has stressed consumer goods and services more. What would be some of the implications of this situation for these countries?

Types of economic systems

In Chapter 2, we identified the three basic economic questions faced by any society: what to produce, how to produce it, and how to divide it up. In order to focus on these basic problems, we placed ourselves in a desert island setting. However, identifying our three basic economic problems is only the first step—next, we will have to devise an *economic system* to decide the answers to these questions. There are only two basic types of economic systems: the **command system** and the **market system**. Actual "real world" economies are almost always some combination of the market and command systems, employing some features of each. In this chapter, we will first consider each of these systems in its "pure" form, then examine how the Canadian economy consists of some aspects of each.

The command system

The command system is a very *centralized* type of economic system, in which *decisions by the government* provide answers to all three of the basic economic questions. In our island mini-economy, it is fairly easy to envision an economy operating in this manner—the leader(s) of the group might take over the task of planning, directing and overseeing all economic activity. They would decide how much of various types of consumer and capital goods to produce, the production methods to be used in producing each and how the output would be divided up among the islanders, as shown in Figure 3-1.

The command system has certain attractions in a situation such as our desert island mini-society. It offers a quick and seemingly simple and effective way to organize resources and people's economic activities according to a plan. The very concept of a plan is attractive, as it seems to provide order to the complex tasks of deciding how best to utilize soci-

FIGURE 3-1   *The Command System*

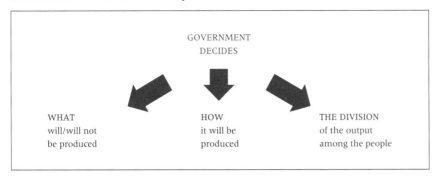

GOVERNMENT
DECIDES

WHAT
will/will not
be produced

HOW
it will be
produced

THE DIVISION
of the output
among the people

ety's scarce economic resources and determining what to produce, how
to produce it and how to share it among the people. In short, the government makes the basic economic decisions, and requires the people to follow these decisions, for their own economic benefit.

PRACTICAL EXPERIENCE WITH THE COMMAND SYSTEM

Actual experience with command systems has been considerably more
complex—and less favorable—than this simple introduction suggests. In
a large, modern industrialized economy, centralizing all major economic decisions through a "command" system is a much more complex task, which
tends to reveal some of the command system's weaknesses.

In the Soviet Union, after the Bolshevik Revolution of 1917, the
Communists established what became the world's most famous command
economic system. The "what to produce" question was decided by government central economic planners. All production facilities (factories,
farms, mines and so on) were owned by the state, and each produced according to *production quotas* determined by the government's central economic planners, in conjunction with a grand economic plan covering the
entire economic system. The production methods and technology in each
enterprise would be determined by the planners, thus answering the "how
to produce it" question. And, finally, since virtually everyone worked for
the state, the central economic planners also decided the incomes that various types of workers would receive, and thus decided how the economic
pie would be divided among these groups. For instance, if the planners
decided that skilled trades workers would be paid twice as much as nurses,
a skilled trades worker's "share of the pie" would be twice as large as a
nurse's share.

Until the late 1960's, the Soviet economy was regarded as the most
outstanding example of the successes possible under a command system.
After that, however, the Soviet command system encountered such increasingly severe problems that it was in effect abandoned in the late

1980's. In examining the Soviet experience, we can gain considerable insight into the strengths and weaknesses of the command system.

ASSESSMENT OF THE COMMAND SYSTEM

In Chapter 2, we saw that the two basic measures of economic performance are *effectiveness* (whether the system produces goods and services that are wanted and needed) and *efficiency* (whether the system produces goods and services in large volumes and at a low cost per unit). We will use these two criteria to assess the performance of the command system, using the Soviet economy for illustrations.

Effectiveness of the command system

With respect to effectiveness, the command system can be regarded as successful in some ways and unsuccessful in others.

From the viewpoint of the government, it can be argued that the command system is quite effective. Because the government controls the economy, it is able to direct economic resources toward goals that it considers important.

The single greatest achievement of the Soviet Union's command system was the transformation of a less developed nation into an industrial power in a remarkably short period of time. The command system could achieve such rapid industrialization because the economic planners could dictate that great emphasis be placed on producing the capital goods (basic industrial facilities, factories, machinery, and so on) that were required for industrial development. Of course, there was another side to this. Because economic resources are limited, the devotion of so many resources to the production of *capital goods* necessarily meant that there must be low levels of *consumer-goods* production, and therefore a low material standard of living for the people.

Other aspects of the economy that were given high priority by the government were military equipment, the space program and athletics and culture, because of their contribution to Soviet national security and world image. Again, the emphasis on each of these was at the expense of consumer-goods production.

With respect to consumer goods, however, the Soviet command system was far from effective. By this, we are not referring to the volume of consumer-goods output, which was low because consumer goods were not a priority of the government. Rather, it is a question of the quality and usefulness of the consumer goods that the command system did produce. Soviet consumer goods were characterized by low quality, poor design, limited variety and limited selection of sizes.

Probably the main reason for this was that plant managers had to please the government economic planners rather than consumers. Faced with the imperative of meeting their production quotas in the face of scarce resources, plant managers sacrificed product quality and variety in order to

> A completely planned economy ensures that when no bacon is delivered, no eggs are delivered at the same time.
>
> Popular Soviet joke

produce the number of products required by their quotas. And if quotas were expressed in terms of weight, plants would produce products such as massive chandeliers and huge armchairs that were of little use to consumers but met the weight quotas set by the planners. And, since most enterprises were state-owned monopolies, they did not have to worry about pleasing the consumer, who had no competing producers as alternatives. As a result, serious flaws in products could go uncorrected for years.

Another problem was the inability of the central economic planning system to cope with the task of planning, directing and coordinating the production and distribution of the vast number of products of a modern industrial economy. While central planning was able to direct the development of the basic industrial facilities of the Soviet Union in the late 1920's and 1930's, the planning and coordination of the millions of products associated with a modern economy is an infinitely more complex task. The task was made more difficult by the fact that the economy's output included many more consumer goods, which by their nature are less suited to planning by a central authority than are basic industrial projects. It is easier to use central planning for goods to be bought by one government than it is for goods that are to be bought by tens of millions of consumers.

As a result, the Soviet economic planning system had increasing difficulty coping with the tremendously complex task of coordinating all aspects of a large modern industrial economy, and increasingly tended to make errors. These errors ranged from the production of large numbers of eyeglass lenses but no frames for them to long delays in the opening of a major electrical generating plant due to the omission of a few vital components. Planning problems were particularly persistent in the consumer-goods sector of the economy because the planners were unable or unwilling to anticipate or cater to consumer preferences. As a result, despite the general shortage of consumer goods, and severe shortages of some, the system produced many consumer goods that were so inappropriate or of such poor quality that consumers would not buy them. Such problems constituted a serious misuse of scarce economic resources.

> The latest index of products has twenty million articles. The plan can't detail that amount.
>
> Official of Gosplan, the Soviet State Planning Committee

Not only were such planning problems quite common; they were also difficult to correct. A master economic plan for a nation is an incredibly complex document that must be drawn up for a considerable period of time (at least one year), making it very rigid. The complexity of the plan causes errors to be quite frequent, while its rigidity makes it difficult if not impossible to correct the errors promptly. This was a fundamental problem of the command system with which Soviet authorities wrestled unsuccessfully for many years.

Efficiency of the command system

Inefficiency is a major weakness of command economies, mainly due to a *lack of incentives*. Workers, including managers, are all in effect government employees who lack incentives to become more efficient. In addition, with most enterprises being government-owned monopolies, the Soviet economy lacked the *competition* that pushes producers to become more efficient. Finally, the command system lacks a *profit motive*—even if an enterprise were to become more efficient and earn a profit, it would have to turn it over to the government. Worse yet, the government would very likely cut that enterprise's budget for next year, on the grounds that because it had earned a profit, its budget must have been too large. As a result of all of these factors, productivity (output per worker) and living standards tend to be low in a command economy.

> We've got the perfect economy. We pretend to work, and they pretend to pay us.
>
> Popular Soviet joke

THE COMMAND SYSTEM IN PERSPECTIVE

The Soviet command economy was characterized by a tremendous unevenness in its performance—rapid industrial growth, great military power, outstanding achievements in space and world-class athletic and cultural performances, contrasted with low living standards, lineups and waiting lists for consumer goods of limited quantities and low quality.

The command system is capable of directing economic resources toward the achievement of the state's goals, such as industrial development, national security and national image. However, the command system has proven to be both ineffective and inefficient in its use of economic resources, mainly because it lacks incentives for enterprises, managers and workers to produce what consumers want and to produce it efficiently. Finally, central economic planning systems tend to have difficulty coping with the volume and complexity of the decisions to be made in a large modern economy. Errors inevitably occur and proliferate, and, due to the rigidity of the plan, the system is slow to correct its errors.

By the 1960's, the weaknesses of the Soviet command system were becoming increasingly apparent, and in the 1970's these became severe. In the mid-1980's, in a belated attempt to deal with these economic problems, the Soviet Union introduced a sweeping reform program intended to invigorate the Soviet economy by reducing the amount of central economic planning. In its place, there was to be a more decentralized system of economic decision-making, in which consumers and plant managers played a larger role. The reforms also included the introduction of elements of private enterprise, in the form of small businesses and increased financial incentives for employees and managers, to promote efficiency. The reforms included many of the characteristics of the market system

KARL MARX (1818–1883)

Karl Marx was a German philosopher who began studying economics seriously after moving to London in 1849, when he became a prominent member of the British classical school of economics. His theories have always been highly controversial.

Marx's views were undoubtedly influenced by the era in which he lived and wrote—the period of the Industrial Revolution, with its extreme exploitation of labor. In his labor theory of value, Marx turned the predominant economic theory of the day—that the value of goods is mainly determined by the amount of labor required to produce them—against capitalism itself, attacking it at its very base.

Marx argued that because labor was the source of economic value, workers should receive the entire value of the products they produced. So, where capitalists view profits as a necessary and justifiable incentive, a reward to producers for supplying desired commodities, Marx viewed them as a surplus value gleaned from the unfair exploitation of other people's labor.

Marx developed an extensive definition of social class, and claimed that, since the capitalist system relied on the exploitation of a particular group (workers), class differences and inequalities could never be abolished under capitalism. In the increasing alienation of workers from owners, Marx foresaw the seeds of a possible socialist revolution, in which the working class would take over the means of production and the economic planning for the whole state, to the equal benefit of all members of the society.

Unfortunately, Marx never set down his ideas on exactly how a post-revolutionary socialist economy would operate. Nevertheless, his ideas have inspired many to attempt to work out a systematic approach to a state-run economy, usually with limited success. Where communist revolutions did occur, the societies were usually agrarian, rather than industrial in nature, and used communism and economic planning to build an industrial state.

which is discussed in the following section. However, before the reform process was complete, the Soviet command system virtually collapsed, and its accompanying system of totalitarian government under the communist party did collapse, as did the Soviet Union itself, which fragmented into a number of separate nation-states.

The market system

Under the command system, all economic decisions are made by the government, in a highly *centralized* manner. The market system operates in a completely different way, with no central government planning or control. Instead, economic decisions are made in a *decentralized* manner, by consumers and producers.

WHAT IS A "MARKET"?

Simply stated, markets are where buyers and sellers come together to exchange goods and services for money, or to buy and sell things. Figure 3-2 illustrates this concept a little more formally, using the market for fradistats as an example.

Figure 3-2 shows that the market for fradistats consists of:

(a) a number of sellers offering to sell fradistats, in competition with each other (economists call this the "supply side" of the market), and

(b) many buyers offering to buy fradistats, in competition with each other (economists call this the "demand side" of the market).

From the interaction between buyers and sellers in the marketplace emerges the price of fradistats ($5.00 each) and the sales of fradistats (100 per day). If the willingness of buyers to buy fradistats or the willingness of sellers to sell them were to change, the price and sales of fradistats would also change.

FIGURE 3-2 *The Market for Fradistats*

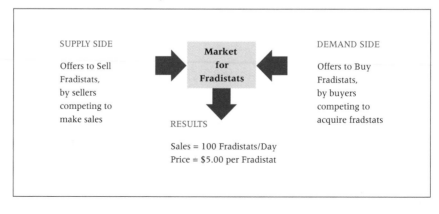

HOW DO MARKETS WORK?

Markets respond to changes in buyers' demand. For instance, if the demand for fradistats increased (because there were more buyers, or buyers had more money, or they just liked fradistats better than before), the increased demand would cause the price of fradistats to increase. This would make it more profitable to produce fradistats, so that more fradistats would be produced in response to the increased demand for them.

DEMAND ↑ → PRICE ↑ → AMOUNT PRODUCED ↑

Conversely, if the demand for fradistats were to fall, this would cause their price to fall, making it less profitable to produce them. As a result, producers would produce fewer fradistats, in response to the lower demand of consumers.

DEMAND ↓ → PRICE ↓ → AMOUNT PRODUCED ↓

Because demand is the most basic force in markets, the market system is sometimes said to be "demand-driven." And because of the key role played by prices and price changes in adjusting production to demand, the market system is sometimes referred to as the "price system."

HOW THE MARKET SYSTEM ANSWERS THE THREE QUESTIONS

The operation of the market system stands in strong contrast to the centralized decision-making of the command type of economic system. In a very decentralized way, without any direction or control from the government, the people of the community—as both consumers and producers—themselves provide answers to the three basic questions.

What to produce is ultimately decided by consumers. Since the fundamental goal of business is to earn a profit, businesses will produce those goods and services that are in demand. This process is described by the phrases "consumer sovereignty" (meaning that the consumer is viewed as "king of the marketplace") and "dollar votes" (meaning that the consumer's purchase of a product is, in effect, casting a vote for the production of that product).

How to produce it is decided by producers, or private businesses, who will strive for the most efficient possible method of producing the product. Lower

PRODUCTION METHODS IN THE CANADIAN ECONOMY

The production methods used in the Canadian economy vary widely, with the greatest degree of mechanization in "capital-intensive" primary industries such as prairie grain, forest products and mining. In the manufacturing sector of the economy, production methods range from technologically sophisticated automobile plants and steel mills to "labor-intensive" industries such as clothing and footwear, which use considerable amounts of labor. Generally, Canadian industries that are capital-intensive are best able to compete internationally, while labor-intensive industries suffer from competition from countries where wages are lower.

production costs mean higher profits, and, in a highly competitive industry, may mean survival. The most efficient method may change as the relative cost and productivity of various inputs changes. For example, rising wages may cause businesses to substitute capital equipment for labor, to "automate." On the other hand, if labor is inexpensive relative to capital equipment, a business would use less capital equipment and more labor in its production processes. Whatever the decision, in a market type of economy it is privately owned producers—businesses—that make the decision.

The *division of the economic pie* among various individuals and groups is influenced by many factors. Obviously, the larger one's income, the greater one's share of the economic pie will be. However, since your income is really the price of your services, the most basic factor here will be the interplay between the supply of and the demand for your productive skills. For example, if computer programmers are in short supply as compared to the demand for them, their incomes (and their share of the economic pie) will be quite high. In the case of low-skilled workers, on the other hand, there may be a very large supply of them as compared to the demand for them, causing them to have low incomes and a small share of the pie.

ASSESSMENT OF THE MARKET SYSTEM

As we did with the command system, we will evaluate the performance of the market system first according to the criteria of effectiveness and efficiency.

In a market system, both *competition* and the *profit motive* provide powerful incentives for producers to be both effective and efficient. With respect to effectiveness, there is no economic system that is more responsive to consumer demand than the market system, which is marvellously flexible in adjusting its production automatically to reflect changes in consumer preferences. And with respect to efficiency, no system provides greater incentives for efficient use of economic resources than the profit motive. Figure 3-3 summarizes the market system's powerful incentives for effi-

ADAM SMITH (1723–1790)

Adam Smith was a Scottish professor of moral philosophy who in 1776 wrote *The Wealth of Nations*, which was to become the most famous and enduring book in the (as yet not founded) field of economics. The essence of *The Wealth of Nations* was that economic liberty, in the form of sellers and buyers competing freely in the marketplace, was the best way to promote the general economic welfare of society. In perhaps the most famous quotation from the book, Smith said, "Every individual endeavours to employ his capital so that its produce may be of greatest value. He generally neither intends to promote the public interest, nor knows how much he is promoting it. He intends only his own security, only his own gain. And he is in this led by an invisible hand to promote an end which was no part of his intention. By pursuing his own interest he frequently promotes that of society more effectually than when he really intends to promote it."

Smith was very critical of monopolies, which restricted the competition that he saw as vital for economic prosperity. He also disliked government policies that protected the monopoly positions of some groups, such as apprenticeship laws restricting the entry of people into certain occupations. By showing how economic freedom could promote the interests of the general public, *The Wealth of Nations* became the rallying point for those who believed in economic liberty and free markets, unhampered by government regulation—that is, "laissez-faire" capitalism.

It is interesting that, more than 200 years after *The Wealth of Nations* was written, similar sentiments again became fashionable. After a long period of growing government regulation of business and the economy in North America, the trend after the mid-1980's was toward "deregulation," on the grounds that competition would promote efficiency and prosperity more effectively than an extensive system of government regulations.

ciency and effectiveness, which contribute greatly to productivity and prosperity.

Figure 3-3 also shows how the basic concepts of effectiveness and efficiency relate to the income statement and the profits of a business. A business that is effective in the sense of producing what buyers want will enjoy a high sales income. If that business is also efficient, it will have low production costs and other expenses. Thus, its profits represent an overall measure of the effectiveness and efficiency with which it uses its economic resources. The more effective and efficient a business is, the higher its profits will be.

On the other hand, the market system is not without its weaknesses and problems. One such problem is *economic insecurity*. Market economies tend

FIGURE 3-3   *Incentives in a Market System*

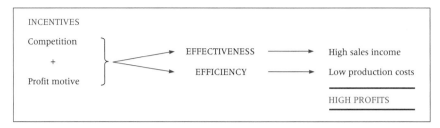

to slump into periodic **recessions**, during which the economy's output falls and unemployment rises. Another problem that can develop in a market system is *market power*, or the development of monopolistic power in some markets. Sometimes, producers may be able to band together and agree among themselves not to compete too strongly, with higher prices and profits the result.[1] To the extent that this happens, the consumer is dealing with an industry that is more like a **monopoly** than the competitive industries we have been describing. In a similar manner, some workers may be able to band together into labor unions that achieve essentially the same result—less competition and higher prices (wages) for their members. In both cases, an organized group (of businesses or workers) seeks to exercise what economists call "market power" by reducing competition for its own benefit at the expense of others. A third problem is the tendency in market economies toward great *inequalities in the division of the economic pie*, with a few people enjoying extremely high incomes while others live in poverty. These wide inequalities can be the result of the forces of supply and demand in labor markets (for example, brain surgeons as compared to retail clerks) and/or the result of the market power of some groups with high incomes.

HOW DOES THE MARKET SYSTEM ORGANIZE THE USE OF ECONOMIC RESOURCES?

On the face of it, the command system provides a highly organized approach towards using economic resources, with a central economic plan as the organizing and unifying force. By contrast, the market system appears quite disorganized—more like an economic "free-for-all" in which people buy whatever they want to, produce whatever they want to, work wherever they want to, and so on. Economic decision-making is spread among millions of consumers and producers in an apparently uncoordinated manner, rather than organized according to a plan. Yet, as we have seen, the market system performs much better than the command system with respect to the key criteria of effectiveness and efficiency, and provides a much higher **standard of living** for its people. What, then, are the forces within the market system that enable it to mobilize economic resources so much more effectively and efficiently?

The *profit motive* plays two vital roles in the operation of a market system. First, **profits** provide incentives for businesses to produce those goods and services that consumers want, and to produce them at the lowest possible production cost—that is, to use economic resources both effectively and efficiently.

The second important role of profits that they provide funds for the *purchase of capital equipment.* While businesses do this to improve their own efficiency and profitability, the result, on a wider scale, is improved productivity across the economy. This productivity is the basic source of higher living standards for society generally. Thus, reinvestment of profits by business makes an important contribution to a society's economic prosperity.

Despite this, there is a great deal of misunderstanding among the public concerning profits. The very word "profit" evokes for many people images of exploitation of workers and consumers. One misconception concerns the level of profits. According to surveys, the public believes that manufacturers' profits amount to 30 or 40 cents per dollar of sales, whereas before-tax profits are actually about 7 to 10 cents per dollar of sales, and after taxes, most manufacturers' profits amount to only 4 or 5 cents per dollar of sales. Ironically, the public believes 20 cents per dollar of sales to be a "fair" profit, indicating that there is a great deal of confusion regarding this matter.

The public also has many misconceptions concerning the uses of profits, which are widely regarded as being hoarded away in corporate coffers or being paid out lavishly as dividends to wealthy shareholders. In fact, roughly one-third of corporate profits goes to taxes and most of the remainder is

---

PROFITS: IT'S ALL IN HOW YOU LOOK AT IT

Suppose a corporation has annual sales of $600 million, profits after taxes of $24 million, 4000 employees and $300 million of shareholders' capital invested in the company.

From the viewpoint of the *employees*, it might seem that they are being underpaid. If the $24 million of profits were divided among them, each would receive $6000 more ($24 million ÷ 4000).

From the viewpoint of *consumers*, $24 million in profits might seem to indicate that they are being overcharged for this company's product. Realistically though, the total elimination of the manufacturer's profits would only reduce prices by 4 percent ($24 million ÷ $600 million).

From the viewpoint of the *shareholders* of the company, their capital invested in the company is earning a rate of return (after tax) of only 8 percent ($24 million ÷ $300 million). Compared to other investments, this is not an attractive rate of return.

Thus, while employees and consumers may complain about this company's high profits, investors could very well be deciding to sell their shares in the company.

reinvested by businesses in capital equipment. Dividends to shareholders generally amount to a modest return on their investment, and these "capitalists" include not only the wealthy but all Canadians who have money in pension funds, bank or trust company deposits, mutual funds and so on, because parts of these are invested in corporate shares. Because of the public's misconceptions about profits and the negative emotional overtones to the word, many companies prefer to call their profits "earnings."

Competition is the other key element in a market system. Competition plays three vitally important roles in a market economy. First, competition forces producers to be responsive to consumers—that is, to give consumers what they want, in order to increase their sales. In this sense, competition promotes effectiveness in the use of economic resources. Second, competition promotes efficiency in the use of economic resources. In order to be able to prosper in a competitive marketplace, a producer must be as efficient as possible, in order to keep production costs low. And third, competition forces producers to keep prices as low as possible, in order to compete successfully for business. Thus, competition ensures that the advantages of higher efficiency/lower production costs are passed

A baffling and contentious concept, profit has been the subject of debate, discussion and misunderstanding for centuries. Eminent men have variously extolled or denied its value to the community. Those who today consider profit as a "corporate rip-off" are, probably unknowingly, echoing the assertion of Michel de Montaigne, the 16th century philosopher, who said: "No man can profit except by the loss of others, and by this reasoning all manner of profit must be condemned." To this way of thinking, it follows, profit is by definition a "rip-off," and the profit motive nothing more than institutionalized greed and covetousness.

On the other side of the question, 19th century economist David Ricardo declared: "Nothing contributes so much to the prosperity and happiness of a country as high profits."

Reprinted from the Annual Report of the Royal Bank of Canada, 1974

THE MARKET AND COMMAND SYSTEMS COMPARED

To demonstrate the different ways in which the market and command systems operate, let's consider how each would address an everyday economic problem such as a shortage of bicycles. By a shortage of bicycles, we mean that at the current price, consumers are prepared to buy more bicycles than producers are manufacturing.

In a *market system*, as the demand outran the supply, the price of bicycles would increase, making it more profitable to produce bicycles. In response to this incentive, production of bicycles would increase, as existing manufacturers (and possibly new firms) increased their output. Manufacturers would order more bicycle parts from suppliers, who would order additional parts and materials as needed from their suppliers. At each stage of this process, decisions would be made by the business(es) involved, without central direction or control. The end result would be that, as quickly as possible, more bicycles would become available to consumers at the retail level, but at a higher price than before.

In a *command system*, changes would only be made if the central economic planners directed that this be done. We will assume that the planners have been made aware of the shortage of bicycles, although this is not a certainty, due to the lack of feedback from consumers in this system. The planners must then decide whether to increase bicycle production or not. Again, this is not a certainty—increasing the resources devoted to bicycle production means reducing the resources available for the production of other goods, and the planners may or may not decide that bicycles are sufficiently important to divert resources from other products to bicycles.

Assuming that the planners decide to increase bicycle production, they would have to re-do the economic plan for next year (at the earliest). They would have to instruct bicycle plants, through increased quotas, to produce more bicycles. (At the same time, they would have to reduce the quotas for those products of which less would be produced.) The quotas of all plants that supply parts to the bicycle plants would be increased, and instructions given as to how much of each part to deliver to each bicycle plant, as well as when and how the parts would be delivered. Similar adjustments would be made to the plans of all enterprises that supply parts and materials to the parts suppliers—quotas would have to be changed, and instructions for delivery provided. Increased numbers of workers would have to be allocated to each enterprise that required them under the new plan; again, the planners would have to decide which enterprises would lose workers due to the new emphasis on bicycles, and how the plans and quotas of these enterprises should be adjusted.

Finally, if there were any errors in these detailed plans, or any enterprise could not fulfill its quota, the entire plan to increase bicycle production could be jeopardized. For instance, a shortfall of rubber production could mean too few bicycle tires, as available rubber is allocated to higher-priority products such as army vehicles. To correct such problems would require changes to the plan for the next year, at the earliest, leaving manufacturers with many tireless bicycles for a year.

along to the consumer, so as to be enjoyed by the maximum possible number of people.

In summary, competition serves to "police" private profit-making producers so as to push them to serve the interests of consumers by being effective and efficient and by keeping prices down. By contrast, in situations in which there is little or no competition, producers tend to be less responsive to consumers' preferences, to become less efficient than they could be, and to charge consumers excessive prices. This can occur not only in industries in which there is only one producer (a monopoly), but also in some cases where there are only a few producers, who sometimes agree not to compete strongly against each other. In such situations, the advantage in the marketplace shifts from the consumer to the producers, who are said to possess "**market power**," or the power to raise their prices. Producers in this position will sometimes hold down the supply of a product in order to keep prices high.

Thus, the two incentives of profits and competition tend to push producers to use economic resources both effectively and efficiently. The ability of this economic system to automatically coordinate the decisions of millions of businesses and individuals in response to changes in consumer demand has been referred to as "the miracle of the market." Adam Smith, the earliest advocate of this system, described businesspeople as being led by an "invisible hand" (the profit motive) "to promote (the interest of) the society more effectually than when they really intend to promote it."[2] For these reasons, the most prosperous economies in the world are market economies, and several former "command" economies are seeking to either adopt key features of the market system or to convert entirely to it.

THE MARKET SYSTEM IN PERSPECTIVE

A basic difference between the market system and the command system is the high degree of *economic freedom* for both consumers and businesses in the market system. This freedom underlies the key strengths of the market system, such as the ways in which its incentives of the profit motive and competition drive producers to be both efficient and effective managers of economic resources. The result is that market economies tend to be the best at generating high levels of productivity and a high standard of living.

Ironically, this freedom also underlies the most serious weaknesses of the market system. Because consumers and businesses are free to spend—and not spend—as they see fit, there are times when spending is inadequate and the economy slides into recessions and high unemployment. Because producers are free to dominate industries and markets if they can, the problem of market power (or monopoly power) tends to arise in some situations. And, because individuals and groups are free to earn (take?) as big a share of the pie as they can get, some can wind up with a very large share and others with very little. These weaknesses of the market system may lead governments to take corrective action of various sorts, which brings us to the "mixed" type of economic system.

The "mixed" economic system of Canada

In the previous sections, the "command" and "market" types of economic system were described in their "purest" form. The command system was described as one in which the government made *all* economic decisions, while in the market system, government played *no* role at all. However, these were just models of the two basic *types* of economic systems, neither of which really exists in such a pure form. In the real world, countries' economies consist of some *combination* of "market" (or "free enterprise") and "command" elements.

Canada's economic system is best described as a "mixed free enterprise" system, because it contains a great deal of both "market" and "command" features.

Basically, and for the most part, Canada's economy is of a market nature. Most goods and services are produced by—and most Canadians work for—privately-owned businesses operating in a market environment, producing goods and services for sale at a profit. However, there are also extensive elements of government involvement, or the command approach, in the Canadian economy.

First, governments are major *providers of services* to the public. From education, health care and law enforcement to public transit and postal service, Canadian governments provide the public with a wide range of services. This is done in various ways. In most cases, such as health care, police protection and elementary and secondary education, the public pays for these services with its taxes. In effect, then, the government is buying these services collectively on the public's behalf, from the government employees and others (such as doctors) who provide the services. In addition, governments operate enterprises that provide services, including Crown Corporations such as Canada Post, the Canadian Broadcasting Corporation and Canadian National, and public commissions that provide services such as public transit and hydro electricity. In many cases, such as public transit and postsecondary education, governments subsidize public services. Such **subsidies** use tax revenues to pay part of the cost of the service, making the cost to the user lower. The grand total of these government-provided services is impressive—when the services of all government employees are counted as government purchases, Canadian governments buy about one-quarter of all the goods and services produced by the economy.

Second, governments *regulate* in many ways the operations and practices of businesses. For example, government laws or agencies set standards for many products, regulate advertising practices, set employment standards such as minimum wage rates and safety standards, set rules for the conduct of employer-employee/union relations, regulate the competitive practices of businesses, including the prohibition of monopolistic practices, and set environmental protection standards. In the case of some farm products, government marketing boards regulate the amount that farmers can produce. In addition, many prices are regulated by government, including electrical rates, tobacco and alcohol prices, some transportation rates and apartment rents in some areas. It has been estimated that about 25 percent of all the prices in the Consumer Price Index are government-regulated prices.

A third major area of government involvement in the economy is *redistribution of income* through programs that transfer income from those with higher incomes to those with lower incomes. Such programs include unemployment insurance, welfare, old age security allowances, assistance to farmers and other groups, and various features of the income-tax system (tax credits) that reduce the taxes payable by those with lower incomes.

Taken together, these amount to a great deal of government involvement in the economy, giving the Canadian economy substantial aspects of both the market and command systems and making the term "mixed free-enterprise system" an appropriate description of the Canadian economy.

The "traditional" system

To complete our discussion of economic systems, we should briefly consider the *traditional* system. Under this system, all economic decisions are made according to historic tradition. Today, this type of system is quite rare, existing mostly in tribal societies in remote regions, such as the Amazon region of Brazil. In such societies, a person's economic activities and status are dictated by tradition. People perform the same economic activities (hunting, fishing, cultivating) as their parents did, using the same production methods and dividing up the economic pie into the traditional shares for various groups. This is a very static economic and social system that is of little interest to economists.

DEFINITIONS OF NEW TERMS

Command System An economic system in which economic decisions are made mainly by the government, in a centralized manner.

Market System An economic system in which economic decisions are made mainly by consumers and privately owned producers, in a decentralized manner.

Profit(s) Those funds left from a business' sales revenues after all expenses have been paid; such funds are therefore available (after taxes have been paid) for dividends to shareholders and reinvestment in the business.

Standard of Living A measure of the economic prosperity of the people of a society, usually expressed in terms of the volume of consumer goods and services consumed per household or per person per year. Also referred to as *material* standard of living, because it ignores other factors that influence human welfare.

Monopoly The control of an industry or a market by a single seller.

Market Power The ability to raise one's price; usually associated with a dominant or monopolistic position in a market.

Recession A situation in which the economy is producing considerably less than its potential·output, and unemployment is high.

Subsidy Payment by the government of part of the cost of a service, so as to reduce the cost to the user of the service.

CHAPTER SUMMARY

1. There are two basic types of economic system—the command system and the market system.

2. In a command system, the government's central economic planners decide what to produce, how it will be produced and the division of the economic pie.

3. The main strength of the command system is its ability to concentrate economic resources on particular objectives, such as industrial growth, while its main weaknesses are inefficiency due to a lack of incentives and ineffectiveness due to a lack of responsiveness to the consumer and due to the errors and inflexibilities associated with the complex task of planning in detail the operations of an entire economic system.

4. The market system (also called the price system and the free enterprise system) operates in a decentralized manner, through markets. In these markets, what to produce is decided by consumer demand, how to produce it is decided by producers, and the division of the economic pie is decided by people's incomes.

5. Profits play a vital role in the operation of a market system. Profits provide incentives for the efficient and effective use of economic re-

sources and are a major source of funds for capital investment, which contributes to economic prosperity by increasing output per worker.

6. Competition is essential to the effective operation of a market economy. Competition polices producers, keeping prices and profits down and forcing producers to be both efficient and responsive to consumers.

7. The main strength of the market system is its high living standards, which are the result of the strong incentives this system provides for efficient and effective use of resources. The main weaknesses of the market system are its tendency toward periodic recessions, a lack of competition in some markets, and a tendency for incomes to be distributed very unevenly.

8. Canada's economic system is a mixed free-enterprise system: while it is basically a market or free-enterprise system, it includes significant elements of government involvement in the economy, or "command."

QUESTIONS

1. Three of the following are essential to the operation of a free-enterprise market economy. Which one might such an economy operate without?

   (a) the profit motive

   (b) markets

   (c) corporations

   (d) prices

2. Not all economists agree that we in North America have "consumer sovereignty." Some economists argue that big business is able to control the consumer to the point where the situation would be better called "producer sovereignty." Do you agree or disagree? Why?

3. Our economic system is not purely a free-enterprise market system because the government (command) is involved in the economic process to a significant degree.

   (a) Regarding the role of government as regulator of economic activity, what are some of the "rules of the game" that the government sets and enforces?

   (b) To what extent does the government (that is, command) play a role in deciding what to produce, how to produce it, and the division of the economic pie?

4. Do you agree with de Montaigne's statement that "No man can profit except by the loss of others, and by this reasoning all manner of profit must be condemned"? Does every economic transaction necessarily involve a winner and a loser?

5. If you were a government central economic planner in a "command" economy:

   (a) how would you make decisions about what to produce (and not to produce)?

   (b) how would you decide which consumer goods to produce (and not produce)?

   (c) how would you decide to divide the economic pie (that is, the wages and salaries to be received by each type of occupation)?

   (d) how would you encourage your workers and managers to work efficiently?

6. In the early 1990's, Russia faced the task of converting an economy that had been centrally planned for over 60 years to a more market-oriented system. What obstacles do you think Russian economic reformers would face in attempting such a basic change?

7. When the government subsidizes a service, it uses taxpayers' money to reduce the cost of that service to the people who use it. What justification might there be for using taxpayers' money to subsidize:

   (a) users of the Toronto Transit Commission?

   (b) students taking postsecondary education?

   (c) users of campsites at provincial parks?

   (d) a city's symphony orchestra?

NOTES

[1] This is most likely when there are only a few producers in an industry, making it more feasible for them to band together into an agreement.

[2] Adam Smith, *The Wealth of Nations* (1776).

Introduction to macroeconomics

The operation of a market system economy as described in Chapter 3 can be represented by the diagram in Figure 20-1.

The upper flows in Figure 20-1 represent markets for tens of thousands of different types of goods and services. In most such markets, products and services are bought and sold by millions of buyers and many sellers and producers. In microeconomics, we are concerned with the market for *each particular* good or service in this upper flow, and its price and the amount purchased. Thus, microeconomics may examine quite closely the market for wheat, or oil, or automobiles, or restaurants. In macroeconomics, we deal with similar matters but on a much broader scale—the *grand total* of all goods and services produced in the economy (which is known as the "Gross Domestic Product"), and the average level of the prices of these (the largest part of which is known as the "Consumer Price Index"). In other words, macroeconomics deals with the *total size* of the upper flow of goods and services in Figure 20-1, on an *economy-wide scale*.

Similarly, the lower flows in Figure 20-1 show producers, or businesses, buying the productive inputs that they need in order to produce the goods and services in the top flows. The most important of these productive inputs is labor, or the wide range of productive services needed by a modern enterprise, ranging from unskilled workers to skilled trades workers to professionals. The lower flows in Figure 20-1 show this wide range of productive skills being "sold" to businesses by the people who possess those skills, in exchange for wages and salaries. As with goods and services, there are markets for each type of labor, or each particular skill. Microeconomics examines the market for *each* of these skills, and the wage rate and the number of workers hired in each market. For instance, in microeconomics, we might study the market for part-time student labor, or

FIGURE 20-1 *The Operation of a Market Economy*

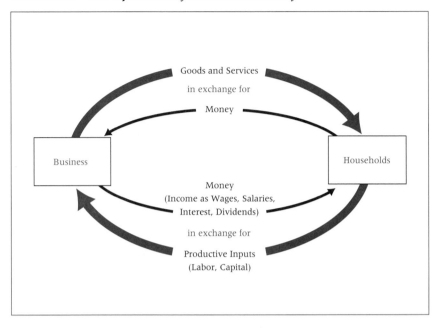

for skilled trades workers, or for computer programmers or for professional hockey players. Again, in macroeconomics, we are concerned with similar matters, but on a much wider scale—the levels of *total employment (and unemployment) and total incomes* in the economy as a whole, or the *total size* of these flows in the lower loop, on an *economy-wide scale*.

Markets on a microeconomic scale

Before considering these larger macroeconomic matters, we will briefly review the way in which markets operate on a microeconomic scale. In Chapter 3, we described markets for individual goods and services as consisting of:

- a **demand side**, or offers by buyers to purchase the item; and
- a **supply side**, or offers by sellers to sell the item, as shown in Figure 20-2.

The key to the demand side of the market is *the ability and willingness of buyers to purchase fradistats*, and the key to the supply side of the market is *the ability and willingness of businesses to produce fradistats and offer them for sale*. And it is the interaction of the demand side of the market and the supply side of the market that determines the price and the sales of fradistats, or any other good or service.

In a real sense, the most basic factor is the supply side's ability and willingness to produce fradistats, because if society is to *have* the volume of

FIGURE 20-2 *A Microeconomic Market*

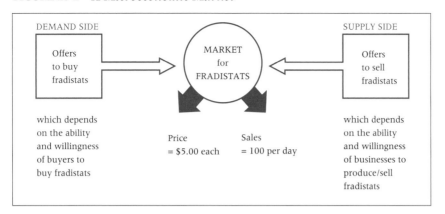

fradistats that it needs or wants, the fradistat industry will have to have the ability to *produce* them in sufficient volume and at a low enough production cost/price. In large part, this will depend on the amount and the quality of labor, capital equipment and other productive inputs that are available to the fradistat industry, although there are several other important factors, as we will see later.

However, the demand side of the market also plays a critical role. The key on the demand side is the ability and willingness of people to buy fradistats. If the demand for fradistats is low, production and prices will be low and fradistat workers will be laid off and suffer unemployment. Higher demand for fradistats would cause higher production, and more workers would be employed. And, if the demand for fradistats were so high that the producers could not keep up with it, the price of fradistats would rise rapidly.

Markets on a macroeconomic scale

In macroeconomics, we are concerned with how the economy operates on a much larger scale; that is, the grand total of all the goods and services produced in the whole economy rather than particular goods or services. However, the basic approach to analyzing macroeconomic issues is very similar to those used to deal with markets on a microeconomic scale. In both cases, the basic economic forces are supply and demand.

As with microeconomic markets, we can divide the economy on a macroeconomic scale into a *supply side*, in which the key is the ability and willingness of producers to produce goods and services and offer them for sale, and a *demand side*, in which the key is the ability and willingness of buyers to purchase goods and services. These are the same "supply side" and "demand side" forces that we saw in our microeconomic analysis, but on a much larger, economy-wide scale.

FIGURE 20-3   *Macroeconomic Supply Side Factors*

Skills and education of the work force
Quality of management
Quantity and quality of capital equipment
Incentive of economic gain
Incentive of competition

ABILITY/WILLINGNESS
TO PRODUCE GOODS AND SERVICES
EFFICIENTLY

On the *supply side*, we have to consider the ability and willingness of the entire economy—all producers, large and small, private and government—to produce goods and services efficiently. The key aspect on the supply side will be *productivity*, or output per worker in the economy as a whole. Thus, analysis of the supply side will take us into examining the skills of the nation's labor force, including its managers, the quantity and quality of its capital equipment, incentives such as economic gain (the "profit motive") and competition for both producers and individuals to be efficient, and various other factors. These are summarized briefly in Figure 20-3; we will consider them in detail in Chapter 22.

And on the *demand side*, on a macroeconomic scale we have to take into account the total of all spending on goods and services in the entire economy, by all buyers. For purposes of analysis, it is helpful to divide these buyers into four basic types: consumers, businesses, governments and foreign buyers. The total of spending o goods and services by all of these groups is known as "aggregate demand." This is summarized in Figure 20-4; we will consider these factors in detail in Chapter 23.

FIGURE 20-4   *Macroeconomic Demand Side Factors*

Consumer spending on goods and services
+ Business investment spending on capital goods
+ Government spending on goods and services
+ Foreign spending on Canadian goods and services

TOTAL SPENDING ON
("AGGREGATE DEMAND" FOR)
GOODS AND SERVICES

The operation of the economy on a macroeconomic scale

Figure 20-5 shows these "supply side" factors and "demand side" factors organized into what economists call a "model" of the economy.

While it is much larger and considerably more complex than the market for a single item, the macroeconomic model of the economy shown in Figure 20-5 operates in certain basic ways like the microeconomic markets covered earlier. For instance, if demand in the economy were low, output would be low and employment would be low—there would be a **recession**. If demand were to increase, output and employment would rise to high levels—there would be an **economic boom**. And if demand were to rise to such high levels that output could not keep up with demand, prices would rise rapidly—there would be **inflation**. Each of these situations is covered in much more detail in the chapters that follow.

AN ILLUSTRATION OF A SMOOTHLY FUNCTIONING MARKET SYSTEM

Figure 20-6 expands upon the concepts in Figure 20-5 to show the operation of a smoothly-functioning market system.

On the supply side of the economy, there is a strong ability to produce efficiently the goods and services that are in demand. The economy possesses all of the productive inputs necessary to produce goods and services efficiently: a capable labor force, good capital equipment and ample natural resources or raw materials. In addition, the economy provides producers with strong incentives to use these inputs as efficiently as possible,

FIGURE 20-5 *The Economy on a Macroeconomic Scale*

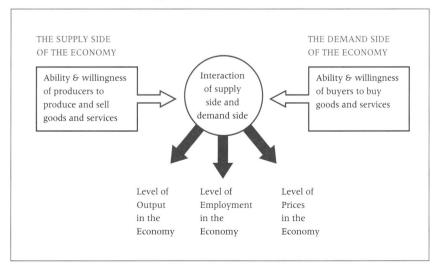

FIGURE 20-6 *A Smoothly Functioning Market System*

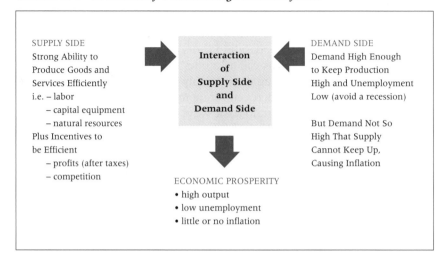

in the form of the "carrot" of profits (after taxes) and the "stick" of strong competition. In short, the supply side of the economy is capable of efficient and effective production. However, for the supply side to be able to achieve its potential, there has to be an appropriate level of demand.

On the demand side of the economy, what is an appropriate level of demand? This depends on the volume of goods and services that the supply side is capable of producing. If demand were well below this level, low sales would cause producers to reduce output and lay off workers. The economy would be producing less than it was capable of producing (its "capacity" output), factories and equipment would be idle and workers would be unemployed—there would be a **recession**. On the other hand, if demand grew too rapidly, the output of the supply side would be unable to keep up with demand. This would cause the prices of goods and services in general to rise very rapidly; that is, there would be inflation.

We have learned through hard experience that the extremes of both recession and inflation should be avoided if at all possible. Ideally, then, the amount of demand would be neither too low nor too high relative to the ability of the supply side to produce goods and services. In other words, the demand side would generate high enough demand to prompt the supply side to produce as much output as possible, but not excessive demand that will only cause inflation.

If the economy has a strong supply side and neither too little nor too much demand on the demand side, the results will be as shown at the bottom of Figure 20-6:

- high output of goods and services (i.e., at or near the economy's potential output),

- high levels of employment (or low unemployment), and

- little or no inflation.

Of course, market economies do not always perform as well as the smoothly-functioning economy shown in Figure 20-6. There are three basic types of problems that a market economy can develop:

- *weaknesses on the supply side* that prevent it from producing goods and services efficiently, such as a poorly-trained labor force or outdated capital equipment,
- *inadequate demand for goods and services* on the demand side, which will cause unemployment and a recession, and
- *excessive demand for goods and services* on the demand side, which will cause inflation (rapid increases in prices).

The problem of weaknesses on the supply side are covered in Chapter 22. The problems of inadequate demand and recessions are dealt with in Chapters 24 and 30, while excessive demand and inflation are the subject of Chapters 28 and 29.

Preview of macroeconomics

The organization of this part of the text follows the model of the economy shown in Figure 20-6. In Chapter 21, we will examine the goals that we want to achieve on a macroeconomic scale in terms of output, employment and inflation, and how we measure the economy's performance with respect to these goals. In Chapter 22, the supply side of the economy will be covered, and in Chapter 23 we will analyze the demand side of the economy. In the chapters that follow, we will examine the problems of recession and inflation, as well as government policies to deal with them. Finally, we will look at the importance of international trade to the Canadian economy, and Canadian trade policy.

DEFINITION OF NEW TERMS

Supply Side (on a Macroeconomic Scale) Consists of the production and offering for sale of goods and services in the economy as a whole; depends on the ability and willingness of producers in general to produce goods and services and offer them for sale.

Demand Side (on a Macroeconomic Scale) Consists of total spending on (demand for) goods and services in the economy as a whole; depends on the ability and willingness of buyers in general to purchase goods and services in general.

Recession A condition of low demand in the economy as a whole, the result being low output of goods and services and high unemployment.

Economic Boom A condition of higher demand in the economy as a whole, bringing output and employment to high levels.

Inflation A condition of excessive demand in the economy as a whole, the result being that output cannot keep up with demand, causing prices in general to rise rapidly.

CHAPTER SUMMARY

1. On a macroeconomic scale, the economy consists of:

   (a) a supply side, in which the key is the ability and willingness of producers to produce goods and services and offer them for sale, and

   (b) a demand side, in which the key is the ability and willingness of buyers to purchase goods and services.

2. Low demand on the demand side of the economy will cause output to be low and unemployment to be high, or an economic recession.

3. Higher demand will cause output and employment to be high, or an economic boom.

4. If demand were so high that output could not keep up with demand, the prices of goods and services would rise rapidly—there would be inflation.

QUESTIONS

1. From the information conveyed through the media, would you say that the Canadian economy is presently in a condition of recession, economic boom or inflation? On what specific information and facts did you base your conclusion?

Our basic economic objectives and how we measure them

Basic economic objectives

In the final analysis, economics is about people, and improving people's lives in material terms—jobs, incomes and goods and services to buy with them. Thus, in the most basic sense, the success of an economy can be measured in terms of how well it achieves the following three objectives:

- *Wealth creation*, as reflected in a high level of output. As we saw in the desert island economy of Chapter 3, the most basic task of any economic system is to provide its people with the goods and services that they need and want. Thus, a successful economy will produce goods and services both efficiently and effectively.

- *Job creation*, as shown by a low level of unemployment. Another fundamental economic objective is to provide jobs for people who want them, or "full employment." An economy with high unemployment is not only failing to meet this need of its people, but also is leaving unused a significant proportion of its most important economic resource—its people. Ever since the extremely high unemployment of the Great Depression of the 1930's, minimizing unemployment has been a high-priority economic objective.

- *Stable prices*, or a minimal amount of inflation. If the 1930's ingrained low unemployment as a basic economic objective, the experience of the 1970's established the dangers of allowing inflation to become too rapid, as we will see in Chapters 28, 29 and 31. Since this experience, the goal of minimizing inflation, or keeping prices as stable as possible, has gained considerable importance.

These three goals—high output, low unemployment and low infla-tion—are, of course, the three most basic ways in which we measured the performance of our ideal, smoothly-functioning economy in Chapter 20.

Economic statistics

The task of economic statistics is to keep track of how the economy is per-forming with respect to output, employment, inflation and a variety of other criteria. By providing up-to-date information as to the performance of the economy and economic trends, such statistics can be of consider-able assistance to policy- and decision-makers in business and govern-ment. A great number of economic statistics (relating to output, employ-ment/unemployment, prices/inflation, money supply and interest rates, productivity and costs, wage rates, government finances, exports and imports, flows of capital between nations and the value of nations' cur-rencies) are used to monitor the performance of the economy, depending on the particular matter of interest. In subsequent chapters, many of these statistics will be introduced as we look into different aspects of the economy. However, in this chapter we will consider only those that measure the economy's success in achieving the three objectives referred to earlier. These are:

- *Gross Domestic Product*, which measures the economy's output of goods and services,
- *the unemployment rate*, which measures the economy's success in providing jobs, and
- *the Consumer Price Index* and *the rate of inflation*, which measure the performance of the economy with respect to prices and inflation.

THE TASK OF ECONOMIC STATISTIC-GATHERING

In Chapter 20, we examined how markets work, as the supply of goods and services is produced by businesses to meet the demands of consumers. This economic activity produces macroeconomic flows of spending, goods and services between the business sector and the household sector of the economy, as shown by the upper loops in Figure 21-1. In addition, this activity generates employment and investment and flows of income (wages, salaries, interest, dividends) arising from these, as shown in the lower loops in Figure 21-1, Obviously, the more economic activity that is occur-ring within the economy, the more output will be produced, the more jobs there will be, the more income will be earned (and spent), and the greater the economic prosperity of the society will be. This will be reflected in larger flows of goods, services and incomes in Figure 21-1, and in the eco-nomic statistics used to keep track of these developments.

FIGURE 21-1 *Macroeconomic Flows in a Market Economy*

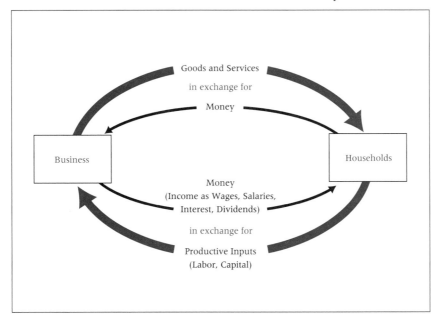

Goods and Services

in exchange for

Money

Business

Households

Money
(Income as Wages, Salaries,
Interest, Dividends)

in exchange for

Productive Inputs
(Labor, Capital)

431

*Our basic economic
objectives and how
we measure them*

Monitoring the performance of the economy in this way is not a simple task—it involves keeping track of the production and sale of hundreds of billions of dollars worth of countless numbers of goods and services and the prices of these, as well as the activities of a labor force consisting of about 14 million individuals.

Measuring output: Gross Domestic Product

Measuring the total flows of output and income in an economy is a massive task, and there are several statistics that can be used to do so. The most commonly-used of these is known as the **Gross Domestic Product** or **GDP**.

The Gross Domestic Product measures the grand total of economic activity across Canada by estimating the annual output of all the sectors of the nation's economy—consumer goods and services, capital goods, government goods and services, exports and imports. This includes a tremendous volume and diversity of goods and services. The only way to add together such a diversity of goods and services into a grand total is to add up their values, or prices, expressed in dollars. The total figure which results is the Gross Domestic Product, which is defined as *the market value of the total annual output of final goods and services produced in the nation.*[1]

Note that the Gross Domestic Product includes *final goods* only: it does not include goods that are used only as inputs in the production of other goods. An example of this distinction is the production of bread, as shown

FIGURE 21-2 *Intermediate and Final Goods*

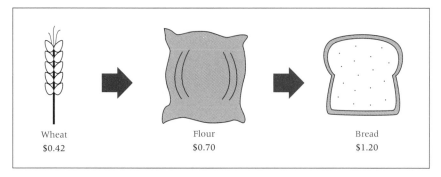

Wheat	Flour	Bread
$0.42	$0.70	$1.20

in Figure 21-2. The final good here is obviously the bread; the wheat and flour are only intermediate products which go into the production of the bread.

The contribution to GDP made by this process is obviously the value of the final product: $1.20. If we had counted the flour and wheat into the GDP, we would have concluded that the contribution to GDP was $2.32—almost twice the actual figure. The GDP would have been badly overstated because we had "double-counted" some items. To avoid double-counting, the GDP is calculated in such a way as to include only the final goods and services produced: in our example, only the value of the bread would be included.

SUBDIVISIONS OF GROSS DOMESTIC PRODUCT

The Gross Domestic Product consists of a vast number of diverse goods and services—all of the automobiles, televisions, haircuts, entertainment, houses, factories, machinery, roads, military equipment, police services, education, wheat, minerals, lumber and so on that are produced in one year. For purposes of understanding and analyzing these statistics, it is helpful to organize them into four major categories according to their destination, or purchaser.

(a) Consumption (C)

This category consists of all *consumer goods and services* purchased by households. This includes a wide range of items, from nondurable goods that are used up quickly, such as food and clothing, to durable goods such as cars and appliances that last several years, to services such as travel and entertainment.

(b) Investment (I)

This category of production includes all additions to society's stock of privately-owned capital equipment, buildings and inventories of products. The major part of the investment category is business spending on plant and equipment. Additions to business inventories of products and new housing construction are also included in the investment statistics.[2]

(c) Government (G)

Governments (federal, provincial and local) constitute another major purchaser of goods and services. Some of these purchases, such as police services, are of a *current consumption* nature because they are used up quickly. Others, such as schools and roads, are really *capital investment*, in that they build assets that provide social benefits over long periods of time. The government sector of the economy is also known as the "public sector."

(d) Net Exports (X – M)

So far we have accounted for all purchases by Canadian households (consumption, or **C**), business firms (investment, or **I**) and governments (government spending, or **G**). Now we must account for two facts arising from Canada's trade with foreign nations:

(i)   Products and services produced in Canada and sold to foreign buyers (Canada's exports) must be added to our figures.

(ii) Some of the Canadian purchases (C + I + G) that we have recorded include purchases of imports of foreign-made goods. While these were *purchased* in Canada, they were not *produced* in Canada. Therefore, these imports should not be included in Canada's GDP, which measures Canadian production.

To correct our GDP figures to allow for these effects of foreign trade, we must add to our C + I + G total the value of all Canadian exports (X) and *deduct* from our C + I + G total the value of all imports (M) purchased by Canadians. By making this adjustment, we ensure that we are measuring what was *produced* in Canada, as distinct from what was *sold* in Canada. The net effect of these adjustments (**X – M**) is called *net exports*. It may be a positive or negative factor, depending on the relative size of imports and exports in any particular year. This sector of the economy is also referred to as the "foreign sector."

CALCULATING GDP STATISTICS

There are two different approaches that can be used to calculate GDP statistics: the expenditures approach and the incomes approach.

The expenditures approach calculates GDP by adding up all the *expenditures* of consumers (C), businesses (I), governments (G) and the foreign sector (X–M) on goods and services. The result is expressed in the equation

$$GDP = C + I + G + (X - M)$$

The use of this approach is illustrated in the calculation of the statistics in Figure 21-3.

FIGURE 21-3 *GDP Statistics—Expenditures Approach*

	($ Billions)	1992
Consumption		
Consumer expenditure on goods and services		419.5
Investment		
Business investment in plant and equipment	69.4	
Residential construction	44.0	
Addition to inventories	−2.6	
Total investment		110.8
Government		
Government expenditure on goods and services		164.9
Exports and Imports		
Exports of goods and services	181.9	
Imports of goods and services	185.8	
Balance		−3.9
Gross Domestic Product		688.5

Note: Totals do not always add up because of statistical discrepancies.

Source: Department of Finance, *Economic and Fiscal Reference Tables,* August 1993

The second approach (the incomes approach) is based upon the fact that every expenditure included in the above approach represents an *income* to someone. That is, every cent that is *spent* on goods and services represents *income* received by someone—mostly the people and businesses involved in the production and distribution of the goods and services, but also to governments whose taxes are included in the price of the goods and services that have been bought. Thus, GDP statistics can also be calculated by adding up all of the incomes received in any given year. This approach is illustrated in Figure 21-4.

FIGURE 21-4 *GDP Statistics—Incomes Approach*

	($ Billions)	1992
Wages, salaries and supplementary labor income		$392.4
Corporation profits before taxes		31.9
Interest and miscellaneous investment income		56.5
Accrued net income of farm operators from farm production		3.7
Net income of non-farm unincorporated business including rent		37.1
Inventory valuation adjustment		−3.2
Indirect taxes less subsidies		84.8
Capital consumption allowances		82.4
Gross Domestic Product		$688.5

Note: Totals do not add up due to statistical discrepancies.

Source: Department of Finance, *Economic and Fiscal Reference Tables,* August 1993

These two approaches to calculating GDP reflect the fact that GDP statistics measure the total amount of economic activity in any given year, and that this activity can be looked at as either the *total output* produced or the *total income* received. The "statistical discrepancy" reflects the fact that because these are estimates of GDP for the year, they are not precise and do not exactly coincide with each other.

GROSS NATIONAL PRODUCT (GNP)

Until 1986, Statistics Canada used a different statistic, known as the **Gross National Product (GNP)**, as its measure of total economic activity. Since references are still made to GNP, we will examine the difference between GDP and GNP.

GDP measures the value of all goods and services produced in Canada—$688.5 billion in 1992. GNP measures the total income of Canadian residents, whether this income was earned in Canada or in other countries. The major difference between GDP and GNP arises from investment income (mostly interest and dividends) earned by Canadians on their investments in other countries and by foreigners on their investments in Canada.

This means, as Figure 21-5 shows, that to calculate the GNP we have to add to the GDP figure of $688.5 billion the $8.9 billion of investment income earned by Canadians on their investments abroad. However, the other side of this adjustment is that we must subtract the $33.1 billion of investment income paid to foreigners on their investments in Canada, because, while this income was earned in Canada (and counted in the GDP), it was earned by non-residents, not by Canadians. The result is a GNP of $664.3 billion, smaller than GDP by $24.2 billion, or the amount of net investment income paid to non-residents.

FIGURE 21-5 *Gross Domestic Product and Gross National Product, 1992*

	($ Billions)	
Gross Domestic Product		$688.5
+ Investment income earned by Canadians on investments abroad	$8.9	
− Investment income paid to foreigners on investments in Canada	−33.1	−24.2
= Gross National Product		$664.

Source: Department of Finance, *Economic and Fiscal Reference Tables,* August 1993

Due to the large amount of foreign investment in Canada, and the resultant large outflow of interest and dividends to non-resident investors, Canada's GNP is regularly slightly smaller than its GDP, as reflected in Figure 21-5. The GDP is considered to be a more complete measure of economic activity in Canada, because it includes all incomes earned in Canada, by both residents and non-residents. On the other hand, the difference between GDP and GNP is not large—in recent years, GDP has been larger than GNP by only about 3 or 4 percent. The main advantage in using GDP instead of GNP is that this is consistent with the practice in most other industrialized nations.

THE LIMITATIONS OF GDP STATISTICS

Gross Domestic Product and other economic statistics that measure the performance of the economy are followed closely by governments, business and the media. While these statistics are important, we should always remember that they do not represent a simple and perfect measurement of the nation's economic prosperity. Like any statistics, GDP figures have certain limitations, some of which are examined in the following sections.

(a) The problem of price changes

The main problem in using GDP at market prices as a measure of total output is that price changes tend to distort the figures. Since GDP is the sum of the price tags of all final goods and services produced, GDP statistics can rise for two quite different reasons.

(I) INCREASED PRODUCTION OF GOODS AND SERVICES (HIGHER "REAL OUTPUT") If society's *output* of goods and services rises, GDP will tend to rise. This is called "real economic growth," because the society has a higher level of real output (of goods and services) at its disposal.

(II) HIGHER PRICE LEVELS If the *prices* of goods and services rise, GDP will tend to rise too, because it is stated in terms of current market prices. For instance, suppose that real output were exactly the same as last year's level but the prices of all these goods and services were 8 percent higher—in such a case, the GDP would register an eight-percent increase over last year. This is obviously not "real economic growth"; in fact, real output has not increased at all. However, because the GDP is higher it *looks like* economic growth has occurred. Increases in the general level of prices such as this are called *inflation*, and cause the GDP in dollar terms to rise faster than the real output of goods and services is rising.

We call these inflated GDP statistics "GDP at market prices," or "money GDP." The problem with such statistics, as we have seen, is that they are not particularly meaningful. For instance, a 10 percent increase in money GDP could mean that:

(a) real output has risen by 10 percent and prices have not risen,

(b) prices have risen by 10 percent and real output has not risen, or

(c) both real output and prices have risen, with the combined effect of a 10 percent increase.

The key to interpreting money GDP figures is to know how much prices have risen—then we could readily estimate the increase in real output. For instance, if money GDP rose by 10 percent and prices rose by 6 percent, the increase in real output would be about 4 percent. The 4 percent increase in real output is a much more meaningful representation of the growth of the economy than is the 10 percent increase in money GDP. On the other hand, if prices had risen by only 3 percent, the same 10 percent increase in money GDP would mean that real output had risen by about 7 percent.

Thus, by adjusting money GDP statistics to eliminate the effects of price increases, we can develop a much more accurate statistic that measures only the real output of the economy and changes in it. This adjusted statistic is known by several names, including "**real GDP**," "GDP in constant dollars," and "GDP in 1986 dollars."[3]

Because prices have risen considerably since 1986, the statistics in Figure 21-6 show a considerable difference between the inflated money GDP figures and the adjusted real GDP figures in 1986 dollars.

FIGURE 21-6   *Money GDP and Real GDP, 1970–93*

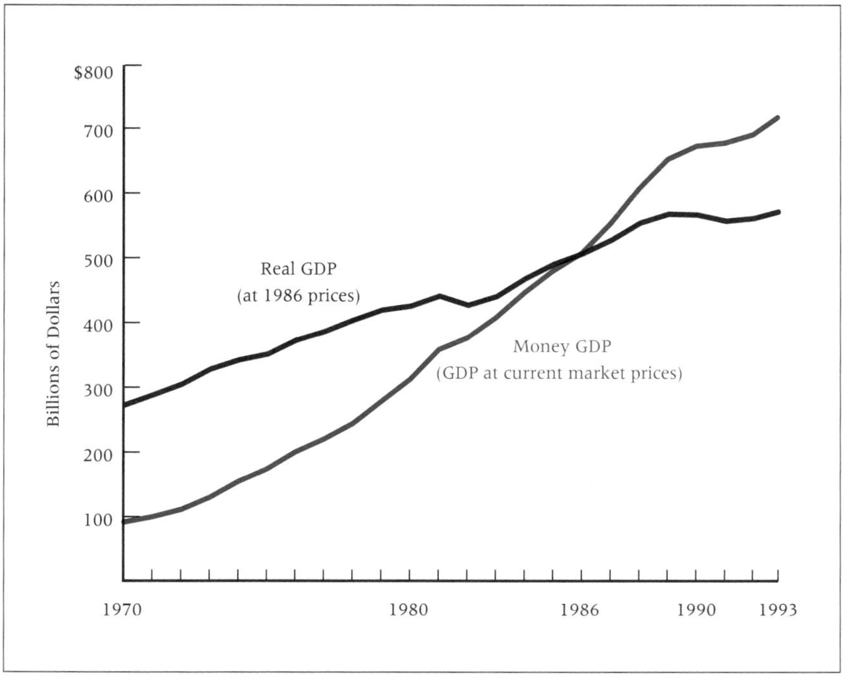

Source: Statistics Canada, *National Income and Expenditures Accounts* (13-001)

In reading and interpreting economic statistics, it is important to be sure whether you are using statistics that have been adjusted for the effects of inflation or not. Generally, the adjusted (real) statistics are more useful because they reflect the level of and changes in real production rather than price changes. For example, from 1990 to 1991, Canada's *money GDP* increased by $6.6 billion, or 1.0 percent—an apparent gain. However, *real GDP* actually fell by 1.7 percent ($9.6 billion) during the same period, indicating a serious economic recession. Because prices rose in 1991 the money GDP statistics made it look like economic gains had been made when in fact real output had fallen, as shown by the real GDP figures.

(b) GDP statistics omit many items

GDP statistics omit a considerable amount of economic activity, either because it is not reported or not marketed. For example, it is estimated that there is a significant "underground economy" in operation in which people buy and sell goods and services for cash (or even barter) in order to avoid paying income tax and the Goods and Services Tax. This underground economy is especially active with respect to many services, such as home contractors and repairs, hairdressers and auto repairs. While these services are rendered and paid for, they are not included in the GDP because the earnings from them are not reported to the government. The extent of this underground economy is unknown but is believed to be considerable—by some estimates, as much as 10–15 percent of GDP, or over $100 billion per year. Another major source of economic activity that goes unreported is income from illegal activities such as gambling, prostitution and the production and distribution of illicit drugs.

Another omission from GDP statistics arises from the fact that not all goods and services that are produced are marketed and, lacking price tags, such items cannot be added into the GDP. Probably the largest of such items is the work done at home for free. Others include volunteer work, do-it-yourself projects and food grown for personal consumption.

(c) Total GDP does not measure living standards

While the Gross Domestic Product does estimate the *total output* of the economy, it does not necessarily measure the *standard of living* of its people. A nation like India or China may have a large GDP, but its population is also large, making the GDP per person relatively low. Thus, GDP *per capita* is a more meaningful measure of economic performance for some purposes. Even this statistic may not measure a society's living standards very accurately, though. For many years, the former Soviet Union reported significant increases in GDP and in GDP per capita; however, its consumers did not benefit from this because the economic planners concentrated on increased production in the capital goods and military sectors of the economy rather than in the consumer goods sector.

For measuring living standards, *real disposable income per capita* (that is, after-tax income per person, adjusted for inflation) is generally considered to be the best statistic.

(d) GDP does not measure the "quality of life"

GDP statistics, however adjusted to reflect real income, production or consumption per person, measure only one aspect of human welfare—material prosperity in terms of the *quantity* of goods and services produced and consumed. No attempt is made to assess the *quality* of particular products in terms of whether they contribute to human welfare or not—the only test applied is whether someone is prepared to buy them. Thus, the total value of GDP includes (as if they were of equal social value) health food, medical care, cigarettes, handguns and even economics texts.

While economists place importance upon GDP statistics, they do not claim that GDP is the measure of human happiness, or that more GDP is always better. In fact, it may well be that other factors are more important, even if having more of these involves having a smaller GDP. Two illustrations should help to emphasize this point.

The first involves *leisure*. In the twentieth century, the average work week has declined from over 60 hours to less than 40 hours. By working fewer hours per week, Canadians accepted that they would be producing—and consuming—less goods and services (real GDP) than they could have had. However, they willingly chose this increase in leisure, because they valued it more highly than the higher GDP per person that they could have had by working longer hours. In effect, they were saying that higher consumption per person is not everything.

The second involves *the environment*. One way through which we have increased our material prosperity to such high levels is by dumping the by-products of our production and consumption into our environment. This practice has increased our material prosperity significantly. Businesses have avoided spending money to prevent or clean up their pollution, and consumers have not had to pay the costs of pollution prevention and cleanup through higher prices for the products they use. By not paying higher prices to cover the costs of making the production and use of our products environmentally sound, we saved vast amounts of money that we could spend on other goods and services, all the while ignoring the environmental effects of our actions.

However, over the years these practices have taken a costly toll on the environment, not only in terms of air and water pollution, but also in new and larger-scale environmental problems such as acid rain, the greenhouse effect and damage to the ozone layer. To deal with these problems, we will have to accept the fact that higher production and consumption are not everything. Just as we accepted the trade-off of lower GDP for more leisure, we will have to accept lower material prosperity in exchange for a better environment.

Thus, GDP is not a measure of human welfare, but only a useful estimate of the material prosperity that is one part of that welfare.

Measuring prices: The Consumer Price Index

Earlier in this chapter, we saw how price changes can affect the accuracy of GDP statistics, and how adjustments can be made to GDP statistics in order to eliminate the effects of price changes. Obviously, then, it is just as important to measure *prices* and price changes as it is to measure the economy's output. Since there are too many prices to monitor all of them, representative samples of prices have to be combined into some kind of average, called an *index*. There are various price indexes. Some cover very broad areas of the economy while others are quite specific, such as indexes for food prices, for energy prices and for housing prices. However, the price index with which most people are most familiar is the **Consumer Price Index (CPI)**, which measures only the prices of consumer goods and services.

The Consumer Price Index is an average of the prices of the goods and services bought by representative or typical urban households. A common way of expressing this is to say that the CPI is the cost of a "basket" of goods and services bought by a typical household. As the prices of these goods and services rise, so does the CPI. To determine what types of goods or services should be included in this "basket" and in what quantities, Statistics Canada undertakes a nationwide survey of spending habits concerning about 600 goods and services. The most recent such survey was completed in 1986. To determine the CPI for each month, survey takers in 64 cities record the prices of nearly 500 goods and services in the "basket." By feeding these prices into a computer, Statistics Canada is able to calculate an average of them that represents the CPI for that month, for various cities and for Canada as a whole.

In calculating the CPI, it is essential to take into account that some items in the "basket" are more important than others, in the sense that consumers spend much more on them. For instance, because consumers spend much more on gasoline than on broccoli, a 10 percent increase in the

---

THE CPI AND YOU

A ten-percent increase in the CPI does not affect all Canadians equally, because individual household's patterns of consumption may differ substantially from the weights used in the CPI. For instance, an increase in the CPI caused by increases in tobacco and alcohol prices will have no effect on people who neither smoke nor drink.

FIGURE 21-7   *Weights of the Major Components of the CPI, 1986*

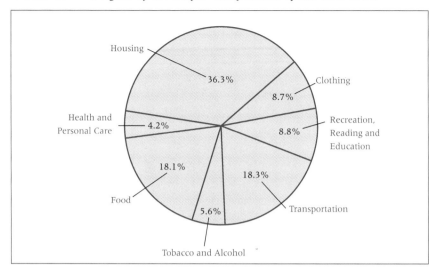

441
*Our basic economic
objectives and how
we measure them*

price of gasoline would have a far greater impact on the consumer—and the CPI—than a 10 percent increase in the price of broccoli. To recognize this, each item in the "basket" is given a *weight* in the CPI, based upon the proportion of the typical household's income that is spent on it. Thus, if a typical household spends fifty times as much on gasoline as it does on broccoli, gasoline would be given a "weight" in the index fifty times as large as the weight given to broccoli, and a 10-percent increase in gasoline prices would have fifty times the impact on the CPI as a 10-percent increase in broccoli prices. Figure 21-7 shows the weights assigned to each broad category of items in the CPI, such as housing, transportation, food and so on. However, it is important to remember that within each of these categories, there are dozens of individual goods and services, each with its own weight. For instance, the transportation component of the CPI includes car prices, gasoline prices, insurance rates, public transit fares, airline and train fares, and so on.

Rather than express the CPI in terms of the actual cost of the "basket" of goods and services in terms of dollars and cents, the CPI is expressed in terms of how much it has changed from a *base year* (1986 at the time of writing) in which the CPI was 100. This is illustrated in Figure 21-8, which shows not only the CPI in general ("all items"), but also the various major components of the CPI. In the "base year" of 1986, the CPI (and all its components) are 100.0. Thus, a CPI of 104.4 in 1987 means that the index (the cost of the "basket") was 4.4 percent higher in 1987 than it was in 1986. Similar calculations can be made for the various components of the CPI. For instance, in 1987, the cost of the clothing items in the "basket" was 4.2 percent higher than in 1986. It is not necessary to use 1986 as the base year for such calculations. For example, from 1991 to 1992 the CPI rose from 126.2 to 128.1, an increase of 1.5 percent (128.1 − 126.2 ÷ 126.2).

FIGURE 21-8   *The Consumer Price Index by Categories, 1961–93*

(1986 = 100)

Year	All items	Food	Housing	Clothing	Trans- portation	Health and personal care	Recre- ation and reading	Tobacco and alcohol
1961	23.9	20.7	24.3	34.2	24.0	24.0	29.6	21.6
1962	24.2	21.0	24.6	34.5	24.0	24.4	29.9	21.9
1963	24.6	21.7	24.9	35.4	24.0	25.1	30.3	21.9
1964	25.1	22.1	25.3	36.2	24.2	25.9	30.8	22.3
1965	25.7	22.6	25.7	36.9	25.2	27.1	31.3	22.7
1966	26.6	24.1	26.4	38.3	25.7	27.9	32.2	23.2
1967	27.6	24.4	27.6	40.2	26.8	29.4	33.8	23.8
1968	28.7	25.2	28.8	41.4	27.6	30.5	35.5	26.0
1969	30.0	26.3	30.3	42.6	28.8	32.0	37.6	27.0
1970	31.0	26.9	31.8	43.4	30.0	33.4	38.9	27.3
1971	31.9	27.2	33.3	44.0	31.2	34.1	40.2	27.8
1972	33.4	29.2	34.8	45.1	32.0	35.7	41.3	28.5
1973	36.0	33.5	37.0	47.4	32.8	37.5	43.0	29.4
1974	39.9	39.0	40.3	51.9	36.1	40.7	46.8	31.0
1975	44.2	44.0	44.3	55.0	40.3	45.4	51.7	34.8
1976	47.5	45.2	49.2	58.1	44.7	49.3	54.8	37.2
1977	51.3	48.9	53.8	62.0	47.8	52.9	57.3	39.9
1978	55.9	56.5	57.9	64.4	50.6	56.7	59.6	43.1
1979	61.0	63.9	61.9	70.3	55.5	61.9	63.7	46.2
1980	67.2	70.8	66.9	78.6	62.6	68.0	69.7	51.4
1981	75.5	78.9	75.3	84.2	74.1	75.4	76.8	58.0
1982	83.7	84.6	84.7	88.9	84.5	83.4	83.4	67.0
1983	88.5	87.7	90.4	92.5	88.7	89.2	88.8	75.5
1984	92.4	92.6	93.8	94.7	92.5	92.7	91.8	81.6
1985	96.0	95.2	97.1	97.3	96.9	95.9	95.6	89.4
1986	100.0	100.0	100.0	100.0	100.0	100.0	100.0	100.0
1987	104.4	104.4	104.0	104.2	103.6	105.0	105.4	106.7
1988	108.6	107.2	108.6	109.6	105.6	109.6	111.3	114.6
1989	114.0	111.1	114.3	114.1	111.1	114.4	116.2	125.2
1990	119.5	115.7	119.5	117.3	117.3	120.0	121.3	136.1
1991	126.2	121.2	124.7	128.4	119.4	128.4	130.2	159.5
1992	128.1	120.8	126.4	129.5	121.8	131.3	131.9	169.0
1993	130.4	122.8	128.0	130.8	125.7	134.8	135.3	171.7

Source: Statistics Canada, *The Consumer Price Index* (62-001); Reproduced by permission of the Minister of Supply and Services Canada

THE RATE OF INFLATION

The upper part of Figure 21-9 shows the level of the CPI since 1961. However, it is of more interest and importance to know how rapidly the CPI is rising in any given year. The lower part of Figure 21-9 shows us how fast (in percent terms) the CPI has risen since the previous year, or the **rate of inflation**. This graph shows that the rate of inflation was quite low in the

443

*Our basic eco-
nomic objectives
and how we
measure them*

FIGURE 21-9 *The Level and the Rate of Increase of the Consumer Price
Index, 1961–93*

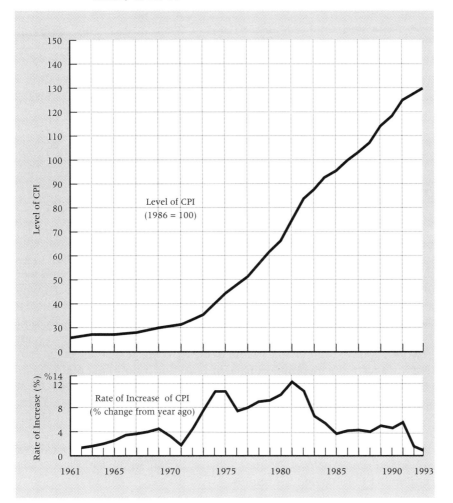

Source: Statistics Canada, *The Consumer Price Index* (62-001);

1960's, but increased sharply during much of the 1970's, declined considerably to the 4 percent per year range after 1982 and again in the early
1990's to about 2 percent per year—the rate that prevailed in the early
1960's.

In summary, we measure consumer prices with the Consumer Price
Index, and the rate of inflation is how fast the CPI rises in any given year.
In this chapter, we have been concerned only with how the rate of inflation is measured. In Chapters 28 and 29, we will examine the causes of
inflation, the effects of it and what can be done to combat it.

> **THE CONSUMER PRICE INDEX IS NOT A "COST OF LIVING" INDEX**
>
> While people commonly refer to the CPI as the "cost of living" index, this is not correct. One reason for this is that the CPI does not include *income taxes*, which represent a major part of most people's cost of living. Another reason is that the CPI only measures the cost of a constant "basket" of goods and services; it does not allow for the fact that consumers tend to adjust to rising prices by buying less of those products whose prices are rising most rapidly.

Measuring unemployment: The unemployment rate

Another important aspect of the performance of the economy is how successful it is in providing jobs for Canadians. The most commonly used measure of this is the **unemployment rate**, which is the percentage of the labor force that is unemployed. The **labor force** refers to those Canadians who are either employed or unemployed and available for work; thus, it is an estimate of *the pool of labor available for work* in Canada. Thus, the unemployment rate can be viewed as an estimate of the percentage of Canadians who want to work but have been unable to find work, or as the percentage of the economic resource represented by the labor force that is not being utilized.

The statistics on employment, unemployment and the unemployment rate are obtained monthly by Statistics Canada through its Labour Force Survey, which is a sample survey of about 56 000 representative households across Canada.[4]

The survey asks a number of questions that are designed to classify respondents as "employed," "unemployed" or "not in the labor force," according to the following definitions:

Employed: all persons who, during the survey week, did any work at all or had a job but were not at work due to their own illness or disability, personal or family responsibilities, bad weather, a labor dispute or vacation.

Unemployed: those persons who, during the survey week,

(a) were without work, had actively looked for work during the past four weeks and were available for work,

(b) had not actively looked for work in the past four weeks but had been on layoff for 26 weeks or less and were available for work,

(c) had not actively looked for work in the past four weeks but had a new job to start in four weeks and were available for work.

Labor Force: that portion of the civilian non-institutional population 15 years of age and over who are employed or unemployed. People who are not looking for work are not counted as employed or unemployed, and are therefore not included in the labor force.

From this survey, estimates are made of the numbers of Canadians who are employed and unemployed (and thus of the labor force, which is the total of these) for the particular month. The unemployment rate is then calculated as the number of unemployed expressed as a percentage of the labor force. For example, if the survey indicated that there were 9 100 000 Canadians employed and 900 000 unemployed, the labor force would be 10 000 000 and the unemployment rate would be nine percent (900 000 ÷ 10 000 000). The results of this survey for the period 1966–93 are shown in Figure 21-10.

FIGURE 21-10   *Labor Force Statistics, 1966–93*

Year	Labor force	Employed	Unemployed	Unemployment rate
	(	000's of persons	)	%
1966	7 493	7 242	251	3.4
1967	7 747	7 451	296	3.8
1968	7 951	7 593	358	4.5
1969	8 194	7 832	362	4.4
1970	8 395	7 919	476	5.7
1971	8 639	8 104	535	6.2
1972	8 897	8 344	553	6.2
1973	9 276	8 761	515	5.5
1974	9 639	9 125	514	5.3
1975	9 974	9 284	690	6.9
1976	10 203	9 477	726	7.1
1977	10 500	9 651	849	8.1
1978	10 895	9 987	908	8.3
1979	11 231	10 395	836	7.4
1980	11 573	10 708	865	7.5
1981	11 899	11 001	898	7.5
1982	11 926	10 618	1 308	11.0
1983	12 109	10 675	1 434	11.8
1984	12 316	10 932	1 384	11.2
1985	12 532	11 221	1 311	10.5
1986	12 746	11 531	1 215	9.5
1987	13 011	11 861	1 150	8.8
1988	13 275	12 245	1 031	7.8
1989	13 503	12 486	1 018	7.5
1990	13 681	12 572	1 109	8.1
1991	13 757	12 340	1 417	10.3
1992	13 797	12 240	1 556	11.3
1993	13 946	12 383	1 562	11.2

Sources: Statistics Canada, *Historical Labour Force Statistics* (71-201)

SEASONAL ADJUSTMENTS

One problem with unemployment-rate statistics is that some jobs (such as farming or fishing) are seasonal in nature. As a result, seasonal factors tend to push the unemployment rate upward each winter, as work in some sectors of the economy is temporarily discontinued until spring. This can make unemployment statistics more difficult to interpret: does an increase in the unemployment rate in January and February mean that the economy is slipping into a recession, or is the increase simply the result of seasonal factors? To make the statistics easier to interpret, Statistics Canada makes a "seasonal adjustment" to them, by eliminating the seasonal elements from the data. Such seasonal adjustments would reduce the unemployment rate in winter by the estimated extent of seasonal unemployment. Such "seasonally adjusted" unemployment-rate statistics are a better indicator of the actual state of the economy with respect to unemployment, because an increase in them is clearly not due to seasonal factors. Figure 21-11 shows unemployment rates in Canada from 1966–1993.

FIGURE 21-11 *Unemployment Rates in Canada, 1966–93*

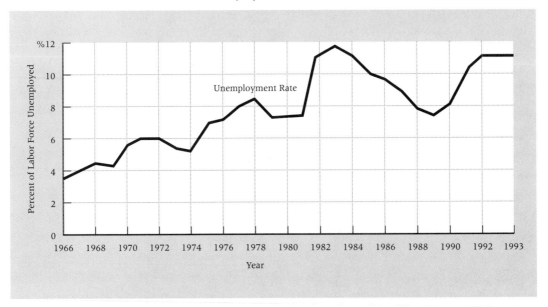

Sources: Statistics Canada, *Historical Labour Force Statistics* (71-201)

THE LIMITATIONS OF UNEMPLOYMENT-RATE STATISTICS

There has been considerable debate in recent years over the *accuracy* and the *significance* of these unemployment-rate statistics. Most of the debate revolves around the fact that unemployment statistics are derived from people's responses to a survey, one of the key questions of which is whether they have been looking for work in the previous four-week period. Some observers argue that the official statistics underestimate the extent of unemployment due to a phenomenon known as "hidden unemployment," while others assert that the official statistics overestimate unemployment, due to something called "voluntary unemployment."

Hidden unemployment

Those who believe that the official statistics underestimate unemployment base their argument on what is called **hidden unemployment**. According to their argument, large numbers of Canadians can be described as "discouraged workers"—people who have given up looking for work, mainly because they believe jobs are not available. As a result, such people are excluded from the unemployment and labor force statistics altogether, and are missed when the jobless data are gathered.

Some critics have claimed that by excluding these people, Statistics Canada is underestimating unemployment by a large amount, perhaps by 400 000 people or more. These criticisms have in the past prompted Statistics Canada to take the unusual step of publicly defending the validity of its statistics. Statistics Canada argues that the unwillingness of the hidden unemployed to hunt for work shows that they have little attachment to the labor market, or little desire to work. The agency also noted "the labor force survey counts as 'active job search' anything done to find out about jobs in general, to collect information about particular jobs, or to attempt to obtain a specific job." People who had not done any of these things, StatsCan said, should not be counted as unemployed.

While there is disagreement over the nature and extent of hidden unemployment, it is generally agreed that it is greater in regions of chronically high unemployment (such as the Atlantic provinces) and during recessions. In such circumstances, even people who want to work may give up looking for work, and thus not be counted among the unemployed.

A similar argument can be made concerning the many people who accepted early retirement with reduced pensions during the recession of the early 1990's—while officially retired and not looking for work, many would probably prefer to be working and perhaps should be counted as unemployed. Finally, it is argued that the official statistics underestimate unemployment because a person who only works a few hours per week is counted as "employed," even if that person wants to work full-time and could therefore be considered as mainly unemployed rather than employed.

Voluntary unemployment

Other people argue that the official unemployment statistics can be a misleadingly high indicator of the number of Canadians who are unemployed, because the statistics include people who report themselves as unemployed in the survey but who are not really interested in taking jobs that are available. It is argued that this is usually related to the availability of unemployment insurance benefits—because they are entitled to UI benefits for up to a year, some UI some recipients are encouraged to be more selective regarding the jobs that they will take, prolonging their period of unemployment and adding to the unemployment rate. This type of **voluntary unemployment** is more likely to occur in multi-income households, which have become much more common since the early 1970's. In such households, total family income could still be substantial even if a second- (or third)-income-earner was on UI of 57 percent of their previous income. Critics argue that another source of difficulty with the unemployment statistics is that regardless of whether they are working or not, people on welfare or UI have little choice but to report themselves as unemployed, for fear of jeopardizing their benefits.

It is difficult to measure the extent of voluntary unemployment, but those studies that have been done estimate it to be between 1.0 and 1.5 percent of the labor force. Viewed from another perspective, this would be between 10 and 15 percent of total unemployment in Canada in recent years, or up to 200 000 people.

INTERPRETING CHANGES IN THE UNEMPLOYMENT RATE

An increase in the unemployment rate is generally interpreted to indicate layoffs, lost jobs and deteriorating economic conditions, such as a recession. While this may usually be the case, it is not necessarily the case, as Figure 21-12 shows.

FIGURE 21-12　*Two Different Reasons for the Same Increase in the Unemployment Rate*

Year	Labor Force	Unemployed	Employed	Unemployment Rate
19X1	100 000	9 000	91 000	9.0%
19X2 (a)	100 000	10 000	90 000	10.0%
19X2 (b)	101 100	10 100	91 000	10.0%

In year 19X1, the labor force is 100 000, 91 000 of whom are employed and 9 000 of whom are unemployed; thus, the unemployment rate is 9.0 percent. Suppose that, in year 19X2, the unemployment rate rises to 10.0 percent. This could reflect lost jobs and a recession, as shown in case (a), in which employment has fallen by 1000 to 90 000 and unemployment has risen by 1000 to 10 000. However, as case (b) shows, it could also be the result of an increase in the number of people looking for work. In case (b), the number of people working is still 91 000, the same as in 19X1; however, 1100 more people are looking for work and not finding it. As a result, the labor force increases to 101 100 and the number of unemployed rises to 10 100, pushing the unemployment rate up to 10.0 percent. In both cases, the unemployment rate increases from 9.0 percent to 10.0 percent; however, in the first case this is due to *fewer jobs*, while in the second case it is due to *more job-seekers*.

It is particularly important to interpret unemployment-rate statistics carefully when the economy is recovering from a recession. During such a period, the number of jobs may be increasing quite rapidly, as economic conditions improve. However, those improving economic conditions usually cause more people to become interested (again) in working, increasing the number of job-seekers and keeping the unemployment rate high, making economic conditions appear to be worse than they are. Conversely, in some months during recessions the unemployment rate goes down, not because there are more jobs, but rather because some people gave up looking for work.

In conclusion, unemployment-rate statistics are the best available *estimates* of the employment/unemployment situation, not the precise, correct-to-one-decimal-point data that they appear to be. Most economists agree that the unemployment-rate statistics probably underestimate unemployment during recessions, when people stop looking for work and "hidden unemployment" rises, and overestimate unemployment during booms, when "voluntary unemployment" keeps the unemployment rate relatively high in spite of jobs being available.

DEFINITIONS OF NEW TERMS

Gross Domestic Product (GDP) The market value of the total annual output of final goods and services produced in the nation. Also called "GDP at current market prices" and "money GDP."

Gross National Product (GNP) The total incomes earned by Canadian residents, whether the income is earned in Canada or not. Because considerable investment income generated in Canada is paid to non-resident investors, GNP is typically 3–4 percent smaller than GDP.

Real GDP GDP statistics that have been adjusted to eliminate the effects of price increases, the result being a statistic that measures only changes in real output. Also called "GDP in constant dollars" or "GDP at 1986 prices."

Consumer Price Index (CPI) A weighted average of the prices of a "basket" of goods and services purchased by a typical urban family.

Rate of Inflation The percentage increase in prices, usually measured by the CPI, compared to prices a year earlier.

Unemployment Rate The percentage of the labor force that is unemployed. Sometimes "seasonally adjusted" unemployment-rate statistics are used, to eliminate fluctuations in unemployment-rate data that occur merely due to seasonal factors.

Labor Force Those Canadians who are either employed or unemployed and available for work.

Seasonal Unemployment Unemployment of a temporary nature due to seasonal factors in industries such as farming and fishing.

Hidden Unemployment People who are unemployed but are not counted in the unemployment statistics because they have given up looking for work.

Voluntary Unemployment People who report themselves as unemployed and looking for work but are not (seriously) seeking employment.

CHAPTER SUMMARY

1. The Gross Domestic Product, which measures the total output of the economy, consists of four components: consumption (C), investment (I), government (G) and net exports (X – M).

2. The Gross Domestic Product can rise either because the output of goods and services is higher or because their prices have risen. These inflated money GDP statistics can be adjusted to eliminate the effects of increased prices, the result being "real GDP" statistics that are more meaningful because they measure only real output.

3. The importance of GDP statistics is probably overrated, as these are far from perfect measures of the welfare of a society. Nonetheless, GDP statistics are a useful approximation of the overall output of the economy.

4. The Consumer Price Index is the most commonly used and well-known measure of prices. It is a weighted average of the prices of goods and services bought by a typical urban family.

5. While most people think of the CPI as a cost of living index, this is not correct. The CPI is a useful approximation of changes in the prices of consumer goods and services and is used to measure the rate of inflation, which is the percentage increase in the CPI from one year earlier.

6. The most commonly used measure of the ability of the economy to provide jobs is the unemployment rate, which is based on the Labour Force Survey, which gathers data on the number of people who are employed and unemployed.

7. Due to factors such as hidden unemployment and voluntary unemployment, and the fact that the unemployment rate is affected not only by the number of people who are unemployed but also by the number who are seeking work, it is necessary to interpret unemployment rate statistics carefully.

QUESTIONS

1. If a working couple were married and both decided one should stay at home and renovate their house, what would happen to

   (a) society's output of goods and services?

   (b) the Gross Domestic Product?

2. Can you think of some examples of the "underground economy" referred to in this chapter?

3. Over the past year, which components of the Consumer Price Index have increased

   (a) the most rapidly, and

   (b) the most slowly?

   Why?

4. Over the past year, what change has occurred in the unemployment rate? What might explain this trend?

5. (a) If money GDP has increased by 5.3 percent over last year's level, can we conclude that the economy's production of goods and services has risen?

   (b) If the general level of prices has risen by 3.2 percent over the same period, what can we conclude about the economy's production of goods and services?

   (c) If the general level of prices increased by 7.6 percent over the same period, what has happened to the economy's output of goods and services?

6.

Year	Consumer Price Index	Annual Rate of Inflation
1986	100.0	_____
1987	104.0	_____
1988	108.6	_____
1989	114.0	_____
1990	119.5	_____
1991	126.2	_____
1992	128.1	_____
1993	130.4	_____

   (a) Calculate the rate of inflation for 1987, 1989, 1991 and 1993.

   (b) Draw on a graph the Consumer Price Index over the 1987–1993 period.

   (c) Draw on a graph the rate of inflation over the 1987–1993 period.

   (d) What explains the different trends shown by the two graphs?

7.

Year	Civilian Labor Force (000)	Employed (000)	Unemployed (000)	Unemployment Rate (%)
1987	13 011	11 861	_____	_____
1988	13 275	12 245	_____	_____
1989	13 503	12 486	_____	_____
1990	13 681	12 572	_____	_____
1991	13 757	12 340	_____	_____
1992	13 797	12 240	_____	_____
1993	13 946	12 383	_____	_____

(a) Calculate the number of Canadians unemployed in each of the years shown.

(b) Calculate the unemployment rate for each of the years shown.

(c) In 1990, the number of Canadians employed rose; but the unemployment rate also rose. What explains this apparent contradiction?

8. Suppose that statistics indicated that the standard of living of Canadians, as measured by real consumption per person, had risen by 10 percent over a five-year period. These statistics *measure* the size of the increase in living standards, but what do you think would have *caused* such an increase?

NOTES

[1] A simpler and probably clearer way of saying the same thing is "the sum of the price tags of all final goods and services produced in the country in that year."

[2] If a manufacturer's inventory of finished products increases by $2 million over last year's inventory, this represents $2 million of production during the year that must be included in the GNP statistics. However, it cannot be counted as "consumption," since it has not yet been purchased by consumers, so we add it into the "investment" statistics instead. While construction of new housing is purchased by households, rather than being counted as a consumer item, it is included in the investment statistics mainly because of its nature as a long-term asset.

[3] This reflects the fact that the adjustment has the effect of calculating, for example, 1994's GDP as if prices had not changed from their 1986 levels.

[4] There is a widespread belief that unemployment statistics are based on the numbers of people receiving Unemployment Insurance. However, this is not the case—many of the unemployed are not receiving UI benefits, either because they do not qualify for them or because their benefits have run out.

Sources of economic prosperity: The supply side

Why are some nations so much richer than others? This is a very complex question involving considerations of natural resources, education levels of the population, climate, social attitudes, capital equipment and many other factors. However, societies that have achieved a high material standard of living do tend to have one thing in common: they have what economists refer to as a strong **supply side** to their economies. That is, they have high productivity, or the ability to produce goods and services efficiently.

The key to a strong supply side is the ability to make efficient use of economic inputs (labor, capital equipment and natural resources) so as to achieve high levels of **productivity**, or output per worker. Such high levels of *output per person* are a key factor underlying the ability to enjoy high levels of *consumption per person*, or a high material standard of living. In addition to enjoying high living standards, nations that achieve high productivity tend to be more successful in international competition. For a country such as Canada, with both exports and imports that represent a high proportion of its GDP, this is a very important consideration.

Income and output are intimately related. Real income (that is, income unaffected by inflation) depends on output, so that any growth in real income requires growth in output.

Economic Council of Canada, *Twelfth Annual Review*

The nature of productivity

Productivity is not a word with a single simple meaning. In its broadest sense, it refers to all three productive inputs (labor, capital equipment and natural resources) and the efficiency with which they work together to produce goods and services. However, the most commonly used definition of productivity—as well as one that is easier to understand and to measure—is labor productivity or *output per worker per hour* (output per worker-hour). A similar measure of productivity is *real GDP per employed person*.

> Labour productivity is probably the most telling measure of economic performance. Unless productivity grows, living standards stagnate.
>
> *The Economist*, February 13, 1993 (page 67)

Defining productivity in terms of output per worker seems to imply that productivity depends on how hard people work. While this is one factor that influences productivity, there are many more important ones, which are considered in the following sections.

FACTORS AFFECTING PRODUCTIVITY

The major factors affecting productivity that we will discuss in this chapter are: (a) capital equipment; (b) education and skill levels of the labor force; (c) management; (d) size of market and scale of operations; (e) the incentive of after-tax gain; and (f) the incentive of competition. In the sections that follow, we will consider the nature of each of these factors, Canada's performance with respect to productivity and each factor, and government policies that can improve productivity performance.

(a) Capital equipment and the saving-investment process

The amount—and quality—of capital equipment per worker is a key factor in determining workers' productivity. Generally, the more and better capital equipment workers have to work with, the higher output per worker and living standards can be. Therefore, a fundamental factor influencing productivity is the amount of *capital investment* by a society in plants, equipment and machinery.

BUILDING CAPITAL EQUIPMENT: THE SAVING-INVESTMENT PROCESS
The process whereby a society acquires capital equipment is so fundamentally important that we will examine it in detail. To emphasize the basic economic concepts involved in the process of capital investment, we will use a simple illustration. Suppose you are alone on a desert island

and must find food to survive. Since the most accessible food is fish from a nearby stream, you set out to catch some.

The only productive inputs available to you are your labor and the stream and fish (natural resources)—you have no capital equipment at all. So you use your hands, with only limited success, and find that you are able to catch two fish per day. This is just enough to feed you for a day, but to catch the two fish takes the entire day, or all your available labor. You have no time available for any other productive activities, such as cultivating vegetables or building a shelter. Your low productivity is limiting you to a subsistence-level standard of living.

Before long, you decide that you have to become more efficient at catching fish, and set out to build a spear to do so. The problem that you face is this: the time that you spend building the spear cannot also be spent catching fish. In other words, in order to obtain the capital good (the spear) that you want, you will have to do without, or sacrifice, some consumer goods (fish) that you also want. It takes an entire day—leaving you very hungry—but you are able to fashion a spear.

Now you have a piece of *capital equipment* to help you produce consumer goods (catch fish). Using the spear, you can now catch six fish per day—a significant improvement. This piece of capital equipment has increased your productivity greatly, and by doing so has widened your economic choices considerably. Because you can catch enough fish to feed yourself in less than half a day, you have in effect released your time (or your labor) to do other things. You could:

- produce other consumer products, such as shelter or other types of food, or

- produce more capital goods such as a net, or a plow, or traps, in order to increase your efficiency further, or

- enjoy some leisure time.

Suppose you decide to build a net. This is a more complex two-day project, but because you can now catch all the fish you need in a few hours each day, you can spread it over a period of four half-days. You could have caught twelve fish in this period of time, but have decided instead to acquire another piece of capital equipment—a net. Using the net, you are able to catch enough fish to feed yourself for a whole day in about half an hour. Your productivity regarding fishing is now so high that you have a great deal of free time (or released labor) to do other things. You then use this available time to fashion some primitive tools—a hammer, a saw, a knife and so on, with which you can construct more capital equipment. After a few weeks, you have a ladder for picking fruit from trees, traps for catching animals, a bow and arrows for hunting, a clearing and a plow for cultivating vegetables, a house for shelter and a boat for transportation, not to mention a several hours per day of leisure time and a comfortable hammock in which to spend it.

Your standard of living has increased tremendously from its original subsistence level. The key to this process is, of course, the *capital equipment* which you have made and thereby increased your productivity. But how was this capital equipment obtained? To make the spear, you had to forego one day's consumption of fish—the two fish you could have caught instead of working on the spear. Making the net also involved a sacrifice of consumption: twelve fish you could have caught in the two days' time it took to make the net. Similarly, to acquire all the other pieces of your capital equipment, you had to *forego consumption*; that is, *forego present enjoyment.*[1] You were willing to do this because you expected that the capital equipment, by increasing your productivity, would *increase your future consumption*. Thus, you were making a decision to trade off a lower standard of living in the present against a higher standard of living in the future. Each time you made a piece of capital equipment you were in effect saying. "I'll accept less consumption than I could have had today in order that I can have more in the future." At first, this process was quite painful—you had to go a full day without food. Later, as your productivity increased, the sacrifices in the present became less harsh, because you could feed yourself quite readily and build additional capital equipment in the remaining time each day.

CONSUMPTION, SAVING AND INVESTMENT   These basic ideas are sufficiently important to be given names and defined carefully. **Consumption** refers to consumer goods and services that are produced to be used up by the consumers for present enjoyment. Consumption includes all such goods and services, from automobiles to manicures. The production of capital goods, which will make possible greater production of goods and services in the *future*, is called **investment**. As we have seen, one key to a society's economic prosperity is the amount of investment it does in capital equipment, which increases productivity.

However, the basic economic problem of scarcity forces upon us a difficult choice: the more of our output we devote to investment (for future prosperity), the less of our output is available for consumption (for present enjoyment). This trade-off, which is illustrated in Figure 22-1, is the same decision we faced regarding the building of the spear and net: to gain the *future benefits* of these tools we had to sacrifice some present consumption.

FIGURE 22-1   *The Consumption/Saving/Investment Relationship*

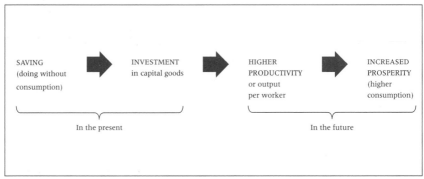

This basic concept of doing without (foregoing) consumption that could have been enjoyed in the present is known as **saving**. Saving is obviously of great importance, since it is essential if there is to be the investment necessary for economic progress.

THE DILEMMA: CONSUMPTION VS. SAVING   Consumption is the end goal of economic activity—the satisfaction of the wants and needs of the consumer. To increase future levels of production and consumption it is necessary to engage in investment, which adds to society's stock of productive capital equipment and increases productivity, while to achieve investment it is necessary to have saving, or the foregoing of some consumption in the present to make productive inputs available for building capital equipment.

These concepts apply to all societies and all economies. Whenever resources are used to construct capital equipment (be it a fishing net or a steel factory) to produce more goods and services in the future, it is true that the resources used to build the capital equipment could have been used to produce more goods and services for consumption in the present. This is true for market economies and for command economies, and for highly industrialized nations as well as Third World countries.

It is, however, much easier for a wealthy nation, which has high levels of output, to save, invest and grow economically. In such societies, consumption is sufficiently high that foregoing some consumption in order to have more investment is not painful. Poor societies are much less fortunate—they may need to consume nearly all of their present output merely to survive. Thus, they may be unable to save and therefore unable to invest. In such a situation, economic progress can be virtually impossible without outside assistance.

(b) Education and skill levels of the labor force

Obviously, the better-educated and more highly-skilled a nation's labor force is, the more likely it is to be highly productive. Over the course of the twentieth century, economic activity has shifted steadily away from the physical work associated with agriculture and factories and toward service industries and high-technology industries that employ large numbers of well-educated and trained "knowledge workers." These changes, which have been accelerated in recent years by advances in computer technology, have made it essential for a modern society to have a well-educated and highly-skilled labor force.

In addition to changes in technology, recent changes in the international economic environment have added to the importance of Canada's having a highly-qualified labor force. In recent years, many more nations, from Eastern Europe to Asia, have adopted the market system, and have begun to seek to attract business investment capital from other nations. At the same time, reduced restrictions on international trade and finance, together with advances in transportation and communications technology,

THE INDUSTRIALIZATION PROCESS

The process of industrialization—of changing a nation's economy from an agricultural one to an industrial one—is a formidable task that requires massive amounts of investment over a prolonged period of time. What is required is no less than a major redirection of the use of the society's economic resources, with capital-goods production emphasized at the expense of consumer-goods production. This involves massive sacrifices in terms of foregone consumption, perhaps over several generations of people. How can this be achieved?

First, the burden will necessarily fall mainly on the masses of the people—the "working class." This is the case because the sacrifices of consumption are so large that they must mainly be borne by the most numerous groups, or the masses. For them, industrialization will mean long hours of work for low pay, as their efforts go mainly to building capital goods for future prosperity rather than consumer goods for themselves today. Second, it is likely that this sacrifice will have to be *imposed* on them in some way—they are unlikely to accept it gladly.

Two interesting examples of this process are the industrialization of Great Britain (during the Industrial Revolution, 1760–1830) and the Soviet Union (following the Bolshevik Revolution of 1917).

In Russia's "command economy," the saving was imposed on the people in a relatively simple way—the Soviet economic planners decided to produce a great deal of capital goods (hydroelectric facilities, roads, factories, steel mills and so on) and relatively few consumer goods (such as appliances, automobiles and housing). Thus, the government decided to divert production away from consumption toward investment. With relatively little available for consumption, the people had no choice—they "saved," in the sense of doing without consumption.

In Great Britain's "market system," the process was somewhat different. During the Industrial Revolution, an exodus of people from the agricultural sector generated a tremendous surplus of labor in the industrial centres. As a result, employers were able to force wages to very low levels and profits rose to high levels. Consequently, the working class was not able to consume much (or was forced to "save," in the sense of accepting very low levels of consumption) and businesses had high profits which they used to expand their businesses through high investment.

While the *process* in Great Britain was very different from that used in Russia, the *results* were essentially the same: high levels of investment were made possible by the economic sacrifices (saving) that were essentially forced upon an unwilling public that had no choice. And, of course, both societies subsequently reaped the economic benefits of the investment, in the form of economic growth and power.

> Increasingly, educated brainpower—along with the roads, airports, computers and fiber-optic cables linking it up (to the rest of the world)—determines a nation's standard of living.
>
> Robert B. Reich, *The REAL Economy*, in *The Atlantic Monthly*, February 1991

have made it much easier for businesses to invest in nations outside of their home country. In this environment, increasing competition between nations for business investment makes it increasingly important that nations be able to attract that investment in order to be prosperous. And, given the growing importance of knowledge workers in most industries, this means that one key to attracting investment is to have an educated and skilled labor force.

In the past, a nation's prosperity might have depended mainly on its natural resources or its massive investments in facilities to process resources into manufactured goods. In the future, prosperity will be much more dependent upon its ability to attract investment with the education, training and skills of its labor force. This is why spending on training and education is regarded as a key strategic investment in the economic future of a nation, and is often referred to as an "investment in human capital."

(c) Management

The level of managerial ability is an important contributor to productivity, since it is ultimately management that is responsible for the efficiency with which productive resources are combined to produce goods and services. This involves management skills well beyond the traditional skills of planning, organizing, directing and controlling work activities. In a sophisticated economy that utilizes many knowledge workers, the abilities to communicate effectively, to lead people and to solve problems are critically important management skills. Furthermore, the quality of employer-employee relations, much of which depends on management, influences employee morale and productivity.

(d) Size of market and scale of operations

Generally, as the size of a production operation increases, it becomes possible to develop more sophisticated and specialized capital equipment and more specialized tasks for workers, and thus to achieve higher efficiency

> We are using Russian engineers living in Israel to design (computer) chips that are made in America and then assembled in Asia.
>
> Peter J. Sprague, chairman of National Semiconductor Corporation

through *mass-production techniques,* or what economists call **economies of scale.**[2]

Economies of scale are more important in some industries than in others. In most service industries, such as restaurants and barber shops, production methods are labor-intensive, and there are few efficiency advantages to large-scale operations—as a result, such service operations tend to be small-scale. In manufacturing industries, on the other hand, large-scale capital equipment and mass-production techniques can bring substantial gains in efficiency and production costs.

As a result, in many manufacturing industries, in order to be competitive, firms must be able to produce—and sell—on a very large scale. This means that they must have access to quite large markets, either domestically or through international trade. Economists estimate that in many such industries, producers need access to markets of at least 100 million people in order to be able to operate on a scale that will permit their efficiency, production costs and prices to be internationally competitive.

(e) The incentive of after-tax economic gain

All four of the aforementioned factors—capital equipment, quality of labor force and management, and size of market—are physical factors that will make it possible for a nation to be efficient. In order to actually achieve this potential productivity, there must be *incentives* in the economic system that push producers to become more efficient. There are two such basic incentives—*economic gain* and *competition.*

Economic gain is a key incentive for both producers and individuals to improve productivity. For businesses, this is the profit motive, which creates incentives for efficiency in at least two ways. First, higher productivity means lower costs and thus higher profits. Second, higher productivity can also make lower prices possible, which can help to increase sales and the growth of the enterprise. On an individual level, managers and employees will be more inclined to improve productivity if there is personal economic gain for themselves in doing so, in the form of pay raises or bonuses based on productivity or profits.

It is important to note that by economic gain, we mean the *after-tax* gain of the business or people involved. This means that government taxation policies can have important effects upon a nation's productivity and prosperity. If tax rates are too high, the after-tax gains will be smaller and the incentive to improve efficiency can be reduced.

The key to economic incentives is the **marginal tax rate**, which is defined as the percentage of any *additional* income (over and above one's present income) that is taken by taxes. If Fred, a musician, earns a salary of $20 000 per year for playing in an orchestra and pays $4000 in income taxes on this salary, he is paying a 20 percent tax rate on his income. This, however, is his tax rate on his *total* income, whereas his marginal tax rate is the percentage of any *extra* income that he earns that would be taken by taxes. For instance, if Fred earns an extra $1000 for playing the piano in a marching band on weekends, and he must pay $400 in income taxes on this $1000 of additional income, his *marginal tax rate* is 40 percent. Because he is probably in a position to decide whether or not to do this extra work, his marginal tax rate will be an important factor affecting Fred's incentive to do such additional work. If the marginal tax rate is too high, Fred will be left with so little after-tax income from such additional work that he may decide that it is not worthwhile. High marginal tax rates can discourage people from working to earn additional income in various forms such as bonuses, profit-sharing plans, overtime and pay raises for promotions.

A more subtle but more important problem occurs if high marginal tax rates impair the *saving-investment process*. If high marginal tax rates make the after-tax returns to investors on income from interest, dividends and capital gains too low, people will be discouraged from saving and less capital will be available for business capital investment. Similarly, high tax rates on business profits can discourage capital investment, not only by leaving business with less funds for capital investment but also by reducing the incentive for businesses to invest in additional production facilities.

Finally, if a nation's tax rates on profits and investment income are too high relative to tax rates in other countries, there is a risk that investment funds (and, to a lesser extent, people) will leave the high-tax country and locate where taxes are lower. This is a particularly important consideration for Canadian tax policy, due to the opportunities for investment in the United States.

In conclusion, in establishing their taxation policies, it is essential that governments take into account not only their revenue needs, but also the effect of marginal tax rates on economic incentives to work, save and invest.

Unfortunately, political considerations may lead governments into setting high tax rates which in turn discourage saving and investment. Governments are usually under political pressure to increase their spending and in seeking sources of additional tax revenue, they sometimes turn to business profits, high-income groups and investment income, none of which are particularly sympathized with by the general public. Many economists consider such taxation policies to have been one of the major causes of Great Britain's economic decline following the Second World War. The government financed heavy spending programs with very high taxes on business profits and higher-income people whose savings had contributed much of the funds for capital investment. These high tax rates contributed to Britain's poor productivity performance and economic decline by discouraging saving, investment and work.

(f) The incentive of competition

The other main incentive in a market system is *competition*. Both theory and experience indicate that when competition is absent or weak, producers can become inefficient and charge higher prices because there are no competitors to whom consumers can turn. Generally, competition is stronger in industries in which there are many competing producers and it is relatively easy for new producers to start up.

As a general rule, the most efficient economies are those characterized by a strong profit motive and strong competition. It is significant that, in seeking to improve the productivity performance of Russian industry, the government has been introducing elements of both profit and competition into their command system to replace the previous system of monopoly producers that were owned and subsidized by the government.

Canada's performance regarding productivity and factors affecting it

Much concern has been expressed about the poor productivity performance of both the Canadian and American economies in recent years. In actual fact, as of the early 1990's, the level of overall productivity in the US economy was still the highest in the world, and Canada's productivity was second-highest, about 7 percent below the US level. This is reflected in Figure 22-2, which also shows most other industrialized nations' productivity well behind US and Canadian levels. However, as Figure 22-2 also shows, the other nations were gaining on both Canada and the United States in productivity. Furthermore, Japan had surpassed the United States in productivity in several major manufacturing industries, including automobiles and electronics.

The problems concerning Canadian productivity performance are not related to the overall level of Canadian productivity, which is second-highest in the world, but rather to two particular aspects of Canadian productivity:

- the low productivity of the Canadian *manufacturing sector*, which was less than 70 percent of US manufacturing productivity and about 80 percent of Japan's in the early 1990's, and

- the *slow growth* of Canadian productivity since the late 1970's. This is reflected in Figure 22-2, which shows the productivity of all other major countries gaining on both Canada and the USA in recent years.

Obviously, with Canada's weak productivity in manufactured goods that are heavily traded internationally, and with other nations' productivity improving faster than Canada's, these factors raise serious concerns about the ability of Canadian manufacturers to compete internationally.

FIGURE 22-2 *International Productivity Comparisons*

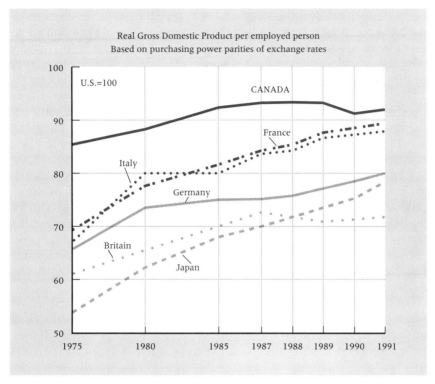

Real Gross Domestic Product per employed person
Based on purchasing power parities of exchange rates

Source: U.S. Bureau of Labor Statistics

THE PRODUCTIVITY SLOWDOWN

Canada is not alone in experiencing a slowdown in productivity growth since the mid-1970's—this has been a problem in most industrialized economies. While the productivity slowdown is one of the most important economic trends of recent years, there is a lack of general agreement as to its causes. In fact, only about one-half of the productivity slowdown can be explained with reference to known factors, leaving about half of this problem unexplained.

Most economists agree that one cause of the productivity slowdown was a weakness in business capital investment spending during much of the 1970's and the early 1980's. The severe inflation and high interest rates of much of the 1970's depressed business capital investment spending by making borrowing very expensive, and the recessions of the early 1980's and early 1990's held investment down during those periods. As noted earlier, capital investment is a key driving force behind improved productivity.

Other economists believe that *demographics* have played a role in the productivity slowdown. In the 1970's, the Canadian and US economies had to absorb into their labor forces the bulk of the "baby boomers" born during the 1946–66 period. According to this view, the addition of so many new workers into the economy depressed output per worker. This would be particularly likely if the sluggishness in capital investment discussed in the previous paragraph meant that the economy's stock of plant and equipment failed to grow as fast as the labor force, leaving workers on average with less capital to support their efficiency. This demographic explanation of the productivity slowdown is supported by the fact that during the 1970's, productivity performance was particularly weak in several years in which employment grew exceptionally rapidly. This factor diminished in importance in the 1980's, when the baby boomers had been integrated into the labor force and the growth rate of the labor force slowed to below two percent per year, reflecting the lower birth rates after 1966.

Other observers believe that *changes in the composition of the industries of the industrialized nations* is a fundamental factor contributing to slower productivity growth. Generally speaking, it is easier to apply productivity-increasing technology to the production of goods than to services. For instance, mass-production technology can be readily used to produce goods such as appliances, whereas the provision of services such as restaurants, health care, legal counsel and education does not lend itself as readily to productivity-increasing technological advances.

As the world's industrialized economies have matured and grown wealthier, an increasing proportion of consumer demand—and thus output and employment—has been for *services,* such as restaurants, entertainment, travel, health care, education and so on. For instance, from 1950 to 1992, the proportion of Canadians working in the service-producing sector of the economy increased from less than 43 percent to over 73 percent; similar trends were evident in the other industrialized economies of the world. This dramatic increase in the proportion of the labor force employed in service industries, which are less suited to productivity-improving technological advances, is seen by many as an underlying cause of slower productivity growth. A contributing and related factor could also be the *growth of part-time employment* associated with some service industries, such as retail trade and food service, which have to cater to periods of peak demand. Simply because they work fewer hours per week, part-time workers drag average output per worker statistics down. Finally, even in service and office workplaces where there was a significant increase in technology, employers did not generally reduce employment as might have been expected or might have been possible. Not until the recession of the early 1990's subjected them to severe economic pressures did employers in many service and office environments reduce employment and thus increase productivity.

Factors such as those discussed in the previous section help to explain much of the productivity slowdown that occurred in all of the major industrialized nations. However, the fact remains that, since the mid-1970's, Canada's productivity performance has been weaker than that of almost all other industrialized nations.

Canadian productivity problems

This is a serious problem for at least two reasons. First, only if productivity rises can Canadians' standard of living rise in the way that they want and expect it to. And second, if Canadian industry fails to improve its ability to compete internationally by improving its productivity, jobs in export industries and industries that compete with imports will be threatened. Canada exports over one-quarter of its GDP, making the economic prosperity of its people unusually dependent on its ability to compete internationally. For these reasons, many economists regard poor productivity performance as the most fundamental and most serious weakness of the Canadian economy.

In the following sections, we will look at some of the reasons for this weak productivity performance by examining Canada's situation with respect to each of the factors affecting productivity that were discussed earlier in this chapter. The discussion of these factors is necessarily in general terms only, which may or may not apply to the productivity performance of individual industries or firms.

(a) Capital investment

On the whole, the Canadian economy has quite high average levels of capital equipment per worker. However, this is partly because the very heavy capital investment in the natural resources sector keeps up the average for the economy as a whole. In the manufacturing sector, neither capital investment nor productivity performance has been as strong. Some observers believe that the poor productivity of much of Canada's manufacturing sector has been due to the fact that Canadian manufacturers have often been slower than their foreign competitors to adopt the most up-to-date production technology, such as robotics and computer-assisted design and manufacturing (CAD/CAM). These observers also point to the fact that Canadian industries and governments invest considerably less in research and development (R&D) as a proportion of GDP than other industrialized countries.

(b) Education and skill levels of the labor force

As a percentage of GDP, Canada spends more on education than any other major industrialized nation, and Canadians' high average levels of educational attainment reflect this. However, there is widespread agreement

---

The lack of a clear, strong upward trend in national productivity over the long term is alarming, because the international competitiveness of Canadian businesses will be a critical determinant of living standards at home

Economic Council of Canada, *Twenty-Fifth Annual Review*, 1988 (page 62)

> One reason that Canada's productivity performance has been poor in recent years is that its technology performance is weak compared with that of its major trading partners.
>
> Economic Council of Canada, *Twenty-Fifth Annual Review*, 1988 (page 63)

that Canada is not getting good economic value for these high expenditures on education.

Most of the criticisms of the educational system are well-known. Because there is inadequate emphasis on the "basics," even many secondary school graduates lack the literacy and numeracy skills to function effectively in the types of jobs that are available in a modern economy. Also, there is a mismatch between what employers need and what the educational system provides. A modern "postindustrial" economy such as Canada's needs relatively few people with academic university-level education, many people with middle-level technical and business skills and relatively few with low skills. Canada's educational system, which has tended to be predominantly academic and university-oriented, has produced the opposite of this—too many university graduates regardless of their practical job skills, too many high-school dropouts who lack any skills and too few people with the middle-level technical and business skills most needed by employers and the economy.

Furthermore, Canadian businesses have failed to fill these gaps with training programs of their own. In the early 1990's, spending on training by Canadian firms was only 0.6 percent of payroll—about half the level of spending by American businesses. Finally, there is a lack of apprenticeship programs in Canada, in large part because employers and governments have found it easier and cheaper to import skilled workers rather than train them in Canada.

A noteworthy symptom of the education and training problems of the Canadian economy is provided by the fact that even in 1992, in the depths of a serious recession and with over 1 500 000 Canadians unemployed, 300 000 jobs remained unfilled and employers were bringing in skilled people from other countries to fill jobs for which qualified Canadians could not be found.

(c) Management

As noted earlier, management skills are particularly important to the development of high productivity. As with job skills in general, the main problem with management skills lies at the critically-important middle level.

Canada has large numbers of university graduates in business and management to fill senior positions, but a shortage of well-trained, practical and competent middle managers to handle the management of operations. One possible symptom of this problem is that even after investment spending in the Canadian economy strengthened after the mid-1980's, productivity growth did not. According to the "new growth theory," this suggests that people's knowledge and skills in the management of resources are more important than ever to productivity growth.

Canadian managers have also been criticized for being slow to adapt to the rapid changes in the world economy, particularly the growth of international trade and competition known as "globalization." According to the Swiss-based World Economic Forum, a weakness in Canada's international competitiveness has been the lack of outward orientation of Canadian management. This may in part be related to Canada's traditional government policy of protecting Canadian manufacturers from foreign competition, as discussed in the next two sections.

(d) Size of market and scale of operations

As noted earlier, a market size of 100 million is widely considered to be necessary for many manufacturers to be able to realize the full benefits of economies of scale. For Canadian manufacturers, with a market of only 27 million,[3] this means that export sales into larger markets are a key to achieving high productivity. Historically, however, many Canadian manufacturers have produced primarily for the small Canadian market and have therefore been relatively small, inefficient and high-cost operations.

The main reason for this has been Canada's tariff policy. Canada has traditionally sheltered its manufacturing sector from foreign competition with protective **tariffs**. While this protection from foreign competition helped Canada's manufacturing sector to survive and grow, it did not help it to become efficient. Not only was it sheltered from the competition that was making other nations' manufacturers more efficient, but also it was largely producing for the small Canadian market of less than 30 million people. This was partly because most Canadian manufacturers were not efficient enough to compete in export markets, and partly because some foreign nations placed restrictions on Canadian access to their markets in retaliation for Canada's tariffs on their exports to Canada. As a result of producing mainly for the small Canadian market, many Canadian manufacturers had small plants that limited their use of mass-production technology, and thus their efficiency. In other cases, a large plant might exist but it would have to produce several different products due to the small size of the Canadian market. To switch over from one product to another takes time and adds costs, making the operation less efficient than it would be if longer production runs of a single product were made. In either case, producing for the small Canadian market limited the economies of scale and the productivity that many Canadian manufacturers could achieve.

(e) The incentive of after-tax economic gain

As noted earlier, the tax rates payable by businesses and individuals influence their incentives to improve efficiency and earn extra income. Overall, in the early 1990's Canada's taxes (including social security contributions) as a percentage of GDP were slightly higher than the average for major industrialized nations. Canadian taxes on business profits were reasonably comparable to (or competitive with) tax rates in other major industrialized countries. For individuals, however, a combination of high and rising personal income taxes and sales taxes had made the situation less attractive by the early 1990's. In 1993, a senior Department of Finance official warned that Canada had become "close to the highest" taxed nation among the seven largest industrialized countries, and that further increases in personal income taxes risked driving Canadians "offshore or out of the formal economy" (i.e., out of the country or underground). This supported the view that Canadian tax rates, at least on personal income, could not be increased much further without risking problems with incentives.

(f) The incentive of competition

There is general agreement that productivity in the Canadian economy has suffered from a lack of strong competition, for at least three reasons. First, there has been Canada's *tariff policy*, as discussed in the previous section, which has protected many Canadian producers from foreign competition.

Second, the Canadian economy has been characterized by a quite high degree of *oligopoly*, or domination of industries by a few large firms. Under these conditions, it is possible that these few dominant firms will reach an agreement or an understanding that it is in their interests not to compete vigorously against each other in a "fight to the finish," but rather to "live and let live" (often by "price-fixing," or agreeing not to compete on prices) so that all can enjoy high profits. Obviously, such a situation greatly reduces the competitive pressure to continually improve productivity. While such agreements not to compete are illegal, until 1986 Canada's legislation against such anti-competitive practices (the former Combines Investigation Act) was remarkably ineffective, so that there was little if any legal pressure for oligopolists to compete. Finally, many of Canada's industries are subject to a variety of *government regulations*. Some of these regulations restrict who can operate in a particular field (such as taxis and airline routes) or restrict how much producers can produce (such as farm marketing boards); some establish prices, often in a way that guarantees producers a certain rate of profit (such as cable television). Thus, many of these government restrictions have the side-effect of reducing competition and the incentive to improve productivity in parts of the Canadian economy.

GOVERNMENT POLICIES TO STRENGTHEN PRODUCTIVITY AND THE SUPPLY SIDE OF THE ECONOMY

While government policies sometimes weaken productivity, they can also do much to improve productivity, prosperity and the international competitiveness of a nation's industries. In the following sections, we will consider some policy directions that have been taken and could be taken to improve the productivity and competitiveness of Canadian industry.

(a) Re: capital investment

By providing tax incentives that make it financially attractive for people to save and invest money and for businesses to invest in capital equipment, governments can promote the *saving/investment process* that is the key to capital formation. Additional support for technological improvements can come from government support for *research and development* (R&D), in the form of tax allowances or other financial support.

(b) Re: education and skill levels of the labor force

Given the importance of human capital in a modern economy, governmental education and training policies have become very important to a society's economic prosperity. Most observers believe that the education system should place more emphasis on basic skills and should be linked more closely to the needs of the workplace in which graduates must function. In addition, there is general agreement that more emphasis should be placed upon the development of middle-level technical and business skills, and upon apprenticeship programs, and that employers should devote more resources to employee training and retraining. Finally, governments have shown increased interest in reforming social welfare programs by linking unemployment insurance or welfare benefits to training or retraining, either by requiring benefit recipients to undertake training or by providing financial incentives for them to do so.

(c) Re: management

At the strategic level, many Canadian managers should shift their focus more toward the global economy, and to how trends and developments in the international economy provide both opportunities and challenges for their firms. At the operational level, Canada's educational system and business community need to develop increased numbers of well-trained middle managers who are capable of managing for the increased productivity that is needed by both businesses and the economy at large.

(d) Re: market size and scale of operations

Without access to larger foreign markets, many Canadian producers would be unable to achieve the economies of scale needed to be competitive internationally. By the mid-1980's, with much of the world moving toward freer international trade, and with the United States—Canada's largest trading partner—becoming more restrictive regarding foreign imports, Canada was feeling strong pressure to secure access to larger markets for its products. As a result, Canada entered into free trade agreements, first with the United States in 1989 and later with Mexico and the USA in 1994. These agreements, details of which are included in Chapter 33, are intended to provide Canada with more secure access to larger international markets.

(e) Re: the incentive of after-tax economic gain

Both the federal and provincial governments face severe financial problems (budget deficits), which will require reductions in government spending and programs and/or increases in taxes. While there is public pressure to maintain the level of public services, it is also true that taxes in Canada are higher than those in most of the major industrialized nations with which Canada trades and competes. In dealing with their financial problems, it is important that governments ensure that the marginal tax rates on business and personal income do not become so high that they impair economic incentives to work, save and invest, or drive investment capital out of the country.

The most recent major tax-reform measures were undertaken by the federal government after the mid-1980's. These reforms included lower marginal tax rates on personal income and higher taxes on consumption spending in the form of the Goods and Services Tax. One key goal of these reforms was to shift the tax burden toward consumption spending and away from productive activities such as work and investment, so as to maintain incentives to work, save and invest.

(f) Re: the incentive of competition

Probably the single most important step taken by government to increase competition in the Canadian economy was the Canada–US Free Trade Agreement of 1989. In 1994, the North American Free Trade Agreement (NAFTA) added Mexico to the North American free trade area. Under these agreements, the degree of import competition will gradually increase as tariffs are reduced.

Second, we have seen that much of the Canadian economy is dominated by large firms, and that the legislation prohibiting anti-competitive practices (such as price-fixing) by such firms was not very effective. In 1986, new competition legislation (the Competition Act) was introduced that has proven considerably more effective than the old legislation against anti-competitive practices such as price-fixing and mergers of firms in order to dominate a market or an industry.

Finally, as noted in the previous section, government regulation of an industry often has the effect of reducing competition. After the mid-1980's, the federal government undertook to "deregulate" to varying degrees various sectors of the economy, including oil and gas, airlines, communications and financial services, in order to promote increased competition, higher productivity and lower prices.

Summary of the supply side of the economy

So far we have discussed several factors which have an effect upon the productivity, or the production potential—the *supply side*—of the economy:

(a) *Capital equipment:* To the extent that the economy has large amounts of up-to-date capital equipment, and an effective saving-investment process for building it, its potential productivity (output per worker) will be greater.

(b) *Education and skill levels of the labor force:* Efficiency of production is also increased by having a greater number of skilled, educated workers; this is especially important in modern economies that utilize high-technology production methods.

(c) *Management:* Ultimately, it is management that is responsible for the efficiency with which productive resources are utilized.

(d) *Size of market and scale of operations:* In many manufacturing industries, it is necessary that producers have access to large markets in order to be able to produce on the scale required so as to be able to realize the economies of scale associated with mass-production techniques.

(e) *The incentive of after-tax gain:* In order for businesses and individuals to have an economic incentive to improve efficiency by working, saving and investing, it is important that the after-tax gains to them from doing so be sufficient.

(f) *The incentive of competition:* Competition, either from other domestic producers or from foreign producers, plays an important role in pushing businesses to be more efficient.

Together, these factors determine not only the efficiency with which the economy can produce goods and services, but also its potential total output: the *supply side* of the economy.

The potential total output of the economy increases gradually over time, as the size of the labor force grows and output per worker (productivity) increases. In recent years, the size of the labor force has grown by about 1.5 percent per year, and output per worker has increased by about 1.0 to 1.5 percent per year, with the result that the potential output of the economy has risen by some 2.5 to 3.0 percent per year, as reflected in Figure 22-3. These are approximate figures and can change to some degree from year to year. For instance, if productivity growth were to become faster, the potential output line in Figure 22-3 would rise more rapidly, and vice-versa. Notwithstanding this, the impression conveyed by Figure 22-3—that the supply side of the economy grows at a fairly slow and steady pace—remains accurate.

FIGURE 22-3   *The Growth of the Supply Side of the Economy*

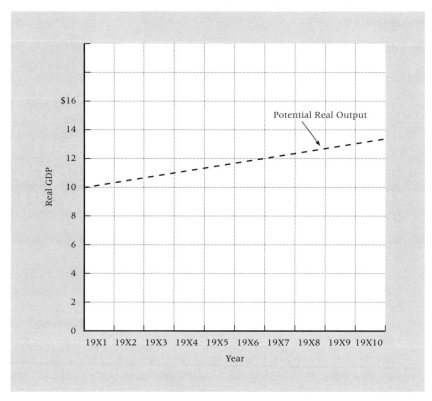

The concept of aggregate supply

The supply side of the economy can be represented by an **aggregate supply** curve, as shown in Figure 22-4, which shows how the level of total output ("aggregate supply") is related to the cost per unit of producing that output.

When operating at *capacity* (that is, at its highest production level), this economy is capable of producing 100 units of output per week. The farther we move to the right on the aggregate supply (AS) curve, the closer we get to this capacity output. The higher the curve goes, the more costly it is to produce goods and services. Up to about 80 or 90 units of volume, we can increase output without experiencing increases in production costs per unit, because the economy has plenty of inputs (labor, capital and resources) available, or unemployed. It should, therefore, be possible to obtain more inputs without having to pay higher wage rates or prices to attract them. Beyond this level, however, it is no longer possible to increase output further without some increases in production costs per unit.

In some industries, production *bottlenecks* will occur, due to shortages of production capacity, skilled labor or other inputs. Thus, output can only be increased by means which will also increase production costs per unit:

FIGURE 22-4 *Aggregate Supply Curve*

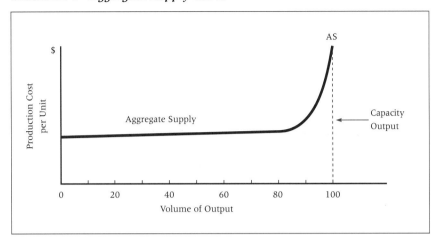

higher wages for overtime or extra shifts, or to attract additional workers, higher prices for increasingly scarce materials or other inputs, and so on. In Figure 22-4 this means that we can move to higher levels of production, but only by accepting higher costs per unit as the AS curve slopes upward.

The closer we get to the economy's capacity output, the more severe these problems of shortages and production bottlenecks become, and the faster the AS curve rises. Finally, at capacity output of 100 units per week, the economy is simply not capable of producing at a faster pace, and the AS curve becomes vertical. The economy is using all of its inputs and the pace of production cannot be increased further, even at sharply higher costs per unit.

CHANGES IN THE AS CURVE

Figure 22-4 represents the AS curve at a particular point in time. If the economy's *potential to produce* were to increase next year as its labor force and stock of capital equipment grew, the AS curve would shift to the right, as shown by AS_1 in Figure 22-5.

AS_1 reflects the fact that the economy is now capable of producing a higher volume of output (110 units) than last year, at about the same cost per unit. Efficiency (productivity) has not improved, as shown by the fact that production costs per unit are the same as last year, but the greater volume of inputs available makes possible a higher volume of total output.

If *overall productivity* in the economy were to improve, so that it was using its inputs more efficiently, not only would its potential (capacity) output rise, but production costs per unit would also fall. This is shown in Figure 22-6 in which AS_2 represents the new situation, with production costs per unit lower than before and capacity output higher than before.

FIGURE 22-5 *AS Curve Illustrating Increased Production Potential*

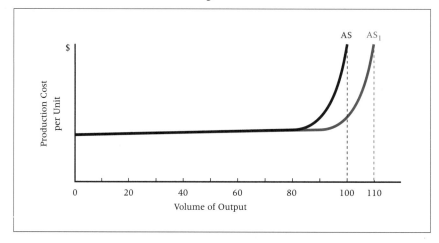

FIGURE 22-6 *AS Curve Illustrating Increased Overall Productivity*

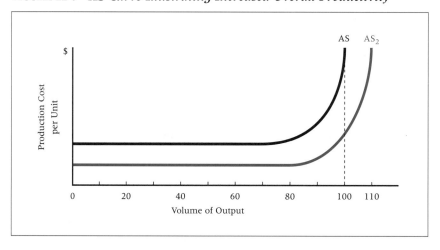

Can saving be too great? A preview of the demand side of the economy

In this chapter, we have stressed the importance of the *supply side* of the economy—its ability to produce goods and services efficiently. Without this ability to achieve high productivity, economic prosperity is not possible. Furthermore, we have stressed the desirability of saving, to make possible the investment that increases the economy's productive potential. However, productive capability alone is not enough to ensure prosperity. If this productive capacity is to be used, there must be sufficient demand for its output. This raises the possibility that saving could be too high—that excessive saving by households could depress consumption spending (demand), leaving business with low sales and little or no incentive to invest in new plant and equipment.

Ideally, then, there would be a *balance* between consumption spending and saving. Saving would be sufficiently high to finance adequate levels of capital investment, while consumption spending would be sufficiently high to provide business with an incentive to invest in additional plant and equipment. Such a balance between spending and saving is essential for economic progress.

In summary, economic progress and prosperity depend on the interaction between the *supply side* and the *demand side* of the economy. Not only must the economy have the ability to produce efficiently, but also there must be sufficient demand for its output to ensure that the economy will actually produce to its fullest possible capabilities. In Chapter 23, we will consider the demand side of the economy more fully.

DEFINITIONS OF NEW TERMS

Supply Side The ability of the economy to use its productive resources efficiently to produce goods and services.

Productivity A measure of productive efficiency, usually measured in terms of labor, as output per worker-hour or output per employee.

Consumption Refers to consumer goods and services that are used up by consumers for present enjoyment.

Investment Refers to the production of capital goods that make possible increased production in the future.

Saving Doing without (foregoing) consumer goods; saving is essential if there is to be investment.

Tariff A tax, or import duty, levied by a nation on products imported from foreign countries.

Marginal Tax Rate The percentage of any *additional* income received that goes to taxes; an important factor influencing incentives to work, save and invest.

Aggregate Supply A representation of the supply side of the economy (usually graphically), showing how production cost per unit changes as the level of output is increased toward its potential.

CHAPTER SUMMARY

1. The key to economic prosperity is high productivity or output per worker-hour.

2. The main factors affecting productivity are:

   (a) capital equipment and the saving-investment process that builds it; this requires foregoing current consumption in order to do the capital investment that will increase productivity (and consumption) in the future,

   (b) the education and skill levels of the labor force,

   (c) management,

   (d) size of market and scale of operations,

   (e) the incentive of after-tax economic gain, and

   (f) the incentive of competition.

3. Canada's *overall* productivity performance is second-highest in the world, about 7 percent below the US level.

4. However, there are certain *particular* concerns regarding Canada's productivity performance and ability to compete internationally; specifically:

   (a) the low productivity of Canada's manufacturing sector, and

   (b) the slower-than-average growth of productivity since the mid-1970's.

5. Most nations experienced a slowdown in productivity growth after the mid-1970's. The reasons for this are not fully understood but are believed to include a slowdown in business capital investment, rapid growth of the labor force in North America, and a shift in all economies of output and employment from goods-producing industries to service industries, in which it is more difficult to apply productivity-improving technology.

6. Canada's below-average productivity performance during this period is attributed to various factors, including a slowness to adopt up-to-date production technology, weak R&D, a labor force (including managers) not educated and trained to match the economy's needs, a small domestic market and a lack of competition due to factors such as tariff protection of manufacturers, domination of industries by a few producers and government regulations that reduce competition.

7. Government policies that could help to improve productivity include policies to encourage saving, investment and R&D, education more attuned to the needs of the economy, agreements to gain/secure access to larger markets (such as the Canada-US Free Trade Agreement), keeping marginal tax rates on business and personal income from becoming too high, and policies to strengthen competition such as freer trade, stronger competition legislation and reduced regulation of business.

8. In recent years, the potential output (supply side) of the Canadian economy has been growing at about three percent per year.

9. Developing the ability to produce more efficiently does not by itself guarantee economic prosperity; there must also be sufficient demand for the economy's output to ensure that the economy actually produces to its fullest possible capabilities.

QUESTIONS

1. If a group of farmers store away some food to eat during the winter, they could be said to be "saving" that food. Is this the same idea as was discussed in the text with respect to saving and investment?

2. In 1992, the highest marginal tax rate on personal income in Canada was about 53 percent; it was payable by people with a taxable income of more than $59 180 per year. Do you regard this as excessively high, or as a fair contribution for a person with an income that high?

3. Some people believe that the productivity slowdown that has occurred since the mid-1970's is largely the result of the decline of the "work ethic." Do you agree that Canadians are becoming lazier?

4. Canada's provincial governments have over the years erected various barriers to trade across provincial borders, such as government purchasing policies that favor suppliers from within the province and preferential licensing and hiring practices favoring residents of the province. What effects would such policies have upon productivity and the economic welfare of Canadians generally?

5. **(a)** Donna teaches accounting in a community college for a salary of $40 000 per year, and pays income tax of $10 000. The average percentage of Donna's income paid to income tax is, therefore, ___ percent; this is Donna's average tax rate.

   (b) If Donna teaches night school, she will earn an additional $1600. The income tax payable on this additional income will be $600. The marginal tax rate paid by Donna on her additional income is ___ percent.

   (c) How would Donna's incentive to work be affected by a significant increase in her:

   (i) average tax rate?

   (ii) marginal tax rate?

6. Fill in the remaining average and marginal tax rates.

Income	Income Tax	Average Tax Rate	Marginal Tax Rate	
$20 000	$4000	20.0%	—	
21 000	4300	20.5%	30.0%	($300/$1000)
22 000	4650	—	—	
23 000	5050	—	—	

7. As an illustration of how a recession can affect labor productivity (output per employee), consider the following case: You are the owner/manager of a small firm that produces kadiddles with the following labor force:

   - 1 president/manager (you)
   - 2 office staff: your secretary/receptionist and a bookkeeper/clerk
   - 1 sales representative
   - 1 plant supervisor
   - 20 plant workers

   The total number of employees is 25, and presently you are producing 5000 kadiddles per week, for an average productivity of 200 kadiddles per person employed.

   Suppose a recession cuts your sales, causing you to reduce output by 20 percent to 4000 per week.

   (a) How many employees will you probably lay off?

   (b) What will "labor productivity" (output per employee) be after the layoffs?

   (c) What is the percentage change in labor productivity, and why has this change occurred?

   (d) When the recession ends and sales and production increase again, what will happen to productivity?

8. People who are working overtime sometimes say that they work "the first two hours for the government then the next three for themselves." Explain what they mean by this.

9. In the early 1990's, Americans were saving about 5 percent of their take-home pay, Canadians about 10 percent and the Japanese about 15 percent. What implications might this have for the potential future growth of these three economies?

10. Under federal tax regulations, the amount of money that Canadians can contribute to tax-deductible Registered Retirement Savings Plans (RRSP's) was increased substantially during the first half of the 1990's. Make an argument that this policy is beneficial, not only to the individual Canadians who can take advantage of this opportunity to save on taxes while saving for their retirement, but also to the Canadian economy as a whole.

11. The graph below shows the aggregate supply curve for an economy that can produce a maximum (capacity) output of 100 units per week. Explain how the AS curve would be changed if:

    (a) the economy had 20 percent more of all productive resources, which could be utilized with the same efficiency as its existing resources.

(b) the efficiency with which the economy's existing productive resources could be utilized increased by 20 percent.

(c) the economy had 20 percent less of all productive resources.

(d) the efficiency with which the economy's existing productive resources could be utilized decreased by 20 percent.

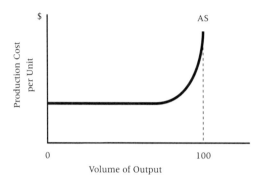

NOTES

[1] This is the concept of *opportunity cost* explained in Chapter 2. The opportunity cost of building capital equipment to increase prosperity in the future is reduced consumption of goods and services in the present.

[2] This does not mean that bigger is always better, though: beyond a certain size, vast operations become difficult to coordinate and manage effectively, and can become less efficient. Ideally, then, manufacturing plants should be of an *optimum size*—the size at which their efficiency is maximized.

[3] Even Canada's small market of 27 million is not a single market. Geographical factors and a variety of provincial laws that restrict the movement of people, capital and products between provinces have the effect of dividing Canada into several smaller markets, further restricting the scale and efficiency of many Canadian industries.

Sources of economic prosperity: The demand side

In Chapter 22, we considered the supply side of the economy—the factors that determine the economy's ability to produce goods and services. Generally, this ability depends on the amount of the society's economic resources (such as labor and capital equipment) and the efficiency with which they are employed. Of particular importance to an economy's ability to produce is the process of capital investment, which contributes not only to total output but also to output per person, and thus to the society's standard of living.

While these factors determine the *potential* output of the economy, they do not decide how much output *actually will* be produced. In a market system, output will only be produced if there is a demand for it. Thus, the total actual output of the economy—the Gross Domestic Product—will depend on the *level of total spending on goods and services* in the economy, or what economists call the **demand side** of the economy.

The level of total spending on goods and services in the economy is known as **aggregate demand**. The level of aggregate demand is critically important to the operation of the economy on a macroeconomic scale: if aggregate demand is too low, there will be a *recession*, with the economy's output well below its potential level and unemployment high. Rising aggregate demand will generate higher levels of both output and employment, or an *economic boom*. However, if aggregate demand becomes too high, output will be unable to keep up with demand and *inflation* will occur, as prices rise rapidly.

Aggregate demand: purchasers of the economy's output

For purposes of analysis, aggregate demand can be divided into the same four categories into which we divided Gross Domestic Product in Chapter 21.

(a) *Consumption spending* by households on consumer goods and services, which buys about 60 percent of the economy's output.

(b) *Investment spending* by businesses on capital goods, which usually amounts to 11–15 percent of GDP.[1]

(c) *Government spending* on goods and services, which accounts for the purchase approximately 25 percent of the economy's output of goods and services, including the services of government employees.

(d) *Net exports* (exports minus imports): A very high proportion of Canada's GDP—between 25 and 28 percent in recent years—consists of exports that are bought by foreign purchasers. From these exports we must subtract Canadian purchases of imported goods and services, so as to determine the net effect of international trade on the level of aggregate demand in Canada.

In the following sections, we will examine each of these components of aggregate demand in more detail, so as to develop a fuller understanding of the demand side of the economy.

(A) CONSUMPTION SPENDING BY HOUSEHOLDS

Consumption is defined as spending by households on consumer goods and services. These can be divided into three categories: *nondurable goods*, such as food and clothing, which are used up quite quickly; *durable goods*, such as cars and appliances, which last considerably longer; and *services*, such as entertainment, medical services and travel. Consumption spending is the "workhorse" of the demand side of the economy, in the sense that it is by far the largest single purchaser of the economy's output. As Figure 23-1 shows, consumption spending buys about 60 percent of the goods and services produced by the economy.

Generally, advanced economies such as the United States, Canada and Western Europe are able to devote a relatively high share of their GDP to current consumption because they have already built a strong base of productive capital through past investment. Countries that are in earlier stages of development tend to devote less of their output to current consumption, and more to investment in building their base of capital.

What determines the level of consumption spending?

The amount of consumption spending done by any particular *individual* household in any given year may be influenced by various factors peculiar

FIGURE 23-1   *Consumption and Gross Domestic Product, 1968–93*

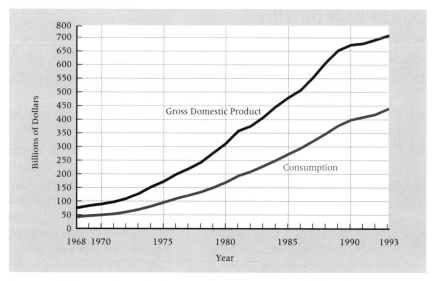

Source: Statistics Canada, *National Income and Expenditure Accounts* (13-001)

to that household. However, when we consider the level of *total* consumption spending in the economy as a whole in a given year, a few key factors stand out.

The most important factor influencing the level of total consumption spending in the economy is the level of total **personal disposable income** (personal income less personal taxes), which is the amount of money

FIGURE 23-2   *Consumer Income and Spending, 1968–93*

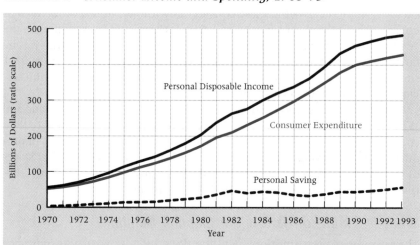

Source: Statistics Canada, *National Income and Expenditure Accounts* (13-001)

households have available to spend. As illustrated in Figure 23-2, consumer spending rises as personal disposable income rises.[2]

Another important factor influencing consumption spending is **consumer confidence**, or the degree to which consumers feel optimistic—or pessimistic—about their future economic prospects. If consumers feel confident about their job and income prospects, they will be inclined to spend more of their disposable income, and save less. More importantly, though, they will be willing to *borrow more*, in order to make larger purchases such as houses, cars, furniture, appliances and vacations that are difficult or impossible to finance out of current disposable income. On the other hand, when consumer confidence is low, consumers tend to borrow and spend less, and may hold down their consumption spending in order to pay off their debts. Figure 23-3 shows the fluctuations in consumer confidence since the late 1970's, as indicated by the Conference Board Survey of Consumer Attitudes. As Figure 23-3 shows, consumer confidence fluctuates considerably from year to year, depending largely on the condition of and outlook for the economy. During recessions, when the fear of unemployment is high, consumer confidence tends to be low. During booms, when job and income prospects are good, confidence tends to increase considerably.

Also, **interest rates** can affect the level of consumer spending. Low interest rates can encourage borrowing and spending, especially on "big-ticket" items such as houses, cars, appliances and furniture. On the other hand, high interest rates can discourage consumers from borrowing and thus depress spending on items such as these.

A related factor affecting consumers' willingness to spend is the level of **consumer indebtedness**. The strong consumer confidence of the mid-to-late 1980's led to quite heavy borrowing that increased the level of household debt from less than 70 percent of disposable income in 1984

FIGURE 23-3 *Conference Board of Canada's Index of Consumer Attitudes*

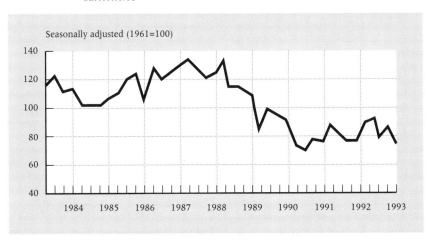

to over 90 percent by the early 1990's. Such high levels of debt made many households reluctant to borrow further; in fact, many concentrated more on repaying their debts and undertook to reduce their debts by spending less on consumption. This depressed level of consumption spending was considered to be a major factor in the slow economic recovery of the early 1990's.

Saving by households

Of course, households do not spend all of their disposable income; they save some of it. **Personal saving** is defined as personal disposable income not spent on consumption. For instance, if total personal disposable income were $500 billion and consumption spending were $450 billion, personal saving would be $50 billion.

Saving by households takes many forms. Much of it is done in savings accounts in banks or trust companies. Other people prefer guaranteed investment certificates, bonds or mortgages because they pay higher interest, or corporate stocks because their value may rise.

How much do Canadians save? This is best measured by the **personal savings rate**, which is the percentage of personal disposable income that is not spent. Using the example from two paragraphs earlier, if personal saving were $50 billion and disposable income were $500 billion, the personal savings rate would be 10 percent ($50/$500). As Figure 23-4 shows, the personal savings rate of Canadians has fluctuated considerably over the years. In the 1960's, personal saving by Canadians averaged about 5 percent of personal disposable income. During the 1970's the personal savings rate rose to levels of about 10 percent, and in the early 1980's it rose again, to about 15 percent. After that, the savings rate declined considerably, into the 9–10 percent range.

Most Canadians, who have little if any money left in the bank by the end of the month, find it difficult to believe that an average household saves 10 percent of its disposable income. However, it must be remembered that saving includes not only bank deposits and securities such as stocks and bonds, but also two other items. These are *pension fund contri-*

QUESTION

If Fran's disposable income is $1600 per month, and she spends $1360 of it on consumer goods and services, puts $180 into a trust company savings account and uses the remaining $60 to buy high-risk "penny-mining" stocks,

(a) How much does Fran *save* per month?
(b) Does this represent a higher or lower saving rate than the average Canadian?

(ANSWER ON NEXT PAGE)

FIGURE 23-4 *Personal Saving as a Percentage of Personal Disposable Income, 1968–1993*

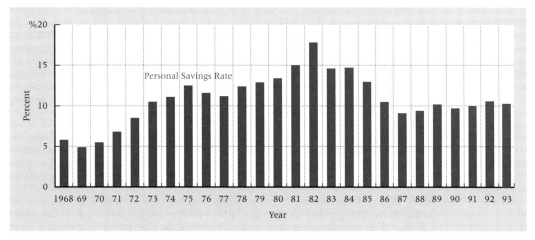

Source: Statistics Canada, *National Income and Expenditure Accounts* (13-001)

butions which are deducted from paycheques regularly; and *mortgage repayments* (excluding interest).[3]

Both of these factors add significantly to saving, although most people do not regard them as saving. However, when many Canadians reach retirement age, their two largest assets are their pension rights and their home—assets for which they have saved for years through their pension contributions and mortgage payments.

What determines the level of personal saving?

As with consumption spending, the most important single factor influencing the level of personal saving is the level of *personal disposable income*: as disposable income rises, so does the volume of saving. However, the level of personal saving is also influenced by other factors, including *consumer confidence*. It seems that consumer confidence is influenced not only by the economic outlook and thus the job and income prospects of consumers,

---

ANSWER

(a) $240—the amount *not spent* on consumption. The fact that some of the savings have been put into a less secure form (stocks) is not relevant here. All of the $240 is saving, and is available for capital investment.

(b) Higher—$240 is 15 percent of $1600, as compared to average saving rates of around 10 percent (and this doesn't even include Fran's pension contributions).

but also by the level of *household wealth*: studies indicate that as the value of household assets (mainly real estate) rose sharply in the 1980's, consumers felt less of a need to save. A different but related factor is the level of *household indebtedness*. The higher the level of household indebtedness, the higher the personal savings rate will likely be, as consumers become more reluctant to take on additional debt and more anxious to pay off some of their debt. In addition, *interest rates* can have an effect on saving, as higher interest rates encourage saving, while lower interest rates encourage borrowing and spending. In addition, *habit* is a factor in saving as many people budget so as to save a certain amount regularly, for security or for a "rainy day"). Finally, *government taxation policies* can influence the saving decisions of households: for instance, the introduction of registered retirement savings plans, which allowed tax deductions for contributions to personal retirement funds, led to a significant increase in the personal savings rate of Canadians. Finally, *demographic factors* can influence the personal savings rate—as the bulk of the baby boomers grow older, their saving rate is expected to increase, pulling up the savings rate for the country as a whole.

How Canadians invest their savings

While Canadians save a considerable portion of their disposable income, this does not automatically mean that Canadian business has ready access to all of these savings, through selling shares and bonds to the public. Canadians tend to be relatively cautious regarding the investment of their savings, preferring safe investments such as bank deposits and guaranteed investment certificates, government bonds and Canada Savings Bonds, and real estate in the form of property or mortgages on property, all of which are seen as more secure than investment in businesses, through purchases of shares. In 1985, the federal government introduced additional tax incentives for investment in shares to encourage Canadians to invest more of their savings in corporations. The purpose of the government's policy was to make more savings available for capital investment, as well as to ease the heavy debt burden carried by many Canadian corporations at that time.

As noted earlier, Canadians do a great deal of saving through their *pension plans*, into which they make contributions by payroll deduction every payday. Figure 23-5 shows the tremendous growth since 1973 of Canadian pension plans, the assets of which grew from $16 billion in 1973 to over $197 billion in 1990. Pension funds are invested in a variety of securities, mostly government bonds and corporate shares and bonds. At the end of 1990, approximately 39 percent of pension fund assets were invested in government bonds, 29 percent in corporate shares and 7 percent in corporate bonds.

FIGURE 23-5 *Assets of Trusteed Pension Plans, 1976–90*

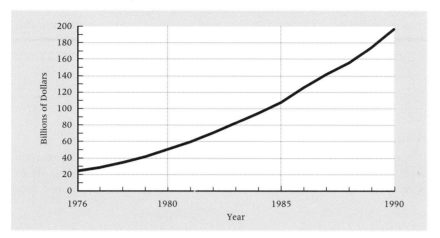

Source: Bank of Canada *Review*, Autumn 1993

(B) INVESTMENT SPENDING BY BUSINESSES

Investment is defined as spending by business firms on capital goods ("producers' goods"). This includes all types of capital goods—factories, machinery, equipment and tools, computers and office equipment and so on. Investment spending includes both additions to society's stock of capital goods and replacements for capital goods that have worn out or depreciated.[4]

Investment includes a great deal of *construction*—not only of factories, but also of warehouses, retail stores and offices. Also, residential construction is classified as investment. When all these types of construction are considered—industrial, commercial and residential—and government construction of roads, public buildings, schools and so on are added, construction has in most years amounted to about one-half of all investment spending in the economy.

Business investment spending on plant and equipment amounts in most years to about 11–15 percent of the GDP—much less than consumption spending. However, business investment spending is a particularly important economic process because the addition of capital goods to the economy increases output per person, or productivity, thus making possible a higher standard of living and improving the international competitiveness of Canadian producers.

The same product can be classed as either a consumption or an investment item, depending on how it is used. For example, if a consumer buys a car for personal use, this is classified as consumption, while the purchase of an identical car by a business for use by one of its salespersons would be investment.

To monitor and forecast investment spending, the federal government twice yearly conducts a survey of business investment intentions. From this survey of a sample of businesses, the government can estimate the future trend of business investment spending in the Canadian economy.

What determines the level of business investment spending?

While there are many factors influencing the level of investment spending by business, these can generally be classified into two categories: (1) expectations regarding the profitability of investments and (2) interest rates.

EXPECTATIONS REGARDING THE PROFITABILITY OF INVESTMENT PROJECTS Business investment decisions are very future-oriented. Since the plant and equipment involved are costly and will typically last for many years and must earn a profit to justify themselves, the *expectations* of businesses regarding the future financial performance of such investments are of great importance. If the outlook for the future of such investments is favorable, investment spending will be high; if it is uncertain or unfavorable, investment spending can be quite low.

Probably the most important considerations underlying business investment decisions in general are:

- how high sales and production are relative to production capacity, and

- whether sales are expected to increase in the future.

If production is at or near capacity levels and sales are expected to rise further, there will be great pressure on businesses to expand through capital investment spending projects. On the other hand, if sales are expected to be stagnant or to fall, capital investment spending is likely to be quite low. Due to these factors, economic forecasts play a significant role in business investment decisions—if good economic conditions are forecast, investment spending is likely to be high, and vice-versa.

In addition, there are various other considerations that will influence business expectations and investment decisions. Will competition increase or diminish? Will our present production facilities have to be upgraded with new equipment in order to remain competitive? Will government trade policy change, facing us with new competition from imports or new opportunities in export markets? Will taxes change? Will interest rates and/or construction costs rise next year? (If so, maybe we should build now.) Will interest rates fall next year? (If so, maybe we should wait, and borrow money then, at lower rates.) Will technological changes occur, making our present facilities obsolete? Do government programs provide tax or other incentives that encourage investment? Will government regulations make new investments unprofitable?

FIGURE 23-6   *Conference Board of Canada's Index of Business Confidence*

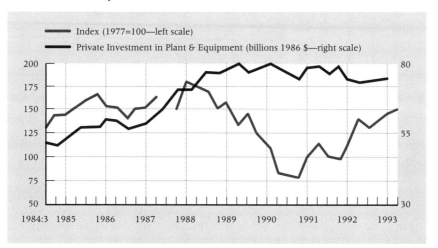

Sources: Statistics Canada; The Conference Board of Canada

Because they are so complex and so specific to individual firms and industries, expectations are difficult to analyze with any precision on a macroeconomic scale. Still, they are the most important factor influencing the level of investment spending. Figure 23-6 shows the Conference Board of Canada's Index of Business Confidence, which is based on surveys of Canadian business firms.

INTEREST RATES   Quite frequently, capital investment projects are financed with borrowed money, which the company usually raises by selling bonds to the public. To be profitable, an investment project (say, a plant) must *earn* a higher rate of return on the money invested in it than the rate of interest that the business must *pay* on the borrowed funds. For instance, if a company must pay an 8 percent annual interest rate on money borrowed through a bond issue, it would be quite profitable to borrow money to build a plant that earned a 12-percent-per-year rate of return. However, if the company had to pay a 13 percent interest rate, the same investment project would not be profitable. For this reason, when interest rates are lower, investment spending by business would tend to be encouraged, while higher interest rates should be expected to discourage capital investment.

Investment in the Canadian economy

Investment has historically played a vital role in the Canadian economy, often amounting to 14–18 percent of GDP.[5] This emphasis on investment has in part been the result of Canada's unusually large investment requirements, which arise from Canada's low population density (which requires proportionately more investment in transportation and distribution facilities) and the fact that many of Canada's industries (especially natural resource industries) are capital-intensive; that is, they use a great deal of capital equipment as compared to labor.

Financing capital investment: the saving-investment process revisited

In Chapter 22, using the illustration of fishing on the desert island, we examined the saving-investment process through which capital equipment is built. We saw that in order to invest in capital goods (spears and nets) that would increase their future prosperity, people had to "save" in the sense of doing without consumer goods (fish) for a while. The key to that process was that investment was not possible without *saving*.

This basic economic principle applies equally to a modern economy such as Canada's. In the early 1990's, Canadian businesses were spending approximately $80 billion per year on capital investment. This required that they have access to about $80 billion of savings, to finance these investment projects. These savings come mainly from three basic sources: *personal savings*, *business savings* and *foreign savings*.

Personal savings have been a significant source of funds for business investment, partly because Canadians, as we have seen, tend to save a relatively high proportion of their disposable income. These savings can be made available for business investment when they are used to buy stocks and bonds issued by businesses. Some of these stocks and bonds are purchased directly by households, but for the most part this is done on their behalf by pension funds and financial institutions such as banks, trust companies and mutual funds, which invest the savings of households. In the early 1990's, personal saving by Canadian households amounted to roughly $45–50 billion annually.

Another key source of funds for capital investment is **business savings**, or **retained earnings**, or profits retained in the business after taxes have been paid and dividends have been paid to the shareholders. Figure 23-7 shows a simplified illustration of the calculation of the retained earnings of a business. In this example, after all expenses, taxes and dividends have been paid, $4 million of additional retained earnings becomes available for reinvestment into the business in the year shown.

FIGURE 23-7 *Retained Earnings: an Illustration*

	Sales income	$100	million
	Expenses	92	
=	Profits before tax	8	
−	Taxes	3	
=	After-tax profits	5	
−	Dividends to shareholders	1	
=	Addition to retained earnings	$ 4	

FIGURE 23-8   *Corporation Profits, 1968–93*

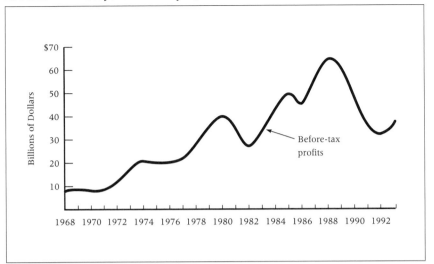

Source: Department of Finance, *Economic and Fiscal Reference Tables*, August 1993

As Figure 23-8 shows, profits and retained earnings are a quite variable source of savings, rising rapidly in some years but actually falling in others. While many factors influence the overall level of profits in the economy, the most important factor is the state of the economy itself: in periods of prosperity and rapid economic growth, profits rise rapidly, while economic slowdowns usually bring declines in profits.

Finally, Canada has also traditionally imported large amounts of **foreign savings**, or foreign capital (mainly from the United States), to finance its capital investment. According to the Economic Council of Canada, "Although Canadians direct a high proportion of their private and business income into savings, Canada has historically needed to supplement its domestic savings with foreign borrowings in order to achieve rates of investment consistent with the desired growth of the economy and employment." When we add the profits of foreign companies in Canada that are reinvested in Canada to the foreign borrowings referred to by the Economic Council of Canada, we see that foreigners have historically tended to provide nearly 20 percent of the savings used for capital formation in Canada.

Business investment in Canada in recent years

Figure 23-9 shows business investment spending in Canada in recent years, in both current dollars and the more meaningful real terms (that is, adjusted for inflation). These statistics show that capital investment tends to fluctuate considerably more than consumer spending (compare Figure 23-9 with Figure 23-2), as business expectations and interest rates fluctuate.

FIGURE 23-9   *Business Investment in Plant and Equipment,ᵃ 1968–93*

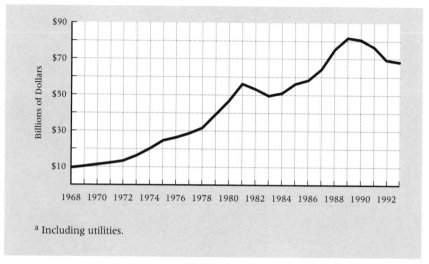

ᵃ Including utilities.

Source: Statistics Canada, *National Income and Expenditures Accounts* (13-001)

(C) GOVERNMENT SPENDING ON GOODS AND SERVICES

Another major purchaser of the economy's output is government. Purchases of goods and services by governments—federal, provincial and local—have amounted in recent years to 22–23 percent of Canada's GDP.[6] Of this, the vast majority (about 20 percent of GDP) has consisted of current expenditures, with only a small amount (2–3 percent of GDP) going to capital expenditures.

The bulk of current government expenditures on goods and services consists of the wages and salaries of government employees who provide a wide range of services to the public, such as health care workers, teachers, social workers, law enforcement workers, civil servants and the military.

(D) NET EXPORTS (EXPORTS MINUS IMPORTS)

As we have seen, purchases of Canadian exports by foreign buyers constitute an important component of aggregate demand in the Canadian economy, buying about 25–28 percent of Canada's GDP in recent years. While export spending adds strongly to aggregate demand in Canada, Canadian purchases of imported goods and services have the opposite effect—they reduce the level of spending within Canada. Therefore, to obtain the net effect of international trade, we must *add* to aggregate demand foreign purchases of Canadian exports and *subtract* Canadian purchases of imports. For instance, if Canadian exports were $170 billion and imports were $150 billion, net exports (exports minus imports) would be +$20 billion and the net effect of international trade would be to add $20 billion to the level of aggregate demand in the Canadian economy. Conversely, if exports were $160 billion and imports were $170 billion, net exports would be –$10 billion, and the net effect of international trade would be to reduce aggregate demand in the Canadian economy by $10 billion.

While this component of aggregate demand is very important to the performance of the Canadian economy, it depends on complex international factors that are quite different from the other components of aggregate demand discussed in this chapter. Therefore, we will cover the international sector only briefly in this chapter, and return to it in more detail later.

The demand side of the economy in review

Aggregate demand, or total spending on goods and services in the economy, is the total of spending by the four sectors of the economy discussed in the previous sections: the consumer sector, the business sector, the government sector and the international (trade) sector. For example, if spending by each of these sectors were as shown in the illustration below, aggregate demand for that year would be $680 billion.

Consumption spending		$400 billion
Business investment spending	$80	
Residential construction	40	120
Government spending on goods and services		150
Exports of goods and services	170	
– Imports of goods and services	–160	
= Net exports		10
Gross Domestic Product		$680

The demand side and the supply side

In the illustration above, is $680 billion a "good" or "bad" level of aggregate demand for the economy in this year? The answer to this question depends on the supply side of the economy, or how much the economy is capable of producing.

If the supply side were capable of producing $800 billion of goods and services and aggregate demand were only $680 billion, then production—and employment—would be 15 percent below their potential levels. The economy would be in a *recession*, and unemployment would be very high.

On the other hand, if the economy's supply side were only capable of producing $600 billion of goods and services, aggregate demand of $680 billion would be too high. Supply could not keep up with demand, with the result that prices in general would rise rapidly, generating rapid *inflation*.

From these illustrations, we can see that ideally, there would be a rough balance between the supply side and the demand side of the economy. That is, the level of aggregate demand would be close to the capacity of the supply side to produce goods and services, and not so low as to cause a recession nor so high as to generate serious inflation.

Does the economy have a natural tendency toward recession?

An idea that gained some popularity during the Great Depression of the 1930's was the Social Credit Party's theory that there was a fundamental flaw in the economic system. According to this theory, the incomes received by households, businesses and governments were simply not large enough to purchase the entire Gross Domestic Product. As a result, the Socreds argued, there was a persistent inadequacy of aggregate demand in the economy, leading to a continual tendency toward an economic downturn and high unemployment. Unable to sell all they had produced and faced with rising inventories of goods on hand, businesses would reduce production and lay off workers. This, in turn, would reduce households' total income further, generating worse declines in sales and more layoffs, causing the economy to spiral downward into a depression. According to Social Credit theory, this was a chronic tendency of the economy.

While the Social Credit theory provided a simple and therefore attractive explanation of, and answer to,[7] the perplexities of the Depression, it was not an accurate theory. In fact, there *is* enough income generated in the production of the GDP to purchase the entire GDP. The incomes of households

FIGURE 23-10 *GDP and Total Incomes*

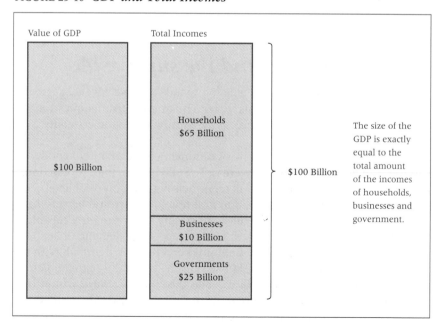

(personal disposable income), businesses (retained earnings plus depreciation allowances) and government (in the form tax revenues) are exactly the same in size as the Gross Domestic Product, as shown in Figure 23-10.

If we regard the value of the GDP as a sort of "super price tag" representing the total of the price tags of all goods and services produced over the year, we can see that each cost of an item that is covered by or included in that price tag represents an income to someone. Labor costs go to households as wages and salaries, profits and depreciation allowances are income to businesses,[8] and sales and other taxes included in the price tag become income to governments.

If each of the three sectors of the economy (households, businesses and governments) were to spend all of its income ($65, $10 and $25 billion respectively in Figure 23-10) on goods and services, the entire GDP of $100 billion would be bought. Thus, there is no automatic purchasing-power problem as envisioned by Social Credit theory. The only way the economy could head into a downturn would be if part of these incomes were *not spent*.

THE PROBLEM OF SAVING

As we have seen, not all income *is* spent: households save some of their disposable income, and this *personal saving* could cause problems for the economy, by creating a *shortage of spending*. If, in Figure 23-10, households saved $5 billion, total spending would amount to only $95 billion, $5 billion short of the value of the GDP, as Figure 23-11 shows.

FIGURE 23-11 *The Problem of Saving*

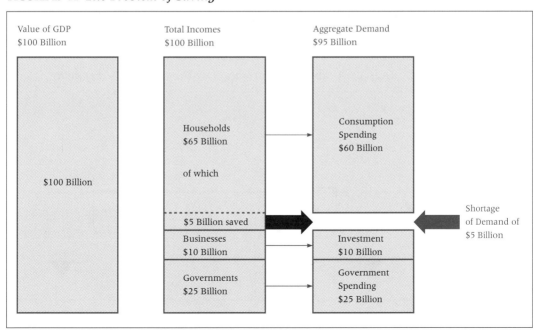

In addition to personal saving, there may also be *business saving*, in the sense of retained earnings not reinvested in capital goods. The result would be an even larger shortfall of demand than that shown in Figure 23-11.

Thus, savings by both households and businesses pose a potential threat to the economy. If money saved by both households and businesses were to lie idle rather than be used to purchase goods and services, it could drag the level of aggregate demand down, generating an economic downturn, or recession.

Models of the economy

In order to demonstrate the dynamics of how the economy operates on a macroeconomic scale, economists construct "models" of the economy. Ideally, such models manage to simplify the complexities of a modern economy by focusing on the key factors that influence how well the economy performs, without becoming so simplified that they omit important factors. Economic models range from simple pen-and-paper representations to intricate computer-based econometric models that utilize highly sophisticated mathematical equations and relationships among various economic variables. In the following, we will consider three such models: a simple *income-flow model*, a simple *supply side/demand side model* and a more sophisticated *aggregate demand/aggregate supply model*.

AN INCOME-FLOW MODEL OF THE ECONOMY

An income-flow model of the economy is particularly useful for analyzing the operation of the demand side of the economy. The flows of income, spending and saving in the economy can be illustrated with a simple income-flow diagram, such as Figure 23-12.[9]

FIGURE 23-12 *A Simplified Income-Flow Diagram of the Economy*

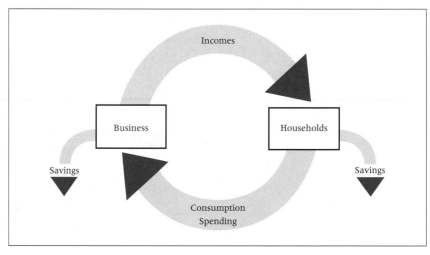

This diagram shows some of the major flows, or streams, of money in the economy. One major flow is the payment of *incomes* (mostly wages and salaries) to households by the business sector, as shown in the top loop. As the bottom loop shows, households spent most of this income on *consumption* (consumer goods and services). However, the diagram shows that households do save some money, and businesses may save, too, in the form of *retained earnings*.

In the economy shown in Figure 23-12, the level of output would fall. The money saved by households and businesses causes a drag on the economy, because it does not buy goods and services. Because of this saving, businesses would be unable to sell all of their output, and would cut production and lay off workers, causing a recession.

Economists use the word **leakage** to describe this effect. If we think of the diagram as an inner tube, with spending and incomes as the air, then saving tends to drain air from the tube, deflating the tube because it reduces spending. Thus, saving is described as a leakage from the spending stream, which reduces spending and slows down the economy.

Offsetting saving: Investment

However, saving need not cause a recession—it is still possible for the entire output of the economy to be bought, despite saving by households and businesses. This can happen if the money that is saved is used by business to buy additional capital goods. The use of business savings for capital investment in this way is simple, as businesses already possess these funds. Indeed, capital investment is the most common use of businesses' retained earnings.

The use of the savings of households to finance capital investment by business is somewhat more complicated, because these funds must first be transferred from the households that have saved them to the businesses that will use them to buy capital goods. In exchange for these savings, businesses issue, or sell, *stocks and bonds*, either directly to households or indirectly. In the latter case, the stocks and bonds are bought by institutions such as trust companies, banks, insurance companies, mutual funds and pension funds into which households have deposited their savings. Such institutions are known as *financial intermediaries* because they act as a go-between to transfer savings from households to businesses.

This is the process referred to as *financial investment* earlier in this chapter. Financial investment does not by itself help to offset the shortage of demand caused by saving—it does not buy any of the economy's output. However, by transferring the savings of households to businesses, it sets the stage for businesses to spend those savings on capital goods—the process of *real investment*. In Figure 23-13, the dotted lines show how funds that have been removed from the spending stream by saving can be returned to the spending stream as real investment.

FIGURE 23-13 *Offsetting Saving: The Return of Savings to the Spending Stream Through Capital Investment by Business*

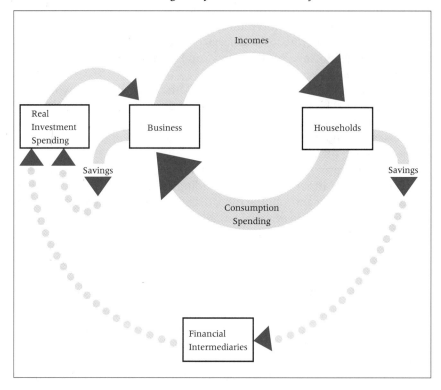

Leakages and injections

The effect of business investment on the economy is just the opposite of the effect of saving. While saving is called a *leakage* from the spending stream because it reduces spending on goods and services, business investment spending is called an **injection** into the spending stream because it adds to aggregate demand, by purchasing capital goods. In effect, the money that was not spent on consumer goods and services can be returned to the economy as spending on capital goods.

To save or not to save?

We have seen how saving can pose a threat to economic stability by creating a shortage of aggregate demand, which could cause an economic slowdown. On the other hand, it is also true that saving presents the economy with a great opportunity—if savings are used for capital investment, the economy can benefit in two important ways. On the demand side of the economy, when savings are invested in capital goods, aggregate demand will be supported, so that a recession can be avoided. And on the supply side of the economy, business investment in capital goods will improve productivity, the living standards of Canadians and the international competitiveness of Canadian producers.

To illustrate the role of saving in the economy, imagine two very different economies—one in which households saved a very large proportion of their income, and another in which they saved none of it. The economy in which saving was very high would suffer from a serious shortage of consumer spending. Without this demand to support current production, there would be a recession, as producers cut output and laid off employees. Such a high-saving economy would experience severe *demand-side* problems in the present.

The second economy, with no saving, would not have that problem—there would be no shortage of consumer spending with a saving rate of zero. However, without saving, this economy could not invest in capital goods. It would not be able to increase its productive efficiency and total output—in short, it would experience *supply-side* problems that would severely limit its future prosperity.

Neither of the two above scenarios will result in good economic performance. What is required for good economic performance is an appropriate *balance* of consumer spending, saving and investment. Consumer spending should be high enough (and thus saving low enough) to support output, employment and prosperity *in the present*, while saving should be high enough to support sufficient capital investment to generate the higher productivity and economic prosperity that is desired *for the future*.

The paradox of thrift

The foregoing suggests that saving alone is less important than the balance of saving and investment. Suppose a nation's people decided, for some reason, to increase substantially the amount that they saved, and that this increase in households' savings was not offset by an increase in business investment spending.[10] Under these circumstances, the public's attempt to save more could actually result in less saving, because it would cause lower levels of aggregate demand, thus generating reductions in output, employment and income—and at these lower levels of income, there would be less saving. This perverse effect, whereby an attempt by the public to increase its saving can actually result in reduced saving, is known as the *paradox of thrift*.

Some observers believe that the Canadian economy suffered from similar problems during the recessions of both the early 1980's and the early 1990's. They pointed out that in both recessions, the personal savings rate rose, and argued that this contributed to the sluggishness of business investment spending by depressing consumer demand. According to this view, the economy would benefit if consumers spent more and saved less. Ironically, the personal saving rate was lowest in the late 1980's, when aggregate demand was already very high and the economy did not need additional consumer spending.

Saving, investment and the performance of the economy

The income-flow model shown in Figure 23-12 can be used to illustrate the relationship between saving, investment and the performance of the economy.

The level of aggregate demand—and the performance of the economy—depend in large part on businesses' plans regarding investment and households' plans regarding saving. If these plans were to coincide, so that businesses were planning just enough investment to offset exactly the saving that households were planning, the *injections* into the spending stream from investment would match the *leakages* from it due to saving. With injections equal to leakages, the level of aggregate demand in the economy would remain unchanged; and the economy (and GDP and total incomes) would neither expand nor contract. Rather, it would remain in a state of **equilibrium**, as shown in Figure 23-14.[11]

There is, however, no reason to expect that plans regarding saving and investment will always coincide in this way. Personal saving depends mainly on personal disposable income. However, it is influenced by many other factors, including consumer confidence, interest rates, the age composition of the population, habit, and government taxation policies concerning income (interest, dividends and capital gains) from savings. On the other hand, businesses make their investment spending plans largely on the basis of their expectations concerning the future profitability of those investments, with the level of interest rates also playing an important role.

With saving and investment plans depending on such different factors, it is very likely that sometimes planned investment will exceed planned saving. At other times, planned investment will be less than planned saving. We will look at each case in turn.

FIGURE 23-14 *The Economy in Equilibrium When Planned Investment Equals Planned Saving*

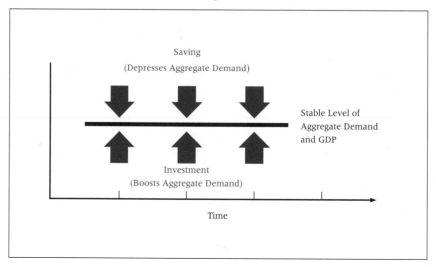

If planned investment is less than planned saving

Suppose that the economic outlook is uncertain at best, unfavorable at worst, and that interest rates are high. Under these circumstances, households may be less inclined to spend freely and more inclined to save, while businesses will likely engage in less capital investment than usual. Thus, planned investment would be less than planned saving, so that injections into the spending stream would be less than leakages from it, *causing aggregate demand to be depressed*. The result would be that the GDP would be depressed, for two reasons.

(A) REAL OUTPUT OF GOODS AND SERVICES WILL BE DEPRESSED   Faced with sluggish sales, businesses will reduce their output of goods and services and lay off some workers. Thus, the most direct effect of depressed aggregate demand would be an economic slowdown, or *recession* as shown in Figure 23-15.[12]

(B) PRICES OF GOODS AND SERVICES WILL BE DEPRESSED   Depressed levels of aggregate demand will have a second effect: they will depress the prices of goods and services in general. In response to sluggish sales, business generally will raise prices less rapidly, and may even reduce them, to encourage sales and thus reduce their excessive inventories of goods.

By "depressed," we refer not only to actual declines in output and prices, but also to slower-than-usual rates of growth of these. During a typical economic slowdown, however, even a slower rate of output growth (and employment) will cause higher unemployment rates, as the economy fails to generate enough new jobs for the growing labor force. Thus, a typical economic recession is characterized by slow economic growth, rising unemployment and relatively slow increases in prices and wages.

FIGURE 23-15 *The Economy in Contraction When Planned Investment is Less Than Planned Saving*

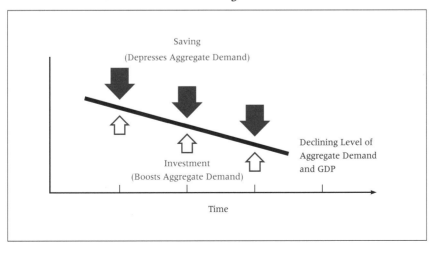

If planned investment exceeds planned saving

Suppose that economic forecasts are encouraging, production is near capacity levels and interest rates are relatively low. As a result, businesses are spending considerable amounts on capital investment, while householders feel less of a need to save and are spending a greater proportion of their disposable income. Under these circumstances, planned investment by business would be greater than planned saving, so that *injections* into the spending stream would exceed *leakages* from it, and *aggregate demand would increase*, as shown in Figure 23-16.

The increase aggregate demand shown in Figure 23-16 could have two quite different effects on the economy:

(A) INCREASED OUTPUT OF GOODS AND SERVICES   Rising aggregate demand will stimulate businesses to increase their production of goods and services, and to hire additional workers. As these workers spend their new incomes, the demand for goods and services will be increased further. Increases in real output and employment such as these are called **real economic growth**, because they add to society's output of goods and services.

(B) INCREASES IN THE PRICES OF GOODS AND SERVICES   However, rising aggregate demand could also cause the prices of goods and services in general to rise; that is, it could generate **inflation**.[13] The risk of inflation is greater, the closer the economy is to its maximum (capacity) level of production. Under these conditions, the supply side of the economy is more likely to have difficulty keeping up with rising aggregate demand, with the result that prices will rise more rapidly. Generally, then, the higher the level of aggregate demand relative to the productive capacity of the supply side is, the greater the likelihood of inflation will be.

FIGURE 23-16 *The Economy in Expansion When Planned Investment is Greater Than Planned Saving*

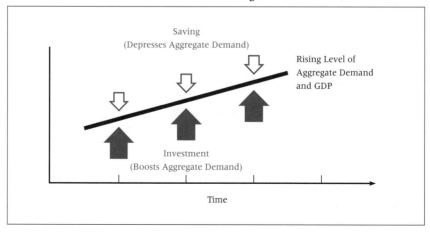

Thus, increases in aggregate demand may cause increases in real output or they may cause inflation, or they may cause some of both.[14]

If the supply side of the economy can increase output in response to the rising aggregate demand, the main result will be increases in output (and employment); however, if the supply side cannot keep up with rising aggregate demand, inflation will result. One limitation of the income-flow model is that it does not show the supply side of the economy, making it impossible to determine whether a given increase in aggregate demand will cause higher output or generate inflation. However, the other two models that we will consider do include both the demand side and the supply side of the economy.

Other leakages and injections

So far in our income-flow model, we have considered only one leakage from the spending stream (saving) and one injection (business investment spending). However, saving and investment do not constitute the only important leakage from and injection into the spending stream; we must also consider the *government sector* and the *foreign trade sector* of the economy.

ADDING THE GOVERNMENT SECTOR   So far, we have omitted the government sector from the picture, so as to develop the basic concepts without unnecessary complications. Now, however, the government sector can be added without any difficulty. As Figure 23-17 shows, the addition

FIGURE 23-17 *Income-Flow Diagram of the Economy Including the Government Sector*

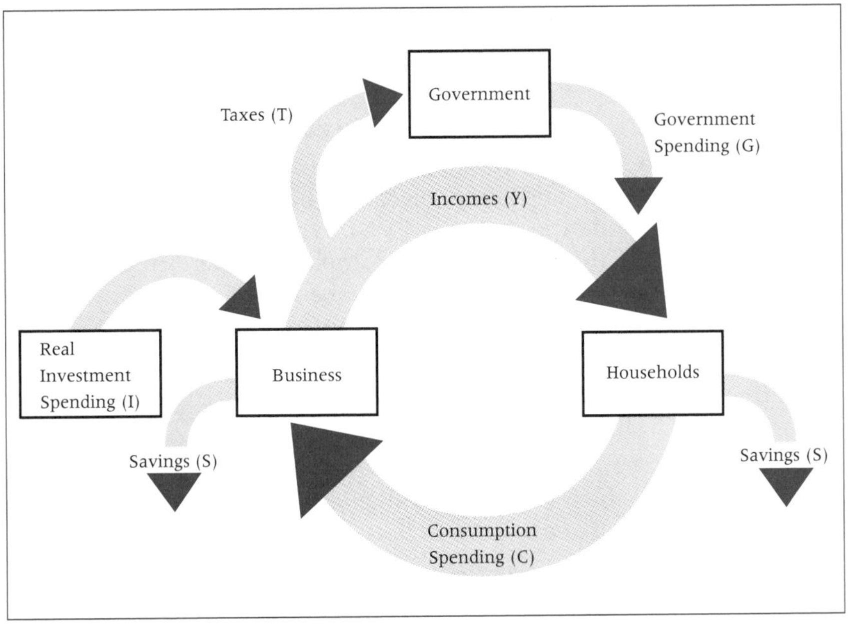

of government (meaning all three levels of government—federal, provincial and municipal) simply adds another leakage (taxes) and another injection (government spending) to our diagram. The effect of taxes is similar to the effect of saving—by removing money from the spending stream, taxes act as a drag on aggregate demand, or a leakage. The effect of government spending on goods and services is just the opposite—it acts as an injection, stimulating aggregate demand and the economy as a whole.

Figure 23-17 is quite oversimplified—it shows taxes coming out of income alone, while in fact there are taxes on other things (such as sales taxes on consumption spending). Also, it shows government spending going only into the income flow, while in fact some goes to business and some to households, in various ways. In addition, it does not show how the government sector (as well as business) can borrow and spend the savings of households. Nonetheless, this diagram does show the basic elements of the role of the government.

The addition of the government sector makes no difference to the way in which the levels of GDP and incomes are determined—this still depends on the relationship between leakages and injections. Now we have one more leakage and one more injection.

Figure 23-17 also shows the abbreviations commonly used for various economic terms: **C** for consumption spending, **I** for investment spending, **Y** for income (Y_d is disposable income), **S** for saving and **T** for taxes.

ADDING THE FOREIGN TRADE SECTOR Finally, we must add exports (**X**) and imports (**M**)—the foreign trade sector—to our analysis. Because they add to aggregate demand in the Canadian economy, exports are considered an injection into the spending stream, and because money spent on imports is removed from the spending stream (in Canada), imports are considered a leakage.

LEAKAGES, INJECTIONS AND THE ECONOMY

In summary, then, we have considered three leakages (savings, taxes and imports, or S + T + M), and three injections (investment spending, government spending and exports, or I + G + X). While the additional leakages and injections make the situation more complex, the performance of the economy still depends on the balance between leakages and injections, just as it did when we considered only saving and investment.

(a) *If leakages exceed injections:* (S + T + M > I + G + X), aggregate demand, output, employment and prices will all be depressed—the economy will go into a slump.

(b) *If injections exceed leakages:* (I + G + X > S + T + M), aggregate demand, output, employment and prices will tend to rise, as the economy experiences a period of expansion.

(c) *If injections are equal to leakages:* (I + G + X = S + T + M), the economy will be in equilibrium, with the levels of aggregate demand and GDP stable.

A SUPPLY SIDE/DEMAND SIDE MODEL OF THE ECONOMY

Figure 23-18 summarizes the supply side of the economy as covered in Chapter 22 and the demand side of the economy as discussed in this chapter.

Figure 23-18 is a *static representation* of the two sides of the economy and the factors that influence each. However, it is the *dynamic interaction* between the supply side and the demand side of the economy that determines the performance of the economy regarding output/real GDP/employment and prices. This interaction is shown in Figure 23-19.

The dotted line in Figure 23-19 represents the supply side, or the potential (capacity) output of the economy. As we saw in Chapter 22 (Figure 22-3), the economy's maximum potential output increases only gradually from year to year, as the number of workers in the labor force and output per worker (productivity) both gradually increase. In recent years, the economy's **capacity output** has increased at about three percent per year, as reflected by the gradual rising trend of the dotted line representing the supply side.

FIGURE 23-18 *The Supply Side and Demand Side of the Economy*

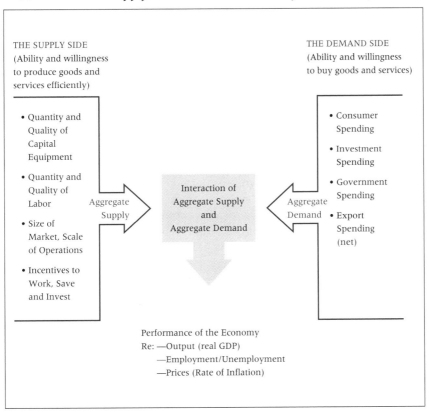

FIGURE 23-19 *A Supply-Side/Demand-Side Model of the Economy*

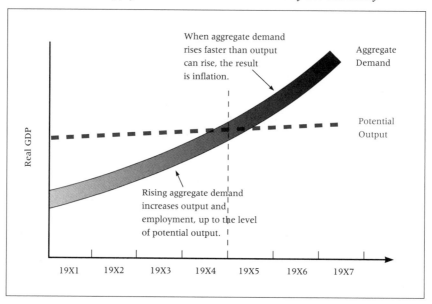

This type of model is most useful for illustrating the interaction be-tween the demand side and the supply side of the economy over a period of time. The wide solid line shows changes in aggregate demand over a period of time, from year 19X1 to 19X7. In 19X1, the economy is in a re-cession. Aggregate demand for goods and services is well below the econ-omy's capacity production level, leaving production and employment well below their potential levels.

As aggregate demand rises in years 19X1 through 19X4, output in-creases quite rapidly. Because production has been below capacity levels, it can temporarily rise by more than 3 percent per year, as previously un-employed labor and plant capacity are brought into production. In fact, when the economy is recovering from a recession, it is possible for out-put to rise by as much as five or even six percent per year.

Such rapid increases in output cannot continue indefinitely, however, because before long the economy's output will reach its capacity level, as shown by the dotted line. From this point forward, output can only in-crease as rapidly as the productive capacity of the economy increases, which we have seen to be about three percent per year. By the end of year 19X4, the economy has reached its potential output, and output can-not increase as rapidly as before. If aggregate demand continues to rise after year 19X4 as it has in the previous three years, output will be phys-ically unable to keep up with demand.

In Figure 23-19, after year 19X4, the output of goods and services (as shown by the dotted line) is unable to keep up with the rapidly rising de-mand (as shown by the solid line). As a result, the prices of goods and ser-vices in general will rise quite rapidly as they are bid up by the excess of demand over available supply—there will be a growing problem of *inflation* in the economy.

In actual fact, the effects of rising aggregate demand on output and prices are not as separate and distinct as this analysis may suggest. Rising aggregate demand tends to cause both output and prices to rise simultaneously, with the effect on prices being stronger, the closer the economy gets to its potential output. This is shown by the grey area in year 19X4 in Figure 23-19: the darker the line, the more rapidly prices are rising as higher demand pushes the economy closer to its limits. Thus, a period of economic expansion tends to be characterized not only by rising output and employment, but also by inflation, and the closer output gets to capacity levels, the more rapid inflation will become.

AN AGGREGATE DEMAND/AGGREGATE SUPPLY MODEL OF THE ECONOMY

Our third model of the economy uses aggregate demand and aggregate supply curves to illustrate the performance of the economy under different conditions, ranging from severe recession to rapid inflation. In doing so, it illustrates clearly how and why inflation becomes more severe, the closer the economy moves to its capacity level of output.

Aggregate demand graphed

Figure 23-20 shows the relationship between aggregate demand (AD) and the *level of prices* in the economy. At high price levels (in the upper range of the AD curve), aggregate demand is relatively low, while at low price lev-

FIGURE 23-20 *Aggregate Demand*

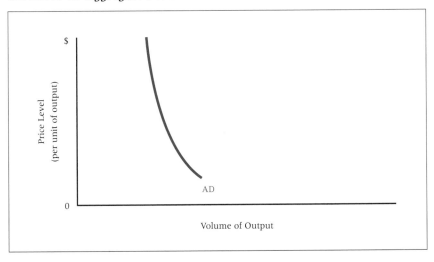

FIGURE 23-21 *Changes in Aggregate Demand*

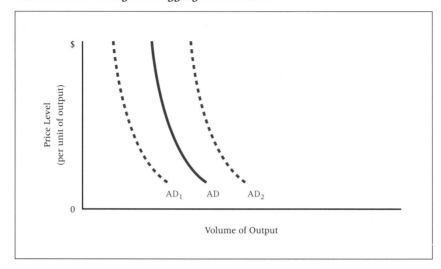

els (in the lower range of the AD curve), aggregate demand is higher. This is mainly because of the fact that if the prices of Canadian products are higher, foreigners buy fewer Canadian products and Canadians buy more imports, both of which depress the demand for Canadian products. On the other hand, if Canadian prices are lower, the demand for Canadian goods and services will be higher both in Canada and abroad. The level of prices could also affect the purchasing behaviour of Canadians: higher prices of goods and services may cause Canadians to postpone their purchases, holding aggregate demand down, while lower prices could have the opposite effect, increasing aggregate demand. The result of these factors is that the aggregate demand curve is shaped as it is in Figure 23-19, with aggregate demand higher at lower levels of prices and lower at higher levels of prices.

We have seen that the level of aggregate demand can fluctuate from time to time, being low in periods of recession and high during periods of boom and inflation. These fluctuations are shown in Figure 23-21. AD is the same curve as in Figure 23-20, while AD_1 represents the low levels of aggregate demand typical of a recession. Note that, at any given price level, AD_1 indicates a lower demand than AD. On the other hand, AD_2 represents a higher level of aggregate demand, with more output being demanded at any given price level.

Aggregate demand and aggregate supply combined

Figure 23-22 adds the aggregate supply curve (AS) from Chapter 22. As we saw in Chapter 22, the AS curve shows that up to an output of 80 units, output can be increased without significant increases in production costs and prices. This is because the recessionary condition of the economy makes the plant capacity, labor and materials needed to increase output readily avail-

FIGURE 23-22 *Aggregate Demand and Aggregate Supply Combined*

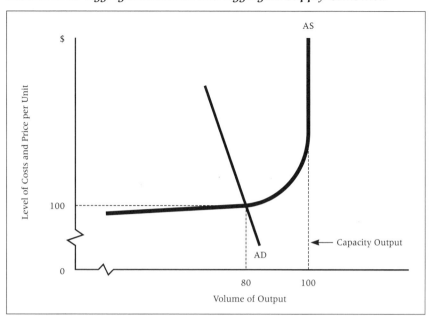

able. However, as output is increased beyond 80 units, production "bottlenecks" begin to appear in the form of shortages of plant capacity, labor or materials that make it more difficult and costly to increase output. And the closer the economy gets to capacity production, the more severe and costlier these bottlenecks will become. As a result, increases in output beyond 80 units will come at a higher production cost—and price—per unit, and these increases in costs and prices will become greater as capacity output is approached. This is shown by the upward swing in the AS curve as production nears its capacity level of 100 units.

Figure 23-22 shows the interaction of the aggregate supply curve from Chapter 22 and the aggregate demand curve from this chapter. With the AD and AS curves intersecting at E as shown, the level of output will be 80 and the level of prices will be 100: the economy is in a recession, with output well below its capacity level of 100 and unemployment quite high due to inadequate aggregate demand. With aggregate demand so weak, the level of prices is quite low.

If aggregate demand were to increase to the level shown by AD_1 in Figure 23-23, output would rise to 95 and unemployment would be lower. However, this higher level of demand would also bring more inflation, as the price level on the vertical axis rises to 110. If aggregate demand were to move still higher, to the level shown by AD_2, the economy would be producing at capacity and unemployment would be minimal; however, AD_2 represents an excessive level of aggregate demand. Because demand exceeds the economy's capacity to produce, inflation becomes very severe, as shown by the movement to a price level of 150.

FIGURE 23-23 *The Effects of Rising Aggregate Demand*

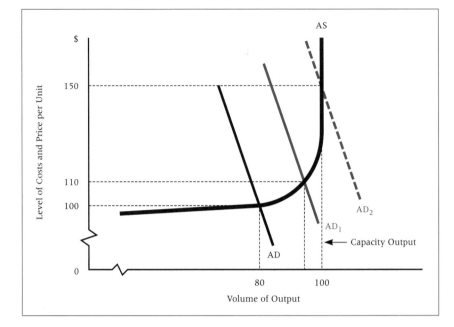

Thus, increases in aggregate demand can have quite different effects upon the performance of the economy (output, employment and prices), depending on the circumstances. If the economy is operating well below capacity and unemployment is high, increased aggregate demand (up to the level shown by AD in Figure 23-22) will have mainly *beneficial* effects. Output and employment will increase considerably and prices will increase only slightly, as the summary in Figure 23-24 shows.

If the economy is closer to its capacity level of output, a similar increase in aggregate demand (from AD to AD$_1$ in Figure 23-23) will have *mixed effects* on the economy. Output and employment will increase, but not as rapidly as before, while prices will rise more rapidly. If aggregate de-

FIGURE 23-24 *The Effect of Increases in Aggregate Demand on the Economy Under Different Conditions*

(See Figure 23-23 for graph)		
	Effect upon	
Increase in Aggregate Demand	*Output and Employment*	*Prices*
Up to AD	Major gains	Very small increases
AD to AD$_1$	Lesser gains	More rapid increases
AD$_1$ to AD$_2$	Quite small gains	Quite rapid increases
Beyond AD$_2$	No gains	Very rapid increases

mand were to be increased further (from AD_1 to AD_2 in Figure 23-23), there would be only small gains in output and employment at the cost of rapid increases in prices, as the economy is *overheated* by aggregate demand that is so high that aggregate supply has difficulty keeping up with it. Beyond AD_2, further increases in aggregate demand cannot boost output and employment any higher, and therefore will result only in more severe inflation.

In summary, it is the interaction between aggregate demand and aggregate supply that determines how well the economy functions regarding output, employment and inflation. Aggregate demand can be too low relative to the economy's productive capacity, causing a recession and high unemployment. Higher levels of aggregate demand can bring worthwhile gains in output and employment, although they will also increase the rate of inflation. Excessively high levels of aggregate demand will generate much more severe inflation but only small gains in output and employment. Thus, it is desirable to seek to maintain a rough balance between aggregate demand and the economy's capacity to produce, or between the demand side and the supply side of the economy.

However, it is not always possible to maintain such a balance between the demand side and the supply side of the economy. In Chapter 24, we will examine how and why these two sides of the economy can get out of balance with each other, and look at the consequences that this imbalance can have on the performance of the economy.

DEFINITIONS OF NEW TERMS

Demand Side The purchasers of society's output of goods and services.

Aggregate Demand Total spending on goods and services, consisting of consumption spending, investment spending, government spending and net exports $(C + I + G + X - M)$.

Consumption Spending by households on consumer goods and services.

Personal Disposable Income Personal income less personal taxes, or after-tax personal income; may be spent or saved.

Personal Saving Personal disposable income not spent on consumption.

Personal Savings Rate The percentage of personal disposable income that is saved.

Real Investment Spending by business firms on capital goods.

Financial Investment Purchases of stocks and bonds issued by businesses; through this process business firms raise capital for real investment.

Retained Earnings Profits retained in a business after taxes have been paid and dividends have been paid to shareholders; another source of capital for real investment. (Also known as **business savings**.)

Leakages Factors that reduce aggregate demand in the economy, consisting of savings, taxes and imports (S + T + M).

Injections Factors that increase aggregate demand in the economy, consisting of investment spending, government spending and exports (I + G + X)

Equilibrium Condition of the economy in which leakages are equal to injections, causing aggregate demand and real GDP to remain stable.

Recession Formally defined as two consecutive quarters (a quarter being three months) of declining real output; commonly used to describe economic slowdowns of less severity than this.

Real Economic Growth A situation characterized by rising levels of output and employment.

Inflation An increase in the general level of the prices of goods and services.

Capacity Output The maximum annual real output of which the economy is capable of producing in any given year.

CHAPTER SUMMARY

1. While the supply-side factors discussed in Chapter 22 determine the *potential* output of the economy, the *actual* level of output depends on the level of aggregate demand for goods and services.

2. Aggregate demand consists of consumption spending, investment spending, government spending on goods and services, and net export spending—or exports minus imports.

3. Consumption spending, which purchases about three-fifths of GDP, depends mainly on the level of personal disposable income, although it is also influenced by consumer confidence, interest rates and the level of consumer indebtedness.

4. Personal saving, which amounted to about 10 percent of personal disposable income in the early 1990's, also depends mainly on the level of personal disposable income, although it too is influenced by the other factors in #3 above.

5. Business investment spending on capital goods usually amounts to 11–15 percent of GDP. Business investment, which is vital to prosperity, depends mainly on expectations concerning the future profitability of investment projects and on the level of interest rates.

6. The main sources of funds for investment in Canada have been personal savings, retained earnings (or business savings) and foreign savings, in the form of foreign investment in Canada.

7. Government purchases of goods and services, which consist mainly of the wages and salaries of government employees who provide public services, amount to about 23–24 percent of Canada's GDP.

8. Exports usually account for 25–28 percent of the GDP; however, when Canadians' purchases of imports are deducted from exports, the net effect of international trade on aggregate demand in Canada is much smaller.

9. In an income-flow model of the economy, the level of aggregate demand is depicted as depending on the balance of leakages from the spending stream (saving + taxes + imports) and injections into the spending stream (investment + government spending + exports).

10. If leakages and injections are equal, the levels of aggregate demand and output will remain stable and the economy will be in a state of equilibrium.

11. If leakages exceed injections, aggregate demand, output, employment and prices will all be depressed, and the economy will slump into a recession.

12. If injections exceed leakages, aggregate demand, output and employment will all rise as the economy expands.

13. If aggregate demand is well below capacity output, increases in aggregate demand will cause output and employment to rise quite rapidly, but will not generate much additional inflation.

14. As output approaches its capacity level, higher aggregate demand will still increase output and employment, although less rapidly than before, and will tend to generate more inflation than before.

15. If aggregate demand rises above the economy's capacity output, the result will be severe inflation.

16. Ideally, there would be a rough balance between the demand side and the supply side of the economy, with aggregate demand close to the economy's capacity to produce goods and services, and neither so low as to cause a recession nor so high as to generate severe inflation.

QUESTIONS

1. There has been a long-term tendency for an increased proportion of consumer spending to go to services (as opposed to goods) and to durable goods (as opposed to nondurables). What do you think accounts for these changes in consumer behavior?

2. One of the most variable components of consumer spending from year to year is spending on durable goods, especially new automobiles. Why do you think this is so?

3. Figure 23-3 shows that consumer confidence was low during the recessions of the early 1980's and early 1990's. Make an argument that this low confidence was:

   (a) a *result* of the recessions, and

   (b) a *cause* of the recessions.

4. *Total* consumption spending in the economy depends mainly on personal disposable income, but the level of consumption spending by *individual households* can be influenced by several factors. What are some of these factors that may cause individual households to spend more or less on consumption (and thus save less or more) in any given year?

5. If there were a period of quite rapid inflation, which you expected to continue for some time, would you change your saving habits? How and why?

6. During the Great Depression, there was actually *dissaving* by households, as consumption exceeded disposable income (which made saving a negative amount). How can a society have negative saving? Why do you suppose this was done?

7. As Figure 23-4 shows, the personal savings rate tends to rise during recessions and fall during periods of economic boom. While these changes in the personal savings rate may seem small, they can have a significant effect on the economy. It is estimated that a one-percentage-point increase in the personal savings rate slows the growth of real GDP by roughly one-half of one percent. In 1991, the savings rate was 10.3 percent; if instead it had been at the 1987 level of 9.1 percent, consumer spending in 1991 would have been about $5.6 billion higher, helping to boost a weak economy in that year.

   (a) Why does the personal savings rate tend to rise during recessions and fall during economic booms? What are the effects of the changes in the savings rate on the economy's performance during booms and recessions?

   (b) The personal savings rate increased in 1989, a year *before* the recession began. What might explain this?

   (c) Since 1992, has the personal savings rate changed significantly? If so, what might have caused such a change? Also, what are the likely economic consequences of this change?

8. (a) As Figure 23-9 shows, business capital investment spending weakened during the early 1990's. What might account for this trend?

   (b) Has the trend concerning business capital investment spending changed since 1992? If so, how has it changed and what might explain the change?

9. As the text notes, the economic progress of Japan and West Germany since the Second World War has required heavy emphasis on capital investment. This, in turn, involved considerable sacrifices of current consumption. Today, Eastern European countries face a similar challenge as they move toward rapid industrialization. What could these countries do to ease the burden of shifting the use of their economic resources away from current consumption and toward capital investment?

10. Following is a list of potential business capital investment projects, showing the expected rate of return on the capital that could be invested in each, and the amount of capital investment for each project, arranged in descending order of expected rate of return.

Investment Project	Expected Rate of Return	Amount of Investment
		($100 millions)
A	20%	$5
B	18%	2
C	16%	8
D	14%	7
E	12%	10
F	10%	9
G	8%	6
H	6%	3
I	4%	4

(a) As the rate of interest on funds that must be borrowed for capital investment decreases, more of these potential investment projects become economical. For example, if the rate of interest is 19 percent only project A is profitable, so there will be $500 million of capital investment. If the rate of interest were to fall to 17 percent, both projects A and B would be economical, making the level of capital investment $700 million.

Complete the following table showing the volume of capital investment that will be economical at various interest rates.

Rate of Interest	Volume of Capital Investment
19%	$5 hundred million
17	7 hundred million
15	
13	
11	
9	
7	
5	

(b) Draw a graph showing the relationship between the rate of interest and the volume of capital investment.

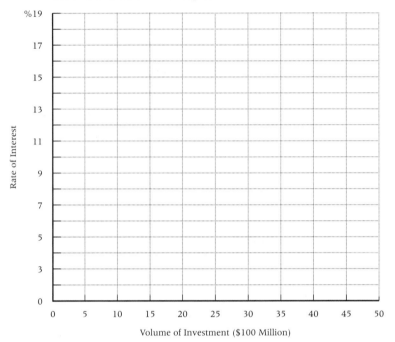

(c) The graph shows an *inverse relationship* between interest rates and capital investment spending; that is, as interest rates rise, the volume of capital investment spending _____.

(d) If interest rates fell from 11 percent to 9 percent, capital investment spending would _____ by $ _____ hundred million.

11. To remedy the "purchasing-power problem" that the Social Credit Party saw as the basic issue facing the economy, the party in effect proposed printing additional money and distributing it to the public. In view of the fact that there is already enough income each year to buy the total GDP, what effects would such a policy have on the economy?

12. During an economic boom, when output is rising, why does the rising supply of goods and services not cause the prices of them to fall?

13. During an economic recession, when output is depressed, why does the depressed supply of goods and services not cause prices to rise?

14. Suppose that widespread rumors of a depression caused people to save more, in an attempt to protect themselves against the event. What effect would this have on the economy?

15. Suppose that rapid inflation caused people to reduce their saving and spend more of their income in anticipation of higher prices in the future. How would this affect the economy?

16. Suppose the economy is in the situation shown in the graph below, near its capacity level of output.

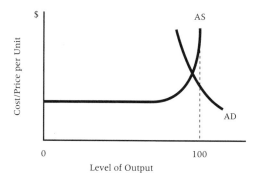

If a major increase were to occur in the price of imported oil which:

(a) reduced the level of aggregate demand by withdrawing large volumes of funds from the economy to pay for the oil, pushing the AD curve to the left, and

(b) raised production costs throughout the economy by making energy much more expensive, making it costlier to produce any given level of output, thus pushing the AS curve upwards to higher levels of cost per unit,

draw the new AD and AS curves and explain the effects of the new situation on the levels of output, employment and prices in the economy.

17. In this graph, the AS and AD curves represent the situation in 19X1, with output and prices both at levels of 100. AS_1 and AD_1 represent the situation in 19X3, two years later, when output is 120 and prices are at the same level as in 19X1.

Ordinarily, such a rapid increase in aggregate demand and output would be accompanied by a significant increase in the price level. Why, in this example, has there been no increase in prices?

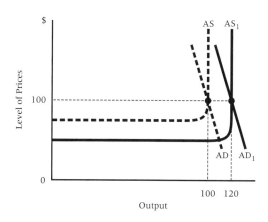

18. (a) At the level of aggregate demand represented by AD_1, the economy is operating at approximately _____ percent of its capacity output (potential GDP), and is in a condition of _____.

(b) AD_2 represents a(n) _____ in the level of aggregate demand that has brought the economy to approximately _____ percent of its capacity output. Describe the effect that this change in aggregate demand has on:

(i)   output and employment, and

(ii)   the general level of prices

and explain the reasons for these effects.

(c) To get the economy to 95 percent of its capacity output requires a level of aggregate demand as represented by AD_3. How does the effect of this change in aggregate demand differ from the change from AD_1 to AD_2 and why?

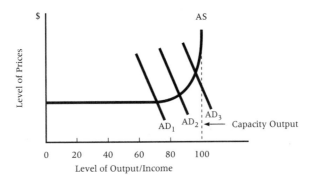

NOTES

[1] Spending on new residential housing, which usually amounts to 5–7 percent of GDP, is usually treated as an additional category of the "investment" figures, as it is considered to be "capital formation" rather than "consumption."

[2] Also, as personal disposable income rises, *saving* rises. That is, people as a whole do not spend all of an increase in their disposable income; they save some of it.

[3] Repayments of the *principal* on mortgage loans are counted as saving because they represent income not spent on consumption in that year. Rather, such repayments represent money saved to pay the mortgage on a house purchased in the past. Mortgage *interest payments*, on the other hand, represent a current consumption item—payment to the mortgage-holder for the service of loaning the money to the home-buyer (like rent paid for the use of someone else's money).

[4] This definition sometimes causes confusion for students because many people associate the word "investment" with purchases of stocks and bonds. The two meanings are obviously related because business often finances its capital-goods purchases (investment) through issues of stocks or bonds to the public (in which the public "invests"). One useful way of resolving this unfortunate—but very im-

portant—confusion of terms is to call the purchase of capital goods **real investment**, because it involves real productive assets, and to call the purchase of stocks and bonds **financial investment**, because it involves financial assets, or securities. Most references to "investment" in the text are to real investment, even if this is not specified. Where confusion may occur, the terms "real" and "financial" will be used.

5 This figure includes government investment projects, in addition to the private business investment spending of 11–15 percent of GDP referred to earlier, but excludes residential housing construction. If the latter were included, the figure would be 20–25 percent of GDP.

6 It is important to note that these figures include only purchases of goods and services by governments, including national defence. *Total* government spending, including transfer payments such as unemployment insurance and welfare and interest payments on government debt, amounted to close to 50 percent of GDP.

7 The Socreds' proposed solution to the problem was, in effect, for the government to print more money and distribute it to the public, to make up the shortfall in aggregate demand.

8 Depreciation allowances can be regarded as a form of income to business because, while depreciation expenses are deducted from revenues as an expense, no money is actually paid out, so that the business has the amount of money deducted as depreciation expense *in addition to* its reported profit. This was the factor the Social Credit theory overlooked—that depreciation allowances are a form of business income.

9 This simplified diagram includes only the *business* and *household* sectors of the economy. The *government* and *foreign trade* sectors will be added later in this section, and fuller consideration will be given to both of them in subsequent chapters.

10 A large increase in personal saving could itself depress business investment spending, by reducing consumption spending and thus businesses' sales, making it less attractive for businesses to invest.

11 It should be noted that the concept of "equilibrium" tends to be a misleading one, since it seems to convey the idea of the economy reaching an equilibrium level and then remaining there. In fact, the investment and saving plans of businesses and households are constantly changing and so is the equilibrium level of the GDP. Thus, increases in investment will increase the equilibrium level of the GDP, and vice-versa.

12 The proper definition of *recession* requires two consecutive quarters of declining real output (a quarter is three months). However, the term is often used to describe economic slowdowns generally, including those less severe than specified in the proper definition.

13 While the basic cause of inflation is generally considered to be excess aggregate demand, its causes are more complex than those considered here, and are considered more fully in Chapter 28.

14 At first glance, this may seem like a contradiction: if the output, or *supply*, of goods and services *rises*, should their prices not *fall*? This would happen if supply

increased and demand did not—if there is a big apple crop without any increase in the demand for apples, the price of apples will fall. However, what we are discussing here is an increase in output that was *caused by an increase in (aggregate) demand*, and the same increase in demand that caused output to rise is also likely to cause prices to rise.

CHAPTER 24

The problem of economic instability

While the Canadian economy has generally enjoyed strong growth over the years, this growth has not occurred in a steady manner. During periods of economic boom, output and employment have risen very rapidly. However, in other years, output and employment have grown slowly or even declined, causing periodic major increases in the number of Canadians unemployed. Figure 24-1 shows that in some years, real GDP has increased

FIGURE 24-1 *Percentage Change in Real GDP, 1948–93*

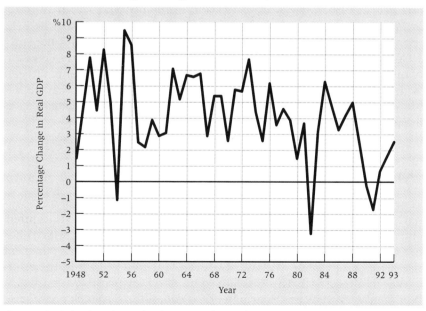

Source: Statistics Canada, *National Income and Expenditure Accounts* (13-001)

521

FIGURE 24-2   *Percentage of Labor Force Unemployed, 1926–93*

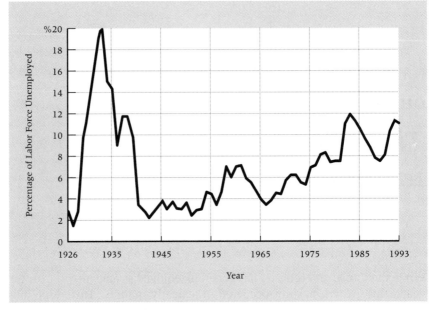

Source: Statistics Canada, *Historical Labour Force Statistics* (71-201)

by as much as 25–9 percent, while in others it has decreased, in one case by more than 4 percent.

While the most famous economic downturn was of course the Great Depression of the 1930's, several other slowdowns, or recessions, have occurred: in 1951, in 1953–54, in 1957–58, in 1960–61, in 1970, in 1974–75, in 1981–82 (sometimes called the "Great Recession") and in 1990–92. In terms of both their depth and their duration, the recessions of the early 1980's and the early 1990's were the most severe since the Great Depression of the 1930's. All of the recessions since the Second World War have been far less severe than the depression of the 1930's, but they have nonetheless caused economic and human hardship, as the unemployment rates in Figure 24-2 show.

Phases of the business cycle

The term **business cycle** is used to describe the fluctuations of the economy between prosperity and recession. A typical business cycle is pictured, and its phases labelled, in Figure 24-3. In the *contraction* phase, which ends in a *trough* when economic activity is at its slowest, output and employment rise more and more slowly, and may even fall: in other words, the economy is in a recession. This is followed by a *recovery* phase, during which economic growth begins to resume. Next comes the *expansion* phase (also known as a **"boom"**), which usually involves quite rapid increases in out-

FIGURE 24-3   *A Typical Business Cycle*

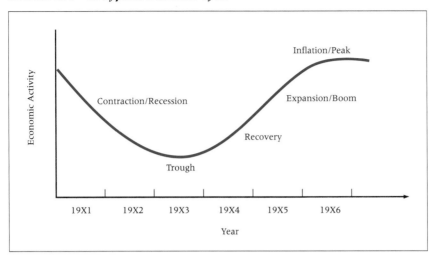

put and employment as economic conditions improve. This continues until the *peak* (which may involve increasingly rapid inflation) is reached, after which the economy goes into a downturn and the cycle repeats itself. Since the Second World War, recessions have occurred on average every five or six years; however, the period between recessions has varied from one and one-half years (in the early 1950's) to nine years (in the 1960's). Thus, while business cycles do not repeat themselves on a fixed timetable and may vary in length and intensity, they do tend to follow one another in a repetitive pattern.

Our free-enterprise economic system is successful in many respects, but this tendency toward periodic slowdowns with increased unemployment

DEPRESSIONS AND RECESSIONS

The severity of the recessions of the early 1980's and early 1990's led some people to describe them as "depressions." While "recession" is formally defined as two consecutive quarters (three-month periods) of declining real GDP, there is no similar definition of what constitutes a "depression," leaving "depression" to be rather loosely defined as "a really bad recession," with the Great Depression of the 1930's as the only example of one.

How severe, then, was the recession of 1990–92 as compared to the Great Depression? The Great Depression lasted for four years (1929–33), during which real GDP shrank by an estimated 28 percent and the unemployment rate soared from 3 percent to 19 percent. The recession of the early 1990's lasted for about two years, during which real GDP fell by 3.6 percent and the unemployment rate rose from 7.2 percent to a peak of 11.8 percent.

and hardship for many people has been one of its traditional weaknesses. In fact, Karl Marx predicted that the capitalist system would eventually collapse in a terrible depression, which would cause a revolution of the working class against capitalism. While Marx's prediction has not come true, it is important for us to try to understand why business cycles tend to occur, so that we can try to take steps to reduce their severity.

THEORIES OF BUSINESS CYCLES

Business cycles have been observed for centuries and many theories have been advanced in attempts to explain them. There are many factors that can stimulate or slow down economic activity. For example, wars cause high levels of government spending, which generate boom-like conditions with high levels of economic activity and very low unemployment, although the military output produced does not add to the prosperity of the people as consumer and capital goods do. Certain inventions, such as the railroad and the automobile, can stimulate the economy by giving rise to surges of capital investment spending. Seasonal factors and variations in weather (such as droughts) can affect the economy, too, although these were regarded as more important in the past, when a greater proportion of economic activity was agricultural. In the past, when gold was used as money, the discovery of new gold mines helped the economy by increasing the money supply. Failure to discover gold for some time could result in economic stagnation. Another theory saw the origin of business cycles in periodically recurring sunspots, which were presumed to affect agricultural production and possibly people's moods, and thus their spending behavior.

While factors such as these may affect the economy, they tend to occur at random intervals and therefore are not a convincing explanation for business cycles, which tend to repeat themselves more or less regularly. For the causes of these economic fluctuations, we will have to look elsewhere.

Fluctuations in aggregate demand

Business cycles involve periodic fluctuations of output and employment across the entire economy. From our analysis of the operation of the economy in Chapter 23, the most likely source of such widespread swings in economic activity would be fluctuations in aggregate demand, or total spending on goods and services in the economy. An upward surge in aggregate demand would boost virtually all sectors of the economy, while a decline in aggregate demand would tend to drag the entire economy downwards.

However, analyzing fluctuations in aggregate demand is not a simple matter, since aggregate demand is a vast and complex factor that consists of various diverse elements: consumption spending, business investment spending, government spending and net export spending. As a result, untangling the more detailed causes of business cycles is a somewhat complex problem that requires careful analysis.

In addition, there is the tendency of the economy to gain "momentum" in whatever direction in which it is moving; that is, for booms to feed on themselves and grow stronger, and for recessions to deepen and become more severe. Again, the answer to this tendency seems to lie in the dynamics of the economic system itself, and particularly in the complex interactions between consumption spending and investment spending from which the economy gains "momentum," in either an upwards or downwards direction.

This chapter deals with the problem of economic instability in two stages. In the first part of this chapter, we will separate the causes of economic instability into the following four factors:

(a) *fluctuations in business investment spending,* the effects of which spread through the economy due to

(b) *the multiplier effect,* whereby fluctuations in investment spending touch off fluctuations in consumption spending, and

(c) *the accelerator effect,* through which changes in consumption spending cause changes in business investment spending, and

(d) *fluctuations in exports,* which are a separate and important source of instability in the Canadian economy.

In the second part of this chapter, we will examine the various stages of a typical business cycle, and how the factors listed above interact in ways that cause aggregate demand and the economy to be unstable, swinging the economy from boom to inflation to recession and back again.

(A) THE INSTABILITY OF INVESTMENT SPENDING

As Figure 24-4 shows, business investment spending has historically tended to fluctuate considerably, rising rapidly in some years and stagnating and even declining sharply in others. In fact, capital investment by business is clearly the most volatile of the components of aggregate demand. Unlike consumption spending, investment does not tend to advance year after year, more rapidly in some years and more slowly in others. Rather, investment tends to surge ahead very rapidly at some times and slow drastically, or even decline considerably, at other times.

This historical pattern is continued in Figure 24-5, which shows the level of business investment spending since 1975. While business capital spending was relatively low at the beginning of the period, it increased strongly in the late seventies, and stayed high until the recession of 1981–82, when it fell sharply. Then, after the recession, businesses began to increase their investment spending quite strongly again, particularly in the second half of the eighties. However, in the early 1990's, real business investment spending declined again.

FIGURE 24-4 *Business Fixed Investment Spending (1971 Dollars), 1926–75*

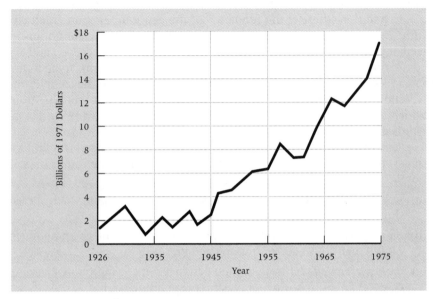

Source: Statistics Canada

FIGURE 24-5 *Business Investment in Plant and Equipment,[a] 1975–93*

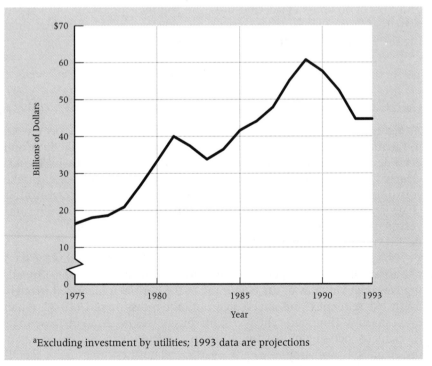

[a]Excluding investment by utilities; 1993 data are projections

Source: Department of Finance, *Economic and Fiscal Reference Tables,* August 1993

FIGURE 24-6 *Housing Starts, 1970–92*

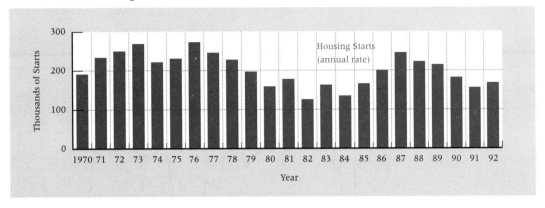

Source: Department of Finance, *Economic and Fiscal Reference Tables,* August 1993

Figures 24-4 and 24-5 show fluctuations in business spending on plant and equipment, which comprise the majority of capital investment spending. However, two other types of investment should also be considered as well. The first is *residential construction*—the homebuilding industry. For various reasons, the demand for homes is quite unstable—in some years, home-builders cannot keep up with soaring demand, while at other times they cannot find buyers for houses they have already built. Figure 24-6 illustrates the fluctuations in housing starts caused by these fluctuations in demand.

The final category of investment spending to be considered is *additions to businesses' inventories*. When a business buys inventories, this is classed as investment, or producer's goods, because the products have not yet been sold for consumption. While it is not very large, this particular type of investment spending—additions to inventories—is the single most variable type of investment spending. Thus, investment spending on additions to business inventories is subject to spectacular swings, as Figure 24-7 illustrates.

Why does investment spending fluctuate so much?

As we saw in Chapter 23, the level of business capital investment spending depends mainly on two factors: businesses' *expectations* concerning the future profitability of investment projects, and the *rate of interest* that businesses must pay on money borrowed to finance such projects. And, since both expectations and interest rates can change considerably from year to year, business investment spending tends to vary considerably from year to year. At times, the economic outlook is favorable and interest rates are low: under these circumstances, business investment tends to rise briskly. At other times, uncertain or poor expectations and/or high interest rates can cause businesses to reduce investment spending, in some cases quite drastically. In fact, investment spending can actually collapse, as it did during the Great Depression of the 1930's, when economic conditions were so bad that few businesses were willing or able to consider capital investment projects.

FIGURE 24-7   *Change in Inventories, 1970–93*

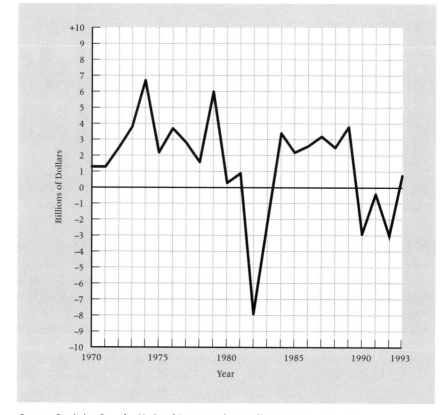

Source: Statistics Canada, *National Income and Expenditure Accounts* (13-001)

Expectations and interest rates also explain most of the fluctuations in the residential housing market. There are times, particularly when mortgage money is readily available and the economy is favorable, when activity in this industry is frantic—buyers want to buy, and they will pay high prices now, because they fear that prices will rise again shortly. Builders and suppliers are barely able to keep up with the demand. But periodically, the situation reverses itself—mortgage interest rates become high and people may expect an economic slowdown in which interest rates and home prices may actually fall, so prospective homebuyers do *not* buy, but rather wait. As a result, the residential construction industry goes into a slump.

Finally, expectations explain much of the fluctuations in businesses' inventories. If retailers and wholesalers expect sales to be strong, they will spend a great deal more than usual on inventory, and inventories will rise rapidly. On the other hand, if sales turn out to be unexpectedly slow, many retailers will expect this trend to continue and may order virtually nothing for inventory, so that inventories will actually decline sharply.

How fluctuations in business investment affect the economy

The fluctuations in investment spending that we have been discussing have an important effect on the performance of the entire economy, which can be illustrated by Figure 24-8. As we saw in Chapter 23, saving is a *leakage* from the spending stream that tends to slow down the economy, because saving involves *not* buying goods and services. Also, investment is an *injection* into the spending stream that can offset saving and stimulate the economy, by buying capital goods.

While the saving rate does vary from year to year, in most years saving tends to be a relatively *steady leakage* from the spending stream—it tends to occur quite regularly. On the other hand, as we have just seen, investment tends to fluctuate greatly, thus constituting a *variable injection* into the spending stream.

Since saving tends to occur more or less regularly, the key factor is really investment spending. If investment spending is high, so that the investment injection exceeds the saving leakage, there will be a net injection of additional spending into the economy. The effect of this additional spending will be to *stimulate* the economy: output and employment will rise, and so (probably) will prices, and the economy will experience more-rapid-than-average growth.

However, if investment is in one of its periodic downturns, the investment injection will be smaller than the saving leakage, causing a net leakage from the spending stream. As a result, total spending on goods

FIGURE 24-8 *Leakages From and Injections Into the Spending Stream*

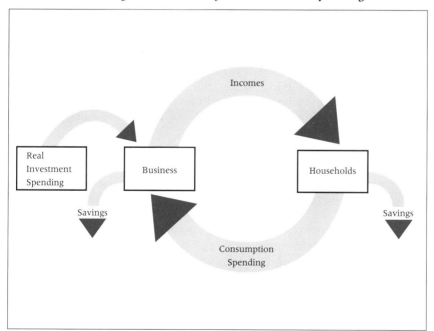

and services will be *depressed*. With aggregate demand depressed, output will rise less rapidly, or even decline, and unemployment will rise as the economy slides into a slowdown, or recession. Wages and prices will also be depressed (rise less rapidly than usual) due to sluggish demand in the economy.

Thus, fluctuations in business investment spending are one important factor in economic booms and recessions. To fully understand the causes of business cycles, however, we must go beyond the capital investment sector of the economy, and examine how these variations in investment spending interact with the much larger consumption spending sector, through effects known as the "multiplier" and the "accelerator," so as to have a much stronger impact on the economy.

(B) THE MULTIPLIER EFFECT

We have seen how investment spending by businesses tends to fluctuate, and how this tends to contribute to the economic ups and downs known as the business cycle. But investment is only about one-sixth of GDP and normal variations in investment amount to only one or two percent of GDP. How can such small fluctuations in investment explain fluctuations across the entire economy, including consumption spending by households?

The answer to this question is suggested by the following illustration. Suppose that a new family moves into a town and builds a $100 000 house, using local labor and materials. Obviously, this will add $100 000 to the incomes of the townspeople involved. While some of this increase in incomes will go to taxes, and some will be saved, the people who receive it will spend a good deal on consumer goods and services, such clothes, home repairs, restaurant dinners and so on. To those who receive this money— the tailor, plumber and restaurant owner and employees—it represents an increase in their income. They, too, will respend a large part of it on a variety of goods and services, generating additional income for the suppliers of those items, who, in turn, will increase their spending. This respending effect will continue as increases in income are respent; however, it will grow weaker at each stage because not all of the increase in incomes is respent at each stage. The result is similar to the ripples on a pond caused by a thrown stone: the original $100 000 spent on the new house is the initial splash, and the respending of the increases in income at each stage creates a series of ripples, each weaker than the previous one, spreading out from the centre and through the economy.

Just as the thrown stone disturbs the pond by much more than the initial splash, the *total* economic effect of the spending of the $100 000 on the house will be much greater than the original $100 000, because as the money is respent, total spending—and incomes—will increase in a series of stages following the initial spending. In effect, the impact of the original $100 000 will be magnified, or *multiplied* by this respending effect. For this reason, the respending effect is known as the **multiplier**

A numerical example of the multiplier

The principle that was shown in the previous illustration can be applied to the entire economy. Suppose total investment spending in the economy increases by $100 million over last year's levels, causing the incomes of people in the capital-goods industries to be $100 million higher than last year. Not all of this $100 million will be spent on consumption—part will go to taxes, part will be saved and part will be diverted to foreign nations through purchases of imports. While it is true that each of these leakages can return to the spending stream, it is not completely certain, so we will consider them gone, if only temporarily.

Assuming that these leakages absorb one-half of the increase in incomes, consumption spending would rise by $50 million over last year's level. This increase in consumer spending represents a $50 million increase in GDP and income to those who receive it. Assuming that they will also respend half of it, this will give rise to a further increase in consumption spending of $25 million, which boosts GDP incomes by another $25 million. Of this $25 million of increased incomes, $12.5 million would be respent as the cycle continues, increasing *both GDP and total incomes* at each stage, as shown in Figure 24-9.

Obviously, the respending effect means that the initial investment project of $100 million has a much more far-reaching effect on the economy (that is, on GDP and total incomes) than its size suggests. To calculate the total impact of the $100 million of investment spending on the economy, we would have to add together all of the increases in spending, GDP and incomes at each stage of the process: $100 million + $50 million + $25 million + $12.5 million, etc. If we did this, we would find that the $100 mil-

FIGURE 24-9   *The Respending Effect Underlying the Multiplier*

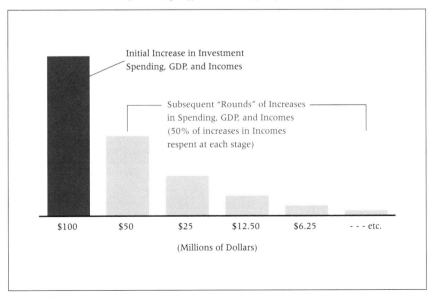

FIGURE 24-10 *The Respending Effect with a Multiplier of Two*

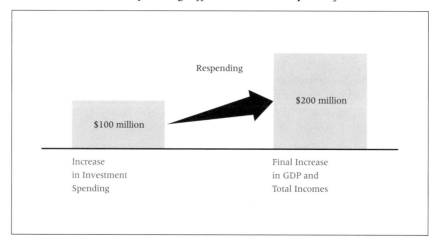

lion of investment spending caused GDP and total incomes to rise by $200 million, as shown in Figure 24-10. In this example, the size of the multiplier is two, because an increase in investment of $100 million caused the GDP to rise by $200 million.

Calculation of the multiplier

So far, we have simply stated that the size of the multiplier in our example was two; next we will see how the size of the multiplier can be calculated. Obviously, the size of the multiplier depends on how much of each increase in income is respent at each stage. If a greater fraction is respent, the respending effect will be greater, and the multiplier will be larger. Once we know what fraction of increases in income will or will not be respent at each stage, we can calculate the multiplier from the following formula:

$$\text{the multiplier} = \frac{1}{\substack{\text{the fraction of } \textit{increases} \\ \text{in income that is } \textit{not} \text{ respent} \\ \text{at each stage}}}$$

In our previous example, 50 percent of increases in income was respent, which of course means that 50 percet was *not* respent (or went to leakages), so the multiplier would be calculated as follows:

$$\text{the multiplier} = \frac{1}{0.50} \text{ or } \frac{1}{1/2} = 2.0$$

The size of the multiplier is not fixed at 2.0 or any other size; it depends on the proportion of increases in income that is respent at each stage. If 60 percent of increases in incomes is respent, the multiplier would be 2.5, or 1 divided by 0.40. This larger multiplier reflects the fact that the respending effect is larger in this case (60 percent respent, rather than 50 percent). On the other hand, if a smaller proportion of income were respent, the multiplier would be smaller.

The Canadian multiplier

In the Canadian economy, the multiplier tends to be smaller than in the above examples, due mostly to the large proportion of income spent on imports (another leakage from the Canadian economy). Various economic models and studies, using different assumptions, have developed varying estimates of the size of the Canadian multiplier. The Economic Council of Canada has estimated that, for government spending on capital formation (such as public works projects), the size of the multiplier is 1.6 over a one-year-period.[1] That is, a $1 million increase in expenditures on public works will boost GDP and total incomes by $1.6 million over the next year. Other studies have estimated the multiplier to be as large as 1.8 and as small as 1.0. These studies tend to agree that the multiplier is higher during periods of economic boom, when people are inclined to respend a greater proportion of any increases in their income, and smaller during recessions, when the opposite is true. Finally, there was a tendency for the Canadian multiplier to become smaller in the 1980's, when growing imports reduced the respending effect within the Canadian economy.

The downward multiplier

So far, we have applied the multiplier only to *increases* in investment spending. However, the multiplier also works in reverse. Suppose that investment spending *fell* from its previous level. This would *reduce* incomes by the same amount, with the result that consumer spending would be cut back. These spending cuts would reduce other incomes, which would cause further spending cuts, and so on. This process is known as the *downward multiplier*. Obviously, it can contribute seriously to recessions and depressions, by increasing the economic impact of reductions in investment spending. For instance, if the multiplier were 1.4, a reduction in investment of $3.0 billion would lead to a $4.2 billion decline in GDP and total incomes.

The multiplier and economic instability

The multiplier effect contributes to economic instability, because it magnifies the impact of any fluctuation in spending on the economy. For instance, with a multiplier of 1.4, fluctuations in investment spending (or any other type of spending) of a magnitude of $5 billion will cause the GDP and total incomes to fluctuate by about $7 billion. The multiplier effect also magnifies the impact of changes in other types of spending besides investment: it is through the multiplier effect that the entire Canadian economy feels the effects of seemingly local developments such as increased exports of British Columbia resource products, falling wheat sales on the Prairies, an investment boom in central Canada and rising unemployment in the Atlantic Region.

(C) THE ACCELERATOR EFFECT

The multiplier effect shows how an increase in investment spending can generate increases in consumer spending by means of the respending effect. The **accelerator** effect operates in the other direction; that is, through the accelerator effect, changes in *consumption spending* cause changes in *investment spending*.

Specifically, increases in consumer spending can generate increases in investment spending, as businesses spend on plant and/or equipment in order to increase their productive capacity so as to be able to meet the rising level of consumer demand. Rising consumer spending will not always cause investment spending to rise in this way. During a recession, when a business may be operating at only 80 percent of capacity, an increase in consumer demand will not cause it to invest in new plant and equipment because it has idle capacity that can be used to increase output. However, when rising consumer demand pushes output to near-capacity levels, further increases in consumer spending will cause an increase in investment spending in order to raise capacity to meet the anticipated demand. When rising consumer spending affects investment spending in this way, the resultant investment is called **induced investment**, and the effect on the economy is called the *accelerator effect*.

Consequently, when there is an economic boom in which many industries are operating near their capacity levels of output, increases in consumer spending will kick off a *surge* of investment spending, which will create a *strong boom* in the capital-goods industries (construction, machinery, steel, building materials, and so on), as shown in years 19X1 and 19X2 in Figure 24-11.

However, this boom in the capital-goods industries may well prove to be temporary. Manufacturers will now have enough capital equipment for their present level of consumer sales, and will not order any more new capital equipment unless *consumer spending* (that is, manufacturers' sales) *increases further*. Year 19X3 of Figure 24-11 illustrates this point: the slowdown of consumer spending has a drastic effect on manufacturers' orders for new capital equipment, so that a mere *slowdown* in consumer spending causes a *drastic decline* in induced investment. Thus, induced investment is a particularly fragile component of investment spending—for induced investment to be merely maintained, consumer spending must *keep rising continuously*. And, when consumer spending merely slows down or levels off, induced investment will fall sharply.

Ironically, in year 19X3 of Figure 24-11, consumer spending, while barely rising, is nonetheless at record-high levels, whereas induced investment has declined sharply from its previous levels. This helps explain why, while the economy in general ("consumer spending" on the graph)

FIGURE 24-11 *The Operation of the Accelerator*

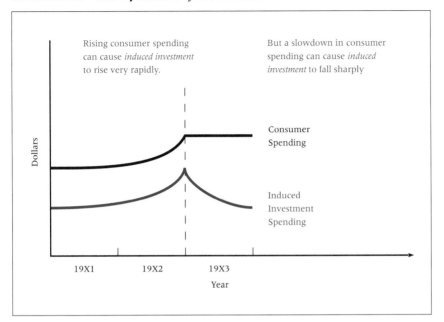

Rising consumer spending can cause *induced investment* to rise very rapidly.

But a slowdown in consumer spending can cause *induced investment* to fall sharply

Consumer Spending

Induced Investment Spending

Dollars

19X1 19X2 19X3

Year

is prosperous, there can be a serious slump in the capital-goods industries ("induced investment" on the graph). Thus, industries such as construction, steel, and building products can experience slumps *simply because consumption spending isn't rising fast enough.* As a result, induced investment is very unstable. This is one reason why capital-goods industries tend to experience feast or famine cycles, and one further reason why the economy tends to experience ups and downs. To aggravate the situation even further, the decline in induced investment can drag the level of consumption spending down with it, via the multiplier effect.

(D) EXPORTS AS A SOURCE OF ECONOMIC INSTABILITY

With 25–28 percent of its GDP sold in export markets (seven-tenths of this to the United States alone), Canada is particularly exposed to international economic fluctuations. When other nations, particularly the United States, have economic booms, their demand for Canadian exports adds significantly to aggregate demand in Canada, boosting the economy. And, when these nations experience economic slowdowns, their demand for Canadian products (especially resource products) slumps significantly, with serious effects on the Canadian economy.

The effects of such slumps in exports are not, however, confined to regions and industries linked directly to Canada's resource industries, such as forest products and mining. Rather, the effects spread, through the mul-

THE MULTIPLIER AND ACCELERATOR EFFECTS COMBINED

We have seen how the multiplier and the accelerator operate separately. During an economic upswing, however, the multiplier and accelerator can *combine* so as to give even greater momentum to a boom.

In the diagram, an economic boom is in progress. Rising investment spending is boosting incomes and consumption spending, through the respending effect of the multiplier. However, the process may not end here. If the increase in consumption spending pushes production to near-capacity levels, the increased consumption spending will induce increased investment, through the process known as the accelerator. This further increase in investment spending will boost the economy to even higher levels, as the multiplier and accelerator effects are combined.

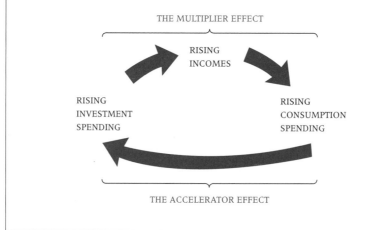

tiplier effect, throughout the economy, and can contribute to a general economic boom or slowdown.

Thus, economic trends in other countries, especially the United States, are an important source of economic fluctuations in Canada. Unlike the other causes of instability examined earlier in this chapter, the source of this problem lies outside Canada. We will consider the matter of Canada's international trade more fully in subsequent chapters.

The dynamics of business cycles

We have seen how several factors can play a role in causing the economy to swing between boom and recession—fluctuations in investment spending, the multiplier effect, the accelerator effect and fluctuations in exports.

In the next section, we will examine the actual dynamics of economic instability—how these and other factors interact so as to cause the economy to undergo swings between booms and recessions, and how those swings, once started, tend to gain momentum, making the fluctuations of the economy more severe. No two booms or slumps are the same, but the following will show the typical kinds of interactions that occur in the economy as it swings upward and downward.

To illustrate the dynamics of business cycles, we will use the "supply side-demand side" model from Chapter 23. This model is shown in Figure 24-12, in which the supply side of the economy is represented by the dotted line which shows potential output rising gradually, and the demand side is represented by the solid line showing the level of aggregate demand in the economy. We will start at the stage of the cycle at which the economy is beginning to recover from a recession.

(A) THE RECOVERY PHASE

In year 19X1 in Figure 24-12, the economy is in *recession*, with aggregate demand well below the potential output of the supply side of the economy. As a result, businesses are operating well below their capacity output level, and unemployment is high.

In years 19X2 and 19X3, the economy is in its *recovery* phase from the recession. Aggregate demand is rising, causing output and employment to rise. Demand could be rising in this way for various reasons, including the following:

FIGURE 24-12 *The Economy in the Recovery Phase*

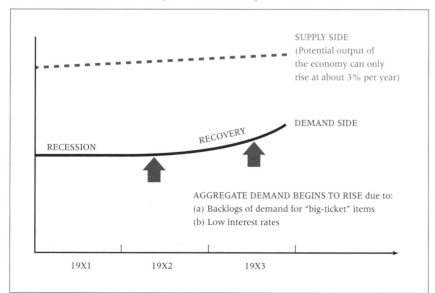

(i) *Backlogs of demand* for certain consumer goods probably exist. In particular, during the recession, consumers have probably postponed purchases of "big-ticket" items such as cars and houses, and the appliances and furniture that are often bought with a new house.

(ii) *Low interest rates* could be making it more attractive to borrow money for such purchases. Interest rates tend to be lower during recessions, to encourage borrowing.

As factors such as these cause aggregate demand to increase, output and employment will start to recover from the recession. At this point in the recovery, the rising level of aggregate demand will not generate much inflation in the economy, because the supply side of the economy can readily keep output rising to match the level of demand.

(B) THE EXPANSION (BOOM) PHASE

In Figure 24-13, the economy has in years 19X3 and 19X4 moved into the "boom" phase of the business cycle, as rising aggregate demand is driving output and employment to quite high levels.

During the boom phase, the increases in demand are gaining momentum, pulling output and employment upwards at a faster pace. The economy *gains momentum* in this way for various reasons:

FIGURE 24-13   *The Economy in the Expansion (Boom) Phase*

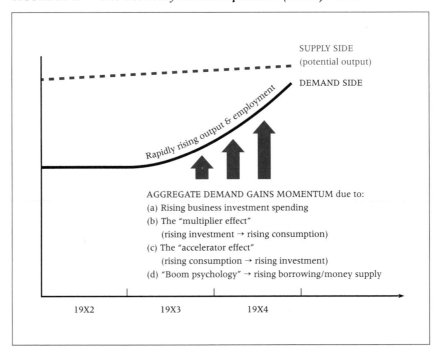

(i) *Rising business investment spending:* As the economic outlook improves, and with interest rates still low, business investment spending can be expected to increase, generating additional increases in employment, incomes and aggregate demand.

(ii) *The "multiplier effect":* Through the "multiplier effect" explained earlier in this chapter, rising business investment spending means higher incomes for people associated with the capital-goods sector of the economy. When these increases in incomes are partially respent on consumption, a chain reaction of respending will be generated that will boost consumption spending by more than the initial increase in investment spending.

(iii) *The "accelerator effect":* As was explained earlier in this chapter, rising consumer spending can cause business investment spending to increase. If consumer spending increases to the point where businesses have to buy additional new equipment to expand their operations, the "accelerator effect" is said to be occurring. The accelerator effect will add further to demand during a boom, as induced investment spending pushes aggregate demand, output, employment and incomes even higher. And, of course, the multiplier effect will magnify the effect of these increases in induced investment, as well.

(iv) *"Boom psychology":* As the economic boom progresses, consumers and businesspeople will feel more confident about the economic future. This "boom psychology" will make them more willing to borrow money for the purpose of buying houses, and "big-ticket" consumer durable goods such as cars, appliances and furniture, and capital goods for businesses. As this borrowed money is spent, spending can rise faster than income, driving the level of aggregate demand to even higher levels.

The combined effect of these factors can become quite strong. Together, they can cause aggregate demand, output and employment to rise rapidly in an economic boom, as shown in years 19X3 and 19X4 in Figure 24-13. However, such high levels of aggregate demand can bring not only an economic boom, but also a troublesome side-effect—*inflation*.

(C) THE PEAK OF THE CYCLE: HOW A BOOM CAN BECOME A DOWNTURN

With aggregate demand gaining momentum and growing at such a rapid pace in the boom phase of the cycle, it is quite possible that demand will rise to the point where it exceeds the economy's ability to produce goods and services. If this happens, the general level of prices of goods and services will increase—there will be inflation.

This situation is shown in Figure 24-14: in years 19X5 and 19X6, aggregate demand has outrun the ability of the supply side of the economy to produce goods and services, generating inflation.

FIGURE 24-14 *The Inflation Phase*

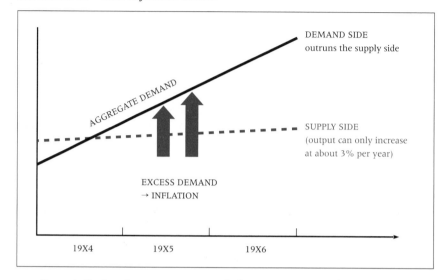

Once inflation becomes severe, it has a strong tendency to lead toward an economic downturn, or recession. The main reason for this is that *rapid inflation causes high interest rates*, which in turn slow down borrowing and spending.[2]

This problem is shown in Figure 24-15, in year 19X7. High interest rates are:

(i) depressing consumer spending on "big-ticket" items such as houses and cars because consumers are reluctant to borrow at such high interest rates to buy these, and

(ii) depressing business investment spending, because:

- businesses are reluctant to borrow at high interest rates to finance investment projects, and

- with consumer spending slowing down due to (i) above, businesses do not need to expand as they had been doing in the previous few years. This is really the operation of the accelerator effect as described earlier in this chapter, at the point at which a slowdown in consumer spending leads to a cutback in induced investment.

As a result, by the end of year 19X7, aggregate demand begins to weaken, the period of boom/inflation comes to an end, and the economy hovers on the edge of a recession.

(D) THE RECESSION PHASE

Figure 24-16 shows the economy sliding into recession in years 19X8 and 19X9. Aggregate demand is falling, output is decreasing, and unemployment is rising.

HOW INFLATION CAUSES HIGH INTEREST RATES

Suppose that someone offers to borrow $100 from you for one year and to pay you 6 percent interest for the year. Is this an attractive investment for you or not?

It all depends on the rate of inflation over that year.

If the rate of inflation were 3 percent,
    you would gain $6   (6% of $100)
    in the interest you receive:
    while inflation would reduce the
    purchasing power of your $100
    by 3 percent, or $3, causing you to lose: <u>3</u>
              for a net gain of: <u>$3</u>

On the other hand, if the rate of inflation were 9 percent,
    you would gain
    in the interest you receive: $6
    while inflation would reduce the
    purchasing power of your $100
    by 9 percent, or $9, causing you to lose: <u>9</u>
              for a net loss of: <u>$3</u>

Clearly, the second case would be unacceptable to lenders. To protect the purchasing power of their savings, they would insist upon a higher rate of interest. For instance, an interest rate of 12 percent would leave them with a net gain of 3 percent, the same as in the first example.

  And, if the rate of inflation were expected to be 13 percent, lenders might well want an interest rate of 16 percent.

Thus, the higher the rate of inflation is expected to be, the higher interest rates will be. Or, put differently: High rates of inflation cause high interest rates.

We have seen how inflation and high interest rates will have already slowed down consumer spending and business investment spending. Once the economy *starts* into a recession, factors tend to come into play that cause the recession to *gain momentum*, and become more severe. These are the same factors that operated during an economic boom, but in a recession, they work in the opposite direction:

(i) *Weak business investment spending:* In a recession, business investment spending tends to fall especially rapidly. This is because expectations and business confidence tend to be particularly low during recessions.

(ii) *The accelerator effect:* With consumer spending levelling off, many businesses will not need to buy as much additional new capital equipment

FIGURE 24-15 *How Inflation Turns to Recession*

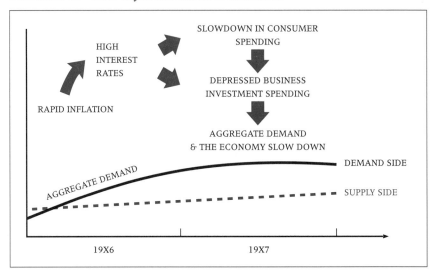

as in the recent past. As a result, their purchases of capital goods will tend to decrease. This is the "accelerator effect" operating in reverse; that is, depressing investment spending rather than boosting it.

(iii) *The multiplier effect:* In a recession, the "multiplier effect" also operates in reverse. As business investment spending decreases, incomes in the capital-goods sector decrease as workers are laid off. This causes reductions in consumer income, which in turn lead to declines in con-

FIGURE 24-16 *The Economy in Recession*

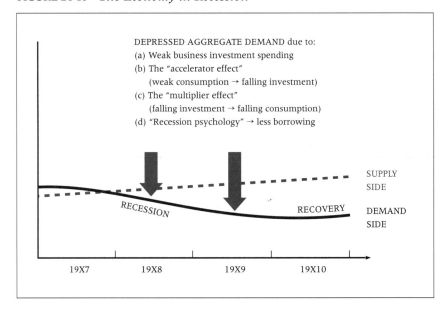

sumer spending. In a chain reaction effect, these decreases in consumer spending spread through the economy, dragging down incomes and consumer spending. The overall result is that aggregate demand and output are reduced by considerably more than the decrease in investment spending that started the process.

(iv) *"Recession psychology"*: Fearing unemployment, consumers tend to borrow and spend less during a recession. Similarly, since businesses expect slow sales, they tend to borrow and spend less because there is no need to expand production capacity or to increase inventory. This drags aggregate demand down even further, taking with it output, employment and incomes.

In addition, many consumers and businesses could by now have become concerned about the high levels of debt that they have accumulated over the previous few years. With already-heavy debt loads and interest payments, and facing increasingly uncertain prospects for the economy, both consumers and businesses may decide to avoid further borrowing, and concentrate instead on repaying part of their debts. This decline in borrowing and new stress on debt repayment will create an additional drag on aggregate demand, slowing the economy further.

The factors discussed in the previous sections will tend to cause the recession to deepen, and become more severe. Finally, the recession will "bottom out" and another recovery can begin. This is shown in year 19X10,

The boom of the second half of the 1980's and the recession of the early 1990's provide an illustration of the role that borrowing and debt can play in the business cycle. During the boom of the second half of the eighties, Canadian consumers borrowed heavily, mostly in the form of mortgage debt for real estate purchases, increasing their debt loads to record levels by the early 1990's. Undoubtedly, this borrowing helped to make the boom stronger. However, during the recession and the very slow recovery from it, consumers' preoccupation with their very heavy debt loads depressed consumption spending, making the recession longer and more severe, and the recovery from it slower.

Commenting on these developments, *The Economist* magazine wrote: "It is no coincidence that the most protracted recessions have been in places where households and firms have piled up the biggest debts," and "Worries about their shrinking wealth and ability to service debts have encouraged consumers to save and repay what they borrowed."

The Economist, "In the Valley of the Shadow of Debt," November 7, 1992
(page 97)

when a backlog of consumer spending, with the help of low interest rates, mark the beginning of another cycle.

The business cycle in review

Figure 24-17 shows a typical business cycle such as has been covered in this chapter, from the recovery stage, through boom, inflation and recession and back to the recovery stage.

Economic forecasting

Obviously, it would be very useful for strategic economic decision-makers in business and government to have advance notice of future economic conditions, so that they could make timely preparations for them. Unfortunately, however, it is easier to appreciate the value of accurate economic forecasts than it is to actually prepare them.

Economic forecasting is a hazardous undertaking at best, as it involves attempting to predict the behavior of millions of consumers and businesses, various levels of government, as well as countless foreign buyers of Canadian exports. Furthermore, the decisions of these various groups are often interrelated (for instance, stronger spending by consumers may induce businesses to increase their capital spending), making the forecasting of the overall situation that much more complex and prone to error.

One approach to economic forecasting is to forecast the various components of aggregate demand—consumer spending, business investment spending, government spending and net export spending. By considering past trends and likely future developments, it is possible to estimate the future levels of these types of spending, and thus of aggregate demand itself, as shown in Figure 24-18. This approach to forecasting generally uses a computer model of the economy that attempts to incorporate into the forecast the numerous interrelationships among the variables in the forecast. Figure 24-18 merely shows the results of such a forecast; it does not reveal the complexity of the process by which the forecast was developed.

Another way to gain advance notice of changes in the direction of the economy is through the use of **leading economic indicators**. These are economic statistics that tend to rise or fall *before* the pace of the economy increases or decreases, and can therefore help to predict future economic

> The experience of being disastrously wrong is salutary. No economist should be denied it, and not many are.
>
> John Kenneth Galbraith

FIGURE 24-17 *The Business Cycle in Review*

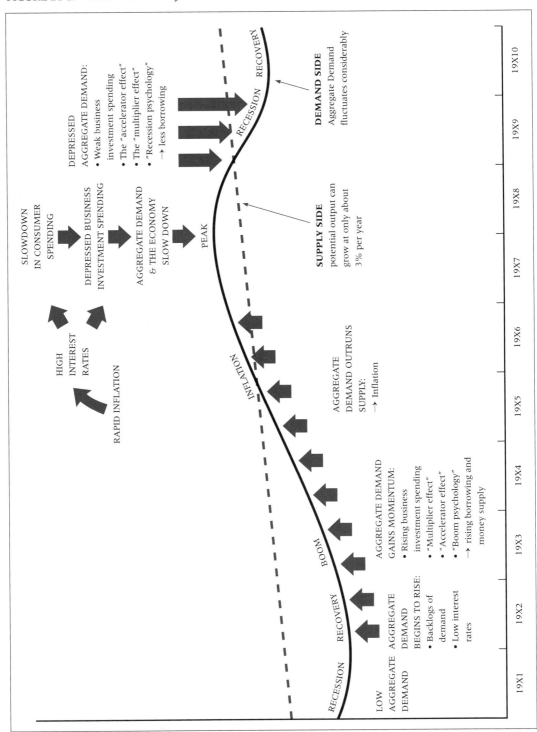

FIGURE 24-18   *Forecasting Aggregate Demand*

		Forecast 1994 ($ billions)
Consumer Expenditure		$463
Investment Spending		
Business investment in plant and equipment	$84	
Housing expenditure	53	137
Government Spending on Goods and Services		203
Net Exports		
Exports of goods and services	$251	
Imports of goods and services	264	(13)
Aggregate Demand		$790

trends. Through a combination of theory and experience with statistics, economists have been able to develop several such leading indicators.

One of the better-known tools used for economic forecasting is the Royal Bank's "Trendicator," which is a composite of seven leading economic indicators. The indicators used to compile the Trendicator are

- the volume of money in circulation (the money supply)
- the ratio of new orders to inventories of consumer durable goods
- primary steel production
- the Toronto Stock Exchange price/earnings ratio (one measure of stock prices)
- the residential construction index (a measure of housing construction activity)
- the ratio of new orders to inventories in export-oriented industries
- the average hours worked (weekly) in manufacturing.

Each of these statistics has tended to give advance notice of economic trends; by combining them into a single statistic such as the Trendicator, a more effective forecasting tool has been developed which is not affected by peculiarities that might make any one (or more) of them ineffective or misleading at any particular time. Figure 24-19 shows both the Trendicator and the trends of the economy since 1963. The bottom graph shows the extent (percentage) by which the growth of real economic activity deviated in each period from the long-term growth trend. Bar graphs on the vertical axis show periods in which growth was faster than the long-term trend, while bar graphs below show periods in which growth was slower than the long-term trend. Growth slowdowns are indicated by the shaded periods on both graphs.

The upper graph shows the composite of seven leading indicators known as the Trendicator. Note how, in most cases, the Trendicator moved down *before* a slowdown started and moved up again *before* the slowdown had ended. By careful examination and interpretation of leading indexes such

FIGURE 24-19 *The Trendicator*

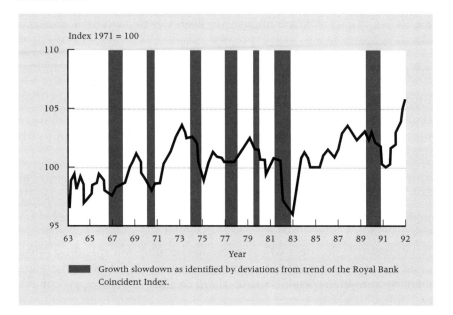

Index 1971 = 100

Growth slowdown as identified by deviations from trend of the Royal Bank Coincident Index.

as the Trendicator, economists can make better economic forecasts. As can be seen from Figure 24-19, leading indicators do not always give accurate advance notice of trends, and are essentially short-term forecasting tools; that is, they do not give long advance notice of changes in the economy.

CONCLUSION

Free-enterprise economies, in which consumers and businesses are free to spend—and not spend—as they see fit have a natural tendency toward instability. At times, consumers and businesses will spend strongly, pushing aggregate demand upwards and generating economic booms, while at other times demand will be weak and the economy will experience recessions.

Whether a particular economic boom or recession was *started* by changes in consumption spending or investment spending often amounts to a question of "which came first—the chicken or the egg?" The causes of business cycles are so complex, involving so many interrelationships between a large number of variables, that it is often very difficult to determine with certainty the origins of economic trends. Regardless of whether a particular boom (or recession) has its origins in the behavior of consumption or investment spending, however, once a boom (or recession) gets started, it tends to *gain momentum* for some time, with the result that the entire economy tends to alternate between periods of rapid growth and slowdowns.

The problem of economic instability, and particularly the periodic recurrence of recessions and depressions, has historically been one of the most serious weaknesses of the free-enterprise type of economy. In this chapter, we have examined the causes of this problem; in the next chapter, we will see what governments have been able to do to try to correct it.

DEFINITIONS OF NEW TERMS

Business Cycle The fluctuation of the economy between prosperity and recession.

Boom The expansion phase of the business cycle, characterized by rapid increases in output and employment.

Multiplier The effect whereby fluctuations in spending (for instance, investment spending) spread by means of the respending effect through the economy, with the total impact on GDP and incomes being considerably larger than the initial fluctuations in spending.

Accelerator The effect whereby rising consumption spending causes rapid increases in induced investment, and a slowing down or levelling off of consumption spending causes sharp declines in induced investment.

Induced Investment Capital investment spending undertaken by business in response to increases in sales that have brought production to near-capacity levels and that are expected to continue.

Leading Economic Indicator An economic statistic that tends to increase or decrease in advance of increases or decreases in the pace of economic activity, thus giving advance notice of changes in economic trends.

CHAPTER SUMMARY

1. Free-enterprise or market economies are prone to economic fluctuations, alternating between periods of rapid expansion (booms) and slumps, or recessions.

2. There are various complex and interrelated factors in the economy that cause these business cycles by generating *fluctuations in aggregate demand*. These include:

    (a) fluctuations in investment spending, which is the most variable major component of aggregate demand,

    (b) the multiplier effect, whereby fluctuations in investment spending, through the respending effect, cause much larger fluctuations in aggregate demand, GDP and total incomes,

    (c) the accelerator effect, through which fluctuations in consumption spending cause much sharper fluctuations in induced investment, and

(d) fluctuations in exports, an important separate source of fluctuations in the Canadian economy, since exports amount to about 25–28 percent of GDP.

3. In the *recovery phase* of the cycle, the economy has been in a recession, but aggregate demand is starting to grow, perhaps with the assistance of backlogs of demand for "big-ticket items" and low interest rates.

4. In the *expansion (boom) phase*, aggregate demand is rising and gaining momentum, as consumption spending and investment spending boost each other through the multiplier and accelerator effects, and growing confidence on the part of both consumers and businesses ("boom psychology") encourages higher levels of borrowing and spending.

5. At the peak of the cycle, aggregate demand has outrun the capacity of the economy to produce goods and services, generating inflation, which in turn causes interest rates to increase. Higher interest rates depress consumer spending on housing and "big-ticket" items, and business investment spending is depressed by higher interest rates and the slowdown in consumer spending. As a result, aggregate demand weakens.

6. In the *recession phase*, aggregate demand falls. The multiplier and accelerator effects operate in reverse, with low consumer spending pulling down investment spending and low investment spending dragging down employment, incomes and consumer spending. "Recession psychology" depresses aggregate demand further, as consumers and businesses fear borrowing, and cut back on their spending in attempts to reduce their debt loads.

7. Economists attempt to forecast the future direction of the economy, by preparing forecasts of the level of aggregate demand and through the use of leading economic indicators.

QUESTIONS

1. In a recession, which *one* of the following industries would likely suffer the greatest percentage decline in its sales, and why?
   (a) Clothing
   (b) Breweries
   (c) Steel
   (d) Agriculture
   (e) Furniture

2. In which *one* of the following industries would you expect annual profits to *vary the most* from year to year, and why?

   (a) Distilling (liquor)

(b) Construction equipment

(c) Banking

(d) Cosmetics

(e) Retail food stores

3. Which *one* of the following would be most likely to experience *periodic* unemployment (from time to time)? Do not refer to seasonal factors in your explanation.

   (a) Teachers

   (b) Managers

   (c) Employees of insurance companies

   (d) Bricklayers

4. Suppose that economists state that, due to a $200 million investment project, GDP will be boosted by more than $400 million. Outline in detail how this might occur.

5. If Canadians imported considerably less from other nations, how would the size of the multiplier be affected?

6. Suppose that there were a sharp increase in interest rates in Canada. Explain how and why this would likely affect the direction of the economy.

7. Suppose that there was a widespread and growing belief among Canadians that the economy was heading into a serious recession. Explain how and why this would likely affect economic developments in Canada.

8. What are the most recent trends in Canada regarding

   (a) capital investment by business?

   (b) new residential housing construction?

   What are the reasons for each of these trends, and what effects are they likely to have on the economy?

9. For each of the seven leading economic indictors used to make up the Royal Bank's composite index, consider what that statistic measures and try to determine logically why that statistic could be expected to increase or decrease *before* the pace of economic activity quickens or slows.

10. Suppose that, on average, consumers will respend 50 percent of any increase in income that they receive.

    (a) If business investment spending increases by $6 billion, GDP and total incomes will increase by $ _____ billion.

    (b) Why do GDP and total incomes increase by this amount rather than by $6 billion?

(c) If consumers respent only 40 percent of increases in income, what difference would this make to the process referred to in (b), and by how much would GDP and total incomes increase?

(d) If consumers respent 60 percent of increases in income, what difference would this make to the process referred to in (b) and (c), and by how much would GDP and total incomes increase?

(e) Record the first three stages of the respending process in each of the above cases on the following table, using the same $6 billion increase in investment spending.

	Percentage of Income Respent		
	40%	50%	60%
Initial Increase in Investment Spending	$6	$6	$6
Stage 1 of respending	—	—	—
Stage 2 of respending	—	—	—
Stage 3 of respending	—	—	—

11. AN ILLUSTRATION OF THE ACCELERATOR

Acme Toy Company needs one machine for every 5000 toys it produces per week. In year 1, as the following table shows, Acme has 20 fully-utilized machines producing 100 000 toys per week. We will assume that this production figure exactly matches the number of toys bought weekly by consumers, so that it also represents consumer demand for Acme's toys. In year 2, consumer demand and toy output increase to 105 000, so that Acme needs 21 machines, as shown in column 2. Since it only has 20 machines (column 3), Acme must buy one new machine (column 4). Since this machine was bought in response to increased consumer demand for toys, we can also regard column 4 as "induced investment" spending.

Now, suppose that in years 3, 4 and 5, consumer demand (toy sales) and toy production are 115 000, 120 000 and 120 000, as shown in column 1.

(a) Complete columns 2, 3 and 4 in the table.

Year	*(1)* Toy Sales and Output *(000)*	*(2)* No. of Machines Needed	*(3)* No. of Machines in the Plant	*(4)* No. of New Machines Bought
1	100	20	20	0
2	105	21	20	1
3	115	—	—	—
4	120	—	—	—
5	120	—	—	—

(b) Summarize the results in the following table.

Year	(1) Consumer Spending (= Toy Sales and Output (000)	% Change From Previous Year	(4) Induced Investment (= Purchases of New Machines)	% Change From Previous Year
1	100	—	0	—
2	105	+5.0%	1	—
3	115	+9.5%	—	—
4	120	—	—	—
5	120	—	—	—

(c) From year 2 to year 3, there was an increase of 9.5 percent in consumer purchases of toys which induced an increase of ___ percent in purchases of new toy-making machines.

(d) From year 3 to year 4, consumer purchases of toys increased by _____ percent, causing purchases on new toy-making machines to _____ by _____ percent.

(e) From year 4 to year 5, consumer purchases of toys remained stable at 120 000; the result of this was that purchases of new toy-making machines _____ by _____ percent.

(f) Show the figures for *consumer spending* and *induced investment* from the table in part (b) on the following graph.

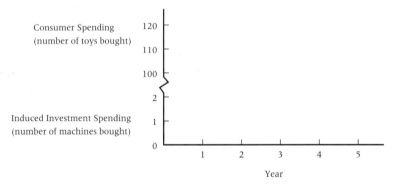

12. Compare the forecasts for the level of aggregate demand and its various components in Figure 24-18 with the actual figures for 1994. How accurate were the forecasts? By what percent did the actual figures differ from the forecasts?

13. Suppose that business inventories increased by $1 billion. How might this statistical fact be interpreted as an indication that:

(a) economic conditions were deteriorating, and

(b) economic conditions were improving?

What might help to determine which of these two possible interpretations was correct?

NOTES

[1] Because the respending effect works through the economy over a period of time, the multiplier effect tends to be larger after a longer period. The Economic Council of Canada also estimates that if government spending is maintained at the higher level (which was not assumed in the estimate of 1.6 for the multiplier), the multiplier effect increases to 2.1 after five years.

[2] Another reason can be that inflation can hurt a nation's exports. For instance, if Canada's inflation were more severe than inflation in the United States, it might become more difficult for Canadian exporters to compete because their prices are too high. This, too, can contribute to a slowing down of aggregate demand and the economy.

CHAPTER 25

Stabilizing the economy: Government fiscal policy

In Chapter 24, we saw that fluctuations in aggregate demand can cause the economy to experience cycles, in which periods of rapid economic growth are followed by recessions and high unemployment. During an economic boom, high and rising levels of consumption and investment spending can feed on each other, driving aggregate demand upwards with increasing momentum, not only boosting output and employment, but also generating inflation. On the other hand, when the economy enters one of its periodic slowdowns, weakening consumption spending depresses investment spending and vice-versa, depressing aggregate demand, output and employment and generating a recession with high unemployment. This tendency to alternate between periods of prosperity and hardship has historically been one of the more persistent and serious problems of free-enterprise economies.

Prior to the 1930's, this tendency for the economy to fall into periodic recessions was not considered by economists to be a major concern. Recessions were generally regarded as temporary adjustments through which the economy periodically passed, somewhat like a manufacturer temporarily cutting its production until it had sold off an unexpected accumulation of excessive inventory. Economists believed not only that governments *could* do little about recessions, but that they *should not even try*, because recessions were believed to be a problem that corrected itself. The prevailing view was that, left on its own and given time, a free-enterprise economy would automatically operate at high levels of output and employment, making intervention by the government unnecessary. This theory was known as **laissez-faire**, which loosely translates into advice that the government should "leave well enough alone," since the economy could be expected to function very well on its own.

However, the Great Depression of the 1930's, in which the economy wallowed for a decade, forced a rethinking of economic theories. The main challenge to the traditional laissez faire theory was advanced by John Maynard Keynes in *The General Theory of Employment, Interest, and Money*, published in 1936. According to Keynes, it could not be safely assumed that the economy would recover from a recession or depression on its own; rather, it might need help from the government. Keynes' basic theory was that the government's control over a major *injection* into the spending stream (government spending) and major *leakage* from the spending

JOHN MAYNARD KEYNES (1883–1946)

The son of two Cambridge University professors, John Maynard Keynes was a child prodigy, working on the economic theory of interest at age four, attending Eton at age fourteen on a scholarship and studying at Cambridge at seventeen. Following graduation, he placed second in a nationwide civil service examination competition. Ironically, he would have finished first if his grade in economics had been higher. He would later comment that this problem had arisen from the fact that he knew more about economics than his examiners did.

Later, while teaching at Cambridge, Keynes served as chairman of the National Mutual Life Assurance Society, editor of the *Economic Journal* and as a director of the Bank of England. He moved in the elite social and cultural circles, organizing Cambridge's Art Theatre and London's Camargo Ballet, and married the celebrated Lydia Lopokova, a prominent Russian ballerina of the era.

In 1936, in the midst of the Great Depression, Keynes completed the most influential of his many writings, *The General Theory of Employment, Interest and Money*, upon which the concept of government fiscal policy is founded. Thirty years later, *Time* magazine would write that this book "had more influence in a shorter time than any other book ever written in economics."

Keynes did not live to see the full extent of his influence. As with all new ideas, his met with considerable resistance initially, and were not widely accepted until after the Second World War. Since then, Keynesian economics has become a key element in government economic policy in industrialized market economies. Nonetheless, his theories and the economic policies associated with them remain controversial: defenders maintain that such policies have saved the free-enterprise system from its tendency toward self-destructive depressions, while opponents argue that these theories have legitimized spendthrift government spending policies that have led to ruinous government borrowing and debt and have fueled inflation, bringing the economy to the brink of ruin.

stream (taxes) gave the government the opportunity to influence the level of aggregate demand for goods and services in the economy, and thus to influence the performance of the entire economy. This use of government spending and taxes to influence the level of aggregate demand and the performance of the economy is called **fiscal policy**. By providing this theoretical basis for fiscal policy, Keynes opened the door to a new era in economic thinking. Eventually, he would come to be regarded as perhaps the most influential economic thinker of the twentieth century.

Part A: Fiscal policy (budget policy)

Keynes believed that during a recession or depression, when the injection of business investment is not sufficiently large to offset the leakage of saving, the government should take steps to correct the situation. One such step could be to *increase government spending*, to create additional injections into the system; another could be to *decrease taxes* so as to reduce that leakage from spending. The common element in both such approaches is that they would *increase the level of aggregate demand* in the economy, with the intention that the increased spending on goods and services would stabilize output and employment, thus making recessions shorter and less severe. This is illustrated in Figure 25-1: in 19X1 and 19X2, the investment injection is smaller than the saving leakage, dragging the levels of aggregate demand, output and employment down, while in 19X3 and 19X4, this is offset by a government spending injection that is larger than the leakage of taxes, the result being that aggregate demand and the economy are boosted out of the recession. Because it involves using the government's budget (the government's expenditures and its tax revenues), fiscal policy is also known as **budget policy**

FIGURE 25-1 *Keynesian Policies to Stabilize the Economy*

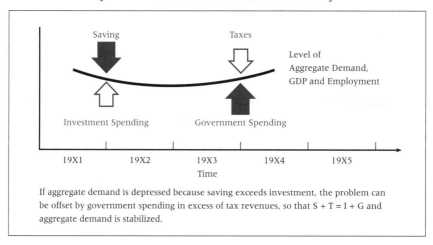

If aggregate demand is depressed because saving exceeds investment, the problem can be offset by government spending in excess of tax revenues, so that S + T = I + G and aggregate demand is stabilized.

Keynes' new ideas concerning the role of the government in the economy created a furor in academic, business and government circles. Conservative thinkers saw such government intervention in the economy as a radical (perhaps even communistic?) threat to the free-enterprise system. To others, his theories represented perhaps the only way to save the economic system from its own self-destructive tendency toward depressions.

While controversy and uncertainty prevented Keynes' proposed policies from being used significantly during the 1930's, the outbreak of the Second World War in 1939 *forced* governments to increase their spending (on the war effort) dramatically without increasing taxes proportionately, a situation which boosted aggregate demand in a "Keynesian" manner. The economic results were dramatic, as the economy recovered quickly from the Depression and unemployment virtually disappeared. For many, the debate had been won—not by theories, but by actual experience.

After the Second World War ended in 1945, a new philosophy developed concerning the role of the government in the economy. *Keynesian economics*, introduced against considerable conservative opposition into university programs, became the basis for the acceptance by governments of their responsibility for the level of employment in the economy. In its 1945 White Paper on Employment and Incomes, the Canadian government accepted responsibility for maintaining a "high and stable level of employment" in the economy and stated that "The Government will be prepared in periods when unemployment threatens to incur the deficits .... resulting from its employment and income policy, whether that policy in the circumstances is best applied through increased expenditures or reduced taxation." Laissez-faire had been abandoned; the government had committed itself to attempting to influence the direction of the entire economy through the use of its fiscal policy.

GOVERNMENT BUDGET DEFICITS

Figure 25-2 shows another feature of Keynesian policy: to stabilize the economy in this way the government must *spend* more than it takes in in *tax revenues*, or run a **budget deficit**. This, too, was considered unthinkable among orthodox economists, for whom the idea of always balancing the budget (keeping expenditures and tax revenues equal) and avoiding debt was virtually sacred.

FIGURE 25-2   *Illustration of a Government Budget Deficit*

if GOVERNMENT SPENDING is	$100 billion
and GOVERNMENT TAX REVENUES are	−90 billion
the GOVERNMENT BUDGET DEFICIT is	$ 10 billion

BUT WHAT ABOUT BALANCING THE GOVERNMENT'S BUDGET?

According to this theory, the government need not follow the traditional rule of always balancing its budget each year; rather, it should use its budget to steer aggregate demand and the economy in the right direction. Keynes, writing during the Great Depression, naturally emphasized the importance of *budget deficits*, because deficits help to stimulate the economy and combat recessions and depressions. However, once the economy had recovered from the recession and was operating at high levels of output and employment, these policies could be reversed. During an economic boom, government spending could be cut back and/or taxes increased, creating a **budget surplus**—an excess of tax revenues over government expenditures. Such budget surpluses would serve two important purposes:

- they would offset the budget deficits of the recession period, and
- the excess of taxes over government spending would hold down aggregate demand, reducing the risk of severe inflation developing as a result of the economic boom.

SHOULD THE GOVERNMENT EVER BALANCE ITS BUDGET?

In any given year, it is unlikely that a balanced budget would be appropriate. As we have seen, if the economy were in a recession, a budget deficit would be in order, while a period of boom/inflation would call for a budget surplus. Only if the economy were operating at a near-ideal balance between these conditions would a balanced budget be appropriate. In these circumstances, a budget that neither stimulated nor depressed aggregate demand would be what the economy needed.

Over the longer run, the budget deficits that are incurred during recessions should be more or less offset by budget surpluses during boom periods, creating a more or less balanced budget over a period of years.

COUNTERCYCLICAL FISCAL POLICY

Properly timed, budget deficits and surpluses can help to smooth out the economic fluctuations associated with the business cycle. In Figure 25-3, the blue line shows how the economy would fluctuate on its own, while the black line represents the milder fluctuations resulting from the effective use of government fiscal policies. As Figure 25-3 shows, budget deficits can support aggregate demand, output and employment during recessions, while budget surpluses can help to ease the pressures of excess aggregate demand during the inflationary peaks of the business cycle. Economists refer to this as **countercyclical fiscal policy**, because the

FIGURE 25-3 *Countercyclical Fiscal Policy*

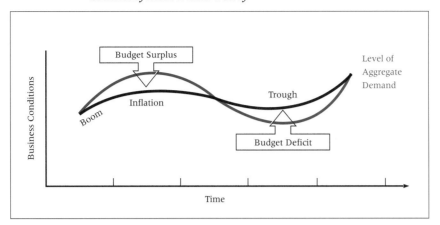

government is deliberately using its budget to offset ("counter") the economic ups and downs of the business cycle, and to smooth out these economic fluctuations.

As noted earlier, ideally the government's periodic budget deficits during recessions would be offset by its periodic surpluses during boom periods. Over the long run, then, the government's budget would be more or less in balance.[1]

The use of fiscal policy in this manner is somewhat comparable to the budgeting practices of people whose incomes fluctuate widely, such as real estate agents. During lean years, when their income is low, such people can cushion the impact by spending more than they earn, provided that they keep their household budget in balance over the longer term by spending less than they earn when times are good.

FISCAL POLICY TO STIMULATE THE ECONOMY

We will now consider in more detail the two approaches by which government fiscal policy can be used to stimulate the economy during recessions: increases in government spending and tax reductions.

(a) Increases in government expenditures

We have seen how increases in government spending can raise the level of aggregate demand and help to lift the economy out of a recession. Traditionally, governments have used *public works* for this purpose, building roads, bridges, parks and public buildings when the economy was slack and the construction industry was particularly depressed. Some programs to increase government spending, such as public works projects or special relief or temporary job programs, must be planned and set up, which creates delays in their implementation. However, there are other types of government spending, such as *unemployment insurance* and *welfare payments*, which tend to rise automatically when the economy slips into a recession, thus providing automatic support to the level of aggregate demand.

(b) Reductions in taxes

While traditional theory would insist that taxes be increased in order to balance the increases in government spending referred to above, Keynesian theory argues that tax increases would only depress spending by consumers and businesses, worsening the recession.

Thus, taxes should not be increased during a recession; indeed, if anything, they should be reduced, so as to help raise the level of aggregate demand. The most popular and effective policy of this type is the *personal income tax cut*, intended to increase personal disposable income and consumer spending, although temporary *sales tax cuts* have also been used for this purpose. To promote higher levels of business investment spending, there are various types of tax reductions, including *cuts in corporate income (profits) taxes* and *increased capital cost allowances*, which permit businesses to depreciate assets more quickly, thus reducing their taxable income and tax liabilities. The operation of these policies is illustrated in Figure 25-4

FIGURE 25-4 *Anti-Recession Fiscal Policies*

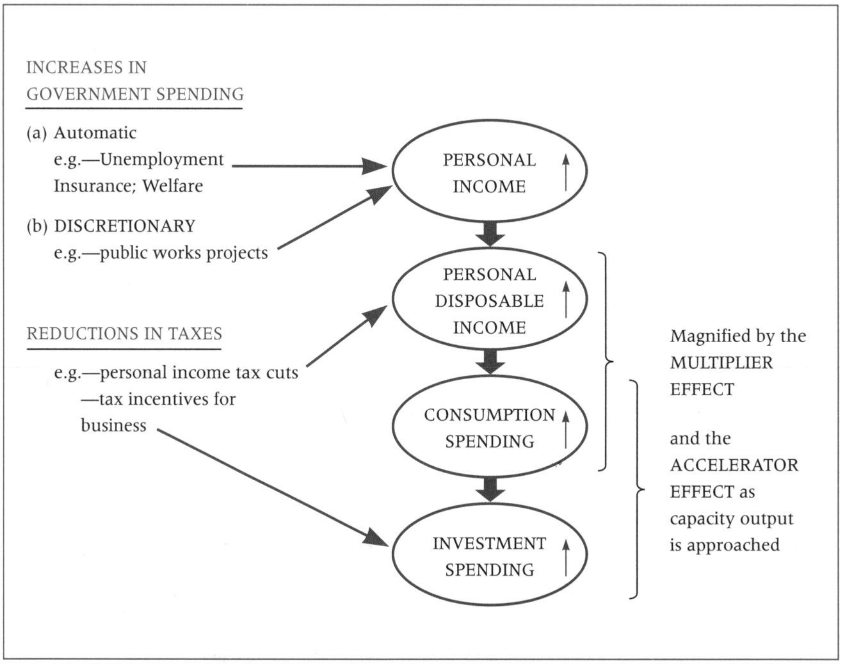

AUTOMATIC STABILIZERS

As noted above, certain types of government expenditures, such as unemployment insurance and welfare, tend to rise automatically during recessions, as unemployment rises. In addition to this, many of the government's tax revenues, such as those from income taxes, profits taxes and sales taxes, tend to be depressed by slower economic activity during recessions. With government tax revenues depressed and expenditures rising, there is an automatic tendency for the government's budget to go into a deficit as a recession develops. This budget deficit will then help to counteract the recession automatically, which is why such government expenditures and tax revenues are called **automatic stabilizers**

THE MULTIPLIER AND FISCAL POLICY

As we have seen, fiscal policy is used to stabilize the economy in recessions by increasing the level of spending on goods and services by government, consumers and businesses. The effect of any such increase in spending will, however, spread through the economy due to the multiplier effect, as increases in income generated by the policy are respent again and again. For example, a government road-building program will increase the incomes of construction workers, who will spend part of their increased incomes on consumer goods and services, starting a chain of respending that will increase total incomes and GDP by perhaps 1.6 times the original increase in government spending. Similarly, personal income tax cuts that boost consumer spending will initiate a respending effect that will ripple through the economy.

PUMP PRIMING

Fiscal policy to stimulate the economy can also involve the accelerator effect. Once the level of consumption spending has risen to the point where it is causing induced investment spending by business, the economy should be able to carry on its recovery without further stimulation from government budget deficits. In fact, further deficits at this point would not help the economy; they would only boost demand to excessive levels and cause inflation. This is the concept of **pump priming**. To get a well to work, you have to pour some water into it first; however, after that is done, the well works without further assistance. Similarly, the economy may benefit from a boost to start it on a path to recovery out of a slump, but beyond a point, no further boosts are needed.

The concept of pump priming views budget deficits as a *temporary stimulus* to the economy rather than as a permanent replacement for business investment spending. Indeed, in a basically free-enterprise economy, government spending cannot replace business investment's vital role of adding to the economy's stock of capital goods, and thus to future prosperity.

Thus, the key to long-term prosperity lies in private-business capital investment, while temporary expansion of government spending and budget deficits can help to combat periodic recessions and thus create the economic conditions that will encourage more private business investment spending.

A NOTE ON CREATING JOBS

Often, when the economy is sluggish and unemployment is high, much attention is given to government efforts to "create jobs," or "government job creation programs." Terms such as these mislead many people into believing that this simply means direct government hiring of unemployed people, often for *make-work programs* ("digging holes and filling them up again").

In fact, creating jobs is a much more positive concept than this—it refers to government efforts to *stimulate the whole economy* (through budget deficits), rather than merely hiring the unemployed to do work of little value. For example, tax cuts increase consumer spending, which stimulates many industries. Also, the effects of government spending (such as on a public works project) will spread, via the multiplier effect, through the economy, increasing consumer spending, too. By generating a more favorable economic climate, these efforts by the government can result in increased business investment spending as well. Thus, the effects of budget deficits designed to stimulate employment will be felt all through the economy, from the toy industry to the construction industry—not merely in the hiring of the unemployed by the government.

FINANCING DEFICITS: WHERE WILL THE MONEY COME FROM?

The use of fiscal policy to stimulate the economy during recessions requires that the government have budget deficits, with government expenditures larger than tax revenues. Where will the necessary money come from to finance such deficits? Basically, there are two possible sources of funds to finance budget deficits.

(a) The government can borrow the money

The government can raise the necessary funds by borrowing them—by selling *government bonds* to individuals, banks, insurance companies, pension funds, investment funds and other financial institutions. By doing this, the government can, in effect, mop up savings that are not being used for capital investment and inject them back into the spending stream as government spending.

(b) The government can "print" the money

Another way to raise the funds for federal budget deficits is to *create new money* (the popular term is *print money*)[2] for the government to spend. While a growing economy requires a larger volume of money in circulation, it is dangerous to increase the money supply too quickly. The inevitable result of such a policy would be severe inflation, as the excessive amount of money in circulation pushes aggregate demand up so rapidly that output cannot keep pace. Thus, while it may be tempting for the government to simply "print money" to finance its budget deficits, this should be done only within strict limits, so as to avoid increasing the money supply by more than the economy can absorb without generating rapid inflation.

Part B: The National Debt

We have seen that the use of government fiscal policy to stimulate the economy during recessions requires that the government borrow money (mostly through bond issues) in order to finance its budget deficits. The total amount of federal government debt thus incurred—the amount of money owed by the federal government—is called the **National Debt**. By 1994 the National Debt was approximately $500 billion, or over 18 000 for every Canadian man, woman and child.[3]

WHAT'S A BILLION?

The sheer size of the numbers involved, expressed as they are in billions of dollars, tends to make it difficult to appreciate the magnitude of the National Debt. For instance, $450 billion is surely a large number, but how large is one billion? One way to explain this is to say that one billion is one thousand million, but this leaves unanswered the question of how large one million is. (It's one thousand thousand, but does *that* really make it all crystal clear?)

A completely different way to try to deal with this problem is to count *seconds*, which are familiar to us as very short durations of time:

- one thousand seconds = 16.7 minutes
- one million seconds = 11.6 days
- one billion seconds = 31.5 years

Thus, a National Debt of $450 billion is the equivalent of over 14 000 years' worth of seconds. And a student who is 21 years old has lived for two-thirds of a billion seconds.

The National Debt has, over the years, been the subject of misunder-standings, fears, myths and political hypocrisy. Many Canadians believe, for instance, that the entire debt is owed to other countries and that Canada may go bankrupt because of it. Both of these ideas are myths. On the other hand, few Canadians appreciate the real dangers concerning the National Debt. In this chapter, we will consider ways in which government bor-rowing and debt can be used beneficially, as well as the real (as opposed to mythical) dangers associated with government debt. First, however, we will take a brief look at the issue of debt in general, so as to provide some context for our discussion of government debt.

THE USES—AND ABUSES—OF DEBT

To many people, "debt" is a four-letter word—something to be gotten into only if absolutely necessary and gotten out of as soon as possible. Debt is viewed by many as synonymous with trouble—the result of past trouble and a source of future trouble.

However, the matter is not that simple. Most households use debt to buy homes, cars and other major items, as well as for credit card purchases. And virtually every business uses debt to finance plant and equipment as well as purchases of inventories. And both households and businesses have found that such debt can be very useful if it is properly managed.

The most common reason for borrowing is to *acquire assets*, such as homes and cars for households and plant and equipment for businesses. Such assets are too costly to pay for out of the current year's income. And, since the benefits from the asset will be received over a long period of time, it is quite reasonable to borrow to buy the asset and to pay for it over a period of years, as the loan is repaid.

For businesses, the main benefit of debt is the prospect of using the borrowed money for profitable investments. For instance, if a business borrowed $100 million through a bond issue to finance the upgrading of its plant, it might cost that business an additional $10 million per year in in-terest payments on those bonds (assuming an interest rate of 10 percent). However, if through lower production costs and/or increased sales as a re-sult of this investment, the business gains $15 million per year, not only will it have no trouble making the interest payments, but also its annual prof-its will be higher by $5 million after the $10 million of interest is paid. The key is that the rate of return on the investment (in this example, 15 per-cent) be larger than the rate of interest on the capital borrowed to finance it (here, 10 percent).

For households, the main benefit of borrowing is that they get the use of the asset sooner. The alternative is to save until enough money has been accumulated to pay cash for the asset, a process which could take a very long time indeed with a large asset such as a home or a car. Therefore, as long as the household's budget can afford the monthly debt repayments with interest, such borrowing and debt can be quite beneficial to it.

There are, however, dangers as well as benefits in debt. The main rules to follow are:

(a) *Don't borrow excessively:* The interest payments on debt are a "fixed cost"; that is they must be paid each year regardless of circumstances. If a business or household falls upon hard times and its income is reduced, or if interest rates rise, heavy debt can be financially fatal, because the interest must be paid nonetheless. Thus, it is wise to be cautious when planning borrowing—in particular, don't borrow too much, and don't make overly optimistic assumptions about your ability to repay the debt, or about interest rates being low.

(b) *Don't borrow to pay current operating expenses:* It is reasonable to borrow to pay for long-term *capital assets* such as a home or production equipment. However, *current operating expenses* such as your food, telephone bill or heating should be paid out of *current income*. Borrowing to pay expenses such as these will only lead to regular monthly borrowing, and an ever-increasing debt with a growing problem of interest payments that will eventually become unmanageable.

There are some important differences between the borrowing and debt of private households and businesses as discussed above and the borrowing and debt of governments. For instance, only the federal government has the responsibility for steering the economy away from recessions, which involves a special reason for budget deficits and borrowing.

Nonetheless, as we will see later in this chapter, the dangers explained in the previous section of excessive borrowing and debt and of borrowing to pay current operating expenses apply to governments as well as to households and businesses.

WHAT IS THE NATIONAL DEBT?

The National Debt is the overall debt of the federal government—most commonly defined as the difference between the federal government's *liabilities* (mostly outstanding bonds) and its *net recorded assets* (mostly those assets which yield interest, profits or dividends). Thus it measures, on balance, *how much the federal government owes to creditors* (mostly the holders of its bonds).

The relationship between the National Debt and the federal government's budget deficits is shown in Figure 25-5. The National Debt is the *total* accumulated federal debt as a result of past budget deficits, while each year's budget deficit represents that year's *addition* to the National Debt.

In Figure 25-5, it is assumed that the government has no debt at the start of 19X1 and at the end of that year, since there is no budget deficit in 19X1. After that, there are deficits in each year, and each year the total government debt (National Debt) increases by the amount of that year's deficit. Note also that even after the government manages to *reduce its deficits* in the last two years, the National Debt *continues to grow*. As long as there is *any* budget deficit, the National Debt will rise.

FIGURE 25-5 *Federal Budget Deficits and the National Debt*

Year	Government spending	Government tax revenues	Budget deficit	National Debt
	(		$ Billions	)
19X1	$50	$50	$0	$0
19X2	60	55	5	5
19X3	70	56	14	19
19X4	80	68	12	31
19X5	83	75	8	39

FEDERAL GOVERNMENT BUDGET DEFICITS AND DEBT UNTIL 1975

Until the mid-1970's, the federal government's budget deficits and debt were of virtually no concern to economists. The federal government had budget deficits in only 11 of the 25 years from 1950 to 1974. These were small deficits, the largest being slightly over one-half billion dollars.

The main reason for the deficits that did occur during this period was to *combat periodic recessions*, especially in the late 1950's and early 1960's. Another reason for government borrowing was to *finance the building of social assets* such as hospitals, schools and roads. Borrowing for both such purposes was considered to be socially beneficial, in that it provided lasting benefits to Canada in the form of a healthier economy and social assets.

Some concerns were expressed about the growth of the federal government's debt, which increased from about $10 billion in 1952 to nearly $25 billion in 1974. However, there was hardly any concern over the size of the National Debt or the government's ability to repay it, for several reasons.

The first of these was that, while the size of the debt was growing, it was growing much less rapidly than the nation's economy as measured by the GDP. As a result, the federal government's debt was only 15 percent of GDP in 1975, as compared to 41 percent of GDP in 1952. Viewed from this perspective, the growth of the government's debt was not alarming.

The second reason was that the vast majority of the federal government's debt was *owed to Canadians*—those individuals and financial institutions such as banks, trust companies, insurance companies and pension funds who had bought government bonds. As a result, the National Debt was an *internal debt*: it was owed by the Canadian public (the federal government) *to* the Canadian public (individuals and institutions owning government bonds). Thus, in a real sense, the National Debt was owed "by us (the government) to us (Canadians holding government bonds)." While repayment of the debt would involve removing billions of dollars from the Canadian economy through taxes, it would also involve returning the same amount of money into the Canadian economy, when the bondholders were paid for their bonds. While money would be *redistributed* by such a transaction, it would involve no net *removal* from the economy, and thus no danger of bankruptcy or burden on future generations. The same principle applies to payment of interest on the debt: it involved a re-distribution of funds from taxpayers to bondholders *within* the Canadian economy rather than a withdrawal of funds *from* the economy. Thus, there was no serious concern about the ability of the federal government to pay off its debt, should this be necessary.

The third reason was that it was not necessary for the federal govern-ment to pay off its debt, in the sense of reducing it to zero. As outstanding bonds became due (matured) and had to be repaid, new bonds could read-ily be issued to raise the necessary funds. This process, known as "refund-ing" a bond issue, is commonplace not only in government finance but also in many large, stable business corporations.

Thus, as of 1975, federal government budget deficits and debt were not viewed as a problem. Rather, they were regarded as generally benefi-cial to society, in that they helped to soften recessions, maintain economic growth and build valuable social assets. In a real sense, they could be re-garded as borrowing in order to provide long-term benefits for society.

FEDERAL GOVERNMENT BUDGET DEFICITS AND DEBT SINCE 1975

After 1974, however, the federal government's budget deficits changed dramatically in nature. The deficits became not only *extremely large*, but also *persistent*: in every year after 1974, the federal government had a large budget deficit, most of them in the $10–30 billion per year range. This noteworthy change is reflected in Figure 25-6, which shows the deficits not only in dollar terms, but also as a percentage of GDP, to eliminate the effects of inflation on the figures. By either measure, the federal budget deficits became massive in a very short period of time.

The federal budget deficits after 1975 were not only large, but also were used for different purposes than in the past. Whereas before 1975 government deficits were used mainly to finance anti-recession programs and social assets, after 1975 the government was increasingly *borrowing to cover its current operating expenditures*, such as health care, income-support pro-grams, education and so on. As we have seen, this generated a stream of very large annual budget deficits.

As a result of this surge of government borrowing, the federal gov-ernment's *debt soared*, from less than 16 percent of GDP in 1975 to about 65 percent of GDP by 1993. As the government's debt grew, from $27 billion in 1975 to about $450 billion by 1993, the *interest payments on the debt soared*. In 1974, about 11 percent of the federal government's revenues went to in-terest payments on the government's debt; by the early 1990's, about 32 percent of federal government tax revenues were being used to pay in-terest. By the early 1990's, interest payments in excess of $40 billion per year had become one of the federal government's largest items of current ex-

FIGURE 25-6 *Federal Budgets, 1970–92*

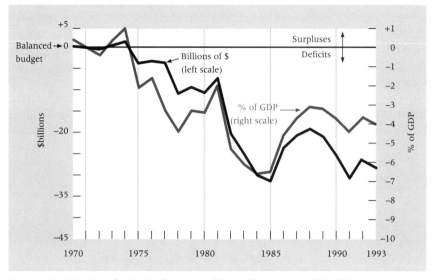

Source: Statistics Canada, *National Income and Expenditure Accounts* (13-001)

penditure, and a major force generating large budget deficits that required further borrowing and thus growing debt. The government was on a treadmill, being forced to borrow more, just to pay the interest on its debt from past borrowings.

Finally, such heavy borrowing involved the sale of massive volumes of government bonds, at times more than could readily be sold within Canada, to Canadian investors. As a result, the government increasingly turned to selling its bonds to foreign lenders. This led to a sharp increase in Canadian government debt to foreign lenders: in 1975, just over 2 percent of federal bonds outstanding were held by foreigners, while by 1992, the proportion was 23 percent and was rising. In the process, a significant part of Canadian government debt ceased to be "internal" in nature (owed to Canadians), and became "external."

FIGURE 25-7 *Federal Budget Deficits Before and After 1975*

Before 1975	Since 1975
• Deficits in 11 of 25 years	• Deficits in every year
• Small deficits (largest = $0.5 billion)	• Very large deficits ($10–30 billion)
• National Debt small; declined from 41% of GDP in 1952 to 16% of GDP in 1975	• Deficits used largely to finance current operating expenditures
• Vast majority of debt was "internal"; only about 2% of bonds held by foreign lenders	• National Debt large and rising rapidly, from 16% of GDP in 1975 to 65% of GDP by 1993
• Interest payments on debt were 11% of federal revenues in 1974	• Large proportion of debt was "external"; 23% of bonds held by foreign lenders
	• Interest payments on debt were 35% of federal tax revenues by 1993

WHY DID THE FEDERAL BUDGET DEFICITS BECOME SO LARGE?

The "short answer" to this question is fairly predictable—the federal government's expenditures increased much more rapidly than its revenues. However, underlying this rather simple reality are some complex political, social and economic factors that need to be examined in more detail. The first of these is some background concerning government spending responsibilities under the Canadian constitution.

SOME BACKGROUND—THE ROLE OF PROVINCIAL AND LOCAL GOVERNMENT SPENDING

The discussion in the previous sections has focused on the *federal* government's spending and budget deficits, mainly because it was at the federal level that serious budget deficits first developed. However, in discussing the reasons for the federal government's budget deficits, it is necessary to examine *provincial and local* government spending, which also played a large role in the overall problem of government budget deficits.

Canada has a very decentralized system of government, under which a great deal of government spending is done not by the federal government, but rather by provincial and local (municipal) governments. At the start of the 1990's, total spending by provincial and municipal governments (excluding interest and payments to other levels of governments) amounted to about $130 billion—more than 50 percent greater than total federal government spending (also excluding interest and transfers to other levels of government). Most provincial government spending is in three areas: *health care*, *welfare* and *postsecondary education*, which, under the Canadian constitution, are the responsibility of the provincial governments, not the federal government. Since these have been three of the most rapidly-expanding areas of government expenditure, provincial and local government spending has increased considerably faster than federal government spending.

While the constitution gives the provincial governments the responsibility for these three major areas of *spending*, it does not give them parallel powers to raise *tax revenues*. The strongest power to levy taxes lies with the federal government, which has the authority to levy various taxes, including the lucrative personal income taxes. The provincial governments' constitutional tax base is much more restricted, consisting mainly of sales taxes.

In order to help the provinces to meet their heavy spending responsibilities in the areas of health care, welfare and postsecondary education, the federal government undertook to transfer considerable amounts of federal revenues to the provincial governments, through various systems of *transfer payments* to the provinces. These transfer payments were substantial, amounting in the mid-1980's to about 20 percent of all federal spending. For instance, by the mid-1980's federal transfer payments to the provincial governments amounted to about 20 percent of all provincial government revenues and $800–900 for every Canadian. And, of course, these transfer payments added to the federal budget deficits and thus to the National Debt.

MORE SPECIFIC REASONS FOR THE LARGE FEDERAL BUDGET DEFICITS

The sharp increase in federal budget deficits since 1975 was the result of certain government policy decisions, certain economic events, and the interaction between these, as described in the following sections.

(a) Government policy decisions

During the 1970's, the federal government made a series of economic and social policy decisions that increased its expenditures and depressed its tax revenues. For instance, the federal government increased benefits under various social programs such as unemployment insurance and pensions, and made commitments to transfer large amounts of federal funds (in the range of $20 billion per year) to the provincial governments to help finance rapidly-rising provincial government spending on programs such as health care, welfare and post-secondary education. At the same time as it was increasing its spending in these areas, the federal government introduced a variety of tax reductions on both personal and business income, which had the effect of depressing its tax revenues.

These divergent trends in federal spending and tax revenues led to a fundamental change in federal government finances. This change is illustrated in Figure 25-8, which divides federal spending into *interest payments* and *"program spending"* (which is all spending except interest, which is not considered to be a spending program like unemployment insurance or national defence).

As Figure 25-8 shows, before 1975 the federal government ran small surpluses on its programs; these surpluses were used to offset (or pay) the government's small annual interest payments. For instance, in 1967, the federal government took in $10.9 billion in revenues and spent $9.8 billion on its programs, leaving a surplus of $1.1 billion that was just about enough to cover its interest payments of $1.2 billion.

After 1975, however, the situation changed dramatically. The federal government ran deficits on its programs rather than surpluses, as Figure 25-8 shows. When each year's interest payments were added to these "program deficits," the result was substantial budget deficits in every year after 1975.

These decisions by the government caused a built-in imbalance to develop between government spending and tax revenues, generating what are known as **structural budget deficits**—large budget deficits that occur each year, whether the economy is in a recession or not.[4]

FIGURE 25-8 *Federal Budget Trends, 1965–85*

Year	Total Revenue	Program Expenditures[a]	Balance on Programs	Interest Expenditures	Surplus (+) or Deficits (−)
			(Billions of dollars)		
1965	$9.1	$7.5	$+1.6	$1.1	$+0.5
1966	10.0	8.6	+1.4	1.2	+0.2
1967	10.9	9.8	+1.1	1.2	−0.1
1968	12.2	10.9	+1.4	1.4	0
1969	14.5	11.9	+2.6	1.6	+1.0
1970	15.5	13.4	+2.1	1.9	+0.2
1971	17.3	15.4	+1.8	2.0	−0.1
1972	19.6	17.9	+1.7	2.3	−0.5
1973	22.8	19.9	+3.0	2.5	+0.4
1974	30.0	25.7	+4.2	3.0	+1.2
1975	31.8	31.9	−0.1	3.7	−3.8
1976	35.5	34.3	+1.2	4.5	−3.3
1977	36.7	38.9	−2.2	5.1	−7.3
1978	38.3	42.7	−4.4	6.4	−10.8
1979	43.4	44.7	−1.3	8.1	−9.4
1980	50.7	51.4	−0.8	9.9	−10.7
1981	65.0	58.6	+6.4	13.7	−7.3
1982	66.1	69.7	−3.6	16.7	−20.3
1983	69.6	77.2	−7.6	17.4	−25.0
1984	76.5	85.6	−9.1	20.9	−30.0
1985	83.2	90.0	−6.8	24.6	−31.4

[a]All expenditures other than interest.

Totals do not always add up due to rounding.

Source: Department of Finance, *Quarterly Economic Review*, Special Report: Fiscal Indicators and Reference Tables (March 1992)

> The hard fact about Canada's deficit is that for more than ten years Canadians have accepted more in services and transfers from the federal government than they have been willing to pay for.
>
> Edward Carmichael, *Tackling the Federal Deficit*, C.D. Howe Institute, 1984

In summary, the federal government was providing Canadians with services (such as health care and education) and transfer payments (such as unemployment insurance and welfare) far in excess of what they were paying for with their taxes, and borrowing heavily to do so, even in years when the economy was not in a recession.

(b) Economic events: the recessions of 1981–82 and 1990–92

When the severe recession of 1981–82 struck, increasing sharply the number of Canadians on unemployment insurance and welfare while also depressing government tax revenues, the federal budget deficits increased sharply, from around $10 billion into the $20 to $25 billion per year range. The less deep, but much longer recession of the early 1990's had a similar effect, driving the federal budget deficit from about $20 billion into the $30 billion range. These recessions, which were the two most severe economic downturns since the Great Depression of the 1930's, added considerably to the federal government's deficits and debt.

(c) Interest payments on the government's debt

By 1985, the factors explained in (a) and (b) had pushed the National Debt to $206 billion. At this point, another factor began to be the dominant force driving the federal budget deficit upwards—*interest payments* on the government's massive debt. Interest payments became the second-largest item of current government expenditure, keeping the deficit high and forcing the government to borrow further.

The result of these forces was a series of large annual federal budget deficits after 1975, which in turn generated the very rapid increases in the federal government's debt shown in Figure 25-9.

FIGURE 25-9 *Net Federal Debt, 1970–92*

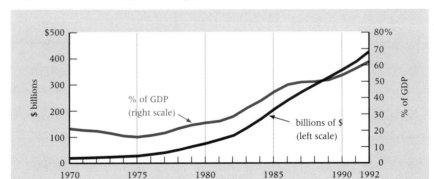

SUMMARY: THE FINANCES OF THE TOTAL GOVERNMENT SECTOR, 1974–85

In summary, from 1974 to 1985, provincial government spending, mainly in the rapidly growing areas of health care, welfare and postsecondary education, rose very rapidly (by 13.5 percent per year, on average).[5]

Provincial tax revenues increased briskly as well (by an average of 13.0 percent per year), which was less rapid than the increases in the provinces' spending; however, rising transfer payments from the federal government filled most of the gap, leaving the provincial governments' budgets reasonably balanced in most years.

FIGURE 25-10   *Government Spending and Revenues, 1974–85*

	Average annual % increase
Gross Domestic Product (for purposes of comparison)	11.0%
Federal government spending excluding transfers to provinces)	13.7%
Federal transfer payments to provincial governments	12.1%
Federal taxes and other revenues	9.7%
Provincial government spending (including transfer payments to local governments)	13.5
Provincial taxes and other revenues	13.0%

Source: Department of Finance, *Economic and Fiscal Reference Tables*, August 1993

Over the same period, federal government spending also increased rapidly. From 1974 to 1985, the federal government's "own" spending (that is, excluding transfer payments to the provinces) increased by 13.7 percent per year on average. Federal transfer payments to the provincial governments grew by an average of 12.1 percent per year. However, the federal government's tax revenues lagged badly, increasing by an average of only 9.7 percent per year, with massive federal budget deficits the result.

Thus, even though it was the federal government that developed massive budget deficits after 1975, a significant part of its spending was due to transfer payments to the provincial governments to support rapid increases in provincial spending in the areas of health care, welfare and postsecondary education. This fact would become very significant after the mid-1980's, when the federal government undertook to reduce its budget deficits through spending restraint.

Concerns regarding federal deficits and debt

As we have seen, since 1975 the federal government has had large annual budget deficits which generated a large and rapidly-growing National Debt. The following section deals with the dangers associated with this situation, and why the federal budget deficit came to be regarded by many economists as one of the most serious economic problems facing the nation. These concerns are of six types:

(a) the rapidly rising interest payments on the debt

(b) future effects on government programs, taxes and Canadians' living standards

(c) the effect on interest rates

(d) the effect on business capital investment

(e) growing indebtedness to foreign lenders

(f) reduced ability to use fiscal policy to combat recessions

In the following sections, we will examine each of these concerns.

(A) INTEREST PAYMENTS ON THE DEBT— A "VICIOUS CIRCLE" OF BORROWING AND INTEREST PAYMENTS?

As interest payments on the government's debt soared (from less than $10 billion in 1980 to more than $40 billion in the early 1990's, concern grew that the federal government's debt would be feeding upon itself in a "vicious circle" in which the government was forced to borrow more just to pay the interest on its debt.

Because of the way in which compound interest operates, there are certain inescapable realities associated with heavy government debt. Assume that the government runs a budget deficit of $10 billion. If interest rates are 10 percent, and the government must borrow $10 billion to finance its budget deficit, it will have additional expenditures next year of $1 billion for interest on the borrowed money. This added expenditure will push next year's budget deficit to $11 billion, which will add $1.1 billion of interest to expenditures in the year after that. That will push the budget deficit from $11 billion to $12.1 billion, which will add $1.2 billion of interest costs, making the deficit $13.3 billion and the interest costs for the following year $1.3 billion and so on, as shown in Figure 25-11.

Note also that each year, the rising interest costs on the past debt add not only to *current spending*, but also to current borrowing and thus to *future debt*. As a result, the process can escalate, or spiral upwards as it feeds on itself.

This effect of compound interest on interest expenditures is not a problem if the government's debt is small and interest rates are low, as was the case until 1975. By the mid-1980's, however, the size of the debt and the fact that interest rates had risen meant the government's interest costs soared: where in 1974, the federal government spent less than 11 percent

FIGURE 25-11 *How Compound Interest Feeds Government Debt*

Year	Government debt	Interest on Debt (10%) (= addition to spending/debt)
1	$10.0 billion	$1.0 billion
2	11.0	1.1
3	12.1	1.2
4	13.3	1.3
5	14.6	etc.

> In each of the past ten years the expenditures of the federal government have exceeded its tax revenues. These continuing deficits have led to an enormous growth in the burden of debt and the (interest) costs of servicing that debt. Moreover, unless we begin now to put our fiscal house in order, the burden of debt will continue to mount rapidly in the future. We are on a very dangerous treadmill.
>
> Hon. Michael Wilson, Minister of Finance, *Economic and Fiscal Statement*, Nov. 8, 1984.

of its tax revenues on interest on its debt, by 1992 nearly 32 percent of its tax revenues went to pay the interest. Total federal expenditures on interest in 1992 were about $39 billion, or $1421 for every man, woman and child in Canada. After 1985, the government's expenditures on interest each year exceeded the government's budget deficit. That is, the government was borrowing in order to pay the interest on its debt, and going yet deeper into debt in the process. Thus, the combination of massive debt, high interest rates and compound interest had set the stage for a potentially serious upward spiral of debt and interest costs unless the government acted to reduce its deficits.

(B) EFFECT ON OTHER GOVERNMENT PROGRAMS, TAXES AND CANADIANS' LIVING STANDARDS IN THE FUTURE

Up to 1985, much of the government's debt was incurred to cover its *current expenditures*, such as health care costs and transfer payments (unemployment insurance and welfare). Borrowing to pay for current expenditures benefited Canadians until 1985, but it postponed paying for these benefits, leaving the burden of debt and the interest on it to be coped with in the future.

There is nothing the government can do to cut the interest payments on its debt—its creditors must be paid. Therefore, as interest payments absorbed a larger and larger share of its revenues, the government was forced to squeeze its spending in other areas. This led to concerns that spending on key social welfare programs such as health care, education and income support (unemployment insurance, welfare, pensions, etc.) would have to be cut back in an attempt to prevent the budget deficit from soaring out of control.

> In its *Seventeenth Annual Review*, the Economic Council of Canada warned that "greater consumption by the present generation of Canadians is at the expense of future generations."

The only other way for the government to reduce its deficits would be to increase taxes, which would also reduce the living standards of Canadians. Thus, the deficit poses a serious threat to the future prosperity of Canadians.

(C) HIGHER INTEREST RATES

Large federal budget deficits could generate higher interest rates in the economy because heavy federal borrowing, in competition for funds with other borrowers such as businesses and home-buyers, could result in *excess demand for capital*, and thus higher interest rates. In addition, high interest rates might be required to induce foreign lenders to continue to buy Canadian government bonds, especially in view of the deteriorating condition of the nation's finances.

Another factor that could keep interest rates high is fear of inflation. Some investors believed that the federal government would never get its budget deficits under control—that political pressures would make it impossible to cut government spending and/or raise taxes enough to reduce the deficits significantly. According to this line of thought, the deficits would continually escalate until the government would have to resort to *printing money* to finance its spending. This would generate serious inflation, which would reduce the purchasing power of investors' savings. To the extent that investors are concerned about such a possibility, they tend to demand *higher interest rates* on their investments, in order to protect themselves. However, higher interest rates can also have negative effects upon the economy, as the next section explains.

(D) DEPRESSING EFFECT UPON CAPITAL INVESTMENT

The most obvious way in which government budget deficits could undermine business investment spending is by generating higher interest rates, as described in the previous section. As we saw in Chapter 23, high interest rates depress business capital investment by making it costlier for businesses to borrow funds for investment purposes.

Another possibility is that the government's deficits would absorb such a large share of Canadians' savings that an insufficient amount would be left over for business borrowing and investment—a phenomenon known as the "crowding-out effect." A more subtle possibility is that chronic massive government budget deficits could undermine the confidence of business—especially foreign investors—in the Canadian economy due to the apparent inability of its government to manage its finances. In such circumstances, business investment spending could be adversely affected.

This would have negative effects upon the economy, not only by slowing the growth of productivity and living standards, but also by making Canadian producers less competitive in international trade.

FIGURE 25-12 *The Three Uses of Savings*

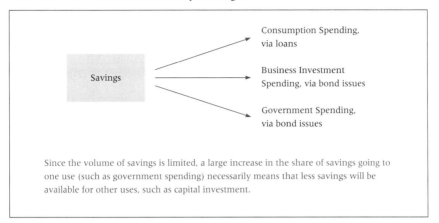

Since the volume of savings is limited, a large increase in the share of savings going to one use (such as government spending) necessarily means that less savings will be available for other uses, such as capital investment.

In broad economic terms, the issue here is the way in which the country allocates its economic resources, particularly its savings, or capital. As we have seen, savings are an essential source of capital for business investment spending, which in turn contributes to productivity and prosperity by building the supply side of the economy. If the government borrows too much of the available savings and uses them for current spending rather than building the supply side, the long-run prosperity of the nation will be undermined.

BUDGET DEFICITS AND ECONOMIC STAGNATION

At first, it seems contradictory that budget deficits, which stimulate aggregate demand and thus the economy, could cause slow growth and economic stagnation. However, the problem concerning stagnation would not arise on the demand side of the economy, but rather *on the supply side*. If continual large-scale government borrowing were to depress business investment spending by absorbing too much of the available savings and driving interest rates up, the supply side of the economy—its ability to produce goods and services efficiently—would be impaired. This is a particularly important consideration in an economy such as Canada's, which must compete extensively with foreign producers.

(E) INCREASING INDEBTEDNESS TO FOREIGN CREDITORS

As the federal government's borrowing needs grew during the 1980's, the government faced increasing difficulty borrowing all of the funds that it needed within Canada. This led to an increasing tendency for the gov-

The large government deficits of recent years have represented a drain on domestic savings that might otherwise have been available to other domestic borrowers (such as the corporate sector), who were forced to raise money outside Canada instead. Thus, further reductions in government deficits would tend to reduce reliance on inflows of foreign capital.

Economic Council of Canada, *Twenty-Fifth Annual Review*, 1988

ernment to sell its bonds to foreign lenders. As a result, the proportion of the National Debt that was held by foreign creditors grew significantly: by 1992, 23 percent of federal debt was held by foreign lenders. Unlike the internal debt referred to earlier, such foreign debt is *external*: the repayment of it, with interest, constitutes a burden on Canadians, now and in the future. And, as noted above, in view of Canada's financial problems, it might prove necessary to offer quite high interest rates to keep foreign lenders buying Canadian government bonds.

In addition to the federal government, Canadian provincial governments and corporations owed a large and increasing amount to foreign lenders. Many observers believe that this was indirectly the result of the federal government's large budget deficits, which absorbed so much of Canadians' savings that provincial governments and corporations were forced to go outside Canada to sell their bonds. By late 1992, Canada's indebtedness to foreign lenders amounted to $300 billion, most of which was owed by Canadian governments. Of the $300 billion of Canadian foreign debt, 44 percent was owed by provincial governments, 27 percent by the federal government and 24 percent by Canadian corporations. Canada's foreign indebtedness amounted to over 40 percent of GDP, by far the highest foreign debt/GDP ratio of any major industrialized nation in the world.

(F) REDUCED ABILITY TO USE FISCAL POLICY TO COMBAT RECESSIONS

Finally, there was concern that the government's budget problems and heavy debt would undermine its ability to use fiscal policy to combat recessions in the manner described in the first part of this chapter. By the late 1980's, the government's budget deficits and debt had become so large that the government was forced to concentrate on containing its deficits. As a result, when the recession of 1990–92 struck, the government was in no position financially to attack it with an aggressive program of government spending increases and tax cuts. In fact, both the federal government and several provincial governments found it necessary to increase taxes during the recession—the opposite of the usual policy. Partly because of this, the recession dragged on much longer than expected, and the recovery from the recession was very slow. Having borrowed so much in the past, the government was not in a position to borrow more when economic conditions called for it.

These concerns regarding the federal government's deficits and debt are summarized in Figure 25-13

FIGURE 25-13   *Concerns Regarding Federal Deficits and Debt*

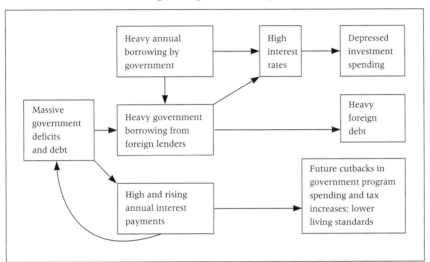

Government attempts to reduce the deficit

Starting in 1984, the federal government set itself the goal of reducing its budget deficits. However, this was no easy task to achieve. About 75 percent of the federal government's total spending consists of social program expenditures (such as health care, education and various income-support programs) and interest payments. Interest payments *must* be made, leaving the big social programs as a logical target for cost-reducing measures. However, Canadians are very attached to their social programs, making it politically dangerous for a government to cut them.

On the other hand, if the government were to try to reduce its deficit by cutting spending on the departments that represent the other 25 percent of federal spending (such as Agriculture, Defence, Energy, Industry, Transport, etc.), it would have to make *drastic* cuts in their budgets, because these are relatively small. So, on the expenditure side of the budget, deficit reduction is not an easy task.

There are real problems on the *tax side* of the budget, too. Increases in personal income taxes involved serious political risks for any government. And Canadian corporate profits tax rates could not be made higher than US tax rates without risking reductions in foreign investment entering Canada and even an outflow of business capital (and jobs) from Canada.

While the business community expressed great concern about the federal government's budget deficits and urged measures to reduce them, the union movement and the New Democratic Party had a quite different view of the matter. In their opinion, the social value of the government's spending programs was too great to be sacrificed on the altar of deficit reduction. In particular, they were concerned about possible cutbacks in spending on the three key elements of Canada's welfare state: *income security programs* (such as unemployment insurance and welfare), *health care* and *education*. In addition, they were resistant to any deficit-reduction measures that would involve higher taxes on Canadians with modest incomes.

Thus, the government was faced with an economically very important but politically very difficult task in reducing its deficit. Even after the federal deficit had fallen to $20 billion per year in the late 1980's, in order to balance its budget the federal government would have had to take an average of *$800 per year* from every Canadian man, woman and child in the form of higher taxes and/or lower benefits from the government. The sudden imposition of such measures would, of course, be politically impossible, making it necessary to implement any deficit reduction program over a period of several years. As a result, the government chose a deficit-reduction program that was gradual in nature, consisting of a variety of relatively small spending restraints and tax increases phased in over a period of several years.

As Figure 25-14 shows, these measures (together with improving economic conditions) had a noticeable effect on federal finances. The spending restraints and tax increases shifted the balance on federal programs from a deficit of $9.1 billion in 1984 to a surplus of $15.7 billion in 1989. Over this period, the federal budget deficit was reduced from 6.8 percent of GDP to 3.3 percent of GDP.

However, Figure 25-14 also shows some real problems with federal finances. Even when the economy was booming in the late 1980's and a balanced budget (or even a surplus) might be expected, the deficit was still in the $20 billion range. This is indicative of a serious fundamental imbalance between federal revenues and expenditures. The source of this imbalance was, of course, the very heavy annual interest payments on the massive federal government debt.

The other problem reflected in Figure 25-14 is the effects of the recession of 1990–92. The recession pushed the federal deficit back up into the $30 billion range as transfer payments such as unemployment insurance and welfare increased sharply at same time as the government's tax revenues were depressed. This led to a deterioration of the federal government's financial position in 1990–93.

Attempting to contain its budget deficits, the federal government implemented a number of measures, ranging from the imposition of the

FIGURE 25-14   *Federal Budget Trends, 1965–92*

Year	Total Revenue	Program Expenditures[a]	Balance on Programs	Interest Expenditures	Surplus (+) or Deficits (−)
		(Billions of dollars)			
1965	$9.1	$7.5	$+1.6	$1.1	$+0.5
1966	10.0	8.6	+1.4	1.2	+0.2
1967	10.9	9.8	+1.1	1.2	−0.1
1968	12.2	10.9	+1.4	1.4	0
1969	14.5	11.9	+2.6	1.6	+1.0
1970	15.5	13.4	+2.1	1.9	+0.2
1971	17.3	15.4	+1.8	2.0	−0.1
1972	19.6	17.9	+1.7	2.3	−0.5
1973	22.8	19.9	+3.0	2.5	+0.4
1974	30.0	25.7	+4.2	3.0	+1.2
1975	31.8	31.9	−0.1	3.7	−3.8
1976	35.5	34.3	+1.2	4.5	−3.3
1977	36.7	38.9	−2.2	5.1	−7.3
1978	38.3	42.7	−4.4	6.4	−10.8
1979	43.4	44.7	−1.3	8.1	−9.4
1980	50.7	51.4	−0.8	9.9	−10.7
1981	65.0	58.6	+6.4	13.7	−7.3
1982	66.1	69.7	−3.6	16.7	−20.3
1983	69.6	77.2	−7.6	17.4	−25.0
1984	76.5	85.6	−9.1	20.9	−30.0
1985	83.2	90.0	−6.8	24.6	−31.4
1986	91.6	89.2	+2.5	26.1	−23.6
1987	100.8	93.7	+7.1	27.8	−20.7
1988	110.8	98.2	+12.6	31.7	−19.1
1989	118.9	102.6	+16.3	37.4	−21.1
1990	127.2	111.0	+16.2	41.5	25.4
1991	132.6	121.5	+11.1	41.9	−30.7
1992	137.7	125.1	+12.6	38.9	−26.4

[a]All expenditures other than interest.
Totals do not always add up due to rounding.

Source: Department of Finance, *Quarterly Economic Review,* Special Report: Fiscal Indicators and Reference Tables (March 1992)

Goods and Services Tax (GST) in 1991 to a 5 percent reduction in Unemployment Insurance benefits in 1992. In addition, the federal government "capped" federal transfer payments to the provincial governments for health care, postsecondary education and welfare.

PROVINCIAL BUDGET PROBLEMS

As Figure 25-15 shows, after 1985, federal transfers to the provinces grew much more slowly than provincial (and other federal) spending, placing growing pressure on provincial government budgets. After the late 1980's,

FIGURE 25-15 *Government Spending and Revenues, 1974–85 and 1985–89*

	Average annual % increase	
	1974–85	1985–89
Gross Domestic Product (for purposes of comparison)	11.0%	8.0%
Federal government spending (excluding transfers to provinces)	13.7%	5.3
Federal transfer payments to provincial governments	12.1%	4.2
Federal taxes and other revenues	9.7%	9.2
Provincial government spending (including transfer- payments to local governments)	13.5	7.0
Provincial taxes and other revenues	13.0%	8.6

Source: Department of Finance, *Economic and Fiscal Reference Tables*, August 1993

federal transfers to the provinces grew much more slowly than in the past, while in 1991–92 the provinces' own revenues barely increased at all, due to the recession, leaving the provinces with a serious revenue short-fall.

Provincial governments responded to this situation with a variety of measures to increase tax revenues and restrain spending. However, most provinces were reluctant to make significant cuts to their key social programs of health care, education and welfare (which was also increasing rapidly due to the recession). The result was a dramatic increase in the budget deficits of the provincial governments in 1990–92, as shown in Figure 25-16.

In effect, the federal budget deficit problems were spreading into the provincial governments' budgets, which were deteriorating at an alarming rate. This led to a serious fiscal crisis in 1993.

FIGURE 25-16 *Provincial Government Budgets, 1970–92*

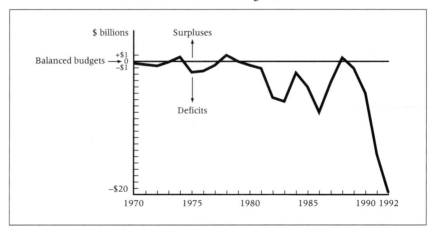

Source: Department of Finance, *Economic and Fiscal Reference Tables*, August 1993

THE FISCAL CRISIS OF 1993–94

By 1993, the situation was becoming critical. The combined budget deficits of all levels of government in Canada amounted to well over $50 billion per year, which was well over double the average for major industrialized nations as a percentage of GDP. The total net debt of Canadian governments was estimated at over 90 percent of GDP, far beyond the 50 percent figure regarded by the World Bank as "critical." Canada's net foreign debt of over $300 billion, three quarters of which was owed by Canadian governments, was by far the largest in the world at about 40 percent of GDP. To place this figure in perspective, Italy's net foreign debt was a distant second at around 5 percent of GDP. Canadian governments, especially the provinces, were increasingly dependent upon foreign lenders to finance their deficits by buying their bonds.

However, some foreign lenders and bond-rating agencies were beginning to express concern over the credit-worthiness of certain provinces. Japanese lenders became much less willing to buy Canadian bonds, and a 1993 report of the C.D. Howe Institute, a private Toronto-based research organization, warned that "continued easy access to financing cannot be taken for granted." As their credit ratings deteriorated, some provinces faced having to pay higher interest rates on their bonds in order to attract buyers. These developments generated renewed and intensified pressure on Canadian governments to deal with their budget problems, forcing them to make some very difficult choices.

WHAT TO DO ABOUT THE DEFICITS?

These considerations placed governments under great pressure to reduce their budget deficits. After several years of federal and provincial tax increases that had made Canadian taxes close to the highest among the seven largest industrialized nations in the world and with Canadians strongly opposed to further tax increases, governments came under strong pressure to cut their spending.

Since 1984, the federal government has implemented a number of relatively modest reductions in certain of its spending programs, including family allowances and old age security (both of which were in effect restricted to people with incomes below a certain level), and Unemployment Insurance, as well as federal transfer payments to the provincial governments. In addition, the federal government was selling some of its Crown Corporations to private investors, and using the proceeds to reduce its deficit.

When these proved insufficient to deal with the problem of government budget deficits, there was growing discussion of more serious modifications to the nation's social programs. With respect to income-support programs such as Unemployment Insurance and welfare, these proposals included "targetting" benefits only to those who really needed them, rather than making them available to all who qualified for them regardless of their income.

THE POLITICS OF DEFICIT CUTTING

According to a 1993 poll by the Angus Reid Group:

- 86% of Canadians wanted the deficit reduced by spending cuts rather than by tax increases
- 74% favoured cuts to the federal civil service
- 70% supported reductions in foreign aid
- 68% wanted cutbacks in defence spending
- 56% would cut funding for the arts and culture

However, these programs are so small that the prospective savings from spending cuts in them would make hardly any impression on the government's budget deficits.

With respect to the big social spending programs such as health care, education and unemployment insurance, there was *virtually no* public support for cutbacks in government funding.

In the area of health care, there were proposals to restrict government payment to treatment that was defined as "medically necessary." There was also growing discussion of user fees as a means of not only raising revenue, but also deterring people from making excessive use of the health care system. And in postsecondary education, there were more severe restrictions on enrollment, larger classes, and tuition-fee increases. At both the federal and provincial level, there were a variety of pay freezes and pay reductions for government employees, as well as layoffs and reductions in government services to the public.

These cutbacks in government spending were very controversial. Opponents of the cuts argued that Canada's social welfare system was being dismantled, that millions of Canadians would suffer from reduced services and transfer payments, and that the cuts in transfer payments and government jobs would undermine aggregate demand, leading to a severe recession. Supporters of the cuts argued that there was no alternative, and that once governments had gotten their finances in better order and the uncertainty that was caused by such large deficits was gone, confidence would return to financial markets, with lower interest rates and stronger consumer and investment spending the result. In late 1993, the deficit for 1992–93 was revealed to be $40.5 billion, far larger than had been

It is estimated that in 1991, the federal government alone paid about $22 billion in benefits/entitlements to families with incomes *above* the national average of $53 900.

> "There is no doubt about our intention to deal with the state of the nation's finances, which are simply of a nature which no one can ignore."
>
> Finance Minister Paul Martin,
> upon the announcement that the federal deficit for 1992–93 was
> $40.5 billion, much larger than had been forecasted.

expected, and as of early 1994, it remained unclear whether the new government would succeed in getting the deficit under control.

ARE BUDGET DEFICITS GOOD OR BAD, THEN?

There is nothing inherently good or bad about budget deficits in themselves; their effect on the economy depends on their *size*, their *timing* and *how they are financed*. At their best, properly timed and responsibly financed budget deficits can help to lift the economy out of the periodic recessions from which it tends to suffer.

There is, however, an important difference between small, periodic deficits and excessive and/or chronically large budget deficits, which can have negative effects on the economy. Excessively large budget deficits that are financed by printing money will cause severe inflation, while chronically large deficits financed by regular heavy government borrowing can cause high interest rates that depress capital investment and generate economic stagnation. At their worst, chronically high budget deficits can have both of these effects, thus contributing to an economic condition characterized by both stagnation and inflation—*stagflation*, which we will consider more fully later.

Despite serious and well-founded concerns about Canada's large and persistent budget deficits since 1975, deficits remain generally accepted as an appropriate policy for dealing with economic recessions. This approach replaces the older view that the government should balance its budget at all times. Balancing the budget every year would contribute to, rather than reduce, economic instability. For example, a recession reduces the tax revenues of the government (such as income and sales tax). To keep the budget balanced, the government would have to either reduce government spending or raise taxes, either of which would make the recession worse. Similarly, if the government were to spend all of its swollen tax revenues during a period of inflation, or cut taxes, it would stimulate demand excessively and aggravate inflation. Rather, the government should try to keep the level of aggregate demand at a reasonable level, supporting it with budget deficits when it is too low, and dampening it with budget surpluses when it is too high, so as to balance its budget over the longer term.

THE PERILS OF BUDGET DEFICITS

Budget deficits can be likened to drinking liquor, in that, at the appropriate time and used in appropriate quantities, they will not be harmful and can in fact be beneficial. However, as with liquor, excessive budget deficits can have severe side effects, including a "hangover" of debt, interest payments and possibly severe inflation accompanied by high interest rates and stagnation, or *stagflation*. And, like a hangover, it can be considerably easier to get *into* this situation than it is to get *out of* it.

DEFINITIONS OF NEW TERMS

Laissez-Faire The theory that the economy functions best without government intervention.

Fiscal Policy The use of government spending and taxes (the government's budget) to influence the level of aggregate demand and thus the performance of the economy. Also known as **budget policy**

Budget Deficit A government budget in which expenditures exceed tax revenues.

Budget Surplus A government budget in which tax revenues exceed expenditures.

Balanced Budget A government budget in which tax revenues and expenditures are equal.

Countercyclical Fiscal Policy Use of fiscal policy (budget deficits during recessions and surpluses during periods of inflation) to smooth out the economic fluctuations associated with the business cycle.

Automatic Stabilizers Government spending and taxation programs that have the effect of automatically supporting aggregate demand during recessions and depressing aggregate demand during periods of boom/inflation.

Pump Priming The temporary use of government budget deficits to boost the level of aggregate demand during recessions, after which the multiplier and accelerator effects can sustain further strengthening of aggregate demand without further boosting from budget deficits.

National Debt The overall indebtedness of the federal government, most commonly measured as the difference between the federal government's liabilities (mostly outstanding bonds) and its net recorded assets (mostly those which yield interest, profits or dividends).

Structural Deficit A budget deficit that is not cyclical (i.e., anti-recessionary) in nature, but rather is built into the government's finances due to a fundamental imbalance between its revenues and expenditures.

CHAPTER SUMMARY

1. "Fiscal Policy" is the deliberate use of the government's budget (tax revenues and expenditures) to influence the level of aggregate demand and thus the performance of the economy in terms of output, (un)employment and inflation.

2. A budget deficit will increase the level of aggregate demand, and thereby combat recessions.

3. During economic booms, a budget surplus can not only offset the deficits incurred during recessions, but also depress the level of aggregate demand, and thus help to combat inflation.

4. The government should not seek to balance its budget every year, but rather have deficits during recessions that are offset by surpluses during periods of boom/inflation, thus roughly balancing the budget over a period of years.

5. Budget deficits can be implemented by increases in government spending and/or tax reductions, some of which (automatic stabilizers) come into effect automatically when the economy slides into a recession.

6. The stimulus to aggregate demand from budget deficits spreads through the economy through the multiplier and accelerator effects, so that a temporary deficit can lift the economy into self-propelled growth again, through an effect known as pump priming.

7. Budget deficits can be financed by borrowing or by "printing" the required funds.

8. Until 1975, government budget deficits and debt were of no real concern. Deficits were periodic and small in nature, and the National Debt was decreasing as a percentage of GDP. As well, interest payments on the federal debt absorbed a relatively small proportion of the government's revenues.

9. Since 1975, Canada's federal government has had very large and persistent budget deficits, which became "structural" in nature. Another factor contributing to the persistence of large budget deficits each year was the rapid growth of the government's interest payments on its accumulated debt from past borrowing.

10. These deficits were the result of federal government policy decisions that depressed federal revenues while sharply increasing spending on both federal programs and transfer payments to the provincial governments for health, welfare and postsecondary education. In addition the recessions of 1981–82 and 1990–92 and rapidly-growing interest payments on the government's debt added to the deficits.

11. These deficits raised several concerns: that rapidly-rising interest payments would add to both the government's deficits and its debt, gen-

erating an upward spiral of interest payments, borrowing and debt, that the government would be forced to cut its spending and increase taxes, reducing the living standards of Canadians in the future, that the deficits would push interest rates up, depressing business investment spending, that Canada's borrowing from and indebtedness to foreign lenders would increase, and that the government would be unable to aggressively combat a recession due to the overriding need to reduce its deficits.

12. After 1984, the federal government tried to reduce its deficits through a series of gradual increases in taxes and restraints on government spending; however, high and rising interest payments on the government's debt kept the deficits high in the late 1980's, and the recession of 1990–92 increased them sharply.

13. This led the federal government to impose additional deficit-reduction measures, including the Goods and Services Tax and spending restraints, including limits on federal transfer payments to the provinces for health care, welfare and postsecondary education.

14. In 1990–92, provincial government deficits soared as the recession increased the spending of provincial governments while depressing their tax revenues at the same time as the federal government was restraining its transfer payments to the provinces.

15. The result was a very serious fiscal situation by 1993, especially at the provincial level, that led to a series of much more aggressive deficit-control measures by provincial governments, including pay cuts for government employees and layoffs and reductions in government services to the public.

QUESTIONS

1. "Useless make-work programs ('digging holes and filling them up again') run by the government can be of economic value under certain conditions." What is the speaker's reasoning? Do you agree or not?

2. "According to Keynesian economics, taxes are no longer a means of raising revenues for the government." Comment on this statement.

3. Which of the following do you believe would have a stronger stimulative effect on the economy: a $100 million increase in government spending or a $100 million reduction in personal income taxes? Why?

4. Which of the two policies in (3) above do you believe would have a faster effect on the economy? Why?

5. "The problem with Keynesian fiscal policy isn't the economics of it, which are reasonable. The problem is the politics of it—democratically elected governments simply can't be trusted to use fiscal policy re-

sponsibly." Why does the speaker believe this? Do you agree? Is this a danger in Canada today?

6. During the 1993 federal election campaign, parties promised to *eliminate* the federal government's budget deficit by as early as 1996 and no later than 1998.

   What is the present size of the federal budget deficit? Has the government succeeded in reducing the deficit from its level of $40.5 billion in 1992–93? Is the deficit still considered a serious concern? Why or why not?

7. If you had to reduce government spending to reduce the deficit, what types of spending would you cut? Why?

8. If you had to increase taxes, which ones would you increase, and why?

9. The following table shows the government as having a balanced budget in year 19X1, and no accumulated National Debt from past budget deficits and borrowing. Given the figures for government spending and tax revenues in subsequent years as shown in the table, fill in the columns for:

   (a) the budget deficit or surplus in each year.

   (b) the total National Debt at the end of each year.

Year	Government Spending ($ billions)	Tax Revenues ($ billions)	Budget Surplus (+) or Deficit (−)	National Debt
19X1	$100	$100	$—	$—
19X2	100	90	—	—
19X3	110	95	—	—
19X4	120	105	—	—
19X5	130	120	—	—
19X6	125	130	—	—

10. (a) At the level of aggregate demand represented by AD_1, the level of GDP and income is $80 billion, or _____ percent below the economy's potential, and the economy is in a state of _____.

    (b) What would be the appropriate action for the government to take regarding its budget?

    (c) Draw a new aggregate demand curve (AD_2) to represent the new situation that might result from the government's action in (b), and show on the graph how this new AD curve would affect:

    (i) the level of incomes and GDP,

    (ii) the level of prices.

    (d) Explain why the effects referred to in (c) will occur.

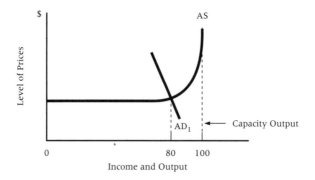

NOTES

[1] The *reality* has turned out to be very different from this ideal situation, as we will see shortly.

[2] The government does not actually physically *print* new money for itself to spend. The process is more subtle than that, and will be examined in detail in Chapter 27. However, the economic effects of such a policy are such that it can reasonably be described as "printing money."

[3] This is only the debt of the *federal* government. With the debts of the ten provincial governments added, the figure was more like $700 billion, or $26 000 for every Canadian.

[4] This is a completely different concept from that of countercyclical budget deficits, which are periodic and temporary anti-recession policies.

[5] These figures *include* provincial government transfer payments to local governments, because local governments spent these funds on public services as well. For comparative purposes, GDP increased by an average of 11.0 percent per year, so provincial government spending grew much faster than the economy as a whole.

Money and the economic system

In the last three chapters, we have emphasized the importance of the level of total spending, or aggregate demand, in the economy. If aggregate demand is too low, the economy will fall into a recession, whereas if aggregate demand outruns the economy's capacity to produce goods and services, inflation will result.

In this chapter, we will examine two factors that are closely related to the level of aggregate demand in the economy and to each other: bank lending and the **money supply**. Clearly, if banks are lending a great deal of money to consumers and businesses, aggregate demand will be increased, while cutbacks in the volume of bank lending would have the opposite effect. A related factor that will obviously have a great effect on the level of aggregate demand is the *money supply*, which is *the total volume of money in circulation*. If there were an insufficient amount of money in circulation, the result would be inadequate aggregate demand and a recession or depression, while an excessively large money supply would generate excess demand and inflation.

In Chapter 27, we will examine how the government tries to keep the money supply at an appropriate level—neither too high nor too low, so as to avoid the extremes of recession and inflation. First, however, in this chapter we will consider what money is, what it does for us and how it is created.

Part A: The nature and functions of money

The most common definition of money relates to its most basic function, which is as a *medium of exchange*—something that people use to buy things.

That is, money is something (indeed, anything, as we shall see) that is generally accepted by people in exchange for (as payment for) goods and services.

As participants in an economy in which people use money, we take it for granted that someone who has an extra horse and wants another cow can simply sell the horse to someone else, and use the money to buy a cow from another person. Without money, transactions would have to be conducted by barter, which is the direct exchange of one product for another. In a barter system, the person with an extra horse who wanted another cow would have to find another person who had a surplus cow and wanted another horse, making a direct exchange possible. Such a system is so awkward as to be virtually unworkable except in the most primitive economies in which there are very few kinds of goods to be exchanged, and few such transactions are made. A barter system would be utterly incapable of handling the billions of daily transactions that occur in a modern economy.

Money is also a *standard of value*, or the yardstick by which we measure the value of a great number of diverse goods and services. If people were using a barter system instead of money, the value of each product would have to be expressed in terms of every other product for which it might be exchanged: a horse might be worth one cow, or four sheepdogs, or fifty bushels of apples, and so on. With money, the value of all items can be expressed in terms of one simple standard—the unit of currency, or the dollar. Thus, a horse and a cow may each be worth $100, a sheepdog $25, a bushel of apples $2, and so on. This makes it much easier to compare the values of different goods and services, and thus to make decisions concerning purchases of each of them.

Money also provides us with a *store of value*—a way to save, or store, purchasing power. Under a barter system, you must accept another good at the time you sell something; however, if you accept money, you can hold it until some time in the future when you choose to spend it. By thus allowing people to store purchasing power, money adds considerable flexibility to people's economic transactions. In this way, money makes it possible to save for things such as future large purchases or for your retirement.

THE ADVANTAGES OF MONEY

We have seen that a barter system is an extremely awkward way of conducting transactions, whereas the introduction of money changes matters materially. The person with the extra horse can sell the horse, say, for $100, then use the money to buy a cow from someone else. There is no need to find another person who has a cow and wants a horse. Clearly, then, money is a great convenience for people who engage in economic transactions.

However, the importance of money goes well beyond being a convenience. As we have seen, the key to a society's economic prosperity is its *productivity*, or output per worker. Generally, people will be more productive if they are *specialized* in a particular kind of work. However, if people are specialized in this manner, there will have to be a tremendous number of exchanges of goods and services amongst them, as each person produces only one product or service and buys everything else from others. By making it easy for people to exchange (buy and sell) goods and services, money makes such specialization feasible, which in turn makes possible higher levels of productivity and thus economic prosperity. Thus, by serving as a medium of exchange, money contributes to our prosperity.

In summary, then, it can be said that money not only adds a great deal of convenience to economic transactions, but also contributes indirectly to specialization and thus to our prosperity.

WHAT CAN BE USED AS MONEY?

We have seen that the introduction of "money" into an economy can be of great benefit to its people. However, we need now to address the question of what might they actually *use* as "money."

The short answer to this question is that people can use *anything* as money, provided that they agree to do so. That is, they must be prepared to accept it as payment for goods and services. Different peoples, in different societies and at different times, have used as money things that seem quite strange to us, including shells, cattle, and heavy stone wheels. In prisoner of war camps in the Second World War, prisoners used cigarettes as money.[1] These examples show that money can be anything that people agree to use and accept as a medium of exchange.

The one essential quality that something must have in order to function as money is *acceptability*: people must be prepared to accept it in exchange for goods and services. Certain characteristics help to make an item acceptable as money, including *scarcity* (which ensures value), *durability* (money that rots in your pocket is of questionable usefulness), *portability* (so that you can carry it around with you) and *divisibility* (for making change when necessary). However, as some of the above examples show, not all these characteristics are essential as long as people will accept the item as money—neither heavy stone wheels nor cattle nor cigarettes are particularly portable, durable or divisible (at least, not easily), yet they have been used as money because people agreed to accept them as money.

THE EVOLUTION OF MONEY

Notwithstanding the exotic examples of money referred to earlier, most major currencies have developed in a similar manner, originating with precious metals and evolving into the more sophisticated forms of money that we use today.

Gold has always played a special role in people's perceptions of "value," and therefore in the monetary systems devised by people. In part, gold's special role arises from its association with *permanence*— gold is a more stable element than almost any other metal, and it never tarnishes or corrodes. The gold recovered from a sunken Spanish galleon of the 1550's still shines like new. And in part, gold's association with value is due to its scarcity—all of the gold ever mined in the entire world could be contained in a single cube with edges only about 18 metres long.

(a) Precious metals

Many currency systems originated with gold or silver. Because they are naturally scarce relative to the demand for them, gold and silver have a naturally high value. This is sometimes referred to as *intrinsic value*, meaning that people automatically associate such metals with value. It was this value of the material itself of which money was made that gave the earliest forms of money their acceptability—someone who was asked to accept money in exchange for something of value (say, a horse) had to be confident that the money was as valuable as the horse. In the early days of money, gold and silver provided the necessary confidence.

At first, pieces of gold and silver of varying sizes were used as money, making it necessary for them to be weighed when used in a transaction. Later, gold and silver were made into coins of standard weights and values, which was more convenient. A much more interesting and important development occurred, however, with the addition of other metals to the contents of the coinage—the *debasement* of the coinage. A king, needing money to finance a war or some other endeavor, would recall all of the currency, which consisted of pure gold coins. These would be melted down and reminted into new coins. During the melting and minting, however, substantial amounts of other metals would be added to the gold, so that more coins could be minted than had previously existed. Thus, all the pure gold coins that had been taken out of circulation could be replaced with "debased" coins that would be returned to the people who had owned them, *and* there would be surplus coins that the king could keep to pay for his war—a convenient, if not totally straightforward, way of raising revenues for the royal treasury.

The debasement of coinage in this way presents an interesting problem—while the *face value* of each coin remains the same, it contains less gold, and has lost some of its *intrinsic value*. What will it now be worth? How much will it buy? The answer to this depends on whether people accept the coins at their face value in exchange for goods and services. If they do, the new coins will be worth their face value, and will function as money just as well as the pure gold coins did, because people have faith that they can spend the coinage at its face value. This is the case with coinage today:

THE ECONOMIC EFFECTS OF DEBASING A CURRENCY

The debasement of coinage raises some fundamental economic issues. Suppose that the king's war will cost the economy ten percent of its annual output for a year; that is, ten percent of the nation's resources and output will have to be diverted from consumer-goods production to military production. Obviously, this will leave consumers with fewer consumer goods, reducing their standard of living.

If the king chooses to raise the money for the war by *increasing taxes*, the people will not only be unhappy that their living standards have declined, but also will know who to blame for this—the king. If, on the other hand, the king debases the coinage, the increase in the money supply resulting from this will drive the general level of prices upwards. Many people will find themselves worse off because of these higher prices—that is, the people's standard of living will decline. However, it will not be clear to them why this has happened, and that the king is really responsible. In fact, they will be more likely to blame the people who are charging higher prices, such as merchants and manufacturers.

The basic economic reality is that the war will reduce the living standards of the people. There may, however, be certain *political* advantages for the king in doing this through debasing the currency rather than raising taxes. In a modern economy, governments do not debase the currency in the manner described here; however, as we will see in the next chapter, they sometimes "print money" to pay their expenses, with similar results.

despite the fact that the metallic content of coins is far less than their face value, they are accepted at their face value in exchange for goods and services. Rather than *possessing* value, they are *representative* of value.

(b) Paper bills (bank notes)

The use of paper bills (bank notes) as money originated with goldsmiths, who performed some of the earliest banking functions. The goldsmith would provide safekeeping facilities for people who would deposit their money (gold) with him. In return, the goldsmith would issue a receipt, or bank note, for the gold as illustrated in Figure 26-1.

At first, when people wanted to buy things, they would return the receipt to the goldsmith/banker and withdraw their gold in order to make the

In England, Henry VIII and his successor tampered with the currency so seriously that by 1551, one penny contained only one-sixth of the silver that it had contained in 1520.

FIGURE 26-1 *An Early Bank Note*

J.R. Goldsmith, Banker
will pay to Fred Flintstone
on demand
Twenty Dollars ($20.00)
in gold
(Signed)

U. R. Stук

J. R. Goldsmith

purchase. However, as they became more familiar with the bank notes, they found it much more convenient simply to exchange the bank notes for goods and services—that is, to use these pieces of paper (bills) as "money." Originally, these receipts, or bank notes, were made out in the name of the depositor, who would have to sign the note over to the person to whom it was being given. Later, however, goldsmith/bankers would make the notes payable "to the bearer" that is, anyone who held the note. This was a more convenient form for bills that would be used as money, and exchanged frequently.

Thus, paper bills, issued by private banks, came to be used as money. These were very special paper bills, however, because they involved a *promise to pay* gold to the holder of the notes. It was because of the *gold backing* of bank notes that people would accept these paper bills as money. As we will see in Part B, however, this did not mean that there was $1 of gold for every $1 of bank notes in circulation.

Later, when governments undertook to regulate currency more systematically, bank notes issued by private banks were replaced by bank notes issued by the government or, more correctly, by government agencies known as *central banks*. Originally, many countries maintained gold backing for the bank notes issued by their central banks, in order to ensure the acceptability of their currency.[2]

As time passed, however, this practice became unnecessary, as people became completely confident in the paper bills. As well, the original system became impracticable, as the volume of money needed by growing economies far outgrew the available stock of gold. Consequently, there is today no gold backing behind the bank notes issued by Canada's central bank, the Bank of Canada.

Bank notes no longer involve a promise to pay, but are instead *fiat money*, meaning that the government has declared them to be "legal tender," so that they must be accepted as payment for debts. This fact was given official recognition in the bank note issue of 1971: the new notes issued no longer said "Will pay to the bearer on demand," but rather simply declared: "This note is legal tender."

The $20 bank note is the most commonly used bill in Canada. In mid-1993, there were about 350 million $20 bills in circulation, worth about $7 billion. The average life expectancy of a $20 bill is about two years.

(c) Cheques (chequable bank deposits)

Are cheques "money"? At first glance, the answer would appear to be "yes." Money is used to buy things, and people do buy things with cheques. In fact, the vast majority of money transacted—over 90 percent by volume—is by cheques. Obviously, then, cheques are widely used to settle transactions.

In actual fact, however, cheques are not themselves "money." If cheques were money, everyone would be able to write their own money without limit. Also, the cheque shown in Figure 26-2 will not stay in Mr. Framish's possession—it will be returned by the bank to Ms. Stuk, for her records. Furthermore, the cheque is valueless if there are not sufficient funds in the account of the cheque writer, which one might suspect to be possible in the case of a cheque writer named "U. R. Stuk." Thus, the cheque itself is not money.

If you read the cheque carefully, you will see that it is really simply a letter to the bank, instructing the bank to pay $25 to Mr. Framish. Figure 26-3 illustrates this fact by showing the cheque rewritten in letter form.

What, then, is the actual "money" to be paid to Mr. Framish? He may cash the cheque, in which case he receives bank notes and coins, which we have already discussed. The more interesting case is that he might deposit it into his own account—what does he receive then? He will receive a *deposit to his bank account*, in the form of *book entries* on the bank's records. When Mr. Framish deposits the cheque, the book entry in his account will be increased by $25 and the book entry in Ms. Stuk's account will be

FIGURE 26-2   *A Typical Cheque*

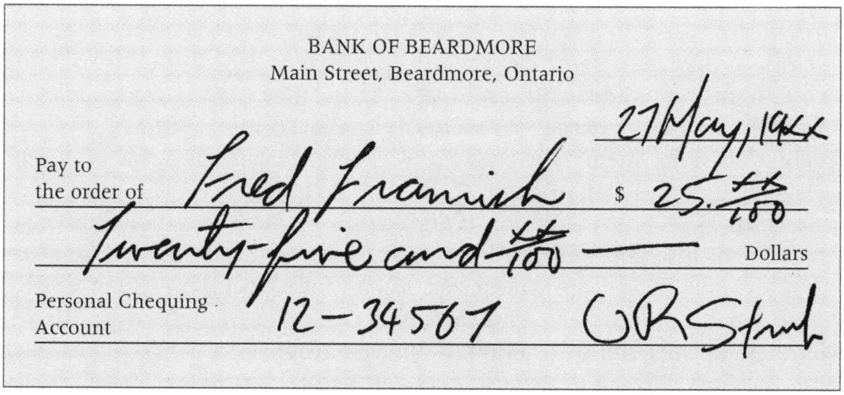

FIGURE 26-3   *A Cheque is Really a Letter*

Bank of Beardmore   May 27, 19XX
Main Street
Beardmore, Ontario

Dear Sirs:

Please pay Mr. Framish $25 of mine. You will
find it in my account #12-34567.

Thank you,

U.R. Stuk

U.R. Stuk

reduced by $25. There is no cash involved in this transaction at all—just book entries.

Are these book entries in the bank's records "money" to Mr. Framish? This can be answered simply by asking if he can *spend* them. Of course he can, by writing cheques on them, as Ms. Stuk did.[3] So these chequable bank deposits (book entries) are "money," and banks can transfer this money between people's accounts as instructed by cheques.

Some people tend to think that the book entries in bank books represent cash deposits (bills and coins) and that bank deposits are not therefore a separate form of money. In fact, this is not true—total bank deposits (book entries) *far exceed* the total amount of bank notes and coins in the economy. Also, these book entries constitute a separate and very important form of money, through which more than 90 percent of the volume of transactions are made.[4] In Part B, we will examine the process by which these deposits are actually created.

CREDIT CARDS AND THE CASHLESS SOCIETY

Credit cards, like cheques, are things that are used to make purchases but are not in themselves money. Credit cards, in effect, give the card-holder access to instant credit, or instant loans for the purchase of goods and services. However, the actual payment of these accounts is usually done by cheque, with the chequable bank deposit being the actual money involved.

A matter of considerable interest and controversy is the concept of the "cashless society," in which *all* transactions would be handled through credit cards and computerized book entries, with no cash used whatsoever. For example, a consumer would pay for a $50 item at Eaton's by processing his or her credit card through a computer terminal, with the result that, on the bank's computer, Eaton's bank account would increase by $50, the Government of Ontario's account would increase by $4.00 (for 8 percent sales tax), the federal government's account would receive $3.50 (for Goods and Services Tax) and the consumer's account would be reduced by $57.50. While such a process represents the most sophisticated form of money yet devised, there are questions as to its practicality—would every parking meter and pay toilet in the nation have to be computerized?—and there are doubts as to whether the public would be willing to abandon cash totally. As well, the concept of the cashless society raises concerns about the invasion of people's privacy, since all their transactions would be available to anyone with access to the computer containing the bank records.

SOME THINGS THAT ARE NOT MONEY

We have said that, in Canada today, coins, bank notes and chequable bank deposits are used as money. To improve our understanding of what money is, we will look quickly at some things that are *not* money.

Stocks (corporate shares) and bonds are transferable financial securities, but they are not money because they are not used as a medium of exchange. This is because their value fluctuates, making their use as money too inconvenient.

Canada Savings Bonds do not fluctuate in value; they can always be cashed in for their face value (plus the interest that has built up to the time they are cashed). However, Canada Savings Bonds are not legally transferable from one person to another, so cannot be used as money. Financial assets such as stocks and bonds are not money: they can be converted into money by simply selling them, but the same thing can be done with any asset, such as a house or car.

Non-chequing bank deposits are not strictly considered to be money for the simple reason that you cannot buy things with them. Unlike deposits in a chequing account, these cannot be transferred to someone else. Of course, you could either shift the money into a chequing account or withdraw it in cash form, but then you would be using these as money rather than the non-chequing bank deposit.

"NEAR MONEY"

Defining what is and what is not money is not a black-and-white issue. For instance, the non-chequing bank deposits, or *savings accounts* referred to above may not by the strictest definition be money, but they can certainly be converted into money very quickly. Similarly, *term deposits* (which the depositor has agreed to leave on deposit for longer periods, such as from one to five years) can be readily converted into chequable deposits, or money. These types of deposits, which are for obvious reasons known as "near money," complicate considerably our attempts to define and measure Canada's money supply.

CANADA'S MONEY SUPPLY DEFINED AND MEASURED

In defining and measuring the money supply we must remember that our main concern is that the size of the money supply is closely related to the level of aggregate demand, which is a major factor determining the performance of the economy. The difficulty is that the vast majority of the money supply consists of bank deposits, and there are many different types of these, as Figure 26-4 shows.

At the one extreme are *demand deposits* (current chequing accounts), which will almost certainly be spent very soon, adding to aggregate de-

FIGURE 26-4 *Various Types of Accounts*

Demand deposits

These are accounts from which funds may be withdrawn without giving notice to the bank or trust company, usually by cheque but also by cash withdrawal. Often called *current chequing accounts*, these are used as a temporary "parking place" for funds that are soon to be spent. Such accounts pay no interest but provide the service of returning cheques to the depositor for the purpose of record-keeping.

Daily interest chequable deposits

These accounts pay interest (usually monthly) which is calculated on the balance in the account each day. Cheques may be written on such accounts, and withdrawals are normally permitted without notice, although the institution may reserve the right to require notice (usually up to 30 days) of withdrawals. Such accounts are also used as a temporary holding account for funds, but one which pays interest on the money each day until it is spent. Cheques are not returned, however, to the depositor.

Other notice deposits

These are savings accounts, which pay higher interest than daily interest chequing accounts (although interest is usually calculated on the minimum monthly balance and paid twice yearly). These accounts do not carry chequing privileges and the depositor may be required to give notice of withdrawals. Such accounts are primarily used for saving money that is not expected to be spent often or soon.

Personal term deposits

These are deposits in which the depositor agrees to leave the funds on deposit for a fixed period of time (a fraction of a year or one to five years). In return, such deposits earn a higher rate of interest than other accounts; however, there is usually a penalty if the funds are withdrawn from the account earlier than had been agreed.

Non-personal notice deposits

These are savings accounts (used mainly by businesses and charitable organizations) which pay interest rates similar to savings-account rates on deposits. Such accounts are often linked to chequing accounts, although depositors may be required to give notice of withdrawals.

mand. At the other extreme are *term deposits*, many of which contain long-term savings that are very unlikely to be spent soon—some of these, in fact, will be part of people's savings for retirement. Between these extremes lie a variety of types of accounts with different probabilities of being spent soon. If we are trying to develop a definition of "money" that relates closely to the level of aggregate demand, which types of bank deposits should we include, and which should be excluded?

Figure 26-5 shows three different measures of Canada's money supply, M1, M2 and M2+. **M1** is the narrowest definition of money, including only funds that are very likely to be spent very soon—*currency* (bank notes and coins) *outside the banks* (that is, in circulation) plus *demand deposits* (current chequing accounts). M1 does not include any accounts that pay interest.

Until 1982, M1 was used as the official measure of the money supply. However, M1 was dropped as the official measure in 1982, because it excluded an increasingly large volume of funds that Canadians had come to use for current spending. In particular, the development and growth of daily interest chequing/savings deposits led many Canadians to start using such accounts in much the same way as they had formerly used their current chequing accounts—as immediately spendable funds for paying bills. The advantage of daily interest accounts is that the account-holder receives interest on the funds in the account, calculated on each day's balance, so that the funds earn interest until the day that they are actually spent. And, as interest rates rose to high levels after the mid-1970's, there was a growing incentive to keep funds in daily interest accounts instead of in traditional current accounts that pay no interest. As a result, the volume of funds in daily interest accounts grew rapidly, making M1 too narrow as a measure of the money supply.

After dropping M1 as the official definition of the money supply in 1982, Canada's monetary authorities considered various alternative mea-

FIGURE 26-5   *Canada's Money Supply, July 1993*

	Billions of Dollars
Currency Outside Banks	$ 23
Demand Deposits	25
Total: M1	49
Personal Savings Deposits and Non-Personal Notice Deposits	271
Total: M2	334
Deposits at Trust and Mortgage Loan Companies, Credit Unions and Caisses Populaires and Money Market Mutual Funds, etc.	235
Total: M2+	569

Note: Totals do not add due to adjustments to figures.

Source: Bank of Canada *Review*, Autumn 1993.

sures of the money supply, two of which are shown in Figure 26-5. **M2** includes *personal savings deposits* (and thus the daily interest accounts that had acquired such popularity) as well as *non-personal notice accounts* that contain the interest-earning savings deposits of some businesses and other organizations which are often directly connected to chequing accounts to facilitate the spending of such funds. As Figure 26-5 shows, these accounts, together with daily interest accounts, contain a large volume of funds, making M2 much larger than M1.

However, many Canadians have deposits at financial institutions other than chartered banks. These funds are included in **M2+**, a more recent addition to the measures of the money supply. M2+ adds to M2 deposits at trust and mortgage loan companies and credit unions and caisses populaires. In addition, M2+ includes money market mutual funds, which in the early 1990's increased rapidly in popularity and size.[5]

The result of these additions is a still larger measure of the money supply—as Figure 26-5 shows, M2+ is considerably larger than M2. In addition, there are still other measures of the money supply, such as M3, which is M2 plus non-personal fixed-term deposits plus foreign currency deposits of residents banked in Canada.

The problem is that as we move farther away from the narrow definition M1, we are including more funds in our definition, but also including more funds that are likely to be *saved* rather than *spent*, at least in the short run. Since a key reason for keeping statistics on the money supply is that the money supply is an important factor in the level of aggregate demand, the real question is which measure of the money supply moves most closely with the level of total spending on goods and services in the economy. M2 and M2+ appear to best suit this purpose: according to Canada's monetary authority, the Bank of Canada, "Among the regularly published aggregates, M2 and M2+ appear to track total spending best over the longer run." However, none of these measures of the money supply is linked sufficiently closely to the level of aggregate demand to have been adopted as the official measure of the money supply. As a result, while the money supply is recognized as being of great significance, we do not have an agreed-upon reliable measure of its *actual size*. Nonetheless, by tracking these various measures of the money supply, it is possible to estimate the extent of changes in the money supply.

THE ACCEPTABILITY AND VALUE OF MONEY IN CANADA

As we have seen, only a small proportion of Canada's money supply consists of coins and bank notes; the vast majority of the money supply is in the form of bank deposits. We have also seen that Canada's money supply is not backed by gold—it functions as money because people have faith in it. People accept money in exchange for goods and services because they believe that they will be able to use the money to buy other goods and services of equivalent value. Ultimately, this confidence in money is really confidence in the monetary authorities of the country—that they will not issue an excessive amount of money, causing inflation that will reduce the value of money so that it ceases to be acceptable. This monetary authority—the agency of the federal government known as the Bank of Canada—has other and sometimes conflicting responsibilities, though, and these are examined in Chapter 27.

While faith is what gives money its acceptability, the *actual value* of a dollar—what it is worth—depends on its *purchasing power*, or how much it will buy. The purchasing power of the dollar, in turn, depends on the general level of the prices of goods and services. If prices in general rise, the value of the dollar will fall, because its purchasing power will be reduced.[6]

Conversely, if the price level were to fall, the value of the dollar would rise. Thus, the actual value of the dollar is inversely related to the general level of prices—the higher the level of prices, the lower the value of the dollar.

Part B: How money is created

We have seen that only a small proportion of Canada's money supply—less than 10 percent—consists of bank notes and coins. It is fairly well known that the bank notes are printed and the coins are minted under close government supervision. Of much greater importance and interest is the vast majority of the money supply, which consists of *bank deposits*. Where do these come from? How are they created? These bank deposits, which far exceed the volume of cash in circulation, are in fact *created by the banking system, when it makes loans*. This is a more complicated process, which requires some explanation.

THE OPERATION OF EARLY BANKS

To illustrate the process by which banks create money, we will use the early banks of the nineteenth century, operating in a simple situation in which money consisted of various types of coins and bank notes (paper bills) issued by privately owned banks—in this economy, book entries are not used as money. Like their modern counterparts, these early banks made loans in order to earn interest income. While borrowers could take their loans in the form of coins, they would much more commonly take *bank notes* such as the one shown in Figure 26-6—paper bills or promissory notes redeemable in coins of gold or silver.[7]

BANK LOANS CREATE MONEY

The creation of money by these banks arose from this fact: a bank could issue *far more* bank notes to borrowers than the amount of coinage, or cash, on hand at the bank to "back" the notes. This was the case for several

FIGURE 26-6 *A Typical Early Bank Note*

Bank of Beardmore
Will pay to the bearer of this note, on demand
Twenty Dollars ($20.00)

Buford McCoy
President

---

reasons. First, relatively few holders of the bank notes would want to redeem them for cash. As people became familiar with the bank notes and accepted them in transactions, the notes would be used as money and would seldom be redeemed for cash. Second, while some holders of the notes would redeem them, drawing coinage out of the bank, other people would be making deposits of coinage into the bank. Therefore, withdrawals of coinage would tend be offset by deposits, enabling the bank to function with relatively little cash to back its notes. As a result, a bank would be able to operate quite smoothly with only a small amount of cash backing up a large volume of bank notes outstanding.

How many bank notes could such a bank issue on the basis of a given level of cash reserves? Obviously, the process is not unlimited: if a bank issued *too many* notes in this way, there would be a high risk that too many noteholders would redeem their notes for cash at one time, causing the bank to run out of cash reserves and collapse. While we have seen that this does not mean that every one of its notes must be backed by cash, the bank will have to back a certain percentage of its notes, to ensure that it

---

The basic realities of banking are sometimes illustrated by the "legendary" story of the clerk of an early bank. According to the story, the banker, who was very conservative, kept a large amount of gold coins as reserves against the notes he had issued. However, since only a small proportion of this gold was actually required to cover daily withdrawals of cash, the vast majority of the bank's gold reserves—about 90 percent—lay unused in a vault in the basement. A much smaller amount of gold that was used to cover day-to-day cash needs of the bank was kept in a smaller vault in the front office of the bank. One night, the bank's clerk made off with the entire contents of the basement vault—some 90 percent of its cash reserves. However, the theft went unnoticed by the banker and the bank carried on business as usual for many years, without any problems.

Many economists feel that even if this story didn't really happen, it certainly *should* have.

FIGURE 26-7 *Creation of Money by Early Banks*

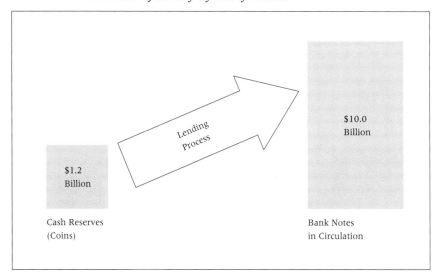

Lending Process

$10.0
Billion

$1.2
Billion

Cash Reserves
(Coins)

Bank Notes
in Circulation

has enough cash to be able to meet cash withdrawals by its customers. The cash kept on hand to cover withdrawals is called the **cash reserves** of a bank. The percentage of its bank notes outstanding kept as cash reserves is called its **cash reserve ratio**. Thus, if the banking system had $10 billion of bank notes in circulation, backed by cash reserves of $1.2 billion, the cash reserve ratio would be 12 percent ($1.2 billion divided by $10 billion). Looked at differently, on the basis of $1.2 billion of cash reserves, the banking system has expanded the money supply to $10 billion, creating money in the process of making loans as shown in Figure 26-7.

THE CREATION OF MONEY BY A MODERN BANKING SYSTEM

In a modern banking system, the nature of money is more sophisticated than in our previous example. Bank notes are no longer issued by the banks, but rather by the government, and, as we have seen, over 90 percent of the money supply consists of bank deposits, or book entries, which are transferred between accounts by cheques. These bank deposits, however, are created in essentially the same way as bank notes were created by the early banks: through the process of making loans. When a modern bank makes a loan, the borrower does not usually get bank notes or coins (cash). Instead, the bank simply increases the balance in the borrower's chequing account, thus giving the borrower more money (book entries) to spend. Using a small amount of cash (bank notes plus coins) as reserves, a modern banking system is able to create a large amount of money (bank deposits), as illustrated in Figure 26-8. Thus, the banking system can, on the basis of a small volume of cash reserves, create a large volume of money.

FIGURE 26-8 *Creation of Money by a Modern Banking System*

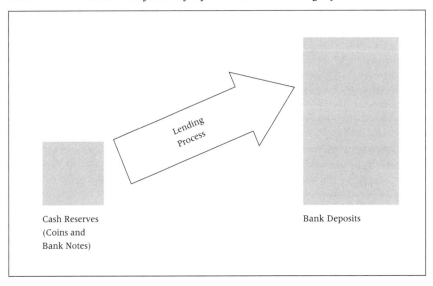

Cash Reserves
(Coins and
Bank Notes)

Bank Deposits

A FORMULA FOR CALCULATING THE CREATION OF MONEY

How much money can the banking system create in this way? This depends on two factors:

(i) the volume of **cash reserves** that the banks have, and

(ii) the **cash reserve ratio** that they maintain.

The extent to which the banking system can create money can be calculated from the following formula:

$$\text{Potential Total Deposits} = \frac{\text{Cash Reserves}}{\text{Cash Reserve Ratio}}$$

Thus, if the banking system had cash reserves of $2 billion and a cash reserve ratio of 10 percent, total assets could be as large as:

$$\frac{\$2 \text{ billion}}{0.10} = \$20 \text{ billion}$$

Note that this represents *potential total deposits*: it is not certain that total deposits actually will reach $20 billion. For this to happen, the banks would have to make every loan that is mathematically possible—they must carry no "excess cash reserves" over and above the 10-percent ratio. Since we cannot know whether this will in fact happen, we must remember that our formula only indicates the potential amount of money that can be created by the banking system on the basis of a given amount of cash reserves and a given cash reserve ratio.

THE CASH RESERVE RATIO AND THE MONEY-CREATING PROCESS

From our formula, it can be seen that the size of the cash reserve ratio has a large impact on the amount of money that the banking system can create. If the cash reserve ratio had been only 5 percent, total deposits (and therefore the money supply) could have reached $40 billion ($2 billion divided by 0.05), or twice the level possible with a cash reserve ratio of 10 percent.

The reason for this is simple: because they have to keep less cash reserves on hand, the banks are able to loan out *more* money, so that total deposits can rise by much more, creating more money. On the other hand, as we will see, there are dangers in keeping too low a cash reserve ratio.

HOW CAN SO LITTLE CASH BACK UP SO MANY DEPOSITS?

How is it possible for a bank to operate safely with so little cash to back up its deposits? We have already seen the answers to this question, but it is worth summing them up here. First, while people and businesses do make cash withdrawals, they also make cash deposits, and there is a strong tendency for cash deposits to offset cash withdrawals. When a bank has a large number of depositors, it can be confident that while some depositors will be withdrawing cash from the bank at any given time, others will be making deposits of cash that will offset those withdrawals, maintaining the bank's cash on hand. Second, and most important, most transactions—over 90 percent by volume—use cheques, so that no cash needs to be taken out of the bank; all that is needed are changes in book entries. This reduces tremendously the need for cash, not only on the part of the public, but also on the part of the banks.

Ultimately, the banking system relies upon the faith of its depositors—the public—in the banking system. If large numbers of depositors were to lose confidence in the banks and demand cash withdrawals, the banks would lack the cash reserves to accommodate them and the banking system would collapse. However, if the banks are able to maintain the confidence of the public, this will not happen and the banking system will be able to operate with a remarkably small amount of cash reserves backing up its deposits.

WHAT SIZE CASH RESERVE RATIO SHOULD A BANK KEEP?

As we have seen, the lower the cash reserve ratio, the higher the level of loans and deposits can be. And the more loans, the higher the interest income of the bank. Accordingly, there is an incentive for banks to hold as few cash reserves as possible.

However, it is also true that it would not be wise to make the cash reserve ratio too low. Since their deposits far exceed their cash reserves, banks can only function successfully as long as they have the confidence of the public. Obviously, if the public's confidence in a bank were shaken, so that depositors wanted all their deposits out in cash form, that bank would run out of cash, and would fail, or go bankrupt. This is known as a *run* on a bank. A run will only occur if public confidence in the bank is shaken, and one way to avoid this is to keep adequate cash reserves so that it can always meet the requests of its depositors for cash. Thus, there is also an incentive for a bank to keep reasonably high cash reserves, for safety.

Banks must strike a balance between lower cash reserve ratios for interest income and higher cash reserve ratios for safety. Statisticians estimate that a 2-percent ratio will suffice for a large bank, but banks generally keep considerably higher ratios than that. In Canada, the law requires the banks to keep cash reserves of 10 percent of demand deposits and 2–3 percent of notice deposits and term deposits.

THE INTERNATIONAL ASPECTS OF BANKING

While the banking system described in this chapter is domestic in nature, there is also an important *international aspect* to banking. During the 1980's, Japan's export success drew large volumes of foreign funds (mostly US dollars) into Japan, making Japanese banks very large and important internationally. By the early 1990's, 8 of the 15 largest banks in the world, including the 5 largest, were Japanese. These banks operated not just in Japan, but rather globally; for instance, by the end of the 1980's boom, 17 percent of total commercial and industrial loans in the United States were from Japanese banks. Generally, foreign banks go unnoticed by the public because they operate in the market for business loans rather than the deposit-taking and consumer loans ("retail" banking) that are visible to the public.

The banking system, the money supply and the economy

We have seen how the banking system, by increasing its lending activities, can cause the nation's money supply to increase. On the other hand, if the banking system were to curtail its lending, the money supply would decline. As outstanding loans were repaid, a decline in deposits, not offset by new deposit-creating loans, would occur.

The creation and destruction of money by the banking system, and the resultant changes in the money supply, are of great importance to the economy. If too much money is created, the result will be *inflation*, as spending is overstimulated and prices rise rapidly. Too small a money supply can slow down spending and economic activity to the point of causing a *recession*. The economy requires the proper money supply and an appropriate rate of increase if there is to be prosperity and economic growth without excessive inflation.

Since banks are privately-owned businesses seeking to make a profit, there is a risk that their lending decisions, while good business from the viewpoint of the banks, may not be suitable for the needs of the economy at certain times. For example, during periods of prosperity, both the banks and borrowers tend to be optimistic. Risks don't look nearly as serious when there are good times, so loans and the money supply tend to increase rapidly, perhaps too rapidly, with inflation the result. On the other hand, during a recession, the situation is reversed. Individuals and businesses are far less ready to borrow money, and banks are far less ready to lend it. Instead, the banks tend to keep some *excess reserves*, for safety's sake, rather than lend them out for interest income. The lack of loans can cause the money supply to shrink and cause a downward economic spiral.

Thus, an unregulated banking system could contribute to economic fluctuations and instability. This is because banking is an industry unlike any other. On the one hand, banks are private, profit-making corporations; on the other hand, they have the power to create and destroy money, thereby influencing the volume of money in circulation, the level of aggregate demand and the performance of the entire economy. As a result, the banks and the banking system are subject to an unusual degree of government regulation, which will be examined in Chapter 27.

DEFINITIONS OF NEW TERMS

Money Supply The total volume of money in circulation, defined variously as M1, M2, M2+ and M3.

M1 The narrowest definition of the money supply, including only currency (bank notes and coins) outside the banks plus demand deposits (current chequing account deposits).

M2 A wider definition of the money supply, including M1 plus personal savings deposits plus non-personal notice deposits.

M2+ A wider definition of the money supply, including M2 plus deposits at trust and mortgage loan companies, credit unions and caisses populaires.

Cash Reserves That amount of cash kept on hand by a bank to cover day-to-day withdrawals of cash.

Cash Reserve Ratio The percentage of total deposits that a bank keeps as cash reserves.

CHAPTER SUMMARY

1. The size of the money supply is of vital importance to the performance of a nation's economy, as too little money in circulation will cause a recession and too much will cause inflation.

2. Money serves three economic purposes: as a medium of exchange, a standard of value and a store of value.

3. The one characteristic that money must have is acceptability; characteristics that tend to make an item acceptable as money are scarcity, portability, durability and divisibility.

4. Money has evolved through various forms, from pure precious metals to impure metallic coins to paper bills (bank notes) to chequable bank deposits.

5. There are various definitions of the money supply, ranging from narrow ones such as M1, which includes only currency plus chequable bank deposits, to wider definitions such as M2 and M2+ which include savings deposits which, while not immediately spendable, are readily converted into chequable deposits and thus represent a potentially very large addition to the volume of spendable funds.

6. The bank deposits that represent over 90 percent of the money supply are created through the lending activities of the banking system.

7. The process of money creation by the banking system is made possible by the fact that banks can operate successfully with cash reserves that represent only a small proportion of their total deposits; thus it is possible to build a large volume of deposits on the basis of relatively small cash reserves.

8. The potential level of total deposits, or money, that can be created through the lending activities of the banks is equal to the banks' cash reserves divided by their cash reserve ratio.

9. Since the banking system's operations can increase or reduce the nation's money supply, they have a strong influence on the performance of the economy and are therefore subject to various government regulations.

QUESTIONS

1. If Canada Savings Bonds were legally transferable, what would be the major obstacle to using them as money?

2. During a war, more of society's scarce economic resources are used for government spending on military activities, leaving less for consumer goods and services. One way for the government to pay for the war spending is to increase taxes, which obviously reduces disposable

incomes and consumer spending. Another method, as we saw in this chapter, is to debase the currency, using newly printed money to pay for increased military expenditures. In this case, does the level of consumption fall? Why? Which method—taxation or debasing the currency—would be politically preferable? Why?

3. What objections do you think people might have to the introduction of the "cashless society" as discussed in this chapter? Why might the banks and government favor this idea?

4. At times, the prices of precious metals have risen rapidly. What problem could this create for coinage containing these metals, such as silver? What would the government have to do about this?

5. Do you think that "near-money" items such as savings accounts and personal term deposits have increased or decreased in size recently as compared to chequable deposits? Why?

6. What effect would a period of rapid inflation likely have on the role of money as a store of value, and on people's attitudes toward money generally? Why?

7. If, as the government, you wished to control the money supply:

   (a) What would be your objectives?

   (b) What would you have to control in order to control the money supply?

8. Under Canada's present economic conditions, do you think the money supply should be increased more rapidly or more slowly than the present rate of increase? Why?

9. Suppose Canada's money supply increased considerably faster than the United States' over a period of several years. What consequences do you think this might have for the Canadian economy?

10. **(a)** If the cash reserve ratio were 10 percent and the banking system had $5 billion of cash reserves, the system's total deposits (and thus the money supply) could be as large as $ _____ billion.

    (b) How can the banks' total deposits be so much larger than their cash on hand?

    (c) Suppose the cash reserve ratio were reduced to 5 percent. How would this affect the potential level of the money supply?

    (d) Explain the process whereby the size of the money supply would change as in (c).

11. From the data below, calculate:

    (a) M1

    (b) M2

    (c) M2+

Personal savings deposits	$45 billion
Deposits at trust and mortgage loan companies	60
Demand deposits	12
Non-personal notice deposits	35
Deposits at credit unions and caisses populaires and money market mutual funds, etc.	10
Currency outside the banks	10

12. The following graph shows currency (bank notes and coins) in circulation as a percentage of GDP. For instance, during most of the 1960's, for every $100 of GDP that was bought, there was about $3.80 to $4.00 of bank notes and coins in circulation.

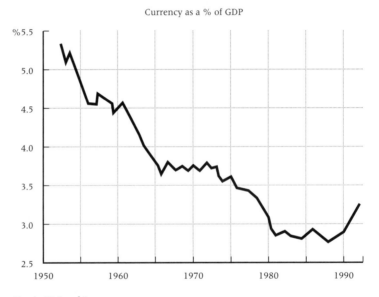

Currency as a % of GDP

Source: Scotia McLeod Inc.

(a) From 1953 to 1990, currency in circulation declined steadily from 5.4 percent of GDP to 2.8 percent of GDP. What would likely account for this trend?

(b) This long-term decline reversed itself abruptly in 1991, when currency in circulation increased sharply to 3.3 percent of GDP, an increase of roughly $3.5 billion in the amount of cash carried by Canadians. What could explain this sudden and sharp reversal of the 37-year trend?

NOTES

[1] Some details of the use of cigarettes as money in prisoner of war camps are provided in Chapter 3.

² The requirement that paper money be backed by gold also had the effect of limiting the amount of paper money that a government could print. Those who feared the tendency of governments to print too much money and cause inflation favored this limitation, while others believed that it would restrict the growth of the money supply too much and thus act as a drag on economic growth.

³ This raises the question of the acceptability of cheques. There are places where cheques are not acceptable (such as liquor stores), and not all cheques are acceptable (such as the personal cheques of strangers). But the vast majority of cheques *are* accepted, and this makes the chequable bank deposits to which they refer "money."

⁴ A little thought leads one to suspect this. Sara's cheque for a new suit is covered by her deposit of a paycheque, written on her employer's account into which have been deposited more cheques (from sales), written on accounts into which people deposited their paycheques, and so on, with cash in each transaction conspicuous by its *absence*.

⁵ Money market mutual funds allow smaller investors to "pool" their funds in order to invest in short-term securities such as Treasury Bills, commercial paper and so on. They offer safety, liquidity and a reasonable return on short-term funds. Money market mutual funds are available through banks, trust companies and other investment institutions, which charge a fee for the purchase of them.

⁶ The value of the dollar referred to here is its value in use *inside Canada*, when used to buy goods and services. The *international value* of the Canadian dollar—its value in terms of other nations' currencies—is a different matter, which will be covered in the chapters on international economics.

⁷ Until the 1930's, Canada had no official uniform currency: the nation's currency consisted of a wide variety of coins and notes issued by various banks.

Stabilizing the economy: Government policies to control the money supply

As we have seen, because the banking system is able to create money, it can have a very powerful influence on the economic system. If too much money is created through the lending activities of the banking system, the money supply will grow excessively rapidly, generating rapid inflation. On the other hand, too little lending and too small a money supply will slow the economy down, causing unemployment and recession. Ideally, the money supply would grow sufficiently rapidly to keep output and employment high, but not so rapidly as to generate severe inflation.

However, we cannot count on this happening. As we saw in Chapter 24, the economy tends to swing between periods of boom, inflation and recession, mainly due to the fact that aggregate demand tends to fluctuate. At the end of Chapter 26 we saw that an unregulated, privately owned banking system can contribute significantly to these economic fluctuations. This occurs because during economic upswings, the banks tend to increase their lending and expand the money supply more rapidly, thus contributing to inflation. On the other hand, during economic downturns, bank lending tends to decrease, leading to slow growth of the money supply and aggregate demand, making recessions and unemployment more severe. In short, a privately owned banking system is not stable enough to be allowed to create and destroy money without the government providing some sort of stabilizing influence. Figure 27-1 shows how, through its lending activities and the size of the money supply, the banking system influences the performance of the entire economy, and why it is important that this process be subject to some kind of government regulation.

FIGURE 27-1 *The Banking System and the Performance of the Economy*

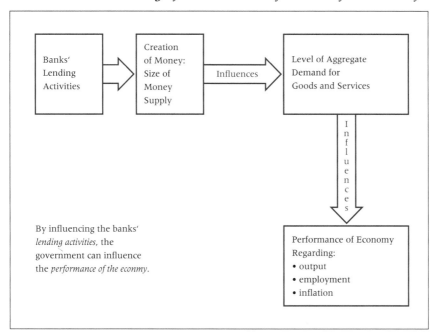

Government regulation of the banking system

Figure 27-2 shows the process of bank lending in more detail, and identifies the following three points in this process at which problems might occur:

(a) *The banks' cash reserves.* If a bank kept inadequate cash reserves to back up its deposits, or made too many loans for its cash reserves, there would be a risk that the bank may not have enough cash reserves to cover withdrawals by its depositors. In addition, if depositors lost confidence in the bank, they might withdraw cash *en masse*, draining the bank of its reserves—a phenomenon known as a "run" on the bank. In either case, the result would be that the bank would "fail" (a polite term used in banking circles for going bankrupt), and many depositors would lose their money.

(b) *The banks' loans and investments.* In investing its depositors' money, it is important that a bank not make loans and investments that are unduly risky. Such investments could undermine the financial stability of the bank, and could also cause depositors to lose confidence in the bank and "run" on it.

(c) *The size of the money supply that results from the banks' lending.* As noted earlier, the lending activities of the banking system affect the entire economy. Excessive lending by the banking system will cause the

FIGURE 27-2 *Government Regulation of Banking*

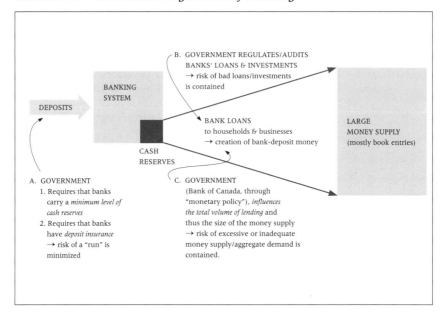

money supply to rise rapidly, generating inflation, while inadequate lending would drag down the money supply and aggregate demand, causing a recession and high unemployment.

To protect against these risks, the government regulates the banking system in a number of ways, including (a) deposit insurance, (b) minimum cash reserve requirements, (c) supervision of banks' loans and investments and (d) the control of the money supply.

(A) DEPOSIT INSURANCE

All banks are required by law to be members of the *Canada Deposit Insurance Corporation (CDIC)*, which provides insurance on depositors' deposits of up to $60 000 per person per institution.[1] The CDIC is financed by contributions by member institutions that are based on the size of their insured deposits. The insurance of deposits (or, more properly, the knowledge on the part of the public that their deposits *are* insured) prevents depositors from panicking and starting a run on the banks. As we saw earlier, even the soundest bank could not withstand a run, because it has deposits far in excess of its cash reserves.

(B) MINIMUM CASH RESERVE REQUIREMENTS

Until 1994, the chartered banks were required by law to maintain a minimum level of cash reserves in the form of cash on hand and deposits at the

Bank of Canada, on which the banks received no interest. The original intent of this requirement was to ensure that the banks carried sufficient cash reserves; however, given the size and stability of Canadian banks, by the 1990's this regulation was no longer considered necessary. In addition, this requirement applied only to banks, and by the 1990's the banks faced competition from trust companies and other lending institutions that were not subject to the same requirement that they set aside (that is, not lend out) a certain proportion of their funds. To provide a "level playing field," the requirement that the chartered banks maintain a minimum level of reserves was therefore eliminated as of mid-1994.

(C) SUPERVISION OF BANKS' LOANS AND INVESTMENTS

The loans and investments of banks are subject to inspection by audit teams of the Inspector General of Banks. The goal of this inspection process is to ensure that depositors' funds are being invested in an appropriately secure manner.

LET'S START A BANK!

It is not as easy to form a bank in Canada as it is to start other types of businesses. Banks are chartered through "letters patent" issued by the minister with the approval of the governor-in-council. Applications for such letters patent are subject to rigorous standards, and may be subjected to a public inquiry. Alternatively, a bank may be formed by a special Act of Parliament.

One purpose of these requirements is to prevent the proliferation of a large number of small banks, many of which could be weak and susceptible to failure. For many years, the Canadian banking system, unlike the US system, has consisted mainly of a small number of large and very stable banks.

(D) THE CONTROL OF THE MONEY SUPPLY

As discussed earlier, it is important that some control be placed on the creation of money by the banking system, so that the money supply grows neither too rapidly nor too slowly for the needs of the economy. The federal government agency responsible for controlling Canada's money supply—the central bank—is the Bank of Canada. We will focus on the most important function of the Bank of Canada: its control of the money supply of the nation through its *monetary policy*.

THE BANK OF CANADA

Canada's central bank, the Bank of Canada, was established in 1934, when the Great Depression caused increased concern regarding economic and monetary management. Part of the central bank's mandate, according to the preamble of the Bank of Canada Act, was to

> " . . . regulate credit and currency in the best interests of the economic life of the nation . . . and to mitigate by its influence fluctuations in the general level of production, trade, prices and employment, so far as may be possible within the scope of monetary action, and generally to promote the economic and financial welfare of the Dominion."

The Bank of Canada is owned by the Government of Canada, and is managed by a board of directors that consists of the governor, the senior deputy governor, the deputy minister of finance and twelve directors. The governor is appointed for a seven-year term by the directors, with the approval of the federal cabinet. The relationship between the federal government and the Bank of Canada will be examined further later in this chapter.

The major function of the Bank of Canada, on which this chapter will focus, is to control the money supply of the nation. Another function is to act as a "bank for banks"—the Bank of Canada accepts deposits from the chartered banks and transfers these funds from the account of one bank to the account of another bank, thus acting as a means of settling debts between the chartered banks. The chartered banks' deposits at the Bank of Canada serve another important purpose: they (along with bank notes and coins held by the chartered banks) count as the cash reserves that the banks are required to hold. In addition to these functions, the Bank of Canada, if necessary, will lend reserves to a bank that is temporarily short of reserves. While Canadian banks very rarely use this service, it is available to them from the central bank.

The Bank of Canada also acts as the sole issuer of Canadian bank notes and as the fiscal agent of the federal government. In this latter capacity, the Bank of Canada operates the deposit account through which government revenues and expenditures flow, handles the sale of government securities and acts as financial advisor to the federal government, as well as having other functions.

Monetary policy

Monetary policy refers to the control of the money supply by the Bank of Canada. In order to control the money supply, the Bank of Canada must influence the process of bank lending through which money is created. To influence the volume of lending done by the banks, the Bank of Canada can influence:

(i)   the banks' *ability to make loans*, by influencing *the level of their cash reserves*

(ii) borrowers' *willingness to borrow*, by influencing *the level of interest rates*

Each of these will be examined in turn.

BANKS' CASH RESERVES

In order to control the money supply, the Bank of Canada must control the lending activities of the chartered banks. The amount of loans the banks can make depends on the level of their *cash reserves;* thus, one key to controlling the money supply is to control the cash reserves of the banks. Should their cash reserves increase, the banks will be able to make more loans, expanding the money supply, whereas a reduction in the cash reserves would lead to a decline in the money supply, since the banks would be able to support fewer deposits and loans.

The most direct way in which the Bank of Canada can influence the level of the banks' reserves is by *transferring government deposits into or out of the chartered banks.* If government deposits are transferred from the Bank of Canada to the banks, they will have more cash available for lending, putting downward pressure on interest rates. Conversely, the transfer of government deposits out of the banks and into the Bank of Canada will leave the banking system with less cash available for lending and push interest rates upward. Government deposits are transferred in this manner on a daily basis so as to "fine-tune" the availability and cost of credit through the banking system.

On a grander scale, the Bank of Canada can use open-market operations, which refer to *purchases and sales by the Bank of Canada of government bonds and Treasury Bills* (which can be thought of as short-term government bonds). Open-market operations are directed toward increasing or decreasing the banks' cash reserves and thus the money supply, in the ways shown in the following sections.

Open-market operations to increase the money supply

Open-market operations to increase the money supply require the Bank of Canada to go into the bond market and *buy government bonds*, by placing a purchase order with a dealer. These bonds may be purchased from a variety of investors, such as banks, trust companies, pension funds, private individuals and so on. To illustrate, we will suppose that the bonds are bought from private individuals. In exchange for their bonds, these individuals receive cheques from the Bank of Canada, which they deposit into their own chartered bank accounts. When the chartered banks in turn present these cheques to the Bank of Canada for payment, the Bank of Canada pays them by increasing their deposits (with book entries) at the Bank of Canada.

Since these deposits at the Bank of Canada count as their reserves, the banks are now in a position to make more loans, thus increasing the money supply. In fact, as we have seen, the banking system will be able to increase its lending, and thus the money supply, by a far greater amount than the increase in its cash reserves. This process is illustrated in Figure 27-3.

Since the chartered banks invest considerable amounts of their deposits in government bonds, some of the Bank of Canada's bond purchases will be from the banks themselves. In this case, the process is somewhat simpler, as the chartered banks receive funds from the Bank of Canada, and these are then deposited into their accounts with the central bank. As in our first example, the banks' reserves rise, enabling them to make more loans and increase the money supply.

FIGURE 27-3 *Open-Market Operations to Increase the Money Supply*

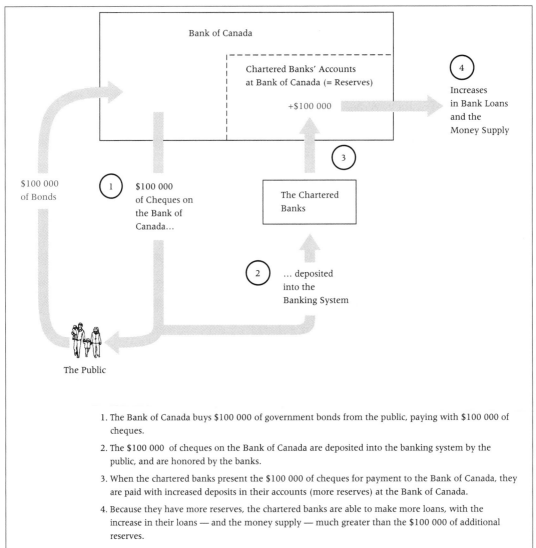

1. The Bank of Canada buys $100 000 of government bonds from the public, paying with $100 000 of cheques.

2. The $100 000 of cheques on the Bank of Canada are deposited into the banking system by the public, and are honored by the banks.

3. When the chartered banks present the $100 000 of cheques for payment to the Bank of Canada, they are paid with increased deposits in their accounts (more reserves) at the Bank of Canada.

4. Because they have more reserves, the chartered banks are able to make more loans, with the increase in their loans — and the money supply — much greater than the $100 000 of additional reserves.

When the Bank of Canada's policies are directed toward increasing the money supply by making loans easier to obtain, it is said to be using **easy money** policies, and the resultant situation is generally referred to as "easy money."

Open-market operations to reduce the money supply

These operations are the reverse of the policies described above. To reduce the money supply, the Bank of Canada *sells government bonds* in the open market. If these bonds are sold to the public, the buyers will pay the Bank of Canada with cheques drawn on their accounts in the chartered banks. When the Bank of Canada presents these cheques to the chartered banks for payment, payment is made by simply reducing the chartered banks' deposits (or reserves) at the Bank of Canada. With their reserves declining, the chartered banks will have to cut back on their lending. The result, as shown in Figure 27-4, is a reduction in the money supply.

Some of the bonds sold by the central bank will likely be purchased by the chartered banks. In this case, payment for the bonds is made simply by reducing the chartered banks' deposits at the Bank of Canada, with the same result: lower reserves and a reduced money supply.

Bank of Canada policies intended to restrict the availability of credit and the growth of the money supply are known as **tight money** policies. Because the economy and the appropriate money supply generally grow from year to year, however, it is not often appropriate for the Bank of Canada to actually *reduce* the money supply, except for quite short periods. Instead, a tight money policy is usually aimed at slowing down the growth of the money supply.

CHANGING THE BANK RATE

The main role of the **Bank Rate** in monetary policy arises from the Bank of Canada's use of changes in the Bank Rate as *signals* of the direction of the central bank's policies. Until 1980, the Bank of Canada would announce changes in the Bank Rate only periodically. An announcement of an *increase* in the Bank Rate was somewhat of an event, which was taken as a signal of tighter money, with loans less available and more costly, whereas an announcement by the central bank of a *reduction* in the Bank Rate was seen as signalling a movement toward easier money, with loans more plentiful and less costly. These periodic announcements of changes in the Bank Rate, which were often front page news, served as a way of reinforcing the monetary policy of the Bank of Canada.

In 1980 the Bank of Canada changed its practice of fixing the Bank Rate at a certain level and periodically announcing changes in it. Instead of a fixed Bank Rate, there would be a *floating Bank Rate* that would change weekly, following fluctuations in the interest rate on federal government **Treasury Bills**

FIGURE 27-4 *Open-Market Operations to Reduce the Money Supply*

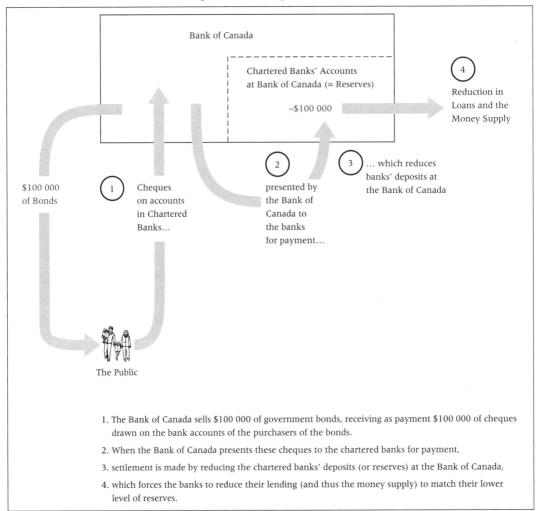

1. The Bank of Canada sells $100 000 of government bonds, receiving as payment $100 000 of cheques drawn on the bank accounts of the purchasers of the bonds.

2. When the Bank of Canada presents these cheques to the chartered banks for payment,

3. settlement is made by reducing the chartered banks' deposits (or reserves) at the Bank of Canada,

4. which forces the banks to reduce their lending (and thus the money supply) to match their lower level of reserves.

Each week, to finance its cash needs until tax revenues are received, the federal government borrows short-term funds through the sale of Treasury Bills. These are Government of Canada promissory notes of various short-term maturities—one month, three months, six months and one year. They are sold each Tuesday by auction, at which they are bought by various institutions, including banks and trust companies, which hold them as one type of investment, and by investment dealers, who resell them, mainly to corporations with surplus cash to invest temporarily and to money market mutual funds.

To borrow these funds in competition with other borrowers, the federal government has to pay the current rate of interest on short-term funds, which fluctuates each week with the supply of and demand for such funds.

THE BANK RATE IN THEORY

We have seen that, in its capacity as "a bank for banks," the Bank of Canada can make loans to chartered banks suffering a temporary shortage of cash reserves. The rate of interest paid by the banks for these loans is known as the *Bank Rate*. In theory, a higher Bank Rate would make the banks keep more excess cash reserves in order to avoid the need to borrow from the Bank of Canada, and would thus restrict the banks' ability to make loans and increase the money supply. In practice, this is not of any real significance, since the chartered banks hardly ever borrow reserves from the Bank of Canada.

The floating Bank Rate is set each week at one-quarter of one percentage point above the rate of interest on Treasury Bills. For instance, if the rate of interest on Treasury Bills was 5.25 percent, the Bank Rate for that week would be 5.50 percent. As a result, the Bank Rate would change each week, depending on changes in short-term interest rates in general and in the interest rate on Treasury Bills in particular.

HOW THE INTEREST RATE ON TREASURY BILLS IS DETERMINED

Unlike bonds, Treasury Bills do not pay a specified rate of interest; rather, *the interest rate (or yield) depends on the price paid by buyers* at the auction for the Treasury Bills. For instance, a buyer who pays $985 for a $1000 91-day Treasury Bill will be repaid $1000, thus earning $15 interest on an investment of $985 over a 91-day period. The formula in Figure 27-5 calculates the effective annual rate of interest on this Treasury Bill as 6.11 percent. If this were the average yield on Treasury Bills at the weekly auction, the Bank Rate would be set for the week at 6.36 percent (one quarter of a percentage point higher than the Treasury Bill rate).

FIGURE 27-5　*Calculation of Annual Interest on a Treasury Bill*

$$\text{Annual Interest Rate (Yield)} = \frac{\text{Interest Received}}{\text{Amount Loaned}} \times \frac{365}{\text{Term of Loan}}$$

$$= \frac{\$15}{\$985} \times \frac{365}{91}$$

$$= 6.11\%$$

Short-term interest rates, and the rate on Treasury Bills, fluctuate with the supply of and demand for short-term funds. If funds are plentiful and not in high demand, interest rates will be lower.

Competing for an opportunity to lend funds to the federal government, lenders will *bid up* the price of Treasury Bills at the weekly
auction. Figure 27-6 shows that, if the price of Treasury Bills were bid
up to $990, the rate of interest on them would fall to 4.05 percent—
which would push the Bank Rate down to 4.30 percent. Conversely,
if short-term funds are scarce and interest rates are high, lenders will
be less anxious to buy Treasury Bills, so their price will be lower,
making the interest rate on them higher. Thus, as short-term interest rates fluctuate, so will the Bank Rate.

FIGURE 27-6   *Higher Treasury Bill Prices Mean Lower Interest
Rates*

$$\text{Annual Interest Rate (Yield)} = \frac{\$10}{\$990} \times \frac{365}{91}$$
$$= 4.05\%$$

So far, we have described a Bank Rate that simply follows the fluctuations of other short-term interest rates. However, the Bank of Canada can
and does influence the level of the Bank Rate. For instance, suppose that the
auction process tends to result in lower Treasury Bill prices—and thus higher
interest rates and a higher Bank Rate—than the Bank of Canada is pre-

FIGURE 27-7   *Short-Term Interest Rates*

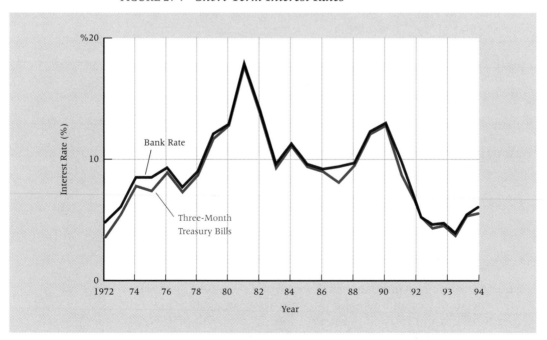

Source: Bank of Canada *Review*, 1994

pared to accept, due to monetary-policy considerations. In these circumstances, the Bank of Canada will enter the auction as a buyer of Treasury Bills, bidding their price *up* and thus pushing the interest rate on them *down*, so as to keep the Bank Rate down to the level desired by the Bank of Canada. It is because the Bank of Canada is known to be able to influence the floating Bank Rate in this way that the weekly movements of the Bank Rate are still regarded as significant by bankers, investment dealers and others who are concerned with interest rates and monetary policy.

As Figure 27-7 shows, the Bank Rate and short-term interest rates have fluctuated widely over the years. At times, rates have been very high as the Bank of Canada has attempted to slow down borrowing and lending in order to curb inflation, while at other times interest rates have been reduced sharply in order to try to stimulate increases in borrowing in order to help the economy out of a recession.

Easy money, tight money and interest rates

During a period of easy money, when the banks have plentiful reserves and are ready to make numerous new loans, interest rates tend to fall, to encourage borrowers to borrow additional funds. Thus, an easy money policy tends to involve two characteristics—increased availability of loans and lower interest rates. By increasing both the banks' ability to lend (with higher reserves) and borrowers' willingness to borrow (through lower interest rates), an easy money policy is intended to stimulate borrowing and spending by consumers and businesses.

During a period of tight money, the scarcity of loans causes interest rates to rise, so that the available loans tend to go to better credit risks and the highest bidders among them. These two characteristics of tight money—reduced availability of loans and higher interest rates—both tend to depress borrowing and spending by consumers and businesses, by reducing the banks' ability to lend and borrowers' willingness to borrow.

How the Bank of Canada's monetary policies affect the economy

THE EFFECTS OF EASY MONEY

Easy-money policies are intended to stimulate bank lending and spending by consumers and businesses at times when the economy is in a recession and unemployment is unusually high. If the easy-money policies cause aggregate demand to increase, real output will rise more rapidly and unemployment will decline, as shown in Figure 27-8.

These beneficial effects of easy money are not automatic, however. If the economy is in quite severe recession and expectations regarding the fu-

FIGURE 27-8 *The Effects of an "Easy Money" Policy*

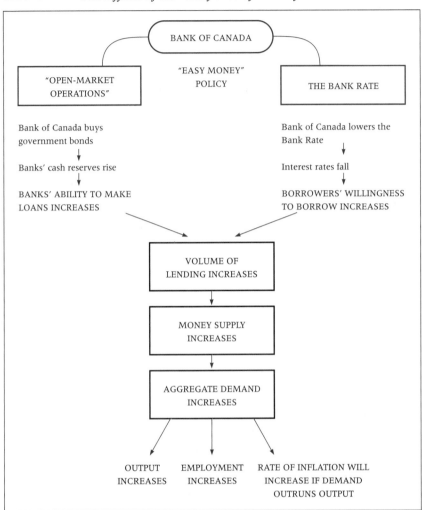

ture are gloomy, consumers and businesses may be reluctant to borrow and spend money. Also, the banks may choose to hold some excess reserves rather than make loans that might prove risky due to poor economic conditions. Thus, easy money merely increases the banks' reserves and makes more loans possible; it does not automatically create money and boost aggregate demand. This problem has been likened to "pushing on a rope," which suggests that easy money by itself may not always be sufficient to lift the economy out of a recession. For this reason, many people believe that easy money should be combined with a *federal budget deficit*, which can provide a more direct boost to aggregate demand and can thereby start the economy on its way toward recovery.

When easy money does generate higher aggregate demand, the results are not totally beneficial: a side effect of the increased total spending may be *more rapid inflation*. While the reduced unemployment from the easy-money policies may make some additional inflation acceptable, this side effect does place a limit on the use of easy money, as excessive use of these policies can result in severe inflation. In Chapter 31, we will examine this trade-off between unemployment and inflation more closely; for now, it is enough to note that while easy-money policies do reduce unemployment, they cannot be pushed too far without causing other problems. Of course, if the economy were already at or near full employment, the added demand could not cause output and employment to rise much further, so it would generate mostly more severe inflation.

In summary, then, easy-money policies can be helpful in lifting the economy out of a slump; however, they may need assistance from fiscal policies (through a budget deficit) and they will likely generate some inflation as a side effect of the higher levels of aggregate demand.

THE EFFECTS OF TIGHT MONEY

Tight-money policies are used to slow down (or even reduce) bank lending and spending by consumers and businesses during periods when excessive aggregate demand is generating unusually rapid inflation. By holding down the demand for goods and services, tight-money policies can help to slow down inflation, as shown in Figure 27-9.

This effect of tight money on the rate of inflation will not always occur automatically, though. If expectations regarding the future are favorable, consumers and businesses may continue to borrow and spend despite high interest rates. This is particularly likely to happen if they expect prices to continue to rise and are prepared, therefore, to borrow in order to "buy now, to beat inflation." Despite having their cash reserves reduced by a tight-money policy, the banks may be able to continue lending. If they were carrying some excess reserves before the tight-money policy, they may still have enough cash reserves left to continue expanding their lending, thus frustrating the tight-money policy. This may force the Bank of Canada to resort to very high interest rates in order to curb borrowing, which can harm the economy in ways described in the following paragraphs.

When tight-money policies do succeed in depressing the level of aggregate demand, their effects are not all beneficial. While such policies will help to slow down inflation, a side effect of the depressed level of aggregate demand will be *slower economic growth* and *higher unemployment*. These tend to be costly politically as well as economically. Indeed, it is fair to say that the major limitation on policies to combat inflation is that they tend to increase unemployment—a problem which we will look into further in Chapter 31.

This is not the only problem associated with tight-money policies, however. Tight money does not affect all sectors of the economy evenly; it hits some much harder than others. Construction is probably the industry most severely affected by tight money, because high mortgage rates and

FIGURE 27-9   *The Effects of a Tight Money Policy*

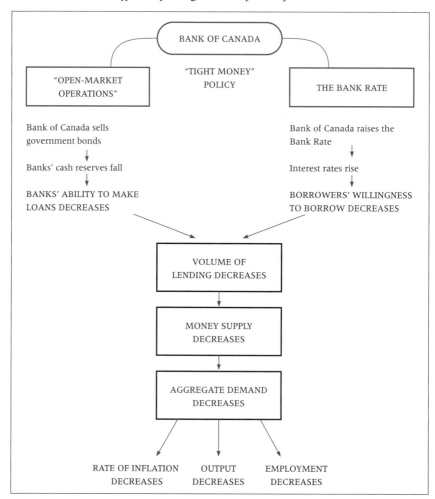

scarce credit discourage the buying of new homes and commercial and industrial buildings. Because investment spending is depressed by high interest rates, tight money also tends to have bad effects on all the capital-goods industries, such as building materials and industrial equipment. In the consumer-goods sector, the effects of tight money fall the hardest on the big-ticket items such as cars and appliances, which involve considerable borrowing and are often tied to sales of new houses.

Small businesses are affected considerably more severely by tight money than are big corporations. Because they tend to have smaller profit margins than large corporations, small businesses are usually more dependent upon borrowing to finance their operations and less able to afford high interest rates. As a result, the scarcity of credit and the high interest rates associated with tight money tend to hurt small businesses more than big corporations.

FIGURE 27-10   *Monthly Payments on a 25-Year $10 000 Mortgage at Various Interest Rates*

Interest Rate	Monthly Payment[a]
5%	$584.59
6%	644.30
7%	706.78
8%	771.82
9%	839.20
10%	908.70
11%	980.11
12%	1053.22
13%	1127.84
14%	1203.76
15%	1280.83
16%	1358.89
17%	1437.80
18%	1517.43
19%	1597.68
20%	1678.45

[a]Assuming interest is compounded monthly.

Governments seeking to combat inflation with tight money often encounter political problems due to the high mortgage interest rates associated with such a policy, which are especially burdensome to prospective home buyers. As the table in Figure 27-10 shows, rising mortgage interest rates have a dramatic effect upon the monthly payments faced by homeowners. While home buyers are hardest hit, all borrowers are adversely affected by high interest rates. This problem is really a political one more than an economic one, but this political reality places a limit on the level of interest rates and, thus, on the effectiveness of tight money as an anti-inflation weapon.

In summary, then, tight-money policies are used to combat inflation by depressing the level of aggregate demand. While these policies will slow down inflation, they also tend to slow down the economy and increase unemployment, and they have particularly severe effects upon certain industries. While these facts tend to make tight money politically unpopular, a tight money policy is widely regarded as essential to any successful anti-inflation program. Indeed, many economists believe it to be the *only* really effective anti-inflation policy.

Monetary and fiscal policy combined

In Chapter 25, we saw how the federal government's Department of Finance uses fiscal policy to influence the level of aggregate demand in the economy. Since the monetary policy of the Bank of Canada discussed in this chapter also influences aggregate demand, we should review briefly how monetary and fiscal policies can interact so as to affect the performance of the economy. (See Figure 27-11.)

During a recession, when aggregate demand is inadequate, a *budget deficit* (achieved through increased government spending and/or tax reductions) is usually combined with an *easy-money* policy consisting of lower interest rates and increased availability of loans. The objective of these policies is to increase the demand for goods and services by households and businesses. This increase in spending will be added to by the respending effect of the multiplier, and will be in large part financed by increases in the money supply resulting from increased bank lending. Also, it is possible that increased consumer spending may cause businesses to increase their investment spending (the accelerator effect), a process which would also be financed by the increased money supply through bank lending, encouraged by reductions in interest rates on loans, which would make business investment projects more attractive. The overall result would be to stimulate output and employment in the economy.

During a period of inflation, aggregate demand for goods and services is so high that the supply of them cannot keep pace, with the result that prices rise rapidly. To combat inflation, a combination of a *budget surplus* (tax revenues in excess of government spending) and *tight money*, with loans relatively scarce and interest rates high, is appropriate. The objective of these policies is to depress the demand for goods and services, so as to relieve

FIGURE 27-11 *Monetary and Fiscal Policy Combined*

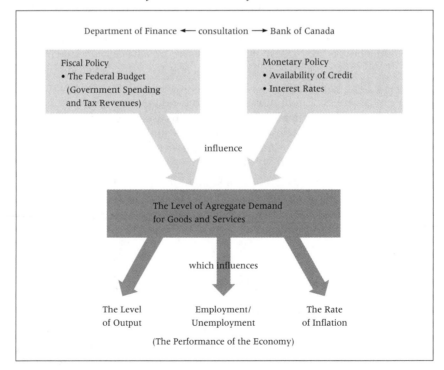

Department of Finance ◄── consultation ──► Bank of Canada

Fiscal Policy
• The Federal Budget
(Government Spending
and Tax Revenues)

Monetary Policy
• Availability of Credit
• Interest Rates

influence

The Level of Agreggate Demand
for Goods and Services

which influences

The Level
of Output

Employment/
Unemployment

The Rate
of Inflation

(The Performance of the Economy)

the pressure of excess demand on the supply and on the prices of goods and services. Government spending will be held down, while tax increases and high interest rates will restrain borrowing and spending by consumers and businesses. With total demand depressed in these ways, the rate of inflation will tend to decrease.

Figure 27-12 shows how the fiscal policy of the Department of Finance and the monetary policy of the Bank of Canada can be combined to affect the economy's performance. By coordinating the two types of policy, the effect can be made considerably stronger than if either were used by itself.

A sometimes confusing aspect of fiscal and monetary policy arises from the fact that both policies involve transactions regarding government bonds. For instance, to combat a recession, the federal government would issue new bonds (sell bonds) to borrow the funds needed to finance its increased spending and tax cuts. At the same time, the Bank of Canada would be buying government bonds (outstanding bonds that were issued in the past) from financial institutions and Canadians, with the objective of increasing the banks' cash reserves to make possible increased lending and thus spending.

In this example, the bond dealings of the federal government and the Bank of Canada are separate—the government is issuing new bonds in order to finance its deficits and the Bank of Canada is buying bonds that were issued in the past, in order to increase the banks' reserves. The Bank of Canada is not buying the new bonds that are being issued by the federal government. That is a different situation, which we will consider in the next section.

FIGURE 27-12 *Coordinated Use of Monetary and Fiscal Policies*

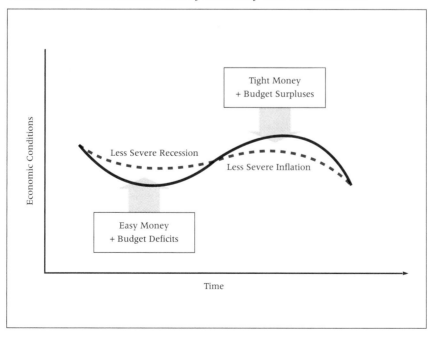

Financing budget deficits by "printing money"

Until now, we have considered federal government budget deficits and increases in the money supply as separate operations, with fiscal policy the responsibility of the Department of Finance and monetary policy the responsibility of the Bank of Canada. In actual fact, however, these two operations can be closely connected because federal budget deficits can be partly financed by increasing the money supply, or by "printing money," as referred to in Chapter 25.

Budget deficits do not always lead to an increase in the money supply. In Chapter 25, we saw that the federal government could finance its budget deficits by borrowing the savings of the public. In this case, the government borrows money from the public, deposits it into the government's account at the Bank of Canada, then spends the money, which finds its way back into the banking system as deposits. This operation, which is illustrated in Figure 27-13, has no effect on the money supply: while money that was already in existence is transferred around, *no new money is created.* Aggregate demand may be increased because money that was in savings accounts and not being spent has been borrowed by the government and

FIGURE 27-13   *Financing Budget Deficits by Borrowing Money*

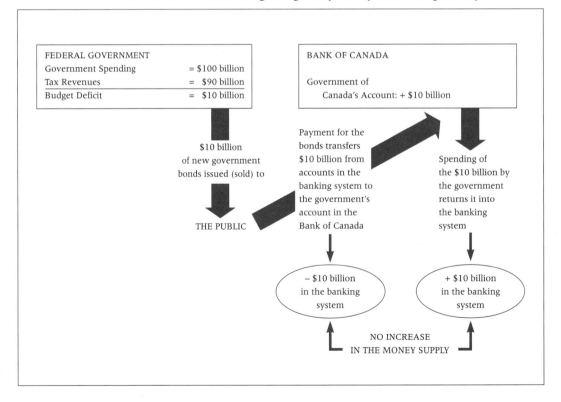

will be spent, but these funds already existed in the form of savings deposits. No new funds are created.

However, not all federal budget deficits are financed in this way—sometimes the federal government sells bonds *to the Bank of Canada* rather than to the public. To pay for these bonds, the Bank of Canada simply increases the amount of the deposits in the federal government's account at the central bank. Thus, the federal government receives in its account *newly created money* (book entries). When it spends these (through cheques), newly created money will be injected into the banking system, and the money supply will rise, as illustrated in Figure 27-14.

When the federal government finances its budget deficits by selling bonds to the Bank of Canada and thus increasing the money supply, it is popularly said to be financing its budget deficits by "printing money." Should the government finance its expenditures in this way? There is no simple answer to this question. During a serious recession, increases in both government spending and the money supply can be beneficial, because they boost aggregate demand, output and employment. On the other hand, as we have seen, excessive increases in the money supply can cause severe inflation. Also, there could be a political temptation for governments to resort to printing money to finance budget deficits: it is politically easier than raising taxes (which is always unpopular) or borrowing money (which must be repaid and involves interest costs).[2] True, the increase in the money supply will contribute to inflation,[3] but the public tends to blame inflation on labor unions and business rather than on government policies.

FIGURE 27-14 *Financing Budget Deficits by Printing Money*

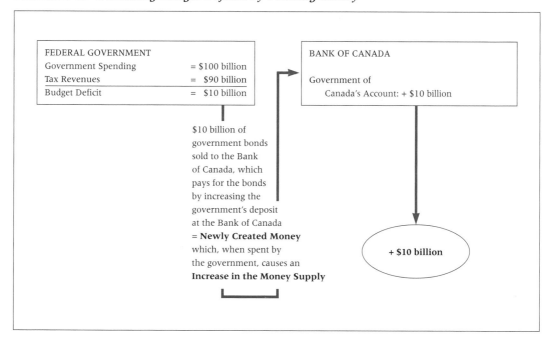

> Too great a growth in government debt puts the Bank of Canada in an awkward position. If the market can't or won't pick up the bond issues on the terms offered then the Bank [of Canada] must. The danger is that money may be created at a faster rate than is probably desirable, and an increase in inflation becomes inevitable at some point down the road.
>
> Bank of Montreal, *Business Review*, June 1980

In summary, financing government budget deficits by "printing money" can have extremely powerful effects on the economy. Because of its potential for generating severe inflation, such a policy should not be used excessively. Finally, this should never be done simply to avoid increasing taxes for political reasons.

Monetary policy: Who should call the shots?

The opportunity for the government to "print money" to pay its expenses raises a fundamental question—who should decide the nation's monetary policy? This is an extremely important question, since a properly conducted monetary policy can be very beneficial, whereas errors in monetary policy can have severe effects on the economy, due to the creation of either too much or too little money.

Some people believe that the financial experts at the Bank of Canada, who possess specialized knowledge of monetary matters, should have the responsibility and the power to decide the nation's monetary policy. Other people argue that such important policy decisions should not be made by the appointed officials at the Bank of Canada, but rather by the government, which was elected by (and is ultimately responsible to) the people.

The worst-case scenario would, of course, be a fundamental difference of opinion between the government and the Bank of Canada concerning the direction of monetary policy.[4] The Bank of Canada Act deals with this matter in two ways. First, the Act requires regular consultation between the Governor of the Bank of Canada and the Minister of Finance (on behalf of the government), the intention of such consultation being coordination of the economic policies of the Bank of Canada and the government. Secondly, the Act provides that in the event of a fundamental disagreement, the government can direct the central bank in writing as to the monetary policy to be followed.

Thus, under the law, the government possesses the final authority over monetary policy, through its power to overrule the Governor of the Bank of Canada. However, the government cannot use this power freely or lightly. First, any government directive overruling the Bank of Canada must be made public, and it is generally understood that following such a directive, the Governor of the Bank of Canada would almost certainly resign. Given the general respect for the Bank of Canada's expertise, such actions on the part of the government could very likely undermine public confidence in the government's own economic policies. For these reasons, a government would be quite reluctant to use its legal power to overrule the Governor.

As a result, the question of who really determines the direction of monetary policy is not a simple one to answer. Through the process of consultation between the Governor of the Bank of Canada and the Minister of Finance, both the expertise of the Bank of Canada and the policy direction of the government play a role in monetary policy.

Monetarism: Another perspective on economics

For many years following the Great Depression of the 1930's, the focus of economics was on *recession*, and the main concern of economic policy was to combat recessions. The key elements of this emphasis were Keynesian fiscal policies, particularly budget deficits to boost aggregate demand and lift the economy out of recessions. Fiscal policy was regarded as the active ingredient of economic policy, whereas monetary policy was seen as playing a secondary role, attracting much less attention.

After the early 1970's, however, the importance attached to the money supply and to the Bank of Canada's monetary policies increased dramatically. This is because the most serious problem of this period was severe inflation, associated with exceptionally rapid increases in the money supply. This drew critical attention to the monetary policies pursued in Canada and elsewhere, which critics saw as having caused severe inflation by allowing excessively rapid growth of the money supply. These critics are often called "monetarists," and their theories **monetarism**—a term subject to varying interpretations. In its milder forms, it refers simply to an increased emphasis on controlling the growth of the money supply in order to restrain inflation. Its more extreme proponents insist that only excessive increases in the money supply cause inflation, that only curbs on money-supply growth can combat inflation, and that the government should never increase the money supply at rates above a specified limit.

MONETARISM IN CANADA

In Canada in the early 1970's, the money supply expanded at a very rapid rate, and the Bank of Canada continued to allow the money supply to increase rapidly even after inflation became rampant, especially in 1974 and 1975. Critics of the Bank of Canada's policies argued that such a sudden ex-

MILTON FRIEDMAN (1912–)

Milton Friedman was born the son of immigrant garment workers in New York, and went on to win the Nobel Prize for Economics in 1976. Given this rise from poverty to celebrity, it is not surprising that his theories reflect a strong belief in economic freedom and the virtues of the marketplace.

After receiving his Ph.D. in 1946 from Columbia University, Friedman returned to teach at the University of Chicago, where he had obtained his M.A. There, he became the leader of what has become known as the "Chicago School"—a group of economists who argue strongly for less government intervention in the economy. According to Friedman, such government regulation usually winds up benefiting certain private-interest groups at the expense of the general public interest. The public interest, the Chicago School argues, would be better served by free and open competition than by well-intentioned but counterproductive government regulations which tend to restrict competition and reduce efficiency.

Friedman is most noted for his work on monetarism, which gained prominence during the inflationary 1970's. According to the Chicago School, monetary policy is a large-scale example of how government intervention in the economy can have disastrous results. They point to both the Great Depression of the 1930's (when the authorities reduced the US money supply by about one-third) and the Great Inflation of the 1970's (when the money supply was expanded extraordinarily rapidly) as examples of the harm that can be done by government intervention in the economy. According to monetarists, it would be in the long-run interests of society if the money supply were allowed to increase at only a certain rate each year, as this would avoid the excesses that are possible under the present system. By preventing monetary instability in this way, they argue, a stable financial and economic environment could be established, in which confidence and longer-run decision-making (especially capital investment) could flourish.

While not all economists would agree with the policy prescriptions of Friedman and the monetarists, many regard their views as a healthy counterbalance to those who see increased government intervention and regulation as the answer to all economic problems.

pansion of the money supply would only worsen an already serious inflationary situation.

By the fall of 1975, inflation was such a severe problem that reassessment of the Bank of Canada's policies seemed necessary. In what was regarded as a landmark speech in September 1975, the Governor of the Bank of Canada, Gerald Bouey, said that, "whatever else may need to be done to bring inflation under control, it is absolutely essential to keep the rate of monetary expansion within reasonable limits. Any program that did not include this policy would be doomed to failure. There is no way of preserving its value if money is created on an excessive scale."[5]

In the view of some, the Bank of Canada had undergone a conversion to monetarism; at the least, the Bank had stated an intention to guard more watchfully against excessive increases in the money supply in the future, by keeping the growth of the money supply within publicly stated limits.

But which measure of the money supply should be used?

Unfortunately, the matter does not end here. As we saw in Chapter 26, there are different definitions of money supply, ranging from the narrowest (M1), which includes only currency plus demand deposits, to broader definitions such as M2 (which includes savings and term deposits) and M2+ (which includes deposits at trust and mortgage loan companies, credit unions and caisses populaires). Figure 27-15 shows the size and growth of the money supply according to each of these three different definitions. Due to the great differences in the sizes and growth rates of M1, M2 and M2+, it is obviously important that the Bank of Canada select the

FIGURE 27-15 *Size and Growth Rates of M1, M2 and M2+*

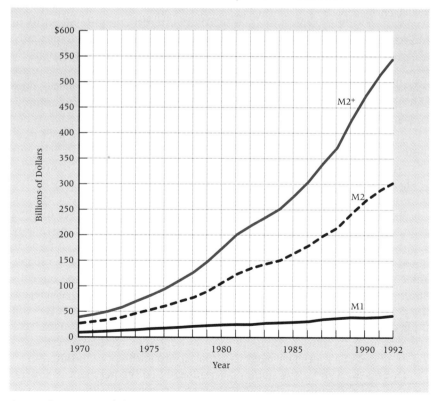

Source: Department of Finance, *Economic and Fiscal Reference Tables,* August 1993

appropriate one as its target for its measurement and control of the money supply.

From 1975 to 1982, the Bank of Canada used M1 as its target for monetary policy. In 1978, the Governor of the Bank of Canada stated that M1 had been chosen because "it moves with the trend of aggregate spending in the economy in a fairly predictable manner and it is susceptible to control by the central bank through the adjustment of short-term interest rates.... Our experience to date in using M1 has confirmed in my mind its usefulness as a proximate target in the conduct of monetary policy." In short, the Bank of Canada regarded M1 as the most relevant measure of the money supply because it includes those most immediately spendable funds (currency plus demand deposits) that have the greatest influence on the level of aggregate demand in the economy.

By 1980, however, M1 was no longer viewed as a reliable measure of the money supply. A combination of high interest rates, computer technology and competition among financial institutions had led to the development of new types of deposits, most notably daily interest chequing deposits. These were attracting large volumes of funds out of current accounts that pay no interest (that is, M1) and into M2, which includes such deposits. Thus, it became accepted that M1 had become a deceptively low indicator of the volume of readily spendable funds and purchasing power in the economy. This is reflected in Figure 27-15.

Most observers would include the daily interest chequing deposits in M2 in their definition of money, but the notice (or savings) deposits of M2 are a more complicated matter, because some of these funds are likely to be spent soon and some are not. To the extent that funds are just being "parked" in interest-bearing deposits (M2) for relatively short periods of time before being spent, that part of M2 is by any reasonable definition money, and should be included in the money-supply figures. Unfortunately, it is not a simple task to determine how much of M2 should be treated as immediately spendable funds: while some of the deposits in M2 will be spent very quickly, others represent longer-term savings with little prospect of being spent for years. Thus, the measurement of the money supply for the purpose of monetary policy is a difficult and complex task.

Because of these problems, the Bank of Canada in November of 1982 abandoned the use of M1 as its official definition and measure of the money supply. In announcing this change, the Governor of the Bank of Canada noted that "M1 has, for some time—more than a year—been a less reliable guide than it was earlier. It is now clear that there have been major and continuing shifts out of M1 as a result of changes in banking practices. As a result, the recorded M1 series is not a useful guide to policy at the present time. In these circumstances I want to make it known that the Bank no longer has a target range for it (but) ... the Bank is continuing to search for ways of making more use of a monetary aggregate than it can at the present time." ·

During the 1980's, the Bank of Canada studied the behavior of several measures of the money supply ("monetary aggregates"). However, as of 1993, the Bank of Canada had not yet found a monetary aggregate that

> Given the close links over the longer run between total spending, inflation and M2 and M2+, these broad monetary aggregates are a source of valuable information for the Bank of Canada.
>
> Bank of Canada *Review*, January 1989

moved sufficiently closely with aggregate demand to be used as the single "official" measure of the money supply.

M2 and M2+ showed the most promise, but the savings deposits included in these caused problems. For instance, an unusually large sale of Canada Savings Bonds in November could cause a large movement of funds out of savings accounts (M2) into CSB's, making it look as if the money supply had declined when in fact all that was happening was that people were shifting their savings from bank deposits to CSB's.

In conclusion, Canada's experience with inflation in the 1970's and 1980's has led to more widespread agreement on the importance of controlling the money supply. However, there are real difficulties and differences of opinion concerning the vital question of how to actually measure the money supply for purposes of controlling it. Canada's monetary authorities will likely continue to grapple with this problem during the 1990's, as they seek improved approaches to their crucially important responsibility to "regulate credit and currency in the best interests of the economic life of the nation."

Regulation versus competition

As we saw at the beginning of this chapter, Canada's banking industry is regulated by the government in many ways. On the deposit-taking side of their operations, banks are required to provide deposit insurance. On the investments side of their operations, the types of investments banks can make are subject to regulation, and the quality of the loans that banks make is checked by government auditors. In addition, restrictions on the formation of new banks and on foreign banks have traditionally protected Canada's banking industry from excessive competition that could undermine the financial stability of banks.

All of these regulations are intended to maintain the stability of the banking system and preserve the confidence of the public in that system. As we saw in Chapter 26, public confidence is essential to the successful operation of a banking system.

On the other hand, these regulations have reduced the degree of competition in the Canadian banking industry. Competition can be beneficial as well, particularly to users of bank services, by spurring efficiency, innovation and the delivery of better-quality services at lower cost. In other words, there is a trade-off between regulation and competition: regula-

> So when we look at any proposed change to our financial system, we have to weigh two fundamental questions. Will the change improve the industry's capacity to develop and deliver its services at least cost? Secondly, what are the implications of any change for the soundness of the system and the confidence users have in it?
>
> John W. Crow, Governor of the Bank of Canada,
> Ottawa, June 9, 1987

tion brings stability and public confidence, while competition brings efficiency and quality.

In recent years, the trend has been in the direction of more competition and less regulation. The government has gradually sought to increase the degree of competition in Canadian financial markets. This has happened in many ways—by allowing other financial institutions such as trust companies to compete with banks, by allowing banks to compete more for mortgage loans, and by allowing increased (although limited) competition from foreign banks. Under the Free Trade Agreement with the United States, competition from American banks was increased. Subsidiaries of US banks in Canada were no longer governed by the limits on the assets of foreign banks, and could open additional branches without the approval of the Minister of Finance.

Some Canadians welcome the shift toward increased competition in financial markets, while others are concerned that in a less regulated environment, the public might have less protection. It still remains to be determined what is an appropriate balance between competition (which promotes efficiency) and regulation (which provides security) in the sensitive area of financial markets. As policy-makers continue to seek this balance, further changes can be anticipated.

DEFINITIONS OF NEW TERMS

Treasury Bills Short-term federal government promissory notes that are sold at weekly auctions.

Monetary Policy The control of the lending activities of the chartered banks, and thus the control of the money supply, by the Bank of Canada.

Open-Market Operations Purchases or sales of government bonds by the Bank of Canada, the effect of which is to increase or decrease the chartered banks' cash reserves and thereby influence the money supply.

Easy Money A situation in which the Bank of Canada's monetary policy is directed toward making loans more available and interest rates lower.

Tight Money A situation in which the Bank of Canada's monetary policy is directed toward making loans less available and interest rates higher.

Bank Rate The rate of interest charged by the Bank of Canada on its infrequent loans to the chartered banks; changes in the Bank Rate are often interpreted as indicative of the direction of the Bank of Canada's monetary policy.

Monetarism An approach to economic theory focusing on the importance of the money supply and of controlling the money supply.

CHAPTER SUMMARY

1. The operations of the banking system are very important to the performance of the economy because it is through the lending activities of the banks that the bulk of the nation's money supply is created.

2. The government regulates the banking system in various ways, the most important of which is monetary policy: the control of the money supply by the Bank of Canada, through its control over the lending activities of the banks.

3. This control is exercised through various means, the most important of which is open-market operations: through these, the Bank of Canada influences the banks' cash reserves and thus their lending activities. The Bank of Canada can also influence the volume of bank lending through changes in the Bank Rate, which affect the willingness of consumers and businesses to borrow.

4. When the Bank of Canada's policies are directed toward faster increases in the money supply and lower interest rates, an "easy money" policy is said to be in effect. "Tight money" refers to the opposite situation.

5. For maximum effectiveness, monetary policy is combined with fiscal policy: together, these can influence the level of aggregate demand so as to attempt to avoid the extremes of either recession or inflation.

6. If the federal government finances its budget deficits by selling government bonds to the Bank of Canada, the nation's money supply will increase, a process popularly known as "printing money" to pay the government's bills.

7. The Bank Act requires regular consultation between the Governor of the Bank of Canada and the Minister of Finance, on behalf of the government. Under the Bank Act, final authority over monetary policy rests with the federal government, which has the power to overrule the Governor of the Bank of Canada; however, a government would be reluctant to resort to such action.

8. The severe inflation of the 1973–82 period drew increased attention to the Bank of Canada's policies concerning the money supply; such emphasis on monetary growth and the importance of controlling it is known as "monetarism."

9. In seeking to control the money supply, the Bank of Canada sought from 1975 to 1982 to keep the growth of M1 within publicly stated limits. However, in 1982, the Bank of Canada stopped using M1 as its official definition of the money supply, because it excludes daily interest chequing deposits and savings deposits, which had grown rapidly.

QUESTIONS

1. Make the strongest possible argument that monetary policy:

   (a) should *not* be decided by the Bank of Canada alone.

   (b) should *not* be decided by the federal government alone.

2. Under the German constitution, Germany's central bank (the Bundesbank) has one key responsibility—to protect the purchasing power of the nation's currency, by keeping the rate of inflation low.

   (a) What would be the advantages and disadvantages of enshrining such a role in law?

   (b) Why do you suppose this was done?

3. In Chapter 25, we saw that Canadian governments tended to finance a significant part of their large budget deficits by selling bonds to foreign lenders. Suppose that the Canadian economy was slipping toward a recession, making it advisable for the Bank of Canada to reduce Canadian interest rates. How could the financial position of Canadian governments complicate the task of the Bank of Canada?

4. In the early 1990's, several trust companies failed, requiring the CDIC to make substantial payments to insured depositors. Following this, all financial institutions covered by the CDIC were required to make much higher contributions to the CDIC. This led to a debate in which the possible effects of deposit insurance on the behavior of depositors and financial institutions were challenged. How might deposit insurance affect the behavior of:

   (a) depositors, and

   (b) financial institutions

   in ways that could be regarded as undesirable?

5. In some of the trust company failures, the federal government reimbursed depositors whose deposits were not insured. Do you believe that the federal government should do this?

6. What effect would a tight-money policy tend to have on

   (a) the stock market (the price of corporate shares)?

   (b) the price of outstanding government bonds (bonds, issued in the past, that have not yet matured and can thus still be bought and sold)?

7. What are the present sizes of M1, M2 and M2+, and by what percentage has each of these increased over the past year? What is the significance of recent trends regarding M1, M2 and M2+ for someone concerned with managing the growth of Canada's money supply? (For statistics, see Bank of Canada *Review*.)

8. What are the present policies of the Bank of Canada regarding the rate of growth of the money supply, and the availability of credit and interest rates? Why has the Bank adopted these policies at this time?

9. Explain the probable effects of each of the following on the money supply and on the performance of the economy in terms of output, employment and inflation.

   (a) The federal government sells $1 billion of bonds to the Canadian public to finance some of its expenditures.

   (b) The Bank of Canada sells $1 billion of government bonds to the chartered banks.

   (c) The federal government sells $1 billion of bonds to the Bank of Canada to finance some of its expenditures.

10. If the cash reserve ratio were 5 percent and the Bank of Canada bought $50 million of government bonds from the chartered banks,

    (a) by how much could the money supply increase?

    (b) Explain the process whereby the money supply would increase.

    (c) What would be required for the money supply to increase by as much as it could as per part (a)?

    (d) What would be the objective of the Bank of Canada in implementing this policy?

    (e) What problems might make it more difficult for this policy to achieve its objective?

11. Suppose that 91-day $1000 Treasury Bills are selling for $970 this Tuesday.

    (a) What is the annual interest rate on these Treasury Bills?

    (b) What would the Bank Rate be for the next week?

    (c) If the Bank of Canada bought Treasury Bills in the weekly auction, bidding their price up to $980 instead of $970, what effect would this have on the Bank Rate?

    (d) What would be the objective of the Bank of Canada in buying Treasury Bills in this way, and how would buying Treasury Bills help to achieve this objective?

NOTES

[1] This coverage can be expanded in certain ways. For instance, a Registered Retirement Savings Plan is considered a separate legal "person," as is a joint ac-

count. In addition, several financial institutions have set up subsidiary companies that also have CDIC memberships, allowing depositors to double their CDIC coverage by placing deposits with both the parent company and the subsidiary.

[2] While by "printing money" in this way, the government still sells bonds, the money is owed and the interest must be paid to the Bank of Canada. Since the Bank of Canada is owned by the federal government, the government, in effect, owes money and pays interest to itself. Thus, the only real effect on the government's finances of selling bonds to the Bank of Canada is that the government obtains newly-created money (in the form of new book entries in its Bank of Canada account).

[3] In effect, the public pays for its apparently "free" government services through higher prices for other goods and services; that is, through inflation rather than taxation.

[4] While such a situation would be unusual, it has occurred. In 1960, the federal government was trying to stimulate the economy with budget deficits at the same time as the Governor of the Bank of Canada, James Coyne, was pursuing an anti-inflationary tight money policy. When Mr. Coyne refused to change the Bank's policy, the government resolved the conflict by replacing him.

[5] Bank of Canada *Review*, November 1980 (page 9).

The nature and causes of inflation

What is inflation?

Inflation is an increase in the general level of the prices of goods and services. The yardstick most commonly used to measure prices and inflation is the Consumer Price Index (CPI), which is a weighted average of the prices of goods and services bought by a typical urban Canadian household, as discussed in detail in Chapter 20. It should be noted that during a period of inflation, wages and salaries (which are the prices of labor services) also tend to increase more rapidly.

The upper graph in Figure 28-1 shows that the level of the CPI (1986 = 100), has risen in every year shown, but rose particularly rapidly from the early 1970's to the early 1980's. Over this period, the CPI more than doubled, meaning that the purchasing power of a dollar was reduced by more than half.

More significant, however, is the bottom graph, which shows the actual **rate of inflation**, or how fast the CPI rose in each particular year. The rate of inflation has varied considerably over the years, with three periods standing out. Until 1973, the rate of inflation was quite low. In the early 1960's, the CPI was rising at less than 2 percent per year, and the rate of inflation remained below 5 percent per year throughout the decade. After 1972, the rate of inflation became very high, in the 8–10 percent per year range. These rates persisted for about ten years, a period which became known as "The Great Inflation." Then, in 1983, the rate of inflation began a decline that was almost as abrupt as its rise in 1973, to a rate in the range of 4–5 percent per year in the second half of the 1980's, followed by

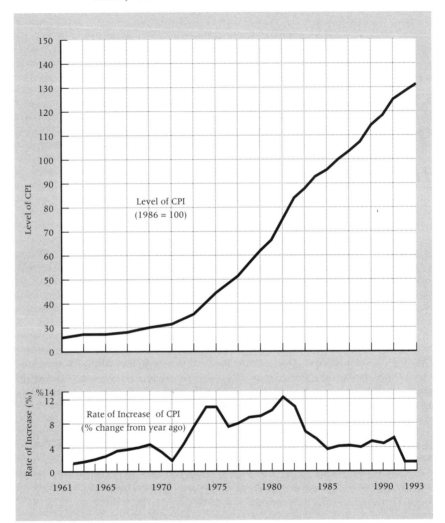

FIGURE 28-1 *The Level and the Rate of Increase of the Consumer Price Index, 1961–93*

Source: Statistics Canada, *The Consumer Price Index* (62-001)

a further decline in the early 1990's back to the below-2 percent per year rates of the early 1960's.

What causes inflation?

Inflation is a complex economic process in which various causes are often intertwined and difficult to disentangle. As a result, there is considerable confusion among the public as to the causes of inflation, with blame being attached variously to labor unions, big business, government, high inter-

Inflation is not a new phenomenon; history contains many examples of outbreaks of inflation. Often, these have been related to wars that governments financed by printing money; the interaction between the larger money supply and reduced availability of consumer goods generating brief but sharp upsurges in prices.

The most notable historical period of inflation is probably provided by Europe in the fifteenth and sixteenth centuries. From 1521 to 1660, the Spanish *conquistadores* brought about 18 000 tons of silver and 200 tons of gold back to Spain from America through official channels. As this money was spent and circulated across Europe, it made a vast addition to Europe's stock of precious metal, and drove prices upwards. By 1600, the general level of prices in Europe was about three times as high as in 1500, an unusual development in that era.

As noted earlier, most historical incidents of inflation have been relatively brief; however, it was in the second half of the twentieth century that inflation became a general and persistent feature of the major economies of the world.

est rates, low interest rates and people's greed, to name a few factors. However, such attempts to assign blame for inflation tend to confuse rather than clarify matters. Instead of looking for villains, we should look to economic fundamentals.

WHY PRICES RISE

In analyzing the causes of inflation, it is helpful to return to the basic concepts of the demand side and the supply side of markets. To illustrate the basic principles, we will use as our example the market for bejuniaberries. Suppose that bejuniaberries are grown by a large number of small farmers. With many competing producers, there is strong competition in the industry (that is, no monopoly power to raise prices). Under these conditions the price of bejuniaberries last year was $0.40 per kilogram. This year, however, the demand for bejuniaberries has increased greatly. Since the farmers are unable (at least in the short run) to produce enough bejuniaberries to satisfy demand, the price of bejuniaberries rises to $0.60 per kilogram, simply because the demand exceeds the supply.

Now let us consider an entirely different possibility. Suppose that Megaberries Inc., a large corporation, were to buy up all the small bejuniaberry farms and establish a monopoly of the bejuniaberry market. Also, suppose that all of the corporation's employees on these farms were to join a powerful labor union, the United Berry Cultivators. Negotiating at harvest time with the threat of a strike, the union is able to secure a big pay raise for the workers. However, because it controls the market, Megaberries Inc. is able to raise the price of its berries considerably. As a result of these two developments, the company's profits and the workers' wages could both rise considerably, with consumers paying the tab through higher prices of $0.60 per kilogram. While sales of bejuniaberries will be somewhat lower due to this higher price, the monopoly producer is in a position to hold down the output (supply) of berries in order to maintain the price at $0.60.

In both cases, the end result was the same—the price of the berries rose from $0.40 to $0.60. However, the underlying cause was quite different. In the first case, the price increase was caused by *demand in excess of supply*, while in the second case the origin of the price increase was the *monopolistic power of producers*—the ability of the company and its employees to push up their incomes.

The example of bejuniaberries illustrates the basic forces that can underlie increases in the price of a particular good or service. While inflation is a much broader concept, involving the general level of the prices of goods and services across the entire economy, the same principles apply— inflationary pressures can come from the demand side of the economy and from the supply side of the economy. The first of these is known as **demand-pull inflation**, in which aggregate demand exceeds the economy's ability to produce goods and services, causing prices to be pulled up by pressure from the demand side of the economy. A second—and quite different—inflationary pressure can come from the supply side of the economy. If labor unions or businesses with monopolistic powers push their wages and profits higher, the result can be upward pressures on prices. Since this inflationary pressure comes from producers and production costs rather than from demand, it is known as **cost-push inflation**. We will consider each of these two basic types of inflationary pressures in more detail in the following sections.

Inflation from the demand side: Demand-pull inflation

When excess demand causes prices to rise, the result is **demand-pull inflation**. This is the "classic" case of inflation, in which aggregate demand (consumption plus investment plus government plus net export spending) exceeds the capacity of the economy to produce goods and services. The economy is only physically capable at any given time of producing goods and services at a certain (capacity) rate; should total spending exceed this level, the only possible outcome is that prices will rise as a result of the excess demand, as illustrated in Figure 28-2.

It is generally agreed among economists that *excess aggregate demand* is the most basic cause of inflation. The most common examples of demand-pull inflation are periods of wartime, when heavy government spending drives prices upward. Another case occurred after the Second World War, when households cashed in their war bonds and went on a spending spree.

FIGURE 28-2   *Demand-Pull Inflation*

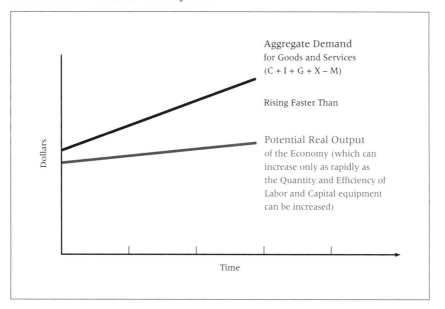

In the second half of the 1960's, US government spending on the Vietnam
War and major domestic social security programs generated increasingly severe inflation, and in the 1972–73 worldwide economic boom—the
strongest peacetime economic boom ever—prices rose at record rates as
output simply could not keep up with booming demand. Each of these
cases of inflation was accompanied by another phenomenon—unusually
rapid increases in the money supply, or the volume of money in circulation.

THE MONEY SUPPLY AND INFLATION

For society in general (consumers, businesses and governments) to spend
on a vast enough scale to drive the general level of prices upwards rapidly,
there must be more money in circulation—the *money supply* must rise. In
fact, any period of rapid inflation is accompanied by rapid increases in the
money supply. And, as we have seen, the growth of the money supply is
controlled by the Bank of Canada, which is ultimately responsible to the federal government. Therefore, the key factor underlying the rate of inflation—the rate of growth of the money supply—is in the final analysis
determined by federal government authorities.

In determining its monetary policy, however, the Bank of Canada is not
concerned solely with minimizing inflation. In particular, we have seen
that increases in the money supply (easy money) can be used during recessions to boost aggregate demand and reduce unemployment. While
easy-money policies can help to lift the economy out of recession, there is
a danger that the government will boost the money supply too quickly or

for too long a time. Of course, this will result in a new surge of inflation, but not immediately—inflation will appear only after a *time lag.*

Experience indicates that if the money supply is increased excessively rapidly, inflation will probably begin to increase after a time lag of about a year and will continue to work its way through the economy for at least another two years, as the increased volume of money is spent and re-spent. Thus, while rapid increases in the money supply may look like a good idea to a government faced with a recession and high unemployment, there is a real possibility that they will generate more inflation in the future.

Generally then, the rate of growth of the money supply and the level of aggregate demand for goods and services are the key factors underlying the rate of inflation. Inflation tends to be most severe during economic booms, when demand is high, and less severe during recessions, when demand is sluggish. While higher aggregate demand is the most basic cause of inflation, the decision of government authorities to allow the money supply to increase in response to the strong demand for loans associated with an economic boom is an integral part of the inflationary process.

FULL-EMPLOYMENT POLICIES AND INFLATION

As pointed out earlier, the full-employment monetary and fiscal policies which the federal government has adopted since the Second World War have usually maintained aggregate demand at high enough levels to avoid prolonged serious recessions. While such policies keep unemployment rates lower than in the past, the maintenance of total spending at such high levels has tended to generate more inflation than occurred prior to the use of these policies. Thus, the commitment of governments to full employment has involved, as a side effect, additional inflation of a demand-pull nature.

GOVERNMENT BUDGET DEFICITS AND INFLATION

While it is commonly believed that government budget deficits cause inflation, most economists think that this is not necessarily the case. Budget deficits are generally used during recessions, when business investment spending is low and there are unused savings available for the govern-

FIGURE 28-3   *The Operation of Demand-Pull Inflation*

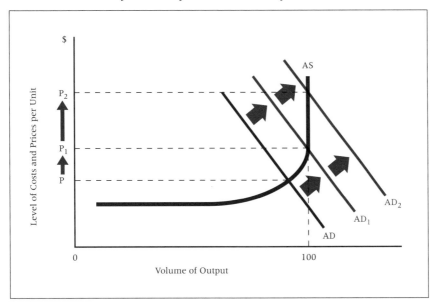

ment to borrow. Borrowing existing funds (savings) from Canadians does not increase the money supply or risk boosting aggregate demand to excessive levels.

On the other hand, if the government were to "print money" to finance its budget deficits (by selling bonds to the Bank of Canada, as in Chapter 27), the money supply would increase and the danger of inflation would be greater.

DEMAND-PULL INFLATION GRAPHED

Figure 28-3 uses the aggregate demand and aggregate supply curves to show the operation of demand-pull inflation. As the level of aggregate demand rises from AD to AD_1, and then to AD_2, the economy is pushed to its capacity output of 100 at the same time, and the level of prices rises from p to p_1, and p_2, reflecting the increasingly severe inflation that results from the high demand.

Inflation from the supply side: Cost-push inflation

While excessive aggregate demand, fuelled by increases in the money supply, is regarded as the most basic source of inflation, there are other contributing factors on the supply side of the economy that can make inflation more severe once it has started. The key to these forces is the ability of some producers—both businesses and employees—to increase their incomes and thus the price paid by the consumer. Because in this case the price is being pushed up by cost factors (profits and wages both representing a cost to the consumer), this process is described as cost-push inflation.

MARKET POWER

Underlying the concept of cost-push inflation is *market power*—the ability of some producers to increase their prices and some employees to increase their wages. At the root of such market power is *monopoly power*—the ability of producers to impose a price increase upon buyers or the ability of unionized employees to impose a wage increase upon employers.

Not all producers enjoy such market power; in fact, most do not. Where producers and/or employees are subject to strong competition (either domestic or foreign) in the marketplace, they lack the power to increase their prices and incomes in this way. On the other hand, there are groups of producers—usually larger corporations and unionized employees—who possess such market power, at least to some extent. Some such industries are monopolistic in nature (for example, postal service), while others are dominated by a few large producers who would prefer to "live and let live" rather than compete ruthlessly and perhaps ruinously regarding prices. Often, these industries, which are dominated by large employers (postal service, telephone service, hydro-electric utilities, steel, automobile manufacturing, petroleum, tobacco, breweries and many others), are also strongly unionized. In these parts of the economy, it is possible for a "wage-price spiral" to develop at times.

THE WAGE-PRICE SPIRAL

When they have to pay more for things, some people like to blame big business, while others like to blame labor unions. Both of these "villain theories" are overly simplistic. It seems to be more correct to say that, rather than one or the other, it is most often the combination of big producers/employers and labor unions that generates large wage and price increases that add to inflation.

During a period of inflation, in bargaining with their unions, such employers may grant above-average wage increases, because they are confident that they will be able to pass these on to the consumer in the form of price increases, due to the lack of competition. However, if many prices are rising in this way, the resultant increase in the cost of living could cause labor unions to demand more wage increases, creating a **wage-price spiral** in which wages and prices chase each other upwards.

Such a wage-price spiral is most likely when the economy is booming, and employers are anxious to avoid strikes because sales are strong. Also, during a boom it is easier for producers to recover wage increases by raising prices, because demand is high. On the other hand, cost-push pressures tend to be less strong during recessions, when weaker demand makes price increases more difficult and employers resist union wage demands more strongly. Recessions, however, are not a complete cure for this cost-push inflation; some producers and some unions possess enough power over their prices and wages to continue to raise them despite sluggish demand. Thus, the wage-price spiral not only aggravates inflation during boom periods, but also helps to keep inflation going (although at a slower pace) during economic slowdowns.

Finally, it should be noted that the wage-price spiral and cost-push inflation are generated mainly by groups who enjoy market power. Many smaller producers in highly competitive industries and non-union employees who lack bargaining power tend to be left behind in the wage-price spiral, and suffer accordingly.

COST-PUSH INFLATION GRAPHED

Figure 28-4 uses the aggregate demand and aggregate supply curves to illustrate cost-push inflation. Essentially, when sellers (producers and workers) are willing to supply their output only at higher prices, the AS curve moves upward to higher cost levels, as shown by AS_1. When the AS curve shifts upward to reflect the higher costs, the price level moves from p to p_1, reflecting the inflation which results.

FIGURE 28-4 *The Operation of Cost-Push Inflation*

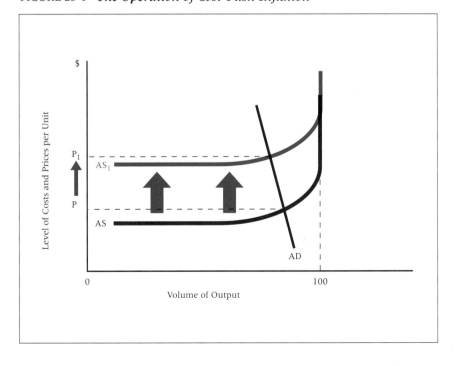

The momentum of inflation

In Chapter 24, we saw how both recessions and economic booms tend to "gain momentum" once they get started. In a similar way, once excess aggregate demand has gotten inflation underway, it can develop a tendency to gather momentum and become more and more rapid. This can occur partly because households and businesses often respond to inflation in ways that make inflation worse, and partly because governments often tend to follow policies that accommodate inflation rather than introduce anti-inflation policies that increase unemployment. We will consider each of these problems in the following sections.

> But after inflation continues for a while its character changes. It becomes seen as endemic, people act in the expectation that it will continue, and it becomes self-reinforcing. That is when the real trouble starts. If inflation is not resisted, if it is accommodated, it will accelerate.
>
> Gerald Bouey,
> Governor of the Bank of Canada,
> Annual Report of the Governor of the Bank of Canada, 1982

(A) FULL-EMPLOYMENT POLICIES AND INFLATION

As we have seen, the political importance of keeping unemployment low can cause governments to use fiscal and monetary policies that increase aggregate demand, generating some inflation as a side-effect. However, this relatively small amount of additional inflation may well be regarded as an acceptable "trade-off" for lower unemployment. At this point, the time lags discussed earlier can become important: if the government increases the money supply in order to reduce unemployment, the inflationary side-effects of this action will progressively work their way through the economy over the next two years or more, adding to inflationary pressures.

(B) INFLATION PSYCHOLOGY

Once inflation gets underway, it can be made more severe by a phenomenon known as **inflation psychology**. This refers to a situation in which people, having experienced inflation for some time, come to expect that rapid inflation will continue in the future. They seek to protect themselves against this expected inflation by seeking exceptionally large wage and salary increases and by spending their money now (before prices rise further), reducing their savings or even borrowing money.

While such actions are a logical way for individuals to respond to expected future inflation, when many people behave this way, they actually

FIGURE 28-5   *Inflation Psychology*

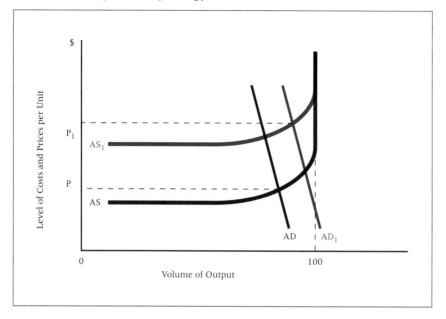

655
*The nature and
causes of inflation*

make inflation more severe, adding not only to cost-push pressures but also to demand-pull pressures on prices.

Inflation psychology graphed

Inflation psychology affects both the supply side and the demand side of the economy. On the *demand side*, aggregate demand rises as people increase their current spending in anticipation of price increases; this is shown in Figure 28-5 by the shift of the AD curve to the higher level of AD_1.

On the supply side, the aggregate supply curves move upward to AS_1, as explained in the section on cost-push inflation. The result is a double impact on prices, which move up from p to p_1. Because people expected inflation, they got inflation.

(C) COST-PUSH INFLATION AND THE MONEY SUPPLY

Once inflation becomes quite rapid, it can become very difficult for governmental authorities to curb it. In fact, it can become easier for them to take actions that not only accommodate inflation, but will make it worse.

To illustrate, suppose that (for the sake of round figures) Canada's GDP in 19X1 was $100 billion, and that there was rapid inflation and strong inflation psychology in the nation that caused strong labor unions, big corporations and other groups to increase their incomes and prices quite rapidly. If these cost-push pressures caused prices in general to rise by 10 percent in 19X2, then the same level of real output that was produced in 19X1 would cost $110 billion in 19X2 (10 percent more than in 19X1). Just to support the *same level* of output and employment that existed in 19X1, at 19X2's higher prices, will require 10 percent more aggregate demand in the economy in 19X2. Viewed differently, to prevent a *decline* in real output and employment in 19X2, aggregate demand must rise by 10 percent, which means that the money supply must also be increased by approximately 10 percent.

This places the Bank of Canada in an awkward position: if it *does not* increase the money supply by 10 percent, aggregate demand will be too low to keep output from falling below 19X1's level—there will be a sharp recession, and unemployment will rise. On the other hand, if the Bank of Canada *does* increase the money supply by 10 percent (or more likely by 12 or 13 percent, to try to stimulate an increase in output), such rapid increases in the money supply, while avoiding a recession, virtually guarantee continued rapid inflation in 19X3 and beyond. Thus, strong cost-push pressures on prices can place the Bank of Canada in the difficult position of having to choose between resisting those pressures at the expense of a sharp recession, or increasing the money supply rapidly enough to avoid a recession, but at the cost of more severe inflation in the future.

In such circumstances, the government and the Bank of Canada could come under strong political pressure to avoid a recession by increasing the money supply sufficiently to accommodate the higher prices set by the powerful unions and corporations. While the result will be a rapid increase in the money supply and more severe inflation, the origin of the inflation problem is not simply demand-pull inflation. It is at least in part a cost-push problem, with the government pushed into participating in the process by increasing the money supply to avoid rising unemployment. A government that accommodates inflation and inflation psychology by increasing the money supply in this way is likely to find itself faced with accelerating inflation, as such a policy feeds not only inflation psychology, but also excess demand.

RIDING THE TIGER

According to an old saying, "It is easier to ride the tiger than to dismount."

One may very intensely dislike riding a tiger, but once one has gotten into this unenviable position, it would seem preferable to remain in it rather than to get off the beast. Once inflation has become severe, government authorities face a similar problem—should they "ride the tiger" by continuing to increase the money supply rapidly, or should they cut back on money-supply growth and "dismount" right into a severe recession?

FIGURE 28-6 *How Inflation Gains Momentum*

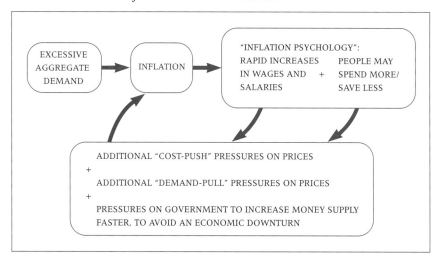

These forces that can cause inflation to gain momentum are summarized and illustrated in Figure 28-6.

Confusing symptoms and causes

While economists emphasize excess aggregate demand as the cause of inflation, the general public tends to blame labor unions and big business. This is probably because the activities of unions and big business—wage negotiations, strikes, price increases—are highly visible, while the role played by excess demand is not visible. Who has seen excess demand bidding up the prices of goods and services? Shoppers are not seen bidding against each other eagerly for roasts or for lumber in stores, thus generating higher prices. Rather, the manufacturers or the stores put higher price tags on them, and explain that their "costs are up." Certainly, this looks more like cost-push inflation than demand-pull inflation.

Yet the underlying economics of the situation are often quite different. If, for example, consumer demand for lumber is very high, lumber stores will find their inventories depleting rapidly and will be anxious to replenish their stocks of lumber. With the purchasers for all the various lumber stores bidding actively against each other for a limited supply of lumber from the sawmills, the price will be bid up at the manufacturers' level and the wholesalers' level.

When the lumber reaches the retail stores, it will have a higher price—which store managers usually describe as an "increase in costs." However, the real origin of the price increases lies in high consumer demand; it is really demand-pull in nature rather than cost-push, as it appears.

People tend to blame inflation on what they can see, such as the increases in union wages and business profits that are its most visible aspects. However, the actions of unions (which represent less than half of employees) and big business (which produces less than half of the economy's output) cannot account completely for inflation, in which virtually *all* wages and prices rise rapidly. The wage and price increases of unions and large corporations are simply the most visible *symptoms* of inflation (or, at most, contributing factors), not its basic cause.

In the view of the vast majority of economists, the basic cause of inflation is excessive aggregate demand. Early in a period of inflation caused by excess demand, prices tend to rise faster than wages, many of which are tied to union contracts that have not yet expired; as a result, profits increase rapidly and the public sees profits as the cause of inflation. Later, as union contracts are renegotiated and wages rise rapidly (the catch-up phase), people blame unions for the inflation. In both cases, public attention is focused not on the basic *cause* of inflation, but rather on the more visible *symptoms*.

The causes of inflation in review

The causes of inflation are complex, interwoven and difficult to separate. The most basic factor determining the rate of inflation is the *rate of growth of the money supply*, which in turn determines the degree of *excess aggregate demand* present in the economy. However, there are different reasons why the money supply might increase rapidly enough to generate rapid inflation. Some people view the basic cause as excessive stimulation of the economy by government monetary and fiscal policies, while others emphasize that cost-push pressures from big business and labor unions can virtually force the government to increase the money supply, in order to avoid a recession, by providing the economy with enough purchasing power to buy all of its output at the higher prices caused by the wage-price spiral. While there are elements of truth in both of these viewpoints, most economists tend to place more emphasis on demand-pull pressures originating in government policies as the basic cause of inflation, and view cost-push pressures as a contributing factor to inflation rather than the basic cause.

Inflation in perspective

On a more basic level, both the demand-pull and cost-push theories of inflation are related to one fundamental factor—the *unrealistic expectations* of people, and their attempts (as workers, consumers, business persons and government leaders) to get more out of the economy than the economy can produce. When such unrealistic demands are placed on the economy—either in terms of excessive spending or in terms of excessive increases in incomes—the result will inevitably be inflation. In this sense, inflation is the economy's way of telling people that their expectations and the demands they are placing on the economy are unrealistic and that they can't have everything they want. Instead, what they get is rapid increases in prices and interest rates, which limit their real economic gains to what is economically possible.

DEFINITIONS OF NEW TERMS

Rate of Inflation The percentage increase in the Consumer Price Index over a period of one year; a measure of how rapidly the CPI is rising.

Demand-Pull Inflation Inflation that is the result of excessive aggregate demand in the economy; that is, aggregate demand in excess of the economy's capacity to produce goods and services.

Cost-Push Inflation Inflation that is the result of the economic power of some large employers and powerful labor unions, which can be used to push up wages and prices.

Wage-Price Spiral An inflationary situation in which cost-push pressures have become severe in the less competitive sectors of the economy, causing wages and prices to chase each other upwards in a spiral.

Inflation Psychology The expectation of continuing inflation in the future, against which people seek to protect themselves by obtaining large wage and salary increases and by reducing their savings.

CHAPTER SUMMARY

1. Inflation is an increase in the general level of the prices of goods and services. It is most commonly measured by increases in the Consumer Price Index.

2. The basic cause of inflation is demand-pull pressures arising from excessive aggregate demand, fuelled by rapid growth of the money supply.

3. Cost-push pressures, generated by the market power of some large employers and powerful labor unions, are generally regarded as contributing factors rather than the basic cause of inflation.

4. Once inflation gets started, it can gain momentum, for various reasons:

    (a) the government may perceive some additional inflation now as an acceptable trade-off for recovery from a recession, and not recognize that due to time lags, inflationary pressures started now will build over the next two years or so;

    (b) "inflation psychology" may develop, causing the public to add to inflationary pressures by seeking large pay increases and by spending more now, before prices rise further;

(c) once wages and prices are rising rapidly, the government may find it easier to continue to increase the money supply rapidly rather than hold down the money supply and send the economy into a severe recession.

5. In the final analysis, inflation is the result of the unrealistic economic expectations of people, whether these take the form of excess demand (demand-pull) or excessive increases in incomes (cost-push).

QUESTIONS

1. The text notes that inflation psychology can make an inflationary situation considerably worse by causing people to spend more, save less and seek large income increases in order to protect themselves against inflation. What could the government do to attempt to reduce such problems arising from inflation psychology?

2. In conclusion, the text describes the fundamental cause of inflation as "unrealistic expectations of people and ... their attempts—as workers, business persons and government leaders—to get more out of the economy than the economy can produce." What could be done in order to make people's economic expectations more consistent with economic reality? How much leadership have governments provided in this matter, and why?

3. Suppose that strong cost-push pressures developed in the economy due to the price and wage decisions of economically powerful employers and unions, and that the Bank of Canada resisted this inflationary trend by refusing to increase the money supply sufficiently rapidly to support these price and wage decisions. What would happen in the economy, and upon whom would the burden fall most heavily?

4. Why should the government not attempt to stop inflation by simply passing a law forbidding price and income increases?

5. Interview several people who have not studied economics to determine their views regarding the causes of inflation and appropriate policies for combating it. How accurate are their views? If their views are representative of the Canadian public, do they make it easier or more difficult for the government come to grips with the problems of inflation?

6. What has the rate of inflation been for the past three years? Has the rate of inflation increased or decreased? What are the possible reasons for this trend in the rate of inflation?

7. Is the rate of inflation forecast to decline or increase over the next year? Why?

8.

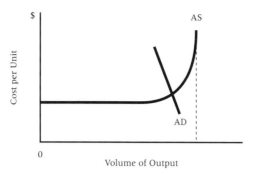

(a) Explain how these aggregate supply and aggregate demand curves (and therefore the rate of inflation) would be affected by each of the following:

    (i)   a significant increase in the level of aggregate demand.

    (ii) the negotiation of significant increases in wages by labor unions in anticipation of further inflation.

    (iii) reduced saving/increased consumption spending by households in anticipation of further inflation.

(b) Draw new AS and AD curves reflecting (i), (ii) and (iii), to show the cumulative effect of all three of these developments on the rate of inflation.

(c) According to the graph, what are the two basic ways to reduce the rate of inflation from that shown in part (b)?

9. According to the federal government, the introduction of the Goods and Services Tax (GST) in 1991 was expected to cause a *one-time* increase in the CPI of about 1.25 percentage points—that is, the rate of inflation in 1991 (only) would be 1.25 percentage points higher than it would have been.

    Others feared that the GST would have a much more inflationary impact, as it could touch off a wage-price spiral, with employees seeking large pay increases to offset it. Which view appears to have been correct? What might explain this?

The "Great Inflation"

The decade from 1972 to 1982 saw a prolonged period of severe inflation that was so exceptional that it became known as the "Great Inflation" (Figure 28-7).

FIGURE 28-7 *The Great Inflation*

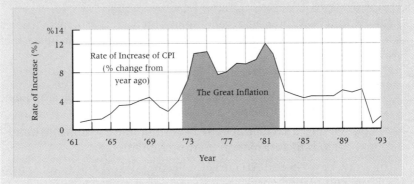

Source: Statistics Canada

Some of the more memorable features of this period were dramatic oil-price increases in 1973–74 and 1979, exceptional increases in wages and salaries, sharp food-price increases and record-high interest rates, followed by the most severe recession since the 1930's. Not surprisingly, the Great Inflation was characterized by unusually strong inflationary pressures from both the demand side and the supply side of the economy.

Demand-pull forces

While the increases in oil prices, wages and salaries were highly visible and well-publicized, there was another underlying force at work that was less visible but more fundamental. This was an exceptional surge in aggregate demand, fuelled by very rapid increases in the money supply. As Figure 28-8 shows, the money supply grew much more rapidly during the 1970's than it had in the 1960's, when inflation rates were much lower. At the same time, there were unusually rapid increases in government spending, which added to aggregate demand.

FIGURE 29-8   *Money Supply^a Growth in the 1960's and 1970's
Compared*

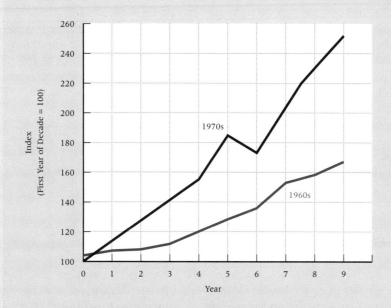

^{a}M1 Cash in circulation and Demand Deposits at Banks

Source: Bank of Montreal, *Business in Review*, September, 1979

WHY DID THE MONEY SUPPLY INCREASE SO RAPIDLY?

(a) The Vietnam War

The origins of the severe inflation of the 1970's go back to the Vietnam War in the 1960's. From the mid-1960's on, the Vietnam War generated excessive demand and inflation in the US economy, as the US government financed the war by massive printing of money rather than tax increases. This led to rapid increases in the money supply of other nations, through the following mechanism.

With the US dollar more plentiful relative to other nations' currencies, the international value of the US dollar tended to fall. Put the other way, the value of other nations' currencies in terms of the US dollar tended to rise—other nations' currencies would become more costly for Americans to buy. For example, from the mid-1960's to the early 1970's, the cost of a Canadian dollar to Americans rose from 92 1/2¢ to over $1.00 US.

This created a serious problem for the nations whose currencies were under upward pressure: if their currencies became costlier to Americans, so would the goods they exported to the vast US market. In short, the rapid increases in the US money supply posed a threat to other nations' exports to the United States and to the jobs associated with those exports. To protect those exports and jobs, many nations undertook to increase their own money supplies at faster rates, making their currencies more plentiful and thus less likely to rise relative to the US dollar. As a result, the rapid increases in the US money supply were matched by other countries seeking to protect their exports to the USA.

While these policies did help to protect exports and employment in the short run, they contributed strongly to inflation in the late 1960's and early 1970's. Thus, the US "Vietnam Inflation" spread throughout most of the industrialized world.

(b) Rapid labor force growth

The exceptionally large number of people born in the decade following the end of Second World came of working age in the decade from the late 1960's to the late 1970's. During this same period, the proportion of women seeking work increased dramatically. These two factors accounted for an exceptional surge in the number of people seeking jobs, which could only be accommodated if the economy grew very rapidly.

Put the other way, these rapid increases in the labor force caused the unemployment rate to rise, placing pressure on the government to stimulate aggregate demand through fiscal policy and more rapid growth of the money supply, to keep unemployment from rising. The resultant surge in aggregate demand added to inflationary pressures.

(c) Rapid increases in government spending

The period from the late 1960's to the mid-1970's saw very rapid increases in federal and provincial government spending in Canada, in areas such as health care, education, civil service payrolls, unemployment insurance and transfer payments (family allowances, welfare, old age pensions and so on), many of which were indexed so that they rose automatically at the same rate as the Consumer Price Index. It is widely believed these rapid increases in government expenditures contributed significantly to inflation in the 1970's, by adding to aggregate demand in the economy.

(d) Political factors

The strong performance of the economy in the second half of the 1960's generated *very high expectations* among the public about what was possible economically and about what government economic policies could and should achieve. In particular, strong economic growth with low unemployment and rapidly rising living standards came to be expected by the public. While these expectations can now be seen to have been unrealistic, they placed great pressure on governments to fulfill them, often by stimulating aggregate demand with unusual strength so as to boost economic growth and reduce unemployment. This problem was particularly important in 1972, which, by coincidence, was an election year in both Canada and the United States, as well as in several other nations. Anti-inflation policies that had been applied in 1969–70 had left considerable unemployment in these economies in 1971, so there was heavy political pressure on governments to stimulate their economies before the 1972 elections. The side effects of these policies, which would be extremely severe inflation by late 1973, were considered secondary at the time. The 1972 federal election in Canada resulted in a minority government until 1974, which made it impossible for the government to impose politically unpopular monetary and fiscal anti-inflation policies. Inflation was, therefore, allowed to gain momentum in 1973 and 1974.

As a result of these factors, government spending, the money supply and aggregate demand all rose at very rapid rates from the mid-1960's to the mid-1970's. Government spending rose from 33 percent of GDP to 43 percent, and the money supply, which had risen by 6 percent per year in the early 1960's, rose by more than 15 percent per year from 1970 to 1975. With real output capable of rising only 4 or 5 percent per year at most, such money-supply increases made severe inflation inevitable.

Cost-push forces

The Great Inflation also saw strong cost-push pressures on prices, most notably from wages and salaries. By 1974, Canadians were firmly in the grip of inflation psychology: expecting continuing severe inflation, they were seeking—and getting—wage and salary increases of 15–20 percent per year in 1974–75. These attempts by people to protect themselves against inflation made inflation worse, by giving it a momentum of its own: Canadians were suffering from continued inflation in part because they expected to experience continuing inflation.

Another cost-push factor which contributed to the Great Inflation was *oil-price increases*. While government subsidies kept Canadian oil-price increases well-below world trends during the 1970's, these subsidies only delayed price increases that were inevitable. When the increases finally occurred in the early 1980's, they added considerable cost-push pressures to the later stages of the Great Inflation in Canada.

Also, *food prices* rose rapidly in several years in the 1970's, which boosted the Consumer Price Index (of which food is the second-largest component). High food and oil costs also added to wage-push pressures, as people sought large income increases to compensate for these added expenses.

Dealing with inflation: Policies and problems

In Chapter 28, we saw how inflation can start slowly, then gain momentum. When the economy is in recession and unemployment is high, inflation tends to be neither a public concern nor a political issue. In these circumstances, governments that are anxious to reduce unemployment may tend to stimulate aggregate demand quite strongly through the use of budget deficits and "easy money" policies. In the political pressure to get the economy growing again and reduce unemployment, concerns about the possible inflationary effects of such policies can be quite secondary. Even if the government's policies are likely to generate inflationary pressures, these will not become a problem for at least a year and probably longer, further reducing their importance. In any event, some additional inflation may well seem a reasonable price to pay for lower unemployment. For reasons such as these, inflationary pressures can be allowed to build up in the economy.

However, as we also saw in Chapter 28, after a certain point, inflation can gain "momentum" and begin to feed on itself. Once consumers and businesses begin to *expect* more inflation, they tend to behave in ways that *cause* more inflation. In particular, employees will demand larger pay increases to protect themselves against future inflation that they expect. Such wage increases may be granted by many employers, especially those that possess the market power to increase their prices in order to recover the increase in their labor costs. Thus, the *expectation* of inflation can add "cost-push" inflationary pressures to the economy. In addition, if people expect prices to rise in the near future, they may tend to buy now—with borrowed money if necessary—in order to beat the price increases; such behavior will only add to "demand-pull" inflationary pressures. Finally, if enough people think and act in these ways, the increased inflation that they cause may push the Bank of Canada in the direction of increasing the money supply even faster, so as to generate sufficient aggregate demand to keep output and employment growing even with the higher prices and wages being generated. Such action on the part of the Bank of Canada can avert a recession (temporarily), but will ensure more inflation in the future. As a result of all of these pressures, once inflation gets started, it can gain momentum, becoming increasingly more rapid.

Why the concern about inflation?

While a society can tolerate moderate inflation, rapid inflation such as was experienced in the 1970's is another matter, for several reasons. Severe inflation imposes hardship on the economically weak; it impairs long-term financial planning; it causes high interest rates and depresses business investment spending; it can undermine a nation's international competitiveness and exports, and it tends to end in a recession with high unemployment. We will deal with each of these problems in the following sections.

(A) INFLATION IMPOSES HARDSHIP ON THE ECONOMICALLY WEAK

For those such as professionals, top athletes, skilled workers and members of strong labor unions, who have the economic power (bargaining power) to increase their incomes, inflation poses no real threat to their living standard. For many others, however, such as unskilled, non-union workers and many service industry workers, it often proves difficult to increase their incomes as fast as prices are rising, so that inflation poses a real threat to their standard of living. Generally, it can be said that inflation falls hardest upon those who are the least able to protect themselves—the economically weaker groups in society.

The people most severely affected by inflation are those on *fixed incomes*; that is, people who receive the same number of dollars of income year after year. As the purchasing power of their fixed income falls due to inflation, their standard of living is driven steadily downward. The largest and most seriously affected such group is, of course, *pensioners*, whose pensions are in some cases fixed for the rest of their lives. Two other groups adversely affected are *welfare recipients* (whose benefits do not always keep up with inflation) and people living off *investment income*, which may not keep up with inflation. This latter group includes not only wealthy investors, but also people such as widows living off the investment income earned through the investment of their spouse's life insurance.

Thus, inflation generally tends to redistribute income within a society, and the economically weak are the losers.

(B) INFLATION IMPAIRS LONG-TERM FINANCIAL PLANNING

By steadily eroding the value of the dollar, inflation will, over long periods of time, drastically reduce its purchasing power, and thus seriously affect long-term financial planning. One example of this problem is *pensions*; another is *life insurance* planning. The objective of life insurance is to provide the survivor (such as a widow) with enough investment income to live reasonably well. Suppose that a widow, age 44, invests the $600 000 of her husband's life insurance benefits in long-term government bonds so as to earn $50 000 per year of interest income. While this may seem quite comfortable, inflation of 6 percent per year would reduce its purchasing power to $25 000 by the time she was 56, $12 500 when she was 68, and $6250 at age 80—one-eighth of its original value. A similar problem can occur for pensioners who have saved for their retirement through contributions to a pension plan—if inflation is too severe, their pensions may prove inadequate, especially if they live to a ripe old age, as more and more people do today.

What can be done about this? By planning for far larger pensions and life insurance, the effects of inflation can be offset—but few people can afford to put aside that much out of today's income in order to protect against the risk of tomorrow's inflation. Consequently, most people cannot protect themselves against this problem, and remain very vulnerable to inflation over the long term. By eroding the purchasing power of money, inflation undermines the role of money as a store of value, making it difficult to plan for the future and to provide for protection against future financial risks. Rather, inflation encourages short-term thinking: "Spend, don't save, and hope that the future will take care of itself."

THE 72 FORMULA

An idea of the impact of inflation on fixed incomes can be gained by using the "72" formula:

> If something (here, prices) is increasing at a compound rate of X percent per year, it will *double* in 72 ÷ X years.

For example, if the Consumer Price Index rises at 6 percent per year, it will double in 12 (72 ÷ 6) years. Put another way, a 6-percent annual rate of inflation will slash the purchasing power of a pensioner's fixed income *in half* in 12 years.

Inflation at the 9 percent and 10 percent annual rates—common since the mid-1970's—has a much more severe impact on fixed incomes, cutting their purchasing power in half in just 7 or 8 years. For a person considering early retirement at age 60, whose life expectancy may be 78, such rates of inflation can ruin a lifetime's planning for a happy retirement.

(C) INFLATION CAN CAUSE ECONOMIC STAGNATION

Ordinarily, inflation has been associated with periods of high aggregate demand, brisk economic growth and low unemployment, as we saw in Chapter 28. In the 1970's, however, it became apparent that very rapid inflation can actually contribute to economic stagnation and high unemployment. This can happen because severe inflation can actually depress capital investment spending by business.

Inflation can have this effect for two reasons: first, inflation causes *higher interest rates*. Fearing that continuing inflation will erode the real value (purchasing power) of the capital that they loan out, savers/lenders will insist on higher interest rates to offset the declining value of their capital.

This is shown in Figure 29-1: if savers/lenders expect inflation to reduce the value of their capital by 2 percent per year, they may accept an interest rate of 5 percent on any loans they make—after inflation, this would leave them with a **"real interest rate"** of 3 percent. However, if they expect inflation of 8 percent, they will have to insist on an interest rate of 11 percent to earn the same "real" (after inflation) interest rate of 3 percent.

Thus, to induce lenders to invest or lend their money, borrowers will have to offer higher interest rates, to offset the effects of inflation.

This is an important (and often misunderstood) point: *inflation* (or, more precisely, savers'/lenders' expectation or fear of inflation) *causes interest rates to rise*. And, the more rapid inflation is, the higher interest rates are likely to be. The high interest rates caused by inflation can, in turn, have certain undesirable effects on the economy. Most importantly, they could discourage the business investment spending that increases productivity and prosperity. Also, high mortgage rates tend to discourage home-buying

FIGURE 29-1 *Inflation and Interest Rates*

$100 invested for one year	With Inflation Expected To Be 2%		With Inflation Expected To Be 8%	
Interest rate	5%		11%	
⟶ Interest income	⟶	$5.00	⟶	$11.00
less: Loss of purchasing Power on the $100 due to inflation	2%	2.00	8%	8.00
equals: "Real" return (after inflation)	3%	$3.00	3%	$3.00

and dampen new home construction. Both of these effects tend to contribute to economic stagnation and unemployment.

Second, contrary to popular belief, rapid inflation is not generally good for business profits. While profits *appear* to be high during periods of rapid inflation, after allowances have been made for inflation and taxes, real after-tax business profits are for many businesses actually *reduced* by inflation. Together with higher interest rates and the increased cost of capital goods, this can, over a period of time, result in depressed levels of capital investment, slower economic growth and higher unemployment.

Thus, severe and prolonged inflation can contribute to economic stagnation and the uncomfortable combination of stagnation and inflation known as "stagflation." This undermining of the critically important saving/investment process is another example of how inflation discourages long-term economic thinking and planning, at the ultimate expense of future prosperity. The future does *not* take care of itself.

(D) INFLATION CAN AFFECT A NATION'S FOREIGN TRADE

For a nation such as Canada, which exports over one-quarter of its GDP, inflation poses another threat to prosperity. By increasing the costs and prices of Canadian products, inflation can impair Canada's competitiveness in international markets. Canadian exports to foreign markets could be reduced, and less expensive foreign imports could penetrate Canadian markets; in both cases, Canadian output and employment would be threatened.

It is important to note that inflation will only have this negative effect on a nation's exports if it is more rapid than inflation in other countries. Obviously, even inflation of 12 percent per year in Canada will not affect Canada's trade if every country Canada trades with also has inflation of 12 percent per year.[1]

(E) INFLATION TENDS TO LEAD TO RECESSION

Periods of severe inflation tend to end in severe recessions. As noted earlier, rapid inflation generates very high interest rates, which in turn depress business investment spending and spending by consumers on housing and "big-ticket" items such as cars and appliances that are financed with credit. The result, as we saw in Chapter 24, is a recession, as aggregate demand is dragged downwards.

In addition, as we will see in this chapter, government policies to slow down inflation invariably include high interest rates and other measures to depress aggregate demand, with the same results: a slowing of the economy, depressed output and higher unemployment.

Thus, for a variety of reasons that are summarized in Figure 29-2, inflation (and especially rapid inflation) represents a threat to the economic

FIGURE 29-2 *The Effects of Inflation*

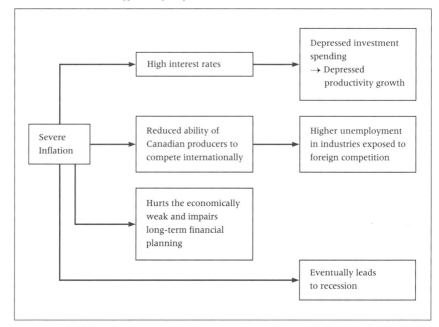

prosperity of society. As a result, governments must make keeping inflation under control another of their policy priorities.

Dealing with inflation

Before examining the policies that governments can use to contain and to
combat inflation, we should first review the causes of inflation.

The basic cause of inflation is *excessive aggregate demand* for goods and
services, which causes prices to rise due to *demand-pull pressures*. This is always accompanied—in fact, preceded—by a rapid increase in the money
supply. *Cost-push pressures* on prices (arising from the ability of some large
corporations and some powerful labor unions to push up prices and
wages) are generally regarded as a secondary cause, or a contributing
factor, rather than as the primary cause of the problem. However, under
conditions of strong inflation psychology, the expectation of future inflation can generate large wage and salary increases that add significantly
to cost-push inflationary pressures, giving inflation a "momentum" of its
own. If inflation is allowed to reach this stage, it becomes much more
difficult to deal with; therefore, it is considered important that governments
prevent inflation from becoming severe in the first place. In this chapter, we will consider:

- first, what governments can do to reduce the rate of inflation once
  it has become too high, and

- second, how governments can keep inflation from becoming severe and dangerous.

Policies to curb inflation

Once inflation has acquired "momentum" in the manner described above, it becomes much more rapid, much more damaging to the performance of the economy and much more difficult and painful to get back under control. In order to combat inflation effectively, government policies must attack its basic causes by restraining the growth of the money supply and aggregate demand, by using its monetary and fiscal policies.

(A) MONETARY AND FISCAL POLICIES

Monetary policy is generally regarded as the key to curbing inflation. To combat inflation, the Bank of Canada will have to impose a *tight-money policy* consisting of higher interest rates[2] and reduced availability of credit. By slowing the growth of the money supply, such a policy will ease the pressures of excess demand on prices and help to restrain inflation. It is generally accepted among economists that no anti-inflation policy can succeed unless it includes control of the rate of growth of the money supply. Whatever else is done to curb inflation, monetary restraint is essential, since if money is created too rapidly, its value will decline (because prices of goods and services will rise).

It was mainly through monetary policy that the Great Inflation of the 1970's was brought under control. Following 1975, the Bank of Canada established publicly stated limits for the growth of the money supply, as measured by M1. Finally, it was a period of very "tight money" in the form of record-high interest rates in 1981–82 that brought the Great Inflation to an end by depressing borrowing and aggregate demand so severely that it also brought on the "Great Recession" of the early 1980's.

Fiscal policy can also be used to combat inflation. The federal government can reduce government spending and increase taxes in order to depress aggregate demand in the economy. The most likely approach is for the government to cut back on government expenditures.[3]

... the fact is that no strategy for dealing with inflation will succeed unless it is well supported by firm and continuing control of the rate of monetary expansion. That proposition is as well established as any general proposition in the whole field of economics, and its acceptance is a basic requirement for any useful debate on how to control inflation.

Gerald K. Bouey, Governor of the Bank of Canada,
in Bank of Canada *Review* November 1980 (page 8)

Such measures will be especially helpful in slowing inflation if they reduce the need for the government to increase the money supply to finance its expenditures.

Serious use of fiscal policy to combat inflation would involve a federal government *budget surplus,* with government expenditures less than tax revenues. However, as noted in Chapter 25, the last federal budget surplus was in 1974.

Side effects of monetary and fiscal policies

The monetary and fiscal policies described above will slow down inflation, but by depressing aggregate demand they will also slow down the economy, causing unemployment to rise. In particular, the high interest rates associated with tight money are likely to depress capital investment spending and the capital-goods industries, as well as the demand for housing and "big-ticket" consumer items. Thus, combatting inflation with monetary and fiscal policies involves the sacrifice of other important economic goals, such as full employment and economic growth.

THE IMPORTANCE OF PRICE AND WAGE FLEXIBILITY

Anti-inflation policies that depress aggregate demand will put downward pressure on either *prices and wages* or on *output and employment,* or on both. The more that prices and wages fall in response to reduced demand, the less that output and employment will have to fall. Monetary and fiscal policies will be more successful in curbing inflation if prices and wages are flexible: that is, in response to lower demand, they should fall (or at least stop rising). Otherwise, anti-inflation policies will not only be less successful in combatting inflation, but will also cause greater declines in output and employment.

Unfortunately, a factor that complicates the problem of combatting inflation in Canada is that many prices and incomes are not flexible in this way, but rather are quite resistant to downward pressure from depressed demand. There are various reasons for this lack of flexibility: many employees in Canada are unionized; much of the economy consists of large corporations or government enterprises which are not subject to strong competition; and the production of many farm products is regulated by producers' marketing boards, the objective of which is to support prices. So when aggregate demand is depressed by anti-inflation policies, many prices and incomes do not decline, and the rate of inflation is not curbed by as much as would be ideal. Consequently, the burden of depressed aggregate demand falls more heavily on *output and employment,* and unemployment tends to rise quite sharply when anti-inflation policies are imposed.

RECENT EXPERIENCE WITH MONETARY AND FISCAL POLICIES

Since the mid-1970's, Canadian fiscal policy has been anything but anti-inflationary, with very large federal budget deficits every year, even in years when inflation was severe. Because of this, the burden of combatting inflation has fallen entirely upon monetary policy and the Bank of Canada. The result has been *unusually high interest rates* in Canada for many years, and especially during the periods of anti-inflation policies in the early 1980's and the late 1980's/early 1990's.

Such high interest rates created difficulties for many borrowers, including home-buyers and businesses, not to mention the federal government itself, which found that very heavy interest payments on its past borrowing were forcing it even further into debt in the late 1980's, as we have seen.

As a result, these anti-inflation policies (high interest rates, scarce credit, cuts in government spending) and their side effects (slower growth and higher unemployment) tend to be economically and socially damaging and politically unpopular, making it difficult for governments to persist in using them for long. Despite their problems, these policies, particularly monetary restraint, are generally regarded as essential to combatting inflation, because only these policies attack the excessive aggregate demand that is the root cause of inflation.

(B) WAGE-PRICE GUIDELINES AND CONTROLS

On rare occasions, when inflation has become very severe and is being made worse by strong "inflation psychology" that is generating large pay increases that are creating powerful "cost-push" pressures on costs and prices, governments may resort to more direct attempts to curb wage and price increases. Governments may do this through wage-price *guidelines* or wage-price *controls*.

Wage-price guidelines

The government may adopt a moderate approach to cost-push pressures, and simply set **wage-price guidelines** to monitor price increases: the guidelines might state, for instance, that wages should not rise faster than 5 percent per year and price increases should be limited to 3 percent per year (the other 2 percent being absorbed by rising productivity). Corporations and labor unions could then be asked to respect the public interest by following these guidelines in their wage negotiations and pricing decisions.

While this approach seems simple in theory, in practice it encounters several serious problems, the basic one being that wage-price guidelines are *voluntary*. As a result, there is a danger that economically powerful corporations and labor unions will not cooperate with the government and will ignore the guidelines, especially if aggregate demand is high enough to be putting upward pressure on wages and prices. In these circumstances, guidelines ask unionists and businesses to voluntarily refrain from increasing their wages and prices as much as they could, forcing the leaders of these organizations to choose between the interests of their union members or shareholders and some vaguely expressed concept of social responsibility. As a result, experience has been that wage-price guidelines generally prove ineffective as an anti-inflation policy.[4]

Wage-price controls

Under **wage-price controls**, it is *illegal* to increase prices and wages more rapidly than as specified by the government. Penalties for doing so range from having the excessive increases "rolled back" to the allowable limit, to fines or (in some countries) even imprisonment or death.

The most extreme form of control is a freeze on all wages and prices, but most control systems do allow wages and prices to rise at limited rates. For example, Canada's controls from 1975 to 1978 allowed wages to rise by 10, 8 and 6 percent in 1976, 1977 and 1978 respectively, and allowed prices to rise enough to offset increases in production costs per unit.

To people who are frustrated by rapidly rising prices and/or who believe in the "villain theories" that portray big business and labor unions as the root causes of inflation, controls seem an apparently simple solution to the problem: why not just stop inflation by making it illegal to increase prices and wages beyond certain limits? However, the vast majority of economists view wage-price controls much less favorably, for three reasons: controls are usually not an effective means of dealing with inflation, they usually have negative side-effects on the economy and they involve severe administrative problems. We will consider each of these problems in the following sections.

The problem of ineffectiveness: attacking symptoms rather than causes

The basic problem with wage-price controls is that they attack the *symptoms* of inflation rather than its *causes*, and therefore cannot succeed. As we have seen, the basic cause of inflation is excess demand for goods, services and labor, fuelled by rapid growth of the money supply. The rapid price and wage increases that result are merely the symptoms of the problem. Unless the cause is attacked (by policies that restrain money-supply growth and spending in the economy), the demand pressure on prices and wages will continue, as willing buyers compete for goods, services and labor.

Under these circumstances, both theory and experience suggest that the controls will not be effective because people will find ways to *evade* them.

JOHN KENNETH GALBRAITH (1908–)

John Kenneth Galbraith, professor of economics at Harvard University, is probably the most prominent Canadian-born economist in the world. Much of his prominence arises from the fact that he disagrees with conventional economists on most matters and writes not for other economists, but for the mass market. Indeed, his books have often been best sellers. He has had a particularly colorful career in politics, which has included acting as an adviser to John F. Kennedy, and serving as US ambassador to India.

Galbraith is particularly critical of economic theories (such as laissez-faire) that place faith in economic freedom, competition and free markets as the best way to promote economic prosperity. These theories, he claims, are from an earlier time characterized by small, independent businesses. They are made obsolete by the rise of the giant corporation, which manipulates the demand side of the marketplace through advertising and, in concert with its supposed competitors, controls both the supply and the price of its products.

Furthermore, he argues, the modern problem of inflation is linked directly to the economic power of the large labor unions and corporations, which generates a continual tendency toward cost-push inflation. The only way to curb inflation, says Galbraith, is through a permanent system of wage-price controls which will prevent the abuse of the power enjoyed by these large employers and powerful unions.

Galbraith's ideas have been less well-received by the economics profession than by the general public. Economists point out that his criticisms apply to only that part of the economy that is dominated by large corporations, and that growing foreign competition (such as in the auto industry) has brought stronger competition to much of that sector. They also point out that the rapid growth of the service industries, which are characterized by many small businesses rather than the industrial giants on which Galbraith focuses, has made his criticisms less relevant today than they were twenty or thirty years ago. Nonetheless, he remains one of the most effective critics of the belief that free competition in the marketplace (laissez-faire) can be relied upon to resolve all economic problems.

There are so many ways of evading controls that only a few illustrations will be listed here. For example, some groups may be able to evade the controls by selling their products or services for cash or other compensation that goes undetected by the government's controllers. Faced with limits on their prices, producers may cut production costs by reducing the quality of the product. This amounts to a sort of "hidden price increase" that allows the producer to make the same profit despite the controls on prices. Also, con-

In 301 A.D., the Roman Emperor Diocletian imposed controls on all important wages and prices. To enforce his controls program, Diocletian used about half the population of Rome. The controls program failed.

trols generally limit increases in the prices of existing products, but allow for new products to be given new prices. Thus, by making minor changes in a product, it can be introduced as a "new" product with a new (and higher) price. In the same manner, previously standard features on a product such as an automobile can be made into options, available at additional cost, or a new feature, such as a warranty, can be added. When they believe controls are likely to be introduced, some businesses increase the list prices of their products, while leaving their actual selling prices unchanged. After the controls are imposed, the selling price (the actual price) can be increased as economic conditions permit, while the list price (the official price being watched by the government) remains unchanged. Regarding wage controls, employers who have high sales may wish to raise wages in violation of the controls, in order to attract and retain workers. One way to raise wages is to reclassify employees, or create new job classifications. For example, a group of Grade C widgetworkers could be upgraded to Grade B (even though they were still really Grade C), and thus given a pay raise in excess of that allowed under the controls.

The result of these evasions of the wage-price controls will be that there will exist a widespread **black market** for goods, services and labor— reflected in the difference between official (legal) prices, and the considerably higher prices that are *actually* paid. As long as there is excess demand in the economy, many people will find a way to charge (and pay) more than the controls allow. Not even the death penalty has prevented the development of such black markets in many instances, mainly because the difficulties that authorities have in detecting violations of the law make the risk of being caught reasonably low.

The examples described above represent only a few of the types of evasion of controls that are possible. These and other evasion techniques present any wage-price control agency with an impossible task of policing not only wage and price increases, but also whether product quality has been reduced in any way, whether "new" products are really new, whether options were standard features last year, whether reclassifications of workers are really justified and so on. Because they can be evaded in these ways, wage and price controls tend to be ineffective as a means of combatting inflation.

The problem of negative side effects on the economy

Monetary and fiscal policies to combat inflation produce the undesirable side effect of higher unemployment. While it may seem that wage-price controls have no such negative side effects, this is not so. In cases where controls *do*

> The historical record indicates that controls have had, at best, only a minor impact on inflation over time; that record is one of the main reasons why a strong majority of economists would argue against their use.
>
> Carl E. Beigie, *Inflation is a Social Malady*, British-North American Committee, 1979

succeed in holding down particular prices and incomes, they can have *negative effects on incentives*. In particular, controls can undermine business confidence, and thereby result in a *reduction in capital investment*, which would slow down the economy and increase unemployment. This danger is particularly great in Canada, because Canadian corporations can readily shift investment to the United States, and American corporations are likely to decide to invest in the United States rather than in Canada, as actually happened during Canada's controls program of 1975–78.

Controls can also have the side effect of reducing *incentives to work*. For example, if a doctor's income cannot be increased beyond a certain limit imposed by the government, he or she may decide to work only four days per week. These disincentives can result in reduced output of certain goods and services, or even in emigration of skilled people to other countries that do not restrict their opportunities in this way.

Related to the problems of depressed investment and reduced incentives is the problem that controls can cause *shortages* of products. For example, there are numerous examples of price controls causing farmers to refuse to bring their crops to market at uneconomical prices, and, more recently, controls on apartment rents have discouraged construction of new apartments, contributing to shortages of apartments.

Other side effects of controls are the development of widespread black markets through which the controls are evaded (as described earlier), a diminished respect for the law and the creation of a vast and expensive government bureaucracy to administer the controls.

The problem of administering wage-price controls

There are tremendous problems in administering controls over millions of prices and wages. One such problem, discussed earlier, is the "policing" of the controls in the face of a wide variety of imaginative methods of evading them. In the attempt to control evasion, what started out as an attempt to hold down prices and wages can broaden into attempts by government to control business decisions concerning product quality, the introduction of new products, product design, classification of employees, and the like. Whether the government *should* involve itself in such matters is strongly disputed by many people. However, the overriding reality is that this task is so vast and so complex that it simply *cannot* be done.

Finally, price controls involve a fundamental dilemma that greatly complicates the problem of administering them. The dilemma is that if prices are subject to simplistic limits, there is the danger that uncontrollable increases in producers' production costs may make it unprofitable to continue producing a product. For instance, if price controls limit the price of candies to a 2 percent increase but the price of key imported inputs such as sugar (the price of which is determined in international markets beyond the control of the Canadian government) rises rapidly, it may prove impossible to produce candies profitably in Canada. The result could be the discontinuing of this product line or even the closing of the company, with many workers laid off.

To avoid this, the rules for price controls would have to allow for producers to increase prices sufficiently to recover increases in their production costs. While this is a simple enough *concept*, the *application* of it in reality is an administrative nightmare. To administer price controls based on production-cost increases would require that the government subject all businesses' claims of increases in production costs to the closest scrutiny—a tremendously large task. Naturally enough, it could be expected that a government agency would develop *forms* for businesses to complete that would require businesses to document in the greatest of detail every aspect of every production cost that they claimed had increased. An example of one such form from Canada's price controls of 1975–78 is shown in Figure 29-3; the reader is encouraged to read it carefully and note that the complete regulations were 60 pages long. This made the task of complying with and enforcing the price controls almost impossibly complex.

Can controls ever be useful?

All of this does not mean that controls are *never* of any use. Notwithstanding the foregoing criticisms of controls, many economists believe that controls can serve a useful (although temporary and limited) purpose as a "supporting actor" in an anti-inflation program, under certain unusual circumstances.

Suppose inflation has become quite severe, and strong inflation psychology is generating very large wage demands that are adding considerable cost-push pressures to the situation. In these circumstances, monetary and fiscal policies will curb inflation only if applied quite severely (and painfully), and even then will only take effect after a year or so. During this period, when the monetary and fiscal policies are taking hold on the economy, controls on wages and prices can be helpful in temporarily holding down the cost-push pressures that are worsening the situation.

An example of an attempt to use controls as a partial, temporary measure is provided by Canada in the mid-1970's: by 1975, inflation rates were in excess of 10 percent per year, incomes were rising at rates of 15–20 percent per year and income expectations had become totally unrealistic. To combat inflation, the government undertook to slow down the growth of the money supply. In addition, it imposed a three-year wage and price

FIGURE 29-3 *One Section of Canada's Anti-Inflation Regulations, 1975–78*

23 (1) The maximum price that may be charged by a supplier in a compliance period for a product in a product line to which this section applies that he commenced to supply more than 182 days before the beginning of the compliance period shall be computed in the following manner:

  (a) determine for the last period that ended before October 14, 1975, or for the first fiscal period that ended more than 182 days after he commenced to supply the product line, whichever is later,

    (i) the total revenue received from the sales of the product line concerned, and

    (ii) the total allowable costs applicable to the product line in question broken into components, such components consisting of at least the cost of direct materials, direct labour and direct and indirect overhead;

  (b) determine, for each cost component referred to in subparagraph (a)(ii), the percentage, if any, by which the cost price of the component, expressed as cost per hour of labour, cost per unit of raw material or cost per unit of other input, has increased or decreased since the last day of the later of the two fiscal periods described in paragraph (a);

  (c) determine the aggregate of the numbers that result when there is added to each cost referred to in subparagraph (a)(ii) the result obtained when the cost is multiplied by the percentage determined under paragraph (b) for that cost;

  (d) divide the aggregate determined under paragraph (c) by the remainder when the target net margin percentage of the supplier in respect of the product line is subtracted from 100 percent; and

  (e) multiply the price of the product on the last day of the later of the two fiscal periods described in paragraph (a) by the quotient obtained under paragraph (d), divide the result by the amount determined under subparagraph (a)(i) and adjust the amount so calculated for variations in fixed costs and increases in volume, where applicable, the result being the maximum price that may be charged for a product included in the product line.

Anti-Inflation Act Regulations, Anti-Inflation Board

Reproduced by permission of the Minister of Supply and Services Canada.

controls program intended to curb inflationary expectations until inflation had been slowed down by the curbs on demand. In effect, the controls were used to treat the *symptoms* of the problem (rapid wage and price increases) while the *cause* (excess aggregate demand) was being attacked with monetary and fiscal policies. In this context, controls can be likened to a wet towel used to keep a patient's fever down while the antibiotics, the real cure, are working on the infection that caused the illness. No one would say that wet towels are a cure for an infection, but they can be of

> Controls are best used as a relatively temporary "shock" measure to curb self-realizing rounds of inflationary pressures and expectations arising from a sudden burst of wage or price increases.
>
> Economic Council of Canada,
> *Fourteenth Annual Review*, 1977 (page 19)

temporary assistance while the cure is being applied. Similarly, wage and price controls are best used as a temporary supplement to, not as a substitute for, real anti-inflation policies. If curbs are not placed on aggregate demand, however, controls on wages and prices cannot be effective in combating inflation.

Policies to keep inflation from becoming severe

The experience of the "Great Inflation" of the 1970's, its negative effects on the economy and the severe recession that followed it have led many observers to the view that with respect to inflation, "an ounce of prevention is worth a pound of cure"—that is, that it is far preferable to *prevent* inflation from becoming severe than to allow it to gain momentum and then have to cure it with policies that cause an economic slowdown and high unemployment.

Before considering ways to keep inflation under control, we should review the fundamental nature of inflation as outlined in Chapter 28. In the final analysis, inflation is the result of people's *unrealistic economic expectations* and their attempts—as workers, consumers, businesspersons and government leaders—to get more out of the economy than the economy is capable of producing. When these unrealistic demands are placed on the economy—in the form of excessive increases in incomes and prices or excessive spending, borrowing and increases in the money supply—the result is inflation. Ultimately, then, the key to keeping inflation from developing is for people to have realistic economic expectations and to *practise discipline* in the demands they place on the economy.

But how is such discipline to be achieved in a free society? Arguably, the key role is that of *the government*, which controls the economic policies that influence the rate of inflation. In particular, the government must exercise a strong leadership role. It must pursue moderate and reasonable fiscal and monetary policies, and resist political pressures to overstimulate the economy with large budget deficits and excessive money-supply growth. Finally, the government must be ready to address an emerging inflation problem early, so as to prevent inflationary pressures from gaining momentum, and to risk reduced short-term popularity in order to achieve the longer-term goal of keeping inflation in check.

As and when inflation begins to rise, the tricky task for central banks and governments is to know when to tighten their policies; in the past they have always acted too late.

The Economist, January 16, 1993 (page 19)

However, governments cannot be expected to carry the entire responsibility for keeping inflation in check. The attitude and expectations of the public are also important, for at least two reasons. First, in order to be elected and re-elected, governments must have the support of the public, and second, the actions of large employers and labor unions with market power can also affect the inflation situation, through "cost-push" pressures.

First, it can be argued that the government's task of containing inflation would be easier if the public had a better understanding of the economic realities of the situation and more realistic expectations as to what was economically attainable. To this end, some suggest that better education regarding economics and economic realities would make people's expectations more realistic. However, skeptics argue that all this would produce would be better-educated unrealistically greedy people (although others see increased sales of economics texts as economically beneficial). On the other hand, it can be argued that it would be easier for governments to pursue more disciplined policies if the public's understanding of the issues were better. Certainly, if the public's economic expectations are unrealistic, the government's task will be much more difficult.

Second, how can discipline be brought to bear upon the price and income decisions of large employers and labor unions that enjoy power in the marketplace? How can their economic expectations and decisions be kept in line with reality so that they do not generate "cost-push" inflationary pressures?

In a market system, *competition in the marketplace* is the key force providing such discipline, by keeping prices and wages in check. Historically, however, many Canadians have been sheltered from such competition, either through tariff protection against foreign competition, or labor unions or professional associations, or by working for large corporations or government agencies that are not subject to severe competition. In the view of many observers, these protections against competition have made the Canadian economy more susceptible than most to cost-push inflationary pressures. In recent years, however, the extent of competition faced by many Canadian producers has been increased considerably by three pol-

"It is imperative that expectations be kept in line with potentials."

Carl E. Beigie, *Inflation is a Social Malady,*
British-North American Committee, 1979

icy changes on the part of the federal government: free trade, stronger laws against price-fixing by business and reduced government regulation of some industries.

Some nations have attempted a form of *economic planning*, in which labor, business and government reach some kind of agreement on the division of the economic pie between wages, profits and taxes. The intention of such *incomes policies* is to avoid an inflationary scramble in which various groups seek to increase their own incomes and shares of the pie at the expense of other groups, with inflationary wage and price increases the result. However, incomes policies such as these do not appear to be feasible in Canada in the foreseeable future, since they require a high degree of co-ordination and cooperation on a nation-wide level between government, business and labor. Canada lacks the institutional framework to implement such an incomes policy. In particular, both business and organized labor in Canada operate in a decentralized manner. There are no nation-wide central organizations capable of speaking for either business or labor in Canada on a national level, much less making commitments for them. Furthermore, the decentralized nature of Canada's governmental system, with political authority divided among the federal government and the ten provinces (each of which has considerable authority over labor relations) is another major obstacle to this type of planning in Canada.

Finally, it can be argued that *more rapid increases in productivity* can help to keep inflation in check. Inflation occurs when people demand more from the economy than it can produce. One way to deal with this imbalance is to reduce demand, through tighter monetary and fiscal policies. Another approach to this problem (and a more positive one) is to take steps to increase the economy's ability to produce goods and services—to increase productivity, or output per worker. Rising productivity can reduce inflationary pressures in two ways: first, by making more goods and services available, demand-pull pressures can be made less severe; second, rising productivity helps to reduce cost-push pressures. For example, a 4-percent wage increase will boost labor costs per unit by 3 percent if productivity rises by only 1 percent, but if productivity rises by 3 percent labor costs per unit will increase by only 1 percent.

The major way in which productivity can be increased is through higher levels of *capital investment*, which in turn require higher levels of saving, both in the form of business profits and personal saving. A society that encourages saving and investment will tend to suffer less inflation than a nation that fails to make provisions for increasing its output in the future. Unfortunately, productivity lagged badly in Canada during the 1980's, which added to inflationary pressures.

Inflation in perspective

The task of containing inflation can be likened to the job of driving a large truck down a steep mountain grade. The truck is capable of gaining so much momentum as to become dangerous, making it necessary for the driver to "gear down" quite early so as to maintain control. If this is done, the grade can be travelled safely, if somewhat slowly. However, if the driver allows the truck to gain too much momentum, it will at some point become necessary to slam on the brakes, risking serious consequences and damage.

Similarly, if the government keeps inflation from gaining momentum, many problems can be prevented. By contrast, government policies that overstimulate aggregate demand and allow inflation to gain momentum will only lead in the longer term to "inflation psychology," higher inflation, high interest rates, depressed business investment and productivity growth, and finally, to the need for the government to stop the inflation by "slamming on the brakes" with a very tight monetary policy, with an economic truck wreck in the form of recession and higher unemployment the results, as happened in 1982–83 and 1990–92.

Keeping aggregate demand, the money supply and expectations within reasonable limits is fundamental to containing inflation. Another worthwhile approach would be to improve productivity, so that the economy is better able to meet the public's expectations. Only by achieving a closer match between a society's expectations and its economic potential can inflation be kept in check.

Ultimately, the answer to inflation lies in *discipline*. Governments must practise discipline in their spending programs and in the creation of money, income earners must practise discipline in their income expectations and income increases, and society in general must practise discipline by accepting sufficiently less consumption today in order to provide the capital investment necessary to increase prosperity tomorrow. The fundamental (and unresolved) challenge underlying the problem of inflation is this: how can this discipline be achieved in a free and democratic society in which political parties must please the public in order to become the government that determines the economic policies that are essential to keeping inflation in check?

DEFINITIONS OF NEW TERMS

Real Interest Rate The rate of return earned by a lender after inflation; for instance, if the rate of interest is 7 percent and the rate of inflation is 5 percent, the real interest rate is 2 percent.

Wage-Price Guidelines Suggested limits for wage and price increases which unions and employers are asked to follow voluntarily.

Wage-Price Controls Legal limits on wage and price increases imposed by governments.

Black Markets The buying and selling of goods and services in violation of the law; in this case the law that sets limits on their prices.

CHAPTER SUMMARY

1. Inflation, especially rapid inflation, has the following negative effects: it imposes hardship on economically weak groups, it impairs long-term financial planning, it causes high interest rates that erode capital investment and thus cause economic stagnation, it can threaten output and employment by reducing exports and increasing imports, and it tends to end in a period of recession and high unemployment.

2. The most basic anti-inflation policies aim at reducing excessive aggregate demand through budget surpluses and, especially, tight money.

3. Such policies have the side effect of causing slower economic growth and higher unemployment.

4. In rare cases, when inflation has become very severe and inflation psychology is generating strong cost-push pressures, wage-price controls can make a temporary contribution to combatting inflation.

5. Unless accompanied by restraints on aggregate demand, controls cannot succeed for more than short periods. Because they attack the symptoms rather than the causes of inflation, controls can be evaded in a wide variety of ways. Also, controls tend to have negative side effects on the economy by impairing incentives to work and invest.

6. It is preferable to prevent inflation from becoming severe rather than to allow it to gain momentum and then have to "cure" it with monetary and fiscal policies that cause an economic slowdown and high unemployment.

7. Keeping inflation in check requires, above all else, strong leadership on the part of the government, especially in its monetary policies and budget policies.

8. In addition, government policies that encourage stronger competition in the marketplace will help to keep prices and wages in check.

9. Also, more rapidly rising productivity would help to keep inflation under control by absorbing wage increases without generating rapid price increases.

10. Ultimately, the answer to inflation lies in discipline: by governments in their spending and creating of money, by the public in its income expectations and by society in general in doing enough saving today to finance the investment necessary to allow the future to meet our expectations.

QUESTIONS

1. By the early 1990's, the rate of inflation was back down to the two percent per year range that had not been seen since the early 1960's. According to some observers, the period known as the "Great Inflation" had come to an end and a new period of sustained low inflation had arrived. Others disagreed, believing that governments would soon again pursue economic policies that would generate another round of high inflation. Which view has proven correct, and why do you think this has happened?

2. The text notes the importance of *expectations* regarding inflation. The "Great Recession" of 1981–82 ended the extreme inflation psychology of the 1970's, and for several years the rate of inflation was stable at around 4 percent per year until it began to rise again in the late 1980's. The severe recession of 1990–92 drove the rate of inflation even lower, to below two percent per year. By 1992–93, job security had replaced inflation as the main concern of Canadians, who settled for very small pay increases at most, and pay cuts in many instances. Since then, has inflation psychology begun to reappear among Canadians or not? Why do you think this is so?

3. In 1989, Canada entered into the Free Trade Agreement with the United States. In your view, would this agreement likely have any effect upon the importance placed by Canada's federal government upon keeping inflation under control?

4. "The government should adopt a 'zero tolerance' policy toward inflation. It should take any and all steps necessary to eliminate inflation from the economy once and for all."

   Do you agree or disagree? Why?

5. Under an arrangement known as "indexing," the government ensures that certain types of income keep up with inflation. For instance, if the Consumer Price Index increased by 3.8 percent, an "indexed" pension would increase by 3.8 percent, protecting the purchasing power of the pensioner from inflation.

   According to some people, government should "index" *everyone's* income to the rate of inflation, so that if the Consumer Price Index rose by, say, 10 percent, the government would guarantee that everyone's income rose by no less than 10 percent. (Some people would be able to increase their incomes on their own by 10 percent or more, but the government would ensure that those who could not keep up with inflation on their own would not fall behind—the government would supplement their incomes so that they would keep up with inflation.)

   Do you agree with this proposal or not? Why?

6. Suppose that all prices in Canada were frozen by law, and that the international price of various commodities imported into Canada rose. What would happen?

7. Suppose that, in an attempt to keep interest costs down during a period of severe inflation, the federal government imposed legal limits on how high interest rates could rise. What would happen?

8. In January 1994, Gordon Thiessen began a seven-year term as the Governor of the Bank of Canada. Prior to his assuming office, an agreement was reached between the federal government and the new Governor that the "target" for monetary policy would be an inflation rate of between 1 and 3 percent per year through to 1998. Has the inflation rate stayed within this range? If not, why was this target not achieved?

9. The cumulative, long-term effects of inflation are much greater than its visible impact in any one year. Using the 72 formula, calculate how long it will take prices to double if the rate of inflation is:

   (a) 1 percent per year

   (b) 3 percent per year

   (c) 6 percent per year

   (d) 9 percent per year

   (e) 12 percent per year

APPENDIX

Dealing with the "Great Inflation"

In Chapter 28, we examined the causes of the "Great Inflation" of the 1970's. In this section, the policies adopted by Canadian governments to deal with this period of exceptionally severe inflation are considered.

While some countries sought to curb this severe inflation as early as 1974 (mostly with *tight money* policies), Canada did not do so, as noted earlier. This reluctance continued until late 1975, when the problem had become so severe that something had to be done. Even then, however, the government did not combat inflation with the same determination shown by some nations.

Still fearful of the high unemployment that would result from all-out attack on inflation, the government aimed instead for a *gradual* slowing down of inflation, through three main approaches. First, and most important, the rate of growth of the *money supply* was to be gradually reduced over a period of time. Second, the government stated an intention to curb the growth of *government spending* in the future. And, finally, to reduce cost-push pressures (especially from wages), the government imposed a temporary three-year program of *wage-and-price controls*.

Canada's wage and price controls, 1975–78

From 1975 to 1978, the federal government imposed a system of wage and price controls on the Canadian economy. The controls were temporary (for a period of three years) and were intended to help contain the very strong inflation psychology that had developed until more basic policies such as a slower growth of the money supply could take effect. The controls were selective, in that they applied only to large corporations (over 500 employees), professionals, government workers and the construction industry: in total, close to 1500 firms and five million people, or about half the labor force, were affected. The allowable increases for wages and salaries were fairly simple, based on increases of 10, 8 and 6 percent in 1976, 1977 and 1978 respectively. The rules for prices, as we have seen, were more complex. To avoid discouraging production and causing unemployment, the controls allowed prices to increase by the same amount that production costs per unit rose.

Canada's controls program of 1975–78 illustrates the basic dilemma of price controls described earlier in this chapter. So that the controls would not jeopardize business incentives to produce output and employ people, businesses were allowed to increase prices to the same extent that production costs per unit increased.[5]

In avoiding the danger that the controls would cause production cutbacks and unemployment, however, the government created another monster: to administer price controls based on cost increases would require very detailed analysis of changes in the production costs of all products covered by the controls. Businesses had to comply with a multitude of regulations by completing masses of forms for an ever-growing federal bureaucracy (the Anti-Inflation Board). The administration of these rules involved bewildering regulations to be followed and forms to be completed (see Figure 29-3), which generated considerable opposition from business and made the enforcement process slow, cumbersome and of questionable validity.

Several products and services were by law specifically *exempt* from the controls, including oil and energy, rents on new apartment buildings, farm prices "at the farm gate" (that is, to the farmer), interest rates and imports. In each case, the exemption was based on legitimate economic concern that the application of the controls would cause *shortages* of these items. Higher oil prices were needed to finance exploration and development; rent controls have traditionally depressed new apartment construction; controls on food prices cause reductions in agricultural output; if Canadian interest rates fell much below US rates, Canada would be left short of vital capital as funds were shifted to the United States; and, finally, import prices are determined in world markets, so that Canada must pay the world price for imports in order to get them. While exempting these items from the controls undermined the credibility of the controls program in the eyes of the public, the results of applying the controls to these items would have been damaging, as serious shortages would have occurred.

The Anti-Inflation Board was most active in its first year (1976), when unions tested it with large wage increases, most of which were rolled back at the order of the AIB. While a few instances of excess profits and price rollbacks occurred, increasingly slow economic conditions depressed most profits anyway, making such cases rare. By 1977 and 1978, the activities of the AIB were much less noticeable, as the sluggish economy depressed both wage increases and profits. Because of these new economic conditions, the disbandment of the AIB in 1978 was not followed by an outburst of wage and price increases, as some people had expected.

On balance, Canada's wage-price controls were more effective in restraining wage increases than in holding down price increases. Wage increases were subject to clearly stated limits, whereas prices could rise to the extent that production costs per unit rose, and many items (comprising a large proportion of the Consumer Price Index) were exempt from the controls. Supporters argued that controls helped to contain wage and price increases until the monetary and fiscal policies could take effect and ease the demand pressures on prices, while their opponents said that controls had a minor effect on inflation at best, and drove capital funds out of Canada at worst. Certainly, they did not succeed in curbing the Great Inflation: the rate of inflation did not decline significantly until 1983, five years after the controls were ended.

The end of the Great Inflation

In the final analysis, the "Great Inflation" was curbed not by wage and price controls, but rather by the "Great Recession" of the early 1980's: a period of severely depressed aggregate demand and high unemployment brought on in large part by very high interest rates in-

ployment brought on in large part by very high interest rates intended to combat inflation. Under the pressure of such high unemployment, even Canada's strong wage-push pressures eased, and the rate of inflation declined from about 10 percent per year to less than 5 percent by the end of 1983. During the next recession in the early 1990's, the rate of inflation fell to below 2 percent per year. Finally, after two serious recessions, the rate of inflation was back down to the levels of the early 1960's, before inflation began to develop momentum and the "Great Inflation" began.

NOTES

1   It can be argued that these problems can be compensated for by a reduction in the international value of the Canadian dollar. For instance, if Canadian prices were 10 percent above our competitors' prices, a 10-percent decline in the international value of the Canadian dollar could occur, leaving our products no more expensive to foreign buyers because the higher prices of the products are offset by the lower price of the Canadian dollar. This, however, is not a painless solution: the lower international value of the Canadian dollar would make the prices of imported products in Canada higher, reducing Canadian living standards. Either way, our excessive inflation would hurt us. Such international matters are covered in more detail in Chapters 32–34.

2   Because interest payments are one of the costs of doing business, some people believe that the way to curb inflation is to reduce interest rates rather than increase them through a tight-money policy. While lower interest rates would have a slight cost-reducing effect on business, the "easy money" associated with lower interest rates would more than offset this gain by increasing the money supply and aggravating the problem of excess demand. In short, reducing interest rates is exactly the reverse of what is needed to combat inflation.

3   In theory, an increase in taxes (for example, personal income taxes) helps to combat inflation by reducing consumer spending and thus aggregate demand. On the other hand, a sharp tax increase could also lead wage-earners to try to increase their incomes more rapidly, causing additional cost-push pressures on prices.

4   Some people argue (cynically, but perhaps correctly) that guidelines are introduced by governments that are anxious to be able to say that they *tried* to stop inflation but that business and labor *refused to cooperate*. Thus, the political blame for inflation can be shifted onto business and labor, and away from the government—even if it was the government's own policies that in fact caused the inflation in the first place.

5   Suppose the production costs of a product were $100.00 and its selling price was $108.50. If the production costs rose to $102.13 per unit, the selling price could be increased to $110.63. Thus, while the controls were intended to prevent profits *per unit* of output from increasing, they allowed price increases sufficient to keep profits per unit constant.

CHAPTER 30

The nature of unemployment

> When somebody asks me what I do, I usually say, "I don't." As far as society is concerned, I don't contribute anything. I'm not a productive member of society.
>
> Unemployed university graduate, quoted in *The Real Costs of Unemployment*, by Richard Spence, *Financial Times*, March 19, 1984

We live in a society that places a high value on working, not only for the income that work generates but also for the contribution to society that it represents. Not surprisingly, then, there is no economic problem that has a more serious impact on people than unemployment. In addition to the economic costs of unemployment in terms of lost income and output, there are human costs associated with unemployment that cannot be measured by economic statistics. According to the Canadian Mental Health Association,

> One of unemployment's most devastating effects is its erosion of self-respect. This is a nearly universal phenomenon. It not only darkens the unemployed individual's image of life, but also puts great stress on the quality of family relations.
>
> Our association's studies have cited numerous investigations that indicate a strong positive correlation between increased rates of unemployment and various manifestations of loss of self-respect, such as increases in depression, anxiety, self-deprecation, fatalism, anger, spouse abuse, child abuse, mental hospital admissions, homicides, rape, property crimes, racism, youth alienation, children's problems in school, and divorce. Almost every painful social consequence known to humankind is related to unemployment. Just as a phys-

ically unhealthy society is costly, so too is one that is socially and psychologically destructive.[1]

Since the Great Depression of the 1930's, the single most basic goal of government economic policy-makers has been the minimization of unemployment, mainly through the use of monetary and fiscal policies. As a result, the thirty years following the end of the Second World War in 1945 were, with some relatively brief exceptions, characterized by lower unemployment rates than in the past. However, in the second half of the 1970's, the unemployment rate drifted upwards again, and when the "Great Recession" struck in the early 1980's, Canada experienced its highest unemployment rates in a half-century, with nearly one in eight Canadians jobless, and nearly one in five young Canadians out of work. Following six years of declining unemployment rates, the recession of the early 1990's brought another period of serious unemployment.

Causes of unemployment

On a macroeconomic scale, unemployment arises from an imbalance between the _supply of labor_ (or the number of people wanting to work) and the _demand for labor_ (or the number of jobs available). Therefore, unemployment can be affected by developments on both the supply side and the demand side of labor markets.

THE SUPPLY SIDE

As Figure 30-1 shows, the number of people available for work (the labor force) depends on two factors:

(a) the size of the population of working age, and

(b) the percentage of this group that wishes to work (the "**participation rate**").

In the example in Figure 30-1, there are 20 million people of working age, 66 percent of whom wish to work, making the labor force 13.2 million.

In Canada since 1970, both of the factors noted above have contributed significantly to unemployment. In the 1970's, there was a very rapid increase in the number of people of working age, as large numbers of baby boomers reached this age. In addition, the participation rate increased sharply, from 57 percent in the mid-1960's to 67 percent by the late 1980's. This was attributable entirely to increased labor force activity on the part of women, whose participation rate increased from 36 percent in the mid-1960's to 58 percent in the late 1980's, adding greatly to the size of Canada's labor force.

FIGURE 30-1 *The Determinants of Unemployment*

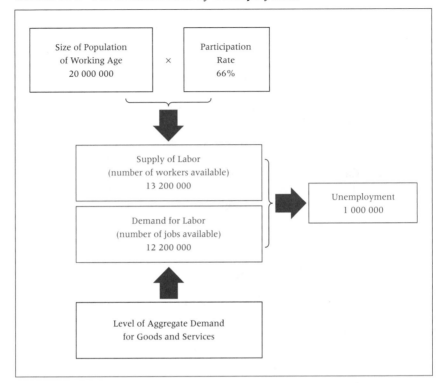

THE DEMAND SIDE

Figure 30-1 also shows that the other major factor influencing the level of unemployment is the *demand for labor*, or the number of jobs available. The main factor determining the demand for labor is the level of *aggregate demand* for goods and services. The level of aggregate demand determines the level of output of goods and services, and thus the number of employees required by employers.[2]

The most common cause of periodic increases in unemployment is a weakening of aggregate demand. This normally happens during recessions or when the government is pursuing anti-inflation policies that depress aggregate demand. On the other hand, when the economy is booming and aggregate demand is high, unemployment declines.

The level of aggregate demand is considered a basic factor influencing unemployment for another reason. While in a dynamic market economy some people will lose their jobs due to factors such as changes in demand, technology and competition, they will be less likely to remain unemployed for long if there is enough aggregate demand in the economy to create other job opportunities for them. Thus, because it is the key to the number of jobs available, the level of aggregate demand is a key to the level of unemployment.

Aspects of unemployment in Canada

Wide fluctuations in unemployment rates from year to year are a characteristic of the Canadian economy. As Figure 30-2 shows, the unemployment rate has fluctuated greatly since the 1920's, with unemployment ranging from less than 2 percent to nearly 20 percent of the labor force. This instability mainly reflects the fact that unemployment has increased whenever the economy has experienced a recession, most notably in the 1930's, the late 1950's to the early 1960's, the early 1980's and the early 1990's. In addition, there are other sources of variations in unemployment, as described in the following sections.

Unlike the "leading economic indicators" discussed in Chapter 24, the unemployment rate is considered to be a "lagging economic indicator," because it usually increases after a recession has begun and declines only *after* the economy is into its recovery phase. The reason for this pattern is that employers tend to delay layoffs until these are necessary, carry some surplus workers through a recession, and when the economy recovers can often get increased production from their work force without increasing the number of workers, at least for a while.

TYPES AND DURATION OF UNEMPLOYMENT

Unemployment can be classified into four basic types, depending on its origin and duration.

FIGURE 30-2   *Unemployment Rates, 1926–93*

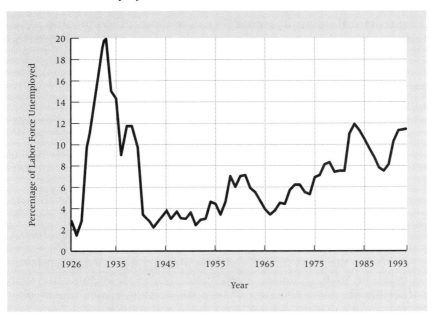

Source: Statistics Canada

Frictional unemployment, which arises when people are temporarily out of work because they are changing from one job to another, is the briefest type of unemployment. Frictional unemployment is considered to be a normal process in a free and dynamic economy, and probably averages about one percent of the labor force. Frictional unemployment tends to be higher in periods of prosperity when job opportunities are more plentiful, and lower during recessions, when fewer people are able to change jobs.

Seasonal unemployment is also relatively short-term in nature. Mainly because of the seasonal nature of economic activity in industries such as agriculture and fishing, unemployment is highest in the winter months of January through March, and lowest from June through October. Such seasonal factors probably add about 200 000 people to the ranks of the unemployed during the winter. Seasonal unemployment usually lasts a few months, during which unemployment insurance benefits reduce the economic costs for many of those who are seasonally unemployed.

Cyclical unemployment, which arises from periodic recessions, is a more serious matter for many workers. The risk of cyclical unemployment is higher in industries that are strongly affected by recessions, including capital goods, construction and consumer durables, such as automobile manufacturing. Depending on one's seniority and the severity of the recession, a layoff due to cyclical forces may be quite short or quite long. While the *average* duration of unemployment during a recession seldom exceeds 20 weeks and thus is covered by unemployment insurance, for *some* workers it can be much longer. In some such cases, the period of unemployment may exceed the one-year time limit on unemployment insurance benefits, forcing the unemployed worker into a very difficult position.

Structural unemployment is an even more serious problem for affected workers, because of its longer-term nature. The major causes of structural unemployment are changes in product demand or production technology. Changes in product demand can cause the decline of not just particular companies, but also entire industries, and changes in technology can leave laid-off workers with inadequate or outdated skills. The result is a *mismatch* of the training and skills required by employers and those possessed by unemployed workers, which can make it very difficult for the unemployed to find work. A contributing factor to structural unemployment is the inadequacy of apprenticeship programs administered by labor unions and industry, which has contributed to the mismatch between the skills of workers and the requirements of jobs. When there is still considerable unemployment even though the economy is buoyant enough for there to be job vacancies, this is considered to be evidence that structural unemployment exists.

Probably the most serious example of structural unemployment in Canada is in Atlantic Canada, where the decline of whole industries such as coal mining, shipbuilding and shipping has left entire communities with high unemployment for many years. Indeed, the most serious aspect of structural unemployment is that it can become very long-term in nature, forcing the unemployed—and in some cases whole communities—to fall back on welfare as a way of life.

THE DISTRIBUTION OF UNEMPLOYMENT BY REGION, AGE AND SEX

There are significant differences in unemployment rates in Canada for different regions and for different age and sex groups. The differences in regional unemployment rates shown in Figure 30-3 are largely the result of structural unemployment as described in the previous section.

The age and sex distribution of unemployment is also noteworthy. As Figure 30-4 shows, unemployment rates are particularly high among *young people* (ages 15–24). Generally, the unemployment rate for the 15–24 age group tends to be about 60 percent higher than the national average un-

FIGURE 30-3   *Unemployment Rates by Region, 1966–93*

		Unemployment Rates				
Year	Canada	Atlantic region	Quebec	Ontario	Prairie region	British Columbia
1966	3.4	4.9	4.1	2.6	2.3	4.6
1967	3.8	5.0	4.6	3.2	2.6	5.1
1968	4.5	5.4	5.6	3.6	3.2	5.9
1969	4.4	5.7	6.1	3.2	3.3	5.0
1970	5.7	5.7	7.0	4.4	5.0	7.7
1971	6.2	6.5	7.3	4.4	5.0	7.2
1972	6.2	7.6	7.5	5.0	5.3	7.8
1973	5.5	7.3	6.8	4.3	4.6	6.7
1974	5.3	8.0	6.6	4.4	3.4	6.2
1975	6.9	9.8	8.1	6.3	4.0	8.5
1976	7.1	10.8	8.7	6.2	4.1	8.6
1977	8.1	12.5	10.3	7.0	4.8	8.5
1978	8.3	12.5	10.9	7.2	5.2	8.3
1979	7.4	11.6	9.6	6.5	4.3	7.6
1980	7.5	11.1	9.8	6.8	4.3	6.8
1981	7.5	11.5	10.3	6.6	4.5	4.7
1982	11.0	14.3	13.8	9.7	7.6	12.1
1983	11.8	15.0	13.9	10.3	9.6	13.8
1984	11.2	15.2	12.8	9.0	9.8	14.7
1985	10.5	15.7	11.8	8.0	9.1	14.1
1986	9.5	14.8	11.0	7.0	8.8	12.5
1987	8.8	13.9	10.3	10.3	8.6	11.9
1988	7.8	12.4	9.4	5.0	7.9	10.3
1989	7.5	12.4	9.3	5.1	7.3	9.1
1990	8.1	12.8	10.1	6.3	7.1	8.3
1991	10.3	14.0	11.9	9.6	8.2	9.9
1992	11.3	14.9	12.8	10.8	9.2	10.4
1993	11.2	15.3	13.1	10.6	9.2	9.7

Source: Statistics Canada, *Historical Labour Force Statistics* (71-201)

employment rate; for example, if the national average unemployment rate were 10 percent, the youth unemployment rate would likely be in the range of 16 percent.

Unemployment rates for the young tend to be higher for various reasons. When the economy slows down, employers tend to reduce or cease hiring, leaving many young people who are trying to enter the labor force unable to find work. Also, layoffs are most commonly done by seniority, and, therefore, hit the young hardest. In addition, young people tend to experience much higher-than-average frictional unemployment, because people move more frequently from job to job early in their careers. Another factor underlying Canada's high rate of youth unemployment is believed to be Canada's minimum wage laws, which require minimum wage rates for younger workers that are the same as or not much less than those for more experienced workers, making it relatively less attractive to employ young people.

As Figure 30-4 also shows, the unemployment rate for males tends to be slightly lower than for females in most years, but higher than for females during recessions such as 1982–83 and the early 1990's. Recessions tend to have an especially severe impact on employment in the goods industries such as construction and manufacturing, in which most employees are males.

The highest unemployment rates tend to be among young males, while males aged 25 and older have historically had the lowest unemployment rates. However, in 1991–92, women aged 25 and over had the lowest unemployment rates, as the recession struck especially hard at the male work force, especially in the manufacturing sector.

The uneven distribution of unemployment in Canada among different age groups, industries and regions creates problems for governments seeking to reduce unemployment by increasing aggregate demand. Even if aggregate demand in the Canadian economy *as a whole* were high enough to reduce the overall nationwide unemployment rate to a quite low level, there would still be substantial *pockets of unemployment* in certain regions and industries and high unemployment rates among certain groups, especially the young.

TECHNOLOGICAL UNEMPLOYMENT?

For many years, improved production technology has reduced the number of workers needed to produce a given level of output, especially in goods-producing industries such as agriculture and manufacturing. In some cases, the introduction of new technology has led to layoffs of workers, leading to an ongoing controversy over whether technological change creates unemployment.

While no one disputes that new technology displaces *some* workers from their jobs, it also has certain job-creating effects that are less visible. The major such effect is that as technology has raised productivity, it has

FIGURE 30-4   *Unemployment by Sex and Age Groups, 1967–93*

| | Unemployment Rate | | | | | | |
| | Males | | | Females | | | Overall |
Year	Total	15–24	25+	Total	15–24	25+	Total
1967	3.9%	7.2%	3.0%	3.7%	5.5%	2.8%	3.8
1968	4.6	8.7	3.5	4.4	6.5	3.3	4.5
1969	4.3	8.3	3.2	4.7	6.5	3.7	4.4
1970	5.6	11.2	4.1	5.8	8.6	4.4	5.7
1971	6.0	12.0	4.3	6.6	9.8	5.0	6.2
1972	5.8	11.9	4.1	7.0	9.6	5.7	6.2
1973	4.9	10.0	3.4	6.7	9.2	5.4	5.5
1974	4.8	9.6	3.3	6.4	8.9	5.1	5.3
1975	6.2	12.5	4.3	8.1	11.4	6.5	6.9
1976	6.3	13.2	4.2	8.4	12.1	6.6	7.1
1977	7.3	14.9	4.9	9.4	13.8	7.4	8.1
1978	7.5	15.0	5.2	9.6	13.8	7.7	8.3
1979	6.6	13.2	4.5	8.8	12.7	7.0	7.4
1980	6.9	13.7	4.8	8.4	12.6	6.5	7.5
1981	7.0	14.1	4.8	8.3	12.3	6.5	7.5
1982	11.0	21.1	8.2	10.9	16.1	8.8	11.0
1983	12.0	22.3	9.2	11.6	17.0	9.6	11.8
1984	11.2	19.3	9.0	11.3	16.1	9.7	11.2
1985	10.3	18.1	8.3	10.7	14.5	9.4	10.5
1986	9.3	16.4	7.6	9.8	13.6	8.6	9.5
1987	8.5	14.8	7.0	9.3	12.4	8.3	8.8
1988	7.4	12.9	6.0	8.3	11.0	7.5	7.8
1989	7.3	12.4	6.1	7.9	10.1	7.3	7.5
1990	8.1	14.0	6.8	8.1	11.4	7.3	8.1
1991	10.8	18.8	9.1	9.7	13.4	8.8	10.3
1992	12.0	20.2	10.4	10.4	15.2	9.3	11.3
1993	11.7	20.2	10.1	10.6	15.0	9.6	11.2

Source: Statistics Canada, *Historical Labour Force Statistics* (71–201)

also raised living standards and disposable income; as a result, aggregate demand has risen, generating new jobs to replace those eliminated by technology. In addition, by making Canadian producers more efficient and more internationally competitive, technology can generate additional jobs. Generally, economists have found that (at least so far), on balance, technological change has not caused unemployment rates to rise (see Figure 30-5).

This is not to say that technological change does not have strong effects on unemployment among specific groups of people, especially when depressed aggregate demand makes alternative jobs scarce. All things considered, however, the level of aggregate demand is a much more important factor than technological change in determining the unemployment rate. Periods of high unemployment have been associated with low aggregate demand rather than rapid technological change.

FIGURE 30-5 *Technological Progress and Employment*

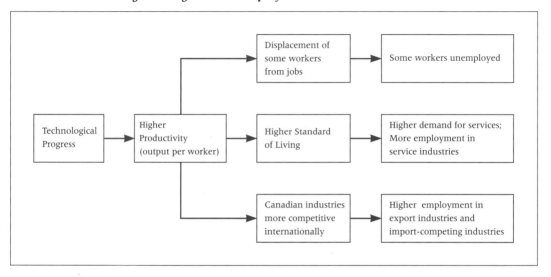

Measuring unemployment

Unemployment rate statistics are not only very important economically; they are probably the most politically sensitive of all economic statistics. However, it is neither easy to define what unemployment is nor to measure it precisely. As a result, unemployment rate statistics are open to different interpretations and are the subject of some controversy. For this reason, we should review the way in which unemployment is defined and measured in Canada, so as to understand the statistics as well as possible.

As described in Chapter 20, unemployment-rate statistics are the product of a monthly survey of about 56 000 households across Canada, which is intended to determine whether respondents are employed or unemployed (and available for work). The **labor force** is the total of the employed and the unemployed, and the **unemployment rate** is the number of unemployed expressed as a percentage of the labor force. Thus, if there were 9 million people employed and 1 million unemployed, the labor force would be 10 million and the unemployment rate would be 10 percent, as the illustration in Figure 30-6 shows.

FIGURE 30-6 *Calculation of the Unemployment Rate*

Labor Force Survey: Employed   :   9 000 000
                         Unemployed :   1 000 000
                         Labor Force :   10 000 000

$$\text{Unemployment Rate} = \frac{\text{Unemployed}}{\text{Labor Force}} = \frac{1\ 000\ 000}{10\ 000\ 000} = 10\%$$

In the labor force survey, a person will be counted as unemployed if, during the survey week, he or she was:

(a) without work, had actively looked for work during the past four weeks and was available for work, or

(b) had not actively looked for work in the past four weeks but had been on layoff for 26 weeks or less and was available for work, or

(c) had not actively looked for work in the past four weeks but had a new job to start in four weeks and was available for work.

Thus, people are counted as "unemployed" if they reply to the survey that they are *out of work* and *available for work* and *seeking work*. There has been considerable debate in recent years over the accuracy and the significance of these unemployment-rate statistics. Some observers argue that the official statistics underestimate the extent of unemployment, while others assert that they overestimate it.

HIDDEN UNEMPLOYMENT

Those who believe that the official statistics underestimate unemployment base their argument on what is called **hidden unemployment**. According to their argument, large numbers of Canadians can be described as "discouraged workers"—people who have given up looking for work, mainly because they believe jobs are not available. As a result, such people are excluded from the unemployment and labor force statistics altogether, and are missed when the jobless data are gathered.

It is generally agreed that hidden unemployment is higher in regions of chronically high unemployment. For instance, in the Atlantic provinces, the highest participation rate ever was 60.1 percent in 1990, as compared to a participation rate of 67.0 percent for Canada as a whole, suggesting that fewer people look for work in this region of high unemployment. Hidden unemployment also tends to grow during recessions, when some people give up looking for work. For instance, the nationwide participation rate fell from 67.0 percent in 1989 to 65.5 percent in the recession year 1992, reflecting the withdrawal of about 316 000 people from the labor force. If those people had been counted as unemployed, the unemployment rate in 1992 would have been 13.3 percent rather than the official rate of 11.3 percent.

VOLUNTARY UNEMPLOYMENT

Other people argue that the official unemployment statistics have become a misleadingly *high* indicator of the number of Canadians who are unemployed, because the statistics include a considerable number of people who report themselves as unemployed but who will not take jobs that are available.

According to this view, the availability of unemployment insurance benefits for up to a year encourages some recipients to be more selective regarding the jobs that they will take, prolonging their period of unemployment and adding to the unemployment rate. This type of **voluntary unemployment** is more likely to occur in households that have more than one income, a situation that became increasingly common after the early 1970's. It is difficult to measure the extent of voluntary unemployment, but those studies that have been done estimate it to be between 1 and 1.5 percent of the labor force. Viewed from another perspective, this would be between 10 and 15 percent of total unemployment in Canada in recent years, or up to 200 000 people.

To the extent that voluntary unemployment exists, the significance of unemployment statistics is obscured somewhat, because some of the unemployed are second (or third) income-earners in a household who are not suffering real economic hardship. Also, the existence of voluntary unemployment would make it more difficult for the government to reduce the unemployment rate beyond a certain point. As a result, it would become necessary to accept a higher unemployment rate than would otherwise be considered acceptable.

INTERPRETING UNEMPLOYMENT RATE STATISTICS

As a result of the factors described above, unemployment rate statistics should be interpreted with some caution. In particular, it is likely that during recessions, the official unemployment rate statistics *understate* the extent of unemployment, due to the growth of hidden unemployment. On the other hand, during periods of economic boom and low unemployment rates, the official statistics probably *exaggerate* the extent of unemployment, because they include those who are voluntarily unemployed.

Canada's unemployment problem

As Figure 30-7 shows, while the unemployment rate fluctuates considerably from year to year, the average unemployment rate has tended to move upwards over the past 25 years. By 1994, Canada was in its fourth consecutive year of double-digit unemployment rates, with little improvement foreseen by most observers. Why has unemployment increased in this way? There is no simple answer to this question. At various times, factors that operate on the demand side of labor markets have increased unemployment, while at other times supply-side factors have added to the unemployment rate.

FIGURE 30-7   *Unemployment Rates, 1960–93*

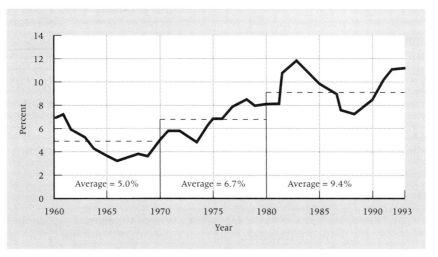

Source: Department of Finance, *Economic and Fiscal Reference Tables*, August 1993

THE 1970'S

The main forces pushing unemployment upwards in the 1970's were on the *supply side* of the labor market. Two developments caused the labor force, or the supply of labor, to increase at exceptionally rapid rates (over 3 percent per year). Firstly, large numbers of the "baby boomers" born in the 1946–66 period came of working age during the 1970's. This *influx of young people* caused the labor force to grow exceptionally rapidly, so that even in years when employment grew strongly, not all these new job-seekers could find work. As a result, there was a great deal of youth unemployment during this period. Secondly, changes in the role and status of women led to a significant increase in the number of *women seeking work* outside the home. Married women, in particular, began looking for jobs, to provide a needed second income for households. From 1961 to 1980, the participation rate for women more than doubled, rising from 23 percent to 50 percent, as women sought work in unprecedented numbers. This move toward fuller economic participation by women added substantially to the growth of the labor force—and thus to *both* employment and unemployment.

Perhaps the most important labor force development in this period (the 1970's) was the increase in the proportion of married women in the labor force.

Industrial Relations Centre, Queen's University,
The Current Industrial Relations Scene in Canada, 1980

Another factor affecting the supply side of labor markets in the 1970's was the 1971 revision of the *Unemployment Insurance Act*. As noted earlier, it is believed that the improvements to UI benefits increased voluntary unemployment by encouraging prolonged and selective job searches by some UI recipients. A study for the Economic Council of Canada estimated that the UI revisions added as much as 1.5 percentage points to the unemployment rate. This finding was supported by the fact that even in the exceptionally strong economic boom of 1973, with aggregate demand at highly inflationary levels, the unemployment rate did not go below 5.5 percent. On the basis of past experience, an unemployment rate of less than 4 percent could have been expected under such boom conditions.

THE 1980'S

In the 1980's, the growth of the labor force slowed to below 2 percent per year, greatly reducing the supply-side pressures that had dominated the picture in the 1970's. However, the average unemployment rate again moved upwards, for quite different reasons: first because of conditions on the *demand side* of the economy, and later because of *structural factors*.

On the demand side, the most dramatic factor driving unemployment higher was of course *the Great Recession*. In 1982, the recession drove employment down by 362 000, unemployment up by 416 000 and the unemployment rate from 7.5 percent to 11 percent in a single year. To make matters worse, the recovery from the recession was slow, so that unemployment remained high for several years.

But there was more to the unemployment problems of the 1980's than simply the Great Recession. By 1987–89, the economic recovery had become quite strong in central Canada and especially Ontario, where the unemployment rate fell below 5 percent at times and the biggest problem was finding people to fill vacant jobs. Despite this, however, the *national average* unemployment rate went no lower than 7.5 percent, because in other regions unemployment was still high, as Figure 30-3 showed.

What was causing this? There was general agreement that the problem was not simply weak aggregate demand—aggregate demand was so high that inflation had become a major concern by 1988. And it was not simply rapid labor-force growth as in the 1970's, because, as we have said, the labor force was growing at less than 2 percent per year. Rather, the persistently high unemployment of the second half of the 1980's seemed to be due to *structural unemployment*.

There was considerable evidence to support the view that Canada was experiencing a problem of structural unemployment:

- a growing number of job vacancies that went unfilled despite the existence of unemployment
- a growing incidence of long-term unemployment (53 weeks or more), which increased from around 4 or 5 percent of job-seekers in 1980–82 to 10 percent in 1983–87.

The matching process is, above all, a dynamic one. The labor market is in a constant state of flux, with workers entering and leaving the labor force, finding and losing jobs, and moving from one job to another.... At any moment in time, however, a certain number of unemployed persons (people without jobs) and a certain number of job vacancies (jobs without people) will coexist. Much of the unemployment, and many of the vacancies, will be short-lived (or "frictional"), reflecting only the time required for the parties to acquire the requisite information and make the necessary arrangements. Mismatches may also persist over a long period of time, however. A considerable body of evidence suggests that it is precisely the increase in the amount of mismatch that explains the rise in structural unemployment rates at the national level, as well as the increasing disparity between regional unemployment rates.

Economic Council of Canada, *Twenty-Fifth Annual Review*, 1988

All of these trends indicated that increasingly, the skills and abilities of the unemployed did not match the requirements of jobs that were vacant.

Studies suggest that two major economic forces contributed to rising structural unemployment in Canada during the 1980's:

(a) The shift from a goods-producing economy to a services-producing economy

(b) Weaker world markets for Canadian resource exports

(a) The shift from a goods-producing economy to a services-producing economy

Over the long term, the proportion of Canadians employed in goods-producing industries has gradually declined, while the proportion employed in the services sector has increased, due to changes in both technology and demand. As technology has increased productivity (output per worker) in goods-producing industries, employment in that sector has grown relatively slowly. In addition, as living standards have risen, the demand for services (such as restaurants, entertainment, travel, etc.) has risen rapidly, generating rapid employment growth in the services sector, which is labor-intensive.

The overall result has been a gradual but important shift in the nature of work, with the service sector's share of total employment rising from 44 to 73 percent from 1951 to 1992, and the goods sector's share declining from 56 to 27 percent over the same period. Such shifts in the nature of work change the skills required of workers, generating some structural unemployment among those who have difficulty adapting to the changes. According to the Economic Council of Canada, the pace of this change increased after 1980, adding to structural unemployment.

> ... The movement from a goods-producing system toward a service-based one quickened. These effects were reflected in an acceleration of the rate at which jobs disappeared, as well as in a radical shift in the nature of the new jobs being offered. The net result was an increase in the degree of structural mismatch in the economy at any given time.
>
> Economic Council of Canada, *Twenty-Fifth Annual Review*, 1988

(b) Weaker world markets for Canadian resource exports

For various reasons (including slower growth of demand, increased competition from foreign countries, and new technologies), world markets for many Canadian resource exports were relatively weak in the 1980's. This depressed the economies of regions that are dependent upon certain resource exports, and increased disparities among regional unemployment rates.

> Whereas resources accounted for 40 per cent of Canada's exports in 1963, that figure had fallen to only 22 percent in 1987.
>
> Economic Council of Canada, *Twenty-Fifth Annual Review*, 1988

Regions dependent upon resource exports, especially British Columbia and the Prairie provinces, experienced more severe problems with structural unemployment than did central Canada. As structural unemployment increased, regional unemployment disparities in Canada worsened and long-term unemployment became more of a problem.

YOUTH UNEMPLOYMENT

Youth unemployment (defined as unemployment among the 15–24 age group) was a particular problem in the 1970's. At that time, such large numbers of baby boomers were entering the labor force that many had trouble finding work, even in years when total employment was rising quite rapidly. As a result, youth unemployment amounted to nearly half of total unemployment in the mid-1970's.

However, youth unemployment became less of a problem in the 1980's, as the numbers of young people entering the labor force actually fell. The youth labor force peaked in size in 1981 at 3 074 000; from then until 1992, the size of the youth labor force decreased by 21 percent to 2 420 000. In 1981, 45 percent of the unemployed in Canada were aged 15–24; by 1992, youths accounted for only 28 percent of total unemployment, making youth unemployment much less of a national political concern than it had been a decade earlier.

THE 1990'S

The early 1990's saw a serious deterioration of the employment situation,
in terms of both the extent of unemployment and the prospects for improvement. From a 1989 low of 7.5 percent, the unemployment rate rose
to 11.3 percent by 1992–93. The official statistics understated the true extent of unemployment, however, for two reasons. First, there was considerable "hidden unemployment" as over 300 000 "discouraged workers"
stopped looking for work. If these people had been counted as unemployed,
the unemployment rate would have been over 13 percent. Second, a growing proportion of the jobs that did exist were part-time jobs. In 1993, 40 percent of all part-time workers really wanted full-time work but were unable
to find it. The numbers of such people had doubled from 1990 to 1993,
meaning that about 880 000 Canadians who were recorded as "employed"
were really partially unemployed. In addition, more of the unemployed
were older workers, and more were unemployed for longer periods of time.
To make matters worse, most forecasts were that unemployment would
remain high, probably in the 10 percent range, for several years.

Reasons for high unemployment

The seriousness of Canada's unemployment picture in the early 1990's
led to considerable analysis of the causes of this problem. In the following
sections, we will examine the findings of this analysis.

ON THE DEMAND SIDE

Obviously, the major problem on the demand side was the *serious recession* of the early 1990's, during which the level of aggregate demand was

quite depressed. However, there were additional demand-side problems that went well beyond a simple recession.

Probably the most basic of these problems was the *financial condition of Canadian governments*, which had ongoing huge budget deficits that were adding to an already-massive government debt, much of which was owed to foreign lenders. Under these circumstances, the government was unable to simply increase its deficit (and debt) in order to boost aggregate demand in the economy, as had been done in the past. To do so would have alarmed its creditors, who would have insisted on even higher interest rates that would have depressed demand in the economy.

Another major factor was the *lack of confidence among Canadian consumers*, whose weak spending slowed the recovery from the recession. This was in large part the result of two factors—many consumers were burdened with *heavy debt loads*, especially mortgage debt, that they had taken on during the boom of the late 1980's, and governments had been *increasing taxes* significantly in their attempt to bring their deficits under control, reducing households' disposable income in the process. Mainly for these reasons, the Canadian economy after 1990 was characterized by weak demand.

ON THE SUPPLY SIDE

On the supply side of Canada's labor markets, there were several problems that can contribute to increasing unemployment:

(a) skills mismatches

(b) uncompetitiveness of some industries

(c) wage rigidities

(d) income support programs

(a) Skills mismatches

There is evidence of a serious "mismatch" between the skills requirements of modern business and the skills of the Canadian workforce. In 1989, with 1 018 000 Canadians unemployed at the peak of the economic boom, there were about 600 000 unfilled jobs—that is, employers were unable to find workers with the skills to perform 600 000 jobs that were available. After two years of recession, with unemployment as high as 1 556 000, there were still about 300 000 unfilled jobs, and some firms were forced to recruit skilled workers from other countries after searching for them in Canada without success. According to most analyses, Canada's educational and training systems were generating too many university graduates without specific job skills and too many high school dropouts, and insufficient numbers of people with "middle level" skills required by a modern economy, from skilled trades to technician/technologist skills to middle-level business skills.

(b) Uncompetitiveness of some industries

During the 1980's, the productivity and competitiveness of the manufacturing sector of the Canadian economy fell behind Canada's competitors, leaving them vulnerable to foreign competition. These weaknesses were exposed by the trend toward freer world trade in the 1980's, including the Canada–US Free Trade Agreement, and by the recession of the early 1990's. As a result, some manufacturers went out of business, and many of those that survived did so largely through extensive "labor-shedding" that reduced employment considerably. This matter is dealt with more completely in Chapter 33.

(c) Wage rigidities

Suppose that either a recession or stronger foreign competition reduces the money that a firm has available for its payroll by 10 percent. To adjust to this situation, the firm could lay off about 10 percent of its employees. However, this would not be necessary if the employees' wages were reduced by 10 percent. While this illustration is somewhat simplistic, it shows that, in general, the more that wage rates are flexible, the more that layoffs can be reduced. On the other hand, if wage rates cannot be reduced, more layoffs will be required.

In Canada, many wage rates and incomes are quite resistant to such downward movements, for various reasons. Many employees' wage rates are specified by union contracts, and Canadian unions have been quite resistant to wage cuts. Similarly, most management staff are reluctant to give themselves pay cuts when times are difficult. And government programs stress income support in various ways, from farm price/income support programs to relatively high legal minimum wage rates. In a broad sense, income reductions are not

---

JAPANESE JOB SECURITY

It is often noted that many large Japanese employers have been able to provide considerably more job security than their North American counterparts. What is less well known, however, is how they manage this. Japanese job security is made possible by various measures, one of which is *income flexibility*. Employees of these enterprises are paid a relatively low base wage rate, but receive very substantial profit-sharing bonuses when times are good, making their incomes quite high. When sales income and profits fall off, however, these profit-sharing bonuses decline, leaving the employees with lower incomes. And, with all employees taking a pay cut in this manner, the firm is able to avoid or at least minimize layoffs. In effect, the employees are engaging in "work-sharing" in difficult times, with each accepting a smaller amount in order to avoid the laying off of some. In the simplest sense, these people have chosen job security over income security—the opposite of the Canadian approach.

part of the culture of a people who have enjoyed unusual prosperity for many years, and *income security* is important to Canadians. The "trade-off" for such income security, however, is reduced *job security* for those who are laid off when employers' revenues are depressed.

(d) Income support programs

Research has repeatedly found that certain features of Canada's income support programs, especially Unemployment Insurance, add to unemployment. In particular, the availability of UI benefits for a year encourages some recipients to engage in prolonged job searches, or even to not search seriously for work until their UI benefits are about to expire. This adds to the duration of their unemployment, and thus to the unemployment rate. In addition, UI benefits are more generous in regions with high unemployment. This encourages some people—with the cooperation of some employers—to work for the minimum period of time required to qualify for UI benefits, then fall back on UI for a year, and then repeat this pattern again and again. By employing people for short periods and then "disemploying" them in this manner, a community can maximize its combined income from employment and UI benefits. One key symptom of this pattern is the large number of UI claims made by people who have worked just long enough to qualify for UI benefits.

Research has indicated that other income-support programs have similar effects on incentives and unemployment. Welfare tends to reduce the incentive to work because, if a welfare recipient earns income, his or her welfare benefits are often reduced by so much that working brings little or no gain. In addition, in some provinces welfare benefits are higher than the income that could be earned from a low-paying job. Also, Canada's quite high legal minimum wage rates tend to discourage employers from hiring workers with limited skills, especially younger ones.

In summary, for various reasons the supply side of the Canadian labor market adjusts rather slowly and imperfectly to changing conditions that call for changes in skills and productivity and more competitive wages and labor costs. As a result, unemployment tends to be generally high in the Canadian economy, and at times particularly high.

Desirable as the UI program may be, it has also been subject to some abuse by workers and employers. The Newfoundland Royal Commission on Employment and Unemployment reported that unemployment insurance can become part of the community culture in regions where there are very high levels of joblessness. In that province, UI benefits have served as a vehicle for sharing work and related income support, to the point where incentives to go to school or to seek a full-time job have been seriously eroded.

Economic Council of Canada, *Twenty-Fifth Annual Review*, p. 33

Government policies to reduce unemployment

In order to reduce unemployment, government policies should generate:

- *more jobs* in the economy,
- *better skills* so that workers can fill those jobs, and
- *improved incentives* for workers to obtain skills and take the available jobs.

To achieve these objectives, government policies can be implemented on both the demand side and the supply side of labor markets.

(A) DEMAND-SIDE POLICIES TO INCREASE THE NUMBER OF JOBS AVAILABLE

The traditional—and most basic—approach to reducing unemployment is by *stimulating aggregate demand* for goods and services. Higher aggregate demand will generate higher output and more jobs, reducing unemployment.

Aggregate demand can be stimulated through fiscal policies or monetary policies. Fiscal policies, as described in Chapter 25, would consist of government budget deficits, created by increases in government spending and/or reductions in taxes. As outlined in Chapter 27, monetary policy to reduce unemployment would be one of "easy money," with increased availability of bank loans and lower interest rates to stimulate borrowing and spending. Both budget deficits and easy money will increase aggregate demand in the economy, reducing unemployment.

However, the higher levels of aggregate demand that reduce unemployment will also generate an inflation problem before unemployment is as low as we would like it to be. This places practical limits on how far policies to reduce unemployment by boosting aggregate demand can be pushed.

In addition, the use of fiscal policy has been limited in recent years by the government's heavy debt and ongoing huge budget deficits that make it difficult for the government to increase its deficits and debt further. And the fact that Canada relies upon foreign lenders to finance much of its government budget deficits limits how low the Bank of Canada can push Canadian interest rates. If Canadian interest rates become too low, foreign lenders could reduce their buying of Canadian government bonds, creating severe financial problems for Canada.

Canada spends four to five times per capita as much as the USA on Unemployment Insurance benefits, and more than any other major industrialized nation.

(B) SUPPLY-SIDE POLICIES TO IMPROVE SKILLS AND INCENTIVES

Skills, retraining and relocation

Higher aggregate demand is not a complete cure for structural unemployment, which involves a mismatch between the skill requirements of jobs and the skills of the unemployed. Even in a booming economy, workers with inadequate or outdated skills will have severe difficulty finding satisfactory work.

To deal with structural unemployment requires policies directed at the supply side of labor markets—policies to *retrain and relocate* unemployed workers to enable them to move into available jobs. While the importance of such programs is obvious in theory, the implementation of effective retraining programs is a complex matter. To plan retraining programs requires reasonably accurate forecasts of the skills required for future jobs, which in turn requires forecasts of:

(a) what will be produced (i.e., what products and services will be in demand)

(b) how it will be produced (i.e., what technology and production methods will be used to produce them).

Experience has shown that it is difficult to make accurate forecasts of these variables. As a result, retraining programs are often less successful than might be hoped; however, retraining programs that upgrade the general skills level of the work force are nonetheless regarded as a key element in any strategy to reduce unemployment.

Getting unemployed people into jobs in Canada often encounters other obstacles besides skills and (re)training. Due to the regional nature of unemployment, getting people into long-term jobs often involves relocating them. For many, this involves much more than the cost of moving (which the federal government often subsidizes); it means a major change in culture and lifestyle. Some people prefer not to make such changes (or attempt unsuccessfully to make them), and end up remaining in their familiar surroundings despite the low employment prospects there, living on income from a combination of short-term employment and UI benefits. The situation is complicated further by language barriers that make it even more difficult for some people to move to available jobs. In the extreme, the problem of combatting structural unemployment could be characterized as "How can the government help an unemployed unilingual Francophone factory worker from Montreal find happiness as a word processor in an office in Calgary?" Notwithstanding these difficulties, however, it is important to provide people with the opportunities for retraining and relocation needed to overcome such problems.

Incentives

As noted earlier, certain features of Canada's income-support programs generate disincentives for people to seek work and employers to employ people. There have been more proposals for reforming Canada's income-support programs in ways that would increase incentives than can be covered in detail in this space; however, some general tendencies can be noted.

With respect to Unemployment Insurance, most proposals would shift the emphasis from simply supporting recipients' income for a year toward retraining them so as to make them more self-supporting in the future. Such proposals usually make UI benefits, or part of them, contingent upon recipients' undertaking retraining and/or taking work that is available. Proposals for welfare reform vary more widely. The most commonly-proposed reforms would allow welfare recipients who also work to keep a greater proportion of their welfare benefits, so as to avoid killing their incentive to work. Other proposals would require welfare recipients to work on community programs or undertake retraining in order to receive full welfare benefits.

As a result of all of these considerations, while there are government policies on both the supply and demand sides of labor markets that can reduce unemployment, there are limits on how far unemployment can be reduced. This problem will be considered more fully in the next chapter.

DEFINITIONS OF NEW TERMS

Frictional Unemployment Unemployment arising from people being temporarily out of work because they are in the process of changing jobs.

Seasonal Unemployment Periodic unemployment arising from the seasonal nature of activity in some industries, such as farming and fishing.

Cyclical Unemployment Unemployment caused by periodic slumps in industries that are strongly affected by recessions.

Structural Unemployment Unemployment arising from shifts in the demand for products or from changes in technology.

Hidden Unemployment Those unemployed who are not counted in the official unemployment statistics because they have given up looking for work.

Voluntary Unemployment Unemployment resulting from people's decisions not to take jobs that are available, due to personal preferences and/or the availability of Unemployment Insurance benefits.

Labor Force The total of employed and unemployed workers.

Unemployment Rate The number of unemployed expressed as a percentage of the labor force.

Participation Rate The percentage of the population of working age participating in economic activity (or included in the labor force; that is, working or seeking work). Participation rates are also calculated for sub-groups of the population, such as men, women, and young people.

CHAPTER SUMMARY

1. Unemployment is a particularly severe problem that imposes major economic and human costs on society.

2. Factors on both the supply side of labor markets (the number of people available for work) and the demand side of labor markets (the number of jobs available) contribute to unemployment.

3. Unemployment fluctuates considerably from year to year, depending on economic conditions (especially the level of aggregate demand).

4. The duration of unemployment varies widely, depending on the circumstances. Frictional unemployment is very short-term in nature, seasonal unemployment is relatively short-term, cyclical unemployment may be of quite short or longer duration and structural unemployment is often quite long-term in nature.

5. Unemployment is higher in certain regions of Canada, especially the Atlantic provinces and Quebec, and among young people.

6. During recessions, the official unemployment rate statistics understate the extent of unemployment because they exclude "hidden unemployment" of discouraged workers. During economic booms, the official statistics overstate unemployment, because they include the "voluntarily unemployed" who will not take jobs that are available.

7. In the 1970's, the unemployment rate increased, mainly due to "supply-side" factors: rapid increases in the labor force as the baby boomers came of working age and the participation rate of women increased, and changes to the UI program that added to "voluntary unemployment."

8. In the 1980's, the unemployment rate increased again. In the early 1980's the weak aggregate demand of the Great Recession caused very high unemployment rates, and during the rest of the 1980's a growing problem of structural unemployment kept unemployment rates high.

9. The early 1990's saw a deterioration in the unemployment situation, mainly due to the "demand-side" factor of a serious recession. In addition, several "supply-side" problems were identified, including a mismatch between the skills of Canada's labor force and the skills required by employers, a deterioration of the international competitiveness of some Canadian industries in the 1980's, the resistance of many Canadian wage rates and incomes to downward movement, and the disincentives of income-support programs to retrain and seek work.

10. To reduce unemployment, policies are required that increase the number of jobs available, improve workers' skills so that they can fill those jobs, and strengthen incentives to seek work. More specifically, the government can use demand-side policies to stimulate aggregate demand and supply-side policies that retrain and/or relocate workers to enable them to move into available jobs, and reforms to income-support programs that improve work incentives.

QUESTIONS

1. The box in the text entitled "The Employment to Population Ratio—Another Perspective" points out that while Canada has a high *unemployment rate*, its *employment to population ratio* is quite high. Why would the job performance of the Canadian economy be so poor as measured by the unemployment rate and so good as measured by the employment to population ratio?

2. What is Canada's current unemployment rate? Has it increased or decreased over the past year? What are the reasons for this trend?

3. Has the distribution of unemployment among Canada's regions changed since the last statistics in Figure 30-3? (A convenient way to check this is to compare the unemployment rate for each region to the national average unemployment rate over a period of time.) If so, what factors might explain these changes?

4. Has the distribution of unemployment among different age and sex groups changed since the last statistics in Figure 30-4? If so, what factors might account for these changes?

5. In 1993, the federal government made the following changes to the Unemployment Insurance program:

   (a) Benefits were reduced from 60 percent of a recipient's previous weekly income to 57 percent. This reduced the maximum weekly UI benefit from $426.00 to $424.65.

   (b) Workers who were fired for just cause or quit their jobs without cause would no longer be eligible for UI benefits. It was estimated that these changes would save the government about $1 billion per year. In 1991, the government had paid benefits to 225 000 people who had quit their jobs.

   Do you agree with these changes to the UI program? If not, what alternatives would you propose?

6. Have any further changes been made in Canada's unemployment insurance program recently? If so, what are they and why were they made?

7. By 1993, there was growing interest in changes to welfare programs that would require welfare recipients to do volunteer community work and/or enroll in training courses in order to receive full welfare benefits. Are you in favor of such reforms or not, and why? Have any such changes in fact been implemented?

8. From your own experience, are you aware of any cases in which income-support programs such as Unemployment Insurance or welfare have caused people to not take jobs that were available? If so, analyze the reasons why the programs provided these disincentives, by looking at the situation from the viewpoint of the person(s) receiving the benefits.

9. "The answer to Canada's so-called 'unemployment problem' is to make UI and welfare benefits so low that people can survive on them and no more. That would get these people off the backs of the taxpayers and out working where they belong."

   Comment on this viewpoint in light of the material in this chapter.

10.

Year	Population of Working Age (millions)	Partici- pation Rate (%)	Labor Force (millions)	Employed (millions)	Unem- ployed (millions)	Unemploy- ment Rate (%)
19X1	20.0	60.0%	12.0	10.8	1.2	10.0%
19X2	21.5	61.5		11.2		

In 19X1, the population of working age is 20 million, 60 percent of whom participate in the labor force, making the labor force 12 million. Of these, 10.8 million are employed and 1.2 million, or 10 percent of the labor force, are unemployed.

Suppose that, in 19X2, the following developments occur:

(i) Employment grows quite rapidly (by 4 percent), to 11.2 million.

(ii) The population of working age increases to 21.5 million.

(iii) The participation rate increases to 61.5 percent.

Calculate the unemployment rate for 19X2.

11.

| Year | Population 15 years and over (000's) | Partici- pation Rate | Labor Force (000's) | Employment | | | Unem- ployment (000's) | Unem- ployment rate |
				Total (000's)	Full- time (000's)	Part- time (000's)		
1985	19 190	65.3%	12 532	11 221	9 484	1 737	1 311	10.5%
1986	19 397	65.7	12 746	11 531	9 742	1 789	1 215	9.5
1987	19 642	66.2	13 011	11 861	10 057	1 804	1 150	8.8
1988	19 890	66.7	13 275	12 245	10 363	1 882	1 031	7.8
1989	20 141	67.0	13 503	12 486	10 597	1 888	1 018	7.5
1990	20 430	67.0	13 681	12 572	10 640	1 932	1 109	8.1
1991	20 746	66.3	13 757	12 340	10 317	2 023	1 417	10.3
1992	21 058	65.5	13 797	12 240	10 182	2 058	1 556	11.3

(a) In 1990, the number of people *employed* increased, but so did the *unemployment rate*. Why did this happen?

(b) What happened to the participation rate from 1990 to 1992? What might explain this change?

(c) Use participation-rate data to estimate the extent of the increase in "hidden unemployment" from 1989 to 1992. (That is, how much higher would unemployment and the unemployment rate have been in 1992 if the participation rate had been the same as in 1989?)

(d) How did the percentage of total employment represented by part-timers change from 1985 to 1992? What might explain this change?

(e) At the peak of the economic boom in 1989, the unemployment rate "bottomed out" at 7.5 percent, and 1 018 000 Canadians re-mained unemployed. Why were so many unemployed under such favorable economic conditions?

NOTES

[1] *Economic Policy and Well-Being*, submission to the Macdonald Commission.

[2] Another factor that can affect the number of employees required by employers is the level of *productivity*, or output per worker. In a simplistic sense, higher output per worker would seem to increase unemployment by reducing the number of employees required to produce a given level of output. However, by reducing production costs, higher productivity can make producers better able to com-pete, and can result in lower prices and higher sales. Both of these effects can in-crease employment, depending on the circumstances.

Economic policy in perspective

We have examined the major macroeconomic problems of recession and inflation, and the policy tools available to the federal government for dealing with them—monetary policy, which is the responsibility of the Bank of Canada, and fiscal policy, which is conducted by the Department of Finance. In short, a combination of easy money and a budget deficit can be used to lift the economy out of recessions by increasing aggregate demand, while tight money and a budget surplus can combat inflation by depressing aggregate demand.

While the *theory* of monetary and fiscal policy is quite straightforward, the *application* of this theory in practice encounters certain practical problems and limitations. In this chapter, we will consider several of these problems and limitations, so as to place the matter of government macroeconomic policy in perspective.

1. The unemployment-inflation policy trade-off

We have seen how the government uses monetary and fiscal policies to influence the level of aggregate demand for goods and services and thus steer the economy toward desired goals. Three goals that the government seeks to achieve with these policies are:

(a) *Full employment:* Since the Great Depression, probably the dominant objective of government economic policy has been **full employment**—the lowest possible rate of unemployment.

(b) *Economic growth:* Another major objective of economic policy is a growing economy, in which a rising output of goods and services will provide not only jobs for a growing labor force, but also a rising standard of living for the population.

(c) *Stable prices:* Economic policy-makers seek the lowest possible rate of inflation, for the reasons outlined in Chapter 29.

Unfortunately, in a basically market type of economy it is not possible to reach all three of these goals simultaneously. A conflict between goals occurs because the high levels of aggregate demand needed to stimulate the economy toward full employment and growth also generate inflation. Beyond a certain point, it is not feasible to increase aggregate demand further in pursuit of the goals of full employment and growth, because inflation would become intolerably rapid.

To see why this conflict between our economic goals arises, we will examine how the economy responds to increases in aggregate demand under each of the three following conditions:

(a) when unemployment is unusually high,

(b) when unemployment is quite low, nearing "full employment," and

(c) when the economy is operating at its capacity, with production at its maximum possible pace and unemployment at a minimum.

Before examining these three situations, it is helpful to recall that in any market, including macroeconomic markets, an increase in demand can have two effects: it can cause an *increase in output* (and employment) or an *increase in prices*, or a combination of these. And the more that output can rise in response to higher demand, the less prices will have to rise. On the other hand, if output cannot rise as fast as demand, prices will rise.

(A) THE EFFECTS OF INCREASED DEMAND WHEN UNEMPLOYMENT IS HIGH

Suppose the economy is in a recession, with unemployment unusually high and output far below its potential. Assume also that with aggregate demand so depressed there is little inflation in the economy, and little is expected in the near future, so that inflation psychology and cost-push pressures are minimal. In these circumstances, if the government uses its monetary and fiscal policies to increase aggregate demand in the economy, the results should be quite favorable. Output and employment should increase, but without a large increase in prices. This increase in output can be achieved without much of an increase in prices, for several reasons. First, businesses should be able to hire unemployed labor at existing wage rates—they should not need to raise wages to attract additional workers. Second, as output increases, production costs per unit will fall, as production facilities are used more efficiently and fixed costs are spread over more units of output. Third, with the economy still sluggish, businesses and unions will be reluctant to seek large price and wage increases, for fear of jeopardizing their sales and jobs.

In short, then, during a period of high unemployment, government policies that increase aggregate demand will have beneficial effects on the

FIGURE 31-1 *How Increases in Aggregate Demand Affect the Economy Under Various Conditions*

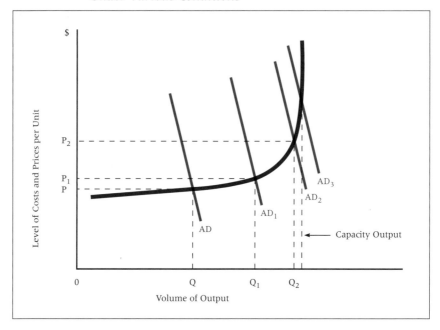

economy by causing quite large increases in output and employment with quite small increases in prices. Such a situation is shown in Figure 31-1 by the increase in aggregate demand from AD to AD$_1$.

(B) THE EFFECTS OF INCREASED DEMAND WHEN THE ECONOMY IS NEARING FULL EMPLOYMENT

As such expansionary monetary and fiscal policies bring unemployment down, however, their effects on the economy will change. With output nearing its potential (capacity) level and unemployment falling to near full-employment levels, further increases in aggregate demand will have *mixed* effects on the economy. Output will still rise, although less rapidly, and prices will begin to rise more rapidly, as inflation speeds up. There are several reasons why inflation appears in the economy before unemployment has disappeared. Despite the fact that unemployment is still quite high in some regions such as the Atlantic provinces and Quebec, demand will be sufficiently high to generate full employment and inflationary pressures in other regions, such as Ontario and the West. Also, as demand rises, shortages of certain productive inputs (such as skilled labor and certain raw materials) will develop, causing their prices to rise despite the fact that the national economy is not yet operating at its capacity output. The price increases resulting from these production bottlenecks will force up production costs, contributing to more rapid inflation. Furthermore, as economic conditions improve, those business firms that are in a position to raise prices will begin to do so, and labor unions will take advantage of the improved bargaining position that low unemployment rates bring, negotiating larger wage increases that add to cost-push inflation.

Thus, as the economy nears full employment, increases in aggregate demand will cause increases not only in output and employment but also in prices, with inflation becoming more severe, the closer the economy gets to full employment. In Figure 31-1, this is illustrated by the shift in the aggregate demand curve from AD_1 to AD_2.

(C) THE EFFECT OF INCREASED DEMAND WHEN THE ECONOMY IS AT FULL EMPLOYMENT

Once the economy has reached full employment, further increases in aggregate demand will bring no additional economic benefits. The economy is already producing goods and services at its maximum possible pace (capacity output level), so producers as a group cannot respond to increases in aggregate demand by increasing the pace of production. Thus, increases in total spending will cause prices to rise very sharply, as aggregate demand in excess of society's productive capacity pulls prices upward. Higher levels of total spending will simply bid up the prices of a fixed real output. Thus, at full employment, increases in spending will cause pure inflation to set in: Prices will rise sharply but real output will not rise at all. In Figure 31-1, increases in aggregate demand beyond AD_3 will have this effect.

Depending on the circumstances, then, increases in aggregate demand can cause increases in output and employment, increases in prices, or both. As the economy moves closer to full employment, increases in aggregate demand become less beneficial, generating smaller gains in output and employment and more rapid inflation, as shown in Figure 31-1. The result is that it is *not possible* to achieve full employment and rapid economic growth simultaneously with stable prices. Therefore, two of our most important economic goals—full employment and stable prices—conflict with each other, and government policy measures that take us closer to one tend to take us farther from the other, as reflected in Figure 31-2.

THE TRADE-OFF CHOICES

The conflict between various economic goals forces difficult choices upon the government in regard to its monetary and fiscal policies. The government is faced with a problem of economic policy *trade-offs*—the closer it approaches one of its goals, the further it gets from another. Under these circumstances, the only practical course of action for the government is to seek a *politically acceptable balance* between its conflicting goals—a situation in which neither inflation nor unemployment is unacceptably severe. In the following sections, we will consider how much inflation and how much unemployment are considered to be tolerable.

FIGURE 31-2   *Inflation and Unemployment Rates, 1966–93*

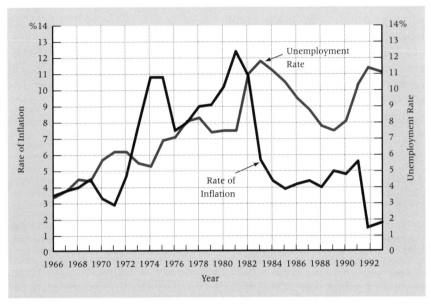

Source: Department of Finance, *Economic and Fiscal Reference Tables*, August 1993

How much inflation is too much? How much is acceptable?

As Figure 31-3 shows, the rate of inflation has varied widely, from less than 2 percent in the early 1960's to over 10 percent in the mid-1970's and early 1980's, then down to around 4 percent for much of the 1980's and back to below 2 percent in the early 1990's. While the Bank of Canada stated in the late 1980's that its objective was an inflation rate of zero,

FIGURE 31-3   *Rate of Inflation, 1962–93*

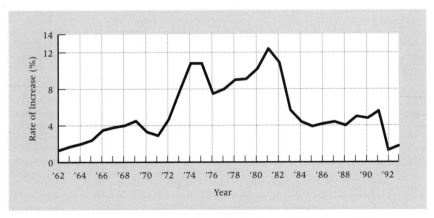

Source: Department of Finance, *Economic and Fiscal Reference Tables*, August 1993

most observers felt that the government would find an annual inflation rate of 2 or 3 percent acceptable. In 1992–93, with the unemployment rate around 11 percent and the inflation rate around 2 percent, the Bank of Canada eased up on its monetary policy considerably, indicating that inflation was no longer considered the main problem.

How much unemployment is too much? How much is "normal"?

Because of the hardship and human costs associated with unemployment, these are controversial questions. There is considerable disagreement over the answers to them, with some people insisting that we can and indeed must reduce unemployment to about 4 percent of the labor force and others asserting that we cannot expect to do better than an unemployment rate of 8 percent—a difference of about 500 000 jobs.

As we have seen, unemployment can be reduced by policies that stimulate aggregate demand; however, the lower the unemployment rate becomes, the higher the inflation rate becomes. At some point, inflation becomes so severe that it threatens the performance of the economy—including employment itself in an economy as dependent as Canada's is on its ability to compete internationally. Beyond this point, it is not advisable to push aggregate demand higher in an attempt to reduce unemployment further. Therefore, *full employment* is considered to have been reached when inflation threatens to become unacceptably rapid.

What unemployment rate actually represents "full employment"? In the 1960's, it was thought that a 4-percent unemployment rate was a reasonable full employment target for policy-makers. In more recent years, however, the task of reducing unemployment has been made more difficult by various factors, including:

(i) a greater degree of "voluntary unemployment," arising largely from the way in which Canada's income-support programs, especially Unemployment Insurance, create disincentives to work,[1] and

(ii) inflationary expectations: with the population more wary of inflation after the experience of the 1970's, government policies to stimulate aggregate demand are more likely to touch off larger wage demands and price increases, causing the stimulus of higher aggregate demand to be dissipated in price and wage increases, rather than to boost output and employment.

Economists believed that by the 1980's, this combination of factors had increased the realistically attainable unemployment rate ("full employment") to as high as 7.5 or 8 percent of the labor force. This was sometimes described as the **Non-Accelerating Inflation Rate of Unemployment (NAIRU)**—the unemployment rate below which inflationary pressures would be strong enough for inflation to begin gaining momentum. Evidence in support of this conclusion was provided by the economic boom of the late 1980's, when the lowest unemployment rate reached was 7.5 percent, and even that rate proved unsustainable as inflation began to gain momentum.

2. The problem of time lags

While everyone would like government policies to bring a quick end to problems such as inflation and recession, this is not possible, due to the problem of *time lags*.

To illustrate this problem, suppose the economy is expanding rapidly, with unemployment low and nearing full-employment levels. The rate of inflation is rising, causing some people in business and government to warn that anti-inflationary policies are in order. However, the situation is not yet completely clear—in some months, the Consumer Price Index barely rises. Other people argue that inflation is not a serious problem yet, and that the government should permit the economic boom to continue rather than slow the economy down. By the time the picture becomes clear enough for those responsible for economic policy to recognize and agree that anti-inflation policies are necessary, a considerable period of time will have passed. This, then, is the first of the lags: the *recognition lag*, or the time between the existence of a problem and the recognition of it.

The policies to attack inflation cannot all be put in place immediately. While the Bank of Canada can move quite quickly to change its monetary policy, changes in fiscal policy involving taxes and government spending can take considerably longer, as they may involve budget or legislative changes. The time lag between the recognition of the problem and the actual implementation of policies designed to remedy it is called the *policy lag*.

Once the government's economic policies are in place, there will be a further time lag before they take effect on the economy. As noted in Chapter 28, changes in the rate of growth of the money supply do not affect the rate of inflation for about a year. Similarly, changes in taxes and government spending do not affect the economy quickly. Higher taxes do not depress consumer spending immediately—despite lower disposable incomes, many consumers will continue for perhaps six months to spend as they have become accustomed to doing. Corporations will complete investment projects that they have started, and the multiplier effect of previous high levels of spending will continue to operate. After a while, the economy will slow down and the rate of inflation will fall. The period between the implementation of policies and the feeling of the effects of those policies is called the *impact lag* (see Figure 31-4).

According to some estimates, the time lags in economic policy in Canada could be as long as two years under certain circumstances. Recessions do not ordinarily last two years. Therefore, it is possible that the policies implemented to combat a *recession this year* may have the effect of worsening a period of *inflation two years from now*, long after the recession is over.

FIGURE 31-4 *Time Lags*

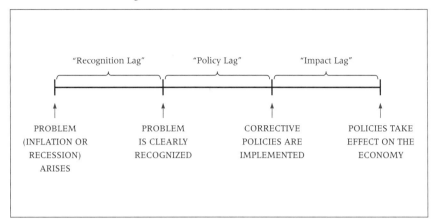

"Recognition Lag"   "Policy Lag"   "Impact Lag"

PROBLEM
(INFLATION OR
RECESSION)
ARISES

PROBLEM
IS CLEARLY
RECOGNIZED

CORRECTIVE
POLICIES ARE
IMPLEMENTED

POLICIES TAKE
EFFECT ON THE
ECONOMY

Together, these time lags can add up to a total of between one and two years. Such long time lags can create serious problems for economic policy-makers. Because of the lags, the problem being attacked (either inflation or recession) can grow considerably more severe and difficult to correct by the time the government's policies take effect. This makes it particularly important for the government to have accurate economic forecasts so that it can implement its policies as early as possible. Unfortunately, economic forecasting is an imprecise process at best, making governments understandably reluctant to base policy decisions on forecasts that may well be inaccurate.

TO FINE-TUNE OR NOT TO FINE-TUNE?

In the late 1960's, following some considerable successes with fiscal policy, some economists grew quite optimistic about the effectiveness of government policies. They spoke in terms of "fine-tuning" the economy with small shifts in policies intended to achieve small and specific policy goals. The economy was likened to a sports car, in that it was seen as being very responsive to directions from its driver (the government). If the economy slowed and unemployment rose, the government could correct the problem with a little pressure on the gas pedal; if inflation started to develop, a touch on the economic policy brakes could correct the problem.

Now, however, it is recognized that because of the time lags involved, such "fine-tuning" of economic policy is unrealistic. Rather than like driving a sports car, managing the economy is more like handling an oil supertanker. These ships operate with such momentum that after their rudder has been turned, they will continue in the same direction for nearly two kilometres before even *beginning* to respond to the turning of their wheel.

3. Political problems: Overstimulation and overreaction

In managing the economy, as in steering an oil supertanker, it is important to do two things:

- look and plan far ahead, and
- avoid sudden or excessive changes in speed or direction, as these will be impossible to correct quickly.

The problem is that government economic policy-makers have to maintain a steady course in this manner while being subjected to harsh criticism and the need to be re-elected every four or five years. As a result, in deciding economic policy, governments are sometimes more responsive to political considerations than to economic ones.

In particular, governments have shown a tendency to be motivated by short-term political pressures to *overstimulate* the economy so as to reduce unemployment, generating severe inflation in the process. Considering the time lags involved, such severe inflation is likely to gain momentum, eventually forcing the government to impose harsh anti-inflation policies. These policies will throw the economy into a recession from which it will take considerable time to recover. History provides many examples of these tendencies: during the second half of the 1960's, the government overstimulated demand, causing inflation that by 1969 led to harsh anti-inflation policies. However, fighting inflation caused quite high unemployment in 1970–71, and the government, facing an election in 1972, reversed the direction of its policies dramatically once again. The result was a very rapid increase in both government spending and the money supply, and the worst inflation in years. In late 1975, the government was again forced to reverse the thrust of its policies, imposing anti-inflation policies that would push unemployment up. However, by the late 1970's and early 1980's, the situation had again reversed itself and inflation had become quite severe. This led to particularly strong anti-inflation policies (including interest rates which peaked around 22 percent in 1981), which ushered in the Great Recession of 1981–82. During the recovery/boom of the second half of the 1980's, inflation again threatened, leading the Bank of Canada to impose another round of very high interest rates that contributed strongly to the severe recession of the early 1990's.

The irony of the situation, of course, is that the monetary and fiscal policies that were designed and intended to *smooth out* economic fluctuations were being used in ways that actually *caused* economic instability. The bad experience with such *stop-go policies* presented a strong argument for a steady hand in the application of monetary and fiscal measures: that is, that the government should manage the economy like a supertanker, not a sports car, and should not allow short-term political considerations to prevail over longer-term economic considerations.

Some people regard these political obstacles to sound economic policy-making as a failing of political leadership, while others blame the public's

> Beyond the short term governments cannot choose to have a bit faster growth in exchange for a bit more inflation. The choice does not exist.
>
> *The Economist*, February 22, 1992

ignorance of or unwillingness to accept economic realities. If the public will elect politicians who promise to reduce unemployment and provide more and more public services while reducing taxes, who is at fault—the public or the politicians? If the public possessed a better understanding of economic realities, sound economic policy-making by governments would be much more likely. However, as long as the public remains relatively uninformed or misinformed on such matters, there is a risk that economic policy questions will be debated and decided more to gain political support than to solve real economic problems.

4. The stagflation trap

So far, we have discussed inflation as a "trade-off" for lower unemployment, and have assumed that at some point the government will have to reduce the rate of inflation through the use of policies that slow down the economy and increase unemployment. However, if the government chooses *not* to fight inflation once it has become rapid, and if inflation is allowed to gain momentum and become ingrained in the economy as described in Chapter 28, a much more difficult economic situation can develop.

Both theory and the experience of the 1970's suggest that if inflation is allowed to become severe and chronic, the "trade-off" of higher output and employment can worsen or even disappear. Instead, the result can be not only severe *inflation*, but also *stagnation*—slow economic growth, high unemployment and weak business investment spending. The uncomfortable combination of stagnation and inflation, which are ordinarily not supposed to occur together, is known by the appropriately unattractive name of **stagflation**. Stagflation is a complex phenomenon

> The idea, once rather popular, that high employment and output could be more readily achieved and sustained by being relaxed about inflation has surely now been demonstrated to be clearly wrong. Inflation and unemployment are not alternatives between which we can choose. Inflationary policies lead to poor economic performance, including high unemployment.
>
> Gerald Bouey, Governor of the Bank of Canada,
> *Annual Report of the Governor of the Bank of Canada*, 1983

that can involve many factors. In the following section, however, we will focus on what many consider to be the most basic cause of stagflation—the depressing effect that severe inflation has on capital investment spending by business.

INFLATION AND INVESTMENT

A major source of funds for capital investment is long-term borrowing, through the selling of bonds that are usually repayable after ten or more years. However, severe inflation makes it much less attractive to corporations to engage in long-term borrowing, by forcing interest rates to high levels. Inflation causes high interest rates in two ways: first, lenders demand an interest premium to compensate them for the declining value of their capital, and, second, the policies used by the government to restrain inflation involve increases in interest rates. In particular, the very high interest rates associated with the severe inflation of the 1970's made many corporations reluctant to raise capital through bond issues that would commit them to paying very high interest expenses for many years.

INFLATION AND SAVING

It seems logical that such high interest rates should at least increase the amount of capital available by increasing the incentive for people to *save*, but this is not so either, due to the effects of inflation and taxation. Figure 31-5 shows the return on $100 of savings invested under two very different circumstances:

FIGURE 31-5 *Inflation, Taxes and Incentives to Save*

Interest Income on $100 invested for one year		
	Inflation of 2%, Interest Rate of 5%	Inflation of 12% Interest Rate of 15%
Interest income	$5.00	$15.00
less: Loss of purchasing power of the $100 due to inflation	−2.00	−12.00
equals: "Real" return	3.00	3.00
less: Tax on the interest income (40%)	−2.00	−6.00
equals: Return after inflation and taxes	+$1.00	−$3.00

- at a 5-percent rate of interest for one year during which the rate of inflation is 2 percent, and

- at a 15-percent rate of interest for one year during which the rate of inflation is 12 percent.

At first glance, the 15-percent investment seems more attractive, because the investment income is much higher—$15 as compared to $5. A second look, however, reveals that inflation takes away much of this apparent gain. For instance, at the end of the year the investor receives $15 in interest income, plus the $100 of capital. However, inflation of 12 percent over the year has reduced the purchasing power, or real value, of this $100 by $12, leaving the investor with an after-inflation ("real") return of only $3. In the other case, the interest rate and inflation rate are different, but the result is the same—a "real" return of $3. After our second glance, then, the two investments appear to be equal.

However, a third look at the situation changes the picture again. Assuming that income tax of 40 percent is payable on the interest income, taxes on the $5 of interest income will be $2 (40 percent of $5), leaving the investor with a return of $1 after inflation and taxes. However, on the $15 of interest income, the taxes will be $6 (40 percent of $15), leaving the investor with a *loss* of $3 after inflation and taxes. As a result, the incentive to save and invest is actually *lower* in the high-inflation/high interest rate situation than in the low-inflation/low-interest rate situation.

INFLATION AND THE SAVING-INVESTMENT PROCESS

We have seen that a key to economic prosperity is an effective *saving-investment process*, assisted by strong incentives both to save and to invest in productivity-increasing capital goods. However, the combination of severe inflation and high interest rates discourages not only capital investment, but also the saving upon which much capital investment depends. By doing so, severe inflation can undermine productivity growth and the supply side of the economy. Figure 31-6 illustrates this problem: after aggregate demand outruns the supply side's ability to produce goods and services, it not only generates severe inflation, but also causes high interest rates that undermine capital investment and slow the growth of productivity and the supply side of the economy, as reflected in the slower increase in the supply side.[2]

5. International limitations on Canadian policies

The Canadian economy has an unusually large exposure to international economic forces. In the first place, Canada is heavily involved in world trade, exporting over 25 percent of its GDP, seven tenths of that to the

FIGURE 31-6 *The Stagflation Trap*

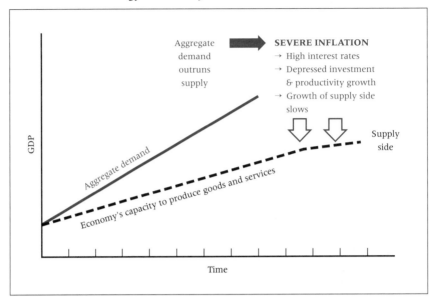

United States alone. Furthermore, Canada has historically received large inflows of foreign capital, mostly from the United States. In the past, this inflow of foreign capital financed a significant proportion of Canada's industrial development; more recently, Canada's federal and provincial governments have relied upon foreign lenders to finance a considerable proportion of their budget deficits by buying government bonds. This reliance of the Canadian economy on exports to and inflows of capital from foreign nations places certain limitations on the economic policies of Canadian governments.

Probably the major international influences on Canadian policies concern monetary policy, particularly *interest rates*. If the Bank of Canada does not keep Canadian interest rates high enough compared to American rates, the inflow of capital into Canada could slow or stop (or, worse yet, capital could flow out of Canada seeking higher returns elsewhere). This would reduce the funds available for capital investment and government programs. Another effect of reduced capital inflows would be a decline in the international value of the Canadian dollar. An important factor influencing the international value (or price) of the Canadian dollar is the buying of Canadian dollars by foreigners for the purpose of investing in and lending to Canada; should this foreign investment decline, the reduced demand for the Canadian dollar would cause its international value to decline. Canadian living standards would, in turn, be reduced, because the prices of imported goods and services would rise due to the reduced purchasing power of the Canadian dollar internationally.[3]

These international considerations significantly limit the freedom of the Bank of Canada in deciding Canadian interest rates—when formulating its interest-rate policy, the Bank of Canada must keep one eye on economic conditions in Canada and the other on the concerns of foreign lenders. Thus, to a large extent, Canadian interest rates are determined not in Canada, but rather in the international capital markets in which Canada borrows quite heavily. At times, this has led the Bank of Canada to increase interest rates in order to match increases in international rates, even when economic conditions in Canada called for lower interest rates.

Canadian authorities are also generally reluctant to allow Canada's *rate of inflation* to significantly exceed US inflation rates for long. If it did, Canada's prices would be significantly higher than US prices, Canada's exports to the United States would decline and imports from the there would rise, threatening jobs in Canada. Thus, if US monetary authorities adopt anti-inflation policies consisting of high interest rates, their Canadian counterparts will come under considerable pressure to follow suit.

The presence of the vast US economy to the south limits the freedom of Canadian authorities to decide *taxation policies*, as well. If Canadian taxes on profits, interest income or dividend income become too high relative to US taxes, there is a risk that the flow of investment capital into Canada will be reduced, and that Canadian businesses will invest in the United States instead of in Canada.

Finally, Canada's high level of imports limits the effectiveness of policies intended to stimulate the Canadian economy. Because so much (about 25 percent) of the respending effect of the multiplier is drained off by imports when Canadian authorities inject additional demand into the economy, the "multiplier effect" in the Canadian economy is quite small. As a result, these policies have less impact on output and employment in Canada than Canadian authorities would like.

In summary, the heavy exposure of the Canadian economy to international economic forces creates special difficulties for Canadian economic policy-makers. In particular, the importance of exports and of foreign capital inflows places significant limitations on Canadian authorities in deciding monetary and fiscal policies, forcing them to consider not only domestic Canadian problems, but also international factors, when formulating policies.

Macroeconomic policy in perspective

Before the Great Depression of the 1930's, the prevailing economic philosophy was *laissez-faire*, which held that the economy automatically moved toward full employment and that there was therefore no need for government intervention in the economy.

The experience of the Great Depression and the war that followed it ushered in a new era of economic policy, in which *Keynesian fiscal policy* to stimulate the economy out of recessions and into growth were the key features. During this period, two fundamentally new ideas were advanced: that the government should actively intervene in the economy on a macroeconomic scale by managing the level of aggregate demand to end recessions, and that the use of government budget deficits to do so was reasonable and legitimate. These new ideas seemed radical at first, and were only used timidly by governments in the 1950's. However, they received a big boost from John F. Kennedy's successful application of them during the 1960's. By openly discussing and using Keynesian policies, Kennedy gave them—and the economists who proposed them—public acceptance and respectability. In many ways, the 1960's were the golden years of Keynesian economics.

Following the late 1960's, however, experience with government demand management policies was much less satisfactory. Excessive stimulation in the late 1960's led to rapid inflation; in response, strong anti-inflation policies were applied, causing unemployment to rise to high levels. Again in the 1970's, excessive stimulation generated very severe inflation and stagflation, with high levels of *both* inflation *and* unemployment.

Clearly, something had gone wrong: the monetary and fiscal policies that were supposed to be used to *reduce* economic instability had been applied in a "stop-go" fashion that actually *created* instability, wrenching the economy from rapid inflation to recession and back again. In addition, they had allowed severe inflation to become ingrained into people's expectations and into the economy, contributing to stagflation. To get this severe inflation out of the system took two periods of strong anti-inflation policies in the form of very high interest rates that led to severe recessions in the early 1980's and again in the early 1990's.

The bad experience with economic policies decisions over this period led some economists to argue that the government should *not* actively manage the level of demand in the economy with its monetary and fiscal policies. They believe that, due to political pressures and the problems of time lags, government attempts at demand management tend to become demand mismanagement, with negative effects on economic stability and prosperity. These economists argue that governments should be required to follow *fixed rules* for monetary and fiscal policy rather than be allowed to adjust the federal budget and rate of growth of the money supply as they see fit. In particular, monetarists argue that the money supply should be allowed to grow at only a certain rate that is not much greater than the potential growth rate of real output, so as to prevent inflationary pressures from building up in the system. Others would apply rules to government budgets in much the same way. The most common proposal concerning budgets is that the government's budget should have to be balanced not each and every year, but over a period of several years. Advocates of such rules argue that they would still allow the government to use deficits periodically to combat recessions, but would require them to offset these deficits with budget surpluses in boom periods, thus preventing governments from using deficits to finance their expenditures on an ongoing basis and building up massive debt in the process. Such rules, it is said, would prevent governments from making major errors in economic policy, especially in the direction of overstimulation and debt, and thus prevent a repetition of the problems of the 1970's and 1980's.

Other economists disagree with this view. They point out that our economic system has a natural tendency toward instability, as discussed in Chapter 24. Therefore, they argue, the government can and should actively intervene in the economy with monetary and fiscal policies to steer the level of demand, stimulating it during recessions and dampening it during periods of inflation. They point to the fact that generally, since such policies came into use after the Second World War, economic growth has been more rapid and recessions less frequent and less severe than before. They also argue that, if mistakes were made in the use of these policies, we should learn from those mistakes rather than abandon the policies altogether in the blind hope that it will all work out somehow.

Which view is correct? There seem to be elements of truth in both views. Management of demand by government can have either beneficial or negative effects on economic stability and prosperity, depending on whether the policies are used with the proper timing and strength. For such policies to benefit the economy, the government must base its decisions on the longer-term *economic* effects of such policies rather than their short-term *political* attractiveness. During the late 1960's and first half of the 1970's, this was not done, and the results were severe instability, rapid inflation and massive accumulations of government debt. Whether this experience has made governments wiser in the use of their policies remains to be seen.

Supply-side policies

Since the 1930's, government economic policy, and debates over policy, have focused on monetary and fiscal policies designed to manage the demand side of the economy; that is, the level of aggregate demand. More recently, there has been increased concern regarding **supply side policies**, or policies designed to increase productivity. This concern has stemmed from Canada's poor productivity performance, which is linked not only to the slow growth of Canadians' living standards, but also to difficulties competing with foreign producers whose productivity has improved more rapidly. These problems have drawn more attention to the "supply side" factors such as business investment, government tax policies, education and training (Chapter 22) that affect our productivity and prosperity.

The need for balance: Perspectives on prosperity

In summary, economic prosperity is the result of a *balanced interaction* between the two sides of the economy:

(a) *the supply side*, through which saving and investment and other factors make higher productivity and living standards possible, and

(b) *the demand side*, because only if aggregate demand is sufficiently high will the economy's potential levels of output, productivity and prosperity actually be reached.

The most basic prerequisite for economic prosperity is *high productivity*—without this, the economy cannot produce the goods and services required for high living standards. Beyond this, however, a reasonable level of aggregate demand is required. Inadequate aggregate demand will result in a recession in which much of the productive capacity of the supply side will remain unused, while excessive aggregate demand will generate rapid inflation that will result in high interest rates that undermine investment spending and productivity growth itself, leading to economic stagnation. The ongoing task of government is to develop policies on both the supply side and the demand side of the economy that will contribute to Canadians' prosperity, while still managing to be re-elected.

DEFINITIONS OF NEW TERMS

Full Employment The minimum possible rate of unemployment that can be achieved without generating unacceptable inflation in the economy.

Non-Accelerating Inflationary Rate of Unemployment (NAIRU) The unemployment rate that is consistent with a low and stable rate of inflation.

Stagflation The coincidence of high unemployment with rapid inflation; also characterized by slow growth of output and productivity.

Supply-Side Policies Government policies aimed at increasing the economy's ability to produce goods and services, or productivity (as distinct from demand-side policies which influence the level of aggregate demand for goods and services)

CHAPTER SUMMARY

1. The economic goals of full employment and economic growth conflict with the goal of stable prices, forcing the government to accept trade-offs between these goals.

2. Because of these trade-offs, full employment cannot mean an unemployment rate of zero. It is believed that it is not possible to reduce the national unemployment rate much below 8 percent without generating considerable inflation.

3. Because of various time lags in the implementation and operation of monetary and fiscal policies, these policies cannot quickly reduce either unemployment or inflation.

4. It is important that the government resist political pressures to over-stimulate aggregate demand, as such policies would result in severe inflation and subsequent severe recessions.

5. If inflation is allowed to gain momentum and become ingrained in the economy, it tends to generate very high interest rates and other problems that depress business capital investment spending and pro-ductivity growth—a condition known as "stagflation."

6. Economic policy in Canada is limited by international factors, partic-ularly the need to keep Canadian interest rates high enough to attract foreign capital.

8. Until the Great Depression of the 1930's, it was believed that govern-ment should not intervene in the operation of the economy as a whole.

9. Following the experience of the 1930's, it became accepted that gov-ernments should attempt to influence the level of aggregate demand in the economy, particularly by using government budget deficits to stim-ulate aggregate demand during recessions. Such policies were used with the greatest success during the 1960's.

10. In the 1970's and 1980's, however, the experience with government eco-nomic policies was much less favorable. One problem was that gov-ernment policies tended to alternate between excessive stimulation of aggregate demand that caused rapid inflation, and severe anti-inflation policies that led to recessions.

11. Another problem was that prolonged rapid inflation generated "stagfla-tion," a combination of rapid inflation and economic stagnation, the lat-ter being largely the result of weak business investment spending as a result of high interest rates caused by rapid inflation.

12. These experiences led to new proposals to limit the discretion available to the government with respect to both monetary and fiscal policy, by establishing fixed rules for the growth of the money supply and the use of government budget deficits.

13. Because productivity growth slowed significantly after the late 1970's, there was also increased interest in "supply-side" government eco-nomic policies that were intended to improve productivity perfor-mance.

14. Economic prosperity is the result of the successful performance and interaction of *both* sides of the economy: the supply side and the de-mand side. The supply side must be capable of strong productivity per-formance, and aggregate demand must be high enough to keep output and employment high, but not so high as to generate rapid inflation.

QUESTIONS

1. Suppose that the government "tightened" the Unemployment Insurance system so as to require that UI recipients engage in serious job searches and take suitable jobs that were available. What effect would such a policy have on the unemployment rate that represents "full employment"?

2. What is the present unemployment rate, and what has been the trend in the unemployment rate over the past two years? Does the present rate of inflation and the trend in inflation over the past two years suggest that the economy is at or approaching a condition of full employment? What are the main causes of this situation?

3. Suppose you are the Minister of Finance. Prepare a statement:

   (a) explaining to a group of unemployed young people why the government has decided to implement anti-inflation policies that will have the side-effect of increasing unemployment, especially among young Canadians.

   (b) explaining to a group of senior citizens why the government has decided to stimulate the economy to reduce unemployment in spite of the fact that inflation is already unacceptably rapid in the view of pensioners, many of whom live on fixed incomes.

4. What is the recent trend in real output per worker employed (productivity) in Canada? What might explain this trend?

5. As noted in the text, people's expectations, or psychology, can play an important role in the performance of the economy. "Inflation psychology" can make the problem of inflation more severe, while its opposite, "recession psychology," can slow the economy's recovery from a recession by depressing demand, especially consumer demand.

   Would you characterize the present time as one of inflation psychology or recession psychology? Why?

6.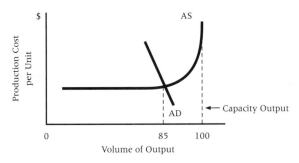

With aggregate demand at the level represented by AD, the economy is operating at only 85 percent of its capacity.

(a) Suppose the government wanted to increase aggregate demand sufficiently to bring the economy up to 90 percent of capacity. Draw a new aggregate demand curve (AD$_1$) and show on the graph the effect of the new situation on output and prices. Explain why these effects occur.

(b) Suppose the government increased the level of aggregate demand further, bringing output up to 95 percent of capacity. Show this new situation on the graph, labelling the new curve AD$_2$. Explain the effects on output and prices.

(c) If the government increased aggregate demand sufficiently to bring output up to 100 percent of capacity, what would happen? Draw another aggregate demand curve (AD$_3$) to represent this situation.

7. Through 1988, the rate of inflation remained quite steady at about 4 percent. Over the year, however, the Bank of Canada raised the Bank Rate from 8.63 to 11.17 percent. In explaining the situation, the Minister of Finance said, "What we are trying to do here is head off the [inflation] problem before it gets to the boom-bust cycle."

(a) Explain what the Minister meant.

(b) What would the Minister have argued would likely happen if the government did not take steps to curb inflation?

(c) With the benefit of hindsight, did this strategy work effectively?

8. Explain what is meant by the following: "The expectations people have about what is going to happen is probably the most important factor in what does happen. So managing people's expectations is a crucial part of economic policy."

What could a government do in order to change people's expectations, and thus make its policies to combat either recession or inflation more effective?

9. Canada's political structure is quite highly decentralized, with provincial governments having extensive responsibilities—and spending powers—in the large and key areas of health care, education and welfare. As a result, the federal government's "own" budget (that is, not including transfer payments to the provinces) in 1992 represented about 43 percent of all government spending in the country, while provincial and local government spending amounted to about 57 percent.

How could this extent of decentralization limit the effectiveness of fiscal policy in Canada?

10. The early 1990's marked a significant development in the Canadian economy, as the rate of inflation declined to the low levels that had prevailed thirty years earlier, before the onset of the "Great Inflation."

In the view of some, the economy had returned to a condition of low inflation, in which interest rates would return to low levels, encouraging business investment spending that would spur stronger growth of productivity, improved international competitiveness and prosperity for Canadians.

Others believed that the economy had sunk into a prolonged period of low demand and high unemployment that would leave it in a state of "semi-recession" for years.

Still others expected that political pressures would force the government to put the economy through yet another round of excessive stimulation of aggregate demand that would generate severe inflation that would end in another serious recession.

On the basis of the evidence available at this time (mainly, trends in unemployment, inflation and productivity), which view seems to be actually developing? What might explain this?

NOTES

1 According to an Organization for Economic Cooperation and Development study in 1991, Canada's UI program alone raised the minimum attainable rate of unemployment by two percentage points.

2 Rapid inflation depresses capital investment in other ways, as well. The main such way is that inflation causes many businesses' profits to be exaggerated because both assets and inventories must be replaced at inflated prices that are not reflected in income statements; the result is that such businesses must pay higher taxes and have less money for investment. In addition, rapid inflation tends to make it more difficult for businesses to raise investment capital through issue of shares, because investors prefer to buy bonds that pay high interest rates rather than shares of companies whose profits are not as high as they appear, especially after taxes.

3 These matters are discussed in more detail in Chapters 32–34.

International trade

International trade is a matter of great importance to the economic prosperity of Canadians. About one in five jobs is directly dependent upon exports, which amounted to nearly $7000 per Canadian and about 25–28 percent of Canada's GDP in the early 1990's. Canada's dependence upon exports is quite high by international standards; for instance, even with Japan's great success in world trade, its exports amount to only about 15 percent of GDP, and the United States exports only about 7 percent of its GDP.[1]

This high exposure to international economic trends has always been of particular concern to those specific regions and communities of Canada that produce *natural resource ("primary") products* for export, such as the coal and lumber products of British Columbia, the grain of the Prairies and the minerals of Northern Ontario and Quebec. Today, however, nearly half of Canada's exports consist of *non-resource-based manufactured goods*, many of which are produced in central Canada. Thus, export industries are major components of the economies of all of Canada's regions.

However, the effects of world economic trends extend well beyond export industries—they affect all Canadians, as the effects of fluctuations in Canada's exports spread throughout the economy due to the *multiplier effect*. Thus, a good year for Prairie wheat farmers means not only higher incomes for the farmers, but also more jobs and income in Ontario's manufacturing sector, as sales of farm machinery rise. There will also be higher sales of consumer goods and services, as the higher incomes of people in both the manufacturing and agricultural sectors are respent. Exports are vital to the prosperity of all Canadians in another way: they are our main means of earning *foreign currency* (mostly US dollars) with which Canadians buy the vast array of imported goods and services that make our standard of living so high. In short, by increasing our exports, we increase our ability to enjoy imports.[2]

Patterns of Canadian trade

Canada relies much more on the exports of its resource and resource-based manufacturing industries than do the other large industrialized nations. As Figure 32-1 shows, Canada's exports consist largely of *natural resources and resource-related products*, such as food, natural gas, lumber, wood pulp, metal, mineral and chemical products, with manufactured goods comprising a relatively small share of exports[3] for an industrialized country. However, the importance of resources as Canadian exports has declined in recent years, from 40 percent of exports in 1963 to less than 22 percent by 1992. Over the same period, exports of manufactured goods grew as a proportion of total exports, reflecting the long-term trend away from primary production and toward manufacturing and services.

Figure 32-1 also shows that Canada's imports consist largely of *finished products*, in the form of both capital goods and consumer goods. Generally, then, Canada's foreign trade still consists in large part of an exchange of resources and resource products for finished products.

As shown in Figure 32-1, Canada's exports exceed its imports in *merchandise trade*. However, on transactions in *services* (such as travel, tourism and interest on debts to foreign lenders), Canada spends much more than it earns internationally. When both merchandise trade and services are considered, Canada regularly spends more on foreign goods and services than foreigners spend on Canadian goods and services.

From Figure 32-2, it can be seen that Canada's trade is overwhelmingly conducted with one nation—the United States. In addition, the importance of the US market to Canada has grown over the recent past—in 1992, over 77 percent of Canada's exports went to the United States as compared to less than 71 percent in 1978. The strong linkage between the two economies seems to be an inevitable result of their geographical proximity.

FIGURE 32-1 *Canada's Major Merchandise Exports and Imports, 1992*

Merchandise Exports			Merchandise Imports		
Commodity Grouping	Value ($ millions)	Per-cent	Commodity Grouping	Value ($ millions)	Per-cent
Fabricated materials	$47 499	30.3%	Other end products	$64 974	44.0%
Motor vehicles & parts	38 014	24.3	Motor vehicles & parts	33 387	22.9
Other end products	35 009	22.4	Fabricated materials	27 398	18.6
Agricultural and fish products (except wheat)	9 545	6.1	Agricultural and fish products	9 127	6.2
Other crude materials	8 654	5.5	Crude petroleum	4 072	2.8
Crude petroleum	5 951	3.8	Other crude materials	3 807	2.6
Natural gas	4 943	3.2	Residual	4 343	2.9
Wheat	3 800	2.4			
Residual	3 150	2.0			
Total	**$156 567**	**100.0**	**Total**	**$147 585**	**100.0**

Source: Statistics Canada, *Summary of Canadian International Trade* (65-001)

FIGURE 32-2   *Canada's Exports and Imports by Area, 1992*

Merchandise Exports to:	Value ($ millions)	Per-cent	Merchandise Imports from:	Value ($ millions)	Per-cent
United States	$121 165	77.4%	United States	$104 390	70.7%
European Economic Community	11 374	7.3	European Economic Community	13 548	9.1
Japan	7 233	4.6	Japan	8 834	6.0
Other countries	16 795	10.7	Other countries	20 905	14.2
Total	**$156 567**	100.0	**Total**	**$147 588**	100.0

Source: Bank of Canada *Review*

Trade and prosperity

> Over much of the post-war period, the main engine of growth in the world economy has been a sharp expansion in trade.
>
> Bank of Montreal *Review*, March-April, 1987

The tremendous expansion of world trade since the Second World War has been of particular benefit to Canada as a major exporting nation, as each additional $1 billion of exports adds about 15 000 jobs to the Canadian economy. While international trade is a major source of Canadians' prosperity, there have also been reasons for concern regarding Canada's trade performance. Canada's share of total world trade fell from 5.3 percent in 1971 to 4.0 percent in the early 1990's, mainly because of a deterioration in Canada's ability to compete internationally. In Chapter 33, we will consider more specific questions of Canadian trade policy and some of the problems and opportunities facing Canada in world trade. First, however, in this chapter we will examine the basic economic principles underlying trade between nations, and the nature of Canada's international trade.

Tariffs and other barriers to trade

The governments of virtually all nations regularly declare that they are "free traders"—that they believe in the economic benefits of international trade, and that barriers to trade should be reduced or even eliminated so that trade may flourish.

When it comes to actually *practicing* these lofty principles, however, governments have a tendency to fall rather short of the ideals that they proclaim. Often, they place *restrictions on imports* of foreign goods into their markets, usually on the grounds that the foreign competitors are "unfair" in one way or another. The most visible of such restrictions on trade are **tariffs** (or custom duties), which are taxes levied on goods imported into a country. The effect (and, indeed, the intent) of a tariff is to increase the price of imported goods, making it more difficult for them to compete in domestic markets, and thus to protect domestic producers against foreign competition.

In addition to tariffs, there are other, often more subtle, restrictions placed on imports by governments. These **non-tariff barriers** to trade include *quotas* on imports, which restrict the quantity of a particular product that may be imported, and *licenses and bureaucratic procedures*, which can involve so much red tape that would-be importers are discouraged. Sometimes, governments practice *preferential purchasing policies*, under which they buy only domestically-produced products, or provide *subsidies* for domestic producers, such as government grants or tax treatment that makes it easier for them to compete with foreign firms. Another non-tariff barrier to trade is *contingent-protection* measures, which allow a government to counter unfair or disruptive trading practices by foreign competitors, such as "dumping" goods at exceptionally low prices. Finally, there are *voluntary export restraints* (VERs), under which one nation agrees to restrict its exports to another country. An example of this is the 1985 Japanese agreement to limit automobile exports to Canada so that the Japanese share of the Canadian market would not increase and disrupt the market. Disagreements over the imposition of such trade restrictions periodically lead to threats of retaliation and talk of "trade wars," a far cry indeed from the ideals of free trade preached by the same governments.

Later in this chapter we will examine the economic reasoning behind free trade, but it should be noted at this point that while many governments advocate free trade *in theory*, what they seem to want *in practice* is freer access to export markets for their own industries while continuing to protect domestic industries from foreign imports. There are obvious contradictions in these positions that make the issue of trade barriers and their reduction or removal a very complex and controversial one. In short, the matter of international trade is a source of many myths, misconceptions and misunderstandings. In order to deal with these, our examination of the topic will take the form of a discussion between a curious citizen and an eminent economist.

> Free trade, one of the great blessings which a government can confer on a people, is in almost every country unpopular.
>
> Lord Macaulay, 1824

How does international trade benefit nations?

CURIOUS CITIZEN: The government favours reducing barriers to trade, but most people I talk to seem to think that, with all the imports coming into Canada, we need higher tariffs, not lower ones. Why do economists and governments tend to favor reducing tariffs?

EMINENT ECONOMIST: Tariffs tend to reduce the volume of international trade between nations because they make it more difficult for imported products to compete with domestically produced products. But international trade is beneficial to all nations, in that it permits nations to specialize their production. Instead of trying to be self-sufficient and produce all sorts of products, many of them inefficiently, nations can specialize in what they can make most efficiently. The result is greater efficiency of production throughout the world, which makes possible a higher material standard of living for all concerned.

Anything that interferes with this process, such as tariffs or other barriers to trade, tends to reduce our efficiency and thus our prosperity. That is why economists and governments believe that barriers to trade should be reduced, and there should be freer trade between nations.

To turn the argument around, if you believe that Canada should have tariffs to keep out foreign goods, then why shouldn't Ontario or Alberta seek to keep out outside goods through tariffs, too? But then why should Toronto or Calgary or Halifax import any goods from "outsiders" ... shouldn't they seek to be self-sufficient, too? And why should your family buy anything not produced by a member of the family? Finally, why should you as an individual have any dealings with other people ... why shouldn't you as an individual seek to be totally self-sufficient?

The answer lies, of course, in the fact that it is economically beneficial for people to *specialize* in something that they do well, to sell it to others, and to buy from others those things that they produce better than you do.

CURIOUS CITIZEN: I can see some cases where this would apply. The Prairie provinces are best suited to wheat production, and southern Ontario specializes in manufacturing—obviously the most efficient arrangement at present. Also, some countries specialize in manufacturing, at which they are

---

It is the maxim of every prudent master of a family, never to attempt to make at home what it will cost him more to make than to buy. The tailor does not attempt to make his own shoes, but buys them of the shoemaker. The shoemaker does not attempt to make his own clothes, but employs a tailor.... What is prudence in the conduct of every private family, can scarcely be folly in that of a great kingdom.

Adam Smith, 1776

very efficient, while others produce raw materials more efficiently. It's obviously beneficial to both Canada and Brazil to specialize in wheat and coffee, respectively, and to trade their products, rather than to try to be self-sufficient.

EMINENT ECONOMIST: Those examples are accurate enough, but it goes much further than that. Surprisingly, the greatest volume of world trade today is not between *dissimilar* countries, but rather between countries that are on the surface quite *similar*—the highly developed and industrialized nations such as the United States, Japan, Canada, Britain, Germany, France and other western European countries.

CURIOUS CITIZEN: That seems rather odd. How do you explain that?

EMINENT ECONOMIST: These industrially advanced economies have pushed specialization to the nth degree. For example, North America exports large automobiles to Europe and Japan but imports small cars from them. These high degrees of specialization create a greater opportunity to benefit from trade.

CURIOUS CITIZEN: But the USA has the highest productivity in the world—it's so advanced technologically that it is more efficient than other countries in the production of most products. Why, then, should the USA trade with other countries—what has the USA to gain through trade?

EMINENT ECONOMIST: That can be explained by what economists call the **theory of comparative advantage**. It is best illustrated by a simple example on a personal level. Suppose the best lawyer in town is also the best typist in town—should she therefore do her own typing?

CURIOUS CITIZEN: Not at all. She may be a faster typist than her secretary, but she can use her time more efficiently by doing legal work. For every hour she spent doing her own typing she might save $10 on secretarial costs, but she'd lose maybe $150 by not using the time for legal work.

EMINENT ECONOMIST: In other words, she can increase her efficiency, her output and her income by specializing in what she does *best of all*?

CURIOUS CITIZEN: Right. By trying to do something else, she loses more than she gains. She has better uses for her time.

EMINENT ECONOMIST: That's right—and the same principle applies to the way nations use *their* productive resources (labour, capital equipment and natural resources). Suppose the USA is 30 percent more efficient than other nations in producing machinery, and 10 percent more efficient in producing shirts. Then the USA should concentrate on producing machinery—it would not make sense to divert scarce productive resources from producing machinery, where they are most efficiently used, to producing shirts, where they are less efficiently used.

CURIOUS CITIZEN: But then the USA would have to buy its shirts from foreign nations.

EMINENT ECONOMIST: That's right, but by selling shirts to Americans, foreign nations can earn the US dollars they need to buy American machinery. And with both the USA and foreign nations specializing in products that they are relatively better at producing, productivity, total output and general living standards are increased. This theory of comparative advantage, then, provides a logical reason why a country such as the USA should import even certain products that it could produce more efficiently than foreigners can. Like the lawyer, it is best for the USA to specialize in what it does best of all.

CURIOUS CITIZEN: So freer trade allows nations to specialize, and that leads to higher productivity, right?

EMINENT ECONOMIST: Right. But that's not all. Freer trade promotes higher productivity not only through *specialization*, but also in two other ways. [See Figure 32-3.]

The first of these is simply through *increased competition*. Industries that are protected by tariffs from foreign competition don't need to become more efficient—management doesn't have to worry as much about productivity, and managers, employees and shareholders can all receive higher incomes, and pass these higher costs along to consumers, through higher prices. On the other hand, free trade creates greater pressure to be as efficient as possible, which is why some don't like the idea of free trade.

The second is through **economies of scale**. When industries and firms have access to larger markets, they can utilize mass-production techniques that in some (not all) industries increase efficiency and productivity. In some mass-production manufacturing industries, it is estimated that the minimum market size needed for fully-efficient production is about 100 million people.

CURIOUS CITIZEN: Okay—I can see how, in theory, international trade permits increased specialization, greater efficiency and a higher standard of living. But, in practice, I see foreign imports causing a lot of trouble for Canadian producers, in areas like cars, clothing, appliances and so on.

FIGURE 32-3 *The Economic Benefits of Trade*

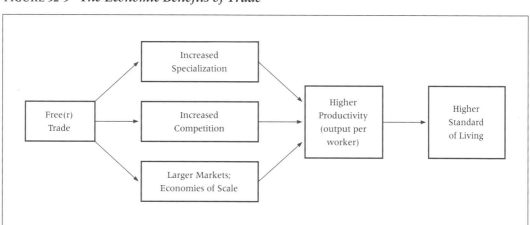

EMINENT ECONOMIST: That's competition, which is what free enterprise is supposed to be all about. It's interesting how many people there are who instinctively favor competition between firms *within* their country, but instinctively oppose competition from *outside* it. Sure, it causes problems for producers, but it keeps them on their toes, and benefits consumers through lower prices. Also, international competition works both ways—Canadian producers sell a great deal abroad, you know—about 25–28 percent of our Gross Domestic Product is exported. In *those* markets, *we* are the "foreign competitors."

UNFAIR COMPETITION?

CURIOUS CITIZEN: I can see how competition can be beneficial in the ways you say, but I also think competition should be fair—and much foreign competition is not fair.

EMINENT ECONOMIST: What do you mean?

CURIOUS CITIZEN: Cheap foreign labor. How can Canadian producers compete with foreign producers using low-wage labor?

EMINENT ECONOMIST: That's a common viewpoint, but it's not supported by the facts. In the first place, many high-wage Canadian firms *do* compete internationally, so we know that this *can* be done. If low wages were the key to being internationally competitive, you would expect the *lowest-wage* industries in any country to be its most successful exporters. In actual fact, the opposite tends to be true—it's usually the *higher-wage* industries that export the most. So higher wages do not necessarily mean that an industry or nation cannot compete internationally, nor do low wages necessarily provide a competitive advantage.

CURIOUS CITIZEN: That seems odd. Why is that so?

EMINENT ECONOMIST: The key to the whole thing is efficiency, or the *productivity* of labor—output per worker per hour. Suppose a foreign worker receives $3.00 per hour for making pencils and, using simple hand tools, produces 150 pencils in an hour. The labor cost per pencil is obviously $0.02 ($3.00 ÷ 150). Now suppose a Canadian worker receives $10.00 per hour for producing pencils, but using modern machinery, produces 500 pencils per hour. The labor cost of each Canadian-made pencil will be $0.02 (10.00 ÷ 500). So, just because Canadian wages are higher doesn't necessarily mean that Canadian production costs per unit must be higher and Canadian producers unable to compete internationally. (See Figure 32-4.)

CURIOUS CITIZEN: So high productivity can more than offset high wages.

EMINENT ECONOMIST: Right. North American workers worry about competition from low-wage foreign workers, but those same foreign workers feel that they cannot possibly compete with North American workers with

FIGURE 32-4 *Productivity and Labor Costs*

	Canadian Worker	Foreign Worker
Hourly Wage	$10.00	$3.00
Hourly Output	500	150
Labor Cost per Unit	$0.02	$0.02

their capital equipment and tremendous efficiency. For instance, it has been estimated that while Mexican workers' wages are about one-fifth those in the United States and Canada, the average output of an American or Canadian worker is about five times that of a Mexican worker.

CURIOUS CITIZEN: Your example of the pencils was rigged to come out in a tie, with the pencils costing the same in both cases. In the real world, who *does* have the competitive advantage?

EMINENT ECONOMIST: It depends on the product. Where production lends itself to mechanization, the North American operation usually has an advantage. For more manual tasks such as making clothing or footwear, lower-wage labor is often more efficient. Some companies produce parts in Canada or the United States, using mechanization, export them to be assembled by hand by lower-wage Mexican labor, and bring back the assembled product to be sold in the US and Canada.

CURIOUS CITIZEN: So some nations are better at some things, and others at other things.

EMINENT ECONOMIST: Yes—and that's why it pays economically to specialize at what you do best, and then trade. Then, everyone can be better off.

BUT WHAT ABOUT UNEMPLOYMENT?

CURIOUS CITIZEN: So far, what you have said makes sense, but I don't see why we should reduce tariffs *right now*, when a lot of Canadians are unemployed.

EMINENT ECONOMIST: Why not?

CURIOUS CITIZEN: More imports would come in, causing more unemployment in Canada, because Canadians would not have jobs producing those imported goods. To protect jobs, shouldn't we *raise* our tariffs, so as to keep out foreign goods and reserve the Canadian market for Canadian-produced goods?

EMINENT ECONOMIST: Is that all there is to it—to solve unemployment, raise our tariffs on foreign products?

CURIOUS CITIZEN: Well, now that you mention it, it seems kind of logical.

EMINENT ECONOMIST: If it were that easy, wouldn't we have solved our unemployment problems long ago? Let's look into this a little further. If we did raise tariffs to try to protect Canadian jobs, what would other nations do?

CURIOUS CITIZEN: I see ... they'd retaliate, by raising *their* tariffs on Canadian goods that we export to their countries. Then our exports to them would fall, and unemployment would increase in *those* Canadian industries.

EMINENT ECONOMIST: Right. What we would gain in employment in *some* industries by raising tariffs, we would lose in *other* industries (our export industries) because of similar retaliatory action by other nations. What many people forget in this connection is that Canada counts upon selling 25–28 percent of its GDP to other countries.

CURIOUS CITIZEN: So if you have an unemployment problem, you shouldn't try to solve it by reducing foreign imports.

EMINENT ECONOMIST: That's right. In fact, that sort of action just makes things worse. During the Great Depression of the 1930's, governments tried to "export unemployment" by raising tariffs. By the time that everyone had retaliated against everyone else in what amounted to a "trade war," tariffs were so high that international trade had been severely reduced. As a result, unemployment had been made much worse than it would have been if tariffs had been left alone. You simply cannot export your economic problems by tossing them off onto other nations. If they depend on you for something, then you depend on them for something else.

CURIOUS CITIZEN: So international trade is a two-way street—you can't just be an exporter, you have to be an importer, too.

EMINENT ECONOMIST: Yes, and that's true for another reason, too. There's the problem of earning foreign currencies. For example, Japan can't buy Canadian goods (our exports) unless Japan has Canadian dollars. But to get Canadian dollars, the Japanese have to sell goods to Canada (our imports). So we must import if we want to be able to export.

For a country as dependent on trade as Canada, matching foreign trade restrictions with domestic ones is not a winning strategy. Canadians would be denied access to an international market large enough to sustain efficient scale production, and an important source of improved productivity and living standards would be foreclosed.

Edward Carmichael
Policy Review and Outlook, 1985: A Time for Decisions,
C.D. Howe Institute

WHO PAYS FOR TARIFFS?

CURIOUS CITIZEN: I can see why international trade is economically beneficial to everyone who takes part in it. Still, taxing foreign imports seems to be a nice way of raising revenue for the government. Canadians already pay so many taxes that it's nice to have some paid by foreigners.

EMINENT ECONOMIST: Just a minute. Who pays the taxes on imports?

CURIOUS CITIZEN: The foreigners ... it's their products we're taxing, isn't it?

EMINENT ECONOMIST: Hold on. Why do we tax imports, anyway? To raise revenue for the federal government?

CURIOUS CITIZEN: Not really. We tax imports to protect our domestic producers from foreign competition.

EMINENT ECONOMIST: And how do tariffs do that?

CURIOUS CITIZEN: By making the price of the imported product higher than it would otherwise have been.

EMINENT ECONOMIST: And how will that affect the price of the same product that is produced by Canadians?

CURIOUS CITIZEN: With less severe competition, Canadian producers will be able to charge higher prices.

EMINENT ECONOMIST: So who really pays, in the final analysis?

CURIOUS CITIZEN: It's the Canadian consumer who pays, through higher prices.

EMINENT ECONOMIST: Right. It is difficult to say with certainty *how much* tariffs cost Canadian consumers, but past studies have put the cost of quotas on clothing alone at one-third of a billion dollars and the total cost in the billions. Of course, as tariffs have been reduced, so have the costs.

In a broader sense, you could say that *everyone pays* in the sense that tariffs reduce international trade, interfere with the process of specialization that increases productivity, and therefore cause us all to have a lower standard of living than we could have had without tariffs. And the cost of tariffs goes further than that, too.

CURIOUS CITIZEN: Why is it that in economics, things can always get worse? Oh well, tell me anyway.

WHAT ABOUT CANADIAN EXPORT INDUSTRIES?

EMINENT ECONOMIST: Suppose the Canadian widget industry, which is not very efficient, gets a tariff to protect itself against imports from Europe, which are of equal quality but less expensive. This tariff will benefit the Canadian widget industry and its workers, who will be sheltered from the effects of foreign competition, but it will hurt the Canadian public, as we have seen, because the price of widgets will be higher than it would have been. However, an equally important effect of the tariff, and one which most people do not see, is its effect on the Canadian fradistat industry, which is a very efficient industry that exports a large proportion of its output to Europe.

CURIOUS CITIZEN: Because the Europeans are likely to retaliate by placing higher tariffs on Canadian fradistats sold in Europe.

EMINENT ECONOMIST: Quite likely. Furthermore, because they can sell fewer widgets to Canada, Europeans will have fewer Canadian dollars with which to buy Canadian-made fradistats.

CURIOUS CITIZEN: So tariffs serve to reward the inefficient producer who can't compete with imports, and penalize the efficient producer who is able to compete in world markets.

EMINENT ECONOMIST: Yes—and this explains why some industries (such as resource industries, and large and efficient agricultural and manufacturing industries) are strongly in favour of free trade, while other industries (such as clothing and footwear) are in favour of continued or even increased restrictions on imports. To some, free trade is an opportunity, while to others, it represents a threat.

THE PETITION OF THE CANDLE MAKERS

The following was written more than 100 years ago by Frederic Bastiat, a brilliant French proponent of free trade.

To the chamber of deputies: We are subjected to the intolerable competition of a foreign rival, who enjoys such superior facilities for the production of light that he inundates our national market at reduced prices. This rival is no other than the Sun. Out petition is to pass a law shutting up all windows, openings and fissures through which the light of the Sun is used to penetrate our dwellings, to the prejudice of the profitable manufacture we have been enabled to bestow on the country.

Signed: Candle Makers

FIGURE 32-5 *The Economic Effects of Trade Restrictions*

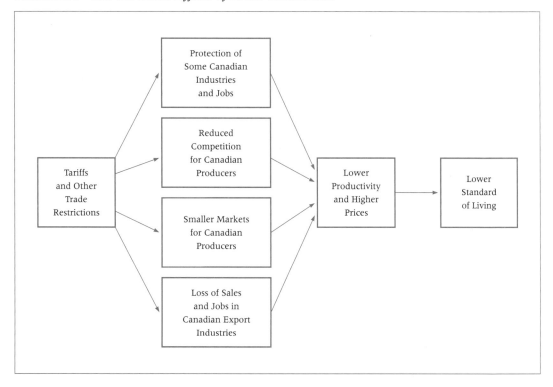

CURIOUS CITIZEN: In summary, then, tariffs and other barriers to trade have a negative effect on our economic prosperity.

EMINENT ECONOMIST: Yes, as a general rule that is true. If you were to summarize what we have said, it would be as follows (see Figure 32-5):

(a) Tariffs do benefit the protected industries and their workers. By protecting them against foreign competition, tariffs permit them to have higher output, employment, profits and wages than otherwise would have been possible.

(b) Because of tariffs the Canadian public as a whole pays *higher prices* for products that it buys. In effect, a tariff takes money from the public in general and gives it to particular industries and their workers. Its effect is very similar to a **subsidy** that is paid by the government out of tax revenues to an industry—except that a tariff has another effect.

(c) It also hurts Canadian industries that *export* to other nations, for the reasons outlined earlier. These industries will have lower output, employment, profits and wages than they otherwise would have had if there had been no tariffs on imports.

CURIOUS CITIZEN: You could say, then, that point (a) is offset by point (c), leaving on balance point (b) as the net effect of tariffs.

IT'S ALL IN HOW YOU LOOK AT IT

As with all things, there are different ways of looking at tariffs. If the government proposed legislation intended to "tax consumers so as to raise funds to pay subsidies to inefficient Canadian industries, the subsidies to be larger the more inefficient the industries are," the public would be in an uproar.

If, on the other hand, the government proposed legislation, the purpose of which was "to protect Canadian businesses and their workers against low-price foreign-made products," many Canadians would quietly accept this as a valid policy.

Both statements are valid descriptions of the effects of tariffs on the Canadian economy.

EMINENT ECONOMIST: Yes, on balance, their effect is higher prices ... or, if you prefer, reduced efficiency and a lower standard of living than we could have had.

CURIOUS CITIZEN: I can see now that, economically, tariffs do not benefit society as a whole. Rather, they benefit some groups at the expense of others. Why, then, do we have tariffs and other barriers to free trade?

EMINENT ECONOMIST: There are two matters to address here: first, the question of why a nation might *establish* tariffs in the first place, and second, why it might *not want to reduce* tariffs that have been in place for long periods of time.

Tariffs as a stimulus to industrial development

EMINENT ECONOMIST: The most common reason for establishing tariffs in the first place is known as the *infant industry* argument. This is based on the idea that certain manufacturing industries could grow in Canada to become fully efficient and competitive with other nations if they were protected by tariffs from well-established foreign competitors during their early years, so that they could become established, efficient and competitive themselves. This argument in favor of tariffs could be particularly important if a nation desired long-term industrial growth. Both Canada and Mexico have used tariffs to promote the growth of the manufacturing sectors of their economies by protecting them against US competition.

CURIOUS CITIZEN: I can see why. They don't want to be merely suppliers of raw materials to industrialized nations forever. Industrial development can benefit them economically.

EMINENT ECONOMIST: There's a second important effect of these tariffs. If a US firm finds that the tariff prevents it from exporting to Canada, it may decide to establish **branch plants** in Canada. By setting up branch plants, the company can avoid having its products taxed by the tariff, because these products are no longer imports; they are produced in Canada. The foreign firm can, in effect, "jump over" the tariff. There are many actual examples of industrial development through branch plants, from the development of the automobile industry in Canada to the building of similar breakfast food plants in Niagara Falls, New York and Niagara Falls, Ontario.

CURIOUS CITIZEN: So, by protecting domestic producers and by attracting branch plants, tariffs can contribute to a nation's industrialization, diversifying its economy away from a dependence on resource extraction and agricultural products, and boosting productivity and employment. All this makes tariffs look like a good thing, rather than a bad thing as you have suggested earlier.

EMINENT ECONOMIST: But it's not that simple—you don't get something for nothing, at least not in economics. Tariffs can stimulate the manufacturing sector of the economy, but this development comes at a cost—the consumer must pay higher prices for the products of these industries. In effect, the public is *subsidizing* the protected industries.

CURIOUS CITIZEN: But the situation should be temporary, shouldn't it? Once the infant industries have matured and become efficient, the tariff protection will be removed.

EMINENT ECONOMIST: That brings us to the second question—having established tariffs, why do governments leave them in force for so long? In theory, the infant industries should mature and no longer need protection, but in fact, it usually doesn't work out that well. Industries that are protected against competition by tariffs tend to remain relatively inefficient, with the result that the tariffs have to be maintained for longer than they were intended to be.

Reduction and removal of tariff protection is made more difficult by the politics of the situation. Once protected industries become established and employers of significant numbers of people, they can become strong political lobbyists for continued tariff protection. While the economic victims of tariffs—consumers—are very numerous, the fact that they are not organized into any kind of effective political lobby means that their political influence is limited. By contrast, those who benefit from tariffs—the protected industries and their employees—are usually well organized so as to have political influence, through organizations such as industry associations and labor unions. Furthermore, they have a more powerful incentive to lobby for protection than consumers have to press for lower tariffs: while the economic costs of protection are spread thinly over millions of consumers, the economic benefits of protectionism are concentrated in the hands of a few in the protected industries. As a result, the political influence of the protected few has often outweighed that of consumers. Largely because of factors such as these, some infant industries tend to have a prolonged and sheltered childhood, and become a drag on the nation's economy.

CURIOUS CITIZEN: So tariffs tend to cause inefficiency.

EMINENT ECONOMIST: Yes, but not just because they shelter industries from foreign competition. Another problem is the *size of the Canadian market*, which is very small by international standards. Many Canadian plants, including the branch plants established in Canada by foreign companies to get behind our tariffs, tend to produce for this small Canadian market only. Consequently, much of Canada's manufacturing sector consists of *small-scale operations* that are less efficient than those in other nations. For example, to be fully efficient, a plant producing television sets should produce between 300 000 and 700 000 sets per year. However, in Canada in the late 1970's, there were *ten* companies producing an average of only about 60 000 *each*. Such small-scale operations make it difficult for producers to become internationally competitive, which in turn requires continued subsidization by the public through tariff protection.

CURIOUS CITIZEN: So tariffs can help to stimulate industrial development, but there are costs and dangers in doing this. How can we tell if it's worth protecting an industry from foreign competition or not?

EMINENT ECONOMIST: There's no simple answer to that question; it's a question of trade-offs, or *costs versus benefits*. The benefits are obviously the industrial development and the jobs associated with it. There are two types of costs to consider, the first being the cost to Canadian consumers. How much extra is the public willing to pay in order to maintain a protected industry and the jobs of its workers?

Let's use as our illustration the kadiddle industry, which is tariff-protected, inefficient and has been declining for years. Suppose that it was estimated that protection of the kadiddle industry "saved" 50 000 jobs and cost the average Canadian family $15 per year through higher prices, for an average cost to consumers of about $3000 per job saved. Many might consider the benefits of tariff protection to outweigh the costs in this example. On the other hand, suppose that only 10 000 jobs were saved and

---

Canada is not the only country facing difficult decisions concerning tariffs. The World Bank's 1986 Development Report put the "efficiency loss" of each job saved by protectionist measures at:

- $71 000 in the US steel industry in 1985
- $124 000 in the European clothing industry in 1980
- $169 600 in the US clothing industry in 1980

The World Bank also pointed out that, because protectionist measures raise prices, they hurt lower-income people the most.

the cost per family was $100 per year. In this case, the cost to consumers would be $100 000 per job saved, which could look like quite a different matter, especially when it is considered that the average job in the kadiddle industry only pays $22 000.

CURIOUS CITIZEN: Sounds simple enough. I'd support the tariff protection in the first case, but the cost is out of all proportion in the second one.

EMINENT ECONOMIST: Unfortunately, it's not quite that simple—there's another type of cost that has to be considered. Because Canada places a tariff on imported products, other nations often retaliate with tariffs on their own that hurt Canadian exports and jobs. Let's go back to that first case, with the 50 000 jobs saved at a cost per job saved of $3000. Suppose that if Canada's tariffs on kadiddles were eliminated, Europe would remove its tariffs on other Canadian exports, resulting in 25 000 additional jobs in Canada's growth-oriented, high-wage export industries. What would you do then?

CURIOUS CITIZEN: I'm not sure. There would be a net loss of 25 000 jobs in the short run, but the kadiddle industry was declining anyway. And there would be 25 000 more jobs in a growing sector of the economy, which could well mean even more in the longer run. Also, consumers would save quite a bit of money. That would be a tough call—I'd seem heartless if I ended the protection of the kadiddle industry, but I'd be a poor strategist if I didn't give our growth industries better access to the European market.

EMINENT ECONOMIST: Be careful—you're starting to sound like an economist.

The evolution of tariff policy

CURIOUS CITIZEN: I hope the condition is curable. We've seen some specifics, but what about the big picture? What is the *general* trend with respect to tariffs and other barriers to trade?

EMINENT ECONOMIST: Since the Second World War, the trend has been to lower them. Perhaps it would be a good idea to run through a brief history of tariff policy, to put the matter in perspective. Sir John A. Macdonald's National Policy, adopted in 1879, used tariffs to promote the growth of manufacturing, especially in central Canada.

During the Great Depression of the 1930's, many nations, especially the USA, increased tariffs to very high levels. While each country was trying to protect the jobs of its people in the face of the depression, the overall result of this "trade war" was a sharp decline in world trade, and higher unemployment in all nations—a bad experience for all.

The General Agreement on Tariffs and Trade (GATT)

Following the Second World War a landmark step was taken when 23 countries, including Canada, signed the **General Agreement on Tariffs and Trade (GATT)** in 1947. The basic purpose of the GATT was to prevent a recurrence of the 1930's experience by agreeing to the principle of negotiating reductions in tariffs among participating countries, with the objective of increasing world trade and prosperity for all concerned. This agreement represented a major shift in policy and began a long trend toward freer international trade. The basic approach of the GATT has been to use *multilateral negotiations* in which all parties to the agreement negotiate mutual tariff reductions, as distinct from trade agreements between specific nations, such as the North American Free Trade Agreement between Canada, the United States and Mexico.

From 1947 to 1993, the members of the GATT met in a series of eight "rounds" of talks to negotiate tariff reductions. The seventh round (the "Tokyo Round") lasted from 1973 to 1979, and expanded the talks to include *non-tariff barriers* to trade. The eighth round (the "Uruguay Round") ran from 1986 to 1993, and included by the time of its conclusion about 116 nations, a great increase from the original 23. It had an ambitious agenda that included trade in *services*, which had grown to almost 30 percent of world trade. This addition represented a further broadening of the GATT's focus, which had traditionally been on trade in *goods*.

In addition to reducing tariffs, the GATT has sought to *establish rules for fair competition* in international trade. For instance, one practice that is considered unfair is "**dumping**," or exporting a product at a price that is below the cost of producing it, or below the price in your home market. It is also considered unfair for a government to give *subsidies* to its industries that give them an advantage in international competition by making it possible for them to sell at prices below their real production costs.

CURIOUS CITIZEN: How successful has the GATT been?

EMINENT ECONOMIST: The GATT has achieved a great deal. By the early 1990's, GATT agreements covered 80–90 percent of world trade in merchandise. As Figure 32-6 shows, from 1947–1990, the GATT reduced tariffs among industrialized countries from about 40 percent to 5 percent. During the same period world trade expanded tremendously, by about 800 percent.

Mexico provides a dramatic illustration of the impact that the GATT can have. After 40 years of remaining outside of GATT in order to maintain its own system of very high tariff barriers, Mexico joined the GATT in 1987. From 1987 to 1992, Mexico's average tariff decreased from 45 percent to 9 percent.

CURIOUS CITIZEN: Sounds like the GATT is an unqualified success.

THE GENERAL AGREEMENT ON TARIFFS AND TRADE

The GATT is best understood not so much as another international organization, but rather as probably the largest contract ever written. Membership in the GATT makes a nation-state a party to a contract, rather than just a member of an organization.

One key element of the GATT contract is *the principle of non-discrimination*, which means that all parties to the contract will be treated equally by all other parties. In practice, this means that a nation cannot set different tariffs on the same good imported from different countries. In GATT terms, this confers "most favored nation" status upon all parties to GATT, meaning that each has the same access to the others' markets.

Another key element is that *all nations that sign the GATT agree to observe its negotiated terms*. While this seems self-evident or even redundant at first, it is in fact quite significant. Under international law, a nation-state can abrogate any agreement with another state or its citizens. Therefore, by signing the GATT, nations agree to forego this basic right of nationhood with respect to matters covered by the GATT. Another basic principle of the GATT is *reciprocity*, which in practical terms means that negotiated reductions in tariffs should be balanced country-by-country.

A fourth key aspect of the GATT is *impartial settlement of trade disputes* between parties to the agreement, through processes provided by the GATT. Under the GATT, trade disputes between nations (such as, for instance, whether a country was unfairly restricting imports from another country) are decided by a tribunal of officials who are knowledgeable about trade and neutral with respect to the parties to the dispute.

In order to make the GATT more flexible, certain exceptions to some of these basic principles are allowed. Probably the most important exception is for trade agreements among specific nations or groups of nations such as the European Community and the North American Free Trade Agreement. The nations involved in such agreements are not required to extend the benefits of their agreements to all other parties to the GATT. Exception to the GATT's principles can also be made if negotiated tariff reductions would cause "serious injury" to a nation's domestic producers—in such cases, a nation can negotiate with the other parties to the GATT to withdraw those tariff reductions, at least temporarily. Nations can impose trade controls if required for their "national security," and Less Developed Countries (LDC's) are permitted to use import quotas to protect and encourage "infant industries," provided that the quotas are non-discriminatory.

FIGURE 32-6　*Tariff Levels, 1940–2000*

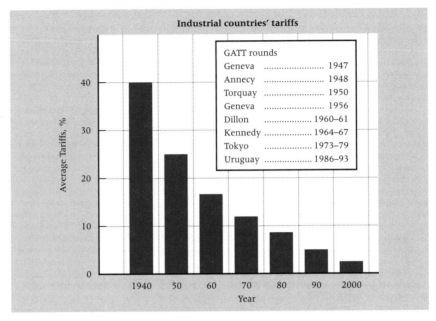

Industrial countries' tariffs

GATT rounds
Geneva	1947
Annecy	1948
Torquay	1950
Geneva	1956
Dillon	1960–61
Kennedy	1964–67
Tokyo	1973–79
Uruguay	1986–93

Source: Centre for International Economics; IMF

EMINENT ECONOMIST: Not completely. After the late 1970's, the GATT encountered growing problems. The larger number of players complicated negotiations, making it more difficult to reach agreements. Also, the inclusion of services and non-tariff barriers in the GATT negotiations added a great deal more complexity to the talks than had existed when they focused on tariffs on goods only. Non-tariff barriers present a particularly difficult problem, as the subtleties of these make it more difficult to establish and enforce rules.

A particularly contentious matter was a bitter dispute between the European Economic Community and the United States over government subsidies for grain farmers. Massive government subsidies to Europe's farmers transformed Europe from one of the world's largest grain importers in the mid-1970's to a huge surplus producer, producing almost 25 percent more than it could consume. European governments then used huge export subsidies to dump this surplus onto world markets, displacing massive amounts of Canadian and US grain exports, in the process depressing wheat prices to below the level of the 1930's when adjusted for inflation. This led to US demands for Europe to end its farm subsidies and threats of US retaliation if the subsidies continued, in a form of a "trade war."

Perhaps the main problem faced by the GATT since the late 1970's, however, has been a quite widespread tendency toward *increased protectionism*, especially in the USA and Europe. Faced with increasingly strong foreign competition from both Japan and many less developed countries as

An International Monetary Fund study concluded in 1988 that US non-tariff barriers against imported cars, textiles and steel were equivalent to a 25 percent tariff, a level not seen since the Second World War.

well as slower economic growth and higher unemployment, some nations were not only resisting further reductions in protection, but erecting *additional* trade barriers, mainly of the non-tariff type. In many cases, one nation would charge another with unfair trading practices, especially "dumping," and take unilateral retaliatory action against these in the form of countervailing tariffs and other actions. In the view of many observers, many of these actions by Europe, the USA and other nations were unjustified by the facts, and were really just increased protection of domestic producers against foreign competition whose crime was not that it was *unfair* but rather that it was *too successful*. In other words, such tariffs were often not really "countervailing tariffs," but rather the kind of restrictions on fair competition that the GATT seeks to reduce and eventually eliminate.

However, the GATT had difficulties in dealing with these tactics because it lacked clear definitions of what constitutes "subsidies" and "dumping," and there was no requirement that nations submit their trade disputes to a neutral body for settlement. Because of this, it was possible for Europe, the USA and others to impose unilateral and arbitrary trade restrictions against competitors. And because such tactics tend to breed retaliation that has a way of escalating into a trade war, such a situation was potentially dangerous.

CURIOUS CITIZEN: Was the GATT able to deal with these challenges?

EMINENT ECONOMIST: After seven years of difficult negotiations, a new GATT agreement was reached in late 1993 that provided considerable grounds for optimism. In general terms, the new GATT agreement:

- lowered trade barriers worldwide
- established the first free-trade rules for trade in services
- gradually brought agriculture and textiles under the new lower-tariff regime
- provided stronger rules to protect exporters, and
- established a much more effective system for the settlement of trade disputes between nations.

More specifically, the new GATT agreement became effective July 1, 1995. The developed countries were to reduce tariffs on industrial goods by 38 percent over six years. For farm products, the troublesome agricultural subsidies were to be reduced and all trade barriers were to be converted to tariffs, which were to be reduced by 36 percent over six years. Various new rules covering trade in services were established, and certain long-established barriers to trade in textiles were to be phased out over a period of ten years, five years sooner than before. In addition, clearer definitions of "subsidies" and "dumping" were established, making the rules for international trade clearer.

CURIOUS CITIZEN: But were these new rules to be *enforced* more effectively than in the past?

EMINENT ECONOMIST: A new Multilateral Trade Organization (MTO) was to be established, the purpose of which would be to administer the new rules for trade and to operate a new and much more effective system for settling trade disputes between nations. According to the GATT, "members shall not themselves make determinations of violations or suspend concessions, but shall make use of the dispute settlement rules and procedures." Potentially, this is an extremely important aspect of the agreement, as it would prevent nations such as the USA from unilaterally declaring that another nation was trading unfairly and imposing retaliatory measures against it.

Instead, trade disputes between nations would be referred to a *panel of three neutral experts* from countries not involved in the dispute, who would make a decision. If the nations involved in the dispute could not agree on who should serve as members of the panel, the MTO would appoint the panel. A panel's decision could be appealed to a seven-member appellate body for a final decision. For each step in the process, there are clear deadlines. If a nation is found to have violated trade rules, it must either change its practices or expose itself to retaliation.

CURIOUS CITIZEN: What is the effect of the new GATT agreement expected to be on Canada?

EMINENT ECONOMIST: In general terms, as a major exporter, Canada stands to gain from freer world trade. In particular, Canadian wheat and grain farmers would benefit as the farm subsidy war between the USA and Europe eased, and grain prices rose. As well, Canadian beef and pork producers expected to benefit from better access to export markets. And, of course, lower trade barriers would mean lower prices for consumers.

CURIOUS CITIZEN: Was the new GATT agreement expected to have any negative effects on Canada?

EMINENT ECONOMIST: In general terms, many Canadian industries would see a gradual increase in foreign competition as tariffs were reduced; however, most of these tariffs were already quite low, so further reduction of them was not in most cases a major threat.

The most serious concerns about the new GATT agreement came from *Canadian farm producers operating under* **marketing boards**, mostly dairy and poultry producers. The objective of these marketing boards is to increase farmers' incomes by increasing the prices of farm products. This is achieved through "supply management"—the marketing board limits the amount that each farmer can produce, so as to hold down the market supply of the product and keep its price high enough for all farmers to make a profit. Largely as a result of marketing boards, prices for products such as milk, cheese, chicken, turkey and eggs in Canada were often 50 to 100 percent higher than in the United States. To keep the supply of these farm products on Canadian markets down and their prices up, however, Canada must also keep out imports of lower-cost foreign products, through strict import quotas. And it was these restrictions on imports that ran afoul of the rules under the new GATT agreement in 1993.

Under the new GATT agreement, import quotas such as Canada's were no longer allowed. Instead, they were to be "tariffied," or *converted to tariffs* providing equivalent protection for Canadian farmers. Initially, these tariffs were to be extremely high—for instance, 351 percent on butter, 283 percent on milk, 280 percent on chicken and 192 percent on eggs. Such high tariffs would act as a virtual ban on imports much as quotas had; however, the GATT agreement required that the tariffs be reduced by 36 percent over six years. This led Canadian farmers to fear that the protection against import competition that they had enjoyed would be eroded, eventually leading to an inflow of imports that would in effect destroy marketing boards by ending their ability to control the supply of food on the Canadian market.

Canadian *food processors* were also concerned about the GATT agreement, but for very different reasons. Food processors that had to buy inputs such as dairy and poultry products produced under Canadian marketing boards and protected by very high tariffs would find themselves at a serious competitive disadvantage relative to US food processors who could buy the same inputs at much lower prices in the USA. These Canadian food processors argued that they might have to curtail operations in Canada, which would not only involve the loss of many jobs but also leave Canadian marketing boards and their farmers without a market for much of their output.

During the 1986–93 GATT negotiations, Canada had been concerned that the new GATT code on subsidies might outlaw many of the subsidies provided to businesses by Canada's federal and provincial governments. However, under the new GATT subsidies code Canada's federal and provincial governments would be able to provide subsidies and incentives for companies for the purposes of regional development, Research and Development and environmental protection, as well as subsidies that are generally available to all industries as under previous GATT rules.

CURIOUS CITIZEN: Was there any estimate of the overall impact of the new GATT agreement?

EMINENT ECONOMIST: Such estimates are difficult to make because of the very broad scope and long term of the GATT agreement. The best estimates were that the agreement would increase world trade in goods by about $745 billion per year by 2005 (a 12 percent increase) and that world income would be increased by at least $230 billion per year.

CURIOUS CITIZEN: Overall, then, it sounds like the GATT has been doing a good job.

EMINENT ECONOMIST: Yes, but the GATT is far from the only important trade agreement in operation. As mentioned earlier, the GATT is a multilateral agreement, involving a great many nations. In addition to the GATT, some nations have reached smaller-scale trade agreements among themselves, known as **trading blocs**.

Trading blocs

CURIOUS CITIZEN: What are trading blocs?

EMINENT ECONOMIST: These are separate trade agreements negotiated outside of the GATT. The most noteworthy ones are the European Economic Community (or EEC, also known as the European Common Market) and the North American Free Trade Agreement. Other such agreements include another group of European nations known as the European Free Trade Association (see Figure 32-7) and Australia and New Zealand. According to the International Monetary Fund, there were in 1992 at least nine other regional trading arrangements in Latin America, Africa, the Caribbean and the Middle East.

CURIOUS CITIZEN: What is the "1992 program" for Europe?

EMINENT ECONOMIST: For many years, there have been no tariffs between members of the European Economic Community; however, various other barriers to trade have existed, especially different government regulations and product standards in different countries. By dealing with most of these obstacles, the "1992 program" unifies 12 European countries economically into a single integrated market without trade barriers. The objective is a unified market of about 340 million consumers, with goods, services and capital moving easily across national borders. Officially, the "1992 program" came into effect when the Maastricht Treaty came into force on November 1, 1993, almost a year late. By the end of the century, it is planned to have one currency for all nations that are party to the agreement, although this is the single most difficult issue faced by the nations involved.

CURIOUS CITIZEN: What would be the effect of all this?

FIGURE 32-7 *European Trade Blocs*

EMINENT ECONOMIST: A study sponsored by the Commission of the European Communities projected that the creation of a unified market would add about 5 percent to the Community's Gross Domestic Product.[4] In the medium term, the study projected that the 1992 program would add as many as 2 million new jobs and keep average consumer prices 6 percent lower than in a divided market.

CURIOUS CITIZEN: And what does this all mean for Canada?

EMINENT ECONOMIST: To some, an economically unified Europe represents an opportunity, since it means the development of a very large and wealthy market. In 1992, Canada's exports to the EEC were over $11 billion, and while this was less than one-tenth of Canada's exports to the USA, the 1992 program might present an opportunity to increase this trade. Others are concerned that Canadian producers will face stronger competition from European companies that are able to gain major economies of scale by operating in a domestic market of 340 million consumers. The EEC is a pow-

> The single market (has given) EC companies a large home market to match the domestic markets of the United States and Japan that have enabled their companies to benefit from enormous economies of scale.
>
> Bruce Barnard, Brussels correspondent for *The Journal of Commerce*

erful force in world trade, representing about 16 percent of all world exports as compared to 15 percent for the USA and less than 4 percent for Canada.

A greater concern is that the new unified Europe could enact protectionist measures against imports from outside, becoming an economic "Fortress Europe." The European Community has stated that these concerns are unfounded and that it will maintain a liberal trading policy. However, Europe's increasingly aggressive use of anti-dumping measures and voluntary export restraints in the early 1990's caused concern among its trading partners. Europe is an important market for Canada, so European trade restrictions would be quite damaging to Canada.

CURIOUS CITIZEN: So are these trading blocs good or bad, then?

EMINENT ECONOMIST: It all depends on how they are used, and the relationships that develop between them. At their best, regional trading blocs could lead the way toward freer trade worldwide, by establishing freer trade within themselves and then extending this principle to trade between blocs.

At the other extreme, trading blocs could increase the risk of trade barriers or even trade wars between the blocs. For instance, trade relations between the United States and Europe have been very strained over the issue of agricultural subsidies, as have relations between the USA and Japan.

If major trade blocs wound up trading mostly *within themselves* rather than *among each other*, the situation could be dangerous. If you divide the nations of the world into four groups—North America, the EEC, Asia-Pacific and "The Rest"—annual trade at the start of the 1990's between countries *within* these groups was $1.5 trillion, while trade *between* the groups was $1.6 trillion. Thus, if the GATT were to break down and regional trading blocs take over, more than half of all world trade could be somewhat at risk. The biggest losers would be "The Rest"—mostly poor nations—who would never in reality be able to unify into an effective trade bloc and would be at the mercy of the powerful blocs.

"Globalization"

CURIOUS CITIZEN: What's all this talk about "globalization"?

EMINENT ECONOMIST: Over the past two decades, and especially in the 1980's, the structure of the world economy has undergone a major transformation. Due to various factors, including lower trade barriers, the spread of the

> Throughout the world, we are coming to terms with a new reality: the borders of the economy are no longer the borders of the state.
>
> Marshall Cohen, president and CEO of Molson Cos. Ltd., to the Canada-UK Chamber of Commerce Joint Committee annual conference in London, 1991

market system into many nations, and especially due to improved communications technology and falling transportation and communications costs, much more business is now conducted on an international basis, rather than within the borders of any one country. This growing *internationalization of business* is described by the term "globalization."

For instance, a Toronto department-store buyer of high-fashion clothing orders a line of dresses from a New York designer. Within an hour of the order the designer sends via satellite the drawings and specifications for making the dresses to a fibre-optic link in Hong Kong, where they appear on a high-resolution computer monitor, ready for a manufacturing engineer to transform them into prototype garments. The prototypes are then reproduced in a Chinese factory. The designer, the engineer and the factory supervisor conduct a video teleconference to work out details, and the finished garments arrive in Toronto less than six weeks after the order was placed.

CURIOUS CITIZEN: To me, "globalization" seems like just another aspect of freer trade, with some fancy high-tech equipment thrown in. Earlier in the century, it was the intercontinental telephone; now it's satellites and computers.

EMINENT ECONOMIST: Many economists believe that the implications of this technology go far beyond that kind of analogy. By allowing buyers and sellers to communicate quickly and effectively all around the world, the technology expands the very concept of a "market" for many items from your local area or country to the entire globe. This adds tremendously to the number of sellers that buyers can choose from, *extending competition* in more fields to a global basis. Hence the term "globalization."

CURIOUS CITIZEN: What are the implications of "globalization" for Canada?

EMINENT ECONOMIST: Many Canadian producers will face *stronger competition* as "globalization" brings more players into the marketplace. The other side of the coin is that these emerging producing countries will provide *growing markets*, especially for the infrastructure and capital goods that they need to build. Canada is a world leader in some of these fields, such as telecommunications and engineering services.

Another implication of "globalization" for Canada is that it will increase the cost to Canadians of pursuing protectionist trade policies. The costs to consumers are increased by the fact that we would be keeping out of Canada goods that were becoming even less expensive due to "globalization," raising the cost per Canadian job saved to very high levels.

> The dynamic developing regions thus constitute a two-edged sword: on one side, new markets and high-return investment opportunities; on the other, a real and increasing threat to the living standards of large groups of workers in the developed world.
>
> Peter Nicholson, Facing the Future, in *The Financial Post 500*, 1993

And, as other nations retaliated against our protectionism, Canada would lose access to the most rapidly-growing markets in the world. All of this means increased pressure on Canada to reduce tariffs and other trade barriers and to become more efficient and competitive.

Adjusting to freer trade

CURIOUS CITIZEN: Still, not all Canadian industries will find it easy to do so. What are the implications of some of these international economic forces for the Canadian economy?

EMINENT ECONOMIST: Canada's traditional strength in *natural resources* will continue, along with products linked to our resource base. However, Canada is quite capable of competing internationally in many other areas as well, as shown by companies such as Northern Telecom and our automobile industry. Generally, Canadians' manufacturing successes tend to be in *high technology* or specialized fields, in which output per worker (productivity) is high enough to make Canadian products competitive despite our high wage rates. However, if past trends continue, *labor-intensive* industries (those that require a lot of labor, such as clothing and footwear) will experience difficulty competing with imports, and production of such products will tend to relocate in lower-wage countries such as Mexico, Hong Kong, Singapore, Taiwan and Korea.

CURIOUS CITIZEN: So free trade would bring not only benefits but also some pretty serious problems for the Canadian economy, too. Some of our industries would expand greatly with access to foreign markets, but others would contract severely due to foreign competition. This would be a tremendous adjustment for our economy to have to make—in the process, many workers might be laid off, businesses may go bankrupt, and so on. I know that's only the dark side of the story, but layoffs and bankruptcies would likely happen if free trade became a fact.

EMINENT ECONOMIST: That's true, which is why it is generally agreed that governments should *reduce tariffs gradually*, and *provide long advance notice* of planned tariff reductions to industries that will be affected by them. The gradual approach would give these industries time to make adjustments, in either their production methods and efficiency, or in their actual product lines. In some cases, it makes more sense to switch to new products rather than to try to compete with the imports.

CURIOUS CITIZEN: Those things would certainly help, but the fact remains that some industries and workers in all countries would be very adversely affected economically—shouldn't something be done for them?

EMINENT ECONOMIST: Many people would agree—tariff reductions are undertaken for the economic benefit of people, so it seems unfair to sacrifice the minority that is hurt by tariff cuts. There is a logical as well as moral argument for government assistance of some sort to those industries and workers that are hurt—the basic idea being that the majority that benefits economically from tariff cuts should in some way assist the minorities that are hurt economically.

CURIOUS CITIZEN: You say "assist in some way"—but surely you don't mean government subsidies to prop them up and keep them producing the same products that were proving uncompetitive and unsuccessful.

EMINENT ECONOMIST: No—generally, the proposed assistance would take the form of *retraining programs* for workers, and *loans and technical assistance* to help businesses to convert to other lines of production. The idea is not just to help those who are adversely affected by tariff cuts, but also to promote more rational and efficient specialization of production among countries, for the general economic benefit of all concerned, which is what international trade is all about. There is little doubt that freer trade involves significant long-term economic benefits for all. The transition period would be difficult, as long-established industries declined or even vanished, but the economics of the situation dictate freer trade as the long-run approach, as the government says (see Figure 32-8).

FIGURE 32-8 *Adjusting to Reduced Tariffs*

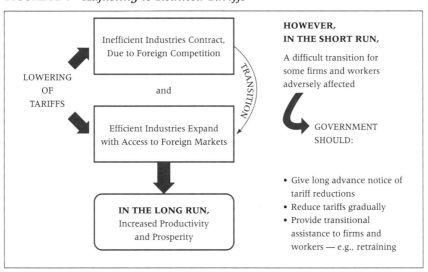

CURIOUS CITIZEN: What you say is logical, but it all sounds so difficult. Wouldn't it be easier to continue as we have in the past, with our natural resource exports earning our way in the world, and our manufacturing industries protected against foreign competition?

EMINENT ECONOMIST: Circumstances are changing. Canadians can no longer count on their natural resources to carry them economically for an indefinite period of time. There is growing competition from Third World countries anxious to sell their resources as a base for their economic development. Also, many forecasters believe that world demand for our natural resources

---

YOU DECIDE

Import quotas on footwear, which have been in effect for eight years, are scheduled to expire in one month. The Canadian Import Tribunal (a government agency) has recommended that the government should drop import quotas on all footwear except women's and girl's casual footwear, and that quotas on these should be phased out over the next three years. The Import Tribunal bases its recommendation in part on estimates that shoe import quotas are costing Canadian consumers $100 million annually, and that perhaps 350 to 700 jobs have been saved by quotas at an annual cost to consumers of $120 000 to $240 000 per job saved. The Consumers Association of Canada and the Canadian Shoe Retailers Association have both argued that the quotas should be removed, pointing out that even without quotas, footwear imports are subject to a tariff of approximately 20 percent—the highest Canadian tariff.

The Shoe Manufacturers Association of Canada claims that domestic manufacturers' share of the market has declined over the past four years from 47 percent to 33 percent. It has asked the government to extend the quotas for a minimum period of five more years and to reserve 50 percent of the Canadian market for Canadian producers. The industry employs about 15 000 people, mainly in Ontario and Quebec. Over the past few years, the federal government has invested quite heavily in financial support for the industry. Political support for the government in Quebec and Ontario, which was crucial to its success in the last election, has been weakening lately. The labor union movement has clearly stated its opposition to any move that would threaten jobs, and a recent public opinion poll indicates that Canadians are nervous about foreign competition.

Finally, the European Economic Community has warned that if the Canadian footwear quotas are extended, it will retaliate against Canadian exports, including methanol, styrene, polyethylene, acetate, kraft paper, wire rod, steel coils and cold-rolled sheets and plates. The value of these exports is about $170 million per year.

If you were the government of Canada, what would you decide?

will not grow as it has in the past, as the direction of economic growth shifts from physical products toward services, information processing and more sophisticated manufactured products, such as electronic equipment. To succeed in these fields, Canada needs access to larger markets, which means export markets. Attracting export markets would, in turn, mean opening Canadian markets more to foreign producers, and accepting the kinds of adjustments we have been discussing here. The world is changing, as markets become globalized and international trade expands rapidly. Canada can choose to resist change, by sheltering its established industries indefinitely, or to adapt to change by looking outward to new markets and opportunities.

DEFINITIONS OF NEW TERMS

Tariff A tax, or import duty, on goods imported into a country, the effect of which is to increase the prices of those imported goods.

Non-Tariff Barriers Other methods (besides tariffs) of restricting imports, including quotas and licenses for imports, preferential purchasing policies and subsidies for domestic producers.

Import Quotas Legal limits on the volume of particular types of goods that may be imported into a nation.

Theory of Comparative Advantage The theory that even if one nation is more efficient in the production of all items than another nation, it can still be to the economic advantage of both nations to specialize in what they produce most efficiently (items in which each has a "comparative advantage"), and trade with each other.

Economies of Scale The achievement of increased efficiency as a result of larger-scale productive operations.

Subsidy Government financial assistance, through measures such as grants, loans or special tax treatment, to an industry.

Dumping The practice of exporting a product at a price below the cost of producing it, or below the price charged in the country in which it is produced.

Branch Plant A manufacturing plant established in a nation by a foreign-owned firm in order to avoid tariffs on imports by producing its products inside that nation.

The General Agreement on Tariffs and Trade (GATT) An international agreement under which many nations have since 1947 negotiated reductions in tariffs in order to promote freer trade.

Trading Blocs Groups of countries that have made trade agreements among themselves outside of the GATT.

Marketing Board Government agency that increases the incomes of farmers by restricting the production/supply of particular farm products so as to increase their price.

Canada–US Auto Pact Agreement between Canada and the United States since 1965 that provides for free trade in automotive vehicles, products and parts together with guarantees that employment in Canada in the industry will be proportional to the volume of cars sold in Canada.

CHAPTER SUMMARY

1. International trade is of great importance to Canada, which exports over 25 percent of its GDP. About one in five jobs in Canada is directly dependent upon exports. About three-quarters of Canada's trade is with the United States.

2. To a large extent, Canada's trade still consists of an exchange of Canadian resources and resource products for imports of foreign manufactured goods.

3. Free trade between nations promotes economies of scale, international specialization and competition, all of which increase productivity, making a higher standard of living possible for all concerned.

4. While it is widely believed that low wages give a country a competitive advantage, this is not necessarily the case, if that country's labor productivity is also low.

5. The results of tariffs and other barriers to trade are reduced specialization and competition, lower productivity, higher prices and lower living standards.

6. Canada has used tariffs to promote the development of manufacturing industry in Canada. Consequently, much of the nation's manufacturing sector came to consist of relatively small-scale plants (including many branch plants of foreign firms) producing for the small Canadian market only and operating inefficiently by international standards.

7. Since 1947, Canada has been a party to the General Agreement on Tariffs and Trade, which has sought to promote increased international trade through multilateral negotiations to reduce tariffs.

8. For about thirty years, the GATT made great progress in reducing tariffs; however, after the mid-1970's it slowed for various reasons, including the growing number of participants and issues, the growing complexity of issues, and growing protectionism on the part of key players, including the United States and Europe.

9. In 1993, the GATT concluded the "Uruguay Round" of negotiations that had commenced in 1986. Key features of the agreement included lower

trade barriers worldwide, the first free-trade rules for trade in services, gradual reductions in trade barriers in agriculture and textiles, stronger rules to protect exporters and a more effective system for settling trade disputes between nations.

10. In addition to the GATT's multilateral approach, there are separate trade agreements (trading blocs) between nations, such as the European Community and the North American Free Trade Agreement.

11. In Europe, the "1992 program" unifies 12 European countries into a single market of 340 million consumers.

12. "Globalization" refers to a recent trend toward conducting more business on an international basis, with stronger international competition the result. Key factors in this trend have been the spread of the market system to more countries and the development of improved communications and transportation technology.

13. Canadian producers face both greater international opportunities and increased international competition in the future, as international competition intensifies. The likely result is reduced importance of some industries (mostly labor-intensive ones) and the expansion of industries in which Canada has the greatest natural advantage.

14. To help Canadian producers to adjust to these changes, the government can reduce tariffs gradually after providing advance notice, as well as provide transitional assistance to affected workers and firms.

QUESTIONS

1. In the early 1990's, the export sector of the Canadian economy was one of the economy's strongest features. Is Canada's export sector still performing well? Why or why not?

2. Has the "1992 program" in Europe had any significant economic impact on Canada? Is there any evidence that concerns about its becoming a "Fortress Europe" with respect to trade policy are justified or not?

3. Suppose Canada were considering a GATT proposal for totally free trade, under which all tariffs and other restrictions on imports, as well as all government subsidies to producers, would be eliminated. How would this likely be viewed in:
   (a) British Columbia?
   (b) the Prairies?
   (c) Ontario?
   (d) Quebec?
   (e) the Atlantic provinces?

4. In the early 1980's, it was estimated that protection of Canada's clothing industry cost each Canadian family an average of $43 per year. Do you believe that this is too high a price to pay for the preservation of jobs in the clothing industry? Is this the only factor that should be taken into account when deciding whether to maintain protection of the clothing industry?

5. What steps could Canada's footwear industry take to be able to compete more successfully with imported goods?

6. The text notes that many people seem to instinctively favor competition between firms *within* their own country, but instinctively oppose competition from foreign firms *outside* their country. What might explain this?

7. In the 15 years prior to the new GATT agreement in December 1993, the United States had quite frequently imposed unilateral trade restrictions on foreign imports. Following the agreement, there was concern that the US Congress may reject certain key parts of it, such as the protections provided for exporters through a clearer definition of "dumping" and the requirement that trade disputes between nations be resolved by a neutral panel of experts. Has the US Congress done this?

8. Has the new dispute resolution process in the 1993 GATT agreement been successful in resolving trade disputes between nations?

NOTES

[1] Both the United States and Japan export a great deal, but have huge *domestic* markets in which the vast majority of their GDP is sold.

[2] "Imports" includes not only goods, but also services bought from foreigners, a major one of which is the travel and tourism enjoyed by many Canadians.

[3] A major exception to its concentration on natural resources is Canada's large exports of *motor vehicles and parts*. This case is an exceptional one, however, as the automobile industry has since 1965 operated under a sort of "free trade" between Canada and the United States known as the "**Auto Pact.**" Under the Auto pact, the Canadian and US governments encouraged and supported continent-wide specialization of auto plants, for increased efficiency. Canadian auto plants specialize in the production of a few cars, most of which are exported to the United States. On the other hand, many cars bought in Canada are imported from similarly specialized plants in the United States. This latter fact is reflected in the statistics in Figure 32-1 showing Canada's high *imports* of motor vehicles and parts.

[4] Ceccini, Paolo. *The European Challenge 1992: The Benefits of a Single Market.* Wildwood House Ltd., Gower Publishing Company, Old Post Road, Brookfield, VT 05036.

Canadian international trade and investment policy

As noted in Chapter 32, Canada is unusually dependent upon world trade for its economic prosperity. Canada exports 25–28 percent of its Gross Domestic Product, over three-quarters of which goes to the large and proximate American market. In return, Canada imports large volumes of both consumer and capital goods that support the living standards of Canadians. In addition, *foreign investment* has played an important role in Canada's economic development and growth, and Canadian corporations have invested substantially in other nations.

In short, Canada has historically had a very active economic relationship with other countries, especially the United States. In these circumstances, the policies of the Canadian government with respect to international trade and investment are of particular interest and importance to Canadians.[1]

A brief historical background

EARLY TRADE POLICIES

The first major market for Canada's resource exports was *Great Britain*, under a British tariff policy that gave preferential treatment to imports from British colonies. However, in the late 1840's, Britain abandoned this policy in favor of free trade, leaving Canada (then British North America) in need of new markets for its resources.

Access to the US market was acquired through the **Reciprocity Treaty** of 1854,[2] under which the United States dismantled its tariffs on natural resource imports. This treaty ushered in a period of considerable prosperity for Canada, whose exports to the United States increased considerably.

However, in 1866 the United States repudiated the Reciprocity Treaty, leaving Canada economically isolated.

Looking now to themselves for economic prosperity, several of the colonies united in 1867 into Canada, which originally consisted of Ontario, Quebec, Nova Scotia and New Brunswick. The new Canadian government introduced a nation-building program known as the *National Policy*, the key economic component of which was a system of protective tariffs.

THE NATIONAL POLICY (1879)

The tariffs of the National Policy were of the "infant industry" type described in Chapter 32—they were meant to protect Canada's manufacturing industries, which were just starting to develop at this time. By placing a tariff barrier along the Canada–US border, the National Policy intended not only to develop a Canadian manufacturing sector, but also to shape trade and economic links along east-west lines rather than the north-south links with the United States that would otherwise have prevailed.[3] For over a century thereafter, Canadian manufacturing industries would enjoy considerable tariff protection against competition from imports.

EFFECTS OF TARIFF PROTECTION

As Figure 33-1 shows, the tariff protection initiated under the National Policy had mixed effects.

The protective tariffs certainly fostered the development of a *larger manufacturing sector* than would otherwise have existed. Furthermore, the

FIGURE 33-1 *Effects of Canada's Tariff Policy*

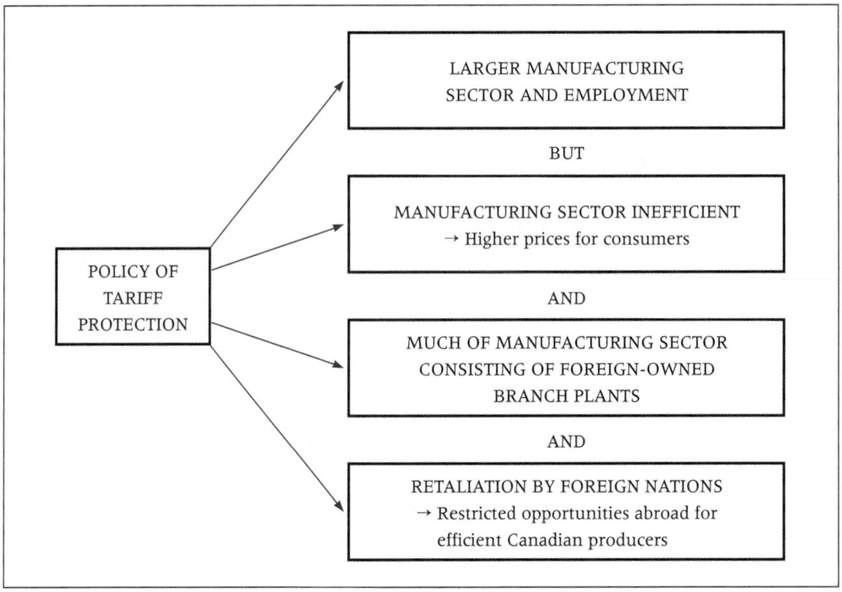

manufacturing sector grew into a major employer, especially in Ontario and Quebec. In this sense, the tariff policy achieved its basic objective.

On the other hand, much of the manufacturing sector that did develop was relatively inefficient and not very competitive internationally. As noted in Chapter 32, productivity in much of the Canadian manufacturing sector is limited by factors such as the small size of the Canadian market and the lack of competition due to tariff protection. Because of this, production costs per unit have tended to be high for many Canadian manufactured goods, and Canadian consumers have in effect been forced to subsidize the manufacturing sector by paying higher prices than they otherwise would have paid.[4]

In addition, there was the question of *foreign ownership* of Canadian industry. Canada's tariff policy led many foreign manufacturers, especially US firms, to establish *branch plants* in Canada. By producing their products in these branch plants rather than importing them into Canada, foreign manufacturers could avoid paying the high Canadian tariffs. In the process, a high proportion of Canada's manufacturing sector became foreign-owned.

In the following sections, we will consider these two questions—(1) the question of the productivity performance and international competitiveness of Canada's manufacturing sector, and (2) the question of foreign ownership of Canadian industry—in more detail.

The productivity performance and international competitiveness question

A key factor underlying the international competitiveness of any industry is its *production costs per unit* produced, since low production costs will enable the industry to be price-competitive in international markets. And, since about three-quarters of Canada's trade is with the United States, the relationship between Canadian and US production costs per unit is particularly important.

In 1980, Canadian manufacturing production costs per unit were only 2 percent higher than US manufacturing costs; by 1990, Canadian production costs per unit were 41 percent higher than US costs. According to the Economic Council of Canada, virtually all of the deterioration of Canada's cost-competitiveness was the result of slower growth of productivity (output per worker per hour) and faster increases in wage rates in Canada's manufacturing sector than in the United States'.

> "The competitiveness of the Canadian economy ... has deteriorated markedly during the past two decades.... productivity growth fell sharply in the 1970's and virtually halted in the 1980's. While most OECD countries also experienced a sharp drop in productivity growth, Canada's performance is among the worst."
>
> *Report of the Organization for Economic Cooperation and Development*, 1992

FIGURE 33-2 *Canadian Manufacturing Productivity as a Percentage of American Manufacturing Productivity, 1950–90*

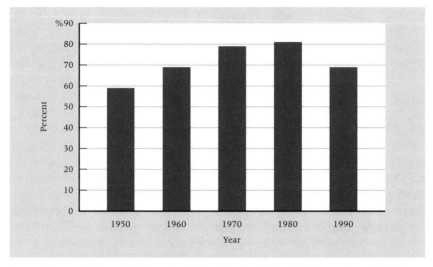

Source: Economic Council of Canada, *Pulling Together: Productivity, Innovation and Trade,* 1992

Figure 33-2 shows Canadian manufacturing productivity as a percentage of US manufacturing productivity from 1950 to 1990. From these statistics, three important facts are apparent:

- Canada's manufacturing productivity has always been considerably lower than American productivity.

- Until 1980, Canada's manufacturing productivity was gaining on its US counterpart, rising from 59 percent of US levels in 1950 to 81 percent in 1980

- From 1980–90, however, Canadian productivity failed to keep up with improvements in US productivity, falling back to only 69 percent of the US level by 1990.[5]

REASONS FOR MANUFACTURING PRODUCTIVITY WEAKNESS

The productivity performance of Canada's manufacturing sector has been the subject of many studies. Virtually all of the research concludes that the weak productivity performance of Canadian manufacturing is mainly the result of Canada's *policy of tariff protection* and the *small size of the Canadian market.*

Tariffs have protected much of Canada's manufacturing sector from foreign competition—and from pressures to become more efficient. Furthermore, due to Canada's tariffs and our lack of a free trade agreement with other nations (until 1989), Canadian manufacturers and foreign-owned branch plants have been geared mostly to the Canadian market, which is very small by international standards. By the mid-1980's, as international trade and competition increased rapidly, Canada remained the only high-income country in the northern hemisphere that did not have something approximating tariff-free access to markets of 100 million people or more, either domestically or through trade.

To make matters worse, even the small Canadian market of only 27 million is not a single market. In some industries, provincial government trade barriers hamper or even ban producers from other provinces. These policies

---

OTHER REASONS FOR LOW PRODUCTIVITY

The studies identified several other reasons for the low productivity of Canadian manufacturing, including the following:

Aversion to change

According to the Economic Council of Canada, "Canadians are too often reluctant to embrace and indeed, on occasion to even accept change. This theme—this aversion to change—emerges from every aspect of our research."[6] The research is critical of Canadian managers, who are often slow to develop and adopt new technology and often take a short-term "cost-cutting" approach to managing rather than the more long-term strategic approach of their Japanese and European counterparts. The result is often underinvestment not only in new technology, but also in employee training and development and in research and development (R&D). Many observers believe that one reason why Canadian managers are resistant to change is that tariff protection for their industries has historically sheltered them from competitive pressures.

Weak performance in science and technology

Canada is generally weak in the fields of science and technology. R&D spending by business is low, and many firms lack qualified scientific and technical staff. Despite this, relatively few young people have taken an interest in careers in science and engineering.

The educational system

According to the Economic Council of Canada, "The large number of dropouts from the Canadian secondary school system (about 33 percent, as compared to 2 percent in Japan and 10 percent in Germany) results in a group of workers who may be functionally illiterate and thus difficult to train. In addition, a recent literacy survey by Statistics Canada indicates that about one third of high-school graduates (about 1.2 million) cannot perform everyday reading requirements. Similarly, 36 percent of high-school graduates (about 1.5 million) experience varying degrees of difficulty in working with numbers."[7]

protect producers within these provinces from competition, but have the effect of subdividing the small "Canadian market" into even smaller regional segments, further restricting competition, economies of scale and efficiency.

The relatively small market available to many Canadian manufacturers has restricted their use of modern mass-production technology. Since the average Canadian manufacturing plant is significantly smaller than its counterparts in the United States, the United Kingdom, France, Sweden and Germany, it is less able to develop the productive efficiency associated with large-scale operations (economies of scale). While this is not a problem in all industries, it is a disadvantage in many.

However, the problems of Canadian manufacturing go beyond small plant size. Because many plants are geared to the Canadian market only, they are unable to specialize in producing one or a few products; rather, they must produce an entire range of products for a market of only 27 million people. The switchovers from one product to another are costly and reduce the plants' efficiency. Studies have indicated that the problem of short production runs could be a greater source of inefficiency in Canadian manufacturing than the problem of small plant size.

CONSEQUENCES OF UNCOMPETITIVENESS

By the late 1980's, the costs of Canada's poor productivity and competitiveness performance were becoming apparent. From 1971 to 1993, Canada's share of total world trade had declined from 5.3 percent to 3.8 percent; this represented the loss of nearly $50 billion of exports and roughly 700 000 jobs associated with them—nearly half the number of unemployed Canadians during the early 1990's. Economic studies indicated that Canada had enjoyed the *opportunity* for export success in the sense of being close to the vast US market and producing an appropriate range of manufactured goods; however, Canada's share of world trade had declined sharply, almost entirely because of a deterioration in Canada's "ability to compete." And, to a significant extent, this was the result of Canada's own policy of tariff protection.

THE SITUATION UNTIL THE 1980'S

Until the 1980's, Canada earned its way in international trade mainly through its exports of natural resources and resource-related products—agricultural and forest products, natural gas, paper, minerals and metals. The earnings from these resource exports financed heavy importation of foreign goods and services (autos, televisions, VCR's, travel and tourism, etc.) that considerably increased the standard of living of Canadians.

Canada also maintained a manufacturing sector that, while a major employer (especially in central Canada), was generally inefficient and uncompetitive by international standards. Many manufacturers were protected against foreign competition by tariffs that required consumers to subsidize them. In addition, Canada's protection of these industries exposed Canada's more successful export industries to retaliatory protectionist measures by other nations. In this sense, Canada's inefficient manufacturers were supported at the expense of more efficient Canadian industries, whose export opportunities were reduced by such retaliatory measures.

Since 1947, through GATT negotiations, Canada had been gradually moving away from this policy stance and toward freer trade. This approach recognized that freer international trade was in Canada's long-run best interests and that to gain access to larger foreign markets, Canada would have to reduce some of its own tariff protection. Still, progress was slow; by the 1980's Canada's tariffs were still relatively high, and the GATT tariff-reduction process seemed to be losing momentum. As the 1980's unfolded, however, several developments pushed Canada to reconsider its trade policy.

Pressures for changes to Canadian trade policy

The key such trend was "globalization"—rapid increases in international trade and competition, generated in large part by advances in transportation and communications technology and the adoption of the market system by a number of nations. The result was a great expansion in world trade—among the main Western industrial nations, the percentage of GDP accounted for by foreign trade almost doubled from 1960 to the late 1980's.

As this trend developed, Canada's protected manufacturing sector came under increasing competitive pressure. On the one side, the newly industrialized countries such as Mexico, Brazil, and the "Asian dragons" (Taiwan, South Korea, Hong Kong and Singapore) provided strong competition in labor-intensive industries such as clothing and footwear, and in assembly activities, such as electronics. On the other side, Canada faced strong competition in high-technology industries from the advanced western economies, such as the United States, Japan and western Europe.

In this new international environment, Canada was under increasing pressure to move toward a new trade policy due to the following factors:

> Changes in the global economy, now as on previous occasions in our history, challenge Canadians to respond positively to a new international environment if we are to have acceptable future growth performances. The necessary response will require significant adaptation in our economy to meet international competition.
>
> Report of the Royal Commission on the Economic Union and
> Development Prospects for Canada
> (Macdonald Commission), Volume One, p. 58

(a) the declining competitiveness of much of Canadian manufacturing

(b) the growing costs to consumers and exporters of protecting uncompetitive manufacturers

(c) outflows of Canadian business investment capital

(d) weaker world markets for Canadian resource exports

(e) growing protectionism in the United States

In the following sections, each of these factors is examined in more detail.

(A) THE DECLINING COMPETITIVENESS OF MUCH OF CANADIAN MANUFACTURING

As outlined above, much of the Canadian manufacturing sector lost competitive ground relative to the rest of the world during the 1980's. While other nations moved toward freer international trade, stronger competition and higher productivity, Canada's manufacturers remained protected by government policies, and oriented mainly to the small Canadian market. In the view of most economists, if Canada's industries were to keep up with their counterparts in other nations, they needed stronger competition.

(B) THE GROWING COSTS OF PROTECTING UNCOMPETITIVE MANUFACTURERS

As its productivity fell further behind world trends, the costs to Canadians of protecting Canada's manufacturing sector increased. These costs took two forms—the costs to consumers of having to pay high tariff-supported prices for goods, and the cost to Canadian exporters of retaliatory measures by other nations.

(i) Costs to consumers

By the mid-1980's, the cost to consumers for each job saved by protectionist measures ranged from $25 000 to *over $200 000*, according to various studies.[8]

Such figures raised the question of whether continued protection of some Canadian industries was economically justifiable, particularly when those industries were continuing to lose ground to foreign competition even with protection that was so costly to consumers.

(ii) Costs to exporters

Second, Canada's more efficient and successful industries needed improved access to larger foreign markets in order to grow and realize their potential. However, it was difficult to gain this access as long as Canada maintained its protection of many of its own industries, often through trade restrictions that were quite questionable (see Figure 33-3). For instance, GATT found Canada's protection of its wine, beer and some food-processing industries to be in violation of international trade agreements, exposing Canada to re-

FIGURE 33-3 *Costs of Canada's Tariff Policy*

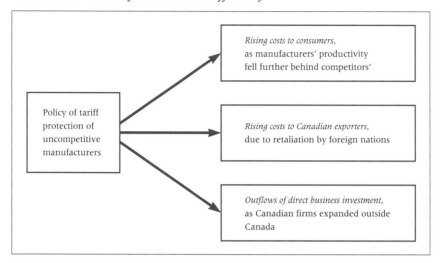

taliatory action by other nations and making it more difficult for Canada to negotiate reductions in other countries' tariffs.

(C) OUTFLOWS OF BUSINESS INVESTMENT CAPITAL

Partly because they could not gain the secure export access that they needed to larger foreign markets, a growing number of Canadian firms turned to establishing branch operations in foreign countries. The result was a significant outflow of job-creating business investment capital from Canada. Historically, Canada had experienced a net inflow of business investment capital; however after the mid-1970's this turned into a net outflow, which became quite large in the 1980's, mainly due to increased investment abroad by Canadian firms.

(D) WEAKER WORLD MARKETS FOR CANADIAN RESOURCE EXPORTS

As noted earlier, Canada had traditionally relied on its exports of natural resources for most of its export earnings. In the 1980's, however, world

> Canadian business has reached a stage where our domestic market can no longer assure our continued growth, and where our access to foreign markets is no longer perceived to be secure enough to stimulate long-term, job-creating investment.
>
> Report of the Royal Commission on the Economic Union and Development Prospects for Canada, (The Macdonald Commission), 1985

markets for Canadian resource exports softened due to a combination of sluggish demand and increased competition from less-developed nations. This was a significant development, as it undermined Canada's traditional main export strength, forcing Canada to look to other sectors of the economy for the export earnings so vital to Canadians' prosperity.

(E) GROWING PROTECTIONISM IN THE UNITED STATES

In the mid-1980's the United States, the market for about three-quarters of Canada's exports, was moving towards *protectionism*. Faced with a large excess of imports over exports, US authorities moved toward restrictions on imports—including imports from Canada—as a means of protecting American industries and jobs.

Under US law, American industries could obtain government protection (usually in the form of tariffs) against foreign (including Canadian) competition or trade practices that were deemed "unfair" by US authorities. As we saw in Chapter 32, under international trade law a nation can impose **"countervailing tariffs"** against imports that are unfairly "dumped" and subsidized by foreign governments.

However, in the view of Canadians, American industries were abusing the US law by obtaining government restrictions on Canadian imports for reasons that were not legitimate under international trade law and customs. Several American industries secured US government action against Canadian imports through the use of inaccurate statistics and economic arguments pertaining to alleged Canadian **subsidies** and **dumping**.[9] It is important to recognize that while such actions appear to be justifiable *defensive* measures against *unfair* imports, they can really amount to unjustifiable *offensive* measures against *fair* competitors whose real crime is their success. Canada could only appeal such actions through US courts, where a sympathetic review of American actions was rather unlikely. As a result, Canadian producers that were successful in the US market faced an ongoing risk of arbitrary and unfair trade restrictions being imposed on them by the US government at the request of their American competitors, with no real opportunity to appeal such restrictions.

To Canada, this posed a particularly serious threat, as the United States was the market for approximately three-quarters of Canada's exports and 20 percent of Canada's GDP. In addition, such American import restrictions (and the threat of them) had been leading a growing number of Canadian firms to invest in building "branch" operations in the United States, rather than in Canada—a reversal of the 1950's, when US firms built branch plants in Canada to get around Canadian tariffs. This outflow of Canadian business capital—and jobs—was a growing concern in Canada.

In the view of many observers, more than any other factor, it was this threat of growing US protectionism that pushed Canada in the direction of a free trade agreement. In addition to all of its other problems as outlined

> ... There is one formidable negative factor we cannot overcome on our own: we have a small market of 25 million people; the Europeans have more than 300 million; the Americans about 250 million; and Japan about 120 million. The rule of thumb among economists is that you need a market of at least 100 million for efficient production. That's why we need a free trade agreement.
>
> Simon Reisman,
> Canada's chief negotiator for the Canada–US Free Trade Agreement

above, Canada could not afford to have its access to the key US market reduced.

As a result of the considerations outlined here, in 1985 Canada announced its interest in negotiating a free trade agreement with the United States.

The 1989 Canada–US Free Trade Agreement

Negotiations between Canada and the United States concluded in late 1988, and, following a bitter Canadian federal election campaign in which free trade was the main issue, the Agreement came into effect on January 1, 1989. The main features of the agreement were as follows:

- Tariffs between the two countries were to be eliminated—about 15 percent of them immediately, about one-third of them over a five-year period and the rest over a ten-year period. These latter tariffs, which applied mainly to the more heavily protected consumer goods, were to be phased out in ten equal stages until they were eliminated on January 1, 1998.

- Canada was to obtain more secure access to the US market, mainly through better protection against unfair restrictions on Canadian exports imposed by the US government at the request of American industries. Under the Free Trade Agreement, such actions by the US government can be appealed by Canada to a neutral board ("panel") consisting of five members drawn from a roster of Canadian and US trade experts. Such panels allow neutral experts to review and overturn decisions by the US government if US law has been applied incorrectly or unfairly. In view of the increasing use of such measures by the United States, this review mechanism was considered by many to be the key feature of the FTA.

- The United States was to obtain some relaxation of Canadian restrictions on foreign investment, as well as assurances that, in times of energy shortages, Canada would not discriminate against American users of Canadian energy with respect to either price or supply.

With respect to investment, the United States would to continue to allow almost-unrestricted Canadian direct investment into the United States, and Canada agreed to subject only very large takeovers of Canadian firms by US firms to government review and approval requirements.[10]

With respect to energy, the United States would improve Canadian access to American energy markets by not applying restrictions on imports of Canadian oil, natural gas and electricity and by ending embargoes on Canadian uranium exports. In effect, the United States agreed to be a reliable customer for Canadian energy.

In return, Canada agreed to something considered to be quite important to the United States—to be a reliable supplier of energy to the United States. In the event of a shortage of energy supplies, Canada would not reduce exports to the USA by more than supplies to Canada itself are reduced. If there were shortages, exports to the USA could be reduced, but the *proportion* of total Canadian production exported could not be reduced. In effect, then, Canada and the United States have agreed to proportional sharing of energy supplies in situations of short supply. In addition, Canada has agreed not to charge higher prices to US buyers than to Canadian buyers in the event of shortages, as this would represent another form of discrimination.[11]

THE ADJUSTMENT PROCESS AND ADJUSTMENT PROGRAMS

The Free Trade Agreement represented a major change in Canadian policy that would result in significant changes to the Canadian economy. And, regardless of which views proved correct concerning the effects of free trade, it was clear that the Free Trade Agreement would generate an *acceleration of change* in the Canadian economy, as some industries expanded and others contracted more rapidly than they otherwise would have. Such changes involved a very important *adjustment process* for both workers and industries, as product lines, production methods and skill requirements would be affected. Some workers would have to move to new industries, jobs or locations. For the Free Trade Agreement to be a success, this transition

---

THE SUBSIDIES ISSUE

In applying anti-dumping and countervail laws, it is very helpful to define just what a "subsidy" is and is not. Both Canada and the United States provide a wide variety of government assistance, or subsidies, to various industries, many of which might be challenged as unfair to foreign competitors. The issue proved too complex for the negotiators to resolve in the time available, so they agreed to try within five to seven years to develop some mutually acceptable guidelines defining what constitutes dumping and unfair subsidization.

FREE TRADE WITH THE USA: NOT A NEW IDEA

While the negotiation and signing of the Canada–US Free Trade Agreement caused a considerable furor in Canada, it was far from the first time that Canada and the United States had considered such a move. As early as 1854, the Reciprocity Treaty gave Canadian natural resource exports tariff-free access to the US market; however, the United States repudiated this treaty in 1866.

In the late 1880's, dissatisfaction with the National Policy led to a debate over the option of renewed reciprocity with the USA. However, after a bitter election campaign (won by Macdonald's Conservatives with the support of the business community, which benefitted from the tariffs), free trade was a dead issue.

The reciprocity issue surfaced again in 1911 when Liberal Prime Minister Sir Wilfrid Laurier surprised the nation by announcing the conclusion of a new free trade agreement with the USA, which had been negotiated behind closed doors in the fall of 1910. Laurier was convinced that the Reciprocity Agreement would secure victory in the upcoming election of 1911. However, during the election campaign, Canadians became suspicious of the deal, and feared that it would cost them their jobs. Laurier lost the election, and once again free trade ceased to be an issue.

Canada again approached free trade with the USA in 1948. Liberal Prime Minister William Lyon Mackenzie King approved secret negotiations with the United States, but cancelled the deal because he feared that Canada could not negotiate on an equal basis with the powerful Americans, that the US media were portraying the deal as a prelude to political integration of Canada with the United States and that it would be costly politically, as it had been for Laurier in 1911.

After 1948, GATT negotiations led to the gradual reduction of Canada/US tariffs as part of a wider process of multilateral tariff cuts. By the mid-1980's, when negotiations for the Free Trade Agreement commenced, nearly 75 percent of Canada-US trade was tariff-free, and tariffs on the remainder were relatively low. However, the United States was increasing its non-tariff barriers to imports as a result of its great excess of imports over exports, which made Canada anxious to obtain more secure access to the crucial US market.

would have to be accomplished as smoothly as possible, and with the minimum possible hardship for the people involved.

The most basic adjustment provision in the Free Trade Agreement is the fact that tariffs are to be eliminated gradually, most of them over a period of five or ten years. This is intended to give companies and workers adequate time to adapt to free trade, which presents both problems and opportunities. In addition, a considerable variety of *retraining programs* are available in Canada, and the Unemployment Insurance program was modified to add a retraining element. Probably, however, the most important element in the adjustment process would be an economic boom that would provide alternative jobs for displaced workers, and this was not to be. After early 1990, the economy slipped into a prolonged recession that made the adjustment process much more difficult for many, and impossible for some.

STRATEGIES FOR SUCCESS I—WORLD PRODUCT MANDATING

It was also very important that Canadian industries adjust effectively to free trade, so as to minimize competitive dangers and take advantage of new trade opportunities.

One of the concerns about free trade was the fate of Canada's foreign-owned branch plants. As we have seen, the small size of the Canadian market means that these are often inefficiently small replicas of their parent operations in the United States. Only because they could avoid paying Canadian tariffs was it economical for US parent firms to establish and operate these plants in Canada. Thus, there was considerable concern that free trade would mean the closing of many Canadian branch plants and the shifting of production back to the United States.

These dire consequences would be much less likely if the Canadian plants were *specialized* in the production of one or a few products so that they could be fully efficient; however, the small size of the Canadian market precluded that for most companies.

An interesting approach to making branch plants more specialized and efficient is **world product mandating.** Under such an arrangement, a Canadian branch plant acquires a mandate to design, manufacture and market a particular product for the world market on behalf of the parent company. That is, branch plants would no longer produce, on an inefficient scale, the full range of their parents' product lines, but rather would concentrate on one or a few selected products for a wider market. With greater specialization and longer production runs, Canadian manufacturers could become more efficient and internationally competitive. Ideally, the Canadian plant would be responsible for all operations associated with its product lines, including research and development, design, production, marketing and exporting, the result being a much more complete indus-

> Since 1978, Du Pont, the US chemical giant, has followed a strategy of investing only in operations that can serve the full North American market and be or soon become competitive with the best in the world. "We thought a branch-plant type of operation is no longer going to work in Canada. We made a corporate decision that we would invest only in facilities that were potentially world-competitive and carve out a place on the world scene. Obviously, free trade gives us very strong support for such a strategy."
>
> Jim Stewart, Senior Vice-President, Du Pont Canada

trial structure than the present branch-plant structure. World product mandating has been successful in a number of companies that have tried it, including Black and Decker Canada Inc., Garrett Manufacturing Ltd., Westinghouse Canada Inc., Litton Systems Canada Ltd., Proctor and Gamble, Gandalf Technologies, GTE Sylvania, Heron Cable, Hughes Aircraft, Kodak, Polymer International and others.

For a nation facing free trade—and increasing foreign competition—world product mandating provides a way to channel the economic resources of foreign multinational corporations into the development of a more specialized manufacturing sector in Canada that is better able to compete not only in domestic markets, but also in export markets.

STRATEGIES FOR SUCCESS II—NICHE MARKETING

One concern regarding free trade was that Canadian manufacturers could not succeed in head-to-head competition with large US mass-production manufacturers. Under a strategy of **niche marketing**, this would not be necessary. Instead, Canadian producers could target smaller volumes of production into relatively small segments, or niches, of the market. For instance, "the market for running shoes" is not really a single market, but rather a series of "market segments" with a large market for medium-quality mass-produced shoes at its centre, but several relatively small segments (niches) as well, such as "high-end" shoes targetted at very specific buyer groups, such as high-income squash players or joggers. In a small market such as Canada's, such niches are often very small; however, in a vast market such as the United States, they can be large enough to offer significant opportunities to niche producers.[12] For example, in the apparel industry, several Canadian firms have been able to do very well by producing high-quality men's suits and high-fashion womenswear for the US market, where they enjoy healthy demand and high prices.

According to Joseph D'Cruz and James Fleck, two University of Toronto professors, there is a significant trend in Canada toward corporate reorganization along lines similar to a combination of world product mandating and niche marketing. In their 1988 book *Yankee Canadians*, they

SLEEMAN'S—AN EXAMPLE OF THE POTENTIAL OF NICHE MARKETING IN THE USA

Sleeman Brewing and Malting Co. Ltd. of Guelph, Ontario is a brewer of premium-quality beer—that is, a small "niche company" in the Canadian market. After signing an agreement with Stroh Brewing Co. of the United States under which Stroh would distribute Sleeman's beer in Michigan, John Sleeman was quoted as saying, "All we have to do is get one percent of the Michigan market and we've got to build a couple more breweries."

interviewed executives in more than 50 leading Canadian subsidiaries of US companies, and found that American parent companies have recently been putting pressure on Canadian subsidiaries to develop specialized, short-run products for niche markets around the world. In most cases, this was done not in anticipation of free trade between Canada and the United States, but as part of the larger process of globalization. As production shifts from national markets to world markets, it is becoming more specialized. To the extent that this specialization has occurred or will soon occur in Canadian subsidiaries, they will be better positioned not only to survive under free trade with the United States, but also to prosper in other world markets.

YOU DON'T HAVE TO BE BIG TO BE BEAUTIFUL

In discussing the benefits of larger markets, economists tend to emphasize the advantages of the mass-production techniques possible in gigantic production facilities. This is certainly the case in many industries, but it is not the only advantage of access to larger markets, as the example of Denmark illustrates. In Denmark, a tiny European nation with a domestic market of only 5 million, the average size of industrial companies is only about 50 workers. Yet Denmark exports 60 percent of its production, mainly to larger European countries. Denmark has become the subcontractor of Europe, turning out subcomponents of large industrial products that are built elsewhere. The Danes are not mass producers, but have become very proficient **niche producers**, who find a small and specialized product area and capture a large share of that market.

The Danish experience illustrates another advantage of large markets besides the opportunity to use mass-production techniques—the creation of a large number of niches, and the opportunity to prosper by specializing in serving these niches.

ASSESSMENT OF THE FREE TRADE AGREEMENT

Five years after the implementation of the Canada–US Free Trade Agreement, the debate over the deal continued. Had it been proven to be a disaster, as its opponents asserted, or was it working out well, as its supporters claimed?

Before examining these claims and the situation, it should be emphasized that it is impossible to reach any concrete conclusions concerning the success of the FTA after only five years. Any free trade agreement is a long-term undertaking, the benefits of which are not expected to be fully realized for ten to fifteen years, or even longer. The situation is complicated further by the fact that for most of those five years, the Canadian economy was in or slowly recovering from a serious recession, as was much of the rest of the world. The high unemployment from the recession made the process of adjusting to freer trade much more difficult, by reducing the number of job opportunities for those displaced from their jobs. The interaction between the recession and the restructuring to make Canadian industry more internationally competitive generated large numbers of layoffs, pay cuts, forced early retirements, and plant closings as many firms failed to make the adjustments and those that adjust successfully often did so by reducing the numbers of their employees.

Opponents of FTA concluded that these developments proved that free trade was a failure; however, in more detailed analysis of the economic situation, advocates of the Free Trade Agreement found support for their views as well, in both trade and investment statistics.

With respect to trade, Canada's export performance in the US market improved following the implementation of the FTA in 1989. Canada's share of the big US market for manufactured goods increased significantly, more than offsetting an increase in the US manufacturers' share of Canada's small market. As a result, in the first few years of the FTA, Canada's share of the overall North American market for manufactured goods increased, with the transportation equipment, food, chemicals, electrical, electronic and paper industries accounting for more than half of Canada's gains.[13]

In the first three years of the FTA, Canadian exports to the USA in areas that were liberalized by the FTA climbed by 33 percent, as compared to 9 percent growth in exports in areas not opened up by the agreement. This was reflected in Canada's merchandise trade statistics. In the first four years of the Free Trade Agreement, Canada's merchandise trade surplus with the United States increased significantly, while Canada's deficit with the rest of the world increased by about the same amount, as Figure 33-4 shows.

With respect to investment, Canada's international position changed even more noticeably. As noted earlier, during the 1980's there was a net outflow of direct business investment capital from Canada, averaging over $3.6 billion per year from 1983 to 1989. In sharp contrast, 1990–92 saw the largest *inflow* of foreign direct business investment capital into Canada ever—over $20 billion in three years, turning the net outflows of direct investment into net inflows averaging nearly $2 billion per year, as Figure 33-5 shows. This change was considered by most economists to be significant, as

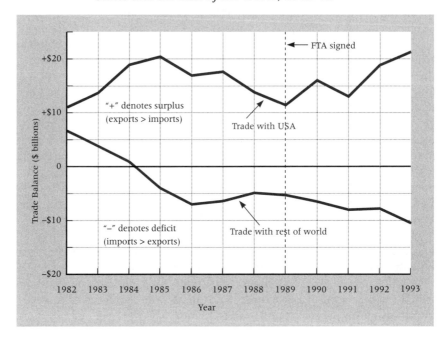

FIGURE 33-4 *Canada's Merchandise Trade Balance with the United States and the Rest of the World, 1982–93*

Source: Bank of Canada *Review*, Summer 1993 (Table J3)

FIGURE 33-5 *Net Direct Investment Flows (Annual Averages)*

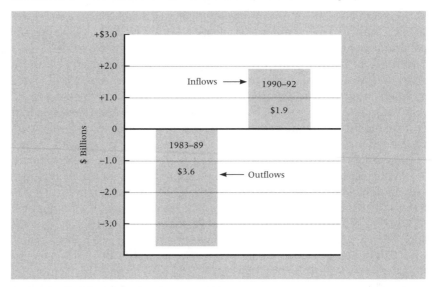

Source: Bank of Canada *Review*, Summer 1993

it represented the assessment of Canada's economic prospects by leaders of the international business community.

Supporters of the Free Trade Agreement claimed that the operation of the all-important disputes resolution mechanism was proving successful from Canada's perspective. As noted earlier, American industries had been harassing Canadian exporters by obtaining US government restrictions on their sales to the United States, often on the basis of questionable arguments and data. Under the FTA, Canadian producers obtained the right to appeal such restrictions to a neutral panel. Canada was successful in the vast majority of such appeals, involving pork, softwood lumber, wheat, autos and other industries. By 1993, there was growing hope that the US government would reduce the harassment of Canadian exporters on the grounds that it was proving not only unsuccessful, but also damaging to relations between the two countries. It is important to recognize that the disputes resolution mechanism has been used for only a very small proportion of the $200–250 billion of two-way trade between Canada and the United States.

Finally, it should be reiterated that all of the statistics and arguments in the previous sections must be considered preliminary in nature—the Canada–US Free Trade Agreement cannot be properly assessed until the turn of the century at the earliest, and probably not for several years after that. And the statistics are interpreted differently by different people—to some, they mean that Canada has been more successful in the US market and at attracting foreign investment; to others, they mean that Canada has become more dependent upon the United States and upon foreign investment. Regardless of the interpretation placed on the data, it is too early to determine the outcome of the FTA, and the Agreement has not yet been tested under good economic conditions, making any assessment tentative at best.

NAFTA—the North American Free Trade Agreement

In 1994, Canada, the United States and Mexico entered into the North American Free Trade Agreement (NAFTA), which in effect extended the Canada–US free trade area to include Mexico. This agreement created the world's largest free trade zone—360 million people and $7.3 trillion of output (1992 data), as compared to 325 million people and $7.0 trillion for Europe.

BACKGROUND ON MEXICO

Like Canada, Mexico had traditionally used high tariffs to protect its "infant industries" from foreign competition, especially from more-advanced industries in the United States. Unlike Canada, however, Mexico did this in the context of a socialist state, based upon what can be regarded as the world's first socialist constitution, in 1917.

The result was an economic system that was not only highly protected from foreign competition, but also highly regulated by its government. One high-profile symbol of this regulation was the "Auto Decree," under which automobile manufacturers were required to export US $2 in product for every US $1 that they imported. Much of Mexican industry was either government-owned or heavily-regulated; in many cases government regulations prevented competition, leaving many key industries under the control of monopolies. With so little competition and so much regulation, productivity and living standards in the Mexican economy were very low.

Not having joined the General Agreement on Tariffs and Trade, Mexico remained for the most part isolated from the trend toward "globalization" in the 1970's and the early 1980's. To a large extent, it staked its hopes for economic prosperity on *oil exports*, and reaped considerable benefits from these when oil prices were very high from 1979–85. However, the collapse of world oil prices in 1986 left Mexico not only with sharply diminished oil-export revenues, but also in near-bankruptcy from its huge foreign debt, mostly from loans made by international banks in the expectation that continuing high oil prices would bring long-term economic progress to Mexico.

At this point, Mexico's government decided upon a fundamental change in strategic economic direction, from an inward-looking, protected and regulated economy to one that was market-oriented and an active participant in the world economy. To this end, the Mexican government began a program of privatizing and deregulating many of the nation's industries in order to improve their efficiency, and in 1987, Mexico joined the GATT. From 1987 to 1993, Mexico's average tariff on imports dropped from 45 percent to 9 percent, and Mexico's international trade grew rapidly, especially with the United States. Mexico signed an agreement with five Central American nations to form a regional free trade zone by 1997, and in 1991, sought a free trade agreement with the United States and Canada.

In the early 1990's, Mexico was exporting about 15 percent of its GDP, with about 75 percent of these exports going to the United States and perhaps 5 percent going to Canada.[14] Mexico's economy was about one-twentieth the size of the economy of the United States.

An interesting exception to Mexico's economic isolation has been the *maquiladoras*, which were established in 1965. These are manufacturing plants located in a strip close to the US border that assemble for re-export components that are imported tariff-free. For instance, a US producer might mass-produce the components for audio cassettes and ship them tariff-free to Mexico to be assembled, then re-exported to the United States. The attraction of the maquiladoras is obviously the cheap Mexican labor for labor-intensive semi-skilled assembly tasks. By 1993, the maquiladoras' sales were in the range of $15 billion.

As the economically smallest and the poorest of the three countries, Mexico certainly has the most to gain from free trade with Canada and the United States. Also, the economic reforms of the 1980's have revitalized much of Mexico's economy. On the other hand, free trade involves significant risks for Mexico and many of its industries. Overall Mexican productivity was not comparable to that of the fast-industrializing nations of Southeast Asia, and it was estimated that only about 40 percent of Mexico's industries had restructured sufficiently to be ready for free trade with the rest of North America. Another 40 percent were considered to be quite ill-prepared for the international competition that would come with free trade.

THE DEBATE OVER NAFTA

The prospect of adding Mexico to the Canada–US free trade area generated intense debate and strong opposition in the United States and Canada. Given the growth of trading blocs around the world, the establishment of a North American free trade zone was in a sense one more step in a logical progression. On the other hand, the greater the differences among the nations involved, the more difficult it tends to be to reach an agreement that does not represent threatening change to many of the industries and workers affected.

Opponents of NAFTA were concerned that competition from Mexican workers whose wage rates were very low by US and Canadian standards would not only put many workers out of work, but also depress the wages of others, especially in labor-intensive manufacturing industries such as clothing, footwear, some auto parts and assembly operations.

Supporters of NAFTA argued that the creation of the world's largest free trade zone would bring economic benefits for all concerned. While it was acknowledged that the biggest winner economically would be Mexico, Canada and the United States would gain economically as well, since the high productivity of their workers would in many industries more than offset the low wages of Mexicans. In particular, opportunities for Canadian producers were seen in Mexico's need for capital goods to upgrade its infrastructure and the capital equipment of its industries. It was argued that as Mexico's prosperity grew in the future, Mexican consumers would buy increasing volumes of Canadian and US imports. Finally, supporters of NAFTA argued that much of the trade between Mexico and Canada and the United States was already tariff-free or subject to quite low tariffs, and that firms that wanted to shift labor-intensive assembly operations to Mexico had been free to do so since 1965, to the *maquiladoras*.

KEY TERMS OF NAFTA

Under NAFTA, tariffs were to be eliminated over periods of up to 15 years; however, virtually all of the tariffs between Canada and Mexico were to be phased out over a maximum of 10 years. On some products, tariffs were to

"Jobs are shifted south by transnational corporations and workers are pitted against each other. It's a process that results in a worse outcome for workers and working people in all three countries."

"The inclusion of Mexico in the FTA would further increase pressure upon Canadians to accept lower wages, to accept lower environmental standards and to accept even more cuts to public and social services."

Canadian Labour Congress President Bob White in *CLC Today*, March 1993

be eliminated immediately, while tariffs on sectors that are more vulnerable to import competition, such as Canada's apparel, most footwear, toys and miscellaneous manufactured articles would be phased out over 10 years. Both Canada and Mexico have the right to take safeguard measures that allow them to re-impose tariffs to protect producers from surges of imports, should these occur.

Most restrictions on investment were also to be phased out over a period of time, although Canada would retain the right to review foreign takeovers of larger Canadian companies as under the FTA. Canada would retain its exemption for its cultural industries under the FTA and its social and health services would be protected as under the FTA.

Finally, the mechanism for resolving disputes over the interpretation of NAFTA would be essentially the same as under the FTA, restructured to accommodate a third party. As under the FTA, disputes could be referred to a panel of neutral trade experts that would have the power to overturn decisions by a country that were contrary to the country's trade laws and NAFTA.

THE LIKELY ECONOMIC IMPACT OF NAFTA ON CANADA

While there was disagreement on whether NAFTA would have positive or negative economic effects on Canada, most experts agreed that the ef-

For the past four decades, America, Japan and the countries of Western Europe, each competing against the others, have grown enormously richer—all of them at once, not some at the expense of the rest.

The same will be true of the Third World. A fast-growing Mexico (or China, or India) will be its own biggest customer. As it succeeds, it will export more—but it will import more, too. Its success will therefore "create" as many jobs in America and other countries as it will "destroy."

The Economist, June 1993

> "The overall macro-economic impact of NAFTA is not going to be big for Canada, but we would have lost a lot if we were not in it."
>
> Daniel Schwanen, senior policy analyst, C.D. Howe Institute

fect would not be large, at least in the short-to-medium term. According to the International Trade Commission, Mexico would gain the most from NAFTA, Canada would gain slightly and the United States would gain the least. Canada's gains would be small for a variety of reasons, the most important of which was that Canada already had a free trade agreement involving the large US market, while its trade with Mexico was much smaller. In the early 1990's, Canada's two-way trade with the United States was over $200 billion per year, as compared to $2–4 billion with Mexico.

In addition, about 85 percent of Canada's imports from Mexico were already tariff-free, and the tariffs on the remaining 15 percent were on average not very high. While Mexican wages were much lower than Canadian wages, Canadian productivity was more than six times as high as Mexican productivity ($24 per worker per hour as compared to $3.70 for Mexico, according to the Conference Board). Also, the Mexican tariffs that were to be eliminated were on average three times as high as Canada's tariffs.

NAFTA would increase export opportunities for a number of Canadian industries, mostly those that could provide goods and services related to the modernization of Mexico, such as telecommunications, engineering consulting and construction, transportation and financial institutions. In addition, under NAFTA Mexico would abandon its Auto Decree that had required automakers to export twice the output that they imported, opening up the large and growing Mexican market to imports of Canadian- and US-built cars. On the other side of the picture, Canada could expect increased competition from Mexico in industries such as apparel, auto parts, textiles and various manufactured goods, and Mexico could provide Canada with competition for US business investment.

While the prospective economic gains for Canada under NAFTA were not large, it was considered strategically important for Canada to be part of the deal. The reason for this is that if the United States had separate free trade agreements with Canada and Mexico, only companies located in the United States would have had free access to the markets of all three countries, giving the United States a significant advantage in attracting business investment capital. Thus, while being in NAFTA would not bring large economic gains for Canada, not being in it could have resulted in significant losses in terms of investment and jobs.

When will there be free trade within Canada?

As the world moved toward large free-trade blocs involving many countries and freer trade on a global basis through GATT, Canada was still far from free trade *within* Canada, that is, among its ten provinces. A web of approximately 500 provincial government regulations designed to protect each province's producers and workers against out-of-province competition restricted the movement of goods, workers and investment capital between provinces. The most common such restrictions required governments and their agencies to buy only from suppliers located in that province, usually at higher costs to the taxpayer. Other restrictions included standards that had the effect of excluding out-of-province products or workers, and simple prohibitions on out-of-province suppliers. Some provinces applied the same rules to each others' products as they applied to imports from foreign nations, and Quebec subsidized "exports" to other provinces as if they were exports to other nations.

According to various studies, these restrictions cost Canadians as much as $6.5 billion annually, or from $500 to $1000 for the average family. Roughly 80 percent of this was due to provincial government procurement regulations that prohibited competition from outside the province. A more subtle cost of these restrictions was that they subdivided the already-small Canadian market into even smaller regional segments, making Canadian producers more inefficient and less competitive internationally.

This placed Canada in the rather bizarre position that there was freer trade *between each Canadian province and the USA* than there was *between Canadian provinces*. In 1993, the federal government established an "Internal Trade Secretariat," the purpose of which was to oversee "free trade negotiations" among Canada's provinces with the objective of reaching an agreement by mid-1994.

The foreign ownership question

As Figure 33-6 shows, foreign ownership of industry is a noteworthy feature of the Canadian economy. Foreign ownership, about three-quarters of which is American, has tended to be concentrated in certain sectors of the economy, such as manufacturing, petroleum and natural gas, and mining and smelting.

WHAT FORMS DOES FOREIGN INVESTMENT IN CANADA TAKE?

Most people think of foreign investment in terms of foreign corporations controlling firms in Canada, but in fact the concept is much wider than that. First, foreign investment can come in two distinctly different forms: debt and equity. **Debt investment** refers to loans made by foreigners to

FIGURE 33-6 *Foreign-Controlled Share of Operating Revenue of Selected Non-Financial Industries, 1992*

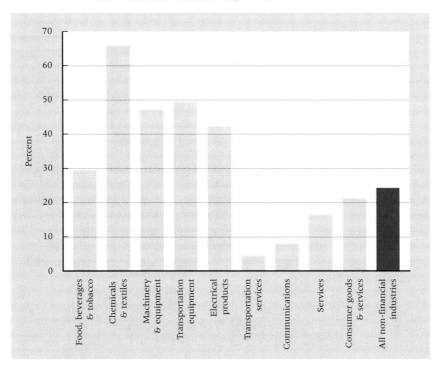

Source: Statistics Canada, *CALURA, Corporations, 1989-1992* (61-220)

Canadian businesses or governments, usually through foreign purchases of bonds issued by Canadian corporations or governments. Many major projects in Canada, including the Quebec Hydro James Bay project and the Ontario Hydro expansion, have been financed in this way. Such investments by foreigners are in effect loans to Canada, and as such involve no foreign ownership or control. **Equity investment** on the other hand, refers to ownership of the shares of Canadian businesses, and often does involve foreign control. Most US investment in Canada is of this type.

Second, foreign investment funds may be used in different ways. They may be used to build new *productive facilities* (capital equipment—plants, machinery and equipment) which did not previously exist. Or they may be used to buy (take over) existing *Canadian businesses*, by purchasing a controlling interest in their stock. Or they may be used to buy *Canadian resources* such as real estate, mineral rights, natural gas, or timber rights.

Third, foreign investment may come from different sources. The funds may come from, say, the United States, to be invested in Canada—in effect, then, Americans would be making their savings available for use in Canada. Or the funds may come from profits earned in Canada and reinvested by US-owned corporations. In recent years, about three-quarters of the growth of foreign investment in Canada has come from the reinvestment of profits earned in Canada.

The varieties of foreign investment indicate that foreign investment is not the simple thing that many Canadians perceive it to be. For instance, the same person may welcome to his or her community a new foreign-owned plant and the jobs it brings, yet feel uneasy about the development and exportation of Canadian resources by foreign corporations, and be strongly opposed to Canadian firms being taken over by foreign companies.

WHY SO MUCH FOREIGN OWNERSHIP?

The most basic reason for the large flows of foreign investment into Canada over the years has been that Canadians wanted it, and sought to attract it. Canadians wanted foreign investment because they wanted industrialization and the economic benefits—higher productivity and a higher standard of living—that it brings. Industrialization required capital investment in excess of our Canadians' ability and willingness to save and invest, so Canada "imported" savings (capital) from more developed countries, especially the United States.

To attract foreign capital, Canada used three basic approaches. First, Canada has had the *least restrictive policy* toward foreign investment of any nation in the western world. Until 1974 there was scarcely any legislation impeding foreign capital inflows. Second, after 1879, Canada imposed *high tariffs* on imported goods, which were a major cause of much foreign investment. These tariffs created a strong incentive for foreign firms to build branch plants in Canada rather than export into the Canadian market. A third measure to attract foreign funds has been Canadian *interest rate policy:* the government has consistently kept Canadian interest rates above those in the United States, so as to make it more attractive for foreign investors to buy Canadian bonds.

Other factors have contributed to the high levels of foreign investment in Canada. The very nature of the Canadian economy—geographically spread out over large areas and concentrating on resource development—has made high levels of capital investment necessary. Furthermore, Canadian investors have not been particularly willing to provide risk capital for Canada's industrial growth, preferring safe, low-yield investments such as residential property, public utilities, and agriculture. The expanding, or growth sectors of the economy—mining, chemicals, electrical apparatus, energy and so on—secured much of their investment capital from foreign sources. Thus, the tendencies of Canadian investors themselves have played a role in the inflow of foreign capital.

On the other hand, as Figure 33-7 shows, the extent of foreign control of Canadian corporations peaked in the early 1970's, and has declined since then. This has been in large part due to the growth of Canadian-controlled corporations, which has reduced the share of foreign-owned ones. Other factors acting to reduce the degree of foreign control have

FIGURE 33-7 *Foreign-Controlled Share of Total Assets and Sales, 1965–92*

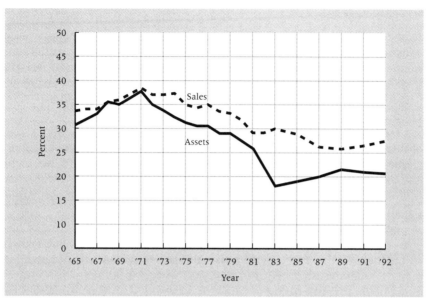

Source: Statistics Canada, Corporations and Labour Union Returns Act, *Report for 1992*, (61-210) and *CALURA, Corporations, 1989-1992* (61-220)

been government policy (which was more restrictive concerning foreign investment from 1974–85) and acquisitions of foreign firms by Canadian corporations.

WHAT HAVE BEEN THE ECONOMIC EFFECTS OF FOREIGN INVESTMENT IN CANADA?

No one doubts that foreign investment has played a large role in developing Canada economically and in providing the prosperity and high standard of living enjoyed by Canadians. If we had had to rely for investment funds on savings generated solely within Canada, our economic development would have been much slower. Furthermore, along with foreign

On the surface, it might seem that Canada's policies with respect to *foreign trade* and *foreign investment* were inconsistent, as Canada restricted foreign imports but welcomed foreign investment. However, both policies served the *same basic objective* of developing Canada's manufacturing sector—the tariff policy by protecting Canadian producers and the investment policy by welcoming foreign investment in Canadian industry.

capital have come managerial and technological expertise, both of which have been of substantial value to Canada. Canadians have gained economically from foreign investment in another way: when foreign firms invest in Canada, they must buy Canadian dollars with their own currency, providing Canada with foreign currencies (mostly US dollars) with which to buy large quantities of imported goods. This process has added substantially to Canadians' living standards. The typical pattern of Canada–US trade has involved heavy purchases of US goods and services by Canadians, paid for partly by Canadian exports and partly by funds provided by US investment into Canada.

On the other hand, foreign investors must be paid for Canadians' use of their capital. The result is a substantial outflow of interest and dividend payments from Canada to foreign holders of the bonds and stocks of Canadian governments and corporations. This gives foreigners a claim on some of the wealth of the Canadian economy, in return for providing Canada with capital.

Over the longer term, the effect of foreign investment in Canada has been that the manufacturing sector of the Canadian economy has grown larger than it otherwise would have, and has provided employment for many Canadians. Still, because of its tariff-inspired branch plant nature, much of the manufacturing sector failed to become the dynamic force that it was intended to be. However, this happened less because it is foreign-owned than that it is the result of tariff protection from competition and the small Canadian market.

GOVERNMENT POLICIES TOWARD FOREIGN INVESTMENT

The basic attitude of Canadian federal and provincial governments over the years has been to *encourage* foreign investment, through tariff and interest-rate policies as well as a lack of restrictions, as noted earlier. While there has been some legislation intended to protect Canada's interests, this legislation has been quite mild by international standards.

Until 1974 the most important approach which the federal government used was the *key sector* tactic—an across-the-board foreign ownership restriction in sectors of the economy deemed to be essential to Canada's political and economic integrity. Through various key sector legislative acts, foreigners have been effectively excluded from control of chartered banks, loan, trust and securities companies, radio and television broadcasting, cable TV companies, magazine publishing and book distribution. In addition, provincial governments regulate foreign investments in certain other ways. For example, there are restrictions on sales of land to foreigners in several provinces, and Ontario requires that a majority of the directors of all provincially incorporated companies be Canadian.

1974–85: a change in policy direction

While Canada has generally welcomed foreign investment, the federal government adopted from 1974 to 1985 a somewhat more nationalistic policy stance. Since foreign ownership peaked in the early 1970's, this shift in policy may have been related to concerns about growing foreign ownership at that time.

In 1974, the federal government passed Canada's most extensive and controversial legislation regarding foreign investment, which led to the creation of the **Foreign Investment Review Agency (FIRA)**. Under this legislation, a federal agency would screen (approve or reject) foreign investment proposals for either the takeover of Canadian businesses over a certain size or for the establishment of new businesses. In making its decisions, the agency was to assess whether or not such investments would be "of significant benefit to Canada." FIRA was quite controversial. It was criticized both for being ineffective in regulating foreign investment and for discouraging valuable investments, due to the red tape involved and the subjective and political nature of the agency's decisions.

The other major piece of economically nationalistic legislation of this period was the **National Energy Program**. One of its goals was to increase Canadian ownership of the oil and gas industry to 50 percent, partly by government policies favoring the growth of Canadian companies and partly by takeovers of foreign firms by PetroCan, the federally-owned oil company.

In 1985, faced with a sluggish economy and the need for more investment spending, the new federal government repealed the National Energy Program and replaced FIRA with **Investment Canada**. While Investment Canada was still to review major foreign takeovers of Canadian businesses, it would do so on a greatly reduced scale. Also, foreign investment creating new businesses in Canada was no longer to be subject to review, but would be required only to provide notification to Investment Canada.

Perhaps more importantly, Investment Canada's basic orientation was to be quite different from FIRA's. While FIRA played the role of *watchdog* to prevent harm to Canada from foreign investment, Investment Canada's role was to be to *promote* both foreign and domestic investment, and to attract foreign investment to Canada. In introducing the new agency, the Prime Minister said, "Canada is on the march to new projects and new prosperity. We have put behind us fears and self doubts that created the National Energy Program and the Foreign Investment Review Agency. Our objective is an economy that is open to new ideas and not afraid of competition."

In summary, economic nationalism, which had always been one facet of Canadians' attitudes toward foreign investment, peaked in Canada from the early 1970's to the early 1980's. These years saw the passage of Canada's most nationalistic economic legislation—the Foreign Investment Review Act, which subjected foreign investment to review and certain limitations, and the National Energy Program, which in some ways was hostile to foreign investment in the oil and gas sector.

Figure 33-8 shows the net flow of direct business investment capital into and out of Canada since 1950 (expressed as a percentage of GDP, to elim-

FIGURE 33-8 *Net Flows of Direct Investment (as a Percentage of GDP), 1950–93*

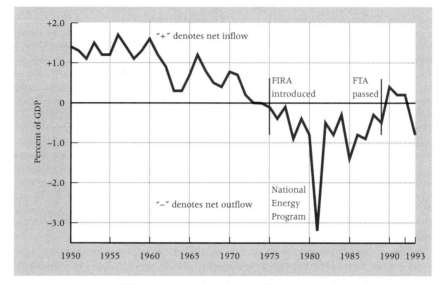

Sources: Department of Finance, *Economic Review*, April 1985; Bank of Canada *Review*

inate the effects of inflation on the data). The heaviest inflows of direct investment occurred in the 1950's; the 1960's and first half of the 1970's saw decreasing inflows, which were followed by outflows during the period of economic nationalism after 1975. After the Free Trade Agreement, there were net inflows of direct investment again. There are different interpretations as to the *causes* of these trends, as economic factors as well as government policies were at work. Also, there are varying interpretations of the *results* of these trends, with some seeing inflows of direct investment as creating jobs for Canadians and others seeing in them increases in foreign ownership and control.

By the mid-1980's, the nationalistic attitudes of the 1975–85 period were being superseded by a new openness to the world in general and to foreign investment in particular. In part, this was probably the result of the fact that the percentage of the Canadian economy that was foreign-owned was declining (more because of the growth of the Canadian-owned portion of the economy than of any reduction in the foreign-owned portion). In addition, as noted earlier, the economic situation in the 1980's was such that investment of any kind, including foreign investment, was much more welcome to Canada.

Finally, the 1980's saw another trend—an accelerating internationalization, or **globalization** of economic activity. The main aspect of this trend was a shift of trade and investment activity from national markets to international markets. Under the Canada–US Free Trade Agreement, restrictions on foreign investment were reduced further, as Canada moved more in the direction of economic internationalism, and away from policies of economic nationalism.

DEFINITIONS OF NEW TERMS

Reciprocity Treaty Free trade between two countries (this term is no longer used).

National Policy A set of nation-building policies introduced in Canada in 1879, the key economic aspect of which was protective tariffs to foster the development of Canadian industry.

Globalization A process of economic restructuring driven by economies of scale based on selling goods in the world market; a shift from national or continental markets to world markets.

World Product Mandating An arrangement whereby a branch plant acquires a mandate from its foreign parent company to design, manufacture and market a particular product or products for the world market, as opposed to producing only for the domestic market of the country in which it is located.

Niche Producer Producer that succeeds not on the basis of mass production for the mass market, but rather by finding a small and specialized product area (niche) in that market.

Dumping The practice of selling goods in export markets for lower prices than in domestic markets; considered an unfair trading practice.

Subsidies In the context of international trade, financial assistance from governments to firms that enables them to practice dumping.

Countervailing Tariff Retaliatory tariff imposed by importing country in response to dumping, intended to neutralize the effect of subsidies and dumping.

Debt Investment Investment in which investors lend capital to a corporation or government, such as by purchasing its bonds.

Equity Investment Investment in which investors buy shares representing ownership (equity) in a corporation, usually acquiring voting rights and thus potentially control.

Foreign Investment Review Agency (FIRA) Federal agency established in 1974 for the purpose of screening (approving or rejecting) foreign proposals for the takeover of Canadian businesses over a certain size or for the establishment of new businesses.

Investment Canada Federal agency that replaced FIRA in 1985, with a much smaller role in screening foreign investment and new emphasis on promoting both foreign and domestic investment.

National Energy Program Federal program established in 1980 that applied various nationalistic measures to Canada's oil and natural gas industry; repealed in 1985.

CHAPTER SUMMARY

1. Under the National Policy (1879), Canada began a long-term program that sought to foster the development of the manufacturing sector of the Canadian economy with tariff protection.

2. This policy led to the development of a larger manufacturing sector, but one that was relatively inefficient and internationally uncompetive and largely foreign-owned.

3. In the 1980's, the international competitiveness of Canadian manufacturing deteriorated, in large part due to weak productivity performance.

4. Factors contributing to this weak productivity performance were tariff protection against foreign competition, small market size, lack of specialization and short production runs.

5. Until the 1980's, Canada earned its way in international trade mainly through exports of resource products, while maintaining its manufacturing sector with tariff protection.

6. During the 1980's, however, pressures for change in Canadian policy arose from various directions: the decreasing international competitiveness of much of Canadian manufacturing, the growing costs to Canadian consumers and exporters of protecting uncompetitive manufacturing, outflows of business investment capital, weaker world markets for Canadian resource exports, and rising protectionism in the United States.

7. On January 1, 1989, the Canada–US Free Trade Agreement came into effect. In broad terms, it provided for:

    (a) elimination of tariffs between Canada and the USA, mostly over a period of 5 or 10 years;

    (b) more secure access for Canada to the US market, through protection against the unfair application of US law;

    (c) relaxation of Canadian restrictions on US investment in Canada;

    (d) assurances that, in times of shortage, energy supplies will be shared.

8. Under the Free Trade Agreement, some Canadian industries expected to benefit, mainly through improved access to the vast US market, while others expected to suffer, due to stronger competition. The expansion of some industries and the contraction of others will involve an adjustment process for both workers and companies.

9. Two business strategies for succeeding in highly-competitive international markets are world product mandating, under which the Canadian branch plants of multinational corporations specialize in the large-scale production of particular products, and niche marketing, in which Canadian producers specialize in the production of smaller-run products targetted at particular relatively small segments ("niches") of international markets.

10. After five years, it was too early to assess the effects of the Free Trade Agreement. Critics pointed to large numbers of plant closings and high unemployment, while supporters of the FTA argued that this was largely due to the recession of the early 1990's and that Canada's export performance in the US market had improved and that Canada was attracting much more foreign business investment.

11. In 1994, the North American Free Trade Agreement (NAFTA) extended the Canada–US free trade area to Mexico.

12. NAFTA's effect on Canada was expected to be quite small due to the low volume of trade and relatively low tariffs between the two nations. Some export opportunities for Canadian firms would open up, especially in industries that could participate in Mexico's efforts to upgrade its public and private capital base, while some Canadian industries such as apparel, textiles, auto parts and miscellaneous manufacturing could expect some increase in Mexican competition.

13. Despite NAFTA's likely small impact on Canada, it was considered important for Canada to be in the deal, so that Canadian-based firms could have the same free access to the markets of all three countries as US-based firms would have if the United States signed a separate free trade deal with Mexico.

14. Foreign ownership of the Canadian economy has historically been quite high, although it peaked in the early 1970's and has been gradually declining as a proportion of the Canadian economy since then.

15. High foreign ownership has been partly the natural result of Canada's need for capital during its development stage, and partly the result of Canada's quite unrestrictive policies toward foreign investment, which has been seen as contributing to Canada's goal of industrial development.

16. The exception to this policy stance was the period from 1974–85, when more nationalistic policies such as the Foreign Investment Review Act and the National Energy Program were in effect.

17. After 1985, Canada took a much more "internationalist" policy direction, reducing restrictions on foreign investment in various ways.

QUESTIONS

1. Overall, is the Canada–US Free Trade Agreement viewed by the Canadian public at this time as having been beneficial to Canada or not? Why?

2. Over the past few years, what have been the trends with respect to:

   (a) Canada's exports to/imports from the USA?

   (b) flows of direct business investment into/out of Canada?

What seem to be the reasons for these trends?

3. A particularly important aspect of the Agreement for Canada was the dispute resolution mechanism, through which Canada could appeal unfair applications of US trade law against Canadian imports. During the first five years of the FTA, Canada used this mechanism on several occasions to appeal arbitrary actions by US authorities, usually successfully. Since then, have there been more or fewer such appeals, and has Canada continued to succeed with most of them?

4. As figure 33-7 shows, the degree of foreign ownership of the Canadian economy decreased after 1971. Under the Free Trade Agreement, Canadian restrictions on US investment in Canada were to be relaxed. Has the degree of US ownership of the Canadian economy increased or decreased since the signing of the Agreement?

5. Some observers predicted that the Free Trade Agreement would reduce regional economic inequality in Canada, by benefitting the eastern and western regions of the country more than central Canada, which had benefitted more from tariff protection. Has this proven correct?

6. Ontario was opposed to the Free Trade Agreement, because a considerable part of Southern Ontario's economy consists of tariff-protected manufacturing industries. Has the Ontario economy suffered particularly severely under the Agreement (for instance, through plant closings and higher unemployment)?

7. How have Canada's farm marketing boards and food processors fared under the Free Trade Agreement?

8. In the late 1980's, Canadian industry engaged in several major mergers and reorganizations, often with the intention of becoming larger and more efficient so as to be better able to compete internationally. Has this trend continued?

9. By 1989, Japan was the only major nation outside of any trading bloc, a potentially serious problem for an exporting nation such as Japan. Since then, has Japan reached a trade agreement with any other major nation(s)?

10. With respect to many "labor-intensive" products such as clothing and footwear, Canada's most serious competition comes not from the USA, but rather from low-wage developing nations. Thus, Canada still has to consider what its policy toward trade with and imports from these countries should be. Do you agree with the following statement concerning that policy, or not? Why?

    Canada might as well negotiate reductions in tariffs on textiles and footwear now, in exchange for reductions in foreign tariffs on Canadian products, because in ten or twenty years, those [Canadian textile] industries will be gone no matter what Canada does, and we'll have nothing to negotiate with.

11. In the interests of preserving Canadian culture and identity, Canada has placed restrictions on foreign activity in fields such as television and radio programming and publishing. Such regulations limit the choices available to Canadian consumers but expand the opportunities for Canadians in these fields. With which of the following views do you agree, and why?

(a) Without these protections, Canadian culture will be swamped by an influx of mass-produced American competition and will eventually disappear. This would be too great a loss for Canada to risk for the supposed economic benefits of free trade, which are only estimated to lie in the range of 1.3 to 7 percent of GDP.

(b) Culture is no different from other inefficient Canadian industries that want consumers' choices to be restricted so that they may continue their protected survival. If Canadian culture is as worthwhile as the nationalists say, it will be able to survive in open competition: if it can't survive, it will be because most Canadians liked something else better. Why should Canadian consumers be forced to support something just because it's Canadian?

12. In the early 1990's, the productivity performance of the Canadian economy in general and the manufacturing sector in particular improved significantly. What has been the trend in productivity since then? What are considered to be the causes of this?

13. The federal government's goal was to have the provincial governments reach an agreement by mid-1994 regarding the reduction or elimination of interprovincial trade barriers. Was this goal achieved? If so, what was the nature of the agreement? If not, what is the current status of this matter?

14. Has the value of the Canadian dollar in terms of the US dollar risen or fallen over the past few years? How has this trend affected Canada's ability to compete in US markets?

15. For many years, Quebec barred construction contractors and workers from outside Quebec from working on Quebec government projects, and severely restricted the right of construction workers from outside Quebec to work in Quebec at all. In September 1993, Ontario announced that it would impose identical barriers against Quebec contractors and workers, in a sort of "interprovincial trade war."

Do you agree with Ontario's action? What do think was Ontario's objective? Has Ontario succeeded in achieving this objective?

16. When the North American Free Trade Agreement was passed in January 1994, opponents predicted that free trade with Mexico would lead not only to higher unemployment in Canada but also to lower wages, increased pollution and deterioration of Canada's social services as Canada was forced to pare these down in order to compete with the Mexicans. Have these predictions proven correct?

NOTES

1 This chapter owes much to *The Canada-U.S. Free Trade Agreement: Background, Overview and Perspectives—What Do You Think? Where Do You Stand?*, Stephanie Currie, Canadian Foundation for Economic Education, 1988.

2 "Reciprocity" is an older term meaning free trade.

3 The tariffs also provided the government with tax revenue, much of which was used to finance the building of the railroad that was crucial to the forging of east-west links.

4 Canada's tariff policy had much stronger political support in Ontario and Quebec, where the protected manufacturing industries were mostly located, than in other parts of the country, particularly the resource-exporting West. Canadians outside of central Canada felt that the tariff policy forced them to subsidize central Canada's manufacturing sector by paying high prices for its products. However, the concentration of population and political power in central Canada was the deciding factor politically.

5 It is important to remember that this applies only to productivity in the *manufacturing sector* of the economy. As we saw earlier, for the Canadian economy *as a whole* (including the large services sector), productivity is about 93 percent of US levels.

6 Economic Council of Canada, *Pulling Together: Productivity, Innovation and Trade*, 1992.

7 Ibid.

8 See for example the study by Glenn Jenkins (Harvard University) cited in *Canadian Consumer*, Oct., 1985.

9 Some US actions went far afield from international trade law and custom—for example, the US Department of Agriculture ruled that the Canadian requirement of dual English and French labelling on packaging constituted an unfair "trade barrier," in total disregard of the fact that Canadian firms are also subject to the same requirement.

10 There are some significant exceptions to these new rules. In cultural industries, such as publishing, proposed takeovers must be reviewed, regardless of the size of the target company. If a US company wants to establish a publishing business, Canadians must have control. Also, the old review thresholds ($5 million annual sales) will continue to apply in the oil and gas, uranium, transportation and financial services industries. And both countries will continue to maintain existing restrictions on foreign ownership in the communications (e.g., broadcasting) and transportation sectors.

11 It should be noted that these provisions apply to other natural resources, and to US exports to Canada as well.

12 With the US market approximately ten times the size of the Canadian market, a one percent share of the US market involves as many sales as a ten percent share of the Canadian market.

13 Statistics Canada, Trade Patterns: Canada-United States, 1993.

14 These figures are vague because official statistics count Mexican goods exported to the USA for re-export to Canada as Mexican exports to the United States, not to Canada.

The Canadian dollar in foreign exchange markets

As we have seen, international trade and Canada's ability to compete internationally are extremely important to the prosperity of Canadians. In Chapter 33 we emphasized the importance of *productivity*, or efficiency, to Canada's international competitiveness, since this affects the price that foreign buyers must pay for Canadian goods and services. However, there is another factor that also has a very strong bearing on Canada's international competitiveness. This is the price that foreigners must pay for the Canadian dollars with which they buy Canadian goods and services—the international value of the Canadian dollar, also known as Canada's **exchange rate**. For instance, it was relatively easy for Canadian exporters to sell to the United States in 1986, when it only cost Americans about $0.72 in US currency to buy $1.00 Canadian. However, by 1991, the cost of a Canadian dollar to Americans had risen to as high as $0.89 US, making it much more difficult for Canadian exporters to sell their goods to American buyers. This rapid increase in the value of the Canadian dollar also generated a sharp increase in cross-border shopping, as Canadians in border communities flocked to the United States to buy consumer goods and services.

Why does the international value of the Canadian dollar fluctuate so much, and what are the implications of these fluctuations for Canadians? To many people, these matters seem as incomprehensible and mysterious as they are important. In fact, however, they can be readily explained and understood in terms of the economic basics involved. In this chapter, we will examine the basic economic forces that determine the Canadian exchange rate of the Canadian dollar. In the next chapter, we will expand our examination of these international matters to a more global scale.

Markets for currencies

International transactions, such as trade, investment and tourism between nations, require that there be some mechanism for converting currencies, or for exchanging various nations' currencies for each other. For example, a Canadian importer of French wine must be able to exchange Canadian dollars for French francs to pay for the wine, and a Japanese corporation buying Canadian lumber must be able to convert its Japanese yen into Canadian dollars to complete the purchase.

These transactions take place in **foreign exchange markets** in which various currencies can be bought and sold. For instance, the Canadian importer of French wine is really *selling Canadian dollars* and buying French francs, while the Japanese importer of Canadian lumber is in fact *buying Canadian dollars* and selling Japanese yen. On any given day, vast amounts of various currencies are bought and sold, for a wide variety of purposes, including imports and exports, investment, tourism and the payment of interest and dividends between nations. These transactions are conducted through banks in each country that have arrangements with banks in other countries for exchanging various nations' currencies.

In short, just as there are markets for goods and services, there are markets for currencies. The marketplace for international currency transactions consists of banks, where currencies are bought and sold. Most people have participated in this market at least in some small way at one time or another—for example, before travelling to the United States, by converting Canadian dollars to US dollars. While we describe such a transaction in terms of "exchanging" or "converting currencies," the reality is that we are *selling* Canadian dollars and *buying* US dollars.

International exchange rates

If currencies are to be bought and sold, there must be prices for them. For instance, when the Canadian tourist exchanges Canadian dollars for US dollars, will he or she get $1.00 US for each Canadian dollar? Or $1.10? Or $0.90? Similarly, how much is a Canadian dollar to be worth in terms of French francs, German deutsche marks, Japanese yen or British pounds? There are no fixed answers to these questions—the international values of currencies, or exchange rates, are prices that fluctuate on a day-to-day basis. Figure 34-1 shows the international price (or value) of the Canadian dollar on November 2, 1993.

These figures can be interpreted in two ways:

(a) If you were a foreigner who was *buying* Canadian dollars on November 2, 1993, the price you had to pay for each Canadian dollar was $0.7661 US, 4.531 francs, 1.298 German deutsche marks, 0.5168 British pounds or 82.372 Japanese yen.

FIGURE 34-1 *International Price (Value) of $1.00 Canadian, November 2, 1993*

$1.00 Canadian = 0.7661 US dollars
= 4.531 French francs
= 1.298 German deutsche marks
= 0.5168 British pounds
= 82.372 Japanese yen

(b) If you were a Canadian who was *selling* Canadian dollars on November 2, 1993, the value you received for each Canadian dollar was $0.7661 US, 4.531 francs, and so on.

WHAT DETERMINES EXCHANGE RATES?

Thus, on November 2, 1993, it took $0.7661 US to buy $1.00 Canadian. What actually *decided* this value of the Canadian dollar? Why was it not $1.03 US, as it had been in 1976, or $0.69 US, as it was at one point in 1986?

Simply stated, the international price of the Canadian dollar, like the price of anything, depends on *supply and demand*. In this market, "supply" means the volume of Canadian dollars being offered for sale in foreign exchange markets, and "demand" refers to the volume of offers to purchase Canadian dollars. It is the balance between the supply of and the demand for the Canadian dollar in foreign exchange markets that determines its value, or price.

For instance, in the early 1970's, strong foreign demand for Canadian exports generated increased buying of Canadian dollars, which rose significantly in value from $0.925 US to over $1.03 US. After 1976, the international price of the Canadian dollar declined sharply for a variety of reasons, including increased selling of Canadian dollars to buy foreign imports and to pay increased interest payments on foreign loans. In the second half of the 1980's, high Canadian interest rates attracted foreign lenders to buy large volumes of bonds issued by Canadian governments and corporations; the resultant high demand for the Canadian dollar drove it as high as $0.89 US. In the early 1990's, this trend was reversed as large volumes of Canadian dollars were sold in order to pay the interest on Canada's large and rising foreign debt.

Receipts and payments

A useful way to summarize a nation's international transactions (and thus the demand for and supply of its currency) is to classify transactions as either **receipts** or **payments**. For example, Canadian exports of lumber to

FIGURE 34-2   *A Summary of Canada's Major International "Receipts"
and "Payments"*

CANADIAN RECEIPTS
(Transactions generating **offers to
buy** Canadian dollars, and thus
increasing the international price of
the Canadian dollar.)

1. **Exports of Merchandise**
   (Foreigners must buy Canadian
   dollars to pay for Canadian
   goods.)

2. **Foreign Tourists Visiting
   Canada**
   (Foreigners must buy Canadian
   dollars to spend while in
   Canada.)

3. **Interest and Dividends
   Received**
   (Foreigners must buy Canadian
   dollars to pay interest and
   dividends to Canadian lenders
   and investors.)

4. **Foreign Investment in/Loans
   to Canada**
   (When foreign funds are
   invested in or loaned to Canada,
   they must first be converted
   into—that is, used to buy—
   Canadian dollars.)

CANADIAN PAYMENTS
(Transactions generating **offers to
sell** Canadian dollars, and thus
depressing the international price
of the Canadian dollar.)

1. **Imports of Merchandise**
   (Canadians must sell Canadian
   dollars to buy foreign currencies
   to pay for imports.)

2. **Canadian Tourists Visiting
   Other Countries**
   (Canadians must sell Canadian
   dollars to buy foreign currencies
   to spend abroad.)

3. **Interest and Dividend
   Payments**
   (Canadian businesses and
   governments must sell Canadian
   dollars to buy foreign currencies
   to pay interest and dividends to
   foreign lenders and investors.)

4. **Investment by Canadians in
   Foreign Countries**
   (Canadian citizens and
   businesses investing in other
   countries must first sell
   Canadian dollars in order to
   buy foreign currencies with
   which to make such
   investments.)

Japan cause Canada to *receive* foreign currency, so exports are classified as a
"receipt" to Canada. Conversely, the winter vacations spent by Canadian
tourists in Florida are classified as "payments," because they involve *payments* from Canadians to a foreign nation. Receipts generate a demand for the
Canadian dollar, because foreigners must buy Canadian dollars in order to
pay Canada, whereas payments generate a supply of Canadian dollars, or offers by Canadians to sell Canadian dollars in order to pay foreign nations.

In summary, Canada's international transactions can be classified as receipts, which increase the demand for and the price of the Canadian dollar, and payments, which depress the price of the Canadian dollar by
causing increased selling (a greater supply) of it on foreign exchange markets. A summary of Canada's major receipts and payments is presented
in Figure 34-2. As the balance of Canada's receipts and payments fluctuates, so should the international value of the Canadian dollar tend to rise
and fall.

FIGURE 34-3 *Major Categories of Canada's Balance of Payments*

RECEIPTS

Current Account

Merchandise Exports
Travel and Tourism
Interest and Dividends
Freight and Shipping
Inheritances and Immigrants'
    Funds

Capital Account

Foreign Direct Investment in
    Canada
Foreign Purchases of Canadian
    Stocks and Bonds
Foreign Purchases of Canadian
    Government Bonds
Foreign Purchases of Canadian
    Short-Term Deposits and
    Securities

PAYMENTS

Current Account

Merchandise Imports
Travel and Tourism
Interest and Dividends
Freight and Shipping
Inheritances and Emigrants'
    Funds

Capital Account

Canadian Direct Investment
    Abroad
Canadian Purchases of Foreign
    Securities and Deposits

Canada's Balance of Payments

The **Balance of Payments** is an annual summary of all of Canada's international financial transactions, classed as receipts or payments. These items, as Figure 34-3 shows, are divided into **current account** and **capital account** transactions. Current account includes mostly day-to-day transactions in goods and services, and capital account refers to flows of investment funds, both long-term and short-term, into and out of Canada.

    The left side of Figure 34-3 shows all of Canada's international receipts. These receipts include earnings from the various current account items shown, plus inflows of capital into Canada, including foreign **direct investment**[1] into Canada, foreign purchases of Canadian stocks and bonds (including corporate bonds and bonds issued by governments), and foreign purchases of short-term Canadian securities (such as Treasury Bills) and bank deposits. The right side of Figure 34-3 shows Canada's payments, which are comprised of payments for the various current account items, plus outflows of capital from Canada, as Canadian businesses and citizens invest funds in other nations.

The Balance of Payments and the exchange rate

As we have seen, foreign exchange markets, in which the currencies of various nations are bought and sold, resemble a "tug of war" between each nation's receipts (which push the international price of its currency up) and its payments (which push the international price of its currency down). There are three possible situations regarding a nation's Balance of Payments and the international value of its currency, which are:

(a) a **Balance of Payments deficit**, when payments exceed receipts,

(b) a **Balance of Payments surplus**, when receipts exceed payments, and

(c) **equilibrium** in the Balance of Payments, with payments equal to receipts.

Using Canada as an example, we will examine the results of each of these situations.

(A) A BALANCE OF PAYMENTS DEFICIT

If Canada has a Balance of Payments "deficit," Canada's payments (offers to sell Canadian dollars) exceed its receipts (offers to buy Canadian dollars). As a result, the supply of Canadian dollars in foreign exchange markets will exceed the demand for Canadian dollars, and the international price of the Canadian dollar will *fall*, as shown in Figure 34-4. An example of such a situation is 1974–75, when Canadian exports slumped and a large deficit developed in trade in goods and services, leading to declines in the international value of the Canadian dollar. Another example is the early 1990's, when deficits arising mainly from outflows of interest payments contributed to a considerable decline in the exchange rate.

(B) A BALANCE OF PAYMENTS SURPLUS

If Canada has a Balance of Payments "surplus," Canada's receipts will exceed its payments, so that the demand for the Canadian dollar will exceed

FIGURE 34-4 *Balance of Payments Deficits and the Exchange Rate*

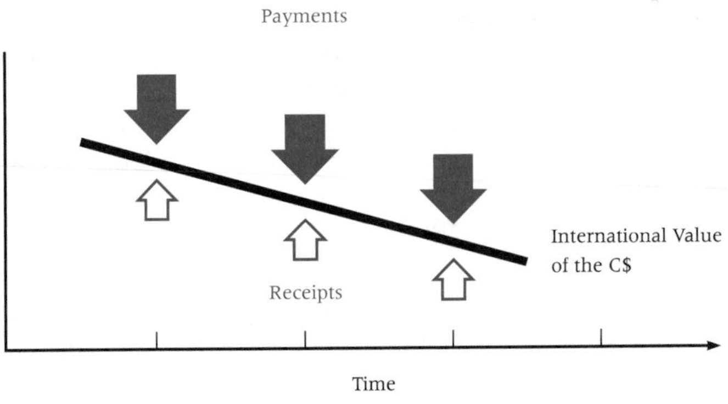

Balance of Payments *Deficit:* Payments exceed receipts. pushing the international value of the Canadian dollar (C$) *down.*

FIGURE 34-5 *Balance of Payments Surpluses and the Exchange Rate*

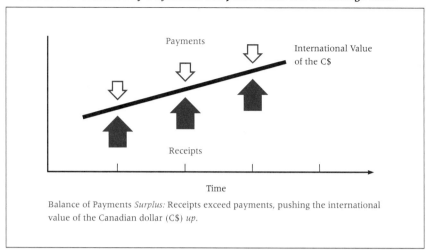

Balance of Payments *Surplus:* Receipts exceed payments, pushing the international value of the Canadian dollar (C$) *up.*

the supply of it, causing the international price of the Canadian dollar to rise, as shown in Figure 34-5. Such a situation occurred in the early 1970's, when strong exports created a surplus on current account, boosting the international value of the Canadian dollar. After 1985, the dollar rose strongly for a different reason: growing surpluses on capital account, due to inflows of foreign capital into Canada as foreign lenders bought large volumes of Canadian bonds.

(C) EQUILIBRIUM IN THE BALANCE OF PAYMENTS

If Canada's Balance of Payments were "in equilibrium," with receipts equal to payments, the supply of and demand for the Canadian dollar would be in balance, and the international value of the Canadian dollar would tend to remain stable at its present level. It is important to appreciate, however, that this does not mean that the Canadian dollar has found its "proper" value, at which it will remain—this stability would last only until receipts and/or payments changed, causing a Balance of Payments surplus or deficit to develop. Given the dynamic nature of international trade and investment flows, such stability is rare and short-lived. In fact, day-to-day fluctuations in currency values in response to market fluctuations are normal.

A floating exchange rate system

We have been examining how the international prices (values) of currencies can rise and fall in response to changes in international receipts and payments. When a nation permits the international value of its currency to move up and down as the supply of and demand for it change, it is said to be operating on a **floating exchange rate** system.

In the following sections, we will examine how a system of floating exchange rates, or currency prices, operates under conditions of (a) a Balance of Payments surplus and (b) a Balance of Payments deficit.

(A) HOW A FLOATING EXCHANGE RATE OPERATES WITH A BALANCE OF PAYMENTS SURPLUS

Suppose Canada is operating on a floating exchange rate system, with the international value of the Canadian dollar at $1.00 US, when Canada develops a Balance of Payments surplus (say, due to increased exports of natural resources). As noted earlier, the Balance of Payments surplus will cause the international price of the Canadian dollar to rise, say, to $1.04 US.

The increase in the price of the Canadian dollar will set into motion an automatic *adjustment mechanism*, which will tend to eliminate the Balance of Payments surplus. Because the Canadian dollar is more costly to foreigners, Canada's receipts will fall: foreigners will buy fewer Canadian goods, travel less to Canada, and invest less in Canada. Also, because the international value of the Canadian dollar has risen, it will buy more foreign currency than before, making it less costly for Canadians to buy, travel and invest in other nations. As Canadians increase their purchases of imports and their travelling to and investing in other nations, Canada's payments will rise. With receipts falling and payments rising, the original Balance of Payments

FIGURE 34-6 *Adjustment of a Floating Exchange Rate to a Balance of Payments Surplus*

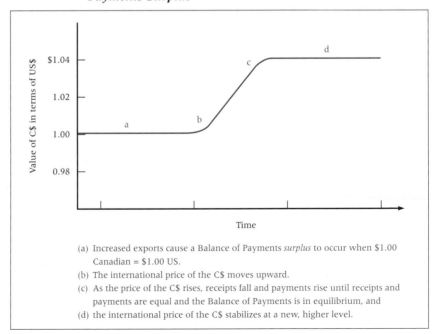

(a) Increased exports cause a Balance of Payments *surplus* to occur when $1.00 Canadian = $1.00 US.

(b) The international price of the C$ moves upward.

(c) As the price of the C$ rises, receipts fall and payments rise until receipts and payments are equal and the Balance of Payments is in equilibrium, and

(d) the international price of the C$ stabilizes at a new, higher level.

surplus will tend to disappear, with the international value of the Canadian dollar having moved to a new higher equilibrium level which is more consistent with the high demand for Canadian exports.

This tendency to move automatically toward equilibrium is illustrated in Figure 34-6. It shows a Balance of Payments surplus causing an increase in the price of the Canadian dollar, which in turn tends to eliminate the surplus.

(B) HOW A FLOATING EXCHANGE RATE OPERATES WITH A BALANCE OF PAYMENTS DEFICIT

In a deficit situation, the adjustments are the opposite of those described above. Suppose Canada develops a Balance of Payments deficit (say, due to increased imports of foreign goods). The increase in offers to sell Canadian dollars will cause the international value of the Canadian dollar to fall, say, to $0.98 US from its original level of $1.00 US.

This decrease in the price of the Canadian dollar will cause the automatic adjustment mechanism referred to earlier to operate in the opposite direction, as shown in Figure 34-7. With the Canadian dollar less costly to them, foreigners will buy more Canadian goods and travel to and invest in Canada more; as a result, Canada's receipts will rise. Also, Canada's payments will

FIGURE 34-7   *Adjustment of a Floating Exchange Rate to a Balance of
Payments Deficit*

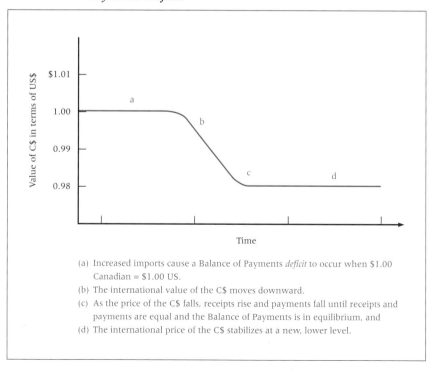

(a) Increased imports cause a Balance of Payments *deficit* to occur when $1.00 Canadian = $1.00 US.

(b) The international value of the C$ moves downward.

(c) As the price of the C$ falls, receipts rise and payments fall until receipts and payments are equal and the Balance of Payments is in equilibrium, and

(d) The international price of the C$ stabilizes at a new, lower level.

CAN A NATION FLOOD ANOTHER NATION'S MARKETS WITH GOODS?

Sometimes, nations fear that they will be unable to compete with goods imported from foreign countries, with the result that large segments of domestic industry will be wiped out by imports. During the 1960's and 1970's, the increasing export success of Japan caused such fears in the United States and Canada.

Under a system of floating exchange rates, could one nation flood another nation's markets to this extent?

ANSWER ON NEXT PAGE

fall: with the Canadian dollar worth less, other nations' currencies will cost Canadians more, making it more costly for Canadians to buy foreign goods and services. Consequently, Canadians will buy fewer foreign imported goods, travel less and invest less in other countries, causing Canada's international payments to decline. As a result of the increased receipts and reduced payments, Canada's Balance of Payments deficit will tend to disappear, and the Balance of Payments will move toward an equilibrium situation with the Canadian dollar at a new, lower equilibrium level.

Thus, a Balance of Payments deficit will cause the international price of the Canadian dollar to fall, which will increase receipts and reduce payments, moving the Balance of Payments toward equilibrium, but at a lower exchange rate.

Summary

Under a system of floating exchange rates, a nation's Balance of Payments will tend to move toward equilibrium, because of the relationship between the Balance of Payments and the exchange rate (or international price of the currency). While the Balance of Payments affects the exchange rate, so also does the exchange rate affect the Balance of Payments.

Specifically, if a Balance of Payments deficit develops, it will tend to be removed by a reduction in the exchange rate, which will increase receipts and reduce payments. Conversely, a Balance of Payments surplus tends to be eliminated by an increase in the exchange rate, which reduces receipts and increases payments. In both cases, the Balance of Payments tends to return to equilibrium through changes in the international price of the currency.

There is not, however, a natural or fixed level which represents *the* equilibrium price for the Canadian dollar, toward which the exchange rate will always tend to move. Nor, having reached its equilibrium level, will the price of the Canadian dollar *stay* at that level. As international trade and investment patterns change, causing shifts in payments and receipts, the supply of and demand for the Canadian dollar—and its equilibrium value—constantly change. The equilibrium price of the Canadian dollar is a moving target, toward which the value of the dollar will tend to move under a floating exchange rate system. Figure 34-8 presents a summary of the operation of a floating exchange rate in the three contexts that we have discussed.

FIGURE 34-8 *Summary of the Operation of a Floating Exchange Rate*

Situation	Effect on Foreign Exchange Markets	Effect on the Balance of Payments
1. Canada's PAYMENTS exceed RECEIPTS (a Balance of Payments deficit)	The supply of C$ exceeds the demand for C$; the price of the C$ falls.	As the C$ falls, receipts will increase and payments decrease until they are equal and the new C$ stabilizes at a new, lower equilibrium level.
2. Canada's RECEIPTS exceed PAYMENTS (a Balance of Payments surplus)	The demand for C$ exceeds the supply of C$; the price of the C$ rises.	As the C$ rises, payments will increase and receipts decrease until they are equal and the C$ stabilizes at a new, higher equilibrium level.
3. Canada's PAYMENTS and RECEIPTS are equal (the Balance of Payments is in equilibrium)	The supply of and demand for C$ are equal; the price of the C$ remains stable.	Payments and receipts remain equal; C$ remains at equilibrium level until payments or receipts change.

ANSWER

No, it could not. Under a system of floating exchange rates, the relative values of the two nations' currencies would change so as to make this impossible. In the case of the Japanese exports, North Americans would have to buy vast amounts of yen (and sell vast amounts of US and Canadian dollars) to buy such large volumes of Japanese goods. As a result, the international price of the yen would rise sharply relative to the US and Canadian dollars, making Japanese goods significantly less competitive in North America.

For instance, from 1952 to 1992, the price of the yen in Canadian dollars rose by 250 percent, and the price of the German deutsche mark rose by 233 percent. While these increases reflected in large part the export gains of those nations, they also made it more difficult for their exporters to continue to achieve such gains.

Foreign exchange speculation

As Figure 34-9 illustrates, the international values of currencies, including the Canadian dollar, fluctuate considerably over time, sometimes quite suddenly and dramatically.

These fluctuations introduce the possibility of making profits through **speculation** in currencies—that is, buying a currency when its value is low and selling it after its value has risen. For instance, there was an opportunity to buy Canadian dollars in early 1986 for $0.69 US and sell them five years later for $0.89 US for a gain of nearly 30 percent. Similarly, a person who anticipated the rapid decline of the Canadian dollar from $0.89 US to about $0.75 US after late 1991 could have converted $10 000 Canadian into $8 900 US in October 1991 and converted this back into nearly $12 000 Canadian just two years later, for a gain of nearly 20 percent.

Of course, hindsight makes this all very clear. At the time that such decisions have to be made, however, the outcome is not at all certain. And, while quick and easy gains can be made through foreign-exchange speculation, equally quick losses can be incurred, if the currency does not move as the speculator anticipated it would. In spite of these risks, speculators will often move considerable volumes of short-term capital out of currencies seen as "weak" (likely to fall in value) and into currencies believed to be "strong" (likely to rise), hoping to make a quick profit by anticipating exchange-rate fluctuations arising from economic or political developments.

As a result, there exists a large volume of speculative short-term funds, known as **"hot money,"** that are capable of moving very rapidly out of

FIGURE 34-9 *The International Value of the Canadian Dollar, 1970–94*

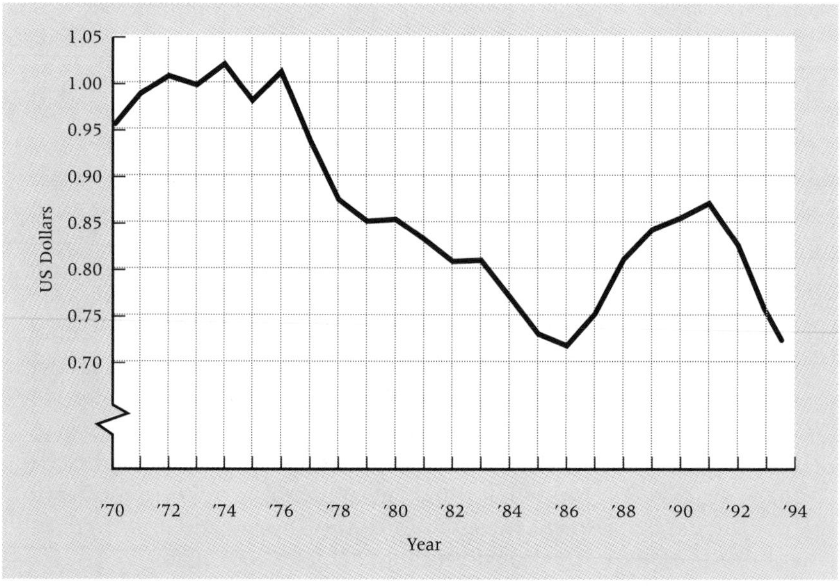

Source: Bank of Canada *Review*

some currencies and into others. Such speculative purchases and sales of currencies can cause their values to fluctuate more dramatically, by forcing "strong" currencies higher and "weak" currencies lower. Such rapid exchange-rate fluctuations can cause considerable difficulties for the economies of the nations involved, as we will see in the next section.

Problems concerning currency fluctuations

We have seen that fluctuations in the international values of nations' currencies are quite normal. In addition, changes in exchange rates can serve a very important purpose, by helping to keep nations' exports and imports in reasonable balance. For instance, if the Japanese yen were at the same value in 1993 as it was in 1952, a Honda Accord would have cost less than $5000 in Canada in 1993—hardly a workable situation.[2]

However, if the international value of a nation's currency changes *excessively rapidly*, that nation's economy can be adversely affected. A rapid increase in the international value of the Canadian dollar could damage the competitive position of Canadian producers by making Canadian exports more expensive and foreign imports cheaper. On the other hand, a sharp decline in the value of the Canadian dollar would cause import prices to rise quickly, which could add significantly to inflationary pressures in Canada.

As a result, governments are often reluctant to allow the international value of their currencies to rise (**appreciate**) or fall (**depreciate**) too quickly. Instead, governments often seek to moderate the currency fluctuations associated with floating exchange rates. When they do so, the situation is referred to as a **dirty float**, because while the exchange rate is floating, it is also being influenced by the government. Government policies that influence the exchange rate are also known as **exchange rate management**

Exchange rate management

> Movements in the exchange rate are of concern because of their potential impact on domestic prices, output and income. Exaggerated changes in the exchange rate that are not consistent with market fundamentals and that threaten domestic objectives may require corrective action.
>
> John W. Crow, Governor of the Bank of Canada, May, 1988

PURCHASES AND SALES OF CURRENCIES

To influence the international value of currencies, governments can simply *buy and sell currencies* in foreign exchange markets. By buying a currency, a government can increase, or support, its price by adding to the demand for it, while sales of a currency by a government will depress its value by increasing the supply of it on foreign exchange markets.

In Canada, exchange rate management is handled by the Bank of Canada. If the Canadian dollar is rising too rapidly as a result of heavy foreign demand, the Bank of Canada may slow down the rise of the dollar by selling Canadian dollars to foreign buyers in foreign exchange markets. In the process of selling Canadian dollars to foreign buyers, the Bank of Canada also buys foreign currencies, mostly US dollars. These foreign currencies are held by the Bank of Canada as part of Canada's *foreign exchange reserves*, or official international reserves, as shown in Figure 34-10. The sharp increase in Canada's international reserves in 1988–90 reflects the fact that the Bank of Canada was making considerable efforts to hold down the value of the rapidly-rising Canadian dollar during this period, by selling Canadian dollars and buying US dollars.

These official international reserves are useful when the Bank of Canada wishes to prevent an excessively rapid decline in the exchange rate. If the exchange rate declines too rapidly, the Bank of Canada can buy Canadian dollars in foreign exchange markets, in order to support its price. Buying Canadian dollars requires that the Bank of Canada sell foreign currencies[3] from its official international reserves, which will reduce its reserves. The decline in Canada's international reserves in 1992–93 re-

FIGURE 34-10 *Canada's Official International Reserves, 1978–93*

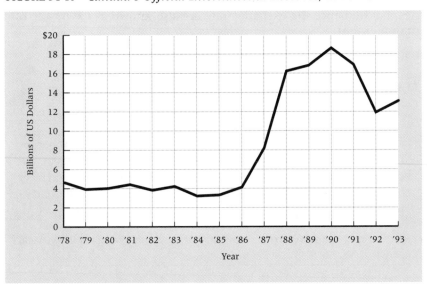

Source: Bank of Canada *Review*

flects the Bank of Canada's attempts to slow down the decline in the dollar during this period by buying Canadian dollars/selling its reserves.

By selling and buying Canadian dollars (and adding to and decreasing its official international reserves in the process), the Bank of Canada can, within limits, prevent excessive fluctuations in the exchange rate and their possibly disruptive effects on the economy.

CHANGES IN INTEREST RATES

Another way in which the Bank of Canada can influence the exchange rate is through its *interest-rate policies*. If the Canadian dollar is declining excessively rapidly, the Bank of Canada can increase interest rates in Canada. Higher interest rates can attract short-term investment funds from foreign nations into Canadian-dollar deposits or securities. To do this, however, their owners must buy Canadian dollars, which will support the international value of the Canadian dollar. This policy can also be used in the other direction: if the Canadian dollar were rising rapidly, the Bank of Canada could reduce Canadian interest rates, holding the Canadian dollar down as Canadian dollars are sold in order to buy those currencies paying higher interest rates.

In summary, by increasing Canadian interest rates, the Bank of Canada can support the international value of the Canadian dollar, and by holding Canadian interest rates down, it can depress the exchange rate. Such changes in interest rates represent another tool for the Bank of Canada for influencing the exchange rate, in addition to purchases and sales of currencies.

Objectives of exchange rate policy—more trade-offs

Is it better for Canadians if the Bank of Canada supports or depresses the exchange rate of the Canadian dollar? While some Canadians believe that a higher international value of their currency is automatically better (perhaps largely because it sounds better), the situation is not nearly so simple. Rather, the answer to this question depends on *one's perspective* and on *economic conditions*.

In part, the answer to this question depends on whether one is a consumer or a producer who is exposed to international competition. To Canadian consumers, an increase in the international value of the Canadian dollar is good news. Because the Canadian dollar buys more foreign currencies, imported goods and trips outside Canada will cost less. However, to Canadian businesses that export or compete with imports, an increase in the exchange rate is bad news. The higher-priced Canadian dollar will reduce export sales by making Canadian exports more expensive, and the relatively lower value of foreign currencies will encourage Canadians to buy imports instead of Canadian products. Conversely, a reduction in the exchange rate would be welcomed by businesses that export or compete with imports, but would mean higher prices for consumers. As a result, exchange-rate policy involves a degree of balancing "trade-offs" between the interests of consumers and the interests of producers.

The answer also depends on the *economic conditions in Canada* at the time. If Canada is in a recession, a lower international value of the Canadian dollar will help to boost the demand for Canadian exports, and thus help to reduce unemployment. On the other hand, if inflation were the main problem in the economy, a falling exchange rate would only make matters worse, by increasing the price of imports. Instead, a rising Canadian dollar would help to contain inflation, by keeping import prices down. In this sense, exchange-rate policy involves the trade-offs between unemployment and inflation that we saw in Chapter 31.

Exchange-rate policy and monetary and fiscal policies

From the foregoing, it can be seen that the Bank of Canada's exchange-rate policy is closely linked to its interest-rate policy and monetary policy as described in Chapter 27. In a broader sense, it is linked to the whole question of "demand management" and the trade-offs between unemployment and inflation that we saw in Chapter 31. As Figure 34-11 shows, government policies to combat recession could include a government budget deficit and lower interest rates to boost spending by Canadian consumers

FIGURE 34-11   *Government Policies to Combat Recession*

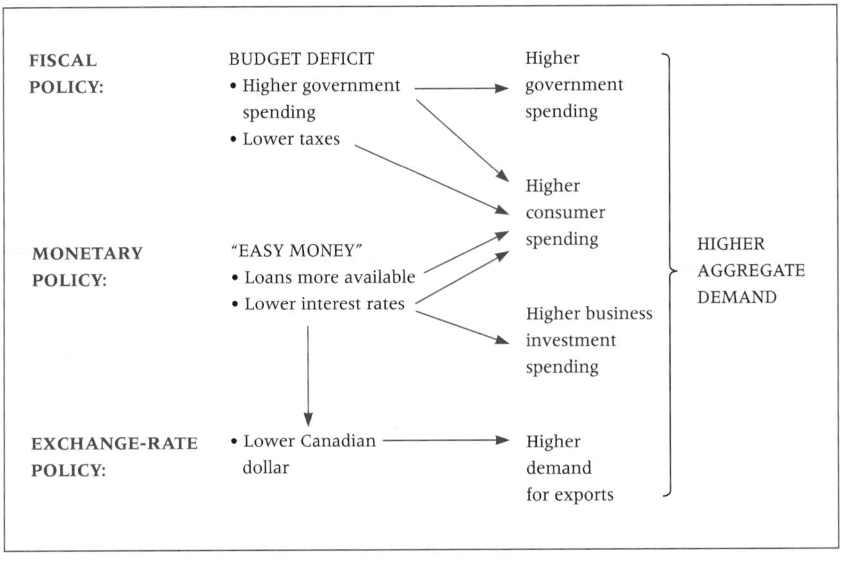

FIGURE 34-12 *Government Policies to Combat Inflation*

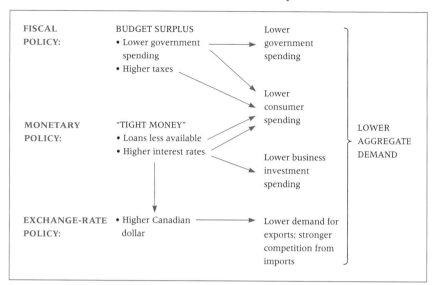

and businesses, with lower interest rates contributing to a lower exchange rate that could also boost foreign demand for Canadian exports. This was essentially the direction of Canadian policy in 1992–93.

Figure 34-12 shows the same policies operating in the opposite direction, to slow down inflation. Cuts in government spending and higher taxes and higher interest rates can depress spending by Canadian consumers and businesses, and higher interest rates could push the price of the Canadian dollar higher, depressing both export demand and the price of imports. From 1988–90, this was the general thrust of Canadian policy.

Finally, as noted in Chapter 31, the use of these policies involves seeking a balance between conflicting objectives—lower unemployment and lower inflation—that is economically reasonable and politically acceptable.

Limits on exchange rate policy

In determining its exchange rate policy, a government cannot ignore the fact that there is at any point in time an *equilibrium international value* for its currency. If a government tries to maintain the value of its currency too far below its equilibrium level, to assist its exporters, it would have to sell vast amounts of its own currency in foreign exchange markets. To sell such quantities of its currency, it would have to borrow (or even print) such large volumes of money that it would damage its own economy, through high interest rates and severe inflation. For example, Japan and West Germany resisted the upward movement of the yen and deutsche mark in the 1960's for fear it would depress their export industries; however, both nations finally found it impossible to prevent their exchange rates from rising.

Similarly, a nation that seeks to keep its exchange rate too far above its equilibrium level will encounter difficulties. To achieve this would require continual large-scale purchases of its own currency, which would mean ongoing large-scale sales of its foreign exchange reserves. Such a policy would eventually deplete its reserves and force it to allow the value of its currency to decline. For instance, as Great Britain's competitive position in world trade declined after 1945, and severe chronic Balance of Payments deficits developed, the British government tried to maintain the international value of the pound at unrealistically high levels, but finally failed because of shortages of foreign exchange reserves. The only other way to keep a currency at a level well above its equilibrium would be through interest rates so high that they would depress the nation's entire economy.

Thus, when we speak of a government "managing" its exchange rate, we do not mean that the government *controls* the international value of its currency. A government can influence its exchange rate, but only to prevent excessively rapid fluctuations around its equilibrium level—it cannot succeed for long in keeping its exchange rate much above or much below its equilibrium level.

The Balance of Payments and the Canadian dollar in recent years

(A) THE 1950'S AND 1960'S

Figure 34-13 shows Canada's Balance of International Payments for 1961, a year that was fairly typical of the 1950's and 1960's. Generally, during this period, Canada had a deficit on current account which was offset by inflows of foreign capital, or a surplus on its capital account. More specifically, in 1961 a surplus on merchandise trade of $173 million (mainly due to resource exports) was more than compensated for by deficits in other areas, especially travel ($160 million), and interest and dividends ($551 million paid out on the considerable amount of foreign capital invested in Canada). The result was a current account deficit of $928 million. The current account deficit was financed mainly by an inflow of long-term foreign capital ($930 million), over half of which took the form of direct investment involving foreign investments in Canadian enterprises. In addition, foreigners provided funds to Canada by purchasing the stocks of Canadian businesses and by lending funds to Canadian businesses by buying their bonds. Canadian governments borrowed a very small amount ($40 million) from foreign lenders by selling government bonds abroad. In the view of some, Canadians were living high on foreign imports, paid for by selling out control of Canadian industry to foreigners and going into debt to foreigners. Others disagreed: they saw Canada as being in a stage of development in which it needed more investment capital than was available within Canada, making it natural and beneficial to import capital from foreign nations such as the United States. Regardless of one's viewpoint, however, it was indisputable that Canadians were enjoying greater economic prosperity than would otherwise have been possible, and that both foreign ownership of Canadian industry and Canada's indebtedness to foreign nations were increasing.

The increase in foreign ownership was not widely regarded as a matter of serious concern. In the process of industrialization, nations often use foreign capital quite extensively in the early years when capital requirements are high. However, after a point, the economy will grow and mature enough that domestic savings become sufficient to finance investment requirements, and the dependence on foreign capital ends. Eventually, the nation will likely become sufficiently wealthy that it will be a supplier of capital to (or lender to, or investor in) other nations. The US economy went through just such a process, with British capital financing the original development.

FIGURE 34-13   *Canada's Balance of International Payments, 1961*

	Receipts (+) (	Payments (−) millions of dollars	Balance Surplus (+) or Deficit (−))
Current Account			
Merchandise	$5 889	$5 716	+$173
Travel	482	642	−160
Interest and Dividends	213	764	−551
Freight and Shipping	486	568	−82
Other			−308
Balance on Current Account			−928
Capital Account			
LONG-TERM			
Direct Investment	$560	$80	+480
Canadian Stocks and Bonds			
Sold (Net[a])	307		+307
Government Bonds Issued (Net[a])	40		+40
Other	103		+103
Balance on Long-Term Capital Account			+930
SHORT-TERM			
Balance on Short-Term Capital Account			+133

[a]After deductions of repayments (retirements) of issues that have matured.

Source: Bank of Canada *Review*, November 1981

FIGURE 34-14 *Canada's Decreasing Dependence on Foreign Capital in the Early 1970's*

	(All figures expressed as a percentage of GNP)			
	Current Account Deficit	*Net Inflow of Foreign Direct Investment*	*Long-Term Bond Issues Abroad (net)*	*Total Capital Inflow (Long-Term and Short-Term)*
1950–59	2.5%	1.3%	0.8%	2.6%
1960–69	1.5	0.8	1.3	1.8
1970–74	0.04	0.3	0.7	0.4

Source: Department of Finance, Economic *Review*, April 1980; Bank of Canada *Review*

(B) THE EARLY 1970'S

In the early 1970's, Canada's dependence on foreign capital appeared to be coming to an end. Figure 34-14 shows that Canada's deficit on current account, inflows of foreign direct investment, long-term borrowing abroad and general reliance on foreign capital of all sorts decreased significantly compared to the GDP. These trends were consistent with the process of economic development described earlier, and it was expected that they would continue as Canada's prosperity increased and its dependence on foreign capital decreased. However, after 1975, this situation would unexpectedly reverse itself, and Canada's foreign indebtedness would increase sharply, as we will see in the following sections.

(C) AFTER 1975

Figure 34-15 shows Canada's Balance of International Payments for selected years since 1975. As Figure 34-15 shows, the period after 1975 saw three major changes from the 1970–74 period:

(i) a reappearance of large current account deficits,

(ii) outflows rather than inflows of direct investment, and

(iii) heavy borrowing abroad by Canadian governments and corporations.

We will examine each of these developments in turn.

(i) Reappearance of current account deficits

As we saw earlier, Canada's current account deficits had been declining more or less steadily, from 2.5 percent of GDP in the 1950's to 1.5 percent of GDP in the 1960's and to nearly zero in the 1970–74 period. After 1975, however, this trend was dramatically reversed, as Canada's current account deficits not only reappeared, but also grew larger—from 1.8 percent of GDP over the 1976–81 period to 2.2 percent of GDP from 1985–89 and 4.1 percent of GDP from 1990–92.

FIGURE 34-15 *Canada's Balance of International Payments, 1976–92*

Current Account	1976	1980	1984	1988	1992
	(		Billions of dollars		)
Merchandise	$+1.6	$+8.8	$+19.8	$ 8.9	$+ 9.0
Interest and Dividends	–3.5	–7.8	–13.5	–18.7	–24.2
Travel	–1.2	–1.2	– 2.1	– 2.9	– 8.1
Other	–1.0	–1.6	– 5.9	– 2.8	– 4.4
Balance on Current Account	$–4.1	$–1.8	$– 1.7	$–15.5	$–27.7
Capital Account					
Direct Investment	$–0.9	$–2.4	$– 1.2	$– 2.1	$+ 1.5
Canadian Bonds Issued and Sold (net of Retirements)	+8.6	+3.5	+ 7.9	+15.6	+15.8
Other	+0.2	+1.7	– 2.2	+ 2.6	+ 6.5
Balance on Capital Account	$+7.9	$+2.8	$ 4.5	$+16.1	$+23.8

Source: Bank of Canada *Review,* Summer 1993

829

The Canadian dollar in foreign exchange markets

As Figure 34-15 shows, the main reason for these large current account deficits was *interest payments* on Canada's debts to foreign lenders. In Chapter 25, we saw how the budget deficits of the federal government grew sharply after 1975, to the point where the federal government was borrowing so heavily in Canada that other borrowers such as provincial governments and corporations often had to borrow outside Canada. Over a period of time, these borrowings caused Canada to accumulate an extremely large foreign debt, the annual interest on which pushed Canada's current account deficits upwards. Canada's international interest payments were further increased by the fact that interest rates during this period were very high due to investors' concerns about inflation and heavy debt.

In addition, Canada had a growing deficit on services, mainly travel and tourism but also freight and shipping, computer services, insurance, consulting, films and broadcasting, advertising and research and development. The high international value of the Canadian dollar in the late 1980's and early 1990's contributed to this deficit by making it inexpensive for Canadians to travel in the United States and buy services there.

On merchandise trade, Canada continued to have considerable surpluses; however, these were not as large as in the past. From 1970–74, Canada's merchandise trade surplus had averaged 2.3 percent of GDP, whereas from 1985–92 it averaged only 1.7 percent of GDP. Various reasons have been advanced for this weakening of Canada's merchandise trade surplus, including weaker world markets for several of Canada's key

FIGURE 34-16 *Features of Canada's Current Account, 1970–93*

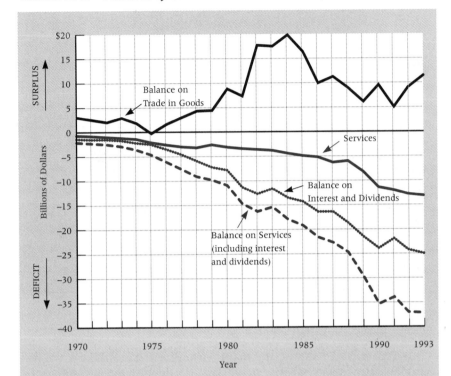

Source: Bank of Canada, *Review*

resource exports such as wheat and energy, and the declining competitiveness of parts of Canada's manufacturing sector over this period. Another—and quite different—theory is that Canada's heavy foreign borrowing generated current account deficits. According to this theory, the heavy inflow of borrowed funds pushed the Canadian dollar to high levels, depressing Canadian exports and boosting Canadians' purchases of imports.

In summary, with sharply higher interest payments, a growing deficit on services and a merchandise trade surplus that was less strong than in the past, Canada's current account deficits grew increasingly large. These developments are summarized in Figure 34-16.[4]

(ii) Direct investment outflows

In every year from 1950 to 1974, Canada received a net inflow of direct investment funds from other nations, mostly the United States. However, from 1975 to 1989, this flow was reversed, as more direct investment funds left Canada than entered Canada, as Figure 34-17 shows.

In part, this reflected reduced interest on the part of foreign businesses in investing in Canada; however, much of the net outflow was the result

FIGURE 34-17 *Flows of Direct Investment Into and Out of Canada, 1970–92*

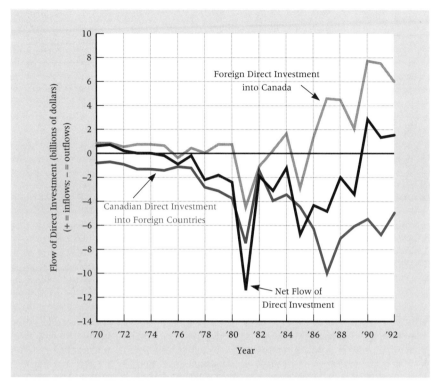

Source: Department of Finance, *Economic and Fiscal Reference Tables*, August 1993

of Canadian businesses investing more abroad. In the view of many economists, the small size of the Canadian market was limiting investment opportunities in Canada, making it more attractive for both Canadian and foreign firms to invest elsewhere. It is interesting to note that following the passage of the Canada–US Free Trade Agreement, which improved Canadian access to the vast US market, the outflow of direct investment capital turned back into an inflow, as foreign firms increased their investment into Canada and Canadian firms reduced their investment outside Canada.

(iii) Heavy borrowing abroad by Canadian governments and corporations

The other major change in Canada's Balance of Payments was a *sharp increase in borrowing abroad* by Canadian governments and corporations. Whereas from 1970–74, net Canadian bond issues abroad amounted to only 0.7 percent of GDP, this increased to 2.4 percent in the second half of the 1970's, averaged 1.7 percent in the 1980's and reached 2.6 percent per year in the early 1990's. This was a very significant change as Canada, one of the richest nations in the world, was borrowing heavily from other

FIGURE 34-18 *Net[a] Canadian Bond Issues Abroad, 1970–92*

Year	By Government of Canada	By Provincial Governments	By Municipal Governments	By Canadian Corporations	Total Bonds Issued Abroad	Total as Percentage of GDP
	(		millions of dollars			)
Average 1970–74	$ –54	$ 774	$ 20	$ 143	$ 879	0.7%
1975	–46	2 993	459	699	4 105	2.4
1976	221	4 630	662	2 565	8 077	4.1
1977	580	2 798	278	1 384	5 037	2.4
1978	2 884	1 467	–64	942	5 233	2.2
1979	1 537	1 200	–203	542	3 077	1.1
1980	939	415	–195	1 231	2 390	0.8
1981	1 538	5 269	205	3 236	10 249	2.9
1982	3 166	5 790	358	2 807	12 120	3.2
1983	282	3 610	13	400	4 305	1.1
1984	288	2 501	528	662	3 980	0.9
1985	3 175	1 691	226	2 691	7 782	1.7
1986	4 420	6 107	189	4 411	15 128	3.0
1987	–504	1 238	–5	4 245	4 970	0.9
1988	520	1 039	178	5 552	7 292	1.2
1989	772	1 171	–57	6 299	8 186	1.3
1990	2 003	6 225	–270	2 794	10 753	1.6
1991	5 238	17 196	84	1 616	24 137	3.6
1992	1 675	13 080	–347	3 067	17 472	2.5

[a] Net of retirements (negative amount indicates retirements exceeded new issues)

Source: Department of Finance, *Economic and Fiscal Reference Tables*, August 1993

nations and in the process accumulating a very heavy international debt. Most of this borrowing was in the form of bond issues by Canadian governments and corporations, as shown in Figure 34-18.

There are different views as to the reasons for this large increase in Canadian borrowing abroad after 1975. In the view of some, Canadians were spending more than they were earning internationally, causing deficits on Canada's current account which required borrowing more in order to cover the shortfall. Others saw Canada as having large borrowing requirements and borrowing abroad simply because of the greater availability of funds at lower interest rates in the United States.

However, other observers saw the causes of Canada's heavy borrowing as more complex, and linked to the large budget deficits of Canada's federal government. In this view, the very large federal government budget deficits were absorbing so much of Canadians' savings (and pushing Canadian interest rates higher in the process) that provincial governments and corporations were crowded out of Canadian capital markets and forced to borrow abroad. According to this view, Canadians' unwillingness to pay for their government benefits through taxes was pushing the country deeper and deeper into debt to foreign lenders. Whatever the causes, there was no doubt that after 1975, Canadian corporations and governments increased their borrowing abroad greatly.

The overall result of these trends, as Figure 34-19 shows, was a significant shift in the basic nature of capital flows, with business direct investment capital flowing out of Canada, and larger amounts of borrowed capital flowing in, with Canada's international debt growing rapidly in the process.

Canada's international debt and the "Twin Deficits" problem

The many years of heavy borrowing abroad by Canadian governments and corporations shown in Figure 34-18 caused Canada's debt to foreign lenders to accumulate to extremely high levels. This is reflected in Figure

FIGURE 34-19   *Flows of Borrowed and Equity Capital, 1970–92*

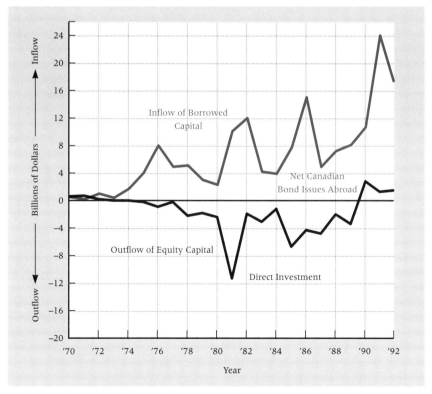

Source: Department of Finance, *Economic and Fiscal Reference Tables,* August 1993

34-20, which shows various countries' net foreign debt as a percentage of their GDP.

Countries below the "0" line do not *owe* debts, but rather *own bonds* issued by borrowers in other nations. For instance, Japanese lenders are shown as owning bonds issued by borrowers in other countries in the amount of about 10 percent of Japan's GDP. Shown in this way, Canada's international debt can be seen to be enormous indeed—about 40 percent of Canada's GDP, as compared to only about 5 percent for Italy, the second most-internationally indebted country.

From 1984 to 1992, Canada's international debt doubled to more than $300 billion ($11 000 for every Canadian), or nearly 44 percent of Canada's GDP. The provincial governments were the largest international debtors, owing 44 percent of the debt, with the federal government owing 27 percent and corporations owing 24 percent. Canada's largest foreign creditors were the United States, which held 43 percent of Canadian foreign debt, European Community nations with 28 percent and the Japanese with 20 percent.

FIGURE 34-20 *Net Foreign Debt as a Percentage of GDP for Various Nations, 1991*

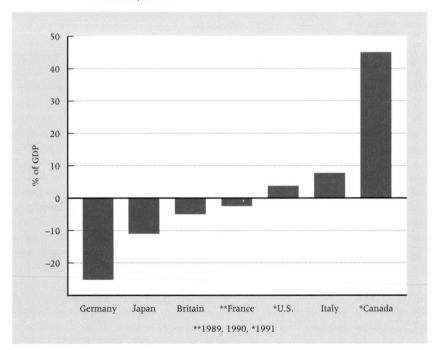

Source: Department of Finance

IMPLICATIONS OF CANADA'S INTERNATIONAL DEBT

Such heavy foreign debt raised various concerns among economists, chief among which were its effect upon the government's freedom to use monetary and fiscal policies and its future effect upon Canadians' living standards. We will deal with each of these concerns in turn.

Effect upon the government's ability to use monetary and fiscal policy

Canada's massive debt to foreign lenders, and ongoing need to borrow more from them, tends to make it very important that Canada maintain their confidence. If foreign lenders' confidence in Canada is reduced to the point that they become less willing to buy or hold Canadian bonds, the consequences for Canada could be quite serious.

For instance, in January of 1990, seeing a recession approaching, the Bank of Canada reduced the Bank Rate by about one-quarter of one percentage point. Senior Bank of Canada officials described the move as a "modest recognition ... of a weakening trend in the economy." Foreign creditors saw it differently. Believing that Canada's heavy indebtedness warranted higher interest rates, they sold off Canadian bonds in large volumes, driving the Canadian dollar down 3 percent in just two weeks and prompting speculative selling of the currency. The Bank of Canada was forced to retract its decision, and to increase interest rates again, even though a recession was nearing.

The same would apply to a Canadian government decision to allow government budget deficits to reach levels that foreign lenders found dangerous—they could insist on very high interest rates on any funds loaned to Canada, or they could even decline to buy additional Canadian bonds, or, worst of all, they could sell bonds that they already held, precipitating the kind of sharp decline in the Canadian dollar as occurred in January of 1990.

The basic reality is that as of 1993, foreign lenders held well over $300 billion of Canadian bonds and the Bank of Canada had less than $10 billion of foreign exchange reserves. If the concerns of foreign lenders caused them to sell even a small proportion of their bonds at one time, the Bank of Canada would lack the reserves required to buy enough Canadian dollars to prevent the dollar from declining sharply, probably forcing interest rates up. As a result of these considerations, Canada's heavy foreign debt severely restricts the ability of governmental authorities to conduct monetary and fiscal policy. In deciding Canadian policy, more consideration might have to be given to the concerns of foreign lenders than to the needs of the Canadian economy.

Impact upon Canadians' living standards

One concern regarding Canada's heavy foreign debt is the *cost of interest payments* on the debt, as these represent transfers of funds from Canadians to foreign creditors. In 1974, interest payments on Canada's foreign debt amounted to 0.8 percent of Canada's GDP; by 1992 this had increased to 3.6 percent, representing nearly $900 for every Canadian. Another way of measuring the interest burden is to compare Canada's international interest payments to its surplus on merchandise trade, the traditional "big earner" of Canada's current account. In 1974, net interest payments amounted to about two-thirds of the surplus on merchandise trade; by 1992 net interest payments were 2.7 times as large as the merchandise trade surplus.

However, concerns about Canada's international indebtedness go well beyond the burden of interest payments. A country with an international debt as large as Canada's faces a high probability of a considerable decline in the international value of its currency, and with it a decline in the living standards of its people. The reason for this lies in the arithmetic of borrowing and debt, as illustrated in Figure 34-21.

Figure 34-21 shows a simplified example of a nation that borrows $10 billion every year for 15 years, and pays an interest rate of 10 percent on it debts. In year 1, its borrowing causes an *inflow* ("receipt") of $10 billion, while the *outflow* of interest ("payments") amount to only $1 billion (10 percent of its total debt of $10 billion). The result is a net inflow (net "receipt") of $9 billion. As we saw earlier in this chapter, this net receipt will

FIGURE 34-21 *Economic Effects of International Borrowing*

Year	Amount Borrowed ("Receipt")	Total Debt	Interest Payable @ 10% ("Payment")	Net Receipt (+) or Payment (−)	Effect on C$ and Living Standard
1	$+10	$ 10	$ −1	$ +9	↑
2	+10	20	−2	+8	↑
3	+10	30	−3	+7	↑
4	+10	40	−4	+6	↑
5	+10	50	−5	+5	↑
6	+10	60	−6	+4	↑
7	+10	70	−7	+3	↑
8	+10	80	−8	+2	↑
9	+10	90	−9	+1	↑
10	+10	100	−10	0	None
11	+10	110	−11	−1	↓
12	+10	120	−12	−2	↓
13	+10	130	−13	−3	↓
14	+10	140	−14	−4	↓
15	+10	150	−15	−5	↓
16	0	150	−15	−15	↓↓↓

push the value of the nation's currency higher, enabling its people to buy more foreign goods and thus raising their standard of living.

This process is repeated throughout the illustration; however, one key change occurs. Each year, the total debt becomes larger by $10 billion, making the interest payments larger by $1 billion and the net inflow of funds smaller by $1 billion. Because the net inflow ("net receipt") becomes smaller, the upward effect on the value of the currency and the living standards steadily diminishes. Finally, in year 10, the outflow of interest exactly offsets the inflow of newly-borrowed funds, leaving no positive impact on the currency or living standards.

After year 10, the situation deteriorates. The debt has by now grown so large that the annual outflow of interest exceeds the inflow of borrowed funds. As a result, there is a net outflow of funds and the value of the currency falls. As the value of the currency declines, so does the living standards of the people, as rising import prices reduce their ability to buy imports.[5] There is nothing unusual in this—it is simply the international manifestation of the well-known fact that steadily going deeper and deeper into debt will for some time add to one's standard of living, but eventually will have the opposite effect.

Dealing with Canada's international current account deficits and debt

As with any debtor faced with heavy debt, Canada faces the problem that dealing with its debt will necessarily require sacrifices in the form of a lower standard of living.

Before considering the alternatives, we should briefly review the nature of the problem. Canada's problem has been described as one of "twin deficits"—a problem of chronic massive government budget deficits that have led to heavy inflows of foreign borrowing that in turn keep both the Canadian dollar and imports at artificially high levels, generating a Balance of Payments current account deficit. The alternatives for dealing with such a problem are few, and none are attractive.

REDUCE GOVERNMENT BUDGET DEFICITS

If government budget deficits can be reduced, the need for the government and other borrowers to borrow internationally will be reduced. This would stop the growth of Canada's international debt, and thus reassure foreign lenders. In these circumstances, there would be much less risk of a sell-off of Canadian dollars by foreign investors and a decline in its international value.

However, all of this is easier said than done. To reduce the budget deficits of the federal and provincial governments would require substantial reductions in government spending and/or increases in taxes, neither of which would be easy for any government to implement. That said, this may be preferable to the main alternative.

CONTINUE WITH LARGE GOVERNMENT BUDGET DEFICITS

If governmental authorities did not adopt the measures discussed above, Canada would continue to have very large government budget deficits. Since this would require further borrowing abroad, Canada's foreign debt would continue to rise quite rapidly. As the outflow of interest payments on this growing debt increased each year, the international value of the Canadian dollar would decline, adding to import prices and reducing the living standards of Canadians. Furthermore, Canada's very heavy indebtedness would bring a risk of foreign investors losing confidence and becoming less willing to buy Canadian bonds, and perhaps selling Canadian bonds, causing a decline in the international value of the Canadian dollar and a decline in the living standards of Canadians.

How far could the Canadian dollar fall in such circumstances? In the view of most observers, most Canadian industries were reasonably competitive in the early 1990's with the Canadian dollar around $0.81–0.83 US. However, the dollar would have to fall low enough to generate a large enough surplus on Canada's trade to cover the deficit on interest. According to some economists, the Canadian dollar might have to fall as low as $0.70 US to create such large trade surpluses. This would impose significant reductions in the living standards of Canadians, who might have to pay more than $1.40 Canadian for $1.00 US.[6]

While such a decline in the international value of the dollar would be costly, it might be considered preferable to the alternative, which would be a considerable increase in Canadian interest rates in order to keep foreign lenders buying and holding Canadian bonds so as to prevent the dollar from falling. Such an increase in interest rates would slow down the Canadian economy, and possibly cause a serious recession.

All of the above outcomes of Canada's foreign debt situation involve a reduction of Canadians' living standards. However, this was made inevitable by the fact that Canadians had since 1975 artificially increased their living standards through government budget deficits financed in large part by borrowing from foreign lenders. Eventually, this would require a downward adjustment to the living standards of Canadians, be it through reduced government benefits, higher taxes, a lower Canadian dollar, higher interest rates or some combination of these.

To reduce this negative impact on their living standards, Canadians could take steps to reduce their reliance on foreign borrowing by attracting inflows of foreign funds in other ways. One such way could be to improve their productivity and competitiveness, so as to increase Canada's export earnings. Another could be to attract more foreign direct investment, so as to not have to rely upon borrowing so much.

DEFINITIONS OF NEW TERMS

Exchange Rate The international price, or value, of a currency in foreign exchange markets.

Foreign Exchange Markets Markets, conducted through banks, in which currencies of different nations are bought and sold (exchanged for each other).

Receipts International transactions in which a nation receives funds from other countries, causing the foreign countries to buy that nation's currency.

Payments International transactions in which a nation pays funds to other countries, causing that nation to sell its currency.

Balance of Payments A summary of a nation's receipts and payments for a given year.

Current Account Balance of Payments items relating to day-to-day transactions in goods and services, including interest and dividends.

Capital Account Balance of Payments items involving flows of investment funds (capital), both long-term and short-term, between countries.

Direct (Foreign) Investment Officially defined as "those investments in business enterprises which are sufficiently concentrated to constitute control of the concern," this term usually refers to investment by foreign firms in plant and equipment for their Canadian subsidiaries; it also includes provision of working capital for Canadian subsidiaries by foreign parent firms, and mergers in which the assets of Canadian firms are purchased by foreign firms.

Balance of Payments Deficit A situation in which a nation's payments exceed its receipts.

Balance of Payments Surplus A situation in which a nation's receipts exceed its payments.

Balance of Payments Equilibrium A situation in which a nation's receipts and payments are equal to each other.

Floating Exchange Rate A situation in which the international value of a currency is allowed to fluctuate freely with the supply of and demand for it.

Appreciation of a Currency Increases in the international value of a currency.

Depreciation of a Currency Decreases in the international value of a currency.

Hot Money Short-term funds that are used to speculate in currencies by being moved rapidly from currencies that are perceived as "weak" to currencies that are perceived as "strong."

Dirty Float A situation in which a government influences the exchange rate by purchases and sales of currencies in foreign exchange markets.

Exchange Rate Management Government policies to influence the nation's exchange rate through purchases/sales of its currency and/or changes in its interest rates.

Foreign Exchange Speculation Purchases and sales of currencies with the intention of earning profits on fluctuations in their values.

CHAPTER SUMMARY

1. The international value of the Canadian dollar is determined by the supply of and demand for it in foreign exchange markets, with Canadian receipts from other nations generating a demand for Canadian dollars, and Canadian payments to other nations generating a supply of Canadian dollars.

2. The Balance of Payments summarizes, for a given year, Canada's international receipts and payments, classifying them into current and capital accounts.

3. Under a "floating" exchange rate, a Balance of Payments deficit will cause the exchange rate to fall, and a surplus will cause the exchange rate to rise. These adjustments will bring the Balance of Payments and the exchange rate automatically toward equilibrium. Thus, fluctuations in a nation's exchange rate are not only normal, but also serve the useful purpose of helping to keep the nation's international trade in reasonable balance.

4. However, excessively rapid changes in exchange rates can cause problems for a nation's economy. A rapidly-rising exchange rate can increase unemployment by making a nation's goods and services less competitive internationally, while a rapid decline in its exchange rate can make inflation worse, by generating increases in import prices.

5. Foreign currency speculation can add to these problems, as speculators buy currencies that are "strong," forcing their values even higher, and sell currencies that are "weak," driving their values down farther and faster.

6. Under a "dirty float" system, the government influences the exchange rate so as to prevent excessively rapid fluctuations. To support a "weak" currency, the government can buy its own currency and/or increase interest rates, and to hold down a "strong" currency, the government can do the opposite.

7. By holding down the international value of its currency, a government can keep unemployment lower, by making its producers more

competitive internationally; however, higher import prices will add to inflation and reduce its people's living standards. If the government supports its currency, inflation will be suppressed and consumers will benefit, but its producers will have more difficulty competing internationally and unemployment will rise.

8. In the 1950's and 1960's, Canada had current account deficits that were offset by surpluses on capital account due to inflows of foreign long-term capital, including substantial foreign direct investment in Canada.

9. From 1970–74, Canada's deficit on current account became very small, and Canada's reliance on foreign capital decreased substantially.

10. After 1974, Canadian governments and corporations borrowed heavily from foreign lenders, causing Canada's foreign debt as a percentage of GDP to become by far the largest of all industrialized nations. On current account, large deficits reappeared, mainly due to large and growing outflows of funds to pay the interest on Canada's massive international debt. Canada's reliance on borrowing from foreign lenders was increased by the fact that Canada no longer received a net inflow of direct investment; rather, there were net outflows of direct investment from 1975 to 1989.

11. One concern associated with Canada's heavy foreign debt was that the government's ability to use its monetary and fiscal policies to stimulate the economy was restricted by the need to maintain the confidence of the foreign lenders upon whom Canada had come to depend.

12. Another concern was that this heavy foreign debt would reduce the living standards of Canadians as the international value of the Canadian dollar would be forced downwards by heavy outflows of interest payments and possibly by reduced confidence among foreign lenders in Canada's ability to deal with its heavy international debt.

QUESTIONS

1. Describe recent trends in the international value of the Canadian dollar, and give reasons for these trends. (Sources of information for this topic include the Bank of Canada *Review* and the Toronto Dominion Bank's *Canada's Business Climate*.)

2. Has the Bank of Canada intervened in foreign exchange markets to influence Canada's exchange rate recently? If so, what were the purposes of the intervention?

3. If you were responsible for Canada's exchange-rate policy, would you favor action to increase or reduce the exchange rate at this time? Why?

4. Would you expect the international value of the Canadian dollar to increase or decrease over the next few years? Why?

5. Has Canada's merchandise trade surplus increased or decreased recently? Why?

6. Has Canada's deficit on interest and dividends increased or decreased as a percentage of GDP? What might explain this trend?

7. From 1975–89, there was a net outflow of investment capital from Canada; however, from 1990–92 there was a net inflow. Has the net inflow continued or not since then? What might explain this trend?

8. If the Canadian government were to increase Canada's money supply much faster than the US government increased its money supply, how would Canada's Balance of Payments and the Canadian exchange rate be affected?

9. Classify each of the following transactions as either a receipt or a payment for Canada, on either current account or capital account:

    (a) Canada exports wheat to Russia.

    (b) Canadian tourists visit Florida.

    (c) A Canadian corporation establishes a branch plant in South Carolina.

    (d) An American investor buys shares in a Canadian oil exploration company.

    (e) An American business ships its products on a Canadian Great Lakes freighter.

    (f) The Canadian subsidiary of a US corporation pays dividends to its US parent company.

    (g) American pension funds buy bonds issued by the Government of Ontario.

    (h) A Canadian company contracts to use computer services supplied by a US firm.

    (i) Canadian provincial governments pay interest to American holders of their bonds.

    (j) US foreign exchange speculators transfer large amounts of money from US accounts into short-term Canadian dollar bank deposits.

10. Suppose that Canada's foreign debt continues to rise rapidly. What would be the likely effects of such a trend on:

    (a) the international value of the Canadian dollar?

    (b) interest rates in Canada?

    (c) Canadians' standard of living?

    (d) Canada's Balance of Payments?

11. The text notes that currency speculators can cause considerable difficulty for a country by forcing the international value of its currency rapidly upwards or downwards when they buy or sell it. In 1978, James Tobin, a highly-respected American economist, advocated an international transfer tax on all foreign-exchange transactions. How could such a tax help to deal with the problems caused by international currency speculators?

12. Re-read the last section in this chapter entitled "Dealing with Canada's current account deficits and debt," which was written in early 1994. Since then, which, if any, of the possible developments outlined in this section have occurred? Try to develop your own explanation of the situation as it now stands and your own predictions as to the course of future events.

13. One concern of foreign lenders is that if they buy bonds denominated in Canadian dollars and the international value of the Canadian dollar falls, their investment will lose value relative to their domestic currency. A way to deal with these concerns would be to make the bonds issued by Canadian governments and corporations *repayable in foreign currencies*.

What do you believe to be the main advantage to Canada of doing this? What do you see as the main *disadvantage*?

14. Suppose that, under NAFTA, Mexican exports to Canada and the United States were to increase dramatically, generating a huge trade surplus for Mexico. Explain the economic forces that would limit the extent to which Mexico could continue to enjoy such a large and growing trade surplus.

NOTES

[1] Direct investment is defined by Statistics Canada as "those investments in business enterprises which are sufficiently concentrated to constitute control of the concern." More specifically, such investments include new plants and equipment built by foreign firms, as well as provision of working capital for Canadian subsidiaries by foreign parent firms and mergers in which the assets of Canadian firms are purchased by foreign firms.

[2] Nor a sustainable one—with Japanese products so low-priced, the demand for yen with which to buy them would drive the yen sharply upward, which is of course what actually happened.

[3] The "foreign currencies" bought and sold are most often in the form of foreign (usually US) government securities.

[4] An exception to this trend occurred in 1982–84, when exceptionally high merchandise trade surpluses carried the current account into surplus. This was an unusual period, during which Canadian imports decreased considerably, adding to Canada's trade surplus. In part, the reduction in imports was caused by the re-

cession, which reduced consumer and business spending. In addition, the early 1980's saw a decline in the inflow of foreign capital into Canada as the federal government's National Energy Program deterred foreign investors, reducing the inflow of funds on capital account which Canadians could use to buy imports on current account.

5   Worse yet, the nation at some point becomes as effectively trapped in its "debt habit" as an addict is in a drug habit. If, for example, the nation somehow managed to completely eliminate its foreign borrowing in year 16, its inflow of borrowed funds would be zero, but its outflow of interest payments would still be $15 billion, causing a large net outflow and a sharp decline in the value of its currency and the living standards of its people—a form of "withdrawal" from prolonged use of debt.

6   This process might have started in 1992–93, when the C$ declined from $0.87 US in 1991 to $0.75 US in 1993. This raised the cost of $1.00 US from $1.15 Canadian to $1.33 ... a 16 percent decline in the purchasing power of C$'s in the United States.

CHAPTER 35

The international monetary system

> What does "globalisation" mean? The term can happily accommodate all manner of things: expanding international trade, the growth of multinational businesses, the rise in international joint ventures and increasing interdependence through capital flows—to name but a few.
>
> Fear of Finance, in *The Economist*, September 19, 1992

As the process described as "globalization" unfolded during the 1980's, the volume of international trade and investment grew dramatically. By the late 1980's, the value of total world trade (in constant dollars) had grown to more than eight times its 1980 level. In 1980, the stock of international bank lending was $324 billion; by 1991 it had reached $7.5 trillion—23 times the 1980 level. The $1.65 trillion of international bonds outstanding in 1991 represented a sixfold increase over ten years earlier, and turnover in foreign exchange in 1992 was estimated at roughly $900 billion *per day*.

As a result of developments such as these, a growing number of people rely upon international transactions for their jobs, more and more consumers and businesses rely upon international transactions for the goods and services they need, and both businesses and governments rely increasingly upon capital provided by foreign lenders.

In order for international trade and investment to continue to increase their contribution to prosperity, there must be an international monetary system that allows exporters, importers and investors to convert one currency into another with convenience and confidence.[1] If a convenient and acceptable system can be established, it will encourage international trade and investment, to the economic benefit of all concerned. However, without such a system, the uncertainties associated with international transactions would increase, international trade and investment would be impaired, and everyone would suffer economically.

In this chapter, we will examine the search for an international monetary system that is stable enough to encourage international trade and investment, yet flexible enough to respond to changing economic conditions, while also being acceptable to the nations that use it. We will start with the unhappy lesson that was provided by the 1930's.

The experience of the 1930's

During the 1930's, exchange rates became extremely unstable under the pressures of the Great Depression. Desperately seeking to reduce unemployment, some nations deliberately reduced the international value of their currencies in an attempt to increase their exports (and jobs) while at the same time reducing imports (which were seen as "stealing" jobs from domestic workers). This led to retaliation by other nations, which reduced their exchange rates in a similar way. The result was widespread *competitive devaluations* of currencies by governments, and a period of chaotically unstable exchange rates as nations engaged in "exchange-rate war" against each other. The effect of these misguided policies was to create exchange-rate instability and uncertainty that further reduced international trade and investment, making the depression even worse. The main contribution of this period was to provide dramatic evidence that the nations of the world had to regard exchange rates as a matter for international cooperation rather than for international competition and conflict.[2]

The postwar system of "pegged" exchange rates

After the Second World War, the nations of the world were determined to avoid a recurrence of the experience of the 1930's. In 1945, they met to set up a system of **"pegged" exchange rates**, in which governments would prevent *any* significant exchange-rate fluctuations. Under this system of pegged exchange rates, nations kept the international price of their currencies at fixed levels, using two approaches:

(a) Basically, they undertook not to use any economic or trade policies that would destabilize international trade and investment, and thereby exchange rates. For instance, they would no longer increase tariffs dramatically, as was done in the 1930's.

(b) In addition, when market forces tended to move exchange rates away from their fixed (pegged) levels, governments would stabilize those exchange rates through *purchases and sales of currencies* in foreign exchange markets. For instance, if the British pound tended to lose value relative to the deutsche mark, the British and German governments would buy pounds and sell deutsche marks in foreign exchange markets so as to support the price of the pound relative to the deutsche mark at the agreed-upon pegged level. As the German government bought pounds, Germany's holdings of foreign currencies (its **foreign exchange reserves**) would increase, and as Britain sold deutsche marks in order to buy pounds, Britain's foreign exchange reserves would decline. In effect, this was a sort of extreme dirty float (as described in Chapter 34), in which the governments' objective was not merely to moderate fluctuations in exchange rates, but rather to prevent them altogether.

To oversee the system, an international agency known as the **International Monetary Fund (IMF)** was established. Its purposes were to provide a forum for the discussion of international financial problems, to promote stable exchange rates (the system of pegged exchange rates), and to help nations to keep the prices of their currencies at their pegged levels. To achieve this latter objective, the IMF would lend foreign exchange reserves (foreign currencies) to nations that had been forced to use up nearly all of their reserves in order to support their currency against downward pressure.

GOLD AND THE US DOLLAR IN THE POSTWAR SYSTEM

Due to the variety of currencies involved in international trade and uncertainties regarding their value, gold has historically played a central role in international finance, either as currency itself or as "backing" for paper currency. Long after gold ceased to play any part in monetary systems *within* countries it was still important in international financial dealings *between* countries—some nations preferred strongly to deal in currencies that they could convert to gold on demand (that is, which were backed by gold), or even in gold itself for some intergovernmental transactions. While placing gold in such a central position is not completely rational—after all, most countries, including Canada, use no gold in their domestic monetary systems—it emphasizes the psychological importance of gold to people, and its association with value and money.

Because of this, currencies that rose to dominance internationally were backed by precious metals—either silver or gold. First the pound sterling, and later the US dollar, were the most acceptable and commonly used currencies internationally. Until 1968, foreigners could demand that the US government convert their US dollars to gold at the rate of $35 per ounce.

Because of this gold backing and the fact that the US economy was strong, the US dollar came to occupy a special place in the international monetary system established after World War II. First, the fact that the US dollar was widely acceptable internationally made it the most widely used currency in international trade. The US dollar became in large part the currency basis for world trade, with other nations often settling accounts between themselves in US dollars, because they were so acceptable. The acceptability of the US dollar led to its second special role—that of *the main reserve currency*. As noted earlier, to maintain a system of "pegged" exchange rates, nations must hold reserves (consisting of gold and foreign currencies) with which to buy their own currency if its value tends to decline. During the postwar period, the US dollar came to be the most important reserve currency held by nations. Finally, the US dollar stood at the centre of the world system of pegged exchange rates—all other nations stated the value of their currencies *in terms of the US dollar* (and thus, indirectly, in terms of gold, since one ounce of gold was worth $35 US. Thus, as Figure 35-1 shows, the essence of the pegged exchange-rate system established in 1945 was that:

(a) the US dollar was pegged to gold at a fixed rate of $35 to the ounce (or $1.00 US = 1/35 ounce of gold), and

(b) other currencies were pegged to the US dollar at various fixed exchange rates.

FIGURE 35-1   *The 1945 Pegged Exchange Rate System*

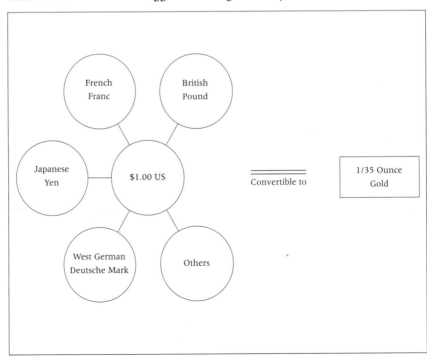

THE INTERNATIONAL MONETARY FUND (1)

In 1945, the same year that the "pegged" exchange rate system was established, 39 nations founded the International Monetary Fund. The IMF had four basic objectives:

(i) to provide a forum in which financial officials could consider and help resolve international monetary problems, through consultation and cooperation,

(ii) "to facilitate the expansion and balanced growth of international trade, and to contribute thereby to the promotion and maintenance of high levels of employment and real income ..." (from the IMF's Articles),

(iii) to help members attain sustainable balance of payments positions, and

(iv) to reduce restrictions on the movement of goods, services and funds between nations.

Originally, the IMF's main task was to preserve the system of "pegged" exchange rates established in 1945. This was done through annual consultations with member nations regarding their balance of payments positions, policies and prospects, including reviews of their domestic monetary and fiscal policies. The IMF would loan reserves to member nations that needed them to maintain their exchange rates at their pegged level; however, it became IMF policy that such loans be made on the condition that the recipient nations undertake economic policies to remedy their balance of payments deficits.

Because of its acceptability and strength (which derived mainly from its gold backing and the economic strength of the United States after the Second World War), the US dollar became the key currency in the international monetary system established in 1945. The pegged exchange rates of this system were intended to eliminate the problems of exchange-rate instability that had plagued the 1930's by holding the values of currencies relative to each other at agreed-upon fixed levels. However, as we will see, the pegged system experienced problems of its own.

STRAINS ON THE PEGGED EXCHANGE RATE SYSTEM

It soon became apparent that it is not possible to peg the international values of all currencies indefinitely. Economic conditions change in ways that make it inevitable that some nations will experience Balance of Payments surpluses (which will push their exchange rates up) and others will have deficits (which will push their exchange rates down). If the surpluses and deficits are short-term in nature and not too severe, governments can offset them by buying or selling currencies; but if they are strong and persistent, it will prove impossible to peg the currency values for long. To attempt to do so would require buying or selling impracticably large volumes of currencies in foreign exchange markets.

Upward pressures on currencies were experienced by nations whose strong internationally competitive positions put their currencies in high demand on foreign exchange markets. For example, West Germany's and Japan's exports grew strongly as they benefited from a combination of rising industrial efficiency, relatively slow inflation and currency values that were pegged at quite low levels after the Second World War. As a result, the values of the yen and the deutsche mark tended to rise. Since higher exchange rates would reduce their exports and increase unemployment, the governments of these nations strove to maintain their currency values at their old, low pegged levels. However, to do so in the face of such high demand for the deutsche mark and yen would require government sales of those currencies on a scale so large as to be impracticable: the governments involved would have to borrow or print deutsche marks and yen to an extent that would be damaging to their own economies. Thus, despite the system of "pegged" exchange rates, governments would eventually prove unable to stop the international price of strong currencies from rising.

Downward pressures on currencies were felt by nations whose weak competitive positions caused their currencies to be in relatively low demand and high supply in foreign exchange markets. A good example is provided by Great Britain, which suffered from a combination of more rapid inflation than most other countries, lagging industrial efficiency and an overvalued currency that was pegged at an unrealistically high value. These factors combined to make Britain's goods uncompetitive in both domestic markets and export markets, causing large trade deficits that generated continual downward pressure on the price of the pound in foreign exchange markets. To maintain the pound at its pegged level, Britain was forced to buy large volumes of the pound, selling off its reserves of foreign currencies to do so. Eventually, Britain ran out of foreign currencies and was unable to continue to support the pound, which fell in value relative to other currencies.

"Devaluation" of currencies

Eventually, nations such as Great Britain and others found themselves in a position where persistent and severe Balance of Payments deficits were forcing their governments to continually buy their own currency, gradually exhausting their reserves of foreign currency and gold. What would happen to a nation that *ran out* of foreign currencies and gold?

A nation in such a situation could no longer buy its own currency. Since government purchases of its own currency are the only force supporting the price of the currency against downward pressures due to payments deficits, the price of the currency would undergo a sudden decline, as shown in Figure 35-2. The process of reducing the international price of a currency that had been pegged is known as **devaluation** of the currency. Under a "floating" exchange rate system such as we saw in Chapter 34, the adjustment would occur gradually, whereas with a "pegged" exchange rate, the adjustment takes place in one big step. Following the devaluation, the currency could be allowed to "float" for a while, so as to find its appropriate "equilibrium" level, then it could be re-pegged at that level, as Figure 35-2 shows.

In certain key ways, devaluation can be viewed as an appropriate step for a nation with severe and persistent Balance of Payments deficits. With its currency at a lower value, its exports will grow and its imports will decrease, bringing its receipts and payments back toward a sustainable equilibrium.

On the other hand, there are complications with devaluation as well. It means higher import prices and thus a lower standard of living for the public, which may cause political problems for the government. More serious, however, are the possible international ramifications. If nation "A" devalues its currency in response to its Balance of payments deficits, this may create deficit problems for its main trading partners, nations "B," "C" and "D." Not only will these nations' exports to nation "A" be reduced, but also their imports from "A" will increase. This could create trade and payment deficits for "B," "C" and "D," and maybe even force some of them to devalue their currencies at some point. In turn, this could spread the problems to even more countries.

FIGURE 35-2 *Devaluation of a Currency*

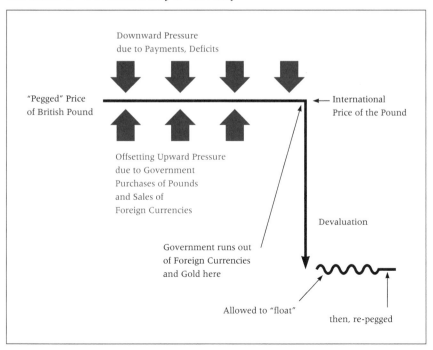

Thus, there were considerable pressures against devaluing a currency, not only from trading partners who would be hurt by it, but also from the world community in general and the International Monetary Fund in particular. To them, the "pegged" system of exchange rates represented the only protection against the chaotic international monetary situation of the 1930's, and devaluations of currencies posed a threat to that pegged system. If nations that were unable to compete, or that allowed too much inflation to develop in their economies, were allowed to deal with their own problems by devaluing their currencies and thus passing their problems on to their trading partners, the world would seem perilously close to returning to the conditions of the 1930's.

Because of these considerations, it came to be generally accepted that devaluation of a currency should be undertaken as a last resort only. For instance, if a nation suffered persistent and severe payments deficits because its currency was **overvalued** (pegged at a level that had become unrealistically high), it was considered reasonable to devalue that currency. For instance, as the United States, West Germany and Japan rose to dominance in world trade, it became totally unrealistic for Great Britain to try to maintain the pound at a pegged level more appropriate for an earlier era, when Britain was the chief manufacturing, trading and financial power in the world. The successive devaluations of the pound since 1945 were, therefore, accepted as a necessary and inevitable adjustment to changing economic realities. However, it was not considered appropriate or acceptable for a nation to devalue its currency simply to gain a competitive advantage in world trade, or because that nation's government had allowed excessive inflation to develop in its own economy. Devaluations for such purposes would only threaten the entire system of pegged exchange rates.[3]

As a result of the strains on the system of pegged exchange rates that have been described, there were several major devaluations of currencies, including the British pound, French franc, Italian lira and Canadian dollar. Under a "floating" exchange-rate system, these adjustments would have occurred gradually, but under the "pegged" system the governments supported the price of their currencies and delayed the adjustment as long as possible. As a result, when the decline in the value of the currency occurred, it happened all at once. Thus, devaluations tended to be quite newsworthy—one of the most dramatic and widely publicized of all economic events.

THE "PEGGED" EXCHANGE-RATE SYSTEM IN PERSPECTIVE

In one sense, the "pegged" exchange-rate system represented a need to *attempt the necessary*—that is, to stabilize currencies so as to avoid a repeti-

A COMPARISON OF FLOATING AND PEGGED EXCHANGE RATES

Floating exchange rate

(a) Balance of Payments Deficit

Exchange rate moves downwards over a period of time causing receipts to rise and payments to fall, until the deficit is eliminated, and the exchange rate stabilizes at a new, lower level.

(b) Balance of Payments Surplus

Exchange rate moves upward over a period of time causing receipts to fall and payments to rise until the Balance of Payments surplus is eliminated and the exchange rate stabilizes at a new, higher level.

Pegged exchange rate

(a) Balance of Payments Deficit

Downward pressure on the exchange rate is resisted by the government's purchases of its own currency and sales of other currencies which can keep the exchange rate pegged unless or until the government runs out of foreign exchange reserves. The exchange rate will then move sharply to a new, lower level, as the currency is devalued.

(b) Balance of Payments Surplus

Upward pressure on the exchange rate is resisted by the government's sales of its own currency and purchases of other currencies which can keep the exchange rate pegged unless or until the government decides or agrees that a higher exchange rate is appropriate. The exchange rate is then allowed to move sharply upward, as the currency is "revalued."

tion of the problems of the 1930's. In another sense, it represented an attempt to *achieve the impossible*—that is, to "freeze" the prices of nations' currencies despite major changes in the economic circumstances of those nations. As a result, the "pegged" system came under periodic strains as some currencies came under downward pressure and others came under upward pressure. Governments were able to resist these pressures by buying and selling currencies, but only for so long. When they were no longer able to do so, there would be a major change in the relative values of currencies, usually occasioned by the devaluation of one or more of them. Thus, it could be said that the actual effect of the pegged exchange-rate system was to *postpone* rather than *prevent* exchange-rate fluctuations. However, on behalf of the "pegged" system, it can be said that between these periodic adjustments, the system did succeed in creating periods of exchange-rate stability.

THE CANADIAN DOLLAR AND THE "PEGGED" EXCHANGE-RATE SYSTEM

Unlike most currencies, the Canadian dollar was not part of the "pegged" system established after the Second World War. Due to Canada's high level of foreign trade and the high level of foreign investment in Canada, the Canadian dollar tends to be subject to strong and variable pressures (such as large increases or decreases in wheat exports or in foreign investment from time to time) that make it very difficult to establish and maintain a pegged level for it. The Canadian dollar floated in the 1950's at levels up to $1.05 US due to heavy foreign investment in Canada, and only after a sharp decline and loss of confidence in the Canadian dollar was it pegged at $0.925 US in 1962. This level was maintained until 1970, when strong upward pressure made it impossible to hold it at its pegged level, and it was again allowed to float. The Canadian dollar, then, was at times part of the system of "pegged" exchange rates established after the Second World War, while at other times it was allowed to "float" apart from that system.

The decline and fall of the "pegged" exchange-rate system

As we have seen, the US dollar occupied a special place at the centre of the international monetary system established in 1945. It was not only the key currency in the "pegged" exchange-rate system, with all other currency values expressed in terms of the US dollar, it was also the most acceptable and widely used currency internationally, and the most widely held reserve currency kept by governments. The key to the US dollar's position was that it was *backed by gold*—foreigners could convert their US dollars to gold on demand at $35 US to the ounce of gold. This fact established the international acceptability of the US dollar virtually throughout the world.

For some time, everything worked quite well—the US dollar was highly acceptable and widely used in world trade, and the United States had ample gold to back up its dollars held by foreigners. During the 1950's, the competitive position of the United States was very strong, largely due to the fact that Europe and Japan had not fully recovered industrially from the war. As a result, the USA was a major exporter, with large payments surpluses and a huge stock of gold reserves. As a result, the US dollar was very strong and highly acceptable; indeed, one concern during this period was that there were not enough US dollars in foreign hands to finance the growing volume of world trade. However, the situation was not to last.

US PAYMENTS DEFICITS IN THE 1960'S

The situation reversed itself dramatically in the 1960's, when the United States had large and regular payments *deficits*. The result was a large outflow of US dollars into foreign hands, to the point where foreigners became concerned that the United States might not possess enough gold to back up its dollars. It is important to understand the reasons for this very significant development.

By the 1960's, Japan and Western Europe (particularly West Germany) had recovered economically from the war. As their industries advanced technologically, these countries provided the United States with increasingly strong foreign competition. Foreign imports to the United States increased greatly in fields previously dominated by the USA, such as automobiles (Volkswagen, Toyota, Nissan), electronic products (Sony, Hitachi, Yamaha) and even steel.

Japan and West Germany were assisted in competing with the United States by the fact that their currencies had been "pegged" at quite low values after the Second World War. Under a floating exchange-rate system, such large increases in their exports would have caused the values of the yen and deutsche mark to rise, making Japanese and German exports less competitive. However, under the pegged system, the yen and deutsche mark remained **undervalued** at the levels set in 1945, giving them a large advantage in competing with US producers.

From the American perspective, by the 1960's the US dollar was *overvalued*, or pegged at too high a level. The pegged level set in 1945 was appropriate to the circumstances of that time, when Japan and Germany were war-torn and faced major redevelopment of their industries, while the United States was the dominant industrial and economic power in the world. However, the rise of foreign competition in the 1960's made the pegged value of the US dollar unrealistically high—20 to 25 percent above its market equilibrium in the early 1960's, according to most estimates. This was a major handicap for US producers and a major advantage for their foreign competitors. As US exports slowed and imports grew, the United States developed increasingly severe Balance of Payments deficits. By the time that imports finally exceeded exports in 1971, there was a massive outflow of funds from the USA that had reached crisis proportions.

PROBLEMS DUE TO THE US DEFICITS

The outflow of US dollars from the United States resulted in vast quantities of US dollars being held by foreign countries. This situation was not altogether bad—these US dollars helped finance world trade, as mentioned earlier, and many nations used them as foreign exchange reserves, to help maintain their pegged exchange rates. However, a problem arose in the 1960's, when the quantity of US dollars in foreign hands grew to the point that it *far exceeded the total US gold stock*, as Figure 35-3 shows.

FIGURE 35-3   *US Gold Stock and Foreign Holdings of US Dollars, 1950–72*

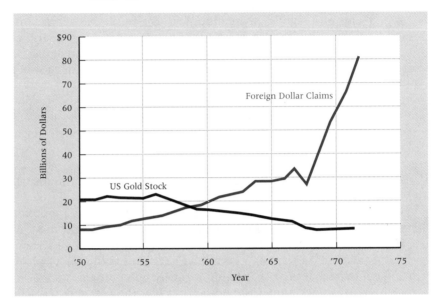

The danger this discrepancy posed was that foreigners might at some point lose confidence in the strength and convertibility of the US dollar, and demand gold for their US dollars. Such a loss of confidence could cause a "run" on the US gold stock,[4] which would quickly be depleted as speculators, frightened by the lack of gold backing for the overly-plentiful US dollars they held, converted those dollars to gold on a vast scale. At times in the late 1960's and early 1970's, such speculative "runs" on the US gold stock did, in fact occur. This reduced the American gold stock even further, raising fears that the US dollar might lose its acceptability, disrupting international trade and investment flows and possibly even leading to a world-wide depression. Finally, it became necessary for the United States to take steps to deal with its Balance of Payments deficits and restore faith in the US dollar.

DEALING WITH THE PROBLEM

The American deficit problems were fundamentally due to a basic shift in world economic power, in which other countries (especially Japan and West Germany) were gaining ground economically and competitively on the United States. While the world marketplace had changed, exchange rates had not. The US dollar remained pegged at the high level established in 1945, and the Japanese yen and West German deutsche mark had not changed in value despite their export success. As a result, the United States had huge payments deficits, and inadequate gold backing for the US dollar threatened the stability of the international monetary system.

Clearly, the solution lay in adjusting currency values to the new economic realities. This could be achieved by either devaluing the US dollar, or **revaluing** (increasing the value of) the yen and deutsche mark.

The United States was reluctant to devalue the US dollar. The dollar was the key currency in the international monetary system, and the maintenance of its value and acceptability was regarded as vital to the success of that system.[5]

There were fears that a major devaluation of the US dollar could lead to devaluations by many other nations, shattering the system of pegged exchange rates and returning the world to the chaotic and destructive conditions of the 1930's. Consequently, due to the special role of the US dollar in the international monetary system, devaluation of the US dollar was seen only as a last resort.

Instead, the United States sought *upward revaluations* of other currencies, particularly the yen and deutsche mark. However, Japan and West Germany resisted such a move, as higher values for their currencies would jeopardize their exports to the vast US market, increasing unemployment in their own countries.

When the situation reached a crisis point in 1971, the United States *forced* other nations to revalue their currencies upward by imposing a heavy surtax on imports, which would only be removed if the exporting countries agreed to increases in the value of their currencies. Virtually overnight, the deutsche mark rose by 31 percent and the yen by 26 percent.

At the same time, the United States suspended the convertibility of the US dollar into gold, so that there was no longer gold backing for foreign-held US dollars. The pegged system was maintained (temporarily) with new pegged exchange rates, but another basic element of the system— gold backing for its key currency—was gone.

It had been hoped that these adjustments to exchange rates would correct the United States' payments deficits, but while the deficits were reduced, they persisted and the outflow of US dollars continued. Finally, in February 1973, the United States took the final step in the dismantling of the pegged exchange-rate system that had existed since 1945. Officially described as an 8.5 percent devaluation of the US dollar, the February 1973 action was much more than that. In reality, the dollar was *not re-pegged* at a lower level, but was *allowed to float* against other currencies. And, since the values of other currencies were expressed in terms of a US dollar that was floating, their values were also floating.

- From 1949 to 1971, the exchange rate for the Japanese yen was 360 to the US dollar, or 1 yen = 0.278 cents US.

- In 1971, the exchange rate went to 1 yen = 0.375 cents US.

- By mid-1993, the exchange rate was about 1 yen = 0.980 cents US ... over three and one-half times as high as its 1949 level.

THE END OF THE PEGGED EXCHANGE-RATE SYSTEM

The pegged exchange-rate system established in 1945 had come to an end. That system had been built upon two foundations:

(a) The backing of the US dollar by gold, or the pegging of the US dollar to gold at a fixed rate of $35 per ounce. This was eliminated in 1971.

(b) The pegging of other currencies to the US dollar. This was eliminated in 1973.

Thus, in February 1973 the pegged system of exchange rates was dismantled. In its place there emerged a *dirty float* system as described in Chapter 34, in which exchange rates could move up and down with market forces, but with governments intervening to prevent such fluctuations from occurring too rapidly. If the international value of a nation's currency tended to decline too rapidly, its government might buy its own currency on foreign exchange markets so as to prevent rapidly rising import prices from generating excessive inflation. On the other hand, if a nation's currency came under strong upward pressure, the government could sell its own currency in foreign exchange markets so as to prevent excessive increases in its exchange rate from jeopardizing the nation's international competitive position or its domestic employment level.

THE INTERNATIONAL MONETARY FUND (2)

After the collapse of the "pegged" exchange rate system and the return of "floating" exchange rates in 1973, some critics argued that the IMF had failed, and others said that there was no further need for the Fund. However, as it had throughout its existence, the IMF adapted to the new circumstances. It amended its Articles to give "floating" exchange rates legal sanction, but also gave itself a mandate to "exercise firm surveillance over the exchange rate policies of its members." Thus, the IMF became a force for stability in the new and potentially unstable world of floating exchange rates. Furthermore, the IMF adapted to meet the needs of the developing countries, which have become the major users of the Fund's resources, by increasing its loan limits and extending its repayment periods. In 1982, the IMF gained recognition as having played a major role in averting a possible world financial crisis arising from the inability of several Third World nations to pay their international debts.

By 1985, the IMF's membership had grown to 148 nations from the original 39. Largely because of its ability to evolve with changing circumstances and needs over the years, it is regarded as one of the more influential and effective international organizations in the world.

Experience with the dirty float system after February 1973

The abandonment of the pegged exchange rate system generated considerable anxiety in international circles. Some feared that a floating US dollar without gold backing would lose acceptability internationally, causing stagnation of international trade and investment. However, these fears were not realized: despite its changed situation, the US dollar remained acceptable and held its place as the key currency in international trade and finance. The basic reason for this stability was probably simply that the world had *no ready substitute* for the US dollar—no other currency was both sufficiently strong and available on a large enough scale to play the role that the US dollar had played in the world.

Others feared that the end of the "pegged" system would return the world to the exchange-rate instability of the 1930's, reducing international trade and investment and causing a recession. However, this did not happen either—most nations behaved quite responsibly in the management of their exchange rates, resisting any temptation to manoeuvre their currency values downward to gain a quick—but almost certainly temporary—competitive advantage.

Americans hoped that with a lower US dollar, the United States could enjoy a merchandise trade surplus that would provide the funds to finance other US activities around the world, such as foreign aid, military spending and investment abroad by US corporations. However, even as the United States was devaluing the dollar, events in the Middle East were moving in a direction that would, within six months, unravel these plans by causing the greatest US trade deficit ever.

OPEC AND THE PETRO-DOLLARS OUTFLOW

In late 1973 and early 1974, the **Organization of Petroleum Exporting Countries (OPEC)**, comprised mainly of Middle East oil-producing nations, finally succeeded in overcoming their mutual suspicion and mistrust sufficiently to unite on the question of oil prices. For years the industrialized nations had bought crude oil at very low prices through the multinational oil companies—prices obtained in part by playing off the oil-producing nations against each other. However, in late 1973 the OPEC nations agreed to present a unified front on oil prices, the result of which was a four-to-five-fold increase in oil prices over a period of a few months.

Because of its position as a large importer of OPEC oil, the United States' payments for imported oil soared, as did its merchandise trade deficit. In 1974, the year following OPEC's oil-price increases, the OPEC nations had a trade surplus on their oil sales of $62 billion; that is, $62 billion of funds—which became known as **petro-dollars** because of their source—flowed from the oil-importing nations to OPEC, in the largest transfer of wealth the world had ever seen.

It was vitally important to the oil-consuming nations that this vast outflow of funds be **recycled** back into their economies. In part, this was done through purchases by OPEC nations of substantial volumes of consumer goods, capital goods and military equipment from the industrialized nations. Further recycling occurred on a large scale through the investment of OPEC funds back into the industrialized nations. At first, these investments consisted mainly of government and corporate bonds and short-term interest-earning securities. Later, petro-dollars were invested in properties and shares of corporations. By the end of 1980, OPEC nations owned more than $340 billion worth of assets around the world.

The outflow of petro-dollars from the oil-consuming nations and the spending and investing of them by the OPEC nations generated a tremendous movement of funds between nations and currencies. This movement put strong pressure on the values of affected currencies, as these were bought and sold in unprecedented volumes. The "dirty float" system, with its flexibility, was much better suited than the old "pegged" system to deal with a situation in which such powerful market forces were exerted on currency prices.

As the price of oil fell in the 1980's under the pressure of oversupply, the flow of petro-dollars diminished sharply. By then, however, another quite unexpected and major international problem had emerged, as the US dollar began a rise to extremely high levels, disrupting international trade flows in the process.

THE SOARING US DOLLAR

While the US dollar was weak relative to other currencies during much of the 1970's, it rose unexpectedly rapidly in the first half of the 1980's. From 1980 to 1985, the US dollar appreciated by about 50 percent against other currencies on a trade-weighted basis,[6] reaching record highs against the Canadian dollar, the French franc and the British pound. By 1985, the strength of the US dollar had reached the point where it was a matter of major international concern, because it was distorting world trade flows.

The origins of the rapid rise of the US dollar lay in the massive budget deficits of the US federal government, which arose from a combination of tax cuts and heavy military spending. These budget deficits generated very large borrowing requirements on the part of the US government. In addition, US industry was borrowing heavily during this period for the purpose of capital investment. At the same time, there was a shortage of capital in the US economy due to a low personal savings rate and a relatively tight monetary policy imposed by US authorities in order to prevent the rekindling of inflation. The combination of a high demand for capital and a limited supply of funds generated very high interest rates in the United States, which attracted large inflows of capital from foreign nations—about $100 billion per year by 1984. The United States was financing a significant part of its federal government budget deficits and its capital investment spending by selling bonds to foreign lenders.

These heavy capital inflows from abroad caused large volumes of foreign currencies to be converted into US dollars, boosting the demand for the US dollar considerably in foreign exchange markets. The result was the exceptionally high US exchange rate referred to earlier, which would cause trade imbalances around the world.

On the positive side, the combination of the brisk US economic recovery and the strong US dollar generated very heavy demand by Americans for foreign goods and services. This rapid growth of exports to the United States gave many nations just what they had wanted—an export-led recovery from the Great Recession of 1981–82. In the words of the London *Economist*, "America has ... pump-primed the world out of the 1980–82 recession" (September 22, 1984).

From 1914 to 1982, the United States built up a net international creditor position of about $200 billion. Three years later, massive foreign borrowing had placed the United States $400 billion in debt to foreign lenders.

US TRADE DEFICITS AND PROTECTIONISM

On the negative side, Americans' strong purchasing of imported goods generated huge *trade deficits* for the United States. During the mid-1980's, the United States was importing about $150–160 billion more in goods than it exported. These massive US trade deficits were paralleled by trade surpluses in other nations, most notably Japan, West Germany and the Asian "dragons" (Taiwan, South Korea, Hong Kong and Singapore). The US protectionist sentiment was especially strong with respect to Japan, which accounted for $37 billion of the United States' $120 billion trade deficit in 1984.

The main cause of these worldwide trade imbalances was the high international value of the US dollar, which boosted Americans' purchases of imports while dampening US exports. And, underlying the strong US dollar were the US federal government's massive budget deficits, which were drawing vast amounts of foreign capital into the United States. The situation is summarized in Figure 35-4.

By 1984, US politicians were becoming increasingly concerned over the loss of American jobs due to the trade deficits, and were leaning toward enacting *protectionist legislation* to reduce imports. The threat of such legislation raised serious concerns in countries such as Canada and Japan, whose economies depend heavily on exports to the United States. By 1985, there was concern that the United States would take protectionist action against imports, and that other nations would retaliate, leading to a *trade war* such as the world had not seen since the Great Depression of the 1930's.[7]

By 1985, there was agreement among the USA's trading partners that the only way to protect themselves against growing protectionism in the

FIGURE 35-4 *The United States' "Twin Deficits"*

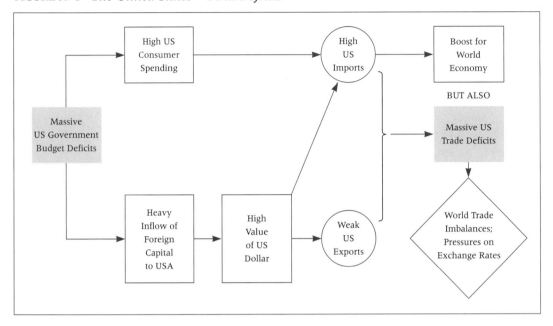

United States was to lower the international value of the US dollar, thereby reducing US imports and the US trade deficits.

THE "PLAZA ACCORD" OF 1985

On September 22, 1985, action was taken to reduce the international value of the US dollar. The **Group of Five (G-5)** nations[8]—the United States, Japan, West Germany, Great Britain and France—agreed to act together in foreign exchange market intervention to "bring the value of the US dollar down and the value of the other currencies up." While the agreement was vague regarding details, its main objective was a reduction in the US exchange rate that could reduce the US trade deficit and, it was hoped, head off protectionist measures.

In a real sense, however, the G-5 agreement dealt only with the symptom of the problem—the high value of the US dollar. Governments could to a certain extent depress the dollar (and increase the value of other currencies) by selling off US dollars and buying other currencies, but correcting the problem of massive world trade imbalances would require more fundamental action, including cooperation among the major industrial nations.

What was required was strong action by the United States to deal with the US government's massive budget deficits, so that massive foreign borrowing by the United States would stop driving both the US dollar and US imports to such high levels. In addition, action by Japan and West

Germany to speed up their economies would help, by increasing purchases of US exports and reducing the US trade deficits. Such a move would require an unusual degree of economic cooperation among the major industrial nations.

What was achieved in the years following the 1985 G-5 agreement was something less than this ideal, although it was helpful. Coordinated efforts by the central banks of the major nations did move the US dollar down significantly; in the eighteen months following the September 1985 agreement, it fell by about 30 percent against the yen and deutsche mark, as shown in Figure 35-5.

THE DIVING DOLLAR AND THE LOUVRE ACCORD

As Figure 35-5 also shows, after 1985, the US dollar resumed its long-term downward trend, but at a faster rate than in the past. By early 1987, there was concern that the US dollar was declining in value too rapidly, and that if the dollar continued its plunge, world trade could be disrupted.

In February 1987, the Group of Seven industrial countries concluded the "Louvre Accord," in which they agreed to try to support and stabilize the US dollar, and keep it within certain (unannounced) limits. In the months following the Louvre Accord, the central banks of the G-7 countries spent well over $100 billion buying US dollars to arrest its decline.

FIGURE 35-5   *Value of the US Dollar Against the Yen and Deutsche Mark, 1960–93*

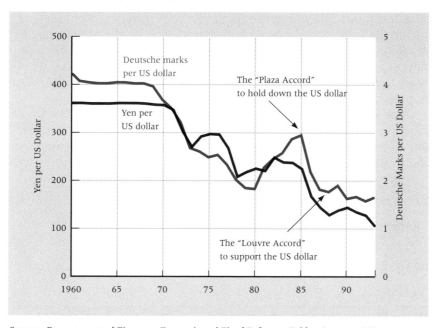

Source: Department of Finance, *Economic and Fiscal Reference Tables,* August 1993

The dollar did stabilize, and even recover, as the graph shows. Whether this was due to the Louvre Accord and central bank support, however, is debatable. The world market for US dollars is so vast—more than $300 billion are bought and sold per day—that it is difficult to influence its price through central bank purchases alone, which seldom exceed $1 billion per day. Unless governments make changes in their basic economic policies such as interest-rate policies and trade policies that support their exchange-rate targets, they are unlikely to be successful in reaching those targets. In the case of the Louvre Accord, this was not done, and the US dollar continued to lose ground to the Japanese yen.

THE HIGH-FLYING JAPANESE YEN

As Figure 35-6 shows, the Louvre Accord provided only temporary relief for the Japanese yen. From 1982 to late 1993, the value of the yen in terms of US dollars increased by almost 135 percent, despite a G-7 agreement in April 1993 to stabilize the values of the main traded currencies. This upsurge in the yen was mainly due to Japan's large *trade surplus*, which generated a strong foreign demand for Japanese currency.

During the 1980's, Japan's corporations had shown remarkable resiliency, continuing to be competitive in world markets despite the rising cost of the yen to foreigners. Certain practices of Japanese corporations helped them to adjust to changing world economic conditions by reducing their production costs. For instance, profit-related bonuses represented about one-third of a typical Japanese employee's take-home pay. When events such as an increase in the value of the yen cut into a company's sales and profits, these bonuses (and workers' incomes) would fall, reducing the company's labor costs and protecting its ability to compete.[9] In addition, Japanese corporations utilize large numbers of part-time employees and contract staff, whose numbers can readily be reduced if necessary to reduce costs and maintain competitiveness. The flexibility provided by practices such as these helped Japanese firms to remain competitive internationally as the yen rose during most of the 1980's. However, as the rising yen continued to put them under pressure, Japanese manufacturers shifted growing amounts of production offshore, to other locations in Southeast Asia and to North America and Europe. In addition, there was a significant shift in Japan's export markets. In the mid-1980's, 40 percent of Japan's exports had gone to the United States; by 1992 this was down to 28 percent as Japanese corporations shifted exports more towards Southeast Asia and, to a lesser extent, Europe.

EUROPE—TOWARD A COMMON CURRENCY—OR NOT?

And in Europe, the search for exchange-rate stability was proving no less difficult. From 1978 to 1992, the currencies of major European nations

FIGURE 35-6 *Value of the Japanese Yen in Terms of US Dollars, 1980–93*

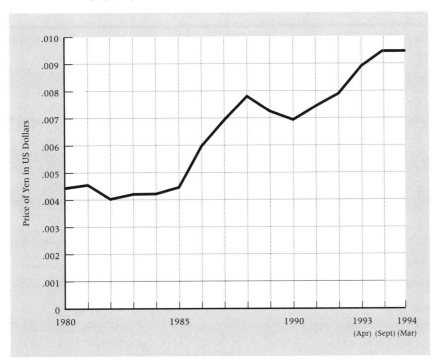

Source: Department of Finance, *Economic and Fiscal Reference Tables*, August 1993

had been relatively stable under an agreement known as the **Exchange Rate Mechanism**, or **ERM**. And, as we saw in Chapter 32, members of the European Community had planned on taking the final step of establishing a common European currency by 1997, or at the latest by 1999. As part of these plans, the Maastricht Treaty required that currencies stay quite stable relative to each other (within bands of 2.25 percent) for two years before moving to monetary union.

However, events overtook these plans. When the Soviet Union collapsed and East Germany was reunited with West Germany, Germany faced a massive task of building up the East German economy. This led to large budget deficits for the German government and unusually high inflation in Germany, a country noted for its low rates of inflation. The result was high interest rates in Germany and upward pressure on the deutsche mark. To keep their currencies in line with the deutsche mark, other European countries were forced to keep their interest rates higher than they wanted, an unwelcome situation because there was a recession at the time. These nations urged Germany to lower its interest rates, in order to keep the deutsche mark's value from rising and to allow lower interest rates across Europe. However, under German law, the first duty of the German central bank (the Bundesbank) is to defend the purchasing power of the deutsche mark; as a result, Germany refused to lower its interest rates. When other countries (most notably France) were unwilling to keep their interest rates high enough to maintain exchange-rate stability, their currencies fell considerably against the deutsche mark and the ERM agreement to keep currencies within "bands" of 2.25 percent broke down in mid-1993.

Under a new agreement, the bands were widened dramatically. Currencies would be allowed to fluctuate by up to 15 percent on either side of their "parity" levels. This would allow a currency to lose up to 30 percent of its value, a system so loose that it virtually amounted to a "floating" exchange-rate system.

This represented a severe setback to Europe's plans of two years of quite stable currencies leading up to a common currency by 1997 or 1999. Once again, governments' attempts to stabilize exchange rates had run afoul of market forces and variations in economic policies between nations.

The international monetary system in perspective

Figure 35-7 provides an overview of the developments in the international monetary system that are discussed in this chapter. As the overview shows, these developments can be broadly divided into three periods. First, there was the exchange-rate instability of the 1930's, which, while partly a re-

FIGURE 35-7 *The International Monetary System: An Overview*

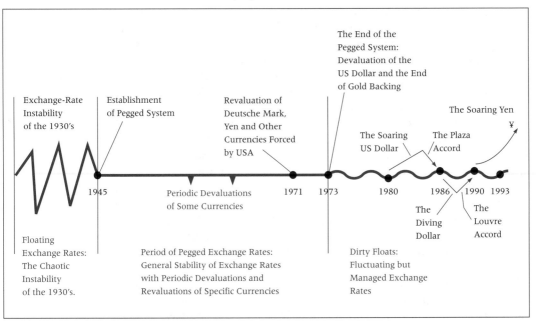

sult of the Depression, also contributed to the severity of the Depression. In reaction to this, the "pegged" system was set up in 1945, to provide international monetary stability. Despite periodic devaluations of some currencies, the pegged system endured until the weakness of its key currency, the US dollar, led first to the revaluation of various other currencies in 1971, then to the end of the pegged system in 1973, when the US dollar was devalued and floated and its gold backing removed. Since 1973, the international monetary system has been characterized by a "dirty float," with exchange rates fluctuating, but under the influence of monetary authorities seeking to avoid excessive instability and with periodic agreements between major nations to "steer" key currencies in directions considered desirable.

The future for the international monetary system

For many years, the US dollar had played a dominant role in the international monetary system, largely because of the dominance of the US economy internationally. And, as the twentieth century nears its end, the United States is still the most productive, prosperous and powerful nation in the world. However, for some time, economic and financial power in the world have been shifting away from the United States and becoming more dispersed among various nations.

During the 1980's, massive foreign capital inflows to the United States, drawn by the US government's huge budget deficits, had changed the United States from a creditor nation to the world's largest debtor and importer of foreign products. The major net creditors and exporters had become Japan, West Germany and Taiwan, but none of these nations were ready to play the world economic leadership role that the United States had provided in the past. Economic power—and financial power—was becoming more dispersed around the world, leaving no one country or currency in a dominant position. Despite doubts surrounding its future value, however, the US dollar remained the most important currency internationally, largely because there was no readily available alternative to it. And the search for exchange-rate stability continued to prove difficult, partly because exchange rates are subject to powerful market forces that are

---

The United States saw its share of world exports drop from about 13 percent in 1960 to less than 9 percent in 1986. Meanwhile, Japan's share rose from 2 to 8 percent, and the share of the newly industrialized countries in Asia also increased—from 2.5 to 6.5 percent between 1973 and 1986.

themselves unstable, and partly because nations were unwilling or unable to coordinate their economic policies in the way that is required for their exchange rates to remain relatively stable.

Postscript: The decline of gold

As noted earlier, key international currencies (most recently the US dollar) have traditionally been convertible into, or backed by, gold. After its gold reserves had been depleted by payments deficits and runs by speculators, the US government suspended the convertibility of the US dollar to gold. The US dollar was no longer backed by gold; its value and acceptability were based on faith.

However, speculators continued to buy gold in great quantities, as they expected that the United States would be forced by other nations to return to gold backing of its currency, and to devalue the US dollar. If the US dollar were devalued, gold would be worth many more US dollars per ounce—the holders of gold would become rich overnight. In anticipation of this event speculators bought great amounts of gold, bidding its price up to very high levels.

While the devaluation of the US dollar did materialize (in February 1973), the anticipated return to gold backing did not. Instead, steps were taken to remove gold from its dominant role in the international monetary system, as the International Monetary Fund began selling off its holdings of gold at a series of auctions, with the proceeds to go to the benefit of underdeveloped nations.

OLD-STYLE TRANSACTIONS

Gold is still sometimes used to settle accounts between governments. For instance, when central banks buy and sell currencies as part of dirty-float operations, payment is sometimes made in gold.

Much of the gold used for this purpose is stored in the Federal Reserve Bank of New York, in a vault carved into the bedrock 25 metres below Nassau Street in lower Manhattan. This vault houses the world's largest store of gold bullion—in 1989, about 12 000 tons, worth over $150 billion US. Almost all of the gold is owned by foreign governments, including countries of the former Soviet bloc.

As an indication of the lasting psychological grip that gold has on people, when one country pays another country, the bank's staff actually *move the gold* on carts to the other country's pile, perhaps only a few metres away. Under the rules of international finance, such action changes the ownership of the gold, and the foreign exchange reserves of the nations involved can be adjusted accordingly.

Despite being phased out of its official role as backing for currencies, gold has continued to attract a great deal of attention from speculators who lack faith in paper money. Believing that governments have a natural tendency to overissue paper money, and seeking protection from the declining value of paper money due to inflation (not to mention profits from rising gold prices), these speculators have on various occasions (such as 1979–80) bought gold heavily, bidding its price up to very high levels. Generally, any event that could add to inflation or shake confidence in paper currencies, such as rumors of war, crop failures, or oil production cutbacks, generates heavier buying of gold and higher gold prices. It is important to note, however, that gold in these cases is being bought as a commodity that is predicted to hold its value better than paper money, not because it has any role as backing for currencies.

DEFINITIONS OF NEW TERMS

Pegged Exchange Rates Exchange rates that are prevented by governments from moving from their fixed levels in relation to each other.

Foreign Exchange Reserves Holdings of foreign currencies and gold maintained by governments for the purpose of stabilizing their exchange rates through purchases and sales of their currencies.

International Monetary Fund (IMF) An international agency established to oversee and maintain the system of pegged exchange rates set up in 1945.

Devaluation A reduction in the level of a pegged exchange rate.

Overvaluation The pegging of an exchange rate at an unrealistically and unsustainably high level.

Undervaluation The pegging of an exchange rate at an unrealistically and unsustainably low level.

Revaluation An increase in the level of a pegged exchange rate.

OPEC Organization of Petroleum Exporting Countries; established to control the supply and price of oil in world trade.

Petro-Dollars Funds (US dollars) earned by OPEC nations through petroleum exports.

Recycling The process whereby petro-dollars are recirculated back into the economies of the oil-consuming nations, through purchases of goods and services and through investments by oil-producing countries.

G-5 The Group of Five nations—the United States, Japan, West Germany, Great Britain and France—who would meet regularly to discuss economic matters. (Now called the **G-7**, since the inclusion of Canada and Italy.)

Exchange Rate Mechanism (ERM) Agreement among members of the European Community to keep the values of their currencies relative to each other within certain limits.

CHAPTER SUMMARY

1. In 1945, to avoid a repetition of the exchange-rate chaos of the 1930's, the major nations of the world established a system of "pegged" exchange rates under the supervision of the International Monetary Fund.

2. The US dollar occupied the key role in this system: backed by gold, it was the most widely used and accepted currency internationally, the main reserve currency and the centre of the system of pegged exchange rates.

3. Strains on the pegged system developed as the competitive positions of nations changed, placing upward pressure on some currencies (such as the deutsche mark and the yen) and downward pressure on others (such as the British pound).

4. As a last resort, the devaluation of chronically weak currencies was considered acceptable, with the currency to be re-pegged at a level that would allow its receipts and payments to be in rough balance.

5. At times, the Canadian dollar was part of the system of pegged exchange rates, but at other times it was allowed to float.

6. After the 1950's, the United States experienced international payments deficits, largely due to increasing foreign competition, particularly from Japan and West Germany.

7. The result of the US deficits was a depletion of the US gold reserves, and concerns about the international acceptability of the US dollar, which was no longer convertible to gold.

8. After a variety of measures to support the dollar, the United States was finally forced to devalue it in 1973. Following its devaluation, the US dollar was not again pegged, so that the "pegged" system was in effect replaced by a "dirty float."

9. The dirty float system was well-suited to the circumstances that followed, as the OPEC oil-price increases of the 1970's generated massive flows of funds between nations and currencies, putting pressure on exchange rates.

10. In the first half of the 1980's, the US dollar was exceptionally strong, largely due to heavy inflows of foreign capital arising from large US government budget deficits and high US interest rates.

11. The strong US dollar contributed to very large US trade deficits. The deficits, in turn, led to protectionist sentiment in the United States, which the G-5 nations tried to stem with a 1985 agreement to reduce the value of the US dollar.

12. By 1987, the value of the US dollar was falling so rapidly that the G-7 nations agreed to try to support and stabilize it through large-scale purchases.

13. From 1980 to 1993, the international value of the Japanese yen increased greatly, undercutting Japan's international competitiveness and forcing Japanese corporations to move production operations offshore and to increase exports to markets other than the United States.

14. The European Community's plans to establish a common currency by 1997 or 1999 suffered a major setback when high German interest rates and a strong deutsche mark forced the EC to allow the value of currencies to fluctuate much more widely than had been planned.

15. Despite the fact that the United States' dominance had declined and that the United States had become the world's largest debtor nation during the 1980's, no other nation or currency was in a position to assume the leadership role played by the United States and the US dollar since 1945.

16. Despite the fact that it is no longer used as a backing for currencies, gold is still bought (sometimes heavily) by speculators who lack faith in paper currencies.

QUESTIONS

1. Has Japan's trade surplus with the United States and the rest of the world decreased in recent years? If so, what has caused this? If not, are measures being proposed to reduce it?

2. "The higher the yen goes, the more likely it is to stop rising." Explain the reasoning behind this statement. Has the yen stopped rising since reaching a level of 0.946 cents US in September of 1993? Why or why not?

3. What does the large and rapid increase in the value of the yen mean to:
   (a) Japanese automobile manufacturers?
   (b) Japanese workers?
   (c) Japanese consumers?
   (d) North American consumers?
   (e) North American producers of auto parts?
   (f) North American auto workers?

4. Has the US dollar continued to decline relative to currencies such as the yen and deutsche mark? If so, why has this happened? If not, what has caused the US dollar to stabilize or increase in value?

5. Have fears of increased US protectionism and possible retaliation by foreign nations proven correct? If so, what measures have been taken? If not, how has this been averted?

6. If the United States printed money on a large scale to finance its budget deficits, what effect would this probably have on:

   (a) long-term interest rates?

   (b) the US exchange rate?

   (c) gold prices?

   (d) the Canadian economy?

7. Have the European Community nations managed to stabilize their currencies within narrow limits and thus resume progress toward a single currency before the end of the century? Why or why not?

8. Suppose that Canada and the United States were considering adopting a common currency. What would be some of the key questions that would have to be worked out, and what obstacles would there be to such a measure?

9. Would Newfoundland be better off if it had its own currency and were able to lower interest rates and increase its money supply in order to stimulate its economy and reduce unemployment?

10. Has the price of gold changed significantly recently? If so, why?

NOTES

1 Some people advocate abandoning national currencies in favor of one world currency. However, this would require each nation to abandon not only its own currency, but also its right to determine its own monetary policy, which presumably would be decided by an international central bank. Generally, sovereign nations tend to be quite reluctant to hand over such crucial economic policy decisions to an international agency.

2 A similar development occurred in the field of *trade policy*. During the 1930's, there were "trade wars," as nations raised tariffs on each others' products so as to keep out imports that were seen as "stealing jobs" from domestic workers. The result was much higher tariffs and a reduced volume of world trade and higher unemployment in all countries. The longer-term outcome of this was a realization that more cooperation was needed in the area of trade and tariffs, which led to the formation in 1947 of the General Agreement on Tariffs and Trade, as discussed in Chapter 32.

3 Before a currency was actually devalued, it was common for various steps to be taken in attempts to avoid it. For instance, the IMF would lend reserves to the na-

tion involved with which to "defend" its currency by buying it. As a condition of such loans, the IMF would often require the nation to invoke a tighter monetary policy. This would not only slow down inflation that might be undermining the nation's competitive position, but also could attract inflows of short-term funds that could support the value of the nation's currency. It would also have the effect of slowing down the nation's economy and increasing unemployment—an uncomfortable form of discipline.

4 There is an interesting similarity between the banks that we studied in Chapter 26 and the United States in the world economy. Both put out into circulation large amounts of paper currency on the basis of only a small amount of cash (gold) reserves. In both cases, the paper currency works well as long as people don't lose faith and try to convert it all to gold (cash). This is why the United States was sometimes called "banker to the world."

5 A devaluation of the US dollar would move its value downward, not only in terms of other currencies, but also in terms of gold. If the US dollar were devalued by 20 percent, it would be worth 20 percent less gold, or viewed differently, the devaluation of the US dollar would mean *an increase in the price of gold*, from, say, $35 US per ounce to $42 US per ounce. People who believed that a devaluation of the US dollar was inevitable therefore had a strong incentive to convert their US dollars into gold so as to profit from the devaluation. Until 1968, foreign speculators could get gold from the US government at $35 per ounce; after 1968, however, the United States refused to convert dollars for foreign speculators, forcing speculators to buy gold in private markets, in which the price of gold was bid up to quite high levels. Such speculative selling of US dollars, of course, only made the problem worse.

6 A method of calculating the average US exchange rate compared to the United States' trading partners, making allowance for the volume of trade the US does with each country.

7 Concern over this rising protectionist sentiment in the United States led to heightened Canadian interest in Canada in negotiating the Canada–US Free Trade Agreement, as discussed in Chapter 33.

8 Later expanded to the **G-7**, with the addition of Canada and Italy.

9 This arrangement also enables Japanese companies to have fewer layoffs in bad times: rather than reduce the number of workers, they reduce the pay per worker, thus helping to provide the job security for which Japanese corporations are famous. In effect, workers traded income security for job security—the opposite of customary North American practice.

Into the future

As the 1990's began, Canada was grappling with some major economic challenges. The nation's ability to address these issues effectively will greatly affect the prosperity of Canadians in the final decade of the century and beyond. The most important challenge facing Canada was the rapidly changing international environment, or the phenomenon known as "globalization." However, in order to cope effectively with these international challenges, Canada would have to deal with important domestic economic issues, in order to become more competitive internationally. Chief among these domestic challenges were *productivity growth* and *government budget deficits*.

Dealing with these challenges would involve fundamental changes in the Canadian economy and in government policies. Before we consider these changes, however, we will review the basic nature of the Canadian economy and government policy orientation that existed prior to the mid-1980's.

The way we were

Traditionally, Canada relied considerably upon exports of natural resources and resource products as a basic source of economic prosperity. These exports, together with substantial inflows of foreign (mainly US) business capital investment, provided Canadians with the foreign currency with which they purchased the large amounts of imported goods and services that supported their high living standards. By making Canadians one of the most prosperous people in the world, these advantages also made it possible for them to afford to support a relatively inefficient tariff-protected manufacturing sector, by paying high prices for its products.

With economic wealth so readily provided by resource exports and foreign investment, government policy tended to be relatively uncon-

> Traditionally, Canadians have lived in a relatively insulated environment brought about by paternalistic government policies, a history of market protection, and the accumulated attitudes and experiences of both individuals and businesses.
>
> This old economic order, as we call it, was a system where many prospered. However, because the old order generally provided insulation from external pressures and fostered limited internal pressures, many of the critical requirements for upgrading to more sophisticated and sustainable competitive advantages in Canadian industry have been missing or are only weakly present.
>
> Professor Michael E. Porter, *Canada at the Crossroads: The Reality of a New Competitive Environment* (October 1991; a study prepared for the Business Council on National Issues and the Government of Canada

cerned about *creating wealth*. Rather, government policies focused on promoting a *fair distribution of wealth* by providing assistance to individuals, businesses and regions that needed it. Over the years, governments established a wide variety of social welfare programs for individuals and families (from education to health care to income support systems such as unemployment insurance, welfare and pensions), an extensive support system for weaker and less efficient producers (including tariff protection for manufacturers, subsidies for farmers and bail-outs of various sorts for many corporations in difficulty) and various forms of assistance to economically weaker regions (including equalization payments, regional development grants and subsidies to people and businesses in those regions).

According to some critical observers, Canada had developed a **"resource wealth mentality"**—the view that wealth is not something that you *create* so much as something that *happens to you* through possessing and selling resources, and the main role of government is to ensure that the nation's wealth is distributed fairly among its fortunate people. As a result, government policy tended to be more concerned with the *distribution* of economic welfare than with incentives for the *creation* of wealth. Thus, while Canadians were generally very prosperous, they were not (with the exception of their natural resource sector) particularly competitive internationally.

The new realities: "globalization" and competition[1]

During the 1980's, a variety of factors combined to generate such a major increase in international trade, competition and investment that this phenomenon came to be known as the "globalization" of markets. Some of the factors that contributed to this change were lower tariff barriers, increasing numbers of "players" as less developed countries adopted market economies, and improved computers, communications and transportation technology that facilitated conducting trade and investment on a global scale. With this technology, designers, manufacturers and retailers in all parts of the world are able to communicate with each other more quickly and more effectively than they used to communicate within one country. And with the increased international competition came higher productivity and lower costs and prices.

> "We are using Russian engineers living in Israel to design (computer micro) chips that are made in America and then assembled in Asia."
>
> Peter J. Sprague, chairman, National Semiconductor Corporation

The new global economy presented Canada with some difficult challenges during the 1980's. As noted above, much of Canada's manufacturing sector was not very efficient and was thus ill-prepared for stronger international competition. To make matters worse, world markets for resource exports—Canada's traditional strength—were depressed. And, despite the importance of trade to its economy, Canadian producers and governments were slow to adapt to this new, more competitive international environment. Rather than look outwards to the opportunities presented by the global economy, Canada sought to maintain the "old order" described above, by protecting its less efficient producers against competition, with tariffs and government subsidies. Partly as a result of this, the efficiency, or productivity, of much of the Canadian economy failed to keep pace with improvements in other nations, causing Canada to become less competitive, especially in manufacturing, as the 1980's progressed.

> The outstanding question at the beginning of 1985 is whether Canada will ride the wave of change or be swamped by it.
>
> Edward A. Carmichael, *Policy Review and Outlook, 1985: A Time for Decisions* (Toronto: C.D. Howe Institute, 1985)

And as Canada tried to continue to protect its producers from foreign competition, the costs of this policy to Canada and to Canadians grew, in terms of:

(a) *costs to consumers*, in the form of higher prices (in many industries, the cost to consumers per job saved by protectionist policies was well in excess of $100 000),

(b) *costs to Canadian exporters*, as foreign nations retaliated against Canadian barriers to their exports with barriers against Canadian exports, and

(c) *lost business investment*, as a growing number of successful Canadian businesses expanded into other countries, in order to avoid the trade barriers described in (b).

In short, Canada was failing to adapt to the new realities of "globalization" by becoming more efficient and competitive, and the costs of this failure were mounting as the decade went on.

The challenge

In this new, "globalized" world economy, business capital searches the world for the most economical locations for its activities. If a country can attract business investment, and the jobs and production that it brings, that country will prosper economically. If it fails to attract investment, it will stagnate economically.

What makes a country an attractive location for business investment? Many people think that the answer is "cheap labor," but the matter is not nearly as simple as that. Cheap labor is important for labor-intensive manufacturing industries such as clothing and footwear; however, in most industries, such low-wage, semi-skilled labor has been replaced to a great extent by technology. To modern, high-technology industries, the key attraction is not cheap labor, but rather *skilled people* with *specialized knowledge*. In addition, a nation needs to have excellent *transportation and communication links* to the rest of the world, in order to be able to function effectively as part of the new world economy. According to this view, a nation's key strategic assets economically are no longer its natural resources or abundant and cheap labor, but rather its education and training systems and its transportation/communications infrastructure ... the knowledge and skills of its people, and the support systems for bringing the productive use of those skills into the global economy.[2]

> Canadians must recapture the pioneering spirit that built our nation and apply it to the challenges that confront us: not merely to survive the new global economy, but to thrive in it; not to turn from competition but to engage it; not to fear the future but to invent it.
>
> Steering Group on Prosperity, *Inventing our Future: An Action Plan for Canada's Prosperity* (1992)

If a country has these attributes, it will tend to gain business investment and prosper economically. Its skilled work force will earn high incomes and its government will have a strong tax base, which can be used to invest further in better schools, research, and transportation and communications systems. These features will attract more investment, and the cycle of prosperity can be continued.

But without the skilled work force and the communications and transportation infrastructure, the opposite kind of cycle can take place. Unable to attract capital with its skills and infrastructure, the nation would be forced to resort to low wages and low taxes as inducements for businesses to invest there. However, such enticements would only undercut the government's tax revenues, making it more difficult to finance good education and infrastructure. This would make the nation a less attractive location for businesses and force the government to drop taxes and social services even further, in a vicious circle.

Into the future

By the mid-1980's, the direction of government policy had changed significantly. Less emphasis was placed on government support for individuals and industries, and increased emphasis was being placed on market forces, private enterprise, entrepreneurship and incentives for work, investment, productivity and the creation of wealth. In short, the policy emphasis shifted from the *redistribution* of wealth to the *creation* of wealth.

In this context, the 1989 Free Trade Agreement with the United States represented a landmark decision for Canada. It signalled Canada's intention to participate more fully in the increasingly globalized markets of the world. As such, it also meant a basic shift in Canadian policy, toward an emphasis on productivity, competitiveness and an outward-looking internationalism rather than on more inward-looking nationalistic policies that sheltered Canadian industries and workers from international competition. The Free Trade Agreement was regarded not as the final step in this direction, but rather as the first step toward Canada's becoming productive and competitive on a global scale.[3]

In support of making Canada more competitive, government policy priorities changed in a variety of areas. Perhaps the most fundamental of these was a new emphasis on *keeping inflation in check*. Nations such as

---

For the first 100 years after Confederation, Canada lived off its resources. For the past 16 years, we have lived off our credit. Now we must live off our skills, our wits, our energy and our initiative.

Hon. Michael Wilson, in a speech delivered to the Centre on Foreign Policy and Federalism, 1984

> In 1966, we could get away with running a closely protected domestic market for manufacturers, and still export our resources. We don't have as good a market for resources anymore, and even with protection, the developing world is starting to take our market away. If we want to maintain our standard of living, we're going to need a more competitive stance in manufacturing and services.
>
> Donald Macdonald in the *Financial Post*, Sept. 14, 1985

Japan and Germany that had been particularly successful in international competition had kept inflation in their economies low. Not only did this help to keep the prices of their products competitive, but also low inflation allowed them to have *low interest rates* that would encourage the business investment spending that would improve productivity, making them more competitive. For these reasons, the government of Canada established the objective of keeping inflation at much lower rates than those that had prevailed in the 1970's and most of the 1980's.

Another key policy in the government's program was *tax reform*. Tax incentives were provided for investment in businesses, and marginal personal income tax rates were reduced somewhat. The tax burden was shifted from income taxes (which reduce incentives to work, save and invest) and toward sales taxes (the Goods and Services Tax), which tax spending rather than the productive efforts of individuals and businesses.

Another aspect of the new policy direction was the *deregulation* of some industries. Over the years, Canada had accumulated a very large body of government regulations of business, many of which controlled prices and production and/or restricted the entry of new competitors into some industries. Many of these regulations had the unintended effect of reducing competition and efficiency in the regulated industries. To improve productivity performance, the government **deregulated** some industries. The most notable examples of such deregulation were the dismantling of the Foreign Investment Review Act, which had restricted foreign investment, and the National Energy Program, which had regulated the operation of the oil industry. Other important areas of deregulation and increased competition were financial services and communications, most notably long distance telephone service.

There were also significant changes to Canada's *competition legislation*— the legislation that is intended to promote competition between businesses. Under Canada's new Competition Act, it became more difficult for businesses to reduce competition through tactics such as mergers with competitors and agreements to avoid price competition, or "price-fixing." And, of course, foreign competition would intensify as tariffs came down under the Canada–US Free Trade Agreement and NAFTA and the GATT.

Along with deregulation came *reductions in government subsidies* to business, which forced businesses to improve efficiency rather than rely on government handouts. Several Crown corporations were sold to private interests ("privatized"), forcing them to operate more efficiently without government subsidies and freeing them from political interference. Changes were introduced to the *unemployment insurance system*, one key aspect of which shifted the nature of UI toward retraining of the unemployed rather than simply supporting their incomes.

Government policy-makers also placed increased emphasis on *encouraging the small business sector* of the economy, which had provided a high proportion of the new jobs created in the recent past and was expected to play a larger role in the future. Unlike resource and heavy manufacturing industries, the emerging high-tech and service industries are not dominated by giant corporations; in fact, small size, innovation and flexibility are seen as advantages in these fields.

More recently, government policy has placed increased emphasis on *investment in human resources*, through education, training and retraining. In the words of Peter Nicholson, "The fundamental determinant of success in the knowledge-based economy is the quality of a nation's human resources.... In the new economy, prosperity will depend less on location and more on networks linked by computer and telecommunications facilities. Here, Canada is at the leading edge of institutional innovation."[4]

These new policies represented a fundamental shift in Canadian economic policy. Government policies had traditionally been directed largely toward *redistributing* economic wealth, through an extensive social welfare system. But to improve productivity and competitiveness, the new Canadian policies emphasized the *creation* of wealth as well as its redistribution. This required incentives for enterprise, entrepreneurship and investment, as well as increased emphasis on competition and efficiency.

The major unaddressed policy problem was government budget deficits. In a real sense, these deficits represented the main link with the policy position of the past, which regarded government spending on extensive social welfare programs for Canadians as the prime responsibility of governments. Until government deficits could be brought under control, concern about inflation and future tax increases would be higher, making interest rates higher and investor confidence lower than was needed for an economy that was meant to develop world-class competitiveness.

A solid foundation for a strong economic performance seems to be in place (for Canada).

International Monetary Fund, *World Economic Outlook* (October 1992)

Strategies for the future

In a broad strategic sense, the new direction of government policy was to shift the emphasis in the Canadian economy from *security and consumption* towards *efficiency and investment*, or from benefits that exist mainly in the present to longer-term gains. The success of such a policy initiative will depend to a great extent on the willingness of the public to support it, which in turn depends partly on how quickly the promised economic benefits appear.

Canadians want a great deal from their economic system. They want prosperity for themselves in the form of high levels of private personal consumption, high levels of government services, including a strong social welfare system, health care and education, economic security and protection of the environment. To provide all of these, the Canadian economy must be prosperous and productive. Only by becoming more productive, more efficient and more competitive will Canadians find it possible to achieve all their economic and social goals. The challenge in this situation is to find an effective balance between the consumption that Canadians want in the present and the investment in not only capital goods, but also human resources, that are essential for longer-term economic prosperity.

DEFINITIONS OF NEW TERMS

Resource Wealth Mentality The view that society's economic wealth is derived mainly from the sale of natural resources, as opposed to efficiency in the production of goods and services.

Deregulation Policies to reduce the extent of regulation of business by government, with the intention of promoting efficiency through increased competition.

CHAPTER SUMMARY

1. Canada had traditionally relied heavily upon natural resource exports to create economic wealth, while government policies had aimed more at redistributing income and providing social welfare programs than at promoting productivity, the creation of wealth and competitiveness.

2. After the early 1980's, Canada was grappling with major economic challenges, the main one of which was the international competition and opportunities presented by the increasing "globalization" of the world economy.

3. In the "globalized" world economy, a knowledgeable and skilled labor force and excellent transportation and communication links to the

rest of the world are keys to attracting business investment and the jobs and economic wealth it brings.

4. Rather than participate aggressively in this new world economy, Canada sought to maintain its old economic order by protecting its less efficient producers from international competition, at considerable cost to Canadian taxpayers, consumers and exporters.

5. In the mid-1980's, in an attempt to improve the nation's productivity and competitiveness, Canadian government policy shifted away from redistribution of wealth and protection of industries, and more toward creation of wealth and economic internationalism.

6. Specific government policies in pursuit of these objectives included:

   (a) the Free Trade Agreement with the United States, so as to secure access to Canada's largest export market,

   (b) the containment of inflation, so as to restore economic stability, reduce interest rates and rebuild investor confidence and business investment,

   (c) various other policies to improve productivity and economic performance, including tax reform, deregulation, new competition legislation, reduction of government subsidies to business, changes to the Unemployment Insurance system, encouragement of small business and increased emphasis on investment in human resources.

7. These policies reflected a change in emphasis from consumption and security to investment (in human resources as well as capital equipment) and productivity, with the objective of longer-term economic gains.

QUESTIONS

1. In October 1993, the Progressive Conservative government that had introduced the change in policy emphasis described in this chapter was defeated and replaced by a Liberal government. Did the new government reverse or change the policy direction established by its predecessor, or did it largely maintain that direction? Why do you think that this happened, and what have been the consequences? What do you think the consequences would have been if the government had done the opposite to what it actually did?

2. Has the government succeeded in keeping inflation under control since 1993?

3. Has the unemployment rate increased or declined since 1993? Why?

4. What is the recent trend in business investment spending? What are the reasons for this, and what are its implications for the economy?

5. Has Canada's productivity performance improved recently? What are the reasons for this trend?

6. Has Canadian industry grown more or less competitive internationally over the past few years? What are the reasons for this trend?

7. Has any progress been made in reducing the size of government budget deficits? Why or why not? Does the public regard government budget deficits as a serious problem or not?

8. Have interest rates risen or fallen since 1993? Why? What are the implications of this trend for the economy?

9. Has the international value of the Canadian dollar increased or decreased since 1993? Why? What are the implications of this for the economy?

10. Have Canadian businesses been able to improve their productivity and international competitiveness in recent years? Which Canadian industries and companies are succeeding in international competition, and why? Which are having difficulty, and why?

11. Generally, how does Canada's economic performance over the past five years compare to that of other industrialized countries? What reasons are given for this trend?

NOTES

[1] This section and the section following it owe a great deal to *The REAL Economy* by Robert Reich, which appeared in the February 1991 issue of *The Atlantic Monthly*.

[2] This assumes that the country does not have specific taxation or other policies that make it an unattractive location.

[3] In 1994, another step was taken as the North American Free Trade Agreement joined Canada, the United States and Mexico into the largest free trade area in the world.

[4] Facing the Future, *The Financial Post 500*, May 1993

INDEX